MARTHA DALLMANN

Professor Emeritus of Education, Ohio Wesleyan University
Professor Emeritus of Elementary Education, St. Cloud State College

ROGER L. ROUCH

Professor of Elementary Education, St. Cloud State College

LYNETTE Y. C. CHANG

Professor of Elementary Education, St. Cloud State College

JOHN J. DEBOER

THE TEACHING OF READING

4th EDITION

HOLT, RINEHART AND WINSTON, INC.
New York   Chicago   San Francisco   Atlanta
Dallas   Montreal   Toronto   London   Sydney

ISBN: 0–03–001306–2
Printed in the United States of America

456789   071   987654321

Preface to the Fourth Edition

Since the publication of the third edition of this book, continued technological and societal pressures have affected the trends in the teaching of reading in the elementary school. This fourth edition reflects those influences.

Increased attention is being paid to two aspects of the teaching of reading (1.) the development of the skills essential to the fluent reader, with the emphasis on diagnosis and prescriptive teaching, and (2.) the encouragement of the voluntary reading program, stressing the importance of the development of permanent interests in reading. Many educators are convinced that the two emphases should go hand in hand, one complementing the other, to help create a reader in whom, because of his skill in reading and his interest in it, a life-long habit of worthwhile reading is being established. That the authors share this point of view is evidenced throughout the book. A chapter has been added on "Classroom Diagnosis of Reading Ability," and the chapter on "Adapting Instruction to the Needs of Individuals" presents suggestions on diagnostic teaching. This emphasis is also highlighted in the chapter on "Developing Children's Interests in Reading," the content of which shows many changes from that of the two chapters on the same topic in the preceding edition.

Research on the relationship between reading and other facets of the

v

language arts is characterizing the efforts of the early 1970s, with attention to the bearing of this relationship on teaching reading to the child from the culturally different home. To acquaint the teacher and prospective teacher of reading with the results of this study a chapter on "Language Development and Reading" has been added. The chapter dealing with "Reading and the Child from the Culturally Different Home" indicates the more recent trends not only in dealing with the factor of a language divergent from that used in textbooks but also with approaches to difficulties in general, encountered when teaching reading to the child reared in poverty and in conditions typically characteristic of such an environment. In the chapter on "Approaches to Reading Instruction" the subject of linguistics is discussed at greater length than previously.

Another trend of the early 1970s is the increase in materials for the teaching of reading with which the market is being fairly flooded. To assist the teacher in the selection of materials suitable to the needs of his pupils, a chapter on "Resources for Teaching Reading" has been added to the book. It should be a particularly valuable reference for teachers in service.

The chapters on comprehension and on reading rates and the chapter on "The Concept of Reading" are among other parts showing major revision. In the chapter on "Implementation of the Reading Program" a more comprehensive treatment, than was included in the preceding edition, is given to procedures for setting up a reading program for a school. Other changes include the updating of bibliographical data and of references to research. As in the two earlier revisions, the aim of the writers has been to retain that from preceding editions which is as valuable now as when it was first written, and to make changes and additions where they add to the worth of the book.

With gratitude the authors acknowledge the assistance of all the persons and groups of persons to whom reference is made in the prefaces of earlier editions—to the writers, editors, and publishers who have permitted us to quote long passages and to the schools and school districts that made photographs available to us. We continue to be grateful to Emeritus Professor Ruth Strickland of Indiana University for her careful reading of the manuscript of the first edition of this book and for her thoughtful commentary on it. Her suggestions have improved the book, but she should not be held responsible for its point of view or for any errors that may appear in it. The authors also recognize their indebtedness to Dr. Walter J. Moore, who wrote two chapters for the third edition and gave other assistance in the writing of that edition. A comparison of it with this revision will clearly show that his contribution is a continuing one.

It is with special gratitude that the authors express their deep indebtedness to Dr. John J. DeBoer, who served as senior author of the earlier editions of this book until his death in 1969. His scholarly insight into the problems of teaching and his all-pervading interest in and affection for boys and girls, helped set the tone for *The Teaching of Reading*. If any one point of view typically characteristic of his philosophy of teaching reading can be cited, it is his overriding conviction that of greater significance than the learning is the learner; that more important than helping develop an efficient reader is helping, through instruction in reading, develop the individual. It is the hope of the writers of this fourth edition that they have been true to the high idealism that is so strongly in evidence in the writings of John DeBoer.

St. Cloud, Minnesota   — *M.D.*
January 1974   — *R.L.R.*
                                                                       — *L.Y.C.C.*

Contents

4th edition

The
Teaching
of
Reading

PART I

Perspective in Reading

Outline for Chapter 1

THE TEACHING OF READING—A CHALLENGE

The Values of Reading
Public Interest in Reading Ability
Efforts of the Teaching Profession
Individual Differences in Reading
The Complexity of Reading
Reading and Knowledge
Reading and Personality
Reading and Citizenship
Need for Improvement in Reading Instruction

CHAPTER 1

The Teaching of Reading —A Challenge

Let us push on and on with more and more vigor in the next decade, and the next decade, and in all of the other decades ahead.[1]

It was with these words that Nila Banton Smith, at the time of the observance of the golden anniversary of the founding of the National Council of Teachers of English, concluded her scholarly review of accomplishments in the teaching of reading during the first half-century of the existence of the Council. Her charge is a fitting challenge for all teachers of reading for whom knowledge of successes and failures in the teaching of reading in the past constitutes reason for ever-increasing effort to provide *every* child with the opportunity to learn to read to the extent of his ability.

It is significant that at present, as never before in the history of American reading instruction, there is such keen interest in the teaching of reading. Especially worthy of note is the fact that increased attention should be given to it in this age of mass communication, with the new technological means of almost instantaneous transmission of sight and sound over long distances, at a time when some voices suggest that the

[1] Nila Banton Smith, "What Have We Accomplished in Reading?" *Elementary English,* 28 (March 1961), p. 150.

new media will soon replace the book. The strong endorsement by educators, in word and deed, of the conviction that reading instruction should be a priority concern of our country is evidence of their faith that technology is not replacing reading. Their faith is justified.

THE VALUES OF READING

In spite of competing mass media, reading in our Space Age is becoming increasingly important. The role of the reading teacher is not less, but more strategic as he guides boys and girls in applying techniques of critical evaluation emphasized in reading instruction to what is seen and heard on the radio and television and through other mass media of communication. As our society continues to change to a technological one, more and more types of employment are requiring skill in reading. Furthermore, as long as competition among nations is based to a large extent on technological achievements, there will be a premium on knowledge that can best be attained through reading. The printed page reaches millions still untouched by electronics; and for those who can take advantage of the newer devices, reading still serves unique purposes. It is many things to many people. It is a telescope, because through it we can look at the distant stars and speculate about life on them. It is a microscope, because through it we can not only examine the chromosomes and the atoms but also infer those minute particles that even the finest lenses cannot reveal. It is a never-ending wide-screen film on which the human pageant passes in review. It is still the only known time machine that can recreate the events of the past and open up the vistas of the future. Primitive man calls reading magic, and he is right.

Reading is essential to the existence of our complex system of social arrangements. But it is more than that. It is the means by which every age is linked to every other. It makes possible man's capacity for "time binding," the ability to perceive himself and the fluid universe around him in the historic process. If all the inventions of a hundred years were destroyed and only books were left, man could still be man, in the sense intended by the idealists, the poets, the great creators. Reading is a humanizing process.

PUBLIC INTEREST IN READING ABILITY

In view of these values it is not surprising that there has always been much concern over the question of whether Johnny is learning to read. In our own country, from the days of the *New England Primer* to the present, adults have eagerly watched their young take their first faltering steps in the world of print. Each year they spend hundreds of millions of dollars to make reading instruction possible. Each year more than 10 percent of all new books published are for children. Today, the public concern with reading ability is reflected in many popular books, magazine articles, pamphlets, newspaper columns, and editorials devoted to the subject. Surely the teacher of reading is engaged in work of vital importance to the public.

EFFORTS OF THE TEACHING PROFESSION

The teaching profession has responded to the public interest by constant intensive efforts to discover ways of improving reading instruction. For example, the National Society for the Study of Education has devoted many of its scholarly yearbooks to the subject. These include *The Report of the Committee on Silent Reading* (edited by Horn, 1921); *The Report of the National Committee on Reading* (edited by Gray, 1925); *The Teaching of Reading* (edited by Gray, 1937); *Reading in High School and College* (edited by Gray, 1948); *Reading in the Elementary School* (edited by Gates, 1949); *Adult Reading* (edited by Clift, 1956); *Development in and through Reading* (edited by Witty, 1961); and *Innovation and Change in Reading Instruction* (edited by Helen M. Robinson, 1968, Part II of the 67th Yearbook of the society).

Conferences devoted to reading and the language arts are sponsored annually by colleges and universities. Many of these schools—for example, the University of Chicago, the University of Pittsburgh, Temple University, and Claremont College—have published or continue to publish regular volumes of proceedings. Numerous organizations—notably the National Council of Teachers of English, the National Conference on Research in English, the American Educational Research Association, the International Reading Association, and the College Reading Association—devote much or all of their attention to problems in the teaching of reading.

The International Reading Association (IRA) publishes the *Reading Teacher,* the *Reading Research Quarterly,* and the *Journal of Reading.* It publishes the proceedings of its annual convention and of its pre- and postconvention conferences and institutes as well as of its world congresses. Reports of convention highlights and bibliographies on specific aspects of reading are part of the IRA program of publications. The College Reading Association publishes quarterly the *Reading World,* which also includes articles of interest to elementary-school teachers and supervisors. It, too, publishes the proceedings of its annual conferences.

The National Council of Teachers of English, founded in 1911, has always concerned itself with the problems of reading. Two of its magazines, *Elementary English* and the *English Journal,* frequently carry articles related to reading.

Agencies other than professional teachers' organizations contribute to our knowledge of the teaching of reading. Independent periodicals, such as the *Journal of Educational Research,* the *Elementary School Journal,* and *Education* are but a few examples.

We are at present on the verge of a great expansion of reading research because of the use of computers and improved means of communication. The number of individual research studies has increased phenomenally in recent years. In the revised edition of this book it was reported that 4,000 research studies in reading had been published in England and America since 1880. Today there are each year so many studies in reading that the annual summaries cannot mention them all, much less evaluate them. Moreover, methods of information retrieval and dissemination are constantly being developed. Thus in 1966 the U.S. Office of Education established the Educational Resources Information Center (ERIC/CRIER), a nationwide information system, with its national office in the National Institute of Education, Washington, D.C., and special clearinghouses—at present, eighteen in number—in universities and other institutions throughout the country. The new ERIC Center for Reading and Communication Skills (ERIC/RCS), established in 1972, is located at the headquarters of the National Council of Teachers of English, Urbana, Illinois. It supersedes the Clearinghouse on Teaching of English (NCTE/ERIC), whose earlier headquarters were with the office of the National Council of Teachers of English, Urbana, and the Clearinghouse on Reading (ERIC/CRIER), formerly located at Indiana University. Documents available through ERIC/RCS are in addition to the various magazines dealing with libraries and literature for children. Here is a source of much information which persons interested in the field of reading can utilize. Tapes, microfiche cards, abstracts, and so on, on reading, as well as on English, speech, journalism, and theater, from kindergarten through graduate school can be obtained from Urbana.

All of these discussions, investigations, and reports have not led to complete agreement about methods of teaching reading. Indeed, the differences of opinion are often sharp and the debates sometimes acrimonious. Nevertheless, there is a substantial body of agreement on many important issues. For example, it seems clear from the research that no one method is best for all children under all circumstances, that children differ widely in the kinds of instruction they need. It seems clear also that a wide variety of approaches must be used in order to get best results with most children. We have learned much about the psychology of reading, about the role of emotion, motivation, home background, and other factors in reading retardation. We have learned most of all, perhaps, about the nature and extent of individual differences in reading.

INDIVIDUAL DIFFERENCES IN READING

Individual differences among children provide, possibly, the greatest challenge to the teacher of reading. Although all teachers know there are differences among their pupils, many are not fully aware of the vast range of those differences. What they need to learn is the fact that these differences are normal, that they exist at birth and increase as the children grow older. Children differ in every identifiable characteristic—in height, weight, color of hair and eyes, intelligence, home background, emotional adjustment, and educational achievement—to name but a few.

The more complex a skill is, the greater the differences in ability are likely to be. Since reading is a highly complex skill, children differ greatly in their reading needs and achievement. They show variation in the extent to which they are prepared to begin reading when they first enter school. The range in reading ability among pupils in any grade is very wide. Indeed, the better the instruction, the greater the probable range in a classroom. Even among pupils who make equal scores on reading tests, the differences in the *nature* of reading problems and of the reading abilities that produced the scores are significant and numerous.

THE COMPLEXITY OF READING

Reading is a challenge to the teacher also because it is such a complex process. Reading is not a general ability but a composite of many specific abilities. It is therefore necessary to break down general comprehension into the specific skills that constitute it. It is necessary to inquire how well the child is able to grasp the general meaning of a passage; how well he can differentiate between fact and opinion; how well he can follow directions; how well he can interpret maps, graphs, and tables; how well he can organize what he reads and classify ideas; how well he can visualize what he reads; and how well he can locate information.

A single reading skill, although a very important one, well illustrates the complexity of reading. Any teacher who undertakes to cultivate, for example, children's critical discrimination in reading finds that he is dealing with a whole cluster of abilities that often need special attention. Among these are classifying ideas, distinguishing between fact and fancy, establishing cause and effect relationships, making generalizations, interpreting idiomatic and figurative language, making inferences, recognizing emotional reactions and motives, judging relevancy, and drawing general conclusions.

READING AND KNOWLEDGE

Reading is an important means of introducing the child to the surrounding world. In this fact we find our opportunity as well as our challenge. Through reading the child can view ever-widening horizons and explore ever-new areas in the world of things, people, and events. School need never be dull as long as there are books to tell about the earth, the sea, the sky, faraway places, events past and present, or the plants and animals and physical phenomena around us.

It must require some ingenuity to turn the study of our wonderful world into a dreary chore, but somehow we at times succeed in doing so. Consider, for example, the plight of the fifth-grade child filling in the blanks of a workbook that demands in what part of New England hay is raised or what the present population of New Jersey is. Very few elementary-school children want to know these facts or have any idea of what to do with them when they find them.

Contrast this picture of an elementary-school child with that of one who has discovered a special issue of the *National Geographic Magazine* dealing with our Eastern states or become absorbed in a book about our national parks or the life of a great hero. The difference is that in the one case the pupil is engaging in an essentially purposeless activity; in the other he is actively reaching out for information to satisfy his curiosity and to find answers to his own questions.

The pupil's knowledge is, in part, the distillation of his impressions gained from abundant reading. The residue left by these impressions keeps growing and changing as his contact with the world of reality through experiences with books expands. For this reason many teachers encourage their pupils to read whole books about important topics rather than merely a few pages in a textbook. The availability of reliable, interesting books for children in nearly all areas of study has fundamentally altered the pattern of instruction in many elementary-school subjects. The key to learning, therefore, is the cultivation not only of the ability to read but also of the love of reading. Young children must be helped to think of reading as an activity with an inherent appeal. The child who loves to read is father to the man who keeps informed through reading.

READING AND PERSONALITY

Reading involves skill and it involves thinking, but considered in its broader sense it affects the entire personality. The world of people and events encountered on the printed page may shape a reader's attitude toward his fellows, toward school, toward parents, and toward life in general. It may heighten his appreciation of the physical world about him or give him a sense of excitement about the future. On the other hand, it may cause perplexity, fear, or anxiety. The teacher bears a great responsibility for exposing the learner to opportunities for selection of appropriate reading matter and for providing expert guidance in the interpretation of what is read.

Especially to the young child in school, successful and happy experiences with reading will determine in great measure his feelings about himself and his social environment. He knows, often before he starts school, that success in reading is essential to success in school. He may be afraid of the reading task or frustrated when he has difficulty or rebellious to all adult authority. It is incumbent on the teacher to make the child feel comfortable and at ease and to give him many opportunities for successful experiences that build self-confidence.

READING AND CITIZENSHIP

Intelligent participation by the citizen of today in the society in which he lives requires an understanding of the forces that in one or two generations have changed the face of the earth. The awakening of the backward nations with their starving populations, the decline and near-disappearance of colonialism, the increase of Communist power in many parts of the world, and the growth of neutralism among the uncommitted nations are factors to be understood if news and commentary in newspapers and magazines are to be intelligible. Along with this understanding must come a keener realization of the dangers of modern war, made infinitely more destructive by the "knowledge explosion" of the last few decades. Our century has already dwarfed all the thousands of years of previous history in its capacity for the destruction of human life and the creation of human misery. All reasonable men and women need knowledge and a sense of moral responsibility to halt the devastating forces in our civilization and to replace them with constructive efforts. Informed discussion, made possible through wide reading, can help to provide these.

To meet the constant demands for great decisions, decisions that affect the future—even the survival—of the human race, we need an informed electorate. But we also need an informed leadership. The greatest of our statesmen have been well-informed men—men with a wide reading background, knowledge, and the ability to use the knowledge of others in specific areas. The future leaders of local, state, and national governments, of industry and finance, are at this moment passing through the most critical stage of their apprenticeship in our elementary-school classes. If their early experiences in school help them to read critically when critical reading is required, to lay the right foundations, we may look to wise and knowledgeable leadership later. The teacher of reading in the elementary school has, indeed, a heavy responsibility.

NEED FOR IMPROVEMENT IN READING INSTRUCTION

As we consider the many values that can be attained through reading, statistics such as these gathered by the U.S. Office of Education spur us on to action:

- One out of every four students nationwide has significant reading deficiencies.

- In our large city school systems up to half of the students read below expectation.

- There are more than three million illiterates in our school population.

- About half of the unemployed youth, ages 16–21, are functionally illiterate.

- Three-fourths of the juvenile offenders in New York City are two or more years retarded in reading.

- In a recent U.S. Armed Forces program called Project 100,000, 68.2 percent of the young men fell below Grade 7 in reading and academic ability.[2]

The correction of this situation, which Allen, formerly U.S. Commissioner of Education, justifiably labels as "shocking," involves teachers of reading in the elementary school. That they are accepting this challenge is evidenced by the devoted interest in improving reading instruction shown by the members of the teaching profession, as they seek to provide the learner with needed reading skills and to instill in him the desire to make reading a worthwhile lifetime habit. It is the purpose of this book to help the teacher meet this challenge through description (1.) of the reading process, (2.) of the ways in which children learn to read, and (3.) of procedures effective in cultivating steady growth in reading.

For Further Study

Allen, James E., Jr., "The Right to Read: Education's New National Priority," *The First R: Readings on Teaching Reading,* Sam Leaton Sebesta and Carl J. Wallen, eds. (Chicago: Science Research Associates, 1972), pp. 7–13.

Allen, James E., Jr., "The Right to Read—Target for the 70's." *Elementary English,* vol. 47 (April 1970), pp. 487–492.

Bond, Guy L., and Miles A. Tinker, *Reading Difficulties: Their Diagnosis and Correction,* 2nd ed. (New York: Appleton-Century-Crofts, 1967), Ch. 1.

Cushenbery, Donald C., *Reading Improvement in the Elementary School* (West Nyack, N.Y.: Parker Publishing Company, 1969), Ch. 1.

Durkin, Dolores, *Teaching Them to Read* (Boston: Allyn and Bacon, Inc., 1970), Ch. 1.

Harris, Albert J., and Edward R. Sipay, *Effective Teaching of Reading,* 2nd ed. (New York: David McKay Company, 1971).

[2] James E. Allen, Jr., "The Right to Read—Target for the '70's." *Elementary English,* 47 (April 1970), p. 488.

Sandberg, Herbert H., "Needed: Teachers to Revitalize Reading." *Proceedings of the College Reading Association: Professional Variety in Reading*, Clay A. Ketcham, ed., vol. VIII, (Fall 1967) (Syracuse, N.Y.: College Reading Association, Reading Center, University of Syracuse, 1967), pp. 135–139.

Smith, Nila Banton, *Reading Instruction for Today's Children* (Englewood Cliffs, N.J.: Prentice-Hall, Inc., 1963), Ch. 2.

Questions and Comments for Thought and Discussion

1. What arguments have you seen in print or heard attempting to indicate that reading is less important now than formerly? How would you answer these arguments?

2. What are values to be attained by the effective reader? Which of these can also be achieved through activities other than reading?

3. You may be interested in reading the book *Need Johnny Read?* by Frederick Goldman and Linda Burnett, published by Pflaum, Dayton, Ohio, in 1971. If you read the book, you may wish to report your reaction to the claims made to your class.

4. That there is a relationship between learning to read and personality has frequently been noted. Teachers and writers have often pointed out that defects in personality are at times a cause of problems in learning to read. Not as often has it been observed that failure to learn to read can be the cause of development of undesirable personality traits. What observations have you made that support the claim that there can be a reciprocal relation between the ability to read and personality traits?

5. What criticisms on the teaching of reading have you heard or read about? To what extent do you consider them justifiable? Unjustifiable?

Outline for Chapter 2

THE CONCEPT OF READING

The Components of Reading
    Word Recognition as a Component of Reading
    Comprehension as a Component of Reading
    Other Components of Reading
The Reading Process
    Reading as Symbolic Behavior
    Visual Shapes, Sounds, and Meanings
    Eye Movements in Reading
      Nature of the Movements of the Eyes
      Comparison of Eye Movements of Effective and
        Ineffective Readers
      Eye Movements, Cause or Symptom?
Elements Important to Growth in Reading
    Physical Health
      Sight
      Hearing
    Mental Health
    Intelligence
    Background of Experience
    Maturity
    Purpose and Interest
    Reading Skills

CHAPTER 2

The Concept of Reading

A teacher's understanding of what reading is determines to a large extent the objectives and procedures employed in instruction and in evaluation. Many definitions and explanations of reading have been proposed, some complementary to one another, others contradictory. The list of quotations which follows is representative of both the similarities among some points of view and the marked differences among others.

Reading means getting meaning from certain combinations of letters. Teach the child what each letter stands for and he can read.[1]

The process of learning to read in one's native language is the process of transfer from the auditory signs for language signals, which the child has already learned, to the new visual signs for the same signals.[2]

Reading is not a simple mechanical skill; nor is it a narrow scholastic tool. Properly cultivated, it is essentially a thoughtful process. . . . It should

---

[1] Rudolph Flesch, *Why Johnny Can't Read and What You Can Do about It* (New York: Harper & Row, 1955), pp. 2–3.
[2] Charles C. Fries, *Linguistics and Reading* (New York: Holt, Rinehart and Winston, Inc., 1963), p. 120.

be developed as a complex organization of patterns of higher mental processes.[3]

Reading thus is the process of giving the significance intended by the writer to the graphic symbols by relating them to one's own fund of experience.[4]

Reading is an act of communication in which information is transferred from a transmitter to a receiver. . . .[5]

Reading is responding. The response may be at the surface level of "calling" the word. It may be the somewhat deeper level of understanding the explicit meaning of sentence, paragraph or passage. . . . It may involve going beyond the facts to the discovery of new and personal meanings.[6]

. . . reading has been described as social interaction between the author of the book and the student.[7]

. . . reading is the meaningful interpretation of printed or verbal symbols.[8]

Reading begins with the management of signs of things. It begins when the mother, holding the child's hand, says that a day is "beautiful" or "cold" or that the wind is "soft." Reading is "signs and portents," the flight of birds, the changing moon, the "changeless" sun and the "fixed" stars that move through the night. Reading is the practical management of the world about us.[9]

The premise on which this book is based is that reading is more than knowing what each letter of the alphabet "stands for," a definition suggested by the first of these quotations. Nor do the authors think of reading as a process as inclusive as that to which Jennings subscribes in the last citation. They limit the use of the term to reading of written material, though they recognize that understanding of "signs and portents"—of the world around us—is essential to reading. They endorse the point of view that reading involves more than word recognition; that comprehension is

[3] Arthur I. Gates, "Character and Purposes of the Yearbook," *Reading in the Elementary School*. Forty-Eighth Yearbook of the National Society for the Study of Education, Part II, Nelson B. Henry, ed. (Chicago: The University of Chicago Press, 1949), p. 3.

[4] Emerald V. Dechant, *Improving the Teaching of Reading*, 2nd ed. (Englewood Cliffs, N.J.: Prentice-Hall, Inc., 1970).

[5] Frank Smith, *Understanding Reading: A Linguistic Analysis of Reading and Learning to Read* (New York: Holt, Rinehart and Winston, Inc., 1971), p. 12.

[6] David Russell, "Personal Values in Reading," *The Reading Teacher*, vol 15 (December 1961), pp. 172–178.

[7] Robert C. Ziller, The Social Psychology of Reading," *The Reading Teacher*, vol. 17 (May 1964), p. 587.

[8] Albert J. Harris and Edward R. Sipay, *Effective Teaching of Reading*, 5th ed. (New York: David McKay Company, 1971), p. 13.

[9] Frank C. Jennings, *This Is Reading* (New York: Teachers College Press, 1965), p. 1.

an essential of reading; that without comprehension no reading takes place; that in reading the reader reacts to what is recorded in writing; that his reaction is determined to a considerable extent by his past experience, both firsthand and vicarious; that what the reader brings to the page is as significant to reading as what is actually written on it. Thus, the emphasis in this book is placed on "reading as a process involving meaningful reaction to printed symbols."[10] Points of similarity between this concept of reading and that expressed by some of the other writers quoted are readily perceived.

THE COMPONENTS OF READING

Insight into the teaching of reading can be gained as one considers the question: "What are the chief components of reading?" The answer will be predicated in part by the definition of reading to which one subscribes. If one thinks of reading exclusively as translation of the written symbols into sounds, then it would follow that word recognition would be the sole component. If one regards reading as "a meaningful reaction to printed symbols,"[11] then comprehension is one of the major aspects of reading.

Word Recognition as a Component of Reading

The conception which for several centuries prevailed in American schools was that reading was a relatively mechanical skill. The degree of excellence in reading was determined by the ability to recognize words. If the highest level in which a pupil could readily recognize words was a fifth reader, fifth-year-reading ability was attributed to him regardless of whether he could comprehend what he was reading. It is little wonder that there should at that time be a dominance of oral reading in the classrooms of this country.

The idea that reading is chiefly skill in recognizing words, particularly during the initial stages of learning to read, is again enjoying support in respectable and influential quarters. Today the favorite expression of adherents to this view of reading is *decoding* the printed page—that is, recognizing the oral equivalent of the written symbol. The principle on which the decoding concept rests is that language is, at base, spoken communication and that writing or print is merely a graphic representation of speech. The process is therefore one of discovering the correspondence between the *grapheme* (the written or printed symbol) and the *phoneme* (the speech sound). In other words, as seen by those who stress reading as decoding, the basic task of the teacher during the initial stage of learning to read is

---

[10] Paul A. Witty, Alma Moore Freeland, and Edith H. Brotberg, *The Teaching of Reading: A Developmental Process* (Boston: D.C. Heath and Company, 1966), p. 8.
[11] *Ibid.*

to teach the child the sound or sounds of each letter of the alphabet and the combinations of some, such as the *st*. It would not, however, be correct to infer that all advocates of decoding are opposed to emphasis on comprehension in later stages of learning to read. Many emphatically assert that after the code of letter and sound equivalence has been mastered, attention should be paid to comprehension skills.

Comprehension as a Component of Reading

The vast majority of teachers do not give endorsement to the claim that the individual who knows the code, who can recognize words, can read. To them, comprehension is an absolute necessity in all reading. They assert that familiarity with the code is not enough to assure any type of activity worthy of being designated as reading. While many argue that reading at all stages of development must necessarily be much more than proficiency of word recognition, they do admit that somehow or other, sooner or later, the effective reader needs to have learned the code used in written communication so that he can translate the written symbols into sound or meaning symbols. Thus, they view both word recognition and comprehension as major aspects of reading.

Other Components of Reading

Many educators have pointed out that word recognition or word perception and comprehension do not comprise the total of the reading act. Gray[12] also includes *reaction* and *fusion*. By *reaction* he refers to the reaction of the reader to what he has read. This aspect of reading may be thought of as critical reading. By *fusion* he refers to assimilation of ideas gained through reading with the reader's former experiences. Like many other specialists in the field of reading who have been interested in determining the components of reading, Gray emphasizes the fact that the four aspects he identifies—word recognition, comprehension, reaction, and fusion—have interactions one on the other and, frequently, when efficient reading is taking place, are not dealt with by the reader as separate components.

Helen M. Robinson[13] agrees with the four aspects that Gray has designated, and she adds a fifth one—rates. David M. Russell[14] designates *utilization* of what is read as the aspect of reading that usually appears as the final step in reading. In fact, he claims that unless most reading is used for a purpose, the act of reading has, in a sense, not been completed. Ac-

[12]William S. Gray, "The Major Aspects of Reading." *Sequential Development of Reading Abilities*, Helen M. Robinson, ed., Supplementary Educational Monographs, No. 90 (Chicago: The University of Chicago Press, 1960), pp. 8–24.

[13] Helen M. Robinson, "The Major Aspects of Reading." *Individualizing Reading Instruction: A Reader*, Larry A. Harris and Carl B. Smith, eds. (New York: Holt, Rinehart and Winston, Inc., 1972), pp. 10–12. Reprinted from *Seventy Years of Progress*, Supplementary Educational Monographs, No. 96 (Chicago: The University of Chicago Press, 1966).

[14]David M. Russell, *Children Learn to Read* (Boston: Ginn and Company, 1961), pp. 110–112.

cording to Russell, reading serves a purpose when, for example, an individual follows directions he has read, when he obtains information of value in solving a problem confronting him through reading, or when he receives enjoyment from what is he reading.

Not all writers concur with either Gray, Robinson, or Russell in their designations of the aspects of reading. There are other classifications of the components of reading.[15] Regardless of which is accepted, it is evident that reading is not a simple activity. Let us, therefore, next consider the reading process itself.

THE READING PROCESS

What happens in reading? The reader is looking at an object in the form of a book or magazine or a billboard or a road sign. Most commonly the object consists of paper, usually white. On the paper appear certain marks, made, as a rule, by the application of dark-colored ink. That is all—just ink marks on white paper. And yet looking at those marks may cause the reader to turn pale, as in the case of a letter containing bad news; or to laugh, smile, cry, or hold his breath in suspense. A laboratory test would reveal that a reader's pulse rate may at times rise sharply when he looks at those curious marks on paper. How can the sight of those marks bring about such mental and physical experiences?

There is no *meaning* on the page, only ink. The meaning is in the reader's mind. Each mark is a signal that arouses some image or concept that is already in the mind of the reader. The order in which these images and concepts are evoked, the context in which they are called forth, and the relations among these concepts and images as revealed by the arrangement of the marks make it possible for the reader to gain new meanings. But the process depends on what the reader brings to the printed page and on the questions he asks.

It has often been said that reading is an *active* process. Good reading is a searching out, a reaching for meaning. The child must go to the printed page with anticipation, with questions, with specific intent. A person turns to a newspaper with the purpose of finding out what has happened recently. He searches the headlines and chooses a story that arouses his curiosity. He reads the story in order to find out what the headline means. He gets real meaning from what he reads because he has asked questions as he has gone along.

Reading as Symbolic Behavior

Man communicates through symbols. A symbol may be a physical act, such as a grimace, a smile, a nodding of the head, or an upraised hand in a dis-

---

[15] Helen M. Robinson, *op. cit.*, pp. 7–9.

cussion. Traffic lights and highway signs are symbols. Spoken language is a complex set of symbols consisting of various combinations of speech sounds. Any representation perceptible to the senses may serve as a symbol.

In reading we employ visual symbols to represent auditory symbols. The basic task in reading is therefore to establish in the mind of the reader automatic connections between specific sights and the sounds they represent. Since the sounds themselves are symbols of meanings, the process of reading involves a hierarchy of skills ranging from sensation (as the eyes via the optic nerve serve as reporters to the brain of what is recorded in writing) through perception (when the mind attaches meaning to what is reported as a sensation). How the mind interprets the visual stimuli will depend primarily on the background of experience of the reader — on what the reader brings to the written material. Mental activities involved in reading include such higher thought processes as association between symbols and meaning, memory, organizing, making inferences, predicting outcomes, judging the accuracy of statements, arriving at generalizations. Thus, reading is both a visual activity and a thinking process.

Visual Shapes, Sounds, and Meanings

In approaching written or printed material the child typically converts the visual shapes of letters and words into their corresponding sounds. At the beginning he probably utters the sounds aloud or to himself. The sounds then evoke in his mind the images and meanings they represent. As he gains proficiency, he depends less and less on the sound "bridge" between visual stimulus and meaning, although a faint awareness of speech sounds is probably always present in reading. If the sound images continue to be prominent in the child's reading, he will develop habits of vocalization and possibly lip movement. Both speed and comprehension may then suffer. The connection between visual stimulus and meaning must become as direct as possible as soon as possible.

Eye Movements in Reading

Through the study of the movements of the eyes while reading, insight has been gained into the reading process. Various methods have been employed in reading laboratories and clinics to investigate the eye-movement behavior of readers. One of the most common methods has been photography. One instrument, the ophthalmograph, makes motion picture records of eye movements in the process of silent reading. The subject is asked to read a passage on a card. As he reads, a ray of light is directed toward his eyes. As the light reaches the eyes, the corneas reflect it on a moving film. The film thus records the movements of the eyes.

Nature of the Movements of the Eyes

The eyes of the efficient reader move across the line of writing in a series of rhythmical leaps referred to as *saccadic movements*. They stop, move, stop, move, as reading along a line of writing progresses. The stops that the eye makes between the saccadic movements are known as *fixations*, and the saccadic movement between fixations is referred to as the *interfixation movement*. The *fixation time* constitutes by far the greatest proportion of the time spent reading — probably over 90 percent of it, while the time of the movement of the eyes from one fixation to the next is less than 10 percent of the total. The part of a line that a reader perceives at a fixation is called the *perception span*. The length of the perception span and consequently the number of fixations per line are determined to a large extent by the difficulty (for the reader) of the material and by the purpose the reader has.

At times a reader makes a backward or reverse movement from a point of fixation to one previously "read." This movement is known as a *regression*, which may be due to a variety of causes, among them problems in vision, lack of establishment of the left-to-right orientation in reading, difficulty of the material. Or regressions may be made to reinforce the message conveyed through the writing. Thus, regressions need not necessarily be undesirable. The efficient reader at times makes regressions to "cinch a point." It is the large number of aimless regressions that interfere with reading efficiency.

Comparison of Eye Movements of Effective and Ineffective Readers

In the initial stages of reading the child's eyes may wander over the page in search of familiar words. As competence grows, under the skilled guidance of the teacher, he learns to confine his observation to one line at a time and to move in a habitual progression from left to right. At first, the duration of each fixation will tend to be relatively long — perhaps as much as nine-tenths of a second. There will be many fixations per line. There will be many regressive movements in which the reader will make return movements to words that were not recognized or comprehended the first time. When a word gives special difficulty, there may be many regressions, and the ophthalmograph film would show a period of confusion. After much experience, and especially when interest is high, the duration of each fixation will decrease and the number of fixations per line will become steadily smaller. Eventually, as the child masters the basic skills and increases his stock of words recognized at sight, he becomes able to read each line in a fairly regular, rhythmical series of fixations, with a minimum number of regressive movements. By the fourth grade the frequency of fixations and the number of regressions commonly tend to level off somewhat (always provided that the material is within the reader's comprehension and the basic eye-movement habits have become reasonably well established.) Some studies seem to show an additional spurt at the beginning of the junior-high-school period and indicate that the normal growth in the rate of reading may continue until grade 10. Individual differences and training will affect each child's rate of growth, and it must be emphasized that improvement in both rate and comprehension may be brought about at any age.

Differences in eye movements of effective and ineffective readers can be summarized by stating that the effective reader, compared with the less effective one:

1. Has more rhythmical (less jerky) saccadic movements,
2. Makes fewer fixations per line,
3. Makes fewer aimless regressions,
4. Has a more accurate return sweep.

Eye Movements, Cause or Symptom?

That there are differences in eye movements between effective and ineffective readers is not a matter of controversy. The point of debate is whether those characteristic of the ineffective reader are the cause of his ineffectiveness. If they are, there would be reason to attempt to help him improve his eye movements. It is on this supposition that many of the pacing devices are based, and it is on this belief that, in general, much of the work in "speed-reading courses" is founded. However, many persons in the field of the teaching of reading, including the authors of this book, regard regular eye movements as symptom rather than cause of effective or ineffective reading. They consider as questionable the efforts that have been made, in many instances, to pace a child's eye movements by means of mechanical devices. Their recommendation is that the reader with ineffective eye movements be given guidance in acquiring improved methods of word attack and greater efficiency in other reading skills. They believe that the basic efforts of instruction should be to focus on meaning and to provide abundant opportunity for contact with the printed word in normal, well-motivated reading situations. Then, as through these efforts, a child improves in ability to read, his eye movements will, without special attention to them, increasingly resemble those characteristic of the fluent reader.

ELEMENTS IMPORTANT TO GROWTH IN READING

To gain further insight into the nature of reading, let us consider some of the elements important to growth in reading. Some of these factors—those described in this chapter—are:

1. Physical health
2. Mental health
3. Intelligence
4. Background of experience
5. Maturity
6. Purpose and interest
7. Reading skills

Fortunately, nearly all children come to school already possessing most of these elements in some degree. A minority of children learn to read in spite of the lack of some of these elements. Blind, deaf, and sick children can learn to read. But to the extent that children are lacking in the elements named, they will be handicapped in the process of learning to read.

The teacher and the school do not bear exclusive responsibility for providing all the necessary conditions. Other agencies, especially the family, bear major responsibility for some of them. The school, however, is inevitably involved, in one degree or another, in helping to create all of the conditions that contribute to growth in reading.

When we specify those factors in child development that are basic to success in reading, we are not suggesting a hierarchy of educational values. Physical and mental health, for example, are ends in themselves. They do not become important merely because they contribute to good reading, as though reading were the supreme purpose of the school. But since this book is concerned with methods of teaching reading, it must necessarily take the broad developmental context into account.

Physical Health

We know that a reasonable measure of physical health is essential to all school learning. Physical discomfort, languor, a low energy level, and similar symptoms of health problems may often interfere with normal progress in reading. Nervous tension and even ordinary physical fatigue can reduce enjoyment and interest in reading, with a consequent decline in efficiency. Vitamin deficiencies and endocrine disturbances have been associated with poor reading. Dechant[16] mentions "hemoglobin variation, vitamin deficiencies, nerve disorders, nutritional and circulatory problems, heart conditions, infected tonsils, poor teeth, rickets, asthma, allergies, tuberculosis, rheumatic fever (or) prolonged illness" as possible factors in reading retardation. Frequent absence from school resulting from illness necessarily retards progress in reading and may produce attitudes of aversion or indifference toward reading.

[16] Emerald V. Dechant, *Improving the Teaching of Reading*, 2nd ed. (Englewood Cliffs, N.J.: Prentice-Hall, Inc., 1970), p. 53.

We must let the clinician determine whether a case of extreme reading retardation may be attributed to physical causes. For our part as teachers we must do all we can in the classroom to promote the physical well being of our pupils. Free and inexpensive school lunches help to provide needed nutrition. (In one school, a pupil who was considered lazy proved to be just hungry.) We can help to provide a healthful physical environment in school —good light, proper humidity and temperature, appropriate seating. We can arrange for periods of rest and exercise.

In addition to attention to the general well being of pupils, both the sight and hearing of those about to learn to read should be checked, and attention paid to these factors throughout the school life of the child whenever there is reason to suspect a problem.

Sight

It has been estimated that about one-fourth to one-half of elementary-school children are in need of visual correction. One of the first questions the reading clinician asks about the nonreader is: "Does this child have satisfactory eyesight?" The child who must strain his eyes to read is not likely to enjoy the process and will usually try to avoid reading. If his vision is so poor that even with considerable effort it is difficult or impossible for him to differentiate between the forms of letters, success in reading will be delayed until he is given reading materials printed in type that he can read comfortably. All teachers should be alerted to signs of visual difficulties among their pupils.

It must not be assumed, however, that poor vision is generally the chief cause of poor reading. Cases of nearsightedness, farsightedness, astigmatism, muscular imbalance, and lack of fusion are found among both good and poor readers. Nevertheless, in good readers, as well as in poor readers, such conditions tend to result in fatigue and consequent loss in reading ability. Quite probably nearly all readers—slow, normal, and superior—who have visual defects would improve in reading ability if their defects were corrected.

Visual handicaps among children may be of many kinds. While the classroom teacher should not undertake to make a diagnosis of the difficulty in any individual case, he should be aware of the common types of visual deficiencies in order that he may know when a child should be referred to a specialist. In addition to the more usual phenomena of nearsightedness, farsightedness, and astigmatism, the eye specialist often encounters cases of monocular vision. In normal vision both eyes receive the image of an object, and the two images are fused in the process of perception. This kind of seeing is called binocular vision. Some individuals, however, ignore or suppress the image received by one eye and consequently "see" with only one eye. In some cases the individual alternates between one eye and the other; in other cases he alternates between monocular and binocular vision.

Since most reading involves near-point vision, it is important for the teacher to recognize the difference between far-point and near-point vision. A child whose vision tests normal when looking at a distant object but who has great difficulty in seeing an object singly and clearly at a distance of fourteen inches or less is in need of attention. Preschool children tend to be farsighted. For this reason, teachers in the first and second grades should place heavy reliance on the chalkboard and on large charts. Children who have visual difficulties should be seated near the chalkboard. Long periods of near-point reading should be avoided.

Hearing

A child who suffers from hearing loss is at a distinct disadvantage. He will, for example, have difficulty in benefiting from the teacher's oral explanations. Especially if the child is taught by predominantly oral-phonetic methods, auditory acuity is important in the process of learning to read. The child with hearing loss will have inadequate or inaccurate auditory images of the words he reads and consequently may encounter difficulty in word recognition.

As in the case of visual defects, hearing loss may be no more common among poor readers than among good readers. Nevertheless, all readers who have deficient hearing ability would probably be aided in reading performance if they received appropriate attention from parents, teachers, and physicians.

Estimates vary as to the number of children who have significant hearing defects. One of the most conservative estimates places the percentage of children with considerable hearing loss at $1\frac{1}{2}$ to $3\frac{1}{2}$ percent of all children. Other findings suggest as much as 30 percent for girls and 50 percent for boys. Whatever the precise figures may be, we are safe in concluding that careful attention should be given to the hearing ability of all pupils.

Mental Health

Among the basic developmental needs of children that affect growth in reading is a feeling of security, of being accepted and loved, and of being adequate to the tasks they are expected to carry out. The importance of an adequate self-concept to growth in learning of various types has been established by research at all levels of learning.[17]

Everyone performs better in any activity if he has self-confidence, a feeling of successful performance, and a strong desire to achieve. One cannot learn well, in reading or in anything else, if he is distracted by anxieties, frustrations, and the sense of failure. For this and other reasons, effort is made in modern schools to build wholesome attitudes in children, to give them a sense of belonging and a feeling of being accepted and re-

[17]Arthur W. Combs, Donald L. Avila, and William W. Purkey, *Helping Relationships* (Boston: Allyn and Bacon, Inc., 1971), p. 151.

spected, and to provide many success experiences. Good reading is best carried on in a classroom atmosphere that is warm, friendly, and relaxed.

To assure success for every child in the process of becoming an efficient reader, the teacher must know the child's capabilities. Expecting either too high or too low an achievement from him will mitigate against a feeling of accomplishment. For the same reason the teacher needs to ascertain the level of reading ability for each boy and girl, and then, in the light of his knowledge, adapt the reading program to the capacity of the learner. It will, in the case of many boys and girls, be necessary to point out to them signs of growth, such as an ability to identify new words, to comprehend better what they read, to read more advanced materials. Though praise needs to be deserved to be effective, the capable teacher, intent on finding the good in every situation, will usually not strive in vain to find reasons for sincere praise.

A success experience need not necessarily be in a reading activity in order to result in growth in reading. Any experience that builds the child's feeling of general adequacy will help to increase his zest in attacking difficult reading situations and to remove the distractions and anxieties that result from the fear of failure in school.

Increasingly, teachers are realizing the significance of the relation between social and emotional factors and beginning reading. They recognize that the child accustomed to the give-and-take of a social group, especially of his peers, will be likely to adjust more quickly to the school situation and consequently will be likely to be ready to read sooner than the child who has lacked contacts with other boys and girls. Also, since reading is taught primarily in group situations, the child who does not feel at ease with others is less likely to be able to attend to the reading. Teachers also realize that such a child is less likely to enjoy what he reads when reading in a group, unlike the child who feels comfortable with his agemates.

Maladjusted home situations or poor family relationships have been shown to be contributing causes in many cases of reading disability. As one writer put it: "Children bring their families to school." They come with all the attitudes and predispositions that were formed in the home and neighborhood during those influential first years of life. Children who are overprotected or the victims of parents who are overambitious for their children, or boys and girls who are unwanted or neglected or insecure because of conflict between parents or because of the loss of one or both of them are often handicapped in their efforts to learn. On the other hand, children who come from stable home situations, who are accepted and loved by their parents clearly approach the reading task with great advantage.

When home conditions are unfavorable to the child, it is the responsibility of the school to take these conditions into account and to compensate for them as much as possible. Some children of normal or superior intelligence fail to learn to read because of emotional difficulty, severe anxiety, or insecurity that develops at the time they are first faced with the reading task. The cause may be the arrival of a new baby, parental hostility, or a feeling of anxiety on the part of the parents concerning the child's reading progress—an anxiety that is easily communicated to the child. Worries of this kind interfere with the concentration so necessary in making the fine discriminations involved in reading. Moreover, children who face serious emotional problems frequently have difficulties with such other aspects of language communication as articulation or listening comprehension. Such shortcomings, in turn, contribute to retardation in reading.

The cause-and-effect relation between emotional and social immaturity and poor reading is sometimes reversed. Often, to be sure, lack of various characteristics of the maturing emotional and social life can have a detrimental effect on reading, but the fact must not be overlooked that frequently inability to read well is a cause of personality defects. The child who cannot read, no matter how normal he was in his emotional reactions when he entered school, is likely to develop undesirable personality traits if he cannot enter into the reading activities that form a large part of the typical elementary-school day. Aggression, withdrawal, irritability, and other forms of unsocial or antisocial behavior are often the visible manifestations of a personality thwarted because it cannot engage in activities satisfying to others in the classroom.

Intelligence

It is known that a fairly close relation exists between intelligence and the ability to read. This relation, however, may be ascribed, in part, to the fact that intelligence tests and reading tests set many tasks that are similar. The fact that the correlation between performance on intelligence tests and reading tests usually tends to be very high may mean merely that a large part of an intelligence test calls for abilities closely related to the ability to read. Moreover, it must be remembered that cultural background and present environment are likely to affect performance on both reading and intelligence tests. Then, too, our general notion of intelligence places a high value on academic learning—including reading. Nevertheless, whatever the reasons may be, it has been demonstrated that in our culture, and under present conditions in American schools, a child has a better chance of success in reading if he has average or above-average intelligence. If we define a child's intelligence as the rate at which he is able to learn, we may assume that the rate of his growth in reading is affected by and limited by his intelligence.

How a teacher defines intelligence is likely to make a difference in the relation he finds between intelligence and reading. It may also affect the results he will achieve with the boys and girls he is teaching. If we define intelligence as the rate at which an individual is able to learn, we may assume that the rate of his growth in reading is affected by his intelligence.

If intelligence is thought of as an inherited ability the role of the school and the teacher is to provide an environment that will help the child function up to his ability. But there is reason to believe that in the early years of a child's life, environment may have a considerable effect not only on learning but also on what is commonly considered as intelligence.

Background of Experience

If it is true that success in reading depends on what the reader brings to the printed page, much significance must be attached to the body of direct and indirect experiences he has accumulated in advance of the reading. The child's prior stock of impressions will determine in large measure how much meaning he will derive from the visual symbols before him. These impressions will include both the things that have happened to him directly and the symbolic experiences he has had with reading, listening, viewing motion pictures and television, and the like.

A simple example illustrating the point that written symbols acquire meaning for the reader because of his previous experiences is that of a reader who encounters what to him is a new word, the word *hogan*. The writer states that a hogan is a circular house used by the Navaho Indians as a dwelling. He may go on to give further details—the materials of which these houses are built, the presence or absence of windows and doors, and similar information. The reader has had previous experience with the letters of which the word is composed and he is able to pronounce it, but he has never before encountered the word *hogan,* nor has he ever seen a hogan. How can this curious visual symbol have meaning for him?

Hogan acquires meaning for the reader because he has had direct experience with other words and ideas in the sentence. These words arouse images in his mind because he has encountered in personal experience the ideas and images they represent. He has seen a circle, and he has had experience with houses. Encountering the concepts of *house* and *circle* in a specific relation to each other, the reader is enabled to create a new image in his mind—an image approximating a hogan—which he has never seen. Thus, through the combination and recombination of familiar words, images, and concepts, the reader builds new meanings, which in turn provide the basis for further understandings.

It becomes apparent that the fundamental elements in reading comprehension derive from direct experience. References to such concepts as anger, love, hate, reconciliation, warmth, pain, light, and dark can have meaning for the reader only in the degree to which he has in one way or another had experience with them. Not only does direct experience facilitate the acquisition of meaning from the printed page but it also creates the conditions for that keen interest in reading that is so essential to reading growth. For example, a person who has visited the headquarters of the

United Nations will read with redoubled insight and pleasure a story in *The New Yorker* about a reporter's visit to the same place; a boy who is assembling a stamp collection will read a book about stamp issues with an intensity of interest that would most likely not exist in a boy who does not pursue this hobby. Thus, the reading of recent history also takes on significance and life as the reader recognizes in historical scenes the flesh and blood realities he knows from his own past. The depth and range of his comprehension will depend in part on the length and richness of that past.

Basic to all the reading experience through which children learn is the direct contact with things, people, and events. It has been argued that the concepts usually encountered in reading material are common to the experience of most or all children and that the instructor's primary task is to teach the recognition of the printed symbol. Such an argument overlooks the wide diversity of the environments of children in the country or in the city, in mining or industrial towns, in slums or wealthy suburbs, in cattle country or fishing villages. For example, consider the difference in the understanding that a country boy, especially one from the West, and a city boy might bring to a passage dealing with the branding of cattle, in which words such as *range, corral, gelding* are used!

Consideration of the bearing of an individual's background on his ability to read with comprehension forces one to recognize the handicaps that a child from a culturally different environment experiences in the process of learning to read. If no adaptation in instruction is made to appreciate and accommodate the language base he possesses when he comes to school, the achievement outcomes are likely to be affected negatively to a marked degree.

Maturity

One of the aspects of maturity for reading is the degree of physical growth and development, which, with most young children, is indicated primarily by age—though there is notable variation in the accuracy of number of years of living as an index of physical maturity. The extent to which age should be taken into consideration in planning the reading program for the learner is a matter of dispute. Undoubtedly physical growth alone cannot serve as reliable determiner of when, for example, reading instruction should begin. Due consideration needs to be given to many other characteristics of the learner discussed in this section of the chapter. Thus, the emphasis to be placed on physical maturity will vary greatly from individual to individual.

While physical maturity is primarily and usually a characteristic not influenced greatly by environmental factors over which the school has much control, there are aspects of maturity, amenable, as a rule, to educational influences, that should figure prominently in reading instruction.

For example, maturity as a condition for success in beginning reading is determined, in part, by the ability of the child to demonstrate persistence at a task and to exhibit attending behavior. His social and emotional development also greatly influence his skill both in working alone and with others in the classroom. His ability to profit from directions or suggestions from his teacher also reveals the extent to which he is oriented to school learning.

Purpose and Interest

The desire to read is the motivating force that leads to reading. It may be the desire to have needed information or to spend a pleasant leisure hour. Some boys and girls in the initial stage of learning to read will want to learn because they wish to identify with adult activities. Others will be eager to learn to read because it has been held up to them at home as a rewarding experience, possibly indirectly through the reading of interesting stories to them. But for still others these are not sufficient motives in the early stages of learning to read. Another motive, emphasized by Busch[18] and many teachers, can be interest in story content.

In any case, whether readers are beginners or are in the later stages of reading development, the desire to read arises from a sense of need for reading. The sense of need can be cultivated by creating the necessary conditions.

Desire eventuates in purpose, which clarifies the direction effort shall take. Thus, the emphasis in reading guidance should be placed not upon arbitrary teacher-direction, but upon the awakening of pupil desire, the release of pupil energy, and the development of pupil self-direction. The teacher's aim is to guide, to lead—not to coerce; but the pupil must supply the voluntary effort if real learning is to take place.

Especially in the initial stages of reading, the factor of good motivation is of prime importance. Motivation is not a mere mechanical preliminary to the reading itself but is the result of the teacher's providing or helping the pupil to discover clear goals. If the child's first experiences with reading are purposeful, he will be started on the road to meaningful reading. We cannot start him with a set of skills, mechanically acquired without reference to meaning, and then expect him later to put them to use in meaningful reading.

The principle of reading with a purpose, of *active* reading, has clear implications for reading assignments. We must not send children to the printed page without adequate preparation for the reading. A good assignment, as a rule, includes a discussion that will orient the pupil to the material he will encounter. It helps him to formulate questions to be answered

[18] Fred Busch, "Interest, Relevance and Learning to Read," *What Children Read in School,* Sara Goodman Zimet, ed., (New York: Grune & Stratton, 1972), pp. 19-26.

and to visualize clearly the uses to which the information is to be put. It gives him some notion of the nature of the material to be read and the manner in which the material is to be approached. It helps him to anticipate some of the key words and perhaps the pronunciation of unfamiliar proper names. In short, the good assignment helps the pupil to establish clear purpose for the reading. Perhaps the best assignments are self-assignments. Such assignments arise out of problems, discussions, and activities that call for further information. The search may be initiated by the individual himself, by a committee, or by the class as a whole.

The reading connected with a unit of instruction may involve various purposes. Reading may be done as preliminary exploration or browsing in a variety of books for the purpose of general orientation to the subject of the unit. This would be a period of "sampling," a get-acquainted period to indicate the nature of the area to be studied. It may be done as differentiated research, where each pupil pursues some special aspect of the main topic. Reading may also be done for the purpose of outlining and organizing what has been read in various sources.

The number and types of purposes for which individuals read are almost unlimited. Children and young adults have many things that they want and need to know. They want to know what the good radio and television programs and movies are, and what makes them good; how to apply for a position and how to behave in an interview; what makes wars and how they might be prevented; how they can be more popular among their friends; what they can believe in the newspapers; how they can get along better at home; where they can get the truth about the trouble spots around the world. They want to know about labor, prices, employment, and new scientific advances. They want to know what they must do to be safe when riding a bicycle, driving a car, or repairing a light switch. They want to know what attitudes they should assume toward sex, courtship and marriage, ethics, and religion.

The task of the school is to assist the reader in carrying out his purposes. If he is frustrated by obstacles too numerous and too great in the form of vocabulary burden or complexity of thought, he will soon give up his purposes or seek to achieve them by means other than reading. Too many young readers have abandoned the spontaneous search for meaning in books because they did not receive appropriate guidance. But if they are given the encouragement and opportunity, they will often avidly explore every aspect of experience, asking more questions than the wisest and most learned can answer.

Closely related to purpose in reading is interest. Children are most likely to read with comprehension those materials that deal with topics of interest to them. In fact, it has been found that some pupils are able to read stories at a level of reading difficulty far beyond their normal abilities if the subject is one in which they are vitally interested. Thus, a boy who follows professional baseball closely may successfully read a sports story in a newspaper even though it is several years beyond him in reading difficulty.

Children's interests are at least in part the result of the experiences they have had. They are closely related to the activities of play and work which constitute their daily living. Many of these interests are common to all boys and girls. Others are common only to boys or only to girls. Some are related to the earlier, others to the later, ages. Still others arise out of individual experience and are affected by the special aptitude or background of the individual. Since interests are learned, rather than inherited, it is possible to extend both their range and their quality. Any activity that will open new fields of exploration to children can help to expand a pupil's reading interests and his mastery of the printed page. Reading should, therefore, be taught in the setting of a wide variety of purposeful enterprises designed to expand the child's range of interests. Radio, television, films, field trips, class projects, group discussion involving the exchange of experiences —all these are methods by which the ground may be prepared for ever more zestful and meaningful reading.

Reading Skills

The omission thus far of a discussion of the specific skills involved in the act of reading itself has been intentional. We felt that because so much of formal reading instruction has stressed the mechanical skills of word recognition and sentence comprehension, a heavy emphasis on the background factors in reading growth was needed here. Nevertheless, no consideration of the development of reading competence would be complete without careful attention to the matter of specific reading skills. Later chapters will discuss these in detail.

Some children acquire the necessary skills without formal instruction. Given the various conditions described earlier in this chapter and an environment that is in every respect conducive to reading growth, they learn from the beginning to get meaning from the printed page and almost unconsciously develop the habits of word recognition and comprehension of sentences and longer units. For such children the analytical reading drills can be more harmful than helpful.

Most children, however, can be materially aided by specific instruction in reading skills. They can make more rapid improvement if they can be shown how to recognize letters and phonic elements; how to discover familiar structural elements in the longer unfamiliar words; how to use context clues; how to note details; how to find the main idea of a longer passage; how to compare, evaluate, and visualize the author's intended message; how to locate and utilize needed information; how to follow printed directions; how to adapt rates of reading both to the nature of the material read and to the purpose of the reader. These skills can be learned through guided practice. In no case must there be neglect of either the factor of interest or the factor of skill in reading. Fortunately the two can go hand in hand since skill development is affected favorably by motivation. The child who recognizes the need for acquiring a skill is more likely to attain his goal than the one who lacks purpose for learning it.

For Further Study

Douglass, Malcolm P., ed., *Reading in Education: A Broader View*. Part I, "On the Nature of the Reading Process," containing articles by R. Van Allen, Peter L. Spencer, Clyde Curran, and Malcolm P. Douglass (Columbus, Ohio: Charles E. Merrill Publishing Company, 1973).

Harris, Albert J., and Edward R. Sipay, *Effective Teaching of Reading* (New York: David McKay Company, 1971) Ch. 1, "What Is Reading?".

Henderson, Richart L., and Donald R. Green, *Reading for Meaning in the Elementary School* (Englewood Cliffs, N.J.: Prentice-Hall, Inc., 1969).

Karlin, Robert, *Teaching Elementary School Reading: Principles and Strategies*. (New York: Harcourt Brace Jovanovich, 1971), Ch. 1, "Emerging Concepts of Teaching Reading."

National Society for the Study of Education, *Innovations and Change in Reading Instruction*. The Sixty-Seventh Yearbook of the National Society for the Study of Education, Part II, Helen M. Robinson, ed. (Chicago: The University of Chicago Press, 1968), Ch. 1, "What is 'Reading'? Some Current Concepts," by Theodore Clymer.

Smith, Frank, *Understanding Reading: A Psycholinguistic Analysis of Reading and Learning to Read* (New York: Holt, Rinehart and Winston, Inc., 1971).

Spache, George D., and Evelyn B. Spache, *Reading in the Elementary School*, 3rd ed. (Boston: Allyn and Bacon, Inc., 1972), Ch. 1, "Ways of Thinking of Reading."

Stauffer, Russell G., *Teaching Reading as a Thinking Process* (New York: Harper & Row, 1969), Ch. 1, "Reading a Thinking Process."

Zimet, Sara Goodman, ed., *What Children Read in School* (New York: Gruene & Stratton, 1972), "Interest, Relevance and Learning to Read" by Fred Busch, pp. 19–26.

Questions and Comments for Thought and Discussion

1. It may be helpful to you to decide on a definition of reading to which you can at the present time subscribe. As you continue the study of how to teach reading, you may want to modify your definition. In fact, it is strongly recommended that you think of the one you now accept as subject to possible change as you gain more insight into the teaching of reading.

2. What are some of the implications for classroom practice that you see in the light of your tentative definition of reading (item 1 above)? Keep an open mind as you continue your study of the teaching of reading, not only in regard to the formulation of a definition of reading which you can accept but also in regard to its implications for classroom teaching.

3. We have noted the significant role of purpose and interest in learning to read. As you recall the early days in your own learning-to-read process, can you find evidence where either purpose or interest or lack of it had a marked effect on your growth in reading? If you were greatly interested in learning to read or in reading, to what causes do you attribute your interest? If interest and purpose were often lacking, can you think of ways in which teachers could possibly have stimulated enthusiasm for reading in you?

4. Have you noted any evidence to support the statement: ". . . what the child is able to learn may be a function of the teacher's expectation of him"? If so, be prepared to present the supporting evidence.

5. If you have the opportunity to observe a classroom while reading is being taught, note ways in which the procedures used indicate that the teacher thought of reading as a cognitive or thinking process.

Outline for Chapter 3

LANGUAGE DEVELOPMENT AND READING

The Interrelatedness of the Language Arts
Language Development of the Child
    Stages in the Development of Language
    Sequence and Timing in the Pattern of Language
      Development
    Factors Affecting Language Ability
Language as a Thinking Process
Concept Development
Dialect Speech
    What Is Dialect Speech?
    Acceptance of Dialect

3

CHAPTER

Language Development
and Reading

As we were referring to elements essential to growth in reading in Chapter 2, we observed that one of the factors in the experience background of the child that he brings to reading is language equipment. Since language development is such an important determiner of the success with which he learns to read, we will next examine somewhat in detail various points concerning language development that warrant careful consideration when planning a reading program for the elementary-school pupil. Implications of their bearing on the teaching of reading will be pointed out.

THE INTERRELATEDNESS OF THE LANGUAGE ARTS

Fundamental to a clear understanding of the process of teaching reading is an awareness on the part of the teacher of the close relationship among all four facets of the language arts—listening, speaking, reading, writing. A reading program that ignores the fact that reading is inextricably interwoven with the other language arts not only defeats, in part, its own purpose but also seriously jeopardizes the success of the programs in oral communication and in writing. Wide experience with all kinds of language, including extensive contacts with words and sentences in meaningful situations, contributes effectively to the improvement of reading. Growth in reading usually is best produced not from a program of isolated drills but from a rich, diversified, and stimulating language environment and a curriculum that provides for many kinds of highly motivated language experiences.

We note the importance of recognizing the interrelatedness between oral communication and reading as we consider a group of children who visit a fire station and see the engines, ladders, fire extinguishers, and other equipment. If they do not hear the words that identify the objects they see, they have not been adequately prepared for later reading about firemen and fire fighting. It is necessary to introduce them to the verbal symbols in association with the observation of the objects and the processes. Much discussion and explanation of terms should therefore accompany the direct experiences the school provides. If direct experience is to be of substantial aid in reading, it must be accompanied by an adequate fund of experience with language.

Linguists—persons who have specialized in studying the science of language—have contributed much to the growing awareness of teachers of the interrelatedness between oral and written communication. One of the tenets on which linguists agree—and there are many points of disagreement among them—is what they refer to as "the primacy of speech" over written communication. They stress the fact that in the development of the child, as in that of races, speaking precedes writing. Linguists interested in the application of their findings to the curriculum of the school point out the importance of building on the child's skill in oral communication when teaching reading.

As the teacher introduces the child to language in print, he relates the child's speech system to written language by using words and voice modulations familiar to the learner. He tries to give him confidence in his ability to express himself orally and then, in turn, to comprehend what he sees in writing. Highlighting each child's linguistic assets in oral communication may, in time, minimize the use of such terms as *disadvantaged, deprived,* and *denied* which are frequently employed to designate the learner who has difficulty in reading due to factors in his background.

The boy and girl with a well-developed speaking and listening vocabulary have an initial advantage in reading, both in word recognition and in comprehension, over the child with a limited vocabulary. To be sure, textbooks for beginners in reading are generally designed so that the meaning of words used is familiar to the average beginning reader. Those boys and girls to whom many words are unknown—as is often the case with children from culturally different homes—are, however, faced with a stupendous task unless the teacher takes into consideration the problems they encounter. (*See* Chapter 14, "Reading and the Child from the Culturally Different Home.") Lack of command of oral language continues to affect the success of a child in many basal reading textbooks even beyond the beginning stages of learning to read, for an increasingly larger proportion of words whose meaning he does not know are typically introduced in these books. Nor is the degree of excellence of the vocabulary of the child the only factor in his oral language that affects reading. His familiarity through speech with the syntax or sentence structure of the language he is learning to read also serves as a determiner of his ability to comprehend what he sees in writing, even if he were not handicapped by unfamiliarity with many of the words in what he is reading. We recognize that a good command of the oral language is one of the greatest assets a child who is learning to read can possess, even though we do not concur with those who assert that writing is merely recorded speech.

What is known as the language experience approach to reading instruction constitutes one of the methods of teaching beginning reading that emphasizes the interrelatedness of the language arts. Typically, in such an approach, after the boys and girls have discussed an experience they have had, they, with the guidance of their teacher, plan the content of a "story" or report, which the teacher records on the chalkboard or on large sheets of paper. The boys and girls receive practice valuable in learning to read through use of the written material they have dictated to the teacher. For example, after the children have had a Halloween party they could discuss it, decide what they want to have recorded about it, and when the teacher has written the report learn to read it.

Recognition by the teacher of the interrelatedness of the language arts is not only essential in the initial stage of learning to read; it is important at all stages of growing toward effectiveness in reading. Procedures such as discussion, oral work on vocabulary, explanation by the teacher can be as valuable in guiding twelve-year-olds in reading a selection as it is with six-year-olds.

Though there is a close relationship between the various facets of the language arts that the teacher of reading should not ignore, there are also many differences among them. Consequently, effective guidance of boys and girls in acquiring efficiency in any one of them requires attention also to the unique problems in learning them. If the teacher of reading, for example, places an undue emphasis on the likenesses, he may slight the many skills specific to effective reading. Although in the past many reading teachers have not made adequate use of the other language arts, teachers should now beware of overemphasizing these other facets in relation to reading. Let us recognize both the similarities and dissimilarities, and teach accordingly.

LANGUAGE DEVELOPMENT OF THE CHILD

We next examine the nature of the development of language as it provides insight into the teaching of reading.

Stages in the Development of Language

Language development begins in earliest infancy. Universally, infants exhibit prelinguistic behaviors, when there is much experimentation with their vocalizing apparatus in cooing, crying, and murmuring. Although the sounds are made with minimal language consciousness or control, they are extremely important in later development, resembling, as they do, vowel and consonant sounds. Generally, between the ages of six months and a year, the baby enters the babbling stage in which he exercises some control, though limited, over the sounds he produces. He converts them from the vocal noises made by all normal babies to those particular components of the speech community into which he was born. When he is about a year old, he makes one-word utterances.

The child's linguistic development continues so that by the time he enters the elementary school his knowledge of language is vast. After approximately six years of listening to speech and five years of expressing himself in words, he has gone far toward mastering the basic structure pattern of English in declarative, interrogative, exclamatory, and imperative sentences. Never in all the later years of his life will the child even dimly approximate the stupendous growth in power of oral communication that he has made in his first five or six years. In subsequent years he will but refine his already acquired skill in oral communication. As he continues this improvement in his command of language, as in earlier stages, he shows a steady development rather than sudden spurts.

Sequence and Timing in the Pattern of Language Development

The sequence in the development of oral communication skills is essentially the same for all normal children. Unfortunately, however, the details of language development as they affect the step-by-step procedures of oral and written communication in the elementary school have not been established. The timing of the appearance of various phases in the developmental sequence shows marked variation from one individual to another. This lack of consistency among boys and girls constitutes one cause for vigorous attempts by the teacher to adapt the language arts program to the differences existing among the individuals whom he teaches.

Factors Affecting Language Ability

Since there exists a close relationship between listening, speaking, reading, and writing, any influences affecting one of these facets is likely to have a significant bearing on the others. Intelligence is one potent factor serving as a determiner of language development. As established by the innate pattern of the individual, intelligence, in that it determines the potentialities for growth, marks the level of development that is possible. However, environment plays a significant role in determining the extent to which these potentialities will be realized and in what manner they will be developed.

One of the major characteristics of language is that it is social at its base. It is the human response that helps stimulate the growth of speech. The tireless care that parents provide the fortunate infant in introducing him to the spoken word gives rise to the very characteristic that helps make him so human; this is speech. But just as the response to and interaction with others encourages speech, so, conversely, the lack of an abundance of speech causes children born into neglect, without favorable companionship, to be deprived of the opportunity to develop into fully functioning human beings until other factors may compensate for this deprivation.

By hearing and gradually comprehending the speech of those around him, the child learns to understand vocabulary before he speaks. Although the usual source of speech stimulation for the young child is the mother, communicative interactions with other adults and with siblings can stimulate verbal growth. Indeed, the role of impersonal sources, such as television and radio, is serving as a significant contributing factor in children's acquisition of words. All these environmental factors have a bearing on the nature of language growth.

The influence of environmental factors affecting language growth is further indicated by the following:

1. A favorable socioeconomic background tends to stimulate language development.
2. The extent and richness of the child's experience background determine in part the development of his communication skills.
3. In general, girls excel boys in language abilities. However, differences within a sex are much more pronounced than those between the sexes.
4. A critical attitude toward the child's power in oral and/or written communication on the part of his associates, either adults or peers, can have a detrimental effect on his progress in language development.
5. Frequently there exists a reciprocal relation between a child's concept of himself and his language ability. A poor self-concept may cause problems in language learning, and conversely, deficiency of language skill may cause personality problems.

LANGUAGE AS A THINKING PROCESS

With the realization, emphasized more and more in recent years, that reading should be viewed as a thinking process, the teacher of reading should be aware of the total language system of the learner as one involving thinking.

Language is essentially a vehicle for transmitting meaning. Through listening and reading an individual can acquire meaning expressed by others; through speaking and writing he can convey it to others. Though meaning is conveyed by words, meanings are not in words themselves. They lie in the interpretation people give to words. Consequently, they may differ from one individual to another. For example, the word *range* may mean something quite different to a boy brought up on an iron range of Minnesota than it does to one who all his life has lived on a cattle ranch on the wide plains of the West. The word *elevator* may not have the same connotation for a city child living in an apartment house that it does for the farmer boy whose father takes his wheat to a grain elevator. Thus, the meaning of a word is often affected by the background of the listener or reader, as well as by the speaker and writer.

Since the transmission of meaning frequently is made through words and since in that transmission a selective process of possible meanings takes place, both in choosing the words to convey meaning and in interpreting those used by another, it is apparent that thinking is frequently, if not always, a concomitant of both oral and written communication. With this point in mind we will not teach reading as a set of mechanical operations but as a skill in which the higher thought processes need to be in operation if comprehension on a level beyond literal translation is to be stimulated. To be sure, there is great variation in the depth of thinking required to comprehend various messages. "The sun is shining" will for most elementary-school children require none of the higher thought processes, but the statement: "The height of the tides along Cook Inlet exceeds that anywhere else along the Pacific Coast" may.

CONCEPT DEVELOPMENT

Concept development constitutes one illustration of how growth in language ability is intimately related to reading. Thinking takes place as vocabulary is developed and concepts are formed through experiences—first-hand or vicarious—which enable an individual to attach meaning to words he sees or hears. Let us consider, as an illustration, the word *silo*. It acquires meaning for a city-dwelling child as he hears about a silo, sees a silo or a picture of one, or reads about one. On the basis of his background of experiences he forms a concept of what a silo is. In time he can differentiate between silos and other farm buildings. Similarly, a child living in the country learns what an escalator is if he is provided with sufficient experience to enable him to differentiate between an escalator and an elevator. If a concept is not fully developed, if as a basis for thinking the learner has insufficient background or fails to utilize all needed factors in that background, he may attach erroneous associations to a word. For example, living in an apartment, a duplex, a cottage, or a bilevel house may lead the child without wide experience—first-hand or vicarious—with homes other than his own kind to form an incorrect concept of the word *home*. The influence of culture on meanings is obvious in the case where the word *home* means an igloo to one child and a twenty-story apartment house to another.

Higher thought processes are required as a child forms concepts by (1.) seeing similarities among situations where there are also differences— as in the case of the word *home*, for example—and (2.) then formulating a generalization from his observations. The larger and more abstract the concept is, the greater the need for wide and repeated experiences to gain insights and for involvement of thought processes. For instance, it would be easier for the child to conceptualize meanings attached to the word *book* than to the word *catechism*.

The teacher's role in the development of concepts is first of all to help supply the child with adequate background. He should also provide guidance, if needed, in inductive thinking, where the learner notes details of similar objects or situations which he perceives and then forms generalizations on the basis of his observations. Let us refer again to the development of a concept of the word *silo*. In inductive learning the teacher may need not only to provide the child with various illustrations and descriptions of silos but also help him in noting what silos have in common, thereby assisting him in making a generalization as to what a silo is and thus guiding him in developing a concept. The development of concepts often requires time on the part of the learner. Yet teachers sometimes become impatient with a child's inability to form these concepts quickly. An appreciation of the complex nature of speech as an expression of meaning and as a facet requiring thought when exercising it will indicate the importance of time in the development of many concepts.

DIALECT SPEECH

During recent decades, as never before, emphasis is being placed on the problems of the child from a culturally and/or economically disadvantaged home. Much attention is being placed on the alleged possibility of improving the child's language skills so that achievement of mobility from a "lower" to a "higher" cultural and economic level will be more readily possible for him. Preschool programs with a language focus such as Head Start, have this as one objective. These programs have not always been conceived with care and implemented with the caution that an individual's language, of which his dialect is a part, is an integral part of him; that it reflects how he has learned to feel, think, and speak as part of the culture into which he was born; that it is inseparable from his evolving self-concept. Teachers, too, have frequently failed to demonstrate these ideas in their classroom conduct, with the result that havoc has often been played with the child's concept of himself. Such failure to take into consideration the crucial need of the child to respect his language on the part of the teacher can interfere seriously not only with the emotional development of the child but also with his school learning.

One of the major points of concern in the focus on the linguistic development of the child from the culturally different or economically disadvantaged home has been his dialect. As in the case of other concerns about his language, it has often not been dealt with judiciously. One problem has been the lack of clarity with which the word *dialect* is often used.

What Is Dialect Speech?

An explanation, rather than a definition, of the term *dialect speech* is probably the most illuminating for our purpose.

Dialect speech has characteristics which are associated with geographical region, social class, or national origin. Typically, the term *dialect speech*, when referring to the speech of children, has been used to designate that of the immigrant child from a non-English-speaking country and that of the American-born child from a non-English-speaking home. Also the speech of many American boys and girls from English-speaking families, whose speech differs markedly from so-called standard English, is usually considered dialect. But, in a sense, all native-born Americans speak a dialect of English. This statement may come as a surprise to some. An anecdote illustrative of the inability of persons to recognize the pervasiveness of dialects in our country is reported by H. Rex Wilson[1] who states:

> A recent addition to American folklore tells of a Texan who welcomed the presidency of Lyndon Johnson with the comment, "At last we have a President who doesn't talk with an accent."

As we ponder the effect that a greatly divergent dialect may have on a child's growth toward maturity in reading, we must not make the error of assuming that the only problem such a child may have, because of his dialect, lies in the sound characteristics of his speech. Dialects differ also in vocabulary and in meaning associated with the words used. Furthermore, syntax or the pattern of phrase or sentence formation of many dialects diverge so much from that of the so-called standard American English and from the English used in most textbooks that the problem lies there too.

Acceptance of Dialect

As people move around more and more from one section of the country to another, they will hopefully come to the conclusion that they themselves

---

[1] H. Rex Wilson, "The Geography of Language," *Linguistics in School Programs*. The Sixty-Ninth Yearbook of the National Society for the Study of Education, Part II, Albert H. Marckwardt, ed. (Chicago: The University of Chicago Press, 1970), p. 64.

speak a dialect. Teachers, too, as their knowledge of language increases, will increasingly recognize that all dialects of American English have rules governing them and that they are legitimate forms of English, portraying, in part, the culture of the social group of which they are representative.

A cause of difficulty in teaching reading to some children may possibly be avoided by the teacher who does not attempt to teach a pupil to speak a different dialect at the same time that the child is beginning to learn to read. Many educators agree — the writers of this book among them — that it is not necessary to change the dialect of an English-speaking child in order to teach him to read. The child speaking a divergent dialect reads the sounds of his own speech as he reads English. The learner's natural dialect, unchanged, can be the immediate bridge to the skills of literacy without forcing him to learn a new dialect as a prerequisite. The issue of whether, during the initial stage of reading instruction, there is evidence enough to support this conclusion is discussed in Chapter 14 of this book.

As we have thus far viewed reading in perspective, we have noted that learning to read is a continuous process, that it is a part of an intricate pattern of growth and development, and that each factor and each specific skill must be considered in relation to all others. These points of view are basic to our discussions throughout the book.

For Further Study

Baratz, Joan E., and Roger W. Shuy, eds., *Teaching Black Children to Read* (Washington, D.C.: Center for Applied Linguistics, 1969).

Bloom, Benjamin S., Allison Davis, and Robert Hess, *Compensatory Education for Cultural Deprivation* (New York: Holt, Rinehart and Winston, Inc., 1965).

Cole, Michael, and Jerome S. Bruner, "Preliminaries to a Theory of Cultural Differences," *Early Childhood Education*. The Seventy-First Yearbook of the National Society for the Study of Education, Part II, Ira J. Gordon, ed. (Chicago: The University of Chicago Press, 1972), pp. 161–179.

Douglass, Malcolm P., ed., *Reading in Education: A Broader View*. Part II, "Reading and Early Language Learning," containing articles by Joan T. Kunz, James L. Hymes, Jr., Ronald Macaulay, Margaret E. Smart, John Downing, Lois Fair Wilson, and R. Van Allen (Columbus, Ohio: The Charles E. Merrill Publishing Company, 1973).

Fishbein, Justin, and Robert Emans, *A Question of Competence: Language, Intelligence, and Learning to Read* (Chicago: Science Research Associates, 1972).

Goins, Jean, "Visual and Auditory Perception in Reading," *The Reading Teacher* vol. 13 (October 1959), pp. 9–13.

Goodman, Kenneth S., E. Brooks Smith, and Robert Meredith, *Language and Thinking in the Elementary School* (New York: Holt, Rinehart and Winston, Inc., 1970).

Lefevre, Carl A., *Linguistics, English, and the Language Arts* (Boston: Allyn and Bacon, Inc., 1970).

Lloyd, Donald, "Subcultural Patterns which Affect Language and Reading Development," reprinted from *Improving English Skills of Culturally Different Youth in Large Cities* (Washington, D.C.: U.S. Department of Health, Education and Welfare, Office of Education, 1964).

National Society for the Study of Education, *Linguistics in School Programs.* The Sixty-Ninth Yearbook of the National Society for the Study of Education, Part II, Albert H. Marckwardt, ed. (Chicago: The University of Chicago Press, 1970).

Shuy, Roger W., "Language Variation and Literacy," *Reading Goals for the Disadvantaged* (Newark, Del.: International Reading Association, 1970, pp. 11–12).

Stauffer, Russell G., *Teaching Reading as a Thinking Process* (New York: Harper & Row, 1969).

Vygostsky, I. S., "Thought and Speech," *Language and Thought*, in *Psycholinguistics: A Book of Readings*, Sol Saporta, ed., Helen Kogan, Eugenia Hanfmann, and Jacob Kasanin, trans. (New York: Holt, Rinehart and Winston, Inc., 1961), Ch. VII.

Zuck, Louis V., and Yetta M. Goodman, compilers, *Social Class and Regional Dialects: Their Relationship to Reading*, an Annotated Bibliography (Newark, Del.: International Reading Association, 1971).

Questions and Comments for Thought and Discussion

1. The interrelatedness of the various facets of the language arts—speaking, listening, reading, and writing—is emphasized in today's reading programs. How can the teacher of reading capitalize on this relationship?

   There are also marked differences among the various facets of the language arts which some teachers in their enthusiastic acceptance of the interrelatedness tend at times to overlook. Can you think of teaching-learning procedures that ignore some of these differences?

2. Can you give an illustration to support this statement: "Thinking takes place as vocabulary is developed and concepts are formed through experiences, first-hand or vicarious, which enable an individual to attach meaning to words he sees or hears."?

3. Emphasis is placed by linguists and by many others on the "primacy of speech" over written communication. What implications for the teacher of reading can this concept have? What problems can arise,

however, if the teacher does not recognize the fact that writing is more than recorded speech?

4. Should boys and girls speaking an English dialect that diverges greatly from the so-called "standard American English" be given, during the initial period of reading instruction, reading materials in their dialect? Name arguments that are or can be proposed on both sides of this question.

5. What are some methods or procedures that you have observed in the teaching of reading that emphasize reading as a "thinking process"? Can you think of additional suggestions for teaching reading as a "thinking process"? Of special interest in relation to this point is the book *Teaching Reading as a Thinking Process* by Russell G. Stauffer, listed under "For Further Study."

6. Do you know of any instances in which teachers have responded to a child's deviation from standard English so as to give him the impression that his dialect is inferior? If so, how might the teacher have responded in an acceptable manner? Can you give instances when a teacher gave the impression to such a child that he considered his dialect different from, but not inferior to, "standard English"?

PART II

Cultivating Growth
in Reading

Outline For Chapter 4A

READINESS FOR READING

CHAPTER

Readiness for Reading

When should reading instruction begin? That is one of the unsettled questions in the teaching of reading.

In the twenties and thirties there were staunch advocates favoring postponement of reading instruction beyond the first grade. Again today there is a small minority of contemporary educators advocating this practice. Their recommendations have, however, never been widely adopted. Typically, in the past it has been assumed that reading instruction should start in the first grade. In fact, until rather recently it was advocated by many persons in the forefront of educational thinking that systematic reading instruction in that grade should be preceded by a so-called reading-readiness period. Often this period extended over a month or six weeks or more for all boys and girls. Frequently, it was even longer for some pupils. It was not unusual for one or more first-grade children in a room to spend the entire year in "getting ready to read." Now, however, educators are seriously questioning the need for a period of reading readiness for many boys and girls in the first grade.

An assumption on which kindergarten programs have been planned ever since the rise of the kindergarten movement is now the subject of marked, at times bitter, disagreement. The argument centers around the role of the kindergarten in teaching reading, as well as its proper place in helping the child to become ready to learn to read.

A more radical position is highlighted as the controversy revolves around the question of whether reading instruction should begin in pre-kindergarten days.[1,2] Of the people favoring prekindergarten instruction in reading some, like Glenn Doman,[3] believe that it should start in the home. Others are of the opinion that provisions for an early beginning in reading should be made through publicly supported agencies.

BASES FOR THE CONTROVERSY ABOUT THE TIME TO BEGIN READING INSTRUCTION

One reason for the debate concerning the optimum time to begin reading instruction is that some commentators refer to formal reading and others to informal reading. There is also lack of unanimity in differentiating between *readiness for reading* and *reading.* For example, some teachers consider learning the letters of the alphabet and the sounds represented by them as part of reading readiness. Others refer to this process as reading. Work with experience charts—records of the experiences of the children—is thought of by some as reading, by others as reading readiness procedure.

Another factor that complicates discussion of the question as to when reading instruction should begin is that teachers differ in the extent to which they will continue into the learning-to-read period some of the types of work begun during the period of reading readiness. One teacher might, for example, at first during the learning-to-read period continue to help boys and girls differentiate between the appearance of letters and words—visual discrimination—a practice he may have emphasized during the reading-readiness period. Another teacher, utilizing a similar procedure before beginning reading instruction, might discontinue it after the children begin to read.

Arguments Advanced for Earlier Instruction

Keeping in mind the difference in interpretation of what constitutes reading readiness, let us examine the arguments advanced for each of the positions favoring earlier instruction in reading to which reference was made in the introductory paragraphs of this chapter.

The Reading Readiness Period in First Grade

Opponents of the practice of having a reading-readiness period as customary procedure in the beginning weeks or months of the first grade point out

[1] Dolores Durkin, *Children Who Read Early* (New York: Teachers College Press, Columbia University, 1966).

[2] Joseph E. Brzeinski, "Beginning Reading in Denver," *The Reading Teacher,* vol. 18 (October 1964), pp. 16–21.

[3] Glenn Doman, *How to Teach Your Child to Read* (New York: Random House, Inc., 1964).

that first-grade children of today differ greatly from boys and girls of a few decades ago in their readiness for reading as far as factors amenable to environmental stimulation are concerned. These persons state that the average six-year old has traveled more extensively, has viewed television programs more frequently, has been in closer contact with people who have seen more of the world, has had more out-of-the-home experiences than children of the preceding generation. Since much of the usual readiness program of the past has consisted of efforts to broaden the pupils' backgrounds, it is claimed that a major purpose for postponement of reading at the beginning of the first grade has already been met by today's entrants to first grade. Furthermore, those favoring elimination of a reading-readiness period at the beginning of the first grade for the average child point out that a greatly increased number of boys and girls now attend kindergarten and that kindergartens avowedly have had as an objective, concomitant with the major aims of the kindergarten, to help boys and girls through ongoing activities to get ready to read. Moreover, many persons opposed to a reading-readiness period for all or almost all beginning first-grade pupils claim that the somewhat formalized instruction boys and girls have often been receiving in the form of reading-readiness exercises—such as discriminating between sounds, between letters, and between words—is either below the learning level of the child or is somewhat irrelevant to the task of learning to read.

The argument as usually advanced against a reading-readiness period in first grade is not against such a period for any one child or group of children in that grade. It is in opposition to a requirement that all or almost all children go through such a stage after they enter first grade. The claim is that only a minority of first-grade entrants are not ready to begin to read. That a sizable number have previously started to read is also pointed out to support the argument against a reading-readiness period for all.

The Role of the Kindergarten in Learning to Read

In the not very distant past it was rather universally conceded that reading instruction had no place in the kindergarten. It was also generally agreed that the activities in the kindergarten that were included, in part at least, to help the child become ready to read should be limited to activities such as helping the child develop emotionally and socially, assisting him in expanding his experiences, and guiding his language development. Efforts to assist him in becoming ready for reading through a systematic program for the development of reading readiness were generally looked on with disfavor. Learning the names of the letters of the alphabet and the sounds they commonly represent was considered entirely inappropriate at the kindergarten level. All these assumptions have been vigorously attacked by educators who support the position that the kindergarten should play a significant role in preparing the child for beginning reading. Many also affirm that a considerable number of boys and girls in kindergarten are ready to learn to read while still on that rung of the educational ladder if the materials and methods are made suitable to their ability. In fact, today the kindergarten in which attention is not given to reading instruction for some boys and girls, as well as to activities closely related to book reading, is probably the exception. The primary concern no longer is: "Should reading be taught in the kindergarten?" Rather, the points of study and debate now focus on these questions:

1. To whom should reading be taught in the kindergarten?
2. What reading should be taught?
3. How should reading be taught?

Reading Instruction in the Preschool Years

Of late, books and magazine articles have been appearing in abundance in which the claim is made that the best time to teach a child to read is in preschool days. An extreme and, on the whole, an untenable position is that taken by Doman, Stevens, and Orem in an article that appeared in the *Ladies Home Journal*, "You Can Teach Your Baby to Read." In it the following often-quoted paragraph appears:

> The best time to teach your child to read with little or no trouble is when he is about two years old. Beyond two years of age, the teaching of reading gets harder every year. If your child is five, it will be easier than when he is six. Four is easier still, and three is even easier. If you are willing to go to a little trouble, you can begin when your baby is 18 months old or — if you are very clever — as early as 10 months.[4]

Doman expanded this article into the book *How to Teach Your Child to Read*,[5] published in 1964.

Evidence Cited

Many books and articles argue for an earlier start in reading by citing evidence that reading has been learned by young children, both on the kindergarten and prekindergarten level.

Studies on the Prekindergarten Level

The work with Montessori[6] materials used in teaching three- and four-year-old children to read in the Whitby School in Whitby, Connecticut, is presented as evidence of effectiveness of early reading (*see* page 504). It must

[4] Glenn Doman, George L. Stevens, and Reginald C. Orem, "You Can Teach Your Baby to Read," *Ladies Home Journal*, vol. 80 (May 1963), p. 62.
[5] Glenn Doman, *op. cit.*
[6] Maria Montessori, *The Montessori Method* (New York: Frederick A. Stokes, 1912).

be remembered, however, that the teaching in Whitby School was not done by parents in the home but by teachers in a school situation. O. K. Moore's work[7] with children of three and four years of age at the Responsive Environment Foundation in Hamden, Connecticut, is also frequently quoted (*see* page 428). The two studies to which reference is made most often in arguing for the effectiveness of reading instruction during the prekindergarten period are a study by Dolores Durkin[8] and the Denver study.[9] A brief report on these studies follows.

A study by Dolores Durkin   Durkin has carried on a longitudinal study with forty-nine children in California who learned to read outside of school. These children were reading at grade levels ranging from 1.5 to 4.6 when they entered first grade. The design of the study was guided by certain general questions, one of which had to do with the frequency of occurrence of evidence of early reading ability. Durkin reported as follows:

> As a way of selecting subjects, a word identification test was individually administered to the beginning first graders ($N = 5,103$) in one city. Children repeating first grade, as well as a small number of children who had been given some instruction in reading the latter part of kindergarten, were not tested.
>
> Following this procedure, 49 first graders (29 girls and 20 boys) were identified as having some ability in reading prior to school instruction. Of these 49 children, 26 (53%) were Caucasian, 12 (24%) were Negro, and 11 (22%) were Oriental. The Oriental background accounted for seven of the ten bilingual children.
>
> Family interview data concerned with socio-economic status indicated that seven of the children in the total group of 49 could be classified as upper-middle class, 15 as lower-middle class, 26 as upper-lower class, and one as lower-lower class. Intelligence test data, obtained from the Stanford-Binet in the second month of first grade, indicated IQ's that varied from 91 to 161, and MA's that varied from 5.1 to 10.7 years. The median IQ for the group was 121, and the median MA was 7.1 years.
>
> Closely following the identification of subjects, and still within the first two weeks of first grade, standardized reading tests were administered. The scores ranged, according to grade norms, from 1.5 to 4.6, with a mean of 2.3. Reading tests administered at the end of the semester and again at the beginning and end of the summer vacation period showed encouraging gains in achievement. By this latter date, for example, the children's grade scores varied from 2.3 to 7.1, while the mean score was 4.0.[10]

[7] Omar K. Moore, "Orthographic Symbols and the Pre-School Child — A New Approach," paper presented at the Third Minnesota Conference on Gifted Children, Minneapolis (October 1960).

[8] Dolores Durkin, *op. cit.*

[9] Joseph Brzeinski, *op. cit.*

[10] Dolores Durkin, "Children Who Read before Grade One," *The Reading Teacher* (January 1961), pp. 163–164. Reprinted with the permission of the author and the International Reading Association.

The boys and girls in Durkin's study initially learned to read at ages varying from three to five. When the children entered first grade the average reading achievement of those who learned at three years of age was 2.6 in terms of grade placement, while that of those who began to read at five was 1.7. At the end of the second grade the group initially learning to read at three was still superior to those who had learned initially at the age of five, but the difference was less than two years before.[11]

Durkin reports the results of her longitudinal studies, which had consumed her attention for ten years, in her book *Children Who Read Early*, a definitive work in the area.[12]

One of the points that stands out in the research by Durkin is that the children were very commonly described by parents, and later by teachers, as persistent, perfectionistic, and competitive children. A majority of them had, their parents and teachers agreed, extraordinary memories and possessed high ability to concentrate. In addition, they were described as curious, conscientious, serious-minded, persistent, and self-reliant. In all instances there were parents who took the time to answer children's questions; and there were older siblings who were both willing and able to teach interested brothers and sisters to read.

The Denver study　Another concern related to early reading instruction —the avowed claim that parents should not teach preschool boys and girls to read—was one of the phases of the teaching of reading investigated by the public schools of Denver under a grant by the Carnegie Corporation. The grant enabled the school system to review and extend its parental instruction program. Much was accomplished in parent education through a series of lessons in the form of television programs and a parents' manual. Brzeinski[13] reports:

> Tests administered to parents showed that they could learn the pilot beginning reading process and use it to help their four- and five-year-olds to read. Also encouraging was the discovery that mothers and fathers who spent a reasonable amount of time [as little as five minutes a day of planned, regular help] preparing their children for reading were quite successful.

Studies on the Kindergarten Level

Arguments for initiating reading instruction in kindergarten include references to experimental studies in which kindergarten children have been

---

[11] Dolores Durkin, "Some Unanswered Questions about Five-Year-Olds and Reading," *Changing Concepts of Reading Instruction*, vol. VI, proceedings of the Annual Convention (Newark, Del.: International Reading Association, 1961), pp. 167–170.

[12] Dolores Durkin, *Children Who Read Early* (New York: Teachers College Press, Columbia University, 1966).

[13] Joseph E. Brzeinski, "Early Introduction to Reading—The Kindergarter." *New Directions in Reading*, Ralph Staiger and David A. Sohn, eds. (New York: Bantam Books, 1967), p. 28.

taught to read. A phase of the Denver studies,[14, 15] with the aid of a grant from the Cooperative Research Branch of the U.S. Office of Education, was designed to ascertain the effectiveness of reading instruction in the kindergarten. Four thousand boys and girls were tested at the end of the kindergarten, as well as at the end of their first, second, and third years in the elementary school. The children who were in the experimental group showed superiority in size of reading vocabulary, in comprehension, and in rates of reading over those in the control group at each of these intervals. Brzeinski, when reporting on the study, also claimed that children who learn to read early enjoy it, and consequently will be more likely to read extensively than other children as a group.

Comments on Arguments for Earlier Instruction

Although an increasing amount of research deals with the question of an early start in reading and a sizable number of experimenters have concluded that on the basis of their work an early start in reading seems desirable, the evidence has not been conclusive. More longitudinal studies will need to be completed before many educators are willing to take anything as a final answer. Evidence undoubtedly shows that children—at least some children—can learn to read earlier than most boys and girls now do. Whether or not it is desirable for many of them to start learning to read at an early age has not been established.

In the Kindergarten

There has been strong opposition by kindergarten teachers and by leaders in the field of child growth and development to systematic reading instruction in the kindergarten. Opponents of reading instruction in the kindergarten argue that because a child of kindergarten age can learn to read is not sufficient reason to conclude that he should be taught reading at that period of his life. James L. Hymes, Jr., for example, sounds this warning: "Everyone loses if we produce early readers but in the process weaken humans. Everyone loses if we produce early readers but in the process kill the joy of reading."[16]

Questions such as these, in addition to those listed on page 52, must be considered in connection with teaching reading in the kindergarten:

1. Does teaching reading require time that should be spent on other types of activities?

[14] Joseph E. Brzeinski, "Reading in the Kindergarten," *Teaching Young Children to Read*, Warren G. Cutts, ed., bulletin 1964, No. 19 (Washington, D.C.: U.S. Department of Health, Education and Welfare, 1964).
[15] Joseph E. Brzeinski, "Early Introduction to Reading—The Kindergarten," *New Directions in Reading* by Ralph Staiger and David A. Sohn, eds. (New York: Bantam Books, 1967) pp. 25–32.
[16] James L. Hymes, Jr., "Early Reading Is Very Risky Business," *Grade Teacher*, 82, (March 1965), p. 88.

2. Are methods used in teaching reading to the beginner in violation of the principles that should govern learning at that stage of the development of the child?

3. Are the children who learn to read in the kindergarten superior in their reading achievement to others by the time they leave the elementary school? (In answering this question care must be taken that children who learned to read early are compared with children equated for intelligence, home conditions, and other factors that may have contributed to making the pupils who learn to read early a selected group, even though it has been claimed that high intelligence is not an attribute of early readers as a group.

4. Is there danger that the child who learns to read early may in later years lose, if he has already acquired, a love for reading?

In Preschool Days

As a group first-grade teachers have been quite vocal in their opposition to teaching reading at home to the preschool child. One argument frequently advanced by teachers is that many parents are not trained to teach reading. However, it would seem doubtful that a child who wants to learn to read before he enters school would be harmed much, if at all, through lack of professional training in the field of reading by his tutor, the parent. Undoubtedly, if preschool reading instruction is proved to be desirable, then it may well be the province of the school or some other agency to provide parents with information on the subject. Some literature is already on the market advising parents as to how to teach their children to read or how to prepare them for reading. The book *Preparing Your Child for Reading* supplements assistance given to parents of kindergarten children in the Denver experiment who listened to a sixteen-lesson television series on the subject. Whether one agrees or disagrees with the methods recommended in any one publication, it cannot be denied that many books could be published to help parents. Furthermore, the schools could sponsor workshops, provide lecture series, give demonstrations, and circulate bulletins designed to assist parents to guide their children in learning to read. One point that should be emphasized in a program of parent education is that no preschool child should be forced to learn to read.

Another contention of many first-grade teachers is that parents should not help boys and girls of preschool age with reading because a parent may use a different method of teaching reading than the one that will be employed in the school. The child may, the argument continues, encounter greater difficulties in reading at school than he would be likely to meet if he had not had parental guidance. However, it seems difficult to imagine that a child taught at home by, let us say, a whole-word method would be handicapped if later at school he were taught by a phonic method, or vice-versa.

Still another reason why many first-grade teachers object to teaching the child to read before he comes to school is that they claim the child will then become bored if he needs to be in a reading group of children without previous reading experiences. That argument is a poor one for the school to offer. A drastic change needs to be made in a lockstep program that requires a child who can read when he enters school to be treated as if he had no knowledge of reading. The school should not discourage a boy or girl from achieving success in any area while he is still at home on the grounds that if the child can read on entrance to first grade the school would not know how to adapt instruction to his needs. If there are others in the room who can read, he can be placed in a group with them alone. If he is the only one who can read, he can be given individualized instruction.

Even though in the preceding paragraphs an attempt has been made to refute the common arguments teachers propose against preschool learning to read, there are serious questions to be raised about preschool reading. Because many preschool children *can* be taught to read, it does not necessarily follow that they *should* be taught to read. "What is to be gained by an early start?" needs to be investigated. More than parental pride in the achievement of a child at an early age must be the underlying purpose. Whether or not the child who learns to read in preschool days is spending time on learning to read that should advisedly be used for other activities is a point to be considered seriously. What effect learning to read at an early age may have on his reading later on, in terms of both reading skills and attitudes toward reading, should also be studied carefully, not only in connection with reading in the kindergarten but also in relation to reading at home on the part of the prekindergarten child.

The extensive research literature on reading readiness now available proves, if nothing else, that the problem related to the time for beginning reading instruction, like all questions associated with human learning in general, is complex and that the need for further investigation is imperative. We must remember, however, when interpreting the research now available and that to be done in the future that we are not dealing with objects on an assembly line but with human beings. The principal object is not to achieve efficiency in putting out a better product, in this case a child who makes better scores on standardized tests. The fullest development, well-being, and happiness of the child is the ultimate end, and reading is but a means to that end. In spite of some of the trends in our national life, we must remember that children are worthwhile for their own sake and that they must not be used to try to prove that our nation and our society are stronger and more intelligent than other nations and other societies. It is a deeply ingrained principle of democracy that the school and society itself exist for the welfare of the individuals who comprise them, not the reverse. This principle has pertinence for the problem of reading readiness.

ASSESSMENT OF DEGREE OF READINESS

When all arguments have been exhausted as to when reading instruction should begin, in the final analysis the decision needs to be made not for boys and girls collectively but for each child individually. In assessing a child's readiness for reading, the question should not be, "Is he ready to read?," but "For what is he ready?" The answer to the second of these questions should then be the key to the instructional program to be followed, so that the child is given help in growing toward achievement of his maximum maturity in reading, regardless of where on that continuum he may be at any time of assessment.

Attitude toward Reading

One significant indication of a child's readiness is his initial attitude toward reading.

On the opening day of school the first-grade teacher will find that his pupils vary greatly in their attitudes toward reading. Probably there will be one or more boys and girls, like Carol, who are already reading material of the difficulty of primers and who are eager to read more and more books. There will be boys and girls like Tommy and Liz who, pencil and tablet clutched tightly, go to the teacher and exclaim enthusiastically, "I want to learn to read. I want to learn to read." Fathers, mothers, and possibly sisters and brothers have been reading fascinating stories to them. So they come to school, wanting to learn to read in order to be independent of others for their stories. They may have discovered, too, that a great deal of information is found in books. They will insist on being taught to read in a hurry.

But not all children in the room will be like Tommy and Liz. There will probably be a Susan, who has enjoyed hearing others read or tell stories to her, but who has not looked forward to learning to read. She prefers not to learn, because she thinks it more fun to have her mother read to her than to read by herself. However, the teacher may wonder whether, in spite of lack of interest at the time, Susan may not become ready for reading before Tommy.

Then, too, there is Carl, who enters school with fear and trepidation because he has heard disconcerting tales about what happens at school. The teacher may ask himself, "If I can get Carl to overcome his fear, will it be wise to put him into a reading group?"

Another familiar figure in a first-grade room at the beginning of the year is Jim, who is greatly disturbed at the thought that now he can no longer spend the entire day playing cowboy. He is in no mood to be interested in what is done at school, for he anticipates only boring experiences.

In the average first grade, then, the children's attitudes toward learning to read may range from disinclination to indifference to anticipation. There are many other respects, however, in which first-grade children reveal great differences. They differ in mental, physical, social, emotional, and other educational or psychological factors of great importance in beginning reading.

Mental Maturity

For several decades after Washburne and Morphett[17] reported that, in the words of Washburne: "It is safer not to try to teach beginning reading to most children until they are mentally six and a half,"[18] their recommendation, though not unchallenged, was widely accepted. It was put into practice in many schools. The validity of the conclusion of the two investigators is now seriously questioned, in fact categorically denied by many.

Whether or not a child is ready to read undoubtedly should be answered not only with reference to his mental age but also in consideration of many other factors. The decision should be based in part on the reading program of the school. Children with mental ages considerably below six years and six months are being taught to read effectively if the methods and materials are suitable to their level of intellectual maturity. For the teacher to know that level is important.

Standardized Tests of Mental Maturity

One method of obtaining information on mental maturity is through the use of dependable mental tests. However, it should be remembered that even the best mental test provides an imperfect measure of native ability or intelligence. A child who has had many rich and intellectually stimulating experiences will do better on an intelligence test than a child of equal innate ability who has been brought up in a very limiting environment.

Perhaps the best-known individual test of mental ability is the *Terman Revision of the Stanford-Binet Intelligence Scale,* available in two forms, published by Houghton Mifflin Company, Boston. Since this test involves some knowledge of language, it may not fully reflect the real abilities of children with language handicaps.

Another frequently used individual intelligence test is the *Wechsler-Bellevue Intelligence Scales,* published by the Psychological Corporation, New York. In it, as in the *Terman Revision of the Stanford-Binet Intelligence Scale,* the factor of language ability is involved. Both the *Stanford-Binet* and the *Wechsler-Bellevue Intelligence Scales* require special training for their administration and interpretation. An intelligence test that can be given and interpreted by the classroom teacher is the *Peabody Picture Vocabulary Test,* published by the American Guidance Service, Circle Pines, Minnesota. However, the information obtainable through use of this

---

[17] Mabel Morphett and Carleton Washburne, "When Should Children Begin to Read?", *Elementary School Journal,* vol. 31 (March 1931), pp. 496–503.
[18] Carleton Washburne, "Individualized Plan of Instruction in Winnetka," *Adjusting Reading Programs to Individuals,* William S. Gray, ed., Supplementary Education Monographs, no. 52 (October 1941), pp. 90–95.

test is much more limited than that which can be derived from the *Stanford-Binet* and the *Wechsler-Bellevue Intelligence Scales.*

Also on the market are individual nonlanguage psychological tests designed to reduce the invalidity of test results that might, with language psychological tests, be due to lack of proficiency in the use of the English language on the part of the person being tested. An example is the *Arthur Performance Scale,* published by C. H. Stoelting and Company, Chicago. It can be used effectively with children from non-English-speaking homes, as well as with children with other language problems. The use of the *Arthur Performance Scale,* however, is not restricted to children with language difficulties.

A much-used group test is the *Pintner-Cunningham Primary Test,* Form A, Form B, and Form C, published by Harcourt Brace Jovanovich. The subtests, which together are devised to examine general mental ability, give an indication of the nature of the abilities tested. They are: Test 1, Common Observation; Test 2, Aesthetic Differences; Test 3, Associated Objects; Test 4, Discrimination of Size; Test 5, Picture Parts (in which the pupil is tested in ability to find among several pictures one like a designated picture); Test 6, Picture Completion (in which the pupil is asked to indicate which of a number of parts is needed to finish an incomplete picture); Test 7, Dot Drawing (in which the pupil is asked to connect dots so that a picture like a given one will be drawn). Although all seven tests are composed entirely of pictures, an understanding of language is required for taking the test, since all the directions are given verbally.

The California Test of Mental Maturity, Pre-Primary Battery, published by McGraw-Hill, New York, is available in long and short forms. Certain of the subtests require a minimum use of language, while other sections reveal how adequately the child understands relations expressed in words. Since a pupil's score in nonlanguage tests may be higher or lower than in language tests, it is of great value to obtain test scores on the types of mental ability tested both by language and by nonlanguage tests. *The California Test of Mental Maturity, Pre-Primary Battery* is concerned with these mental factors: memory, spatial relations, logical reasoning, numerical reasoning, and verbal concepts.

The Pintner Non-Language Primary Mental Test, published by Teachers College Press, Columbia University, New York, can also be used with children with language handicaps.

Other widely used group intelligence tests are the *Kuhlmann-Anderson Intelligence Test, Grade IA,* published by the Educational Test Bureau, Minneapolis, Minnesota, and the *Detroit Beginning First Grade Intelligence Test,* distributed by Harcourt, Brace, Jovanovich, New York.

Subjective Data on Mental Maturity

Intelligence tests are not the only means by which the teacher can gain insight into the child's intelligence. Long before psychological tests were available there were rough methods of estimating a person's intelligence. Although mental tests are probably more reliable indexes of intelligence than more informal methods, the latter should also be used. Informal observation may serve as a valuable check on the accuracy of test scores. If no mental test has been given, the observant teacher may compare the child's reactions with those usually expected of children his age. By consulting books on child growth and development the teacher can find out what types of behavior are characteristic of children at various age levels. Information about an individual child's customary behavior can also be obtained from others who know him well, especially his parents. The teacher should also realize that environmental deprivations may make the child seem less intelligent than he is.

Physical Fitness

The teacher of the beginning reader should always consult such data as may be available in the offices of the school doctor or nurse. Information that can be obtained through conferences with parents is also often helpful. Through observation of the child the teacher can frequently get clues to the child's physical well-being which may alert him to the need for referral to the nurse or doctor. If there is no school nurse, symptoms of illness or handicap may be discussed with the parents, who may be encouraged to consult a physician, dentist, or eye specialist. Rather easily observable factors such as sleepiness, listlessness, irritability, and languor often are signs of difficulties that may seriously interfere with learning to read.

Unfortunately, during the critical period of getting ready to read and of beginning reading, children are often absent from school because of illness. Not much can be done by the teacher to prevent such illness, except to provide frequent rest periods and frequent periods of physical activity, to check room temperature and ventilation, and to suggest that a child be sent home at the first sign of a cold or other illness. Since frequent interruptions are to be expected, the teacher should plan his work accordingly. Much repetition and review of earlier activities are necessary. When a child returns after an absence of several days, the teacher should do everything possible to make him feel that he still belongs, has his own seat, and follows the familiar routine. He should be greeted with pleasure by teacher and class.

Vision

Since probably no phase of the physical well-being of the child affects reading as much as eyesight, the vision of a child who is about to learn to read should be checked as carefully as possible.

The screening test for vision that is most commonly used in schools is the Snellen Letter chart or the Snellen Symbol E chart, which is an adaptation of the letter chart for use with nonreaders. On the letter charts are seven rows of the letters printed in various sizes, decreasing from the top row to the bottom. While the examinee is being tested, he stands twenty feet from the chart and reads as far down the Snellen Letter chart as his vision permits. On the Snellen Symbol E chart the pupil indicates by the fingers of one hand the positions, like **E, ᗰ , Ǝ, ᗡ** , in which the letter *E* occurs on that chart. The Snellen charts test vision only at the far point, at a distance of twenty feet. Since they do not check vision at reading distance, the near point, there is little relationship between a child's performance on these charts and ability to read at the near point. Two of the instruments on the market that screen for visual defects affecting academic success are *The Keystone Visual Survey Telebinocular* (Keystone View Division/Mast Development Company) and *The Master Orthorator Visual Efficiency Test* (Bausch and Lomb Optical Company, Rochester, New York). Both measure such visual functions as binocular vision and fineness of discrimination at both far and near points, skills definitely related to the ability to learn to read. Both also test depth perception and color blindness. Additional screening tests or devices for screening include:

> The Reading Eye Camera (Educational Development Laboratories).
> The Prism Reader (Educational Development Laboratories).
> The A O Screener (American Optical Company, Kansas City, Missouri).
> The Spache Binocular Vision Test (Keystone View Division/Mast Development Company).

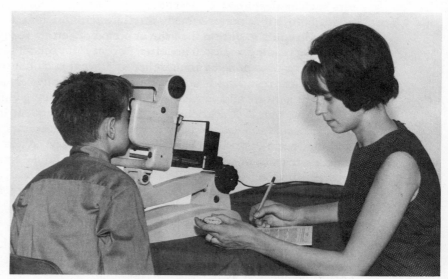

Figure 4.1 This boy is taking a skills test with the Keystone Telebinocular, which is used in vision screening. (Keystone View Division/Mast/Keystone Development Company, Davenport, Iowa.)

Before choosing any test for checking visual efficiency teachers are advised to study carefully the literature furnished by the publishers of the tests to note what they purport to test and how the tests operate. In no case should the teacher or school nurse use vision tests to try to *diagnose* eye defects. The tests should be used in the schools merely as screening tests. If the results of the testing indicate that there is a possibility of a difficulty in vision, a referral for diagnosis and possible remediation should be made to a competent specialist in the field of vision.

Even without tests some symptoms of visual difficulties, such as in-flamed eyelids, rubbing the eyes, confusing similar letters such as the *c* and the *e*, scowling, and frowning can be detected. The distance from the eye at which a child holds his books may also be a sign of trouble. Complaints of headaches after reading are frequently significant in discovering vision problems.

Hearing

Since the hearing ability of a child may have an important effect on his reading, in many schools an effort is made to secure accurate information about children's auditory acuity. In these schools the health service often checks hearing by means of an audiometer. Some audiometers are made for group, others for individual, testing. Audiometers are obtainable from:

Beltone Electronics Corporation, 4201 West Victoria Street, Chicago, Illinois.
The Maico Company, Minneapolis, Minnesota.
Medical Acoustic Instrument Company, Minneapolis, Minnesota.
Dakon Corporation, New Hyde Park, New York.
Otarion Listener Corporation, Ossining, New York.
Sonotone Corporation, Elmsford, New York.
Zenith Hearing Aid Sales Corporation, 6501 West Grand Avenue, Chicago, Illinois.

The use of an audiometer requires specialized training. Moreover, in many schools teachers do not have access to clinics in which audiometers are used. They should therefore be alert to observable signs of hearing loss, which frequently goes undetected and which can seriously interfere not only with reading progress but with learning in general. Inattention, mono-tonous or unnatural pitch, lack of clear and distinct speech, frequent requests for repetition of questions, turning one ear to a speaker, mouth breathing, complaints of ringing in the ear, head tilting, confusion of words with similar sounds, and rubbing of the ear are among the indications of possible defects of hearing.

The classroom teacher can also make a rough check of children's hearing by means of the "watch-tick" test. The examiner holds a watch of medium size and quietness in the palm of his hand and stands behind the child being examined. The child covers one ear with the palm of his hand. The watch is held about three feet from the child and moved closer until the child indicates that he hears its tick. Both ears are tested in this way. By comparing one child's responses with those of others, the teacher knows which children should be examined by a nurse or doctor. Whisper tests and low-voice tests may also offer clues as to whether hearing difficulty should be suspected.

Social and Emotional Development

The social maturity of a child can be determined in part by observing his "at-homeness" in group situations. It is of special importance to note his ability to cooperate with others in a group. Emotional maturity can roughly be gauged by the child's reaction to conditions that to him are unpleasant, his willingness to consider the rights of others, and his ability to sacrifice immediate pleasures for future gains.

To the child in the prereading period school is still a strange place calling for many adjustments which had not been required of him at home or even in the kindergarten. Teachers will often observe signs of fear, anxiety, withdrawal, or belligerence in children as a result. Getting ready to read requires the growth both of self-confidence and of confidence in the teacher.

Language Development

We have referred in Chapter 3 to the bearing of language development on reading. It is of great importance that the teacher consider the factors to which reference is made in that chapter, as he assesses the type of reading or prereading activities for which the child is ready.

Educational Factors

Educational factors that have decided bearing on beginning reading can be measured through the use of tests frequently referred to as reading readiness tests, as well as by means of a variety of nonstandardized procedures.

Reading-readiness Tests

Many, though not all, of the educational factors related to beginning reading are being measured by means of reading-readiness tests. However, such tests are far from perfect predictions of reading success, with some decidedly better than others.

Many reading-readiness tests appraise the child's background of information, either in a subtest so labeled or in one by some other name in which other characteristics of reading readiness are also tested. The breadth of background of a pupil's information, which reflects the richness of experience he has had, is tested by asking him such questions as: "How many cents are there in a nickel?"

The ability to discriminate between objects, words, and letters is also measured in many reading-readiness tests. A common method for evaluating the ability to discriminate among objects is to present a series of four or five pictures in a row, all but one of which is like the first one. The series may consist of pictures of five houses all alike except one in which no chimney is shown. The child is asked to cross out the one that is unlike the first one. Similar exercises are devised for testing the pupil's ability to discriminate between letters or words. Pupils are not expected to read the words or letters; all they are to do is to recognize which letter or word is different from others in the same row, or which are alike.

Comprehension of the meaning of words is also tested in many reading-readiness tests. In some tests the pupil is asked to give words that mean the opposite of the words named by the examiner. If, for example the teacher says *summer,* the pupil is to answer *winter;* if the teacher says *up,* the pupil is to say *down.*

One widely used readiness test is the *Gates Reading Readiness Test,* published by Teachers College Press, Columbia University. It is divided into five subtests which measure specific skills important in learning to read. The skills tested are the ability to follow directions, to discriminate between words that are similar, to differentiate between sounds, and to identify letters and numbers by name. The ability to follow directions is tested by asking the pupil to mark pictures as instructed. Two subtests measure the ability to discriminate between words. One does so by requiring the child to indicate which two words in each group of four are alike. The other asks the child to state which word in a series of four is like the one shown to the child on a word card. In the fourth subtest the pupil marks the picture the name of which rhymes with a word the examiner names. The first four subtests are group tests, but the fifth subtest, in which the pupil names as many of the capital and small letters and the given numbers as he can, must be administered to one pupil at a time.

The Metropolitan Readiness Tests, which are group tests published by Harcourt, Brace & Jovanovich, and available in two forms, consist of six subtests entitled "Word Meaning," "Sentences," "Information," "Matching," "Numbers," and "Copying." All six subtests are made up of pictures which the pupil is asked to mark or copy according to oral instructions by the teacher. The first subtest is one to measure the child's ability to understand words. In the second subtest the pupil's comprehension of phrases and sentences is checked. The informational background of the child is tested in the third. In the fourth test his power of visual perception is measured as revealed by his ability to select the letter, figure, word, or picture that is similar to a specified one. The fifth subtest measures many abilities related to numbers, such as knowing the vocabulary of numbers, writing numbers, recognizing written numbers, understanding number terms, telling time, and knowing the meaning of fractional parts. In the sixth subtest, "Copying," the pupil's power of visual perception and his motor control are tested. One special value of this subtest, in terms of reading skills, is that it helps detect tendencies toward reversing parts of letters or words that may be indicative of difficulties in reading.

The Lee-Clark Reading Readiness Test, published by the California Test Bureau, Los Angeles, is a group test printed in only one form. The three subtests measure the ability to match letters, to follow directions, to understand the meaning of words, and to note similarities among given words.

The Classification Test for Beginners in Reading by Clarence R. Stone and C. C. Grover, distributed by the Webster Publishing Company, St. Louis, is a group test in which the pupil's ability to observe likenesses and differences between word forms is examined. No more than about twenty minutes is required for giving the test.

In the choice of reading-readiness tests, as in the selection of other kinds of standardized tests, attention needs to be given to validity, reliability, ease of administering and of scoring, availability in more than one form, and reasonableness of cost. Since many teachers find it valuable to know a child's achievement in a variety of abilities related to beginning reading, they welcome the fact that many readiness tests are divided into subtests. When averages or norms are computed for the subtests, the teacher can determine in which of the characteristics tested each child is average, above average, or below average.

Although readiness tests alone are far from a perfect means of determining the extent to which a pupil is ready for beginning reading, the use of sufficiently reliable ones can be an asset in evaluation. However, the results must be interpreted with great caution. Readiness tests have fallen short of the goal that it was once optimistically believed they could accomplish. Many of them were constructed on the theory that there is one time at which a child is ready to begin to learn to read. When that hypothesis is not accepted, the tests lose some of their validity.

In spite of the shortcomings of reading-readiness tests it is probably true that a teacher can learn more about a child's readiness for reading by giving him a readiness test than he could learn by spending the same length of time on other means of evaluation. Further value in their use is that the teacher can find them a diagnostic tool by means of which he can plan subsequent work for the child.

Informal Means of Evaluation

Even though standardized tests throw considerable light on factors that are important in deciding whether it is advisable to begin the teaching of reading to a child, much can be done without them in trying to make that decision wisely. Informal tests constructed by the teacher, can also yield information that affords direction in his teaching of individual children in daily instruction.

1. Testing visual and auditory discrimination The ability to discriminate between letter and word forms and between letter and word sounds, which constitutes an essential to reading, can be tested in a variety of ways through teacher-made tests. In devising these tests the teacher must have clearly in mind the meaning of the terms *visual discrimination* and *auditory discrimination* and the importance to reading of the development of these skills. He must not confuse *visual discrimination* with *vision* nor *auditory discrimination* with *hearing*. By *visual discrimination* is meant the ability to *differentiate* between two or more forms, such as objects, written words, or written letters. Although a child's vision may be excellent, he may be unable to make fine differentiations between similar objects, pictures, words, or letters presented in visual form. In order to succeed in reading, the child should be able to differentiate between forms as nearly alike as *m* and *n*. If an individual cannot see such differences readily, he is likely to be greatly handicapped when learning to read. Some entering pupils do not possess this ability to the extent needed for beginning reading, but fortunately it can be developed through training.

By auditory discrimination is meant the ability to note the differences between sounds. A high degree of correlation has been found between auditory discrimination and success in reading.[19] A child's hearing may be excellent, even though he is unable to distinguish or discriminate between the sound of the bells of the Lutheran church and the Catholic church. In order to be successful in reading, pupils should be able to distinguish between sounds as similar as the *b* and the *p* sounds as they occur in words. As in the case of visual discrimination, auditory discrimination may be improved through practice.

To test visual discrimination the teacher may make a test similar to one used frequently in standardized reading readiness tests. He may ask the pupils, for example, which word in the following row is different from the others:

> man   man   man   men   man.

Or he may ask the boys and girls to find the word in a row such as the following that is different from the first one in the row:

> fine   fine   find   fine   fine.

A test of this type can be duplicated for the pupils on sheets of paper containing many rows of words arranged similar to those in the examples.

To test auditory discrimination the teacher can ask the pupils to in-

---

[19] Bertha Boyd Thompson, "A Longitudinal Study of Auditory Discrimination," *Journal of Educational Research*, vol. 56, (March 1963), pp. 376–378.

dicate, for example, which of these pairs of sounds he gives are alike and which are different: m, n; n, m; n, n; m, m; b, p; p, p; p, b; b, b. Or he can ask pupils to name other words that begin with the same sound as the one with which, for example, the word *mother* begins. Another variation is to ask the pupils which pairs of words such as the following begin with the same sound: *mother, man; cat, came; bark, pie.*

2. Testing knowledge of letters   According to John C. Manning:[20] "There is ample evidence to indicate that letter knowledge is indeed predictive of reading success." If it is predictive, we may well ask ourselves which particular aspects of letter knowledge contribute most meaningfully to that prognosis. The classic study by Donald Durrell[21] and others identifies several levels of letter knowledge of which the teacher should be aware, as he tries to determine the child's level on the continuum of being prepared for beginning reading instruction. Following is an adaptation of those listed by Alice Nicholson,[22] a member of Durrell's research force:

Ability to directly match letters (upper and lower case).
Ability to match letters shown (upper and lower case).
Ability to identify letters named (upper and lower case).
Ability to name the letters (upper and lower case).
Ability to relate upper to lower case letters.
Ability to write letters.

Samuels,[23] when summarizing his own and Ohnmacht's[24] studies, points out that they found no positive effect of knowledge of letter names on reading, but that he, as well as other investigators, have found training in letter sounds has a beneficial effect on learning to read.

Arthur Heilman, considered by many an outstanding authority on the question of phonics in reading instruction, states:

Research on first grade reading instruction leaves little room for doubt that pupils exposed to systematic instruction in letter-sound relationships

[20] John C. Manning, "Early Letter Emphasis Approaches in First Grade Reading Programs," *Perspectives in Reading*, no. 5 (Newark, Del.: International Reading Association, 1965), p. 122.

[21] Donald D. Durrell, Alice Nicholson, Arthur W. Olson, Sylvia Gavel, and Eleanor Linehan, "Success in First Grade Reading" Boston: Boston University, *Journal of Education*, vol. 51, no. 3 (February 1958), entire issue.

[22] *Ibid.*, p. 7.

[23] S. Jay Samuels, "Models of Word Recognition," *Theoretical Models and Processes*, Harry Singer and Robert B. Ruddell, eds. (Newark, Del.: International Reading Association, 1971), pp. 24–37.

[24] D. C. Ohnmacht, "The Effects of Letter Knowledge on Achievement in Reading in the First Grade," paper presented at the American Educational Research Association in Language Arts (February 1969).

score higher on "reading achievement" at the end of grade one than do pupils who receive little or no such instruction.[25]

Undoubtedly in some programs of reading instruction—especially those with a synthetic approach to phonics (*see* page 116)—letter knowledge acquired on prereading or reading levels would have a greater bearing on reading than it would in others.

3. Appraising other factors   Through teacher-made tests, often somewhat similar to standardized tests, the teacher can get an approximation of the child's vocabulary, his ability to follow directions, his ability to remember, his power to think critically, as well as of many other skills or abilities related to reading.

Valuable information can also be collected through careful observation of the children. To get insight into a child's background of experience, the teacher may wish to talk with him concerning his interests. A rough measure of his attitude toward reading can be gained by observing how often he looks at books on the reading tables, whether he asks for stories to be read to him, and whether he is interested in finding out what the written word says. Whether he has acquired the top-to-bottom and left-to-right sequence can be determined in part by observing him as he looks at pictures and as he "reads" captions and other labels. An index of his vocabulary can be gained by listening to him talk and by gauging roughly how well he understands what he hears. Many teachers keep a written record of those characteristics of a child that have a bearing on his ability to learn to read. Whether a written record is kept or not, informal observation of children in classroom and playground situations serves as a useful supplement to standardized reading-readiness tests.

Thus, during the first weeks of school the teacher will want to study the characteristics of each child that relate to success in beginning reading. He can do so by means of mental tests, reading-readiness tests, informal observations of children, conferences with children, consultation with parents and others, and examination of records. Some factors that he should consider are intelligence, hearing, vision, visual and auditory discrimination, experience background, vocabulary, emotional and social maturity, ability to remember, ability to follow directions, power to think critically, and interest in reading. On the basis of his judgment, as he weighs all the data that he has collected, the teacher will decide for what prereading or reading activities the individual child is ready.

[25] Arthur W. Heilman, "Research Findings Concerning Phonics in Beginning Reading," *A Decade of Innovation: Approaches to Beginning Reading*, Elaine C. Vilscek, ed., (Newark, Del.: International Reading Association, 1971), Proceedings of the Twelfth Annual Convention of the International Reading Association, vol. 12, Part 3, pp. 100–107.

GUIDELINES FOR ASSISTING THE CHILD IN BECOMING MORE READY FOR BEGINNING READING INSTRUCTION

After the teacher has decided whether some of his pupils are ready to learn to read, he is confronted with the problem of what to do with those who are not ready for systematic instruction in reading. Should he have them postpone participation in all activities that pertain to reading in the hope that as they mature they will overcome their shortcoming? Clearly the answer is "no." There is no justification for the attitude of the teacher who, when asked why one child sat by himself in the back of the room throughout most of the school day, answered: "Oh, he is waiting for his reading readiness."

What then are the guidelines that the teacher should follow when planning a program for the prereading period?

The teacher should recognize that there is probably no one optimum time for any given child to begin to learn to read. We can think of readiness for reading as extending over a continuum on which no point is the most propitious. The "best time" will be determined to a large extent by methods and materials used. Therefore, it is quite understandable that children who vary in their readiness for reading could be started at the same time on the adventure of learning to read, providing attention is paid to individual differences as the reading program is being designed for each of them.

Reading-readiness activities should be an integral part of the total program. By means of many of the activities that the children carry on in any good first-year program many of the goals of the prereading period can be attained. For example, characteristic activities, such as storytelling, the examination of picture books, music and art activities, and excursions can contribute greatly to the development of readiness for reading.

Direct help in the form of practice activities should be provided for some boys and girls. Although many of the activities of a good first-year program, even when not designed specifically to prepare children for reading, are instrumental in fostering reading readiness, some boys and girls seem to require additional practice on certain skills which are essential to beginning reading. For example, practice periods set up to help children gain proficiency in discriminating between word forms are valuable when not enough meaningful repetition can be provided by incidental means. Such practice should not, however, replace abundant incidental instruction, which can be afforded, when the children look for a name on a chart listing those who have special responsibilities for the week. The teacher may at that time say: "No, that word is not *Mark* (as the teacher points to *Mike* and then to *Mark*), although it begins like *Mark*. It is *Mike*. Find Christine's name. Is it longer or shorter than Carol's?"

The activities of the prereading period should provide background for initial reading tasks. Unfortunately, the usual reading textbooks, written for the child population as a whole, do not take account of the many variations in the social, cultural, geographical, and vocational backgrounds of all children. The characters and situations portrayed in most reading textbooks are, therefore, usually drawn from the environments of fairly typical middle-class homes and communities. To be sure, the popularity of television has had an equalizing effect on the background information that many boys and girls have. The city child who watches television has a better understanding of the farm and the farm child of the city than was formerly the case. Nevertheless, this knowledge as obtained through television is often superficial. The ghetto-dwelling child or the child living on a Wyoming ranch or an Indian reservation is still likely to have some difficulty in recognizing the Bob and Sue of the suburbanite family popular in some basal readers. Furthermore, to the country child the incidents may be quite dull in comparison with the killing of a rattlesnake or the rounding up of cattle escaping through a break in the fence. Nor can it be taken for granted that the city child will understand references to a farm. He may not ever have seen a cow, and the illustration in the book may give him a misleading impression of her size.

Preparing the children for the basal reading series can therefore be a formidable task. Storytelling, discussion, and the use of various audiovisual aids may prepare the child for the situations encountered in readers. A rich "experience" program in the prereading period will provide the foundation on which the initial reading skills may be built.

Even in schools where no basal reading series is used and the program is individualized as the teacher attempts to help every child read material on his level, problems similar to those mentioned in relation to the textbook program persist. In such an individualized reading program it is still necessary to provide appropriate experiences in preparation for reading. Experiences such as field trips, discussions, and at times word study can help assure greater effectiveness for an individualized reading program, as well as for one based in part on textbooks.

The length of the reading readiness program period, if one is needed, should vary. Some of the boys and girls will probably be reading when they enter first grade. Others, though not reading, may know the alphabet and the sounds commonly associated with the letters or combinations of letters. Reading readiness activities for these children can often prove to be worse than a waste of time unless preparation can help reduce possible lacks that might persist, even though in most respects the child is ready to read or is already reading.

A child should be taught to read as soon as he is ready. If he is ready before he starts school he should be permitted, even encouraged, to learn to read. The experience of reading, for the child who can read with success and pleasure, enriches his life and contributes to his general development. On the other hand, it is an error to assert, as some writers have done, that it is an established fact that a child who starts to read late has lost one or more years of his life and that he will always be one or more years behind in his capacity to read. First, there are many experiences besides reading that a young child can have to enrich his life. Second, although evidence has been presented indicating that an early reader may be able to maintain his superiority, there is also evidence to show that some children who do not receive reading instruction until the second year of school outstrip their counterparts who learned to read in the first grade, even before the end of the elementary-school period.

A large variety of appropriate materials should be made available during the prereading period. Since one important objective of the prereading period is to develop and maintain an interest in reading, the children should have access to a large number of attractive books. Some of these may be placed on a library table, of height appropriate for the first-year child, while others may be arranged on low bookcases. Included should be books to which the pupils have been introduced as the teacher showed them or talked about them or read from them to the class. The display should not, however, be limited to books with which the pupils are familiar. There should also be some that are new to the children, so that through them interest in exploring books can be developed. To help the boys and girls realize that books are valuable not only for the stories but also for the information they contain, the book collection should include both stories and informational material.

Books that boys and girls have made can also stimulate interest in reading. Large books that other children have made in preceding years may be placed on the library table. For example, if the first grade the year before made a big picture book telling about a visit to a farm as a class project, the children can see how it is possible to share information with others by means of the book. Such a book is especially helpful if there are captions or simple story material accompanying the pictures. The new class, too, might bring pictures on a subject like "Our School" or "Our Pets" and mount them to form a big book. Under each picture the teacher might write a sentence or two suggested by the children. It is easy to interest children in reading a book they have helped to make.

Displays on bulletin boards can be of much value. A bulletin board on which are mounted leaves, with captions telling the kind, may help extend the experiences of some of the children. It can also give them further proof that learning to read is worthwhile, since the words below the leaves give significant information. Pictures of the means of transportation that some of the boys and girls used, like a bicycle, truck, automobile, and airplane, can serve similar purposes.

Many publishing companies that sell textbooks for elementary-school reading also have reading readiness booklets that can serve a helpful purpose for some children. Some of the booklets provide specific preparation for a certain series of readers, while others can be used profitably by some boys and girls regardless of the reading books that will be used later.

Outline for Chapter 4B

DEVELOPING READINESS FOR READING

Fostering Emotional and Social Maturity
Developing Educational Readiness
    Enriching the Child's Background of Experience
    Stimulating Growth in Language Abilities
    Developing Auditory and Visual Discrimination
      Auditory Discrimination
      Visual Discrimination
    Improving in Ability to Remember
      Remembering a Sequence of Ideas
      Following Directions
    Stimulating Growth in Critical and Creative
      Thinking
    Orienting to the Left-to-Right and Top-to-Bottom
      Sequence
    Developing and Maintaining Interest in Reading
Using the Experience Chart in the Prereading Period
    Steps in Making and Using Experience Charts
    Description of Steps in Making and Using Ex-
      perience Charts
    Illustration of Work on an Experience Chart
    Arguments for and against the Use of Experience
      Charts

CHAPTER

Developing Readiness
for Reading

So far we have discussed in some detail the theory basic to a sound prereading program. Now let us see how it can be applied in the classroom.

FOSTERING EMOTIONAL AND SOCIAL MATURITY

As the teacher adjusts his procedures to the emotional and social maturity of his pupils and strives to help them reach higher levels, he will keep certain principles in mind:

1. The teacher himself should act like an emotionally and socially mature person.
2. An atmosphere of calm, courtesy, industry, and happiness should prevail in the room.
3. Respect should be shown for the personality of each person.
4. Restrictions should serve a purpose and be relatively few in number.
5. Directions and suggestions should generally be positive rather than negative.
6. Praise is usually more effective than blame, but praise must be deserved to be of value.

7. In all school activities, the development of the entire child should be taken into consideration.

8. Every individual needs security, approval, success, and means of self-expression.

9. The help and cooperation of parents should be secured whenever possible.

10. The teacher should not necessarily postpone reading instruction until a child is well adjusted socially and emotionally, because success in reading can contribute greatly to a feeling of security.

The teacher will encounter numerous problems of emotional and social maturity which directly affect a child's readiness for reading. Some children are shy, others overaggressive; some are overprotected; others are over-assertive or lacking in self-control or in concern for others. What can the teacher do for them?

Often the shy child is the immature child. Insecurity may result from many causes. One of the common characteristics of the shy child is his fear of not being accepted by his peer group. If he has had little previous experience with participation in group activity, he may need gradual and patient introduction to group enterprises of many types. Certainly he should be made to feel, by every possible means, that he is liked. He should be brought into contact with other children who are friendly to him. He should receive praise for successful efforts at social adjustment. He should be encouraged to contribute constructively to the work of the group and thus secure the approval of his peers.

In the case of the child who cries easily or loses his temper on slight provocation, careful attention should be given to his general physical well being. Has he been getting enough rest and wholesome food? Does he show signs of illness? Where the crying may have become a habit, the teacher should be ready to supply suitable distractions and try to avoid situations that may give rise to crying. The positive approach is usually the more effective. Thus, when a child exhibits self-control in a situation, the teacher, instead of ignoring such desirable behavior, may say: "I noticed that Phyllis did not become angry when George broke her clay bowl. She helped George pick up the pieces and said she would make another bowl."

Although the overassertive child may be the most troublesome, he usually presents a less serious problem than the shy and retiring one. Tactful discussions with the group as a whole about respecting the rights of others may be helpful, and it may be necessary to provide experiences that teach the child he cannot get what he wants through aggressive behavior. Most of the children who manifest such behavior are merely seeking to gain recognition which they cannot get by more constructive methods. They should be given frequent opportunities to obtain such recognition by means that are socially approved.

The teacher will also encounter the overprotected child and the overly self-centered one. Wherever possible, he should seek the cooperation of the oversolicitous parents. The overprotected child, while feeling secure in the affections of the teacher, should be encouraged to assume ever-increasing independence in making and carrying out decisions. The teacher should insist on his doing for himself the things he can learn to do without adult assistance and should praise him when he succeeds. The child who often insists on having his own way should be taught to "take turns" in group activities. He can be made to understand that no one is able to have his own way at all times and that thoughtfulness for others creates pleasant relationships. In extreme cases it may be necessary to isolate the child temporarily from the group, if only for the sake of the other children. Such disciplinary measures should, however, be regarded as exceptional.

The following is a list of ways in which the teacher can help boys and girls develop emotional and social maturity important in the learning-to-read period:

1. Providing the shy child with opportunities to become increasingly involved in activities well graded for him.
2. Helping the overaggressive child take a rightful place in the social scene of the classroom.
3. Using praise when deserved but resorting to criticism sparingly.
4. Adapting the curriculum to the needs of each child so that he is likely to have a maximum of success and a minimum of frustrations.
5. Helping boys and girls appreciate the difference between license and liberty.
6. Giving responsibilities to all pupils.
7. Helping boys and girls in self-evaluation.
8. Helping boys and girls become more self-reliant.
9. Avoiding much competition with others.
10. Placing a child in a group in which he is likely to be happy.
11. Encouraging the child to do without assistance chores that he can do alone.
12. Encouraging a child to express his own opinions.
13. Encouraging every pupil to develop his special talents.

DEVELOPING EDUCATIONAL READINESS

As the teacher pays attention to the emotional and social development of boys and girls, he can at the same time help them grow in other characteristics that have a marked bearing on success in beginning reading. How this can be done through attention to the experience background, auditory and visual discrimination, and other factors is explained in the remaining pages of this chapter.

Enriching the Child's Background of Experience

One way in which boys and girls can be helped to become more ready for beginning reading instruction is through the extension of their experience background. However, experience is important, not merely because children must get ready for reading but because appropriate, wholesome, and varied experiences are an important part of each person's life, at any age. Even for the many children in the primary school who have already enjoyed a wide variety of experiences with places, persons, things, processes, and events, new and interesting school experiences are desirable. The school should provide all children with an interesting environment in which to grow up. Although many—perhaps most—of the children who enter school have a sufficient experience background to learn to read, the school should continue to open new worlds of experience to all children. For those children whose experiences have been severely limited, it may be desirable to postpone formal reading instruction until they have had the opportunity to enjoy a variety of direct experiences.

For all children it is well to make sure that the situations encountered in their first reading books are familiar. Most children's books, especially reading textbooks, present scenes and incidents familiar to the majority of children. A boy and a girl, parents, a dog or a cat, simple toys, and perhaps a tractor or a mechanical crane constitute the major "props" of many primers. Nevertheless, the wider and richer the child's previous experience has been, the greater his chances of approaching the reading with confidence and pleasure. Building background should therefore not be limited to the kinds of situations encountered in the first reading book.

Experienced teachers are familiar with wide variety in the range and types of backgrounds found among school children. They know it is necessary to study the children carefully in order to meet the multifarious individual needs. In some cases it will be possible to distinguish between different groups in the first-grade class. Thus, for example, those children who have not attended kindergarten may be selected for an exploratory trip through the school building. If an individual child has never had a pet, the teacher may talk with him about animals, show him pictures of pets, or better still, arrange for the class to acquire one.

Socioeconomic level will often affect the nature of the child's previous experiences, but not necessarily their extent. Children from middle-class homes have often traveled considerably, some even to distant countries. They are likely to see more movies; have more toys and books at home; and have more opportunity for gardening, experimentation with pencils, crayons, and paper and construction materials than lower-class children. On the other hand, the child from the ghetto knows a world that is quite unfamiliar to his more fortunate classmate. He may have developed, through the necessities of his life, a greater maturity and independence and often even a tragic sophistication about the ways of the adult world.

The ideal school environment for preparing boys and girls for reading, then, is one in which many things are going on. A primary class may be building a large model airplane, operating a store, viewing a film, making a terrarium, or caring for a pet. The child's background of experience can be extended by going on field trips, examining objects, looking at pictures, observing or participating in demonstrations and experiments, and listening to stories.

Going on Field Trips

The eagerness of most first-grade children to learn more about the part of the world near them should be fully utilized. There are many places in or near school that boys and girls enjoy seeing. Trips through the school, examination of playground equipment, walks to gather leaves or stones, trips to look at trees and birds—all can be made real learning experiences, contributing not only to reading but also helping the child find out more about the world in which he lives. But such trips must be carefully planned if the maximum value is to be obtained. Part of the planning should usually involve preparing the pupils for the trip so that they will know better what to look for. For example, before the boys and girls go on a walk to gather leaves, some pictures of pretty leaves may be shown and brief comments made. The purpose of the children in going on the walk, possibly to see how many different kinds of leaves each child can find, should be one that is wholeheartedly accepted by the group. During the trip itself help should also be given frequently in the form of suggestions or questions or directions. At this time the teacher may ask the pupils to notice if many leaves have fallen, and whether more green leaves are on the trees than on the ground. After the trip it is important to have a follow-up, when the pupils may engage in one or more activities such as showing their leaves, expressing rhythmically how the leaves fall, mounting them, drawing pictures suggested by their walk, making up a poem about leaves, or planning the sentences for a chart telling about their trip.

Examining Objects

By means of objects displayed in the room or otherwise brought to the attention of the boys and girls, the pupil's fund of information can be greatly extended. Discussion of material on a science table can be stimulated. The children can be encouraged to bring to school objects in which they are interested, such as stones or model airplanes or toy boats, and to explain them to the other children. Thus, through wise direction many significant facts can be learned as the children show a new doll, a strange-looking acorn, or a knife that was recently received as a birthday present.

Looking at Pictures

Pictures serve as an important means of broadening the experience background of children. If motion-picture equipment is available, the teacher can select films that will fit the needs and interests of his group. Slides and filmstrips, too, some of which are specifically planned for several of the basic reading series, can be used to make concrete the things that might otherwise be rather meaningless abstractions. Mounted pictures, postcards, and snapshots, brought either by the pupils or the teacher, can be a source of pleasure and of learning. Exhibiting them attractively will encourage children to study them and can also serve as a means of teaching them how to display pictures effectively. If the children share the responsibility of arranging the materials in an orderly fashion, they can develop skill in mounting pictures and arranging attractive displays.

Observing or Participating in Demonstrations and Experiments

Demonstrations and experiments are of special interest to many children, and they can be the source of much information. Many experiences in science lend themselves well to use with young children; these include finding out what happens to plants when they have and when they do not have sunlight, discovering what effect salt has on ice, noticing how steam becomes water, and discovering that air is necessary for a candle to burn. Often the teacher can let the pupils take part in experiments.

Listening to Stories

Storytelling at all ages can open vistas to the child. Realistic stories, in particular, are appealing to children of five and six. Although children should share in the storytelling, and self-expression for the child telling a story is important, the welfare of the listener should also be considered. Consequently, the quality of the story and the method of telling it should be matters of concern not only for the sake of the storyteller but also for that of the listener.

Engaging in Other Activities

The teacher has at his disposal many other means of preparing boys and girls for beginning reading through extending their experiences. He can do this by providing records to which the children can listen, encouraging creative expression through music and art, interesting the children in putting on plays or puppet shows, and making provisions for discussions and conversation that is interesting, elevating, and informative.

Stimulating Growth in Language Abilities

Since there is a close relation between reading and other language abilities, much can be done to help the pupil develop in all of the linguistic skills. Both during the prereading period and after the child has begun reading in books, his development in language can be stimulated in a variety of ways, so that he will become more ready for reading or will become a more efficient reader. The teacher can effect growth in reading skill or in abilities related to reading by wisely guiding activities that deal with speech; listening; and writing.

One period of the school day that can contribute richly to the development of language efficiency is the "sharing period." In a large number of primary grades a short period, popularly called "show and tell" time, is set aside daily so that pupils will have an opportunity to "share" some of their experiences with others in their group. They do so by telling their classmates and the teacher experiences of interest to them. During this period many teachers like an informal seating arrangement, often in circular or semi-circular formation.

Typically, during the sharing period one pupil at a time, either while seated or standing at a place where others can see him, tells in a sentence or more something that he thinks will interest others. At times he has something to show to the class as he makes his explanation. A child showing a stone that he found on his way to school may say, "I found a pretty stone." With or without questioning by the teacher or the rest of the group he may add, "I found it on the way to school. I am going to keep it." Other typical bits of information given by pupils are:

We have a new baby. It is a baby sister.
Mother is taking me to the five-and-ten-cent store tonight. I will buy a doll.
I fell yesterday. This is where I hurt my leg. A dog chased me.

In conducting a sharing period these are points many teachers find profitable to observe:

1. Good English should be encouraged but not to the point of inhibition of spontaneity in talking.
2. Participation should be well distributed. Although frequently not every child can have a "turn" during every sharing time, no one shoud be slighted day after day and nobody should monopolize the time.
3. Opportunities to increase the pupils' vocabulary should be utilized. This can often be done if after a pupil has used a word unfamiliar to many the teacher makes the term clearer. For example, if one child says, "I found this piece of marble," the word *marble* can be explained through comments or questions by the teacher.
4. Sharing time should be a happy time.
5. The sharing period should not be a long period, probably not more than about twenty minutes.
6. A good time for a sharing period is the beginning of the day when the pupils are eager to tell what has happendd since they were last with the others.

Many values can be gained through effective use of sharing time, some of which are directly related to reading abilities. Besides having an opportunity to improve the understanding vocabulary, the children can grow in self-confidence, in power to relate events in sequence, in ability to predict outcomes, in attentiveness when listening, in number and complexity of concepts, in interest in reading more about some of the topics discussed, and in many other ways. The relation of many of these learnings to getting ready for reading is evident.

Increasingly, the interrelation between reading and writing is being stressed. One of the major gains possible from the use of the experience chart (discussed in the last part of this chapter) is that it highlights that relation.

Developing Speech

A chief objective of first-grade language arts programs, before and after reading instruction has begun, is to help the pupil express himself well orally.

Skill in speech plays a significant part in learning to read. The child embarrassed by ridicule because of baby talk is not likely to want to participate freely in group discussions based on reading activities. The boy or girl unable to talk in short, simple sentences is frequently unable to anticipate the meaning of a sentence, even of the type found in beginning reading books. In these and other ways skill in reading and in speech often go hand in hand.

The following points should serve as guidelines in the selection of procedures for the development of speech:

1. Lack of a feeling of emotional or social security frequently causes faulty enunciation as well as other poor speech habits.
2. Most speech improvement comes about through informal classroom activities.
3. Provision should be made for a large number of enriching experiences that give opportunity for improved oral expression.
4. Attention should be given to various phases of speech, such as proper enunciation and pronunciation, adequate speaking vocabulary, and interest in speaking with or to others, with an understanding of courtesies and proprieties in speaking.
5. Pupils who need help in speech should be given opportunity for special practice.
6. In oral expression both content and form should be emphasized.
7. Relatively little effort should be made to correct speech defects that are due to the transition from temporary to permanent teeth.
8. The teacher's own speech should be a suitable model for the boys and girls.
9. The teacher should not talk too much.
10. The physical features of the room and the activities carried on by the class should be made so interesting that the children will have vital topics for discussion and conversation.
11. The atmosphere of the classroom should encourage children to converse freely at appropriate times.

The following are some ways in which the teacher can help pupils to improve the pattern of their expression:

1. Providing many opportunities for free discussion during various activities, such as planning a project or making the schedule for the day.
2. Encouraging the pupils to tell stories that they have heard or experienced or made up.
3. Asking pupils to explain pictures they have drawn.
4. Placing on the bulletin board pictures the pupils can interpret orally to others.
5. Setting aside time for dramatizing some of the stories read or told by the teacher to the group.

6. Helping the boys and girls put on simple puppet shows.

7. Providing opportunities for dramatic play—for example, playing house.

8. Helping the children do choral reading or otherwise saying poems in unison.

9. Making provisions for many opportunities for singing.

10. Talking individually to the boys and girls when they come to school in the morning, during the noon hour, when they leave in the afternoon, or during periods set aside for individual or committee work.

11. Encouraging all pupils to participate in a "sharing period."

12. Asking pupils to talk about group experiences, like class trips to the bakery or the post office or the fire station, or to report on trips they have taken when not under the supervision of school.

13. Displaying in the room objects that are likely to stimulate discussion.

14. Setting time aside for the children to tell about what they enjoy doing, like caring for an animal, playing a game, or doing some cooking.

15. Providing practice situations in which the importance of good enunciation is stressed. For example, the pupils might be asked to tell which of a series of sentences given by the teacher illustrate good and which poor enunciation.

16. Setting up some exercises to furnish practice in the correct pronunciation of words frequently mispronounced. For example, the pupils might play a game in which some of the children try to reach the top of a diagram of a ladder drawn on the chalkboard, on rungs of which are words— such as *running, yellow, was*—often mispronounced by the children.

Developing Listening

One aspect of the language arts that has not been emphasized sufficiently in many schools is listening. Frequently it has been taken for granted. Because of its close relation to reading and to many other significant activities both in and out of school, increased attention should be given to this ability.

In trying to help children develop better habits of listening, the teacher should utilize regular classroom activities whenever possible. The following are ways in which children can be assisted in becoming better listeners.

1. As the teacher taps a pencil on a table or claps his hands several times, the children, with eyes closed, give the number of taps or sounds they hear.

2. As the children listen to recordings of sounds characteristic of the home, the street, the farm they identify the sounds.

3. The boys and girls identify sounds they hear as they are in their schoolroom, such as cars passing by, children walking in the hall.

4. The pupils play games in which children, who are blindfolded, try to identify sounds such as the tapping of a pencil on a desk, the crushing of paper, writing on the chalkboard.

5. The children go on a "listening walk" with the teacher, on which they try to discover as many sounds as they can while on the walk. Later a composite list of the sounds heard might be made.

6. As the teacher tells or reads stories to the boys and girls, he stops occasionally to ask questions that test their attentiveness—for example, "Why did Bobby want to get some apples for his mother?"

7. After the teacher has told or read part of a story to the class, he says: "When I have finished the story, see if you can tell what happened to the snowman."

8. Before the teacher reads a story to the class, the pupils are told that after the reading they will be asked to arrange in order pictures that illustrate the action of the story.

9. The pupils are encouraged to listen carefully to stories so that they can tell them to others.

10. The pupils draw up standards for good listening, such as looking at the person talking, not talking while someone else talks, and not playing with anything while someone is talking.

11. Evaluations of how well the pupils are listening, according to standards such as those mentioned in item 10 are made by the class.

12. Listening is encouraged by means of dramatization of stories or incidents.

Developing the Speaking and Understanding Vocabulary

Since the vocabulary of beginning books and the sentence structure used in these books are necessarily below the understanding and speaking level of many of the children, it is important to extend their knowledge and use of words through listening and talking. Although much of the work on vocabulary development may be carried on by incidental instruction, it should nevertheless be carefully planned. Direct practice may sometimes be needed, but it should be in a meaningful setting, not as isolated practice on words. Growth in children's speaking and listening vocabulary can be fostered in many ways, such as:

1. Providing opportunity to engage in work on significant areas of study, such as the farm. New words should be introduced as the need for them arises.

2. Reading or telling stories that include some unfamiliar words. The meaning of new words should be explained.

3. Helping children write a group letter.

4. Asking pupils to dramatize words such as *walked, ran, crept, raced.*

5. Drawing attention to pupil's use of "new" or especially descriptive words.

6. Having children draw pictures illustrating such "new words" as *funnel, burrow, tractor.*

7. Having pupils play games in which they make up sentences that refer to a "new word." A group of sentences might be: "I am thinking of something a

rabbit does. He does it when he makes a hole. The word begins with the sound with which *boy* starts."

8. When showing motion pictures, slides, or filmstrips, drawing attention to the use of words that might advisedly be added to the children's vocabulary.

9. Bringing interesting objects to the room. If a rock exhibit is set up, for example, children may enlarge their vocabulary by learning terms like *marble, granite, sandstone.*

10. Taking children on excursions and helping them become familiar with terms that give more meaning to their trip, like *cash register, sales, customer.*

11. Introducing songs and poems that contain new words.

In helping children to add words to their understanding and speaking vocabulary the teacher may follow these steps:

1. Introduce the word in a meaningful situation.

2. Draw attention to the new word by giving its meaning, asking someone in the group who knows the word to give the meaning, or questioning the others so that they can tell what the word means.

3. Let some of the children use the word in a sentence.

4. Make certain that the pupils pronounce the word correctly.

5. Use the word in later conversation or discussion.

6. Encourage the pupils to use the word.

Developing a Reading Vocabulary

Even during the prereading program the teacher can help pupils acquire a reading vocabulary that will assist them greatly when they begin reading in a book. As in the case of the speaking and understanding vocabulary, the words on which help is given in the development of a reading vocabulary should be those of which a meaningful application can be made. With this point in mind, the teacher may wish to label shelves where articles such as scissors, paste, and crayons are kept. Attaching the children's names to their lockers and desks can also be of value. But merely labeling articles is not enough, for looking at a word, without the intent to remember it, frequently does not result in learning on the part of the child. For this reason, attention should be called to the labels and the children should be given an opportunity for associating the words with objects. At times the pupils may be asked to match the appropriate cards with the labels, or they may name cards containing the words without comparing them with the cards used as labels. Labeling objects like a table, a desk, or a chair is of little value unless a real purpose is served thereby. It may be profitable, for example, to place words on a table to show what is to be exhibited on it.

Picture-word cards—cards on which the picture and the name of the item pictured are given, like *mother, father, sister, brother, cat, dog, school,* and *home*—can be displayed and used in practice exercises for pupils who seem to need such repetition. On the back of the card may be written the word that goes with the picture, so that pupils may practice recognizing words without looking at the illustrations. Sets of small cards like these, possibly four inches by six inches, can be used by the pupils individually. Similarly, both large cards for group use and small cards for individual practice can be made, with the names of the primary and the secondary colors corresponding to the color illustrated on the reverse side.

There are many other means of adding words to the children's vocabulary. The teacher may put on the chalkboard or on large sheets of paper directions often used in the classroom, such as: "Please get your wraps," or "Please form a circle." Instead of giving the directions orally, the teacher can sometimes point to these. Plans for the day may also be written on the board daily before school: "We will take a walk," or "We will hear a good story today." A chart with the names of the children in the room can be used in a game in which one child points to a name while another says it.

Learning to Write

The simple writing experiences of children during the prereading period can be of help in later reading instruction. Usually their writing during this stage is confined to the writing of their names or the copying of sentences from the chalkboard or from sheets of paper. Brief invitations to parents or short sentences to accompany illustrations they have made may be copied. Through writing of this type, children can be made more aware of the function of the written word both as writing and as reading. Moreover, as the pupils are writing they can become familiar with the configuration of words, by noting which words are short, which are long, and which begin or end in the same way. Since many children enjoy reading what they have written, they should have the opportunity to read to others in the room or to their parents the captions under their pictures or the notes they write.

Learning the Letters of the Alphabet and Their Sounds

As indicated in Chapter 4A, some teachers do not believe that part of the reading-readiness period should be devoted to learning the letters of the alphabet and the sounds that they commonly represent. In general it may be said that teachers favoring synthetic methods of teaching phonics, rather than phonics taught through analysis of word forms, will be placing early emphasis on letter sounds and names. Many suggestions for teaching the letters and their sounds are given in workbooks and teachers' manuals of series of readers that emphasize early learning of the "code" (the letter-sound or the grapheme-phoneme relation) on which the English language is based. However, a few suggested procedures are also indicated below:

1. The boys and girls are given cards on each of which is written a letter of the alphabet. As the teacher names a letter, the pupils hold up the card on which it is written.

2. As the teacher or a pupil points to a letter of the alphabet written on the chalkboard, a pupil gives the name of the letter.

3. The children write the letter of the alphabet with which the name of the word representing an illustrated object begins. For example, the pupils write the letter *b* as the beginning letter of the word for a picture of a boy.

Developing Auditory and Visual Discrimination

Among the most important prerequisites for successful reading are the ability to differentiate between sounds of words and letters and the ability to see the differences between written words and between letters. Since improvement in making such discriminations can be brought about through training, suggestions for their development are given in the following pages.

Auditory Discrimination

In helping children to discriminate between sounds they hear, teachers should remember that:

1. *There is great variation among first-grade children in powers of auditory discrimination.* The difference is not necessarily due to degrees of auditory acuity. Two children, for example, may plainly hear the words *walk* and *walked,* but only one may be able to note the difference in the sound.

2. *Instruction in auditory discrimination should take individual differences into account.* Many children will have developed the needed skill in auditory discrimination before they first come to school. For them the exercises in discrimination would be wasteful and stupid. On the other hand, the child who cannot tell whether *dog* and *cat* begin with the same sound or with different sounds needs help in learning to discriminate between sounds that are quite unlike. The same is true of those children who have little difficulty in distinguishing sounds at the beginning of words but have trouble with sounds at the end of words.

3. *Instruction in auditory discrimination should be an integral part of regular classroom activities.* As children take part in the usual classroom activities, like playing with their toys or pets, their attention can be drawn to the differences in sounds. When, for example, a child fails to distinguish between *car* and *cars,* the teacher may try to help him detect the difference. At times there is value in providing separate exercises in noting which pairs of words are alike and which different, as in the case of *car* and *cars* and *car* and *car.* Or a child may be asked to supply the last word of the second line of a jingle in order to make it rhyme with the first line.

4. *Growth in power to distinguish between sounds should continue even after reading instruction is begun.* With the child who is unable to make rather careful discriminations between sounds of letters and between sounds of words that are somewhat similar, it must not be assumed that all efforts to develop this ability need to be completed before initial instruction in learning to read is given. As in the case of many other objectives related to reading that can be attained only in part during the pre-reading period, many methods for securing continuous growth in the ability to distinguish between sounds should be utilized in later stages of learning to read.

Some of the ways in which auditory discrimination can be developed during the prereading period consist of having the pupils do the following:

1. Giving orally words beginning with the same sound with which another word begins. The teacher may write on the board the words named by the pupils, even though the pupils cannot read them.
2. Drawing a circle around each picture in a group, the name of which begins with a specified sound.
3. Telling whether a sound that the teacher specifies is found at the beginning, near the middle, or at the end of each of a group of words named by the teacher.
4. Telling which pairs of words named by the teacher—like *mother, man* or *little, ball*—begin with the same sound.
5. Naming the word in a list given by the teacher—like *mother, man, many, few, market*—that does not begin with the same sound as the others.
6. Telling which pairs of words given by the teacher end in the same sound —like *walks, sings* or *runs, play.*
7. Naming the word in a list—like *at, talk, fit, get*—that does not end with the same sound as the others.
8. Telling which pairs of words—like *rat, sat* or *bat, sit*—are rhyming words.
9. Telling which word in a list does not rhyme—as in *cat, bat, sat, sit.*
10. Naming rhyming words.
11. Telling which pairs of sounds—like *m, n* or *m, m*—are alike.
12. Making up rhymes.
13. Playing the game, "I spy." In this game, pupils guess what object a child refers to in a statement like "I spy something that begins with the same sound as *Mary,*" or "I spy something that ends with the same sound as *took.*"
14. Naming the objects in a picture that begin with the same sound as a word that is named by the teacher.
15. Naming the objects in a picture that rhyme with a word that is named by the teacher.
16. Supplying the last word for a two-line jingle of which the teacher gives all but the last word. The pupils would name the words that rhyme with the last word of the first line.

Visual Discrimination

In planning procedures for the development of visual discrimination during the prereading period, certain general observations should be kept in mind: (1.) Some beginning first-grade pupils do not have enough skill in visual discrimination to undertake the reading task with ease. (2.) Instruction should be adapted to individual differences. (3.) So far as possible, skill in visual discrimination should be furthered in connection with meaningful classroom activities. (4.) Not all deficiencies in visual discrimination need to be removed before reading instruction is begun. As the child learns to read, opportunities for making finer discriminations will present themselves.

Boys and girls can systematically be taught to discriminate visually between letter likenesses and letter differences. Directions for two exercises to promote visual discrimination between letters follow:

1. *Matching letters.* Prepare two sets of 3 x 5 cards on which capital or lower-case letters have been written, one of the twenty-six letters of the alphabet on each of the cards in a set. Limit the number of cards to be used with beginners, possibly to as small a number as four or five. To keep the cards in the duplicate set separated from the others, a different color of ink can be used in writing the letters. To make the exercise self-checking, the two cards with identical letters can be placed on each other and a notch cut through both cards so that when the same letters are matched, the notches are in corresponding position.

2. *Testing visual memory of letters.* Purchase a miniature slate or a magic slate on which you can write letters and erase or remove them at will. Use the sets of cards on which you have written upper-case or lower-case letters (*see* Exercise 1 above). Show the children a card and then remove it from sight by turning it over. Next write several letters on the slate, among which is the one shown earlier. Ask the child to point to or circle the letter you showed him.

Additional suggestions for methods of stimulating growth in the ability to make visual discriminations during the prereading period or later are:

1. Asking the pupils to find the word in a written series—like *big, boy, big, big, big*—which is unlike the other words.

2. Asking the pupils to draw a line under each word in a written series, like the following, which is the same as the first word in a row:

    man   mother   man   man   man.

    At first, practice should be given in differentiating between words that are decidedly different in appearance, like *man* and *mother*. Later, the pupil should be asked to discriminate between words almost alike in appearance, like *man* and *men*.

3. After pupils have dictated to the teacher a record of some experience they have had, like taking care of a pet, asking one child to draw a line under all the words in the story that begin with the same letter as a word indicated by the teacher.

4. Listing two parallel columns of words in which the same words are used but in a different order. The pupils may draw lines connecting like words in the two columns.

5. Asking the pupils to cross out a given word, like *dog,* each time that it occurs in a group of sentences in which the word is used several times.

6. Having the pupils match tagboard cards, on which single words are written, with words as they are written on the chalkboard.

7. Having the pupils draw a circle around a word in a list on the chalkboard that is the same as a word on a card shown to the class.

8. Having the children find on a chart all the names of pupils in the room that begin with a specified letter.

9. Having the pupils arrange cards in groups that end with the same letter.

The words on the cards might be *sing, jump, running, pup, duck, thing, black, dog, back, rug.*

10. Asking the boys and girls to draw a line under the words in a list that contain a given combination of letters such as *in,* for listings such as the following: *tin, tan, it, inside, win.*

11. Asking the pupils to match word cards with words in a cardholder or on the chalkboard.

Improving in Ability to Remember

The ability to remember plays an important role in reading. One cause of inadequate retention in reading is found in poor habits of attentiveness: A child who does not pay careful attention to what is going on cannot be expected to remember. The teacher can attack this problem by assisting boys and girls to become more attentive. Some ways in which children can be helped to attend better, and therefore to remember better, have been discussed earlier in this chapter under the related topic "Improving Listening." Here are some additional suggestions for increasing a pupil's memory span:

1. Making the work interesting enough so that the pupil will have reason to want to pay attention.

2. Making sure that the work is on the level of the pupil.

3. Varying the activities frequently enough so that the child's power of attention will not be overtaxed. At the same time children should be helped to develop an ever longer span of attention.

4. Developing in pupils the desire to remain with an activity until it is completed, unless there is good reason not to do so, through helping them recognize the wastefulness of effort when, for little reason, they discontinue an activity before its planned completion.

5. Keeping reasonable orderliness conducive to good attention in the room.

6. Requiring pupils to keep to the topic of discussion.

7. Keeping each child responsible for remembering the answer to a question that he asked a community worker on a trip to the post office or police station or fire department.

Remembering a Sequence of Ideas

To help the boys and girls remember a sequence of ideas encountered in reading or listening, the teacher may wish to follow some of these suggestions:

1. After the teacher or a pupil has told a story, the teacher may ask such questions as: "What was the first thing Nancy did when she saw that her dog had followed her?" "What did she do next?"

2. After the teacher has given directions for a simple experiment, like showing that plants need light, he may ask the pupils: "What is the first thing we need to do?" and "What do we need to do next?" After the experiment has been completed, the pupils may be asked to enumerate the steps that were followed.

3. Retelling stories can be a helpful means of developing the ability to re-member a sequence of ideas. The pupil should relate the incidents in the correct order.

4. The boys and girls, with the assistance of the teacher, might build a topical outline for the dramatizing of a story. The pupils decide on the events to be included in the dramatization and the teacher lists these on the chalk-board. They could then arrange these events in logical sequence.

5. The teacher might place on a flannel board, in mixed-up order, a series of pictures illustrating a story known to the boys and girls and then ask the pupils to rearrange the pictures in correct order.

6. The group may make a "movie" either to illustrate a story that the teacher has told or read to them or to portray activities in which they have en-gaged. Such an activity furnishes excellent practice in remembering events in sequence and cultivates other abilities important in reading, such as critical thinking, good work habits, skill in following directions, and ability to work with others.

Steps in planning a "movie" on a story told to the class may be these:

1. Discussing the story.
2. Deciding to make a "movie" of the story.
3. Retelling the story.
4. Deciding on pictures to include.
5. Working out a sequence of the pictures to be drawn.
6. Assigning pictures to be drawn.
7. Drawing the pictures.
8. Deciding on captions or longer explanations of the pictures to be written for the "movie" by the teacher.
9. Arranging the pictures and the writing in the proper sequence.
10. Fastening the pictures to a roll.
11. Practicing telling the story of the "movie."

If the story of *The Three Billy Goats Gruff* were made into a "movie," these are pictures that might be drawn:

1. Three billy goats at the side of the hill
2. The green hill that they saw in the distance
3. The stream they would have to cross
4. The bridge they would have to cross
5. The ugly troll who lived under the bridge
6. The youngest billy goat starting to cross the bridge
7. The troll roaring at the youngest billy goat
8. The youngest billy goat talking with the troll
9. The youngest billy goat feeding on the hillside
10. The second billy goat starting across the bridge
11. The troll roaring at the second billy goat

12. The second billy goat talking with the troll
13. The second billy goat going across the bridge
14. The first and the second billy goats feeding on the hillside
15. The big billy goat starting across the bridge
16. The troll roaring at the big billy goat
17. The big billy goat talking with the troll
18. The fight between the big billy goat and the troll
19. The end of the troll
20. The big billy goat going across the bridge
21. The three billy goats feeding on the hillside

The troll roaring at
the youngest billy goat

If there are fewer pupils than pictures to be drawn, some children could draw two. If the number of pictures is less than the number of pupils, two children could draw a picture on the same topic. In that case one of the pictures, not necessarily the better, could be used in the "movie" and the other displayed with pride elsewhere, possibly as part of a big book or on the bulletin board.

Following Directions

The ability to follow directions involves considerable skill in remembering. So many directions are given to children in school that, as a rule, no special exercises are needed for practice in this skill. To facilitate learning, the teacher's directions should be clear. Although at first the directions should be very simple, they should become more complex as pupils develop. At times the teacher may need to demonstrate how to follow a rather involved set of directions. At other times he can help pupils by having the class follow directions together.

Stimulating Growth in Critical and Creative Thinking

An important component of effective reading is the ability to think critically and creatively. Encouragement for the development of this power can and should be given during the prereading period, as well as on all subsequent levels in learning to read.

In Chapter 6A, "Comprehension," a discussion of critical and creative reading as it has bearing on reading in the elementary school is included, and in Chapter 6B, "Developing Comprehension," suggested activities for helping boys and girls increase in power to do reading of this type are listed. For background for the next few paragraphs the reader may at this time wish to refer to those pages. Reference is made below only to a few procedures for stimulating the pupils' power of critical and creative thinking—and subsequent reading—including some that are especially appropriate for use in the prereading and early reading stages.

The teacher can help boys and girls increase in ability to think critically and creatively by asking thought questions when he reads or tells stories to the class. For example, as he reads the story *Millions of Cats* by Wanda Gág, he may ask: "What do you think the little old woman will say when the little old man comes home not with one cat, but with millions of cats?" Or after the teacher has told *The Tale of Peter Rabbit*, he may ask: "Why was Peter Rabbit happy at the end of the story even though his mother had punished him?" After the children have heard the story of *The Three Pigs,* they could be guided in making an analysis of a problem through a question such as: "In what other ways could the wolf have been kept from blowing down the brick house?" Questions about what will happen next also encourage children to think as they listen.

The following are a few additional ways in which the children can be encouraged, through stories told or read to them, to do critical or creative thinking:

1. They can draw a picture of a character in a situation described in the book.

2. They can synthesize or combine their ideas in such a manner that the outcome is novel, though somewhat resembling that of the author who created an imaginary character. For example, after hearing the story *The Funny Thing* by Wanda Gág which tells about a dragonlike creature fed on jum-jills, they enjoy experiences where they are encouraged to be inventive in making up their own strange characters. After hearing about *Chitty-Chitty-Bang-Bang* by Ian Fleming, they may wish to invent a magical car.

3. They can pantomime or dramatize stories, giving reign to the exercise of their interpretative powers.

4. They can compare similar happenings in different books to develop relationships. For example, they can compare the reactions to the snowstorm as described in *White Snow, Bright Snow* by Alvin Tresselt with those evidenced in *The Big Snow* by Berta and Elmer Hader.

To encourage critical and creative thinking, it is not enough that the teacher ask suitable questions; boys and girls, too, should be encouraged to ask thought questions. To provide such encouragement the teacher will need to respect the questions they ask. The teacher can show his respect by providing opportunity for this kind of questioning and by listening attentively to the questions. At times he may wish to help the boys and girls record their questions. Care needs to be taken in any attempt at improvement that the altered question continues to express what the child has in mind. Praising a child when he asks a pertinent question beyond the factual level is another way in which thought questions can be encouraged as well as improved.

Critical thinking can also be stimulated through application of something read to real-life problems. For example, in stories about handicapped children, the class might consider ways in which they have observed individuals with handicaps make adjustments to daily routines of living. Or they might tell of ways in which other people have accommodated those with disabilities.

The teacher can encourage critical thinking by giving the boys and girls a part in planning activities, in deciding on the better course of action in a given situation, in determining why some of their actions were wise or unwise.

Orienting to the Left-to-Right and Top-to-Bottom Sequence

Some children entering first grade require help in directionality; that is, in observing a left-to-right and top-to-bottom sequence in reading pictures or print. Some need to be shown which is their right and which is their left hand. Others, who do know left from right, have not yet discovered that reading, in English, proceeds from left to right and from top to bottom. Special practice in left-to-right and top-to-bottom reading may sometimes be needed.

The following are suggestions for helping children develop this directional orientation to reading:

1. As the teacher reads a book to the class, he can point out where he starts reading and in what direction he progresses.
2. As the teacher or children reread from charts or the chalkboard stories that have been dictated, the teacher can run his hand rhythmically under the lines. Or he can ask a pupil to point to the word with which he should begin reading. In time, a pupil can sweep his hands below the line he is reading from a chart or from the chalkboard. Care must be taken in the latter case that word pointing with consequent "word calling" does not result.
3. At times, when the teacher writes on large sheets of paper or on the board, he can ask the pupils where he should begin writing and in what direction he should proceed.
4. As some pupils are placing a picture story on a flannel board, they should be guided to arrange the pictures from left to right in each row and from top to bottom by rows.
5. To emphasize the left-to-right order, boys and girls could be shown a series of possibly three pictures illustrating different actions, with the pictures not in the sequence of the activity illustrated. For example, the pictures might illustrate a boy leaving his home. The first one might show him outside the door of his home, the second running when he is already

a distance from home, and the third running when he is farther from his home. The pupils could then be asked to arrange the pictures in order in a left-to-right sequence on a chalkboard tray.

Developing and Maintaining Interest in Reading

One of the major objectives of the prereading and early reading stages should be to guide the boys and girls so that they will develop or maintain an interest in reading. Unless boys and girls have strong motivation for reading, many of the other suggestions given in this and succeeding chapters will be futile or almost futile. The power of interest must not be overlooked or minimized.

The importance of access to an abundance of interesting reading materials has already been stressed in this book. Other ways in which the teacher can try to interest the children in books are: taking them to the school or public library where they can browse among the books and where, probably, the librarian will be willing to tell them a story; inviting one or more children from a second or third grade to entertain the first grade by reading an interesting story to them; taking boys and girls to other rooms in the elementary school in which they can see books being used for various purposes; reading stories and informational material to the class.

The sharing period, discussed earlier in this chapter, can serve to interest children in reading. They can be encouraged to show and talk about books they like. Some of these may be picture books for which the child reporting makes up the story. Or the books may contain a simple text, which someone has read beforehand to the pupil reporting.

Use of little booklets containing children's stories, written by the teacher at the dictation of the pupils, gives added incentive to learning to read. In these booklets may be recorded reports planned by the class as a whole on an activity in which they have engaged, such as a trip to a farm. Or the material may consist of individual accounts about each child—for example, reports on the work of each child's father or mother. For recording in these books, some teachers make up stories in which the vocabulary is well controlled. Although making such a book is time-consuming, it is worthwhile in the long run, since the book can often be used not only once with a given group but later on with classes in succeeding years.

Keeping records on charts of some of the experiences of the group, such as visiting the grocery store, can also stimulate interest in reading. How these charts can be constructed and utilized is explained below.

USING THE EXPERIENCE CHART IN THE PREREADING PERIOD

The term *experience chart* ordinarily refers to a written record of an experience a class has had, is having, or is intending to have. An experience chart is planned cooperatively by the pupils and the teacher and, in the primary grades, is usually recorded by the teacher. First-grade children who find pretty leaves may make an experience chart telling about their leaves, or those about to have a party may plan a chart to help remember points about the proposed party. Examples of such charts are given here:

Leaves

We found many pretty leaves.
We found them on our walk.
We found some red leaves.
Some of our leaves are brown.
Some of our leaves are yellow.

Our Party

We will have a party.
We will have the party on Monday.
We will have it in the afternoon.
Mary and Susan will bring cookies.
We will drink milk.
We will play games.

Experience charts serve a variety of purposes. The teacher's objective in helping plan a chart may be primarily to give children an opportunity to learn to express themselves well. Sometimes they are used chiefly to provide an opportunity for cooperative planning. Such charts are frequently referred to as language charts. Experience charts that are used primarily for reading purposes, either to get the child more nearly ready for beginning reading or to supplement the reading experiences that he has already had, are known as reading charts. Various purposes can be served by the same chart. As the pupils construct and use a reading experience chart, they can also improve their ability to express themselves and learn to plan cooperatively. The differentiation between the two kinds is made because in the so-called language-experience chart it is not as important to restrict the vocabulary as in the chart that serves primarily as a prerading or reading experience. The following discussion of experience charts refers essentially to those that help in reading, either in the prereading period or later.

Experience charts are frequently recorded on large pieces of paper, often 24 x 36 inches or 18 x 24 inches. They can, however, be made on smaller sheets, as they often are when they are designed for individual use rather than for group purposes. If the chart is to be preserved for a considerable time, it is often made on tagboard or mounting board. A record that is to be used for only a short time may well be kept on less expensive paper, like newsprint. Sometimes the charts are assembled, punched at the top, fastened by rings, and attached to a chart holder, which often is on a tripod base. On the tripod there is frequently an adjustable metal pole, across the top of which is a crossbar which holds the chart. Some experience records are kept in large notebooks, often made of butcher paper, probably 24 x 36 inches in size. The records kept in a notebook usually are on one theme, such as "Our Pets" or "Our Schoolroom."

Steps in Making and Using Experience Charts

Experience charts are used in a variety of ways during the prereading period. Outlined below are steps similar to those that many teachers follow when detailed study of the chart is done as a prereading exercise. The work is set up for two successive school days, although a shorter or longer time may be devoted to use of it. In considering these steps, the reader must bear in mind that many stories on charts or on the chalkboard have usually been created and utilized in a class before any one chart is given the detailed study that is here described.

First Day

1. The boys and girls participate in an interesting and significant experience.
2. The children discuss the experience.
3. The pupils, with the help of the teacher, plan the title, general content, and the exact sentences for the chart as the teacher does the writing on the board.
4. The chart as a whole is read first by the teacher, then by the pupils and the teacher together, and finally by the boys and girls alone.

Second Day

5. Before class the teacher has copied onto chart paper the writing for the experience chart that he had put on the board the preceding day. The teacher has also copied on separate strips of tagboard each of the lines of the chart, so that they can be matched later with the writing on the chart. These are placed on the chalk tray or in a word-card holder. On word cards made of tagboard the teacher has also written a few of the words on which he plans to give special practice.
6. The new chart is then read by the teacher and pupils together.
7. The teacher reads sentences for the pupils to find, and they point to each one as they read it.
8. After the teacher has read the sentences out of the regular order, the pupils match the sentence strips with the sentences on the chart and then read them.
9. As the teacher shows the boys and girls each of the several word cards, containing those words on which he thinks it is important to provide practice, he pronounces the words and has the pupils say them after him. A pupil then matches the word on the card with the same word on the chart. Further practice on the words can be given if before class the teacher writes these words on the board. In that case the pupils can name the words as the teacher points to them.
10. Review of words used in the chart that the boys and girls have studied earlier can then be utilized.
11. Before the period is over one or more pupils can read the chart alone.

Description of Steps in Making and Using Experience Charts

Since some of the steps already outlined need no further explanation, they are not included in the comments that follow.

1. Motivation for Making a Chart After the pupils have engaged in an experience and have discussed it, there are many ways in which the teacher can interest the pupils in making, and then reading, an experience chart. The teacher may suggest to the pupils that they make a chart so that visitors coming into the room can read, or have read to them, what the class has done. Or the boys and girls may make one so that they can go to other rooms to read the chart to the children.

2. Planning the Chart In planning the chart, the teacher should proceed according to the overruling principle that too much teacher-direction in content to be included, in words to be used, in structure of sentences can defeat the purpose for making an experience chart. In fact, some authorities on the use of the language-experience approach recommend a very low minimum deviation from the children's spontaneous suggestions. Additional guidelines for planning the chart are:

a. Care needs to be taken that many, preferably all, of the children take part in the planning.

b. The teacher can, by questioning, help the pupils suggest significant items.

c. He can be of assistance in helping formulate sentences.

d. He can help decide on the sequence.

e. He can guide the work so that the vocabulary used in the chart is fairly simple.

f. He can give the pupils help in vocabulary building by asking for more colorful or more descriptive words to be substituted for some suggested.

g. After the first draft is written, he can assist the children in revising the sentences so that a more unified composition will be the result.

3. Constructing the Chart Care should be taken to make the manuscript writing as nearly perfect as possible in the time available. Neatness, letter form, alignment, size, slant, and spacing between letters, between words, and between lines should receive adequate attention. If a picture is needed, it can be supplied by the teacher or a pupil or taken from a discarded publication.

4. Making the Sentence Strips and the Word Cards The precautions given in connection with the writing of the chart should also be observed in making sentence strips and word cards. Teachers find it desirable to keep sentence strips and word cards of the same width, often about four inches wide, for uniformity when they are used with other cards and for ease in filing. For the same reasons some teachers also cut most of the word cards the same length, approximately ten inches. Words that cannot be written without crowding on this size of paper are written on longer cards.

Usually no more than three or four "new words" for special study should be included on one chart. These should be selected on the basis of their likely usefulness to the children. Some teachers prefer to choose words from the pupils' first reading books.

5. Follow-up Activities In addition to the culminating activity, already suggested, of reading the chart to visitors or pupils in other rooms, the teacher may make copies available to the children. He may leave space near each of the words that can be illustrated, so that the pupils can draw a picture that goes with the word; for example, opposite the word *leaves*, the pupils may draw a picture of leaves. This activity can help the children recall the word more easily later on. The children can make the sheets into a booklet and draw an appropriate picture for the cover. After a child has learned to "read" the chart, he may take his booklet home and read it to his parents.

Illustration of Work on an Experience Chart

The following is an imaginary description of possible procedures in the development of an experience chart.

Early in the year, after the first-grade boys and girls had been on a listening walk, they made an experience chart on which were recorded some of the sounds they heard while taking the walk. At that time the teacher suggested that they might want to make a chart of all especially interesting activities in which they would take part during the year. The idea received an enthusiastic reception. The teacher pointed out that such charts could help the children remember what they had done during the school year. He also suggested visitors might like to read them. Consequently, the day after the Halloween party, it was easy to interest the boys and girls in making a chart reporting on it.

The teacher helped the boys and girls decide on the title for the chart. When "Our Party" was suggested, he asked if anyone could think of a title that would tell what kind of party it was. When a boy responded by suggesting "Our Halloween Party," he wrote the title on the chalkboard. Then the pupils discussed some of the points they wanted to include in the report. Comments such as these were made:

We will want to tell that we had a Halloween party.
We should tell that we had candy.
We want to tell that we were dressed up.

As the pupils suggested the wording of the sentences, the teacher helped them with sentence structure. Furthermore, he watched the vocabulary used on the chart so that some of the "new words" were repeated frequently enough to assure the pupils' increased likelihood of learning them. He also guided the children so that their thoughts were recorded in logical sequence. Thus, the following sentences, which the teacher wrote on the chalkboard, evolved:

Our Halloween Party

We had a Halloween party.
We had the party in our room.
We played games at our party.
We had candy at our party.
It was Halloween candy.
We also had cookies.
We wore Halloween costumes.

The, a, at, and *in* were words used on the chart that the children had previously acquired as part of their reading vocabulary. "New words," which the teacher planned to teach in connection with the work on this chart, were *we, had, our,* and *Halloween.* These words, excepting *Halloween,* were found in the first-grade reading books that the children would later be reading.

Next followed practice in "reading" the chart. First the teacher read it alone. Then he and the pupils read it together.

For an illustration on the chart several suggestions came from the children. Someone recommended cutting a picture of a goblin out of an old magazine. Another pupil suggested that a picture of a goblin be cut freehand. Still another child thought that drawing a picture of one would be better. After further discussion it was agreed that each pupil should cut out of construction paper, freehand, a picture of something that would go well with the chart. It was also agreed that each pupil could then decorate his cutout as he saw fit. A committee, it was decided, was then to select one for the chart that the teacher agreed to have ready by the following day.

The next day the teacher brought the chart to class with him, along with separate strips of tagboard on which were written the title and each of the sentences used on the chart, and cards on which the "new words"—*we, had, our,* and *Halloween*—and the "review words"—*the, a, at,* and *in*—were written.

Practice was then given in reading the new materials. First the teacher alone read the chart as he moved his hand under each line of writing. After the pupils had read it twice in concert, several children read it alone. Then the pupils matched the sentence strips with the chart, by holding each strip next to the corresponding sentence on the chart and reading it. As the teacher read a sentence out of its normal order in the story, a pupil found the correct strip and read it orally.

To give practice with the words on the cards, the teacher began by asking someone to find the word *our* in the title. Then the pupils pronounced the word *our* as the teacher showed the class the word card for it and as he placed it in a card holder. A pupil pointed to the word *our* as it appeared in some of the sentences of the report and pronounced it. In a similar manner the teacher presented the words *we* and *Halloween.* When he introduced the word *had,* before telling the pupils the word, he wrote *house* and *had* on the chalkboard, explaining that the "new word" began with the same sound as the word *house,* which the class had already learned to read. After the class had identified the *h* sound in *house,* the teacher pronounced the word *had* and asked the pupils to note that both of these words began with the *h* sound. Next, the pupils named other words beginning with the same sound— such as *hat, home,* and *Harry*—which the teacher wrote on the chalkboard. As the teacher showed the cards for the "review words" *the, a, at,* and *in,* the pupils named them and found them on the chart. The word cards containing the new words and the review words were then mixed, and pupils, individually, named them as the teacher showed the cards. Before the period was over several children again "read" the chart.

For follow-up work, on the third day of the lesson the teacher brought to class duplicated copies of the chart, one for each child, on paper 8½ x 11 inches. He also had sheets of paper of the same size on which were the four "new words"—*we, had, our* and *Halloween. Above the word Halloween space was provided in which the pupils then drew illustrations of things that might suggest Halloween. The teacher also distributed to each boy and girl a piece of construction paper on which the pupils could paste the freehand drawings they had cut out of paper two days before. The pupils made all the sheets into booklets, fastening them with brass fasteners. Several children then read the story orally. The rule was made that, as soon as a child could read the story without error, he could give his booklet to his parents and read it to them. The boys and girls who did not have an opportunity to read the booklet orally on that day were given a chance to do so within the next few days, either during class time or at other times. When need for additional practice was indicated, it was provided.

Arguments for and against the Use of Experience Charts

There is disagreement concerning the use of experience charts. Most of the controversy centers on the question: "To what extent should experience charts be used in first-grade reading?"

Some of the arguments given for rather extensive use of experience charts as reading-readiness materials are these:

1. The valuable experiences that boys and girls get can be made more meaningful by basing charts on them.
2. Reading about their own experiences is more interesting to them than using reading-readiness books.
3. The relation between reading and two other language arts, talking and writing, is made evident to the boys and girls.
4. The children acquire a reading vocabulary, the value of which they easily recognize.

Persons who do not favor the extensive use of experience charts try to refute the arguments given for their frequent use by claiming that:

1. The valuable experiences that boys and girls get will enrich their background of information and understanding without their necessarily writing a chart about the experiences.
2. Reading one's own story is not as interesting, in some cases, as reading the published prereading materials.

3. The relation between reading and the other language arts can be made evident to the boys and girls without using experience charts extensively.

4. The pupils are able to recognize the value of the reading vocabulary they acquire when reading well-graded and well-written reading-readiness books.

Among the most significant arguments advanced against much use of experience charts as reading materials is that the words that appear in the charts are not as well selected as those that are found in published reading-readiness books. Writers of textbooks in reading for the primary grades have spent much time and energy in attempts to secure a suitable vocabulary. An effort is made by them to use words that pupils will meet frequently in other reading, to introduce only a few new words in each selection, and to give systematic review of words learned by providing for repetition in the reading, at spaced intervals, both in the book in which the word is presented and in later books in the series. Those favoring the use of experience charts claim that the teacher can help in selecting words for a chart so that it will include those words that the children will be likely to encounter in other reading. However, if the teacher does much of the selecting of the words for a chart, it is evidently the teacher's, rather than the pupils', account.

Another argument against extensive use of experience charts during the prereading or early reading stages is that boys and girls do not get practice of the type needed for independent reading later on. Reading should be, it is argued by persons opposed to the wide use of reading experience charts, a process of thought getting, not a process of "reading" what one already knows—as is the case in experience charts when used as outlined on pages

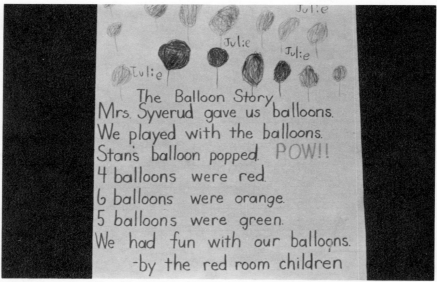

Figure 4.2 The values of language-experience charts are many. (Campus Laboratory School, St. Cloud State College, St. Cloud, Minn.)

97–101. Furthermore, criticism is directed at the fact that there is memorization of what is written on the chart, not reading in the true sense of the word.

A point the teacher must consider when deciding on the number of experience charts to use is the fact that to make many charts is very time-consuming.

No one formula can be given for the proportionate amount of emphasis that should be placed on experience charts. There will, in many classes, be some boys and girls who will need relatively few reading experiences with charts or with published reading-readiness materials before they begin regular book reading. With others it will be advantageous to use either or both types. What the proportion of charts and reading-readiness books should be with those children for whom either type or both are indicated will vary with the skill of the teacher, the books available, and the needs of the pupils.

Although the discussion in this chapter has been limited to the use of experience charts in the prereading period or during initial reading instruction, it should not be assumed that this is their only value. They can also be used to advantage with older boys and girls who are retarded in reading, as well as with those who, because of their language background, have difficulty in reading so-called "standard English." It has been suggested that they serve as a means of giving boys and girls in the inner city access to reading material more relevant to their lives than the typical reading textbook.

Experience charts can also be used, as suggested earlier, as language charts in which the main objective is not reading but one or more of the other phases of communication. For example, a second grade might make a series of charts on interesting experiences the class has had—not to increase their ability to read but to help them to remember important details or to obtain practice in written communication. Or boys and girls could make individual experience charts, with the assistance of the teacher, telling about events important in their lives for the enjoyment of their classmates.

These, then, are some of the ways in which the teacher can help boys and girls become ready for the great adventure of school—learning to read.

For Further Study

Bereiter, Carl, "Instruction of Three- and Four-Year-Old Children," *Child Study* 29 (Fall and winter 1967), pp. 3–11.

Brzeinski, Joseph E., "Beginning Reading in Denver," *The Reading Teacher,* vol. 18 (October 1964), pp. 16–21.

Brzeinski, Joseph E., and Gerald E. Ellege, "Early Reading," *Some Persistent Questions on Beginning Reading,* Robert C. Aukerman, ed. (Newark, Del.: International Reading Association, 1962), pp. 73–74.

Brzeinski, Joseph E., and Will Howard, "Early Reading—How, Not When!," *The Reading Teacher,* vol. 25, no. 3 (December 1971), p. 239–242.

Doman, Glenn, *How to Teach Your Baby to Read* (New York: Random House, Inc., 1964).

Doman, Glenn, George L. Stevens, and Reginald C. Orem, "You Can Teach Your Baby to Read," *Ladies Home Journal,* vol. 80 (May 1963), p. 62.

Durkin, Dolores, *Children Who Read Early* (New York: Teachers College Press, Columbia University, 1966).

Durkin, Dolores, *Teaching Them to Read* (Boston: Allyn and Bacon, Inc., 1970), Ch. III.

Durkin, Dolores, "What Does Research Say about the Time to Begin Reading Instruction?," *Journal of Educational Research,* vol. 63 (October 1970), pp. 52–56.

Enzmann, Arthur M., "A Look at Early Reading," *The Reading Teacher,* vol. 24 (April 1971), pp. 616–620.

Hall, Mary Anne, *Teaching Reading as a Language Experience* (Columbus, Ohio: Charles E. Merrill Publishing Company, 1970).

Harris, Albert J., and Edward R. Sipay, *Readings on Reading Instruction,* 2nd ed. (New York: David McKay Company, 1972), Ch. III.

Heilman, Arthur W., *Phonics in Proper Perspective* (Columbus, Ohio: Charles E. Merrill Publishing Company, 1964).

Herrick, Virgil E., and Marcella Nerbovig, *Using Experience Charts with Children* (Columbus, Ohio: Charles E. Merrill Publishing Company, 1964).

Hymes, Jr., James L., "Teaching Reading to Under-six Age: A Child Development Point of View," *Claremont Reading Conference Yearbook,* vol. 34 (Claremont, California: Claremont College Library, 1970), pp. 79–83.

Karlin, Robert, *Teaching Elementary Reading* (New York: Harcourt Brace Jovanovich, 1971), pp. 73–99.

Lee, Dorris M., and R.V. Allen, *Learning to Read through Experiences* (New York: Appleton-Century-Crofts, 1963).

Lillard, Paul Polk, *Montessori: A Modern Approach* (New York: Schocken Books, 1972).

Montessori, Maria, *The Montessori Method* (New York: Frederick A. Stokes, 1912).

Smith, Nila Banton, "Perspectives: Teaching Young Children to Read," *Issues and Innovations in the Teaching of Reading,* Joe L. Frost, ed. (Glenview, Ill.: Scott, Foresman and Company, 1967), pp. 116–123.

Spache, George D., and Evelyn B. Spache, *Reading in the Elementary School,* 2nd ed. (Boston: Allyn and Bacon, Inc., 1969), Ch. 2.

Staiger, Ralph, and David A. Sohn, *New Directions in Reading* (New York: Bantam Books, 1967).

Stauffer, Russell G., *Directing Reading Maturity as a Cognitive Process* (New York: Harper & Row, 1969), Ch. 4.

Questions and Comments for Thought and Discussion

1. In the book *Predicting Reading Failure: A Preliminary Study* by Katrina DeHirsch, Jeannette Jansky, and William S. Langford (published by Prentice-Hall, 1964), the authors attempt to develop diagnostic criteria

predictive of future failure at early stages. What do you regard as some of the criteria that would help teachers identify at kindergarten level "high risk" children—those in danger of failing when they are exposed to formal education? What suggestions do you have for trying to prevent their failure?

2. At the present time, what is your attitude toward the role of reading or readiness-for-reading programs on the kindergarten level? Give reasons for your stand. What evidence, in addition to that which you now have, will you want or need to obtain either to substantiate or negate your current point of view in regard to reading or prereading activities in the kindergarten?

3. If you were a first-grade teacher, what would you want to do at the beginning of the school year to assess the degree of readiness for reading that each of your children had acquired? Or in the case of those who already were reading, to ascertain the level of their achievement?

4. Some writers have pointed out that what constitutes readiness for reading depends to a degree on what the program in any given school is. Thus, it is believed that a child may be ready for the materials and methods used in one school but not nearly as ready for the program found in another school. How does a teacher deal with the problem of the pupil who has been caught, through no fault of his own, in such a predicament?

5. In this chapter many suggestions are given for developing auditory discrimination (*see* page 87) and visual discrimination (*see* page 88). What additional suggestions on either of those topics can you think of?

6. You may wish to plan a language-experience lesson for boys and girls in the beginning of the first grade. Since you will want to make certain that it is on a suitable topic before you start your plans for the procedure, you may wish to check the suitability of your proposed topic with your instructor. It is suggested that you plan your lesson in the same kind of detail in which the language-experience lesson described in this chapter is planned.

Outline for Chapter 5A

WORD RECOGNITION

Historical Perspective
Skills for Developing Independence in Word Recognition
    Learning Words by the Sight Method
    Use of Context Clues
    Use of Phonics
      Points of Dispute
      Principles of Teaching Phonics
      Elements of Phonics to Be Taught
      Sequence
    Studying the Structure of Words
      Principles of Teaching Structural Analysis
      A Developmental Program
      Sequence and Allocation to Levels of Reading
The Reading Vocabulary
    Description of Word Lists
    Use of Word Lists
    The Vocabulary Burden

CHAPTER

Word Recognition

Reading involves much more than word recognition, although the ability to recognize recorded words is basic to the reading process. Without skill in associating word forms as given in writing with word sounds and meanings, no one can be an effective reader. Persons in the field of reading accept without question that this ability to recognize words is essential to the development of maturity in reading. On this point there is no argument. There are, however, many points of controversy concerning how word recognition should best be taught.

The current debate among those in the reading field primarily focuses on the question of how word recognition should be taught in beginning reading instruction. The issue concerns whether the emphasis in the initial stages of reading instruction should be on learning the sounds represented by the written letters or whether, without much or any attention to the letter-sound relation, the effort should be concentrated on helping pupils to acquire the meaning of the written message. In other words, the point of contention is whether a code approach or a meaning approach to reading instruction should be used.

As suggested earlier, (*see* page 21), the code approach emphasizes the need of the child in beginning reading instruction to learn the sounds represented by each letter or combination of letters. It is so named because the aim of the teacher employing the method is to help the learner acquire facility in the use of the code of the letter-sound relation. The meaning approach, on the other hand, places major emphasis on the meaning of what is read and gives little, if any, attention to developing in pupils skill in recognizing relations between the letters and the sounds they represent. This approach is also known as the *whole-word approach*. There are also various combinations of the two methods, with some placing almost equal emphasis on the deciphering of the code and the acquisition of meaning. In practice, rarely, if ever, is either the code or the meaning approach used to the exclusion of the other.

Many people, both professional and lay, would state that the issue in beginning reading instruction is the *phonic approach* versus the *"look-say" approach*. The phonic is a code approach, since it is by means of phonics that the child learns what sounds are represented by the letters of the alphabet. The "look-say" method refers to the practice by which the pupil, without learning to focus on the letters of the alphabet and their sounds, centers his attention on the whole word. Typically he looks at the word as someone tells it to him and then he repeats it ("says" it), hopefully so he will remember it from its appearance. When the "look-say" method is used, emphasis is usually placed on the meaning of what is read. Consequently, for practical purposes this approach is classified as a meaning approach. Thus, the question of the phonic versus the "look-say" approach can be thought of as roughly paralleling that of the code versus the meaning approach.

HISTORICAL PERSPECTIVE

Gaining an historical perspective on the problem of whether a code or a meaning approach should be emphasized in beginning reading instruction may be helpful in understanding why teachers sometimes fail to see the importance of both these aspects of reading.

In the history of reading instruction in the United States at times one method and at times another has been the prevailing one. In Colonial times and throughout much of the nineteenth century and even into the twentieth, a code-deciphering approach to reading instruction was generally used. The child learned the names of the letters of the alphabet and the sounds they most commonly represented. He combined sounds to make syllables and words of more than one syllable. Thus, a synthetic phonic approach was used, in which the learner synthesized the sounds of a syllable or word as a way of learning to recognize a word.

A strong reaction to the use of phonics then set in. The criticisms leveled against the phonic method were numerous. Important among them were the following:

1. The English language is not based on an easily acquired letter-sound relation, for some letters have more than one sound (for example, *c*,

with its soft and hard sounds) and some sounds are represented by more than one letter or letter combination (for example, the sound of *s*, which is represented not only by the letter *s* but also frequently by the letter *c*).

2. Phonics when used as the initial approach to reading instruction tends to produce slow word-by-word readers.

3. Use of phonics as a beginning method places the emphasis on the mechanics of reading rather than on thought getting.

4. A phonic approach is likely to make learning to read an uninteresting experience.

Beginning about 1915 the whole-word or sight method became popular. Some teachers advocated using a sentence method, in which an entire sentence was read to a child and then his attention drawn to some of the words that comprise it. Others advocated a story-method approach, with a very short story read to the pupil and subsequently his attention directed to some of the sentences and words comprising the story. The experience chart, which the pupils help make (described in Chapter 4B), has been used extensively as representative of the story method. The whole-word method, the sentence method, and even the story method, including the experience chart, became popular during the period when the progressive education movement was at its height in this country. In addition, the word method gained substantiation from research which was interpreted to indicate that since it was as easy, if not more so, to learn a whole word as a part of one, a meaning unit, the word, should be used as the basic element in beginning reading instruction. It was popularly suggested that the beginner should learn about fifty to seventy-five words by the sight method, with someone telling him each word, before beginning work on phonics. It was also recommended that when phonics was used it should be as phonic analysis rather than synthesis. In other words, instead of beginning with the sounds of the letters and combining them into syllables (synthesis), the learner should start with the word and from it derive the phonic elements that make it up. For example, when the child knew the word *mother* because he had been told the word, the teacher might through phonic analysis have him identify the sound with which the word begins and then ask him to name other words that begin with the same sound.

Proponents of the phonic method for beginning reading instruction have not been lacking at any time during the century. However, little attention was paid to them by leaders in the field of elementary school education until the publication of *Why Johnny Can't Read.*[1] In this book, the word method was severely criticized and a phonic approach strongly advocated. Widely read and highly acclaimed by the public, Flesch's book was the target for much criticism by professional educators. It would seem, however, that in

---

[1] Rudolph Flesch, *Why Johnny Can't Read and What You Can Do about It* (New York: Harper & Row, 1955).

spite of the renunciation of the book by various professional persons, it had a significant effect on the teaching of reading. Undoubtedly it has been instrumental in causing phonics to be given greater attention in educational literature even by teachers who strongly disagree with much of the book.

Another factor resulting in the more widespread use of phonics at the present time might well be the fact that in many schools the emphasis, rightly or wrongly, in recent years has become more academically centered and less child centered. What a child learns in terms of subject matter has been stressed in many educational circles—to the regret of a large number of specialists in the area of child growth and development—rather than factors related to the pupil's emotional and social development.

During the last few decades, too, several widely publicized innovations in the teaching of reading, some of which are described briefly in Chapter 15, fit in well with a phonic approach. Undoubtedly some of them have played their part in causing increased attention to be given to code deciphering as a method of beginning reading instruction.

SKILLS FOR DEVELOPING INDEPENDENCE IN WORD RECOGNITION

Consideration of various approaches to reading instruction, not described elsewhere in this book, is also the subject of Chapter 15. Here we will turn our attention to the four major skills for developing independence in word recognition, skills that a reader must acquire regardless of what approach is being made to reading instruction in order to become a proficient reader. These skills can be classified as:

1. Recognizing whole words by means of the sight method
2. Using context clues
3. Studying words phonetically
4. Studying words structurally.

Many persons favoring a code approach to reading deny the value of the first-named skill; and some greatly question the use of context clues as a means of word recognition or identification.

All four skills are discussed in turn, although often more than one is employed simultaneously in an attack on a given word. For example, in the sentence "Dick is playing with his dog," the child may use several clues for recognizing the word *playing*. If the word is not already a part of the child's sight vocabulary, he can use context clues, study the word phonetically, and note the structure of the word as he takes cognizance of the *ing* ending. Nor should the fact that consideration of the use of phonics here precedes that of the study of words through attention to their structure be interpreted as recommendation for teaching most of the phonic word attack skills before teaching those of structural analysis. Some of the latter may well be taught before many of the former type. Similarly, all the emphasis on learning to recognize words through context clues should not precede, in classroom practice, all work on identifying words either through phonics or through the study of the structure of words.

Learning Words by the Sight Method

As noted earlier, the predominant method of teaching reading fifty and more years ago was to teach the child the individual letters first and then to teach him how to combine these letters into syllables and words. The reading of phrases and sentences was presumed to follow naturally. This method seemed the simplest and most logical. In the terminology of today a code approach was used, namely, phonic synthesis. In fact, the approach had marked similarity to code approaches used today by an increasing number of persons.

Justification for teaching words as wholes has been based in part on early research on perception, which many believe revealed that most people tend to recognize the larger visual shapes first and examine details only when the total configuration cannot be readily identified. Thus, advocates of the whole-word method would claim that it is easier for a child to recognize the word *dog* as a unit than to discover the phonetic values of the letters and combine them. The theory is that much as the child recognizes his pet dog without adding up the colors and characteristics of the individual parts—legs, ears, eyes, and the like—so can he learn to recognize a word. Furthermore, the argument would be that only when dogs resemble each other in most details does one look more closely at the parts to make an identification and that similarly the learner needs to analyze the difference between words only when it is not marked.

Confirmation of the value of a whole-word method came from early eye-movement studies in reading by Dearborn, Judd, Buswell, and others. Their investigations indicated that in a single fixation the reader recognizes whole words and even phrases that have become familiar to him through frequent exposure to them. Consequently, many reading systems begin with whole words and introduce the child to them through telling the words, associating the words with pictures, using experience charts, and similar methods. An obvious advantage claimed for this approach is that the child is immediately started on the road to reading for meaning. The words so taught at the outset are said to be taught by the sight method.

Presentation of new words to be added to the pupil's sight vocabulary is generally made both in meaningful context and out of context. The purpose is to make the pupil's response automatic when he sees the word. In this connection the chalkboard and teacher-made or commercial charts are most useful. Labeling of objects in the room is helpful if it is made functional. Thus, the shelves in the cupboard may be labeled *Scissors, Paste, Brushes,* and *Cloths* to aid the child in finding materials. Words learned out of context should as soon as possible be encountered in context. Reading-card exercises in which whole words are presented should be preceded and followed by the use of these words in speaking and reading. The task is made easier if the words are selected from those the child uses in his own speech and from those "service words"—such as prepositions, pronouns, and connecting verbs—that account for a majority of all words read.

The basis of the procedure is repetition of the desired words in different situations. If the child's reading vocabulary is consequently impoverished, as many critics of the sight-word method complain, the use of abundant voluntary reading in children's general books can serve as supplement, the adherents of the meaning approach claim.

It used to be recommended rather universally by persons favoring the sight method that a stock of between fifty and seventy-five words learned by this method is necessary before work in phonics can be successfully begun. However, many people currently who favor the sight method agree that there is no reason why teaching by this method cannot be accompanied earlier by some help from phonics. In fact, many recommend that the sight method be supplemented almost from the beginning with work on one or more phonic elements of many of the words being learned.

It is important that only a rather limited number of new words be presented at one time by the sight method. Individual differences among the children should determine the number attempted, and the teacher should not inhibit the gifted reader in a successful quest for a growing reading vocabulary, whatever the method of teaching. For the average pupil, however, a firmer foundation is laid if only a few words are thoroughly fixed in mind from day to day.

Some persons draw attention to the value of noting the general configuration of a word as an aid to recall. After a pupil has been told a word, it is claimed, he may at times find it helpful to recognize it when he encounters the word again if he observes the outline of the word or other matters of form.

Observation of the configuration of a word can be a valuable procedure, it is asserted, not only during the periods of reading readiness and initial reading instruction but in all stages of reading, including adult reading. In fact, for rapid reading it may be essential. Through noting the outline of the word the reader is saved, it is argued, from the necessity of painstakingly deciphering many words that he meets, especially if this clue is used in conjunction with the verbal context in which a word appears. Frequently, too, people favoring this procedure claim that attention to the configuration can be given to good advantage along with a study of phonics. One way in which the child in the early stages of learning to read can be aided in developing skill in the use of the configuration clues is through questions and comments by the teacher concerning the length of a word. If a child reads *mother* when he sees the word *man,* the teacher may say: "This word could not be *mother,* for *mother* is a longer word than this."

The following cautions should be observed in using the configuration of a word as a method of recognition:

1. Pupils should not be expected to remember a large number of words through configuration clues only, for many words closely resemble one another in general appearance. Overuse of this practice is likely to result in guessing.
2. The teacher should be on guard against making wrong use of the striking characteristics of a word as a means to word recognition. To try to help a child remember the word *monkey* by the "tail" letter on *monkey,* for example, is a most confusing practice, since many words other than *monkey* end in *y.*

One more concern should be mentioned pertaining to the use of a sight method of teaching reading. Recent research tends to refute earlier findings concerning how much a beginning reader can see at a single eye fixation (a stop of the eye while reading). Spache and Spache[2] conclude that contrary to early research a child often needs more than one fixation to see a whole word. Stated in a different way, a beginning reader frequently sees or recognizes less than one whole word at one fixation. If this conclusion is true, we need to reconsider methods currently used and approved in teaching words by the sight method. Undoubtedly more research is needed on this point.

Use of Context Clues

Like the sight method, the use of context clues is severely criticized by many advocates of a code approach to beginning reading instruction. It has been ridiculed as a "guessing" method, but its adherents persistently claim that intelligent guessing is often a desired procedure. Let us note how the method is frequently used.

A teacher may use the sight method plus the method of visual context when he helps a pupil learn the word *mother* as it appears with a picture of a woman. When using both of these procedures in teaching a child to identify the word, he may tell him the word is *mother* and than lead the child to notice that the word goes with the picture. Or he may ask him what the word under the picture might be. If the child says *mother,* the teacher needs to let him know that he is right.

A word can also be presented by the sight method combined with the use of verbal context clues. For example, if the pupils know all the words except *ball* in: "Hit the ball with the bat, Bob," the teacher might tell

[2] George D. Spache and Evelyn B. Spache, *Reading in the Elementary School* (Boston: Allyn and Bacon, Inc., 1969), pp. 7–12.

them that he thinks many of them can figure out the new word in the sentence as they read it to see what word would fit where the new word appears. If the pupils suggest that the word might be *ball,* he will need to tell them that they are right. If the pupils do not name the correct word, the teacher should tell them the word and help them see that *ball* fits with the meaning of the rest of the sentence.

In spite of the critics of the use of context clues, many persons consider skill in making use of verbal context clues significant to all stages of reading instruction, including adult reading. Arguments for use of context clues in word recognition include:

1. In the earlier stages it is of great help in providing boys and girls with needed practice on words they have identified at a previous time but which they still do not recognize instantly without other aids.
2. Before the pupils have learned to identify and remember words through word analysis or synthesis, they can, by means of skill in the use of verbal clues, frequently receive from the context aid in recalling the word that they need.
3. Even after the readers have developed facility in the use of structural and phonic analysis and synthesis, they can be aided in increasing their rate of reading through efficient use of verbal context clues; often through context a reader can recognize a word faster than through analytic or synthetic methods. For example, a person who comes across the sentence: "Geometry is one branch of mathematics in which I am greatly interested"—can use a context clue in recognizing the word *mathematics.*
4. There are many words in English whose pronunciation depends on the context, such as *read, lead, bow, refuse.*

As indicated in the illustration in the preceding paragraph, an adequate background of experience is essential for success in the use of context clues. A person who does not know what geometry is would receive little help from context in the sentence: "Geometry is one branch of mathematics in which I am greatly interested." Consequently, it is the teacher's responsibility to provide sufficient experiences with the subjects about which the pupils will be reading. The teacher can help boys and girls get the needed background by a variety of means—discussions, explanations, demonstrations, experiments, field trips and other visual aids, and reading. Once he has read fairly easy material on a given subject, the pupil can often be helped to understand more difficult reading done subsequently on the same topic. At times, guidance can be given just before the class begins reading a selection in which concepts are discussed with which the pupils are not familiar. At other times, preparation for the reading may have taken place days or even weeks before. A wide background of experience is one assurance that the child will have less difficulty not only in reading in general but also in making intelligent use of verbal context clues.

If a reader is to be expected to get help through the verbal context in the identification of a word, the proportion of unfamiliar to familiar words should be kept small. If a first-grade child comes to the sentence: "The boy has a bat and ball," without recognizing either *boy* or *ball* or *bat*, no intelligent use of context clues can be made. The exact ratio of unknown to known words, as far as recognition of the word is concerned, cannot be ascertained because it will differ according to the difficulty of the concepts discussed, the intelligence, maturity, background, and reading ability of the reader, and the skill of the teacher.

The identification of a word does not necessarily have to take place in context in order that the pupil may recognize it later by context clues. A teacher may write the word *mother* on the chalkboard when he tells the child the word, and later on, when the child again encounters the word in his readings, help him make use of the context to recall the word. Sometimes it is desirable first to present a word in isolation, since more attention can then be given to its characteristics.

Until recently little was done to help boys and girls learn how to use context clues in connected discourse, although advocacy of the techniques dates back for at least half a century. In 1965 Wilber Ames[3] developed a classification scheme of value in comprehending the meaning of unknown words in contextual situations. His classification of types of context clues which might be taught systematically included the following fourteen categories:

1. Clues derived from language experience or familiar expression
2. Clues utilizing modifying phrases or clauses
3. Clues utilizing definition or description
4. Clues provided through words connected or in series
5. Comparison of contrast clues
6. Synonym clues
7. Clues provided by the tone, setting, and mood of a selection
8. Referral clues
9. Association clues
10. Clues derived from the main idea and supporting details pattern of paragraph organization
11. Clues provided through the question-and-answer pattern of paragraph organization
12. Preposition clues

[3] Wilbur Ames, "The Development of a Classification Scheme of Contextual Aids." *Reading Research Quarterly*, vol. II, no. 1 (Fall 1966), pp. 57–82, with quotations from pages 66–67.

13. Clues utilizing nonrestrictive clauses or appositive phrases

14. Clues derived from cause-and-effect pattern of paragraph and sentence organization.

How application of the list can be made is illustrated in Chapter 6B, "Developing Comprehension" (*see* page 200).

Use of Phonics

The place of phonics in reading instruction, as noted earlier, has been the subject of heated controversy and of much experimental research. Not only has the subject been discussed by teachers for many years but it has also in recent times excited partisan interest not only within the teaching profession but among the public at large. This increased participation in the controversy is undoubtedly due in part to the publication of such books as *Why Johnny Can't Read* and the increased and easy availability to the lay public of commercial phonics teaching materials.

Probably few persons in the field of the teaching of reading would disagree with the point of view that no one becomes an efficient reader who has not learned—either by himself or with the aid of another person, most likely the teacher—at least part of the code giving the relation between the written symbols and the sounds represented by them. The dispute about phonics, therefore, is not over the *whether* but over the *how*, the *when*, and the *what*.

Points of Dispute

A point of much debate, as noted earlier, is whether a phonic approach rather than a meaning approach should be the basis for beginning reading instruction (*see* page 107).

A second question is whether the approach to word recognition should be *synthetic* or *analytic*. Advocates of the synthetic method favor teaching letters or graphemes and phonograms, first, and then teaching children to combine the sound elements into words. Those who believe in the analytic method favor presenting children with whole words first and then teaching them to analyze words into the sound elements that comprise them. In other words, the analytic approach starts with sight vocabulary and then makes use of the phonic analysis of words; the synthetic approach starts with the coding system and then synthesizes the sounds into words. Thus, the beginning emphasis in a synthetic approach is learning the sound-symbol correspondence.

Over the years, children have learned to read by various methods, including, both the analytic and synthetic. The problem has been one of finding a general approach that would be effective with the largest possible number of children and that would lead to strong and continuing interest in reading throughout life. Most people will concede that an intelligent, able, sympathetic teacher, one who is flexible enough to adapt his procedure to individual needs, is more important than the method — whether it is the analytic or the synthetic. However, this fact in no way relieves us of the necessity of weighing the relative advantages of one method over another.

Related to the debate as to whether phonics should be taught by the analytic or synthetic method, but not identical with it, is the question whether phonemes (letter sounds) should be taught in isolation or in word context. Linguists, as well as reading specialists, have opposite views on the subject. Research has not firmly established the answer to the question.

Still another point of difference, which arises among those not subscribing to a code approach in beginning reading instruction is the question of whether instruction in phonics should be systematic or incidental. Granted that there is an essential body of phonics skills to be mastered, should these skills be taught sequentially to all children, with whole words deliberately chosen to illustrate a phonic principle? Or should the phonic principles be taught to each child as the need arises in his reading? Many reading specialists and classroom teachers prefer a combination of these two approaches.

An objection to the sequential, isolated teaching of phonic principles is the fact that many alert young readers discover the principles themselves in the course of highly motivated meaningful reading, and for them class instruction in phonics may be wasteful. On the other hand, in guided individualized reading programs there is danger that many children will fail to encounter or to master essential phonic elements.

It is feared by many that prolonged work on phonics independently taught not only diverts the child from the process of getting meaning from the printed page but also reduces the amount of time available for genuine reading. It is also argued that emphasis on phonics may cause lack of interest in reading. It should be noted, however, that Jeanne Chall (*see* page 482) arrived at the following conclusion in her report on her extensive investigation of primary-grade reading:

> Under a meaning emphasis, the child has an early advantage (in the middle of grade 1) on reading-for-meaning tests (standardized silent reading tests of vocabulary and comprehension). However, he has an early disadvantage in accuracy or oral word recognition (pronunciation) and connected oral reading tests (when rate is not included in the score), which ultimately dissipates the early advantage on the standardized silent reading tests. At about the end of the first grade (or the beginning of the second grade), and continuing through about the third grade, meaning-emphasis programs tend to affect comprehension and vocabulary test scores adversely, mainly because the child does less well in word recognition.[4]

[4] Jeanne S. Chall, *Learning to Read: The Great Debate* (New York, McGraw-Hill Book Company, 1967) p. 127.

Figure 5.1 Motivation can be strong in skill-development activities. (Dubuque Public Schools, Dubuque, Io.)

Principles of Teaching Phonics

With the great divergence of opinion concerning the role of phonics in reading instruction, there are but few generalizations having to do with teaching by this method that will be accepted by the two opposing factions other than that phonics is important in learning to read. Other principles, though less commonly accepted, to which, however, a large number of educators adhere, are listed here:

1. Instruction in phonics should be functional Only those generalizations about differences and likenesses of words should be taught which apply to the simple words the beginner encounters in his reading or in presentations by the teacher.

2. For most pupils, instruction in phonics should be systematic The progression should be from the simpler, more widely used elements and generalizations to the more difficult and less generally applied learnings, with well-distributed practice.

3. The work in phonics should be adapted to individual differences Any program in word recognition should be geared to the developmental level of the children. Pupils within a given grade may be expected to be on varying levels in many respects, including the various phases of phonetic analysis. Some will not be ready as soon as others. Some will be able to deal with simple abstract learnings; others will profit more from concrete experiences. Moreover, progress will vary greatly after initial instruction has begun. Some pupils will need practically no help beyond that provided by the material they are currently reading, while others will benefit greatly from additional practice in workbooks or teacher-made materials and games or drills that focus attention on certain needed skills.

4. Rules and generalizations should frequently be taught inductively
By presenting three or more familiar words that have the same initial, medial, or final letter, the teacher can call attention to the similarity and help the pupil to fix the appropriate sound in mind in such a way as to enable him to recognize the same sound in another word. For example, if the pupil has learned the similar beginning of the words *make, mother,* and *man,* he is equipped to attack the work *many* by applying a generalization to a new grouping of letters. Chalkboard, chart, and workbook can supply practice in making such applications, and of course the rule, which the pupil himself has been led to formulate, can then be used in his own "silent" reading. Similar generalizations can be made and applied with the medial vowel in words ending in a silent *e.*

It should be noted that it is probably unwise to expect that all generalizations about phonics should be learned inductively. Children can also learn through deductive teaching. While it seems desirable that often they should be helped in reaching conclusions in the form of rules or generalizations, to follow the inductive procedure at all times may slow the process of learning. Furthermore, much learning in life outside of school takes place without use of an inductive method. Children learn to profit from deductions made from generalizations presented to them.

Elements of Phonics to Be Taught

One major point of disagreement concerning the teaching of phonics is the question of what should be taught. It is not the purpose of the writers to state authoritatively what the phonic content of the reading program should be. Most reading systems emphasizing phonics and most basal readers indicate clearly what they recommend as the minimum of phonics that should be taught. The listing given here includes only those elements that are rather commonly accepted as important.

For convenience in studying the list that follows a few definitions are here given:

1. *Digraphs* are written or printed symbols made up of two letters representing one phoneme or speech sound. They are of two kinds, consonant digraphs—such as *th, ch, sh*—and vowel digraphs—such as *ei, ie, ea, ay.*

2. *Diphthongs* are written or printed symbols representing two vowels so nearly blended that they almost produce a single speech sound—such as *oy, ou, ew*.

3. Consonant blends are combinations of two or three consonants—such as *br, gr, str*—blended in such a way that each letter in the blend keeps its own identity.

1. Outline of subject matter   Included in many programs of reading instruction are the following elements of phonics: (a.) single consonants in monosyllabic and polysyllabic words, found in initial, final and medial positions of words; (b.) consonant blends, such as *st, gr, br, cr, str, pl;* (c.) consonant digraphs, such as *ch, th, sh;* (d.) single vowels ("short" and "long" vowels, vowels modified when preceding *r*, the *a* when preceding *l* or *w*, and other vowel sounds); (e.) vowel digraphs, such as *ea, oa, ai, ay, ee, oo;* (f.) diphthongs, such as *oy, oi, ou, ow;* and (f). silent letters.

2. Generalizations to be learned   It should be noted that several of the generalizations here stated are not without exception as far as the universality of their application is concerned.

A single vowel in a syllable is usually short unless it is the final letter in the syllable. (Examples: *bat, baby*)

If a final *e* in a word is preceded by a single consonant, a single vowel preceding the consonant is usually long and the *e* is silent. (Example: *rate*)

The sound of a single vowel preceding an *r* is usually modified by the *r*. (Example: *color*)

The sound of a single *a* preceding an *l* or a *w* is affected by the *l* or *w*. (Examples: *fall; claw*)

A final *y* in words of more than one syllable usually has the long *e* sound. (Example: *frequently*)

A *c* before *e, i,* or *y* has, as a rule, the soft sound. (Example: *city*)

A *g* before *e, i,* or *y* has, as a rule, the soft sound. (Example: *gem*)

Sequence

One caution needs to be expressed at this point. The listing of phonic elements and generalizations in the preceding section of this chapter is not to be considered as the sequence in which they are to be taught.

Grade levels are an undesirable criterion for determining sequence. Since the accomplishments of boys and girls and their readiness for any phase of reading instruction varies so much from grade to grade, it is better to express the sequence of phonic skills to be studied in terms of levels of achievement.

There is no one best sequence for teaching the various aspects of phonic analysis. Numerous acceptable orders of presentation have been worked out. The succession should be based on principles such as these:

1. There should be progression from the simple to the more complex.
2. Other things being equal, the more frequently used elements and generalizations should be taught before the less frequently used.
3. Provisions should be made on each level for the maintenance of skills acquired, at least in part, on the preceding level.

One of the best sources of suggestions on the sequence to follow in phonic analysis is to be found in the teachers' manuals accompanying series of readers. Any teacher using one of these should acquaint himself with the program outlined in the manuals. However, the suggestions should not be followed slavishly. The recommendations are, for the most part, made in terms of the average child in a grade. The teacher must make adaptation to individual differences. An example of a sequence for phonics instruction follows:

1. Provide needed work on auditory and visual discrimination.
2. Teach the sounds of consonants before those of vowels. Start with the single consonant sounds that have but one sound, namely, *b, h, j, l, m, p, t,* and *v.* Teach them as they occur in initial and then in final positions in words, before teaching them in medial positions. Finally, teach common consonant digraphs, then two-letter consonant blends, then, three-letter consonant blends.
3. Teach the vowel sounds with the short sounds first and then the long.
4. Teach vowel digraphs and diphthongs and silent letters.
5. Teach rules governing long and short vowels.

An excellent publication in the area of phonics is *Phonics in Proper Perspective* by Arthur W. Heilman, published by Charles E. Merrill Publishing Company. The December 1967 edition of *The Reading Teacher* also carries an informative article on this subject—"When Two Vowels Go Walking and Other Such Things" by Robert Emans.

Studying the Structure of Words

Phonic analysis is not the only type of word analysis. A second method of analyzing words is through the use of structural analysis. While in phonetic analysis the reader deciphers a word by means of sounds represented by the letters or combination of letters in a word, in structural analysis he recognizes the meaning or pronunciation units of a word.

Structural analysis deals with both word variants and word derivatives.

By a word variant is meant a word that deviates from the root word according to the case, number, and gender of nouns; the tense, voice, and mood of verbs; and the comparison of adjectives and adverbs. Thus, variants of the noun *prince* are *princes* and *princess;* of the verb *walk* are *walks, walked, walking;* of the adjective *small* are *smaller* and *smallest.* Word derivatives are words formed from root words through the addition of prefixes and/or suffixes—for example, *likeable* and *uncomfortable.* Learning compound words—for example, *something*—through identification or recognition of the parts and polysyllabic words through the aid of syllabication is also part of structural analysis.

The question may be asked: "Why teach structural analysis of word variants or word derivatives when these words could be studied through phonic analysis?" To be specific: "Why should the teacher bother teaching children to use structural analysis when learning the word *unhappy* if they can analyze the word through phonics?" The answer is that phonetic analysis is a slower form of word analysis than structural analysis. The child who has learned to recognize instantly the prefix *un* in *unhappy* does not have to engage in the uneconomical procedure of first analyzing by means of phonics. The reader who can quickly identify the common prefixes and suffixes reads with more speed than the one who has to use phonics in this process.

In succeeding paragraphs the following questions will be discussed:

1. What are the basic principles that should be observed in teaching structural analysis?
2. What should be taught to boys and girls in the elementary school about structural analysis?
3. In what sequence and at what levels should the various elements of word structure be taught?
4. What are some additional suggestions for teaching children to identify and recognize words by means of structural analysis?

The fourth question will be answered primarily in Chapter 6B, "Developing Comprehension," where many specific illustrations are presented.

Principles of Teaching Structural Analysis

The following principles warrant special emphasis in relation to analyzing words by means of their structure.

1. Overemphasis on structural analysis should be avoided   Structural analysis should be seen in relation to other methods of word recognition. When a word can be recalled by means of quicker methods, such as configuration or context clues, the reader should not resort to word analysis. If too much attention has been paid to locating root words, prefixes, and suffixes, it is possible for reading to become ineffective because the reader approaches too many words by trying to locate word parts. Consequently, it is undesirable to have all "new words" analyzed either structurally or through a phonic approach.

2. As a rule, the reader should examine a "new word" to see if he can analyze it structurally before he tries to unlock it by means of phonics This principle is sound because structural analysis is usually a quicker method of word recognition than phonetic analysis. Consequently, rate in reading as well as quality of comprehension can be improved if the more tedious methods involving phonics are employed only when other means fail.

3. The analysis of "new words" should not be isolated from reading as a meaningful process Frequently it is advisable to present in context a "new word" that is to be analyzed structurally. The context can help the reader decide what the word is. For example, if the reader comes across the sentence, "Sam is walking home," and he knows the root word *walk*, he can often tell without really studying the ending that the "new word" is *walking*, not *walks* or *walked*.

4. The sequence in teaching a "new word" by means of structural analysis should, as a rule, be from the whole word to the word part and then back to the whole word Specifically, it is usually desirable to present the word first—for example, *walking*—next to ask the pupils to identify the root word and the ending, and then to have them combine the root with the ending. This procedure is recommended because it more nearly resembles the situation in which the pupil is likely to encounter a word. Nevertheless, occasional special practice in which a child forms variants or derivatives of a word are helpful, as, for example, having the pupils form the words *walks*, *walked*, and *walking* from *walk*.

5. Structural analysis should not be confused with "finding little words in big words" One rather common method used to help boys and girls analyze words structurally is to ask them to "find little words in big words." This practice may be misleading. For example, finding *at* in *mat* could lead a child also to look for *at* in *mate* and therefore confuse him. Furthermore, even in *mat*, if the reader looks for *at*, he is likely to pronounce it *mu-at*. Anyone accustomed to searching for "little words in big words" might easily pronounce *together* as *to-get-her* or *some* as *so-me*, and in the word *furthermore* he might be led to a wrong identification if he isolates *the* or *he* or *her*.

6. Generalizations should be developed with pupils They should not be presented as rules to be memorized. For example, when teaching that words ending in *y* preceded by a consonant change the *y* to *i* before adding *es*, the teacher may write on the board a few nouns ending in *y*, some preceded by a consonant, others by a vowel, like *boy, boys; lady, ladies; day, days; candy, candies;* and *toy, toys.* The pupils may observe how the plural of each of the singular nouns in the list was formed, writing in one column the singular words ending in *y* preceded by a vowel and in the other the singular words ending in *y* preceded by a consonant. Next the pupils may summarize their observation that to the words in the first column ending in *y* preceded by a vowel, an *s* only was added. The teacher may then explain that this summarization holds true in other cases. Similarly the boys and girls may summarize their finding that in the words in the second column—those ending in *y* preceded by a consonant—the *y* was changed to *i* before *es* was added. The teacher may then explain that this summarization, too, holds true in other cases. To make this original learning permanent, the pupils should be helped to note the application of these rules in their later reading and in their spelling. This method of procedure in developing a generalization is much more likely to be effective than that in which the teacher gives the rule and the pupils memorize it.

7. There should be a developmental program that provides for training in structural analysis   Skill in analyzing words structurally is such a significant phase of skill in word recognition that it cannot be left to chance. While incidental methods should be used when they help foster a better understanding of words on the part of boys and girls, the teacher should make certain that all the essential elements of structural analysis are presented and that provisions are made for the maintenance of these skills through meaningful distributed practice. Suggestions as to the elements to include in such a program are given in the next paragraphs.

A Developmental Program

Exactly which elements and generalizations in structural analysis should be taught in the elementary school is a question that has not been determined. In trying to decide on the points to be studied, the teacher should keep these criteria in mind: (1.) the frequency of occurrence of the structural form, (2.) the ease with which the learner can identify the form, and (3.) the value of the element to the development of speed and independence in word recognition.

The following elements in structural analysis of words are frequently considered important enough to be taught somewhere in the elementary school:

1. *Skill in identifying or recognizing words ending in* able, ance, d, ed, er, es, est, ful, ible, ies, ily, ing, ish, less, ly, ment, ness, *and* s *in words in which the root is known to the reader.* Pupils should be familiar with the application of the following generalizations about the endings of words:

Words ending in *y* preceded by a consonant change the *y* to *i* before adding *es* to form a variant of the root word.

Words ending in *y* preceded by a consonant change the *y* to *i* before *ed, er, est,* or *ly* is added.

Many words ending in a consonant double the final consonant before *ed* or *ing* is added.

Many root words ending in *e* drop the *e* before adding *ing* to form a variant.

2. *Skill in identifying or recognizing words with the prefixes* ab, ad, com, de, dis, ex, im, in, pre, pro, re, sub, *and* un *in words in which the root is known to the reader.* The more advanced pupils in the elementary school may also be helped to recognize the fact that a variation of the prefix *im* occurs in words like *illegal* and *illegible,* where instead of the *m* of the prefix *im* the first consonant of the root of the word is doubled so that the consonant preceded by *i* forms the prefix to the root of the word.

3. *Skill in identifying or recognizing compound words where one or both parts of a compound or hyphenated word are known to the reader.*

4. *Skill in identifying or recognizing the possessive form when the word without the possessive ending is known to the reader.*

5. *Skill in identifying or recognizing common contractions like* he'll, I'll, I'm, it's, there's, they're, that's, she'll, we'll, we're, what's where's, *and* you'll *and those ending in* n't, *like* don't.

6. *Skill in identifying or recognizing polysyllabic words partly by means of syllabication.* Syllabication can aid in the identification and recognition of words. It is usually helpful to pupils to understand that there are as many syllables in a word as there are vowel sounds. It is not essential to the recognition or pronunciation of a word to know exactly where some of the breaks between syllables occur. For instance, a child does not have to know whether the division of syllables in the word *tumble* comes before or after the *b* in order to pronounce the word correctly, even though for written syllabication that knowledge is essential. However, if rules for syllabication are to be studied, these are some that may be helpful to elementary-school children:

If the initial vowel in a word is followed by two consonants, the first of the two consonants usually ends the first syllable of the word, as in *big ger.*

If the initial vowel in a word is followed by a single consonant, the consonant usually begins the second syllable of the word, as in *má jor.*

If the last syllable of a word ends in *le,* the consonant preceding *le* usually begins the last syllable, as in *tá ble.*

Sequence and Allocation to Levels of Reading

The order in which the elements significant in structural analysis should be taught cannot be stated authoritatively for all grades or for all individuals within a grade. Factors such as the following will need to be taken into consideration in working out the sequence in which the elements should be taught: (1) The items included in a list of points to be developed in stressing facility in word recognition through structural analysis should not be taken up in the order in which they occur in this book. (2) One factor that should help determine the order of development is the occurrence or presentation in the reading textbook of words representative of the form to be studied. Most reading books for the elementary school provide definite guidance in the teachers' manual for a program of word recognition. (3) The difficulty of a point to be learned should be one of the criteria for deciding the order in which the items should be taught. Other things being equal, those points easier to learn and to apply should be taught first.

THE READING VOCABULARY

Writers of reading textbooks have tried to include only those words in books for the primary grades that are a part of the understanding and speaking vocabulary of the child. Unfortunately, they have not found it possible to include the many dialects and linguistic variations employed by children in so vast and diverse a country as ours. For this reason, the reading textbook necessarily fails to meet the needs of children in the many geographic sections. How, for example, can the youngster on a Nebraska farm, in a New York ghetto, or on an Alabama plantation meet on common terms with a boy or girl who has grown up in a Cleveland suburb? All this is not to suggest that a reading series designed for the children of a large nation must provide a homogeneous reading diet. The effort has been to find a common denominator.

The selection of words for inclusion in the pupil's reading vocabulary, especially in the primary grades, is a matter of considerable consequence. It is for this reason that makers of textbooks in reading have spent time and effort in the selection of words used in their books. They have rightfully insisted that it is unwise to try to teach beginning readers to read words with which they are unfamiliar, when there are several thousand words in their understanding vocabulary that they cannot recognize in print. It is not until the later primary grades that most authors of basal reading books try to introduce words that will extend the child's understanding vocabulary. In order to provide a vocabulary suitable for the child to read, authors of reading series have based their vocabulary selection in part on carefully compiled lists of words.

Description of Word Lists

One of the earliest studies of children's vocabulary was "The Kindergarten Union" list published in 1928 by the International Kindergarten Union, which is now the Association for Childhood Education International.[5] It contains 2,596 words which, according to that study, were used the most frequently by young children whose parents or kindergarten teachers recorded the words the boys and girls used. Although this list does not indicate which words are encountered most in reading by beginning readers, it does throw light on the problem of vocabulary selection for first-grade books, since the words in the early reading materials should be chosen from the words whose meaning presents no problem to the children.

The much-used *A Teacher's Wordbook of 20,000 Words,* compiled by Edward L. Thorndike,[6] contains words selected from a large variety of sources of reading material, some for children, others for adults. Thorndike tabulated these so that the frequency with which each word is used is indicated by its placement in groups of 500 or 1,000. It is of only limited value for work on vocabulary control for the primary grades, however, since the frequency with which words are used by adults in reading is not a good index of the words that can best be used in primary-grade reading. *A Teacher's Wordbook of 30,000 Words,* by Edward L. Thorndike and Irving Lorge,[7] published in 1944, includes not only the results of the research reported in the earlier *A Teacher's Wordbook of 20,000 Words* but also three other counts made of more than four million running words. Since it indicates the frequency with which some of the words are used in reading materials for children, it is more useful than its predecessor for writers of children's books and for teachers who construct some of their own instructional materials.

One of the most widely used lists by makers of textbooks for children in grades one through three is *A Reading Vocabulary for the Primary Grades* by Arthur I. Gates.[8] It is based in part on Thorndike's studies and gives 1,811 words frequently used in primary-grade reading materials. The relative frequency of words arranged in groups of 500 is shown.

Stone's 1941 Graded Vocabulary for Primary Reading[9] contains 2,164 words selected on the basis of a vocabulary study of textbooks from the

---

[5] Association for Childhood Education International, "The Kindergarten Union List" (New York: Teachers College Press, Columbia University, 1935).

[6] Edward L. Thorndike, *A Teacher's Wordbook of 20,000 Words* (New York: Teachers College Press, Columbia University, 1926).

[7] Edward L. Thorndike and Irving Lorge, *A Teacher's Wordbook of 30,000 Words* (New York: Teachers College Press, Columbia University, 1944).

[8] Arthur I. Gates, *A Reading Vocabulary for the Primary Grades* (New York: Teachers College Press, Columbia University, 1935).

[9] Clarence R. Stone, *Stone's 1941 Graded Vocabulary for Primary Reading* (St. Louis, Mo.: Webster Publishing Company, 1941).

preprimer level through the third reader and of other lists compiled earlier. All the readers used in the study were published between 1931 and 1941.

The Author's Word List for the Primary Grades[10] is based on the study of the vocabulary of 84 preprimers, 69 primers, 84 first readers, 85 second readers, and 47 third readers. Among the preprimer and primer words were included only those that were found in one-third or more of all the books studied on that level. The words are graded and their frequency of use is indicated.

A list that is based on words used in writing by children of the elementary school through grade eight is Rinsland's *A Basic Vocabulary of Elementary School Children.*[11] It consists of 14,571 words, each of which occurred at least three times among the 6,112,359 words that the children in the elementary school used in their writing.

A much-used list is the one by E. W. Dolch, *A Basic Sight Vocabulary,*[12] consisting of 220 words, exclusive of nouns, which are used with greatest frequency in reading books for the primary grades. Although no nouns are given in this list, Dolch has compiled a separate list of 95 nouns commonly used in the lower grades in basal reading books. Dolch's study shows that approximately two-thirds of the words in reading material for the primary grades are among the 220 words listed by him. Almost as large a percentage of words found in the intermediate-grade reading books that were examined in the Dolch study are in the list. Because of the frequency of the use of the words, they are words that many teachers think every child should learn to recognize with facility during the initial period of reading instruction.

A more recent word list for use in the lower primary grades has been developed by Dale D. Johnson.[13] Johnson uses 220 words from the Kucera-Francis word list and presents statistical evidence that these words are more commonly used by contemporary children than those on the Dolch Basic Sight Word List.

A recent addition to books containing word lists is *The American Heritage Word Frequency Book.*[14] The following statements indicate in part, the research that went into the word book in the words of the publishers.

First a national survey of public, independent, and parochial schools determined what reading materials are in fact being used today in class-

---

[10] L. L. Krantz, *The Author's Word List for Primary Grades* (Minneapolis, Minn.: Curriculum Research Company, 1945).

[11] Henry Rinsland, *A Basic Vocabulary of Elementary School Children* (New York: The Macmillan Company, 1945).

[12] Edward W. Dolch, *Methods in Reading* (Champaign, Ill.: The Garrard Publishing Company, 1955), pp. 373–374.

[13] Dale D. Johnson, "The Dolch List Reexamined." *The Reading Teacher,* vol. 24 (February 1971), pp. 449–457.

[14] Peter Davies, Barry Richman, and John B. Carroll eds., *The American Heritage Word Frequency Book* (Boston: Houghton Mifflin Company, 1972). (Published jointly by American Heritage Publishing Company and Houghton Mifflin Company)

rooms and libraries for every standard school subject taught from grades 3 through 9.

Next, more than 10,000 samples of 500 words each were selected from the resultant corpus of 5,000,000 words. The selections were carefully balanced to insure representative coverage for each subject at each grade level—from spelling books to histories to sports-car magazines.

Basing their work on *The American Heritage Word Frequency List,* Wayne Otto and Robert Chester[15] compiled a list called the *Great Atlantic and Pacific Sight Word List.* They used as a basis for their list the 500 words that had the highest frequency on the third-grade level, the lowest level of reading materials checked in the compilation of the American Heritage list. The confidence which can be placed in a sight word vocabulary list for the primary grades based on frequency of words used on the third-grade level has been questioned.[16]

The most recent of the lists to which reference is here made is one by Albert J. Harris and Milton D. Jacobson,[17] known as the *Harris-Jacobson Core List.* The authors checked the vocabulary in books for the first six grades of sixteen basal reading series widely used in 1970. They then compiled an alphabetical list of words most frequently used in these readers and another list in which these words were arranged in "difficulty levels from preprimer through sixth grade".[18]

Use of Word Lists

Although a great service has been done by the compilers of word lists, these points should be considered:

1. When making use of word lists based in part or in entirety on occurrence of words in writing of or for adults, the teacher should not conclude that the words used most frequently in writing for adults are the ones that should appear in the books for children in the lower grades.

2. If a word list is based on the material written for adults as well as on some for children, unless the two parts of the study are kept discrete, it is questionable to what extent the list is useful in determining the vocabulary that should be used in reading material for children.

3. Whenever a new reading series bases its vocabulary extensively on a list that expresses current practice in vocabulary selection among mate-

[15] Wayne Otto and Robert Chester, "Sight Words for Beginning Readers," *Journal of Educational Research,* vol. 65 (July–August 1972), pp. 435–443.
[16] Albert J. Harris and Milton D. Jacobson, "Basic Vocabulary for Beginning Reading," *The Reading Teacher,* vol. 26, no 4 (January 1973), pp. 392–395.
[17] Albert J. Harris and Milton D. Jacobson, *Basic Elementary Reading Vocabularies* (New York: The Macmillan Company, 1972).
[18] Albert J. Harris and Milton D. Jacobson, "Basic Vocabulary for Beginning Reading," *The Reading Teacher,* vol. 26, no. 4 (January 1973), p. 394.

rials already in print for children, there is the likelihood that whatever imperfections in vocabulary there are in other books will be perpetuated.

4. There is danger of lack of rich content if the vocabulary is too strictly controlled. This is true especially in books in the content areas like social studies and science. As a rule, the children's books in these fields have a greater vocabulary burden than those in basal reading series. While in many respects this is fortunate, cognizance must be taken of the resulting reading problems.

The Vocabulary Burden

When deciding on the reading materials for boys and girls, particularly in the lower grades, the teacher should consider not only the choice of words included but also the proportion of new words and the amount of repetition provided at appropriately spaced intervals. The tendency has been to reduce the number of different words used in readers during the initial stage of reading instruction. Recently, however, an increase in the number of running words has been advocated. It is claimed that if the words are phonetically regular words, more words can be learned by the child than when he is unable to unlock the new words by means of phonics.

No conclusive research is available on the optimum number of new words per page, but it is questionable whether it is desirable to introduce on the average more than one new word per page in preprimer material and more than two per page in the primer and first reader stages. The number of new words to be presented on a page, however, is dependent on so many factors that it is doubtful whether research can establish the optimum number for any level. It is usually conceded that as the child progresses in his ability to read, he can encounter, without reaching a level of frustration, more new words in proportion to the running words than he could earlier. In this connection it is important to bear in mind that while the number of new words given on a page in an intermediate-grade book is often considerably larger than the number in first-grade books (one reason being that the average length of the page increases from the primary to the intermediate grades), in reality many of the so-called "new words" in the intermediate-grade reader are new only insofar as they have not been used before in the series; they may be words which the pupils have identified through other reading.

A bright child may not need nearly as many repetitions as the average child. Furthermore, the method of presentation of a new word by the teacher determines in part how many repetitions are desirable. It would seem that probably in the books for the primary grades adequate repetition is provided for the average child. However, many reading textbooks for the intermediate grades do not repeat words often enough for many boys and girls to be able to learn them without undue difficulty. This point is particularly serious when the words are new not only to the child's reading but also to his understanding vocabulary. A teacher can, however, solve this problem in part by supplying significant supplementary practice on the words, most of which should as a rule be done in context.

The proportionate number of new words and the amount of repetition desirable should not be determined mechanically, without reference to the individual, to the method of presentation of words, and to the supplementary reading that the child does. The learning of words should not be dependent solely on repetition in a textbook. If considerable emphasis is put in reading instruction on developing power to decipher new words and on meaning, it becomes less important to rely greatly on word lists.

What we have said in the preceding paragraphs is relevant to the determination of words, providing that a basal reading textbook, in which frequently there is a rather rigid vocabulary control, is used. Some authorities question the need even in reading textbooks for as much control over vocabulary as is now exercised in most series. Authors of general books for boys and girls, including those for beginners, have typically seldom shown much concern about word count. And careful count of "new words" in language experience charts would defeat a major purpose of that approach; namely that of providing boys and girls with the opportunity to express themselves in the material they dictate to the teacher for future reading by them.

Outline for Chapter 5B

DEVELOPING SKILL IN WORD RECOGNITION

Teaching Words as Sight Words
Developing Word Recognition through Context Clues
Developing Word Recognition through the Use of Phonics
Developing Word Recognition through the Use of
   Structural Analysis
Using Picture Dictionaries
Games and Word Recognition
     Criteria for Selection of Games
     List of Games Commercially Available
     Other Reading Games
     Distributors of Games

CHAPTER

Developing Skills in Word Recognition

Specific suggestions for classroom practice in developing skill in word recognition are presented in this chapter. As the reader notes them it is hoped he will keep in mind the importance of having the learner see motives for performing suggested activities. Without convincing motivation, felt by the boys and girls, much of their work on the skills of word recognition or on any other reading skill is likely to be of but little value. The reader should also bear in mind that much of the work on word recognition can best be done in meaningful reading situations, rather than through isolated practice exercises.

TEACHING WORDS AS SIGHT WORDS

The following suggestions may be helpful to teachers when using the whole-word method as one of the means of helping boys and girls grow toward independence in word recognition.

1. Presenting new words before reading a selection   Let us assume that the new word to be encountered is *summer*. The teacher has written it on the chalkboard in manuscript and now points to it, saying it clearly. He invites the class to repeat it with him in unison. He turns next to a cardholder or to word cards placed on the chalk ledge and asks individual children or the class as a whole to select the word *summer* from among the words listed. On the chalk-board are several sentences, one or more of which include the word *summer*. Children are called on to select those sentences containing the word and to point to the word. They then find the word in the selection to be read.

2. Studying new words after a selection has been read   At times the teacher may prefer to have the children read a selection before he helps them with the new words in it. He is justified in doing so if he has reason to believe that most of the pupils will be able to figure out the new words by themselves. If the selection to be read contains many new words, however, it is usually advisable not to rely on children's ability to deal with them indepen-dently. After the reading, the children may be asked to identify the words with which they had difficulty, so that the teacher may present them in the manner suggested in the preceding paragraph. When using this procedure, however, the teacher should keep in mind the fact that frequently boys and girls, especially those with many problems in the recognition of words, may not respond to the suggestion that they designate the words they do not know. The teacher will, therefore, frequently want to select for practice words with which he thinks one or more children may have difficulty.

3. Presenting new words before reading a selection and providing further practice on them after the reading   In many instances work on words either before or after reading a selection may be insufficient to assure needed con-trol of the new vocabulary. Consequently, at times the teacher will want to present the "new words" before the reading and then provide additional practice on them after the reading. The latter reinforcement of the learning may frequently be planned in such a way that the boys and girls become more familiar not only with the word in question but also with other forms of the word and of words that have elements in common with it. For example, if the "new word" *walk* has been presented before the reading, after the selection has been read the boys and girls might work on variants of the word, such as *walks, walked, walking.* Or if the word *cat* has been presented, after reading the story or part of it the pupils might work on words similar to *cat* in all respects except the initial letter, such as *hat, fat, pat, rat, sat.*

4. "Telling" the word to save time   After a child has acquired some effi-ciency in analyzing words phonetically and structurally, it may still at times be desirable to present a word to him as a "sight word." Stopping to decipher the sound of a word may interfere seriously with the flow of the narrative and thus produce irritating interruptions in what should be a pleasurable process of getting meaning. In such instances the teacher may want to supply the word so that the pupil can get on with the story.

5. Reading "new words" orally from the board   A list of numbered words written on the chalkboard may sometimes be used as a brief exercise in the building of a sight vocabulary. Members of the class may volunteer to indicate by number the words they know. Thus the presentation of new sight words by the teacher is supplemented by class participation. Such an exercise should be both very brief and relatively infrequent.

6. Distinguishing between words of similar length and shape Words that bear a general resemblance to each other in the eyes of a young child may be placed on the board in a row, with all the words alike except the one that is to be distinguished from the others. Or in the following list of words:

when   where   where   when   where   when

pupils may be asked to draw a circle around each word that "says" *where*. The exercise may be repeated for the identification of the word *when*. Brief exercises may be arranged for other words of similar general appearance, such as *say* and *may, man* and *can, make* and *cake, mat* and *sat*.

7. Distinguishing between words presented in pairs Words often confused by young readers may sometimes be presented in pairs. Thus the following words may be written on the board together:

when, where   thought, through
why, what   on, no
then, there   went, want.

The teacher points to each pair in turn, saying the words and calling on pupils to draw a line under the appropriate word or pair of words. Or he may write an incomplete sentence, calling on pupils to supply the missing words:

I——a new ball.   *(went, want)*

8. Matching words and pictures Both to provide practice in recognizing words and to test the ability to do so, the teacher can provide each pupil with a sheet of paper giving a column of words and another of pictures. Pupils can then be asked to draw lines from the words to the matching pictures. Or, instead of single words, groups of words or whole sentences can be supplied along with matching pictures. For example, pupils may be asked to draw a line from a picture of a girl with a book to the one of three sentences that is illustrated by the picture shown below:

Tom has a book.
Mary has a ball.
Mary has a book.

9. Copying the word to be learned Some children who have difficulty in remembering the appearance of a word by means of the sight method find it helpful to get practice in writing the word. There are many ways in which practice can be provided through a visual-motor approach. For example, the child is presented with the written or printed word *sister*. He is told what the word says and then proceeds to copy it. If he has made an error, he draws a line under the part of the model word that he did not copy correctly. Then he takes a second look at the word, thinking of its sound as he does so. He knows that next he will be asked to write the word without looking at the model. After he has written the word from memory, he compares it with the original copy and takes note of any differences. After a certain amount of such practice, he tries to identify the word in a list and in context. The learner should be helped to recognize purpose for the copying; meaningless copying of words is not likely to lead to the desired growth.

By no means do all children need to use this slow and rather cumbersome method for learning new words. Nevertheless, it has been used successfully when other methods have failed. It is useful also with children who normally respond readily to the sight method but have difficulty with certain words, such as *them, then, why, what, where,* and *when.*

10. Using individual word cards   When pupils have individual cards, similar to the larger ones suitable for group work, for practice on words, they might hold up their word cards that correspond to the ones the teacher shows. Then one of the pupils could name the word on the card.

11. Labeling objects in the room   After the teacher has made labels for various items in the classroom, the pupils can be asked to place the labels with the objects. In some cases the labels may be placed on or near the objects, and in other instances they may be attached to the objects with tape. Labels can be used to designate objects in an exhibit, owners of lockers, contents of shelves or cupboards, library books, and the like.

12. Pantomiming words.   Pantomime can be used effectively for practice on sight words that are difficult to illustrate in some other ways. Verbs and prepositions are among these. The pupils might illustrate by actions, as the teacher points at the written words—verbs such as *hop, walk, run, smile, laugh;* and prepositions such as *under, between, over.*

13. Using a flannel board   To a flannel board might be attached, for practice on sight words, various cutouts illustrating "new words." These may be selected in terms of words "new" in a given story or in terms of those used in connection with a given topic, such as Christmas, Thanksgiving, birds, or space. On a table near the flannel board might be placed word cards (backed by a strip of flannel or felt) to accompany each of the cutout figures. The pupils could attach the cards to the appropriate illustrations. They could check their work by referring to a chart that is provided, on which the words are given next to the illustrations of them.

14. Using "helper charts"   "Helper charts," on which are indicated lists of duties to be performed by members of the class, possibly illustrated, could have a parallel column with names of persons to perform the tasks. For example, the direction *Water plants* in the first column could have a card to the right of it with the name *Sally* attached to the chart. Or the only words on the chart could be the children's names. In that case a picture of a waste basket, for example, could indicate that David is to pass it during the week that his name is on the chart opposite the illustration.

15. Following directions given on a chart Practice in learning some words or groups of words by sight can be provided by listing on a chart some directions that the pupils have frequent occasion to follow, for example: *Get ready to go home; Put on your wraps; Get ready for storytelling.* As the teacher points at a direction, the pupils respond by following it.

16. Illustrating words for a booklet To help pupils remember words that can be illustrated, the teacher might prepare a worksheet for every child on which in each quarter of the sheet is written in manuscript a word to be illustrated. These sheets can be assembled in a booklet.

17. Distinguishing between homonyms The sight-word method can be used in teaching homonyms. To gain practice in using newly acquired knowledge of the words, pupils might be given exercises in which they are to supply the correct homonyms. In sentences such as the following the pupils might be asked to write the correct word given in parentheses.

> John——the ball to the catcher.   *(threw, through)*
> ——you please open the window?   *(wood, would)*

DEVELOPING WORD RECOGNITION THROUGH CONTEXT CLUES

Context clues are often most effective when they are employed along with other methods of word attack. The following suggestions should be read with this point in mind.

Using Picture Clues

Below are ways in which pictorial clues can serve as aids to word recognition:

1. Using pictures in connection with the presentation of a word If the teacher wishes to present the word *ball* to the young child, he may first show a picture of a ball and carry on a brief conversation about it. In this way he is able to create in the child's mind the impressions of reality that give meaning to the verbal symbols. First comes the referent, then the symbol for it. The symbol can then evoke the referent when the reader encounters it in verbal context. To reinforce the context clues, the teacher may call attention to the length and contour of a word and confront the reader with sentences in which it is used.

2. Introducing new words, in advance of reading, with the aid of pictures Before either the class or a single pupil begins to read a selection, the attention of the children may be called to an accompanying picture in the book. Discussion of the picture can naturally lead to the new word in the text, which can be pointed out and emphasized. In such preliminary discussions, the teacher may encourage the class to anticipate the story from an examination of the pictures.

A variation of this method is for the pupils to find the picture that completes a part of a sentence that the teacher has written on the board among various ones placed on the chalkboard. Then the teacher can write the word with the rest of the sentence or show a word card with it.

3. Using picture-word cards Some teachers have quite successfully made extensive use of picture-word cards in teaching word recognition. Sets of cards, each one of which carries on one side a picture with the appropriate label and on the other the word alone, are given to all pupils. Sometimes larger versions of the picture cards are placed along the walls, and the children make a game of matching their own cards with those they find there. It should be emphasized that such games in word recognition should be combined with abundant experience in encountering the words in sentence context.

4. Using picture clues on the bulletin board The bulletin board should be a source of constant pleasure and stimulation to the pupils. Pictures— clipped from magazines, drawn, or contributed by pupils or secured from various other sources—are a most effective means of introducing children to the printed word. For example, a picture of a Christmas tree, attractively labeled, is a powerful device for drawing attention to the appearance of familiar words and for leading into a brief study of the structure of those words.

5. Anticipating meaning through examination of pictures in a series Since logical thinking can be an important aspect of the use of picture context clues, pupils might be provided with exercises in which they tell what they think will happen next in a series of events represented by pictures. For example, the first picture might be of a dog following a boy to school; the second might be of the boy stopping en route to school trying to persuade the dog to return home; the third might be of the boy and his dog approaching the door of the schoolhouse. Then the children could be asked to state which one of two pictures is the more likely to be the next in the sequence, one showing the dog running home as soon as they neared the schoolhouse door or one showing the dog managing to get into the school as the boys and girls enter the building, even though the owner tried to prevent him from entering. A variation of this exercise is one in which the pupils are asked to describe a suitable picture to follow the pictures in the series that were shown.

6. Providing pupils with pictures to complete so that they fit sentences that accompany them Each child could be given a sheet of paper on which there is a series of sentences or groups of sentences, each containing an indication as to what needs to be done to a picture in order to have it fit the sentence containing the new word, which is underlined. For example, one group of sentences might be:

Ted likes to play *ball.*
His *ball* is red.

To the right of these two sentences there might be an outline picture of a ball.

7. Giving the pupils duplicated pictures on which various words that they are learning are illustrated   For example, there could be a picture of a Christmas scene, with these words illustrated in it: *mother, father, tree, book, doll, candy, ball.* The words could be written along the sides and bottom of the picture. The pupils could then draw a line from each of the words to the part in the picture illustrating that word.

8. Using transparencies with an overhead projector   On a transparency the teacher may write before class a series of sentences in each of which a blank has been left for a "new word." To the right of each sentence can be a picture illustrating the word. The children can be instructed to read the part of a sentence given, look at the accompanying picture, and name the missing word. The teacher can then, after a sentence has been taken up in this manner, write the word in color on an overlay so that it completes the sentence on the original transparency. After each sentence has been completed, the boys and girls may be given practice in naming the "new words," first, as they occur when the overlay is placed on the first transparency and then when only the overlay is shown.

9. Using other visual aids   Some reading series are accompanied by films and filmstrips that introduce children to new concepts and new words. Teacher-made slides, based on the reading materials, can also prove to be effective in helping children cope with new vocabulary.

Using Verbal Context Clues

Following are suggestions for using verbal context clues as an aid to word recognition.

1. Using questions to help pupils learn words   If, for example, in the sentence: "Betty bought a present for her mother," all words but *bought* are known by the reader, the teacher may ask: "How do you think Betty got the present that she gave her mother?" If the child says that she found it, the teacher may ask him to name words other than *found* that could fit into the sentence, or he may tell the pupil that the word used begins with the letter *b* as a clue to the "missing word."

2. Anticipating meaning through completion exercises   Pupils can be asked to supply words that might fit in a blank in an incomplete sentence, such as: "Dick——home after school." The word to be supplied is *ran.* If the pupils suggest *walked, ran, hurried,* or *hopped,* the teacher may say: "Yes, all those words would fit into the sentence, but this one begins with the *r* sound. Which word is it?" The correct word is then written in the blank. A variation from this type of exercise is one in which the pupils choose from a group of words the one that fits the meaning, for example:

Sam played ———. *(ball, boy, bat, work, sing)*

3. Anticipating words when listening Training in the use of context clues may occur if the teacher pauses at suitable spots as he reads orally and asks the class to tell what they think the next word is. For example, he may read a sentence such as: "The cat climbed up a ———," and then ask what word might come next.

4. Discussing with the class appropriate techniques of identifying words through context Although the suggestions will necessarily vary with the pupil's stage in learning to read, certain general hints may prove helpful to children in various grades: (a.) Read the entire sentence before trying to determine the meaning of the new word. (b.) Look at the beginning and ending sounds of the word to note whether these match a word that would make sense in the context. (c.) Read for meaning. If your first impression of a word does not make sense, give it a second and more careful look. (d.) If sentence clues do not help, read the whole paragraph. The broader context may provide the key.

5. Becoming acquainted with words related to the theme of the selection If the teacher will introduce children to interesting new words in advance of the reading, vocabulary difficulties may be substantially diminished. Thus, in a story about Eskimos, a preliminary discussion of such words as *igloo, kayak, whale, walrus, glacier,* and *frigid* may markedly reduce the child's word-recognition problems.

6. Learning to recognize synonyms and antonyms Word meanings may frequently be obtained from reference to neighboring words. Thus, in the sentence: "These are the nomothetic, or institutional, dimensions of our goal-structure, as distinguished from the idiographic, or individual dimensions," we have both synonymic and antonymic clues to the unusual words, *nomothetic* and *idiographic.* Phonic and structural clues are essential, and an elementary knowledge of Greek would help us a great deal, but the sentence contains its own built-in keys to the new words. At the child's level, the following sentences illustrate the value of contextual clues in the form of synonyms and antonyms.

The picture showed an *ocelot,* a member of the cat family, in a charming pose.

While the princess moved among the guests with a friendly smile for everyone, the prince offended many with his *dour* expression.

As the game was about to begin, the principal announced over the loudspeaker that the coach and *mentor* of the team would be present, after all.

Unlike the *torrid* winds of his homeland, the cool breezes from this picturesque harbor invigorated and inspired Sapu.

For various and *sundry* reasons, the squire delayed building his new home.

Neither the rich nor the *indigent* failed to find a welcome at the bishop's home.

7. Utilizing expectancy clues   The teacher may wish to present a group of words, asking the pupils to tell in what types of context each is likely to be found. Samples of suitable words, with possible answers in parentheses, are:

> barn (farm)   groceries (store or home or kitchen)
> teacher (school   flowers (garden or home or school).

A variation of this exercise is to have the pupils tell which of a group of words is associated with a specified topic. For example, the pupils might indicate which words of a list such as the following are "farm words":

> silo   cows   airplane   chickens   barn   paper.

8. Having pupils find the word in a group of words which means the opposite or almost the opposite of the first word in the row.

> kind: sad   happy   good   mean

9. Giving riddles, in written form, for the pupils to solve   A number of simple riddles like the following might be written on the chalkboard:

> I give milk.
> I eat grass.
> What am I?

Opposite the riddle might be placed a series of words—like *apples, cow, house*—from which the children are to select the one that answers the riddle.

10. Taking advantage of typographical aids   Among the various types of context clues, some of the most helpful are the mechanical typographical devices. Punctuation marks, italics, bold print, parentheses, indentations, footnotes, and other similar devices provide helps in the recognition and interpretation of new words.

11. Making effective use of context to aid in pronunciation   Children may be given practice in recognizing the one correct alternative pronunciation of a word. In these sentences the context provides the essential clue:

> The *lead* in my pencil is broken.
> *Lead* the way, please.

Boys and girls enjoy making up sentences in which words like the following are pronounced in two different ways, depending on the context: *read, tear, use, wound, wind, bow.*

DEVELOPING WORD RECOGNITION THROUGH
THE USE OF PHONICS

Suggestions given here for the use of phonics in the teaching of word recognition are intentionally confined to a relatively small number. The teachers' manuals that accompany the better reading series contain many excellent suggestions for applying the phonics principles stated in Chapter 5A. These suggestions are based on the special vocabularies which are a part of the developmental programs described in specific series. Methods of teaching phonic skills described in the following paragraphs should be adapted to the specific needs of children, whether a basal reading series is used or not.

1. A child should not receive phonics instruction before he is "ready"; that is, until he is able to make the necessary visual and auditory discriminations with ease. The stage of readiness will vary with different children and with the difficulty of phonics instruction to be given. It is important to remember that the initial experiences with phonics should be successful ones.

2. One of the most elementary of the phonic skills is that of knowing the sounds commonly associated with single consonants in the initial position in a word. In the first work on phonics the teacher should teach consonants that, unless they are "silent letters" or blended with others, can be depended on to have the same sound always—namely, *b, h, j, l, m, p, t,* and *v.* Practice can be provided by means of procedures like these:

   a. After the pupils have had some practice in, for example, associating the letter *m* in the initial position in a word with the corresponding sound, they may name words in addition to the ones already mentioned that begin with the same letter. These words may then be listed on the chalkboard and attention drawn to the letter *m* in those words.

   b. The teacher may wish to write on the board two letters, such as *m* and *h,* with which the pupils have had some familiarity and illustrate them as they occur in initial position in a word. Then a pupil may point to the correct letter as the teacher names words that begin with either the sound of *m* or *h*—for example, *man, mother, hat, hair, many, had, has.* As a variation of this procedure, if the boys and girls can write the letters, each child could number a paper—possibly from 1 to 10— and then write *h* or *m* as the teacher names words beginning with these letters.

   c. The boys and girls might make sentences in which the initial sound is alike in many of the words in a given sentence, like:

   Polly picked peas and put them near the flower pot.

   d. As the teacher names a word the pupils might write the letter representing the sound with which the word begins.

e. As the teacher names a word beginning with a consonant in initial position, the pupils might point at objects in the room, the names of which begin with the same sound. The game "I Spy," in which the leader says: "I spy something that begins with the same sound as the word ———" can be played.

f. A phonic tree may be made by placing a small branch of a tree in a jar of sand. The "tree" could be whitewashed and the stand, if not colorful, painted green. To the top of the tree could be attached a card with a letter to be emphasized. If the letter *t* is used, the boys and girls might hang pictures of words beginning with that letter to the branches of the tree. Similarly, a tree could be used for practice on consonants in ending positions, on blends, on various vowel sounds, and on phonograms such as *ake, air, at.* The children can look for the pictures or they can choose appropriate ones from a box containing many pictures selected on the basis of use for help in phonics. The tree should be changed frequently if maximum learning is to be achieved through use of this device.

3. To get practice in application of what they know about consonants in initial position in a word, as well as about the use of context clues, pupils could tell what word fits into sentences such as this one, where only the initial consonant of the word is given:

Susan fed her d ———.

Or the boys and girls might draw pictures to illustrate words missing in sentences of that type.

Similar types of practice might be provided for pupils to strengthen their recognition of the sounds of consonants in final position in a word.

4. Practice could be provided in making substitutions of consonants in words. For example, if the pupil knows the word *fun,* he has merely to substitute the consonant *r* for *f* to be able to recognize the word *run.* The teacher can ask boys and girls who know the word *man,* when they come to the "new word" *can:* "What word that we know looks the same as this word except for the beginning letter?" When the boys and girls have replied *man,* the teacher can write *man* on the chalkboard directly below the word *can* and then ask with what sound that word (pointing at *can*) begins. He can continue by saying: "Let's name a word that begins with the *c* (hard *c*) sound and rhymes with *man."* Opportunity might also then be given for the boys and girls to name other words that are like *man* and *can* except for the beginning letter, such as *tan* and *ran.* Attention needs to be drawn not only to the possibility of substitution of consonants in initial position but also in ending and medial position in a syllable as a possible means of deciphering a new word. In such cases a similar procedure may be followed. The same method can be used with words in which substitution of a vowel in a syllable is a possible means of identifying a new word, as when *but* is recognized if the word *bat* is known.

If special practice is needed to develop skill in identifying words through substitution of letters, an exercise such as this might be used:

Direction: Draw a line under all words in each row that are exactly like the first word except for the beginning letter.

man: men   can   pan   map   ran.

The following directions might be given with a page consisting of rows of words such as those here listed:

Direction: Draw a line under all words in each row that are like the first word except for the ending letter:

has: hat   was   ham   had   his.

5. Some boys and girls who can use phonetic clues secured through the recognition of consonants at the beginning and ending positions of a word are uncertain what to do when a consonant comes in a medial position within a syllable; for example, in the word *late.* What can be done in the case of polysyllabic words is briefly described later in this section in the part on syllabication in connection with structural analysis of words. As a rule, in the case of monosyllabic words not much practice is needed on consonants in medial position if the pupils know well the role of the consonants in the intial and ending positions. Nevertheless, an indication should be given to the child fairly early in his training in phonics that consonants can occur in other than beginning and ending positions.

6. As boys and girls meet in their reading consonant blends like *st, gr, tr, cr,* and *str,* they should learn that these and other consonant combinations are sounded in such rapid succession that they do not make two entirely separate sounds. They could be asked to name words beginning with whatever blend they are then studying or have studied. A phonic wheel like the one illustrated can help provide occasional practice not only on beginning consonant blends but also on initial single consonants.

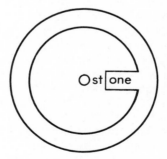

The wheel can be made of two circles of tagboard, one a little smaller than the other, fastened together in the middle by a brass fastener so that the smaller wheel can spin around. Since the wheel here illustrated is to give practice on *st* in initial position in a word, the letters *st* are written on the inner circle next to an indentation in that circle made by cutting out a piece of the tagboard. The cutout part should be of sufficient size so that endings like *ore* (to go with the *st* to form *store*), *one,*

op, and *ick* written on the outer circle can be seen when the slot is moved in such a way that the opening in the smaller circle is opposite the place where the ending in the larger wheel occurs. Then, as the child spins the smaller circle he can read the words that begin with *st*, like *store, stone, stop,* and *stick*.

7. Another phonic device that helps provide practice needed by some pupils is that of listing either consonant blends or single consonants on slips of tagboard about 1 x 1½ inches, with the consonant or consonant blend written at the right of each of these cards. Attached by brass fasteners to the bottom of the pile of these smaller cards could be a larger one, possibly 1½ x 5 inches, that contains all of the letters of a word except the beginning consonant or consonant blend. If, for example, on the longer card the ending *ake* were given, then on the smaller cards might be written, *b, r, c, t, m, f, l, s,* and *w*. To form different words for recognition, the pupils can lift up one card at a time and thereby make a number of words ending in *ake*.

8. After boys and girls have learned the sound of *th*, both voiced as in *there* and voiceless as in *thin*, the teacher may wish to write on the board a list of words beginning with *th*, some with the voiced and some with the voiceless sound, such as *the, that, thick, think*. Then as the pupils pronounce each word they could, for example, put a star in front of every word that begins with the sound of the *th* in *thin*.

9. When teaching vowel sounds the teacher may, for example, ask the pupils to identify the sound of the *a* in words like *at, bat, man, sand*. Or he may ask the boys and girls which words in a series like the following has an *a* with the same sound as the *a* in *at: ate, cat, am, air, can, arm, late, bat*.

    Another, but similar, type of practice could be provided by asking the children to indicate which in a series of words listed on the chalkboard or on paper contains a given sound that is identified as the long sound or the short sound of a vowel. For example, the pupils might select words with the long *e* sound from among a group of words such as the following, included among which are words with the long *e* sound, words with the short *e* sound, words with other sounds of *e*, and words with the silent *e: be, set, late, been, he, she*.

    Another procedure is to have the pupils make new words by changing the vowel in a word to form other words, as when they substitute for the *a* in *hat*, the letters *i, o,* and *u* to form *hit, hot,* and *hut*.

10. Further practice on vowels could be provided through procedures such as the following:

a. After the teacher has written on the board a word containing one vowel, for example, *bell,* he asks questions that involve changing the vowel of the given word so that another word is formed. For example, if the word *bell* has been written on the chalkboard, the teacher might ask the pupils what change would need to be made in that word so that the "new word" names something with which boys and girls play.

b. In two columns words containing various vowel sounds could be listed, with one word in each column having the same vowel sound as a word in the other column. The pupils are to match the words with similar vowel sounds.

take	at
and	end
eat	seat
ten	say

11. To provide practice in identifying the sound of a vowel—for example, the sound of long and short *a*—the boys and girls could be given a sheet of paper on which are drawn squares about 2 x 2 inches. In each of the squares is a picture illustrating a short word containing the long or short sound of the letter *a.* Also in each square the teacher could write four or more words, some of which contain the long *a* and some the short *a* sound. The pupils could then be instructed to draw a line under every word in a square that contains the same sound of the *a* as in the word illustrated by the picture. One row of the pictures with accompanying words might look like this:

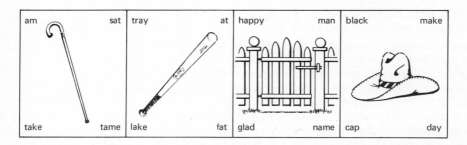

As a variation of the exercise just described, the pupils could indicate which words in a row such as the following have the same sound of the vowel *a* as the first word in this row has:

bat   rat   rate   made   sat

12. The pupils may write on small slips of paper the vowels on which practice is needed, one vowel per piece of paper. If the practice is to be on the vowels *a* and *e,* the pupils may hold up the one of these two letters that is represented by a sound in each word as the teacher names it.

For example, when the teacher says *name*, the pupils will hold up their papers with the letter *a* written on them.

13. To teach the boys and girls the sound of *ar, or, er, ir,* and *ur,* as used in standard American speech, the teacher could have them give the sound of these letters as he pronounces them and writes words such as these on the board: *color, murmur, burglar, fir, orator.* Next the pupils can give the sound of those combinations of vowels with *r.* Then they can name other words containing an *ar, or, er, ir,* or *ur* combination. They should be helped to realize that a vowel preceding an *r* does not necessarily indicate such a combination, as, for example, in the words *rare, figure, mire, deer, clear.*

   In a similar manner the teacher can proceed to develop inductively the generalization about the modified sound of *a* when it precedes a *w* or an *l,* as in *claw* and *fall.*

14. After the boys and girls have learned that in vowel digraphs—such as *ea, oa, ai, ay, ee,* and *ei*—the sound of the first letter forming the digraph is often long and the second silent, the teacher may list on the board examples that the pupils name. Then they can mark words, given on a list distributed to each child, that contain one of the digraphs that follow the rule. Some of the words on this list might be *each, oats, may, eel.* What words are used will depend in part on the reading level of the learner. In a similar manner pupils could practice on diphthongs like *oy, oi, ou,* and *ow.*

   The pupils should be cautioned that the generalization regarding vowel digraphs is not, by any means, an invariable rule.

15. Although it is usually easy to develop the concept that some letters are silent, it is more difficult to teach pupils *when* letters are silent. In this connection it is desirable that boys and girls recognize the difference between vowel digraphs (for example, *ea* in *eat*), in which one letter is silent, and diphthongs (for example, *ou* in *out*) in which two letters together form one sound unlike either of the vowels. Practice may be provided by having the pupils tell in which words, in a list like the following, one of two letters in Roman type is silent: ab*ou*t, *oi*l, b*oa*t, cl*ea*n, c*ow*, r*ai*l.

   To teach inductively the generalization that a final *e* in a syllable preceded by a single consonant is usually silent, the teacher could place on the chalkboard a numbered list of three or four words that are governed by the rule, such as: *rate, tame, hope, rule.* With each word the pupils could be asked to: (a.) pronounce the word, (b.) tell with what letter the word ends, (c.) tell whether the *e* is silent, (d.) indicate what kind of letter—vowel or consonant—precedes the vowel, and (e.) state how many consonants precede the vowel. As a summary the pupils could answer these questions about all the words in this list:

   With what letter does each word end?
   Is the *e* silent?
   What kind of letter—vowel or consonant—precedes the final *e?*
   How many consonants precede the final *e* in each of the words in the list?

Next the teacher could tell the pupils that usually, when the final letter in a word is *e*, the *e* is silent if it is preceded by a single consonant. He could then give the pupils opportunity for applying this generalization. They could tell in which words in a list of words such as these the rule applies: *came, ride, male, riddle, table.*

16. To help pupils remember sounds of letters they could make individual booklets in which there is a page for each letter or letter sound that they have studied. On these pages they could paste pictures illustrating words that contain these sounds.

17. To get further practice in associating the written symbol with its sound(s), a box containing slips of paper with various consonants or consonant blends on them could be used. As a child draws a letter out of the box, he might name it and find objects in the room the names of which begin with that letter. Or the pupils might match the written symbols with pictures arranged around the room that begin with a given sound. Or, as the teacher holds up a picture, the children might hold up a card with the letter or letters with which the name of the object in the picture begins.

18. Rhyming words can be used in teaching phonics with procedures such as the following:

   a. The teacher repeats a nursery rhyme and asks the pupils to listen for words that rhyme.

   b. The boys and girls complete jingles that the teacher makes up, such as:

      At recess time on this day
      All the children will want to——.

   c. The pupils name pairs of rhyming words.

   d. As the teacher names various words in pairs, some of which rhyme and some of which do not rhyme—such as *meat, seat* and *take, talk*—the pupils tell which pairs rhyme.

   e. The teacher presents orally sets of three words, two of which rhyme. The pupils tell which pairs rhyme.

   f. The pupils make card files of rhyming words. For example, one card could consist of words rhyming with *play*, such as *day, hay, lay, may, pay, ray, say, stay, today, way.* Pupils may wish to refer to the cards when writing original poetry.

   g. The teacher places on the chalkboard ledge a series of pictures, the name of each of which rhymes with the name of some other object or person pictured in the collection. For example, he might place on the chalkboard pictures of a boy and of a toy, of a hat and of a bat. As a leader points to one of the pictures, another pupil finds a picture the name of which rhymes with the name of the one at which the leader pointed. These two pictures can then be removed from the collection as practice continues on other rhyming words.

19. To provide practice in becoming conscious of the position of sounds in a word the teacher could tell the pupils, for example, that all the words he will give will contain the sound of *t*. After the teacher has named a word, a pupil tells whether the sound of *t* comes at the beginning or end of a word or within it. Words like these can be pronounced: *hat, Tom, little*.

20. After the boys and girls have had work on blends, the teacher may draw three or more large circles on the chalkboard, on one of which he has written, for example, the word *clock*, on another the word *tree*, and on still another *store*. Then as he gives from a word card the name of a word beginning with the sound of the *cl* in *clown*, a child can take the card and put it on the chalkboard ledge near the circle in which the word *clock* is written. Similarly, when the teacher pronounces the word *stove*, a pupil should place the word card under the circle with the word *store*. When the boys and girls are ready to learn the diacritical markings of words, it is important to begin slowly enough so that the work will not be confusing to them. After they have worked on the long and short sounds of the vowels, the teacher may tell them that there is a way of indicating the sound of a letter in writing. Then he can tell them the marking frequently used for the long and short vowels and provide practice in their interpreting and writing these markings for words. At this time he may also wish to draw attention to the fact that in some systems of marking the short vowel sounds are not indicated by markings and explain that the assumption is that when words are marked diacritically, if no marking occurs over a vowel, the vowel is short. One way in which he may wish to help boys and girls use diacritical marks is by asking them to mark all the long and the short vowels in a list of words of which they already know the pronunciation. Later they can learn to decipher words by means of markings.

Since more than one set of diacritical markings is in common use the system selected for practice should be the one most used in the pupils' glossaries or dictionaries. In the intermediate grades, however, boys and girls should be helped to decipher words when a system different from one they have been employing is used. They should know that at the bottom of the pages of a dictionary the guide to pronunciation that will help them interpret the markings of the words in that book is given.

DEVELOPING WORD RECOGNITION THROUGH THE USE OF STRUCTURAL ANALYSIS

Without resorting to the undesirable practice of having boys and girls "find little words in big words"—like *do* in *dog*—the teacher can in many ways aid pupils in developing through structural analysis a method of identifying and recognizing some words more rapidly than through phonetic analysis.

Study of Roots of Words, Prefixes, Suffixes, and Inflectional Endings

A few ways are suggested here by means of which boys and girls can be helped in the recognition of words through attention to the roots of the words, prefixes, suffixes, and inflectional endings.

1. The boys and girls can make a list of words containing a given root, like *walk, walks, walked, walking.*

2. When the pupils come to a word like *unwise,* if they have had the word *wise,* the teacher can draw a line under *wise* and ask what that part of the word is. The pupils can then give the prefix and, next, combine the prefix with the root of the word. Having the boys and girls make a list of common prefixes—like *mis, im,* and *ir*—with words in which they form a prefix—like *misuse, impossible,* and *irresponsible*—can help them both in word recognition and in word meaning.

3. On a sheet of paper each child can write the base words of a list of words containing either prefixes or suffixes or both that have been written on the board.

4. The teacher may write on the board a list of words with prefixes that mean *not*—like *unhappy, impossible,* and *irresponsible.* Then the boys and girls could name words to add to the list. Next they could draw a line under the different prefixes that mean *not.*

5. The boys and girls can supply the correct prefix for each word in a list, like the following, for which the meaning of the word to be formed has been given:

    ———— known   not known
    ———— like   not to like
    ———— kind   not kind

6. The pupils can be helped in the development of the generalization that many root words ending in *e* drop the final *e* before adding *ing*—like *make, making.* They can give examples of words to which this generalization applies.

7. Each pupil can be given a card with a prefix or suffix or inflectional ending, while the teacher has a series of cards containing root words to many of which a prefix or a suffix on a pupil's card could be added. As the teacher holds up a card, all pupils who have a card with a prefix or suffix that can be combined with the root word stand. Next the pupils who have the appropriate prefixes or suffixes can write on the chalkboard the words that can be formed from the root word with the addition of their prefixes or suffixes.

8. The class might make a chart with three columns in the first of which are listed common prefixes. In the second column could be given a meaning of each prefix, and in the third column examples of words in which the prefix has the designated meaning.

9. The pupils may be given two columns of words, having words with pre-fixes in the first column and synonyms for them, in a different order, with-out prefixes in the opposite column. The instructions would be to draw lines connecting each word in the first column with its synonym in the second.

unhappy	hate
dislike	mean
unkind	sad

10. The pupils could be asked to draw a line from a root word given in one column to a prefix that goes with that word in another column.

form	dis
happy	re
interested	un

11. Another matching exercise is one in which the pupils draw a line from each prefix given in one column to a common meaning of that prefix found in the second column.

un	back
ex	under
re	out
pre	before
sub	not

Attention to Compound Words

To help boys and girls gain facility in recognizing compound words, these suggestions may be followed:

1. As the teacher refers to a compound word on the chalkboard, like *grand-mother,* he may tell the boys and girls that the word is made up of two words and ask them to find these two words.

2. Use can be made of two columns of words in one of which is the first part of a compound word and in the other, the second part. The boys and girls can then draw lines connecting the words in the two columns that together form one word, for example:

grand	basket
worth	room
waiting	while
waste	mother

As a variation of this procedure the teacher may put into a cardholder a group of words in mixed-up order that might be used in forming compound words, such as the following, which pupils will combine into compound words: school, stairs, book, story, up, mother, grand, house.

3. The boys and girls can make a collection of compound words for posting on the bulletin board. To the right of each compound word, the words of which it is composed can be written.

4. A crossword puzzle could be made by the teacher or pupils in which only compound words would serve as answers. Part of each word could be supplied in a numbered list, while the other part could be chosen from an unnumbered list that is supplied with the puzzle.

5. Each pupil in the room might be given a card on which is written part of a compound word that can be combined with the word on another pupil's card to form one word. The children find their word partners and then each pair tells the class what was formed.

Syllabication as an Aid to Word Recognition

As the boys and girls acquire the essentials of syllabication, they should learn to divide words into syllables—first of all, as an aid to word recognition and, second, as a help in writing words when it is necessary to divide them into syllables. Some generalizations about syllabication, of value in word recognition, are given in Chapter 5A (*see* page 125).

1. To provide assistance in syllabication the pupils might be given a list of words, some with one, others with two, and still others with more than two syllables. The boys and girls could indicate after each word the number of syllables it contains.

2. The boys and girls might be given a list of words with more than one syllable, which they are to look up in a dictionary to find out how the words are divided into syllables.

3. After the boys and girls have learned inductively a few important generalizations about syllabication, they could be given a list of them, which they match with words governed by these rules.

Other Means of Studying the Structure of Words

A few other means of word study through attention to the structure are here given:

1. The class could make a list of contractions, with the words that were combined to form each contraction given opposite each.

2. The boys and girls could make or solve a crossword puzzle constructed by the teacher, the answers to which are contractions. The words from which the contractions are formed could constitute the numbered list of words for the puzzle.

3. The boys and girls could be given a list of words, some of which are possessive pronouns and some of which are contractions, such as the following: *its, it's, there's, theirs, I'll, hers*. They can be asked to tell which are possessive pronouns and which contractions. They might also use the words in sentences.

USING PICTURE DICTIONARIES

The term *picture dictionary* usually refers to books in which a picture is used with every word entry to help the child identify and recall words. To illustrate the letter *a,* a large picture of an apple, along with the word *apple,* and a sentence containing the word may be given. Often, but not always, the words are arranged in alphabetical order.

Brief descriptions, quoted in part or in entirety from the publishers, of a few picture dictionaries are given below. They provide added information about these aids to learning.

Courtis-Watters Illustrated Golden Dictionary for Young Readers by Stuart A. Courtis and Garnette Watters, published by the Golden Press.

> This picture dictionary is designed for middle elementary grades. Not all words are pictured, but pronunciation and word division are indicated for all words. A section in the book contains maps, days of the week, months, seasons, holidays, names of oceans and continents, abbreviations, various measures, largest cities in the world, longest rivers in the world, and many other useful items of information.

Cat in the Hat Beginner Dictionary by P. D. Eastman, published by Random House.

> An entertaining picture dictionary with funny pictures similar to those by Dr. Seuss.

Picture Dictionary for Boys and Girls by Alice Howard Scott, published by the Garden City Publishing Company.

> The author is mindful of present-day youthful interest in technical inventions and equipment. Contains over 1,700 lively illustrations in color and over 3,600 words.

Child's First Picture Dictionary by Lillian Moore, published by Grosset & Dunlap.

> It contains words of a child's own world. Only the present tense of verbs is listed. Contains 302 words suitable for first and second grades.

The Golden Picture Dictionary by Lillian Moore, published by Simon and Schuster.

> It contains 800 words for beginning readers. Pictures are well within a child's realm of experience. It is suitable for grades two through four.

My Picture Dictionary by Hale C. Reid and Helen W. Crane, published by Ginn and Company.

It is designed to go along with Ginn's Elementary Reading series in first and second grades. Colorful pictures with no sentence definitions.

Golden Dictionary by Ellen Walpole, published by the Golden Press.

It is geared to second through fourth grades, but pictures are very small for young children. Color is on every page.

The Picture Dictionary for Children by Garnette Watters and Stuart Courtis, published by Grosset & Dunlap.

All pictures are in black and white. It includes pictures, comparisons, context, print, and script in ways that very young readers enjoy. Suitable through the third grade, it contains 2,177 basic words and an index of defined and undefined words compiled to aid teachers.

The Rainbow Dictionary by Wendell Wright, published by the World Publishing Company.

This dictionary is suitable for children five to eight years old. It uses various methods in helping children to learn meanings of words, such as the picture with its caption, the simple explanation of a word, the use of the word in a sentence, the use of the word and a synonymous word or phrase in two otherwise identical phrases, the use of the word with its antonym, or the use of the word in a quotation. Simple pictures are used.

The following are additional widely used picture dictionaries:

McIntire, Alta, *The Follett Beginning-to-Read Picture Dictionary* (Follett Publishing Company).

Monroe, Marion, and W. C. Greet, *My Little Pictionary* (Scott, Foresman and Company).

O'Donnell, Mabel, and Wilhelmina Townes, *Words I Like to Read, Write, and Spell* (Harper & Row).

Parke, Margaret B. *Young Reader's Color-Picture Dictionary for Reading, Writing, and Spelling* (Grosset & Dunlap).

Scott, Alice, and Stella Center, *The Giant Picture Dictionary for Boys and Girls* (Doubleday & Company).

Some suggestions for the use of picture dictionaries are:

1. For younger children, stress simplicity of arrangement of words and of illustrations of the words.
2. Take time to help children in the use of the picture dictionary.
3. Be sure to make ample time available for the use of the picture dictionary.

4. Use the picture dictionary primarily as a self-help device.
5. Make the picture dictionary easily available to the children, display it attractively, and have numerous copies on the reading table.

Pupil-made picture dictionaries are especially valuable, perhaps more than the commercial ones, certainly as supplementary materials. One type of picture dictionary is one in which the children either draw or paste a picture representing an entry word and then write the word, often used in a simple sentence, on the same page with the picture. These pages can be arranged to good advantage in alphabetical order by means of a looseleaf notebook. As the pupil is learning a new word that can be illustrated, he writes it on a sheet of paper and pastes on the same sheet a picture that he has found or drawn himself. Sometimes the picture dictionary is a group project; at other times each pupil makes his own.

A picture dictionary may be in the form of cards, instead of sheets of paper, that contain the words and the illustrations of words. These cards can be arranged in a file, which can be expanded as the class progresses in knowledge of words. Another variation of the picture dictionary is often made in connection with the words that can be illustrated that occur in a story or a section of a book. As the pupil is learning new words that can be illustrated in a given story or unit in a reader, he illustrates each one; he then can refer to the word as he finds the need of doing so. For example, if in a story the child is introduced to the words *rabbit, tree, ran, squirrel*, and *into* he may divide a sheet of paper into four parts, using one of the four parts for the word *rabbit* under a picture of a rabbit and reserving another of the four parts for each of these words: *tree, ran*, and *squirrel. Ran* he may illustrate by a boy, a dog, or a rabbit running. Since words like *into* do not easily present themselves in a pictorial illustration, that kind of word usually is omitted from a picture dictionary. However, in a card file these words might be alphabetically listed as "function words" or "words we often use."

Another teacher-pupil-made adaptation of the picture dictionary deals only with words used in a science or social studies unit.

As the pupil uses the picture dictionary to recognize words, the teacher can help him derive other benefits from it. Some of these values are: (1.) help in spelling, (2.) development of interest in words, and (3.) development of skill in finding words in alphabetical order. If the picture dictionary is pupil-made, these are additional values: (1.) practice in arranging words in alphabetical order, and (2.) development of skill in arranging words and pictures neatly on a page.

GAMES AND WORD RECOGNITION

In connection with the role of games in relation to the development of power in word recognition, these questions frequently concern teachers: (1.) Under what conditions are games desirable? (2.) What are some games that can aid in word recognition?

Criteria for Selection of Games

In determining the role of games in developing power in word recognition, the teacher needs to have his purposes clearly in mind. If the major purpose is to help the boys and girls become more skillful in identifying and remembering words, then a game, to be acceptable, must satisfy the requirements for effective practice or reinforcement. If the chief aim is to furnish recreation, then it is not essential that the characteristics of effective drill be present. Games that are not primarily designed to give help in reading can be scheduled during times of the school day set aside for recreational activities, such as before school, during the noon hour, during recess when better use of the time cannot be made, and during other periods when recreation is the primary aim.

One criterion for effective practice that is often not observed when games are used in learning to read is "Other things being equal, that method of reinforcement is the better of two that provides the more practice on the skill in question in a given length of time." Other criteria for a game used primarily as a learning activity are:

1. The boys and girls should be cognizant of the purpose served by it.
2. The game should be on the interest level of the participants.
3. If competition is an element of the game it should be primarily competition with self rather than with others.
4. The game should be a means to an end, not an end in itself.

List of Games Commercially Available

Some reading games are available through publishing companies, in variety stores, and in department stores. Use of most of these can be justified chiefly as recreational activities that may, however, provide opportunity for growth in reading. Many teachers like to place such games on a reading table, so that they will be accessible to the children in free periods.

The following list of games is merely illustrative of the large number now available.

1. *"Phonic Lotto," by E. W. Dolch (The Garrard Publishing Company).*

"Phonic Lotto," a game for two to ten players, consists of ten cards $7\frac{1}{2}$ x $5\frac{1}{2}$ inches, and sixty smaller cards, $2\frac{1}{4}$ inches square. Each of the larger cards is divided into six squares on which there is printed a vowel or vowel combination accompanied by a picture, the name of which contains the vowel or vowel combination given in the square. The sixty smaller cards show pictures of objects whose names contain one of the vowel sounds found on the squares of the large cards. The sounds on which there is drill are the long and short vowel sounds, *a, e, i, o, u;* the digraphs, *ai, ay, ee, oa;* the diphthongs, *oi, oy, ou, ow, ew, oo;* and the vowels with the letter *r,* namely, *ar, er, ir, or, ur.* In the game the purpose is to match the small cards so that the pictures on them are placed on the pictures on the large card, the names of which contain the same vowel sounds.

2. *"Group Word Teaching Game" by E. W. Dolch (The Garrard Publishing Company).*

   The game consists of nine sets of cards each containing six similar cards. On the cards of each set are listed 24 of the 220 basic sight words compiled by Dolch. The game is played much like "Lotto." As a word from a printed list is read by the leader, the players cover the word on their cards with small oblong pieces of paper.

3. *"Group Sounding Game" by E. W. Dolch (The Garrard Publishing Company).*

   There are six cards, similar to "Lotto" cards, in each of the following sets: Set A—initial consonants; Set B—short vowels, *a, e,* and *i;* Set C—all short vowels; Set D—harder consonants; Set E—blended consonants; Set F—consonant digraphs; Set G—long vowels; Set H—vowels with *r;* Set I—diphthongs; Set J—miscellaneous consonants; Set K—closed syllables; Set L—open syllables; Set M—prefixes and suffixes; Set N—three syllables; and Set O—three syllables. The game can be played by six players, who cover the words the leader calls from a list of words on a given "set" that he is furnished.

4. *"What the Letters Say" by E. W. Dolch (The Garrard Publishing Company).*

   This game, also called "A Beginning Sounding Game," consists of cards on which one sound for each letter is illustrated by a picture and a word. In the game the child gets practice in associating the name of a letter with one of its sounds and with three different words on different cards that illustrate the sound.

5. *"Take," by E. W. Dolch (The Garrard Publishing Company).*

   This is a self-teaching phonics game in which the pupils match the sounds of the beginning, middle, or ending of words with cards on which a picture and the name of that picture are given. This game is for boys and girls in the third grade and up.

6. *"The Syllable Game" by E. W. Dolch (The Garrard Publishing Company).*

   In "The Syllable Game" there are three decks of 64 cards each, with two-syllable words in two decks and with words up to four syllables in the third deck. It is a game that a child can play either alone or with another person while learning to recognize many common syllables.

7. *"Phonic Rummy" (Kenworthy Educational Service, Inc.).*

   "Phonic Rummy," comes in four sets: one for grades one and two; another for grades two and three; still another for grades two, three, and four; and a fourth for grades three, four, and five. In each set there are two packs of 60 cards. With these cards a game in matching vowel sounds can be played.

8. *"Junior Phonic Rummy" (Kenworthy Educational Service, Inc.).*

   This game, similar to "Phonic Rummy," is also a matching game in which words used widely in first-grade readers are matched for vowel sounds.

9. *"Doghouse Game" (Kenworthy Educational Service, Inc.).*

   "Doghouse Game" comes in 12 game envelopes, on the face of each of which are printed 35 phonograms as well as rules for pronunciation and 64 consonants and consonant blends. A variety of games can be played with these cards.

10. *"A B C Game" (Kenworthy Educational Service, Inc.).*

This game—designed for teaching letter, word, and picture recognition—is played by matching the cards in the set, on each of which are a picture, the name of the picture, and the letter with which the word begins. The game is played somewhat like "Old Maid," as the players try to find the mate for every card that they have until every player, excepting the person who has the card entitled "Mr. ABC," has given up all of his cards.

11. *"Phonic Quizmo" (Beckley-Cardy Company).*

This is another game that is similar to "Lotto." The pupils cover on their cards the words beginning with the same letter or letter combination found in words that the teacher reads from a list supplied with the game.

12. *"Phonetic Word Wheel" (Beckley-Cardy Company).*

Various games can be devised with the phonetic word wheel in which the pupils are provided with practice in recognizing vowels, consonants, and blends.

13. *"Make-a-Word Game" (Beckley-Cardy Company).*

With the 65 green cards with consonants or consonant blends and the 65 orange cards with phonograms that are supplied, matching games can be played.

14. *"Go Fish" (The Remedial Education Center).*

"Go Fish," a consonant sound game, consists of a series of three cards for each consonant, of three different colors, with a picture on each, the name of which begins with a consonant sound, the letter for which is also given on the card. Each player is given 6 cards, while the remaining cards are placed into the fish pile in the center. Each player in turn asks any other player for a card that begins with the consonant sound that he gives. If the player is unsuccessful in his attempt to get the desired card from a player, he goes to the fish pile to see if he can draw it from that. If he does not get the card at his first attempt, he loses his turn. Whenever a player has acquired all three cards beginning with the same consonant sound, he places the three cards in a pile in front of him, forming a "book." The person with the largest number of "books" wins the game.

15. *"Vowel Dominoes" (The Remedial Education Center).*

To play this game, cards $1\frac{1}{2}$ inches by $2\frac{1}{2}$ inches, resembling dominoes, are used. On half of each card is a vowel and on the other half a picture of a word containing a vowel sound. For example, on half of one card is the letter *o* and on the other half a picture of a drum, to represent the *u* sound. The game can be played much like dominoes. For example, a card with the letter *a* and a picture of a safety pin can be placed next to a card with the letter *i* and a picture of a top, so that the half of the first card on which the safety pin is drawn is next to the letter *i* of the second card. Thus the picture of a word with the *i* sound is placed next to the letter *i*.

16. *"Phonics-We-Use Learning Game Kits" (Lyons and Carnahan).*
    These kits include a number of games that can be used in teaching or reinforcing decoding skills.

Other Reading Games

Many games other than those produced commercially can be used to develop reading skills. It is hoped that those listed here will suggest to the teacher many others that might be particularly suitable to the needs of his pupils.

1. *Word Baseball.* One way in which to play "word baseball" is to designate one corner of the room as "home" and the other three corners as first, second, and third bases. If the pupil who is "up to bat" can pronounce the word that the teacher shows him, he can go to first base. If he can also say the next word, he may go to second base. If he can go on through third base to home, he scores a "home run." However, if he is unable to pronounce his first word, he is "out" and an "out" is recorded for his team. If he cannot pronounce a word, other than the first one given to him when his turn comes, he proceeds to second base when the next batter on his side has pronounced the first word given to him. A similar procedure determines the length of his stay on third base. Scoring can be done in a variety of ways.

2. *A Reading "Spelldown."* The class can line up in two teams as they do for spelldowns. One child can be appointed scorekeeper. The teacher should have a large number of word cards with words that the pupils have studied but on which they need further practice. As the teacher holds up the first card, the first pupil tries to pronounce it and use it in a sentence. If he is able to pronounce the word and use it in a sentence, he scores a point for his team; he then takes his place at the end of the line. If he cannot pronounce a word and use it in a sentence, he stays where he is and a score is recorded for the opposing team. In that case the card is shown to a member of the other team. If he, too, does not know the word or cannot use it in a sentence, the word "comes back" to the next pupil on the team who was first given the word. Each time a word is missed, the opposing team gets a point.

3. *Action Sentences.* The leader, who may be the teacher, places in a word holder or on a chalk ledge several sentences with directions such as "Get a book from the table." After a pupil has performed one of the directions, another child points to the sentence that tells what the other child did. He reads the sentence as he points to it.

4. *Ten-pins.* Ten-pins can be set up on the floor. From a stack of word cards placed face down, players take turns in picking up the top card. If a player can pronounce the word on his card, he gets a turn at trying to knock pins over with a ball. If he cannot pronounce a word, the person whose turn it is

next pronounces it. Score is kept in terms of the ten-pins that are dislocated. This game is chiefly for recreational, not reading, purposes.

5. *Ring-toss.* A variation of ten-pins is ring-toss. In this game the person pronouncing his word correctly gets a turn at trying to toss a ring onto a hook. The winner is the one who has hooked the most rings by the time the hooks are filled. The chief value of this game is recreational.

6. *Sentence Game.* Each player places his cards on the table or desk, word side up. The teacher reads a sentence using words appearing on the cards. Every child who has a card on which a word used in that sentence is written goes to the front of the room. A pupil designated as "sentence maker" makes the sentence by arranging the children with their cards in the proper order as the teacher repeats the sentence. If a sentence maker forms the sentence incorrectly, another pupil is appointed in his place. The pupil who does not recognize that he has a needed word in his possession, or who thinks that he has one when he does not, can be "penalized" by having to put his card into the center pile from which, with future sentences, the "sentence maker" selects the word if it is again needed for a sentence.

Distributors of Games

Teachers interested in securing reading games may, in addition to canvassing stores, wish to write to publishing companies for catalogues describing their reading games. Some companies that distribute games are:

1. Beckley-Cardy (Benefic Press)
2. The Garrard Publishing Company
3. Houghton Mifflin
4. The Judy Company
5. Kenworthy Educational Services
6. Milton Bradley Company
7. Remedial Education Center
8. Simon and Schuster
9. Whitman Publishing Company.

For Further Study

Fry, Edward, *Reading Instruction for Classroom and Clinic.* (New York: McGraw-Hill Book Company, 1972), Ch. 4 "Basic Vocabulary—The Instant Words", Ch. 5 "Phonics—Sounds of English", Ch. 6 "Phonics Testing and Teaching," Ch. 7 "Phonics Teaching Materials."

Gans, Roma, *Fact and Fiction about Phonics* (Indianapolis, Ind.: The Bobbs-Merrill Company, 1964).

Gray, Wiliam S., *On Their Own in Reading,* 2nd ed. (Chicago: Scott Foresman and Company, 1960).

Harris, Albert J., "Basic Vocabulary for Beginning Reading," *The Reading Teacher,* vol. 26, no. 4 (January 1973), pp. 392–395.

Harris, Albert J., and Milton D. Jacobson, *Basic Elementary Reading Vocabularies* (New York: The Macmillan Company, 1972).

Harris, Albert J., and Edward R. Sipay, eds., *Readings on Reading Instruction,* 2nd ed. (New York: David McKay Company, 1972), Ch. VIII, "Word Recognition and Word Analysis," containing contributions by Stanford E. Taylor, Jack Bagford, Emmett A. Betts, Mary Meighen and Marjorie Pratt, E.W. Dolch, Lou E. Burmeister and Yetta Goodman.

Heilman, Arthur W., *Phonics in Proper Perspective,* 2nd ed. (Columbus, Ohio: The Charles E. Merrill Publishing Company, 1968).

Heilman, Arthur W., "Research Findings Concerning Phonics in Beginning Reading" *A Decade of Innovative Approaches to Beginning Reading,* Elaine C. Vilscek, ed., vol. 12, Part 3 of the Proceedings of the Twelfth Annual Convention of the International Reading Association (Newark, Del. International Reading Association, 1968).

Karlin, Robert, *Teaching Elementary Reading: Principles and Strategies* (New York: Harcourt Brace Jovanovich, 1971), Ch. 5, "Teaching Word Recognition."

Otto, Wayne, and Robert Chester, "Sight Words in Beginning Readers," *Journal of Educational Research,* vol. 65 (July–August 1972), pp. 435-443.

Samuels, S. Jay, "Effect of Letter-name Knowledge on Learning to Read," *Education Digest,* vol. 37 (September 1971), pp. 49–51.

Spache, Evelyn B., *Reading Activities for Child Involvement* (Boston: Allyn and Bacon, Inc., 1972).

Wallen, Carl, *Competency in Teaching Reading* (Chicago: Science Research Associates, 1972), Ch. 6 "Testing Strategies for Phonic Word-attack Skills," Ch. 7 "Teaching Strategies for Phonic Word-attack Skills," Ch. 8 "Testing Strategies for Structural and Syllabic Word-attack Skills," and Ch. 9 "Teaching Strategies for Structural and Syllabic Word-attack Skills."

Zintz, Miles V., *The Reading Process: The Teacher and the Learner* (Dubuque, Iowa: Wm. C. Brown Company, 1970).

Questions and Comments for Thought and Discussion

1. In Chapter 5B many suggestions are given for developing word recognition skills. Try to find suggestions for additional activities that might be of value in teaching word recognition by each of these methods: the sight method, use of context clues, phonics, study of the structure of words. Teachers' manuals or guidebooks accompanying basal readers are one good source for such suggestions.

2. You may find it profitable to examine several picture dictionaries. If you do, evaluate them in terms of what you know about means of developing word recognition.

3. Various commercially obtainable word lists are briefly described on pages 156–159. Of what assistance could a word list be to you in teaching word

recognition? What cautions would you want to observe as you were using any one of several lists?

4. Workbooks are a part of the basic reading program according to some authorities. But from other quarters comes severe criticism, which may be the result of the misuse of the workbook rather than the material itself. How would you use the workbook in your program? If you would not want to use a workbook, be able to state your reasons.

5. Teachers, especially those of children who are beginning to learn to read, often wonder what they should do about teaching the alphabet. They are in doubt as to whether they should set about this task deliberately and at a specified time or delay introducing letters. What would you do about teaching the alphabet? Can you differentiate between teaching the alphabet and the procedures that may be used in other early letter-emphasis programs?

6. Some teachers have been concerned about the use of charts in the primary grades and their relation to the reading program. What do you regard as the proper place of experience charts in the primary program? What purposes might such charts serve and what are their uses as learning instruments?

7. Several factors, which are listed for you, contribute to the simplicity or difficulty of reading material. What are important factors to consider in connection with each?
   a. Familiarity of experience described.
   b. Concreteness of words and concepts.
   c. Length and complexity of sentences.
   d. Effective use of words.
   e. Inclusion of vivid details.

8. Some individuals argue that pictures should be omitted from beginning reading materials. Their assumption would appear to be that children might use the pictures for solving some unrecognized words and thus would not come to grips with the printed symbols themselves. Can a child become overly dependent on pictures? What would you do to prevent this problem if you think it is a possibility? If it did occur, how would you help the child overcome his overreliance on pictorial clues?

Outline for Chapter 6A

COMPREHENSION

Comprehension Skills
    Skills Classified According to Purpose of the Reader
        Reading to Find the Main Idea
        Reading to Select Significant Details
        Reading to Follow Directions
        Reading to Answer Questions
        Reading to Summarize and Organize
        Reading to Arrive at Generalizations
        Reading to Predict Outcomes
        Reading to Evaluate Critically
    Skills Classified according to Structure or Length of
        Reading Unit
        Phrase Meaning
        Sentence Meaning
        Paragraph Meaning
        Comprehension of Longer Selections
Causes of Difficulties in Comprehension
    Limited Intelligence
    Environmental Influences
    Overemphasis on Word Recognition
    Overemphasis on Oral Reading
    Insufficient Background for Reading a Selection
    Failure to Adjust Reading Techniques to Reading Pur-
        pose and Type of Reading Material
    Lack of Appropriate Teacher Guidance
General Procedures for Improving Comprehension
    Improvement through Incidental Means
    Improvement through Practice Exercises
    Use of Cloze Procedure

CHAPTER 6A

Comprehension

The importance of skill in recognizing words has been pointed out in the preceding chapters. While it is impossible for a person to read without being able to recognize words, word recognition does not constitute all of reading. It is merely a tool for reading. Unless the reader comprehends what is recorded on the page, he is engaging in an exercise in recognizing words, not in reading as the word *reading* is used in this book.

Although there are differences of opinion as to how to define comprehension as it refers to reading, there is general agreement that by reading with comprehension is meant getting meaning from what is being perceived in writing. In fact, reading without understanding should not be called reading, for reading necessarily involves comprehending.

A passage can properly be read with varying degrees of understanding. The scale of comprehension ranges from practically no meaning to what might be referred to as complete understanding. The degree of comprehension will depend not only on the physical condition of the reader, on his skill in reading, and on the difficulty of the material but also on his purpose. All he may want as he reads a selection is to get the general idea of what is written. On the other hand, he may set out to read the material in order to test every point made in terms of its applicability to a problem confronting him. He may read every detail of the directions for performing an experiment, but may read the society column of a newspaper only to find out whether anyone he knows is mentioned in it. One of the marks of the efficient reader is the extent to which he can adjust the degree of his comprehension to his objective.

The level on which comprehension takes place can be classified in a variety of ways. One classification recognizes that comprehension may be on (1.) the factual level, (2.) the interpretative level, or (3.) the evaluative level. Reading on the factual level refers to understanding what is actually written on the page. Reading on the interpretative level designates reading in which the reader comprehends the meaning that is not expressed "in so many words," but can be implied or inferred. In evaluative reading the reader evaluates what he reads through mental activities such as judging the authenticity of the material in terms of the qualifications of the author, predicting outcomes, determining the correctness of the conclusions reached by the writer, associating what he is reading with his own experiences, past or contemplated. Sometimes reading on these three levels is referred to as (1.) reading the lines, (2.) reading between the lines, and (3.) reading beyond the lines. The understanding with which a person reads may also be thought of as: (1.) getting the facts, (2.) making inferences from what he reads, and (3.) applying what he reads by means of associational processes. Yet another means of classifying the type of comprehension is to divide it into (1.) the factual level, (2.) the level of generalization, where the reader generalizes on what he reads; and (3.) the critical level, where the reader evaluates what he reads in terms of the purpose of the author and the reliability and validity of the material.

In the classifications given there is no basic contradiction concerning what reading comprehension should include. All of these classifications throw light on the process of reading with understanding. One trend in current thinking, which is reflected in the categories into which comprehension has been divided, is the placing of increased emphasis on the nonfactual phases of comprehension.

COMPREHENSION SKILLS

There is controversy among leaders in the field of the teaching of reading as to whether or not reading is a general ability. Some claim that it is, while others think of reading as a combination of various specific skills, such as getting the main idea or predicting outcomes, which should be identified for the purpose of helping the learner improve in ability to comprehend what he reads. Part of this argument is probably one of semantics, since comprehension could be described as a general ability even by those who believe that there are specific skills that comprise the general ability. Where the point of view does make a difference, however, is in the application to a teaching-learning situation. Those who believe that there are specific abilities that constitute effective comprehension will probably want to pay definite attention to these skills in their instructional procedures; others who do not share this view are likely not to place much, if any, emphasis on the acquisition of these various abilities. To the authors of this book it seems important that help be given to many boys and girls in acquiring such skills as noting details that support the main idea of a selection, judging the authenticity of a report, and making generalizations on the basis of what is read. Rationale for this position lies, in part, in the fact that improvement in ability to perform one of these activities does not necessarily bring about improvement in others. For example, greater skill in noting details significant for achieving a purpose the reader has in mind may not have any effect on judging the authenticity of a report. Consequently, various comprehension skills are here identified and described.

Skills Classified according to Purpose of the Reader

The specific skills that form a part of the ability to comprehend what is read may be classified rather loosely according to (1) the purpose of the reader and (2) the length and nature of the selection read. We consider first the skills dependent upon the reader's purpose.

Reading to Find the Main Idea

One of the most common reasons for reading is to get the general idea of a selection. Reading of fiction is usually done for this purpose. Even in other types of reading, such as science, it may often legitimately be the goal. In that field the primary-grade pupil may, for example, read a page to find out whether it tells about helicopters. The more mature reader in an elementary school may read to find out whether it is advisable to include a certain chapter in a bibliography that he is preparing on "Our Solar System." The ability to determine the main idea of a part read is basic also to many other comprehension skills, such as the ability to summarize and organize. Skill in finding the main idea in a paragraph or a longer selection, and in not mistaking a detail for the major point, needs to be developed in many pupils not only through incidental means but often also through practice exercises.

Reading to Select Significant Details

The ability to note important details is closely related to skill in finding the central thought or main idea of a selection. To be proficient in this respect, the reader needs to do more than differentiate between main points and supporting details; he must also be able to decide what points are important for the purpose he has in mind. In *Miss Hickory* by Carolyn Sherwin Bailey, the story about the little doll whose body is a twig of an apple tree and whose head is a hickory nut, the person who tells the story may want to remember exactly where the story takes place. However, the child who is reading the book solely for his own enjoyment may satisfy his purpose without taking special note of this detail. The reader who gives equal attention to all details that are presented may find himself so encumbered that he loses perspective. Practice may be needed to help him decide which details are worthy of special note and which should be ignored. Their relation to the main idea of the selection will often determine their value; the purpose of the reader will be another determinant. As the pupils work for improvement in noting details, they should be helped to realize that details are of value as they support a main idea or assist in arriving at a conclusion or serve some other purpose of the reader beyond that of merely taking note of details.

Care must be taken that practice in noting details does not decrease the ability to find the main idea or to generalize. Constant emphasis should be placed on the fact that details should be fitted into a setting in which they serve a purpose.

Reading to Follow Directions

The ability to follow directions is usually a combination of many reading skills. The ability to note details, to organize, and to note the sequence of events are among the learnings essential to this type of reading skill.

Reading to Answer Questions

The question that a reader purports to answer may be one that requires merely the finding of a fact specifically stated in written material. It may call for skill in finding the main idea, selecting a series of details of significance in relation to the question, following directions, summarizing, or organizing. Or it may involve the use of such higher thought processes as are essential to predicting outcomes, reading critically, doing associational reading.

Reading to find the answer to one or more questions is one of the common goals for reading in the elementary school. Often the question is asked by the teacher. However, boys and girls also need to develop in ability to formulate significant questions for themselves. Questions from the teacher should, in part, serve as stepping stones to those that the reader decides on for himself.

Reading to Summarize and Organize

Both the ability to select the main idea and to choose significant details are basic to another commonly sought after goal of reading—that of summarizing and organizing. However, to make an adequate summary or to organize what has been read, it is not enough for the reader to know what the main idea is and what the significant details are. He must also be able to sense the relation between the main point and the details, as well as the relation among the details. Furthermore, he often needs to know either how to make these relations clear to others or how to record them for later rereading.

Frequently, the efficient reader makes summaries and organizes what he reads without doing any writing. The person who reads a chapter and then asks himself what the main points are, what material constitutes significant details, and how all these parts are woven together is making a summary and organizing what he reads. In fact, skill in organizing or summarizing is ordinarily put to use without the writing of summaries or outlines. Practice is summarizing and organizing may lead to such skill in these activities that frequently the reader almost unconsciously summarizes and organizes what he reads.

Reading to Arrive at Generalizations

Formulating generalizations is in a sense a specialized form of summarizing. To arrive at generalizations the reader needs to note specific instances and then decide whether the data presented are sufficient to warrant a significant conclusion. If they are of the type on which a sound conclusion can be based, he must determine what the deduction from the instances discussed should be. If, for example, he reads about children in Holland who wore wooden shoes, he should realize that he would be wrong if he made the decision that Dutch children always wear wooden shoes. On the other hand, if a typical scene in a schoolroom in China were described, and if the author indicated that the scene is representative, the reader may correctly conclude that Chinese schools in many respects are unlike the school he is attending.

One danger for the person not skillful in making generalizations is that he may generalize without sufficient evidence. Another is that he will make too broad a generalization. To avoid errors due to both of these causes a teacher can give specific guidance not only with material read but also with observations made in other situations.

Reading to Predict Outcomes

Another important comprehension skill is that of predicting outcomes. This skill may manifest itself in a variety of ways. For example, if the reader sees the sentence: "The farmers set no traps for any of the animals on the grounds, for they like animals," he can anticipate (unless a break of thought is indicated by words like *but* or *however* or *nevertheless*) that the next sentence in the paragraph will not contradict the thought that the farmers were kind to animals. This skill is in effect an aspect of what we call "active" reading, in which the reader assumes an attitude of anticipation.

Skill in predicting outcomes is useful in helping the reader note when he has misread a word or a group of words or a sentence. It is also of value because the person who is adept at predicting outcomes as he reads can usually get the thought more quickly than others. This skill is helpful also in remembering what is read, for it enables the reader to take special note only of those points that are new to him or are different from what he would have expected. The burden of recall is thereby lessened.

Reading to Evaluate Critically

One of the most significant comprehension skills is that of making critical evaluations of what is read. By critical evaluation is not meant the attitude of suspecting every statement read of being false. The power of critical evaluation in reading involves numerous factors. The reader needs to learn to ask such questions as these: Is the material relevant? Can the alleged facts be verified? Is the author qualified to discuss the subject? Do the statements harmonize with what I know to be true? Does the author draw valid conclusions from the facts? Is the author omitting or suppressing any important facts? Are the statements expressions of fact or inferences? Does the material contain any unstated assumptions? Can I accept these assumptions? Should I revise my own assumptions in light of what I have read?

Critical discrimination in reading calls for a wide background of knowledge concerning the subject under discussion. Literally, the word *criticism* means the application of criteria or standards of judgment. Such criteria can come only from some previous contact with the subject. The reader has no way of judging the truth of the statement, "Polio is seldom fatal," if he has not had some earlier knowledge about polio. He must then be entirely dependent on the reliability, competence, and honesty of the author. Moreover, critical reading involves the capacity for making comparisons and appraisals. Critical reading is active, creative reading. Children should begin developing the skills of critical independence in reading at the outset.

The levels of criticism will vary with the age and maturity of the pupil. A primary-school child may be asked to pick out a false statement in a series, such as "Horses can fly," while a sixth-grade pupil may be called on to find editorial statements in a news story. Critical discrimination in reading can be cultivated through skillful training.

A study by Willavene Wolf and others[1] lists the following abilities important in critical reading:

[1] This discussion of critical reading is reproduced by permission from the study of Willavene Wolf *et al., Critical Reading Ability of Elementary School Children,* (Columbus, Ohio: Ohio State University Research Foundation, 1967), pp. 133–135 Project No. 5-1040 supported by the U.S. Office of Information. The section is quoted at length because in our opinion it is one of the best statements available concerning the elements involved in critical reading. It is necessarily theoretical, and students are encouraged to devise creative ways of translating it into specific classroom practices.

I General abilities.

A. The ability to recognize reading material as one important source of ideas or information and to relate other sources such as television, pictures, etc., of the child's own personal observations of his world.

B. The ability to read and understand a variety of reading materials which represent differing interpretations or viewpoints.

C. The ability to question as one reads, to phrase possible answers, and then to read further for the information that will act as a guide for the conclusion that:

1. There is more than one answer to the question.
2. There is no conclusive answer to the question.
3. There is one answer to the question.

D. The ability to continue reading until one has gathered enough information to reach as complete an answer or to make as sound a judgment as he can presently make.

II. Specific abilities.

E. The ability to analyze what is read for the purpose of identifying the author's purposes, point of view or prejudices (and then determine how the purposes, etc., relate to one's own set of values and opinions or to the values and opinions of others).

F. The ability to analyze what is read for the purpose of identifying the publisher's purposes, point of view or prejudices; to determine how these influence the publisher's selection and promotion of materials; and finally to relate these to one's own values and opinions of others.

G. The ability to determine the author's reputation as a knowledge-able and reliable source of information in a specific field or as a recognized writer of quality material.

H. The ability to see relationships while reading that are not directly stated by the author (draw inferences): for example, to read the author's description which indicates but does not directly state that the setting is a spring morning; or, to read the author's subtle wording which hints at but does not directly state his opinion, and then to relate that opinion to the reader's own, perhaps for forming a new opinion.

I. The ability to tell the difference between an author's factual statements and the author's opinion or personal interpretation of fact.

J. The ability to follow the sequence of an author's presentation and to determine how logical or illogical the sequence was.

K. The ability to compare and contrast various (reading) sources in related content areas and determine, on the basis of sound judgment, the worth of each in contributing to one's increase in that area.

L. The ability to form an opinion of what one reads, relating what is read to one's past knowledge, and identifying those areas where one lacks enough knowledge for forming a sound opinion.

M. The ability to locate and select the reading materials that will provide the information related to the topic of the study.

N. The ability to recognize when the author has omitted facts or information that are necessary for an honest and complete understanding of some situation or issue.

O. The ability to identify and analyze the devices authors sometimes use to persuade or influence the reader:

1. Appealing to emotion over reason (name calling, appealing to sympathy).
2. Using glittering generalities.
3. Getting endorsements from some prominent person (testimonial).
4. Inferring a relationship between two objects, or persons, or events which does not exist (identification, transfer).
5. Omitting facts (card stacking).
6. Avoiding source of information.
7. Encouraging one to join the band wagon.
8. Plain Folks approach.

P. The ability to analyze and determine the accuracy and clarity of information presented through such graphic presentations as cartoons, maps, charts, graphs, pictures.

Q. The ability to identify and then analyze the literary form used by the author: fiction, historical fiction, nonfiction, biography, autobiography, fantasy, fable, myth or legend, folk tale, satire, allegory, etc.

R. The ability to analyze and then form a personal opinion about the literary quality of the material read. Such analysis might concentrate on one or more of the following:

1. Story structure.
2. Character development.
3. The story atmosphere, setting, or mood.
4. The author's style or literary devices used: figurative language, symbolism, repetition, understatement, exaggeration, personification, foreshadowing, irony, pun, alliteration.

It should be noted that critical reading is essential, too, to some of the comprehension skills discussed in this chapter, such as reading to find the main idea, reading to predict outcomes, reading to arrive at generalizations.

reading skills in the world will not enable him to read materials involving abstractions beyond the level of his mental development. While we should never underestimate a child's powers, we should adjust the task to his capabilities. The slowest learner can grow in comprehension, but in some cases we must expect the growth to be slow. The reader whose IQ is 65 may learn how to find the answer to a simple question, but he should not be required to interpret a complicated graph.

Environmental Influences

Noisy surroundings, inadequate lighting, high or low temperatures, stimulating or distracting surroundings may interfere with maximum comprehension. The extent to which the environment affects comprehension varies with individuals. The same person may at one time not be bothered by factors that other times decidedly decrease his comprehension. Interest on the part of the learner is one of the determinants of the effect of potential distractions.

Overemphasis on Word Recognition

Methods of teaching that concentrate on the recognition of individual words but neglect attention to meanings that can be derived from connected discourse may account for deficiencies in comprehension. Bright children normally make the transition from word to phrase to sentence to paragraph with ease and with little aid from the teacher. Many boys and girls, however, are baffled by the task of finding meaning in word groups. They need to be encouraged to move rapidly on the line in order to discover what happened or to find the answers to their questions. Exclusive use of phonic methods, for example, may result in mere word calling rather than intelligent reading. The aim is to equip the pupil with a variety of methods of attacking new words and at the same time to develop in him the power to get larger meaning from the printed page.

Overemphasis on Oral Reading

Oral reading can have either a desirable or a detrimental effect on comprehension. At times, oral reading of a selection that is particularly difficult for the reader increases his understanding of it, since he not only sees but also hears what he reads. Furthermore, in effective oral reading, if there is an audience, the reader is required not only to understand what he reads but also to interpret his understanding to others. In this process increased attention needs to be placed on comprehension.

Unfortunately, oral reading, if not done well, can have an undesirable effect on comprehension. The reader can become so conscious of his audience that he will fail to understand what he is reading. Overemphasis on oral reading may also make a child so self-conscious while reading to others that his concentration may be on how, rather than on what, he is reading. There is a point to the familiar story of the child who, after he had read a passage orally, was asked by his teacher a simple question about the content of the selection. His response was: "I don't know. I wasn't listening; I was reading."

Insufficient Background for Reading a Selection

Another frequent cause of poor comprehension is lack of an experience background essential to the understanding of what is being read. A city child who has never been on a farm may have difficulty in fully comprehending a story about country life. A sixth-grade boy who has never worked with science materials may not be ready to follow the directions given for an experiment. Lack of understanding of the concepts involved in reading materials and of the words used is an additional limitation to comprehension. Semantic problems of pupils who know only one meaning of words like *fair, spring,* and *plain* may also cause difficulties in comprehension.

Failure to Adjust Reading Techniques to Reading Purpose and Type of Reading Material

Good reading comprehension requires a flexible approach to the printed page. Stevie, for example, had been reading a great deal of fiction and had derived great pleasure from the experience. However, when he encountered arithmetic problems, he had difficulty because he read them as if he were reading a story and consequently moved too rapidly over the lines. On the other hand, Bobby was a meticulous reader of science materials. When he tried to read stories he failed to derive real satisfaction from his reading because he used the same reading methods for narrative that he was accustomed to employ with factual and expository prose. Similarly, a child may be unable to recognize the main idea of a passage because he is too absorbed in noting concrete details. The need is for versatility in adapting the reading method to the reading purpose and to the nature of the material read.

Lack of Appropriate Teacher Guidance

Difficulties in reading comprehension may frequently be overcome with the aid of a teacher skilled in observing the causes of the difficulties. Some of the possible causes have been suggested in the preceding paragraphs. They are only illustrative.

Alert teachers put forth great effort to find and eliminate or prevent the obstacles to meaningful reading. Problems of comprehension among pupils can sometimes be reduced by the effective use of questioning. By asking suitable questions before the pupils read a selection or after they have completed it, the teacher can help make otherwise obscure meanings clear. However, when teachers are unfamiliar with the nature and extent of the pupil's difficulties, the problems tend to multiply. The use of appropriate standardized reading tests (*see* Chapter 12), informal teacher-made tests such as those suggested in Chapters 7B and 13, as well as frequent oral reading to the teacher by individual readers are the common means of discovering some of the causes of poor comprehension. Careful observation of a pupil's reading behavior may offer valuable clues. The teacher may ask: "What type of material does the pupil read outside of class?" "How much spare time does he spend reading?" "How does he attack new words?" "Does he have a limited vocabulary for his stage of development?" "Does he know how to get the main thought of a passage?"

School records are an essential source of information about the causes of poor comprehension. Attendance records; health records; previous school history; anecdotal records concerning the child's attitudes, problems, and earlier behavior; and similar records can give the teacher insight into his difficulties.

GENERAL PROCEDURES FOR IMPROVING COMPREHENSION

Improvement in comprehension skills can be brought about in the same manner that growth in almost all other reading abilities can be stimulated. It can be achieved through reading in context during the regular reading period, through reading activities during other parts of the school day, and through reading out of class, as well as through the use of practice exercises specifically set up to provide improvement in the skills. Activities other than reading, too, can serve as an important means of improving comprehension in reading. Because of the close relation between comprehension of material presented orally and comprehension of material in written form, some procedures beneficial to the former type are also valuable in the development of the latter. Whatever types of activities are used, the power of motivation should be recognized and provisions made for stimulating purpose on the part of the learner. Without it many of the procedures and activities suggested in this and other chapters might easily turn out to be sterile exercises.

Improvement through Incidental Means

If the term *incidental means* is used to refer to all types of reading situations other than those involving practice exercises, there are many ways in which comprehension skills can be improved during the regular reading period by such means. Much of the reading of beginners, for example, deals with reading to answer questions. The boys and girls may read a story in their textbooks in order to answer a question that either the teacher or a pupil has raised. Or after the pupils have read a story they may practice selecting the main point by suggesting titles for a puppet show that they plan to base on the story. Similarly, practice is summarizing can be given when a pupil who has time to finish reading a selection summarizes the ending of the story for a child who has not completed it. During the process of reading a story there can be discussion as to what the children think will happen next. Skill in predicting outcomes can also be acquired by discussion of why certain developments in a story were the ones likely to take place. If a child reads the story of *The Three Billy Goats Gruff* after he knows how the little Billy Goat Gruff was allowed to cross the bridge, he can be asked what he would imagine the middle-sized Billy Goat Gruff would say when the troll threatened to eat him.

In classes other than reading much opportunity can be given for improvement of comprehension skills simultaneously with learning the content. In the social studies there is almost unlimited chance for meaningful practice in reading maps. Boys and girls can be helped not only in reading political maps but also physical maps, temperature maps, rainfall maps, population maps, product maps, and others. Growing out of the work in social studies may be projects such as this in which one fifth grade engaged. The teacher placed on a big bulletin board a variety of maps and a sheet of paper on which were listed significant and interesting questions under the caption: "Can You Find the Answers to These Questions?" The boys and girls were also encouraged to bring to school other types of maps, which, if appropriate, were posted.

The many tables given in books in the area of social studies can be made to serve an important purpose in comprehension. Boys and girls who need to learn when to use a table and how to use it can be helped to acquire that learning during classes in the social studies and science. In these classes they can learn the importance of noting the titles of tables and the significance of the names of the columns and rows in a table. They may at times be asked to see how many of the questions that they have raised are answered in a table or graph or map in their own textbooks. They may also look into a reference book, such as a young people's encyclopedia, to find out what information bearing on their problems they find there in maps, tables, charts, or graphs. Use of literary maps in phases of literature for children can improve skill in using pictorial materials of that type, and at the same time enhance the study of literature.

There are also many ways in which the teacher can encourage the pupil to acquire skill in various types of comprehension outside of the classroom. He can stimulate the pupil to read widely and extensively. Incentive to note main points and significant details and to organize and summarize can be given by providing the children opportunity to report on some of the outside reading in a variety of ways. The reports may take the form of telling in a few sentences the gist of a book they have been reading or by describing in detail some favorite scene. Planning dramatizations based on books, giving puppet shows or television programs, or making "movies" can all help the learner to read with more comprehension.

The teacher can help the boys and girls develop many of the comprehension skills through activities other than reading. He can ask the children to predict events in stories that he is telling or reading to them. He can encourage them to summarize reports they have heard, to enumerate in order the steps they followed in performing an experiment, to make plans for a project in which they are about to engage, to come to valid conclusions when they have listened to a series of remarks on related topics, and to decide whether certain information given to them orally is factual or a matter of opinion. The teacher's insistence on better concentration on whatever the children are doing can also bring about rewarding results. The individual who is in the habit of not concentrating when not reading is likely to find it difficult to refrain from letting his mind wander while reading.

Improvement through Practice Exercises

For some boys and girls a program of improvement in comprehension skills similar to the type just described will be sufficient. However, many will profit greatly if they are also given direct practice in the form of exercises to help them develop skills in comprehending what they read. Some pupils may need direct practice on all of the major types of comprehension skills, while others will require such help with only some or one of the skills. Ability in diagnosis on the part of the teacher is therefore necessary as she tries to determine which boys and girls need special practice in developing some or all of the comprehension skills.

In the use of practice exercises, the teacher must keep in mind certain basic principles:

1. *The teacher should have a clearly defined goal to be accomplished with each of the practice materials he uses.* He should decide what skills require direct practice and then provide the best type of exercises possible for achieving his goal economically.

2. *The boys and girls should know the purpose of each practice exercise.* Unless they know why they are doing a certain exercise, they are likely to get inferior results and lose interest.

3. *The boys and girls should be helped to see the importance of the skill to be developed by means of a given exercise.* If pupils are not helped to appreciate the worthwhileness of an activity, they may perform it halfheartedly and consequently achieve poorly. In fact, it is often valuable to let them help determine, with teacher guidance, the number and types of exercises they need.

4. *Both the teacher and the pupil should know what, if any, progress is being made.* Knowledge of results, especially if they are encouraging, seems to be a real incentive for learning. Through a study of results the teacher can also profit directly by securing evidence on the effectiveness of methods and procedures used.

Use of Cloze Procedure

A technique to which considerable attention has been paid recently by some persons in the field of the teaching of reading is the cloze procedure. When this technique is used, the reader is confronted with the need of supplying words that have been omitted—words that fit the meaning of the passage. Thus, it requires him to put meanings together in the process of reading as compared with the question-answer technique where conclusions or answers come as a result of reading a passage in its entirety, without any parts omitted.

A teacher can design materials for use with the cloze technique by selecting passages from the pupils' reading materials. Any number of variations of the technique can be used. For example, the teacher can delete every tenth word (in fact, every *nth* word). Or he might decide that only certain words, such as nouns, will be omitted. He can determine the kind of word, the frequency of deletion, the difficulty of the written material, and the responses acceptable.

An example of an item of a cloze exercise in which every tenth word is omitted is as follows:

Since the leaves had fallen and the birds had ————— southward, the day had seemed a dreary one to ————— little girl as she walked slowly to the home ————— one of her best friends.

The same sentence, rewritten with every noun omitted, would read thus:

Since the ————— had fallen and the ————— had flown southward, the ————— seemed a dreary one to the little ————— as she walked slowly to the ————— of one of her best ————— .

The cloze procedure, so far used chiefly for testing purposes and for determining the difficulty of reading material, has also been shown to be of value as a teaching procedure, for use in the development of ability to note details, to determine main ideas, and to make inferences, though seemingly at a sacrifice of rate of reading.[2]

What are the assumptions underlying the use of the cloze procedure? For its use as a testing tool and as a means of checking the readability

[2] Richard H. Bloomer, "The Cloze Procedure as a Remedial Reading Exercise," *Journal of Developmental Reading* vol. 5 (1962), pp. 173–181.

of material, the assumption is that the ability of the performer to determine from the remaining context (sometimes called the "mutilated" material) what words have been deleted is indicative of his power to comprehend. When the procedure is used as a teaching technique the assumption is that practice in supplying the correct words helps the reader increase his power of comprehension.

The reader interested in pursuing the use of the cloze procedure for teaching and testing purposes is referred to the second edition of *Corrective Reading* by Miles V. Zintz (published by Wm. C. Brown Company), and to the following publications obtainable from the International Reading Association, Newark, Delaware:

Goodman, Yetta M., and Kenneth S. Goodman, compilers, *Linguistics, Psycholinguistics, and the Teaching of Reading* (1971), an annotated bibliography.

Jongsman, Eugene, *The Cloze Procedure as a Teaching Technique* (1971).

Robinson, Richard T., compiler, *An Introduction to the Cloze Procedure* (1971), an annotated bibliography.

Outline for Chapter 6B

DEVELOPING COMPREHENSION

Procedures for Developing Comprehension
  Developing Skill in Finding the Main Idea
  Learning to Select Significant Details
  Learning to Follow Directions
  Developing Skill in Reading to Answer Questions
  Developing Skill in Making Summaries and Organizing Material
  Developing Ability to Arrive at Generalizations and Come to Conclusions
  Improving Ability to Predict Outcomes
  Developing Skill in Critical Evaluation
  Developing Skill in Acquiring Word Meanings
  Developing Skill in Getting the Meaning of Phrases
  Improving Skill in Sentence Comprehension
  Developing Skill in Paragraph Comprehension
  Developing Skill in Understanding the Meaning of Longer Selections
Development of Comprehension Skills through Reading Lessons
  Using a Story at the Lower Primary-grade Reading Level
  Using a Story at a More Advanced Reading Level

CHAPTER

Developing Comprehension

This chapter suggests ways in which the ideas on reading with comprehension presented in Chapter 6A can be put into practice. The fact that a long listing is given for various skills to be developed should not indicate to the teacher that he should use many of them at one time. Rather, the lists should be used as a reference from which those that appear appropriate for use at the time can be selected. It is hoped that many of these ideas will suggest to the teacher additional practices that might be valuable for use in the classroom. Some of the suggestions can be followed when systematic or incidental instruction in reading is given; others are of value primarily during the phases of the reading program that deal with the development of skills. In all cases, however, if the activities are to be of maximum value, boys and girls should see purpose in them—purpose that they can accept as worthwhile.

PROCEDURES FOR DEVELOPING COMPREHENSION

Suggestions for developing the following types of skills are given:

1. Finding the main idea.
2. Selecting significant details.

3. Following directions.
4. Answering questions.
5. Making summaries and organizing material.
6. Arriving at generalizations and coming to conclusions.
7. Predicting outcomes.
8. Evaluating critically.
9. Developing skill in acquiring word meanings.
10. Getting the meaning of phrases.
11. Comprehending sentences.
12. Comprehending paragraphs.
13. Reading longer selections with comprehension.

Developing Skill in Finding the Main Idea

Activities such as the following may help the learner to find the main idea of a passage:

1. Matching a series of pictures with the paragraphs they illustrate.
2. Stating the main idea of a selection.
3. Selecting from a list of sentences one that best expresses the main idea of a paragraph.
4. Selecting from a list of questions one that the entire paragraph answers.
5. Writing below a paragraph the question answered by the entire paragraph.
6. Selecting the best title from a list.
7. Naming a title to fit a given paragraph or longer selection.
8. Following directions, such as:
   a. Find the sentence that gives the main idea of the article.
   b. Draw a line under the words in the second paragraph that give the topic of that paragraph.
   c. Draw a line under the words that best describe the character discussed in the selection.
9. Reading a story to find out whether it is suitable to tell or read to others for a given purpose or to dramatize.
10. Reading a story a second time in order to determine what scenes should be dramatized.
11. Skimming a series or a group of trade books to decide which one to read, either for pleasure or some other purpose.
12. Making a "movie" or mural showing the main events in a story.
13. Noting certain phrases such as *the first* and *the most important* to see if they point out a main idea.
14. Matching a picture that illustrates a main idea with a paragraph that it illustrates.

15. Locating topic sentences in paragraphs that contain topic sentences.
16. Changing each of the side headings of a longer selection to a question answered by the part following.

Additional Activities

The following are illustrations of practice exercises based on the preceding suggestions:

1 *Direction:* After you have read the story, write an x on the line to show which one would make the best title.

> We made plans for our book fair. We decided to decorate our classroom. Each boy and girl will make a book cover. We also decided to have a parade of book characters. We will march into the other classrooms. We will invite other children to our book fair. When they come to our room, we will tell them stories.

——(a) Our Plans for Our Book Fair
——(b) Our Parade
——(c) Our Book Covers
——(d) Reading in Our School

2 *Direction:* On the line below the story write a good title for it.

> Sir Edwin Landseer was one of the greatest animal artists of modern times. When he attended art school, he divided his time between his classes and the zoo, where he studied animals and drew pictures of them. Although Landseer drew pictures of many animals, probably his most famous ones are those of dogs. The best-known one undoubetdly is the one named "The Old Shepherd's Chief Mourner." It is the picture of a devoted dog sadly guarding the coffin of his master, a shepherd.

Learning to Select Significant Details

By performing activities such as the following, boys and girls can get practice in noting details and choosing those that are significant for their purposes.

1. Indicating which of a series of ideas listed are brought out in a given selection.
2. Telling which of a series of details support the main idea of a selection.
3. Reading to note as many details as possible that support a main idea.
4. Making a list of details included in a selection.
5. Answering questions on details in a sentence, paragraph, or longer selection.
6. Completing sentences, copied by the teacher from a reading selection, in which blanks were left for words that test the comprehension of details.

7. Matching a series of details with a list of main ideas.

8. Giving a list of words to describe a character whose actions have been discussed in a story.

9. Taking special note of details of a story to be told to others.

10. Showing which word in a series of sentences or paragraphs does not belong in a paragraph.

11. Checking a list of materials to indicate which are needed for an activity or project.

12. Studying the regulations for use of equipment for the playground, the reading table, or the playhouse.

13. Looking at a picture and then describing it.

14. Drawing a picture illustrating details of what has been read.

15. Deciding what actions in a story should be performed by characters in a "movie" or play that the class plans to put on.

16. Making a list of details that occur in a story, as preparation for dramatizing the story.

17. Composing a paragraph by supplying details to support a main idea that has been selected as a theme.

18. Deciding which details are important to remember in terms of a stated purpose.

19. Preparing charts based on material that has been read; for example, a chart showing the growth in population in a state.

20. Taking notes on points read in order to report them to others in a group in connection with a unit of work.

21. Reading reference materials to answer questions raised by the class or by a committee in order to get information needed for a project.

22. Showing through outlining the relation between details and a main point.

23. Indicating which details belong and which do not belong in an outline that has been made on a selection.

24. Reading material in science and mathematics in which careful note needs to be taken of many points in order to comprehend the meaning, and then answering questions on the material or using it in other ways.

25. Doing editorial work on a class newspaper.

26. Deciding whether the facts given by a reporter include sufficient details to justify a given headline in a newspaper.

27. Discussing whether the author relates details through his own comments, by the characters' actions, or by reports from characters as to what happened.

28. Listing the details in a description of a room, a landscape, or some other setting, in preparation for making a drawing.

29. Writing a main idea for a paragraph and then writing details to support it.

30. Writing a paragraph describing a given object, which other pupils are to guess.

Additional Activities

Two types of procedures that can be used in order to develop skill in selecting details are illustrated in the following exercises:

1 Directions: After you have read the following paragraph, write *M* on the line to the left of the topic listed that expresses the main idea of the paragraph. Write *D* to the left of each topic that expresses a detail mentioned in the paragraph. Write *O* to the left of any item not mentioned in the paragraph.

One of the most interesting animals in the world is the great gray kangaroo, found in great numbers in Australia. One of its characteristics of special note is its size and shape. It is sometimes 10 feet in length from the tip of the nose to the end of the tail and weighs as much as 200 pounds. Its long, strong tail is used as a prop when the kangaroo stands on its two hind legs. The kangaroo is a very swift runner. It can clear as many as twenty feet at one leap. It runs on its hind legs only. The development and care of the young is very interesting. Upon birth the baby kangaroo is only about an inch in length. It is then taken care of in the pouch to the front of the mother's hind legs. In this pouch it receives its nourishment from the milk of the mother. After the baby has lived in the pouch for about four months, it leans out of the pouch to eat grass while its mother, too, is grazing. Then for months thereafter, usually till the baby is about ten months old, the young kangaroo returns to the protection of the pouch even though it spends much of its time in the world outside. In fact, the baby likes the pouch so much that it stays in it until its mother refuses to carry it any longer.

———(a) The claws of the kangaroo.

———(b) The kangaroo, an interesting animal.

———(c) Australia, the home of the kangaroo.

———(d) How the kangaroo takes care of its young.

———(e) The leap of the kangaroo.

———(f) The value of the kangaroo.

2 Directions: The main topic of a paragraph is the food of the camel. Some of the sentences that are listed below are on that topic. Others do not deal with the topic and therefore should not be included in a paragraph on the food of the camel. Write *yes* on the line to the left of each sentence that can correctly be included in the paragraph and write *no* on the other lines.

———(a) The camel eats thistles that grow in the desert.

———(b) The camel is a lazy animal.

———(c) The mother camel is very tender toward her baby.

———(d) The camel can live for a long time without food.

———(e) The camel likes to eat baskets or saddles or newspapers.

Learning to Follow Directions

These methods may be helpful for an individual who is trying to improve his skill in following directions:

1. Repeating directions.
2. Observing written directions, such as: "Make one ball yellow. Make the other ball blue."
3. Following directions that the teacher has written on the chalkboard or on cards, such as: "Get ready for music" or "Come to the reading circle."
4. Answering questions about a set of directions, such as: "What should you do after you have cut the paper the correct size?"
5. Acting out an individually assigned sentence from a reading selection and then having the rest of the class tell which sentence it is.
6. Following written or oral directions for making things, such as a folder for papers or a papier-mâché globe.
7. Drawing a picture from directions given.
8. Drawing pictures based on descriptions that the boys and girls read.
9. Carrying out plans made by the class or committee for work on a unit.
10. Writing directions for doing or making something.
11. Reading directions for a game and then following them.
12. Reading directions for doing tricks and then performing them.
13. Arranging in correct order the sentences for directions to do or make something.
14. Reading directions for work-type activities in various subject fields and then following them.
15. Finding directions for experiments and carrying them out in front of the class.

Additional Activity

This type of exercise may be helpful to persons having difficulty either in giving or following directions for going from one place to another.

Directions: Draw a diagram showing how a person who is at the post office could get to city hall.

> From the post office walk north until you come to the end of the block. Then turn left and walk west for two blocks, crossing the street before you again turn right to walk another half-block north. There in the middle of the block you will find city hall.

Developing Skill in Reading to Answer Questions

Proficiency in finding the answer to a question can be helpful in a variety of reading situations. It is important at times in order to choose the main idea, to note details, to predict outcomes, to form generalizations, to follow directions, and to perform other activities connected with reading.

Answers are relatively easy to find when the questions are partly couched in the exact words of the writer. With the immature reader or the one who has difficulty in reading to find the answer to a question, this type of question may be used at first. If the writer says: "Susan's father gave her a kitten for her birthday," the teacher may ask: "What did Susan's father give her for her birthday?" A sample of a question to which the answer can be found less easily is: "What reasons can you find for the actions of the heroine?" or "Why do you think the heroine acted as she did?" The formulation of questions the teacher asks can encourage or discourage critical thinking.

Not only should the pupils gain skill in finding answers to questions that are stated by others but to avoid overdependence on the teacher they also need to develop in ability to formulate significant questions for themselves as purposes for reading. Questions by the teacher should serve chiefly as steppingstones to questions that the reader raises himself.

Practice that can be of value in developing skill in answering questions can be secured by performing activities such as the following:

1. Reading to answer questions stated by the teacher.
2. Indicating which of a series of questions listed by the teacher are likely to be answered in a given selection and then checking the responses after reading the selection.
3. Stating questions the reader would expect to find answered in a given selection and then checking to find the responses after reading the selection.
4. Indicating which of a series of questions that may possibly be answered in a given selection are formulated clearly, and rewording those that are not.
5. Reading to answer questions stated at the end of a selected reading.
6. Reading to answer questions brought out by viewing a film or filmstrip.

Additional Activities

The following exercises indicate two ways in which pupils can get practice in deciding which questions are likely to be answered in a given selection. Since frequently it is important that the pupil rather than the teacher ask a question or questions that he hopes will be answered in a selection, an exercise like the first one given below is often of value.

1 Directions: Before you read this selection on [title stated], make a list of questions that you may expect to find answered in it. Then read the selection to find the answer to as many questions as you can. After you have read it, on the lines provided after each question, write the answer to the questions that were answered in the paragraph. If a question was not answered, write the words *not answered.* (The selection may be chosen from the pupils' textbooks in social studies or science.)

1. Question   1. _____
    Answer: _____
               _____

2. Question   2. _____
    Answer: _____
               _____

3. Question 3. _____
   Answer: _____
               _____

4. Question 4. _____
   Answer: _____
               _____

2 Directions: Which of the following questions would you expect to find answered in the article on [title stated] given below? Before you read the selection, write *yes* on the line to the left of each question that you think may be answered. On the other lines write *no.* After you have read the selection, correct your *yes-no* answers by putting an *x* to the left of each of your answers that is incorrect. Then write the answer to each question that was discussed in the paragraph. Write it on the lines provided below the questions. (The selection may be chosen from the pupils' textbooks in social studies or science.)

1. _____ (Question 1 by the teacher is listed here.)
   Answer: _____
              _____
              _____

2. _____ (Question 2 by the teacher is listed here.)
   Answer: _____
              _____
              _____

3. _____ (Question 3 by the teacher is listed here.)
   Answer: _____
              _____
              _____

Developing Skill in Making Summaries and Organizing Material

Skill in summarizing and organizing what is read can be developed through activities such as these:

1. Telling which of several summaries best summarizes a paragraph or longer selection.
2. Answering questions like these: "What explorers helped Spain establish her claims to the New World? What did each of them do to give her a claim to the Americas?"
3. Taking note of words like *first, second,* and *third* as they occur in context.
4. Classifying materials in the room for functional purposes; for example, putting all the books on one topic on a specified table or assembling, for use on two or more bulletin boards, pictures on different topics.
5. Telling what items belong in classifications like *food, clothing, shelter.*

6. Drawing pictures to tell what are the main events in a story.

7. Arranging pictures in the order in which events illustrated by them occurred in a story.

8. Organizing steps in a process demonstrated on a field trip, under topics such as "Steps in Baking Bread" or "The Manufacture of Flour."

9. Filling in main topics and subtopics of a selection when suggestions are given as to the number of main topics and the number of subtopics under each main topic.

10. Listing the questions on which information is needed to solve the problem of a unit, and then grouping the questions on similar topics.

11. Listing the topics on which information is needed to solve the problem of a unit, and then putting the list into outline form.

12. Placing subtopics, which are given in mixed-up order, under a list of main topics that are specified.

13. Learning the form for making outlines, including numbering and lettering, indentation, and capitalization and punctuation.

14. Making an outline, either in a group or individually, of parts of a story that one of the pupils will tell to another group of boys and girls.

15. Telling what is wrong with an incorrect outline that some pupil has made or one that the teacher has intentionally written incorrectly.

16. Arranging in correct order paragraphs dealing with one topic given in mixed-up order.

17. Selecting the sentences that do not belong in a paragraph that is set up so that it contains some irrelevant sentences.

18. Writing headlines for a class paper.

19. Making a list of actions of characters to show what traits they possess.

20. Making charts giving information about topics studied, such as "Our Community Workers," "How We Travel," "Famous Americans," "Greek Contributions to Civilization."

21. Studying the table of contents to note the organization of a book.

22. Learning where, in a well-constructed paragraph, a topic sentence, if there is one, is often found.

23. Reading to plan a dramatization.

24. Planning pictures for a "movie" or mural on a story or article read.

25. Telling under which of a series of circumstances outlining is of value.

26. Checking a series of true-false statements such as the following, to indicate which give good advice for making notes: (a) "Take your notes in your own words, not in those of the writer." (b) "If you do not understand what something means, be sure to include the point in your notes."

27. Before a child is able to write an outline, drawing illustrations to use as notes when planning a report or story; for example, as illustrated notes on the story of *The Three Little Pigs* sketches illustrating topics such as these might be made:

The three little pigs.
The houses of the three pigs.
The wolf blowing in the first house.
The wolf blowing in the second house.
The wolf trying to blow in the third house.
The wolf trying to catch the third pig.
The death of the wolf.

28. Taking notes on points needed for a report.

29. Making an outline, such as the following, of points to be included in book reports:

The title and author of the book.
What the book is about.
Two or three interesting parts of the book.
How the reporter liked the book.
Where the book can be found.

30. Checking a list of notes to determine which are appropriately recorded and which are not.

Additional Activities

Three additional ways in which practice can be given in summarizing or outlining are shown in these exercises.

1   *Directions:* Make an outline that will give the information shown in this chart.

Purposes of Settlement

For religious freedom	Jamestown
To help debtors	Plymouth
For commercial reasons	Pennsylvania
	Georgia
	New Amsterdam

2   *Directions:* The sentences in this paragraph are not in the correct order. Write *1* on the line to the left of the sentence that should come first. Write *2* on the line to the left of the sentence that should come second. Number the rest of the sentences in the same way.

——— Stephen heard something call, "Caw! Caw!" ——— There lay a baby crow. ——— Stephen looked around. ——— One day Stephen went to the woods with his father. ——— When Stephen saw that the crow could not walk, he took it home with him. ——— The crow had a broken leg. ——— Stephen always took good care of his crow.

3   As the boys and girls are studying about the Missouri Compromise, they could be asked to fill in subtopics in this beginning of an outline:

The Missouri Compromise

A. Events leading up to the compromise.
1._____
2._____
B. Provisions of the compromise
1._____
2._____
C. Effects of the compromise.
1._____
2._____.

Developing Ability to Arrive at Generalizations and Come to Conclusions

In addition to the following suggestions for activities that can be valuable in developing the ability to arrive at generalizations and come to conclusions, some of those recommended under "Making Summaries and Organizing Material" can be used:

1. Making and guessing riddles.

2. Checking which ones of several conclusions are warranted by data given, and explaining why the unsound conclusions are invalid.

3. Stating as specific a conclusion as possible after reading data presented in a paragraph or longer selection and explaining, in some cases, why no broader conclusion could be reached.

4. Matching a fable with a proverb it illustrates.

5. Discussing questions such as the following after reading a story: a. "Why do you think——made his decision to go West?" b. "Under what conditions do you think——would have been friendly to strangers?"

6. Telling which of a list of statements are generalizations and which are specifics.

7. After making a generalization based on what has been heard or read, checking it against experiences or finding additional support for it or experimenting to see if the generalization applies.

8. Discussing the effect that certain events in a story or in history had on individuals.

9. Stating the generalization that is justified on the basis of given facts.

10. Discussing the ideas contained in several stories to see if they give generalizations that were brought out in a story.

11. Formulating titles that indicate the generalization brought out in a series of stories.

12. Drawing a series of pictures that illustrate points leading to a generalization developed in a story or article.

These exercises indicate how some of the above suggestions can be carried out:

1   After the teacher has read the following paragraph to the class, he asks the pupils: "What was Sally holding in her arms?"

> It was Christmas Eve. Everybody in the family—Father, Mother, Bobby, and three-year-old Sally—were in bed, or were supposed to be in bed. Suddenly Mother awoke. She thought she heard the creak of a stair. Then she heard nothing. So she fell asleep again. Later she heard a sound that seemed to come from the living room. She thought she heard a thin voice say, "Ma-ma! Ma-ma!" It was not Sally's voice. It was not Bobby's voice. Then all was quiet again. But this time Mother did not fall asleep. She awoke Father. Father went downstairs to see what was happening. When he opened the door into the living room, he saw that the big Mamma-doll that Santa Claus had left for Sally to find the next morning was gone. Then he looked into Sally's playroom. There he saw Sally sitting in her little rocker holding a bundle in her arms.

2   Pupils can make up and guess riddles like the following:

> a. I have two legs and two wings. I can fly high into the air. I sing songs. I lay eggs. What am I?
>
> b. I lived in Minnesota when I was a boy. I am an aviator. I made one of the most famous airplane flights that has ever been made. My wife enjoys flying. Who am I?

3   *Directions:* Below the following paragraph is a list of statements in the form of conclusions. On the blank to the left of each statement write *yes* if you think the reader can correctly come to that conclusion after reading the paragraph. Otherwise write *no.* If a conclusion is not correct for the paragraph, in the space provided state why you think it is not a sound conclusion. When you give your reasons, make certain to write the number of the conclusion to which you are referring.

> On my last visit to the zoo, I spent part of my time watching two mother camels and their little colts. Both of the mothers stood near their young as if they wished to protect their babies from all harm. It seemed to me that there was a look of tenderness on the mothers' faces as they were looking at the little camels. I then remembered that my father had told me that the mother camel is often very kind to her young.

——— 1. The camel is very gentle toward other animals.

——— 2. The camel is very gentle toward people.

——— 3. The mother camel is often very kind to her baby.

——— 4. The mother camel is a very gentle animal.

Reasons:_____

_____
_____
_____
_____
_____
_____

Improving Ability to Predict Outcomes

Some of the suggestions given under "Developing Ability to Arrive at Generalizations and Come to Conclusions" may be added to the following list of activities for improving the ability to predict outcomes:

1. While looking at the pictures of a story, stating what the outcome of the story is likely to be.
2. Telling what is likely to happen next in a story or article, with or without the help of multiple-choice questions.
3. Discussing why things happened as they did in a story or other account.
4. Making up endings for stories, orally or in writing.
5. Estimating the answer in some types of arithmetic problems.
6. Comparing our present situation with a previous one in history and deciding what might happen as a result of present conditions.
7. Indicating what is likely to happen at the time when work on a science experiment is begun.
8. Evaluating plans the class is making, in terms of expected outcomes.
9. Predicting what will happen next after having listened to part of the account of an experience another pupil has had.
10. Listing on the board known points about a situation and possible outcomes and then discussing the probability of certain results and the unlikelihood of others.
11. Arranging in order pictures illustrating a story that the pupils have not heard or read in its entirety.
12. Predicting, after reading a current news report, what will happen and then the following day checking to see if the prediction was correct.

Developing Skill in Critical Evaluation

The ability to evaluate critically what is read may require any one of the following skills:

1. Distinguishing between fact and opinion.
2. Telling what is real and what is fanciful.
3. Determining the qualifications of the author and his purpose and attitude.
4. Noting the up-to-dateness of the information presented.

5. Deciding whether propaganda is being spread.
6. Examining critically the generalizations made.

For a discussion of the last-named of these skills the reader is referred to page 193. Below are suggestions for developing each of the other skills already listed. It should be noted that some suggestions applicable to critical evaluation of what is read are listed on preceding pages under other topics dealing with the development of comprehension. The reader is also referred to the quotation from the book, *Critical Reading Ability of Elementary School Children,* by Willavene Wolf and others given on pages 171–172.

Fact or Opinion

To gain proficiency in distinguishing between fact and opinion, the pupils might do the following:

1. Analyze newspaper reports to determine whether they present facts or opinions.
2. Study news reports and editorials to determine the essential differences in the two types of writing.
3. Locate statements of opinion found within a given selection.
4. Indicate which of a series of statements express facts only and then rewrite those that are not purely factual so that they do not express an opinion.
5. Rewrite statements of fact that are mixed with statements of opinion in such a way that instead of showing sympathy toward a person or event they will show antipathy (and vice-versa).
6. Delete from paragraphs or longer selections statements that are not entirely factual.

Additional Activity

Directions such as the following may be given to provide practice in discriminating between statements that are based entirely on facts and those that are based, in part at least, on opinion.

Directions: Some of the following sentences are statements of fact; others are, at least in part, expressions of opinion. On the line at the right of each sentence, that is only a statement of fact, write an *F,* for *fact.* Write an *O,* for *opinion,* on the line if the statement is, at least in part, an expression of an opinion. Then, in the space following the last sentence in this exercise, rewrite those sentences which reveal the writer's opinion. Rewrite them in such a manner that the rewritten sentences are statements of fact only. Number your sentences to correspond to the numbers of the printed sentences.

1. Lake Michigan cuts the state of Michigan in two parts.   1. _____
2. The best place to be in winter is Florida.   2. _____
3. The road from here to the next town is a gravel road.   3. _____

4. The most beautiful place in the United States is Mount Rainier.   4. _____
5. The best vacation spot in the northwest is Portland, Oregon.   5. _____

_____
_____
_____
_____
_____

Real or Fanciful

In order to become more adept at judging whether or not written material is of a fanciful nature, pupils might perform activities such as these that follow:

1. Find examples in stories of means by which the author indicated that the story is fanciful.
2. Draw up a list of expressions often used in stories to show that the stories are fanciful, for example: "Once upon a time."
3. Decide whether a story is real or fanciful and indicate the reason for the decision.
4. Read a story that is fictional but based in part on fact and then determine which statements are likely to be true and which are more likely to be fictional.

The Author

In order to become more able to decide on the qualifications of an author or his purpose or point of view, the pupil might engage in activities such as these:

1. Deciding how each of two persons, both qualified to speak or write on a given subject but with a different experience background, might express themselves on that subject.
2. Discussing which of two authors whose qualifications are stated would be better qualified to write on a given topic.
3. Deciding with classmates on questions that, if answered, might help a reader decide on the qualifications of an author, for example: a. Does the author have much information about the subject? b. Has he a good reputation as a writer? As a person? c. Is there a reason why he would be likely to push one point of view over another?
4. Deciding on the purpose of an author in writing a given selection.
5. Indicating which sentences in a list reveal a sympathetic attitude and which an unsympathetic one toward a person or a situation.
6. Writing two paragraphs giving the qualifications of an imaginary author on a topic such as "Life in Harlem" or "Our First Lady." One of the paragraphs should indicate sufficient background of the imaginary author for writing with authority on the topic, and the other should be lacking in evidence that the author has adequate background.

Up-to-Dateness

Activities such as these might be of value in helping boys and girls decide on the up-to-datedness and the need of up-to-datedness in regard to writings:

1. Noting the copyright date of books.
2. Indicating which books written long ago are valuable for a stated purpose and which are not.
3. Finding an item of information as it is reported in a book with an old copyright date and in one with a recent copyright and comparing the two.
4. Making a list of questions on which information in a book with an old copyright date would be as useful as one with a recent copyright.
5. Answering questions or following directions such as these, when pupils have available to them a number of books, including those to which reference is made in the directions or questions, some with old and some with recent copyright dates: a. Is your social studies book written recently enough so that it can report on events that occurred during the past four years? b. What is the copyright date of Virgil Hilyer's book, *A Child's Geography of the World?* c. Find two items of information in the book, *A Child's Geography of the World,* that now are out of date. Find two items of information given in that book that are still true today.

Propaganda Techniques

Activities such as the following may help a person detect propaganda when he sees it in print or hears it:

1. Indicating which statements present only so limited a part of the truth that an incorrect impression is given.
2. Indicating which of a series of words—such as *native land, house, home folks*—arouse emotion.
3. Noting types of words often used to arouse emotions of sympathy or love or anger.
4. Finding an example of some of the following types of propaganda techniques, which are among those identified by the Institute for Propaganda Analysis, New York:

    + *Name calling,* such as calling a person a Communist without justification.
    + *Glittering generalization,* such as "We will not be undersold."
    + *Testimonials,* such as an advertisement indicating that a movie star endorses a certain toothpaste.
    + *Plain folks device* used often by politicians to show they are "one of us."
    + *Bandwagon,* such as when a girl tries to convince her mother that everybody is wearing the kind of sweater she wants her mother to buy for her.

5. Writing a paragraph using one or more propaganda techniques.

6. Noting how an author who says he is presenting both sides of a controversial matter slights one side of the question.

7. Reading a report on an event in two newspapers, one of which is known to be sensational, and then comparing the reports.

8. Writing headlines that might be included in a newspaper or magazine known for sensationalism, and rewriting these headlines as they might appear in a paper or magazine not given to sensationalism.

Additional Points

The following are additional suggested activities for increasing the power to evaluate critically what is read:

1. Indicating which of a series of statements are relevant and which are irrelevant to a given purpose.

2. Locating inconsistencies in a series of paragraphs or longer selections.

3. Matching a series of abstract statements with items in a list of incidents that illustrate the abstractions.

4. Asking or, in other cases, answering thought-provoking questions about something that has been heard or read.

5. Choosing from a list of chapter titles those chapters that are most likely to be valuable in connection with a given problem.

6. Setting up standards for a story to be chosen, such as listing points to consider when selecting a story to be read to a given group for a stated purpose.

7. Giving book reviews in which emphasis is placed on the evaluation of the book rather than on the story itself.

8. Checking the validity of a statement in terms of agreement with other statements in the same book.

9. Determining how to decide on the likely truth when two contradictory statements are found.

10. Bringing to class an editorial from a newspaper and a news item and then listing the differences in writing style, giving reasons why each type is written as it is.

Developing Skill in Acquiring Word Meanings

While in the early stages of learning to read the words in the reading material should be some that are in the learner's understanding vocabulary, there comes a time when reading should serve as a means of developing growth in word power. To stimulate such development, activities by the pupils such as the following can be provided by the teacher:

1. Before reading a selection, finding the meaning of words through class discussion, studying the words written in context on the chalkboard, looking up the words in the dictionary.

2. Illustrating through pictures or models some of the words that lend themselves to this kind of activity, such as the words *portage, cataract, fall line.*

3. Constructing a bulletin board with illustrations of some of the terms used in connection with a unit of study. With the study of Switzerland, for example, words such as *glacier, chateau, alp* might be illustrated.

4. Making class or individual word files in which cards are kept for the "new words" acquired that the class decides to include or that an individual (in case of a personal file) wishes to include in his list. The type of information that the pupil will want to give on a file card will depend in part on his stage of development. For less advanced readers nothing more than the word, an explanation of it, and a sentence with the word illustrating a common meaning of it might be included on a card. For more adept readers the phonetic spelling, the plural form of nouns, various explanations of the word, and sentences containing the word showing different meanings could also be recorded.

5. Deciphering the meaning of words in exercises constructed by the teacher illustrating some of the points in Wilbur Ames' classification scheme, which categorizes types of context clues that might be taught systematically (*see* page 115). An illustration of three of his fourteen types is given below.

   + *Synonym clues or appositives.* A *peccary,* a wild pig native in both North and South America, is a blackish animal with whitish cheeks and an indistinct white collar.

   + *Clues utilizing definition or description.* His behavior was *inexplicable.* No one could explain why he was tardy.

   + *Comparison of contrast clues.* She was much more gregarious than her friend who preferred being alone much of the time.

6. Giving illustrations of some of the types of context clues identified by Ames (*see* item 5 above).

Developing Skill in Getting the Meaning of Phrases

Skill in the comprehension of phrases can be developed by means of the following activities:

1. Giving the meaning of expressions used in sentences.

2. Matching phrases in one column with words with similar meaning in another column.

3. Finding in a selection phrases that answer certain questions such as: "What group of words tells that Frank is happy?"

4. Discussing the meaning of commonly used idiomatic expressions.

5. Interpreting figures of speech.

6. Underlining the complete phrase in an exercise where the first word of the phrases is underlined.

7. Playing a game in which pupils read what is written on a phrase card.

8. Locating a phrase that is illustrated by a picture.

9. Making up a phrase that expresses the meaning of a given phrase.

10. Completing sentences by matching the beginnings of sentences given in one column with appropriate endings in a column of phrases.

Additional Activity

Directions: Each sentence in this exercise contains an expression in italics. To get the meaning of the expression, note the meaning of each word in it and study the context. If necessary, consult your dictionary. Then, in the space provided, explain what the expression means.

1. When the explorers came to the end of the path, they saw *a veil of spray* coming down from the falls more than a hundred feet in height._____

_____

2. General Grant asked his opponents for *unconditional surrender.*_____

_____

Improving Skill in Sentence Comprehension

Some pupils may find the following activities of value in improving their comprehension of sentences.

1. Drawing a line under one of a series of sentences that is illustrated by a picture in a workbook or teacher-made practice exercise.

2. Picking out in connection with an illustrated story the sentences that are well illustrated by a picture.

3. Arranging in correct order the parts of scrambled sentences.

4. Listing the sentences in a selection that help prove a given point.

5. Indicating which sentences in a series mean almost the same as specified sentences.

6. Making up sentences that describe a picture.

7. Finding in a book a sentence that suggests an appropriate title for a story or picture.

8. Answering with *yes* or *no,* questions on which readers will agree if the meaning is clear to them, such as: a. Is winter a colder season than summer? b. Do all good people live in warm houses?

9. Making sentences that show variety in structure, such as: a. "Quickly the boys ran home." b. "The boys ran home quickly."

10. Studying the thought of sentences in which the subject and predicate are in inverted order, and constructing some of that type.

11. Finding sentences that answer given questions.

12. Making up sentences that describe the same idea in different ways.

13. Studying sentences in which many adjectives or adverbs or phrases or clauses modify the subject and the predicate.

14. Interpreting the meaning of conjunctions and prepositions as they are used in sentences.

15. Answering questions about a sentence with which the pupils have difficulty and indicating which part of a sentence answers each question.

16. In connection with a long sentence that presents comprehension difficulties, making a sentence for every idea contained in it.

17. Establishing the relation in meaning among the parts of a sentence.

18. Deciding on the meaning of some sentences through the study of punctuation marks.

Additional Activity

The boys and girls can be provided with practice in reading for meaning by using cloze techniques or variations of the cloze procedures (*see* page 180). Two cloze items for each of six categories based on Wilbur Ames' classification of context clues (*see* page 115) are given here as examples.[1] A practice exercise containing many cloze items can be made for each of the categories of context clues. It should be noted that cloze items can be used for either practice or testing purposes.

1. *Definitions and descriptions*

   + The boys were playing a game of ——————— in the park. It was very exciting when a player caught a high pass and made a touchdown.

   + She was always ——————— . She meant well and had a good clock, but somehow she could never get started on time. Something always seemed to happen at the last minute to delay her.

2. *Words connected or in series*

   + The two children never minded the three-mile walk to school. The forest always offered them something new to ———————, hear, smell, or touch.

   + Forests are important. They provide lumber and things made from it. And think of all the birds and animals that need the forest for their ———————, home, and protection.

3. *Direct referrals*

   + She was bothered about something. She tried to think that the something did not matter. She was going to laugh and forget about it. But she couldn't laugh and she couldn't ———————.

   + The name *raccoon* comes from an old American Indian word that means *one who scratches with his hands.* Raccoons have front paws that look like little ———————, and they often scratch around on the ground looking for insects to eat.

[1] Lynette Y. C. Chang, *The Ability of Sixth-grade Pupils to Use Certain Verbal Context Clues in Listening and Reading,* unpublished doctoral dissertation (Minneapolis, Minn.: University of Minnesota, 1968).

4. *Modifying phrases/clauses*

+ Jim lost his lunch money because there was a hole in the ———————
of his old blue jeans.
+ Since we're probably ———————— , I wonder if anyone else has arrived yet.

5. *Familiar expressions*

+ We wanted to give Tommy a surprise birthday party, but someone let
the ———————— out of the bag and told him about it.
+ When John had done something well and someone told him about it,
Grandpa used to say that he was as ———————— as a peacock.

6. *Comparisons or contrasts*

+ Neither the reader who reads everything rapidly nor the one who reads
everything ———————— is really a good reader.
+ George was very sure that he was right, even when everyone else knew
he was ————————.

Developing Skill in Paragraph Comprehension

Many suggestions for improved comprehension of paragraphs have been
given under various skills listed earlier in this chapter as, for example, under
"Developing Skill in Finding the Main Idea" and in "Making Summaries and
Organizing Material." A few additional ones are given here:

1. Locating a paragraph on a stated page by means of directions such as:
"Place a finger under the paragraph that begins with the words 'Evelyn
ran home as fast as she could,'" or "Read the last sentence of the first
paragraph on page ———."
2. Finding the paragraph that answers a question or contains a specified
thought.
3. Finding the topic sentence of paragraphs that contain topic sentences.
4. Studying the topic sentence of a paragraph to help get the main idea of the
paragraph.
5. Using the topic sentence of a paragraph as an aid when organizing, as well
as when skimming.
6. Writing paragraphs on specified topics.
7. Arranging in order paragraphs that are not in the correct sequence.
8. Matching a series of paragraphs with summaries of these paragraphs.

Additional Activities

The following two exercises can be of value to some pupils in improving
their skills in paragraph comprehension:

1 An exercise such as this one can be particularly helpful, since it is

based on reading in the pupils' books. At least one of the paragraphs used in this exercise should have a topic sentence and at least one should not.

Directions: Read the three paragraphs in your (name of textbook supplied) on page —— to answer these questions and to follow these directions. (The same questions as those given for the first paragraphs should be asked about the other paragraphs.)

Paragraph 1. Does it contain a topic sentence? —— If so, write the first three words of the sentence: ——————

If there is a topic sentence in the paragraph, do all the details given in the paragraph support the topic sentence? ——

If the paragraph does not contain a topic sentence, would the paragraph be improved if it had one? —— Give reasons for your answer.__

If the paragraph has no topic sentence and if the paragraph could be improved if it contained one, write a sentence that would make a good topic sentence for the paragraph.——————————————

In this paragraph, demonstrating use of the cloze procedure, every tenth word has been omitted. The boys and girls should be instructed to fill the blanks.

Steamboats could not come right up to the landing —————— the channel did not go over there and the —————— was not deep enough. Passengers paid to have their —————— hauled ashore or onto the boat and for a —————— for themselves. Abe did not look on his small —————— as a ferry, and so he did not try —————— get a license. Some fellows on the Kentucky side, —————— Dill brothers, were running a ferry.[2]

Developing Skill in Understanding the Meaning of Longer Selections

Since many suggestions for development of skill in comprehending longer materials were given under a variety of topics earlier in this chapter, we list here only the following additional types of activities that some pupils could profitably perform to gain more skill in comprehending materials of this type.

1. Finding the place in a story or article or book where specified parts begin.
2. Reading a story or article to decide where it can be divided into parts.
3. Taking a pretest, before reading a selection, on questions based on the selection and then, after reading it, taking the test again.

Additional Activity

To help boys and girls make adequate use of center heads and sideheads, an exercise like this may prove of help.

[2] Edith McCall, *Frontiers of America: Pioneer Traders* (Chicago: Childrens Press, 1964), p. 107.

Directions: Read the headings given in this exercise. Study them to find out what questions you would expect to find discussed under each. Then in the space to the right of each question write the number of the center head and the letter of the sidehead under which you would expect to find the question discussed. Write an *N,* for *not discussed,* in the space to the right of each question that you do not expect to find discussed under any of these headings.

Center head: 1. *The Boyhood of Columbus*
Sideheads: a. Birthplace
                    b. Work of his father
                    c. His early interest in the sea

Center head: 2. *The Plan of Columbus*
Sideheads: a. His beliefs about the shape of the earth
                    b. His disbelief in the stories of the dragons of the sea
                    c. His belief that India could be reached by water

Center head: 3. *Columbus in Search of Aid*
Sideheads: a. Refusal of Spain to help him
                    b. Plan to ask France for aid
                    c. The help of the abbott
                    d. Promise of help by Queen Isabella and King Ferdinand

Center head: 4. *Getting Ready for the First Voyage*
Sideheads: a. Getting men
                    b. Getting ships and supplies

Center head: 5. *First Voyage*
Sideheads: a. Fears of the sailors
                    b. Scarcity of food
                    c. Length of the voyage
                    d. Threat of mutiny
                    e. Seeing land
                    f. The landing
                    g. Exploring the land
                    h. Return to Spain

Center head: 6. *Later Voyages and Death*
Sideheads: a. The second, third, and fourth voyages
                    b. Return to Spain in chains
                    c. Last days and death

1. Why were the sailors afraid they would fall off the edge of the earth?———

2. How did the Spanish court treat Columbus upon his return after his fourth voyage?———

3. Did the Norsemen discover America?———

4. What did Columbus believe, even before 1492, was the shape of the earth?———

5. Why did Spain at first refuse to give aid to Columbus?———

6. Why was it hard to secure good men for the first voyage?———

7. How many ships did Columbus have with him on his first voyage?———

8. When was land first seen?——

9. What did Columbus do to keep his men from mutinying on the first voyage?——

10. Where did Columbus die?——

11. What parts of America did the French explore?——

DEVELOPMENT OF COMPREHENSION SKILLS THROUGH READING LESSONS

All of the comprehension skills can be developed in part through reading lessons without recourse to definite practice exercises. This section of the chapter is devoted to demonstrating how growth in the various skills can be encouraged in these lessons. The suggestions are based on selections from two reading series, one for boys and girls reading on a lower primary-grade level and the other for those on a more advanced level. The comprehension skills that a teacher will decide to develop in either of these lessons will depend on the total developmental reading program based on the needs of the boys and girls. The suggestions enumerated in connection with any of these lessons are not necessarily the ones to be used. They are merely suggestive of the many possible ones from which a selection may be made. Nor should nearly all of the recommendations be used for any one selection, for the number is too large and there is overlapping among them. Excellent suggestions for the development of power in comprehension are also listed in the manuals for the teacher accompanying the basal textbooks.

Using a Story at the Lower Primary-grade Reading Level

For an example of how various comprehension skills can be highlighted in a story on the lower primary-grade *The Three Little Pigs*[3] as retold by John Lowell.

Finding the Main Idea

The pupils may read the story to decide whether it would be a good one to read to another group or whether it would be suitable for using for a dramatization or a home-made "movie," if they had been planning to engage in one of those activities.

Selecting Important Details

If the pupils decide to dramatize the story or to give a puppet play or to make a "movie" of it, they may read the story carefully in order to decide what scenes to include in the play or "movie."

Summarizing and Organizing

Although most work in writing summaries is usually postponed till boys and girls are on a higher reading level than the one for which this story is

[3] Leo Fay, Ramon Ross, and Margaret LaPray, *Red Rock Ranch,* The Young America Basic Reading Program, Level 6 (Chicago: Lyons and Carnahan, 1974), pp. 106–117.

geared, some children who read it might wish to include a brief summary of stories they like particularly well in a large looseleaf notebook, possibly 18 x 24 inches. For such a notebook the group could cooperatively plan a brief summary on this order: "Three little pigs built their own houses. One little pig made his house of straw. Another little pig made his house of sticks. The smart little pig built his house of bricks. The wolf blew down the straw house. He blew down the house made of sticks. He could not blow down the brick house. The wolf went down the chimney of the brick house. He fell into some hot water. That was the end of the big bad wolf."

If the pupils decide to put on a play, they can help determine what the parts of the play should be. The division might be as follows:

1. The mother pig tells her little pigs to build houses.
2. The little pigs build their houses.
3. The wolf blows down the house of two little pigs.
4. The wolf tries to blow down the house of the third little pig.
5. The wolf falls into hot water.

Then the pupils can decide on the details to be portrayed in connection with each part.

Arriving at a Generalization

After the group has discussed how the first two little pigs showed they were foolish and how the third little pig showed he was wise, the teacher might ask the boys and girls what lesson they think the first two pigs learned from their experiences with the bad wolf.

Predicting Outcomes

During the course of reading of the story, the teacher may at appropriate places make comments and ask questions such as these: (1.) The wolf had no trouble blowing down the straw house. Do you think he will be able to blow down the house made of sticks? (2.) Why did the little pigs put some hot water in the fireplace and more wood on the fire when they saw that the wolf was coming down the chimney?

Evaluating Critically

The pupils may name ways in which they can tell that this is a "make-believe" story.

Answering Questions

After the boys and girls have read the page that tells the reader the big bad wolf said, "Ummmmm, I like little pigs," the teacher might ask the class what they think the big bad wolf meant when he said that. Or after the boys and girls have read the first two sentences of the page where the wolf said, "I will get the three little pigs," the teacher might ask them what they think the wolf's plans were.

The teacher may write on the chalkboard directions such as these:

1. Read the rest of the story.
2. Write the word *wolf.*
3. Write the word *pig.*

Sentence Comprehension

If the pupils have difficulty in comprehending the rather long sentence: "Please, man, give me some of your bricks to build a 'house,' said the little pig," the teacher may ask them to tell in their own words what the little pig asked the man. Practice in formulating good sentences as they discuss what they read or as they make a summary can also indirectly help boys and girls in the comprehension of the meaning of written sentences.

Comprehension of a Longer Selection

On the basis of a story such as this pupils can be helped in learning to read longer selections more effectively by performing such activities as these: (1.) finding where each of the parts of the story that were enumerated earlier in connection with this story under "Summarizing and Organizing" begins, or (2.) telling the story to another group of boys and girls.

Using a Story at a More Advanced Reading Level

In *Joys and Journeys*[4] one of the upper-level books of the *Read* Series, is the selection "Benny by the River," the story of the boy Benny, son of a displaced family that had escaped from behind the Iron Curtain. Requested to "be nice to Benny" by the parents of the gang to which the boy who is the narrator of the story belongs, the boys in the group tried but all they did was to tolerate him and let him tag along with them. To the boys Benny seemed queer because of his speech, his clothes, his haircut, his shyness. They looked on him with disdain after, shaken with terror, he had sobbed when he approached the bridge that led to the boys' swimming place. Then when Benny's mother had explained to the narrator of the story that Benny's fear stemmed from the day when, as they were fleeing from behind the Iron Curtain, guards shot and killed his brother who had helped him across a river, the narrator planned to tell the other boys the terrible story, so that they would understand why Benny had acted as he did. But the explanation was not necessary, for that very evening, as the boys were skating on the river, Benny, endangering his own life, saved one of the group who had broken through the ice.

Finding the Main Idea

After the boys and girls have read the story, they may suggest other titles for it. Or they may be given a series of possible titles from which they can

[4] Marjorie S. Johnson, Roy A. Kress, John D. McNeil, and Pose Lamb, *Joys and Journeys. The READ Series,* Level J. New York: American Book Company, 1971, pp. 280–290.

choose the most appropriate, such as: (1.) Leaving the Iron Curtain Behind Us, (2.) Ridiculed by the Gang, (3.) Courage Undaunted.

Selecting Important Details

Pupils may enumerate the details which indicated that the boys' attitude toward Benny before his heroic act had been one of tolerance or less than tolerance.

Arriving at Generalizations or Coming to Conclusions

The story provides excellent opportunities to help boys and girls develop in their ability to make generalizations. Attention can be drawn to the fact that the boys had come to an incorrectly inferred conclusion that Benny was cowardly. The importance of deferring generalizations until enough evidence is available can be stressed. The class might also discuss the appropriateness of the conclusion stated in the last sentence of the story: "That Benny Wlodarski is some guy."

Predicting Outcomes

After the pupils have read to the point where Benny, terrorized at the thought of crossing the bridge, left the other boys, pupils could be asked how they imagined the boys would treat Benny after that episode.

After finishing reading the story, they could predict how the boys would treat Benny in the future. They could base their prediction in part on the sentences: "Benny didn't need any help. He'd won a place for himself without it."

Evaluating Critically

The ability to evaluate critically what is read can be developed by considering the true-to-life quality and the justifiability or wrongness of actions portrayed by sentences such as the following: (a.) If he had been anyone else, we would have yelled the roof down at the stunts he did—but we remembered too clearly that day by the river. (b.) My mom always called Benny "that poor little foreign boy," and she'd told me to be nice to him. The other kids heard the same from their folks, so we let Benny tag around with us; but we weren't really friendly to him.

Word Meaning

This story provides much opportunity to help boys and girls develop their reading and speaking and understanding vocabulary. They can probably learn the meaning of some of the words, like those underlined in the following sentences through context: (a.) "November had been as cold as October'd been *balmy*." (b) "I *peered* toward the shadows, and I could see Benny's figure."

Phrase Meaning

The story contains many idiomatic expressions, the meaning of which the class could discuss. In some cases they might like to substitute other words for a phrase and then compare the forcefulness of the sentences in the book with that which they suggested. Some of the phrases that might be studied are: (1.) the water's edge, (2.) yelled the roof down, (3.) strike out.

Sentence Meaning

Developing skill in sentence comprehension could be brought about through questions and directions such as these:

1. What did Benny's mother mean when she said: "And is all. Paul, my son"?
2. Give in your own words the meaning of the statement by Mrs. Wlodarski: "We have not say much about when we leave old country."
3. Why are complete sentences not necessary to give the thought of the last six words of these comments made by the narrator: "I thought of Benny that day with us, crying. Remembering another bridge. Remembering a bullet"?

Outlining and Organizing

The boys and girls might think of this dramatic story as a play and determine what scenes could be portrayed in a dramatization. The following is one possible plan of organization:

1. Treatment of Benny by the boys before the bridge episode.
2. The bridge episode.
3. The changed attitude of the boys following Benny's reaction at the bridge.
4. The mother's visit.
5. The rescue.
6. A change in treatment of Benny.

For Further Study

Beery, Althea, Thomas C. Barrett, and William R. Powell, eds., *Elementary Reading Instruction: Selected Materials* (Boston: Allyn and Bacon, Inc., 1969), Ch. 7, "Comprehension—Cognitive Dimensions," containing articles by J. P. Guilford, Irving Lorge, Frank J. Guszak, Amelia Melnick, Carl Sailer, and Althea Beery.

Boyan, Catherine S., "Critical Reading: What Is It? Where Is It", *The Reading Teacher,* vol. 25 (March 1972), pp. 517–522.

Caskey, Helen J., "Guidelines for Teaching Comprehension," *The Reading Teacher,* vol. 23 (April 1970), pp. 649–654.

Culhane, Joseph W., "CLOZE Procedures and Comprehension," *The Reading Teacher,* vol. 23 (February 1970), pp. 410–413.

Dawson, Mildred A., compiler, *Developing Comprehension* (Newark, Del.: International Reading Association, 1968).

DeChant, Emerald V., *Improving the Teaching of Reading,* 2nd ed. (Englewood Cliffs, N.J.: Prentice-Hall, Inc., 1970), Ch. 13, "Advancing the Pupils' Comprehension Skills."

Durkin, Dolores, *Teaching Them to Read* (Boston: Allyn and Bacon, Inc., 1970), Ch. 14, "Teaching Comprehension Skills."

Harris, Albert J., and Edward R. Sipay, eds., *Readings on Reading Instruction,* 2nd ed. (New York: David McKay Company, 1972), Ch. X, "Reading Comprehension," containing articles by Nila Banton Smith, Amelia Melnik, Sarah W. Lundsteen, Charlotte Agrast, and Dorothy Burrus.

Herr, Selma E., *Learning Activities for Reading,* 2nd ed. (Dubuque, Iowa: Wm. C. Brown Company Publishers, 1970), Ch. 8, "Comprehension Skills" and Ch. 11, "Critical Reading."

Schell, Leo M., "Promising Possibilities for Improving Comprehension," *Journal of Reading,* vol. 15 (March 1972), pp. 415–424.

Spache, George D., and Evelyn B. Spache, *Reading in the Elementary School,* 3rd ed. (Boston: Allyn and Bacon, Inc., 1973), Ch. 14, "Developing Comprehension and Critical Reading."

Stauffer, Russell G., *Directing Reading Maturity as a Cognitive Process* (New York: Harper & Row, 1969), Ch. 7, "Concept Development."

Stauffer, Russell G., *Teaching Reading as a Thinking Process* (New York: Harper & Row, 1969), Ch. 10, "Concept Development."

Sullivan, Joanna, "Liberating Children to Creative Reading," *The Reading Teacher,* vol. 25 (April 1972), pp. 639–642.

Zintz, Miles V., *The Reading Process,* (Dubuque, Iowa: Wm. C. Brown Company Publishers, 1970), Ch. 8, "Comprehension Skills."

Questions and Comments for Thought and Discussion

1. In some instances children can ascribe no meanings to terms that are used in materials at hand. Or they may ascribe wrong, vague, or partially correct meanings to such words. Thus, what has been termed verbalism develops. What harm can verbalism do as both teacher and pupil strive for meaning?

2. Some writers think of meaning-getting skills in reading as falling into three levels: literal comprehension, interpretation, and critical reading. Precisely what do these terms mean to you?

3. In the past, teachers and research workers in reading have given a great deal of attention to word perception and general reading comprehension skills on the literal and interpretative levels. But in recent years the development of critical reading skills has come to be of increasing concern. Do you believe that critical reading can be taught in the early grades? If so, can you describe a situation in which conditions would appear to be conducive to the development of critical reading ability during one of the first years in the elementary school?

4. The term *creative reading* has come to mean many things. For one writer it means an attitude of suspended judgment with regard to reading materials, the ability to read above and beyond the obvious, the ability to see or perceive relations, the ability to recognize authors' intentions. At what level would you try to develop such abilities? How would you embark on such a venture?

5. Some suggestions are given in this chapter (*see* page 198) for assisting boys and girls in recognizing propaganda techniques. In what additional ways could the teacher assist his pupils in becoming aware of the use of such techniques as they are reading or viewing television or listening to the radio or to people talk?

6. Many suggestions are given in this "B" chapter for developing various comprehension skills, and some examples of exercises are included. You may wish to plan an exercise to help boys and girls, on any level of reading development, to improve in any one of these skills—such as predicting outcomes, recognizing propaganda techniques, judging the qualifications of an author.

7. If you have access to teachers' guidebooks or manuals to be used with basal readers, examine them to find helpful suggestions for improving comprehension.

Outline for Chapter 7A

READING AT APPROPRIATE RATES

Reading Rate and Comprehension
Causes of Problems Related to Reading Rates
    Lack of Skill in Word Recognition
    Vocalization
    Pointing to Words
    Overemphasis on Oral Reading
    Lack of Sufficient Practice in Reading at Different
      Rates
    Lack of Interest and Purpose
Appraisal of Reading Rates
Controlled Reading
"Speed Reading" Courses
Guidelines for Improved Reading Rates

CHAPTER 7A

Reading at Appropriate Rates

"How fast should I be able to read?" is one of the questions about reading most frequently asked of teachers. It is asked from the elementary school through college. Not only are pupils and students concerned about the rate of reading but parents, too, want to know how many words a minute their child reads and how he compares with the average for his grade. Inquiries concerning the reader's rate of reading are often accompanied by the question: "How can I improve my rate?"

The concern about rate of reading is understandable. The person who can read a selection rapidly and still accomplish his purpose has a distinct advantage over the one who cannot. In school the slow reader is often unable to do the work required of him. In the professional and business world the ability to perform activities quickly — and these include reading — is an important asset. The individual who always reads slowly will not have time to read as much interesting and significant material as the one who reads rapidly. The sheer volume of printed matter available today, much of it essential to a knowledge of new developments in the world of ideas and events, makes extensive reading mandatory for the educated person and the responsible citizen.

Ideally, one's rate of reading would approximate one's rate of thinking. Obviously such a standard would be unrealistic in the case of difficult material, but serious lag between rate of reading and rate of thinking not only results in waste of time but tends to reduce a person's pleasure and interest in reading. Slow, cumbersome methods of reading start a vicious circle from less reading to less efficient reading to still less reading.

Professional interest in speed of reading first rose sharply in the 1920s with the shift of emphasis from oral to silent reading. It was discovered that the average child entering the intermediate grades could read more rapidly silently than orally. At first it was widely believed that reading speed was a unitary ability and that improvement in rate was automatically reflected in all kinds of reading. Only gradually did the relation between rate and type of reading material come under intensive study.

The difference in rate between oral and silent reading was dramatically illustrated in the eye-movement studies of Judd, Buswell, and others. Buswell's study of the eye-voice span (the distance between the word the reader pronounces and the point on which his eyes fixate), for example, showed that in oral reading the eyes of the effective reader run well ahead of his voice. When reading silently he is not delayed as in oral reading by the mere physical act of articulation. Obviously the silent reading rate of the efficient reader exceeds that of his oral reading. In the later elementary school years the average pupil may read silently from one and a half to twice his oral reading rate, or even more.

READING RATE AND COMPREHENSION

Much discussion has centered on the question of the relation between rate of reading and comprehension. The question would be clarified if we substituted the term *rate of comprehension* for *rate of reading*. Reading without adequate comprehension cannot properly be called reading. Therefore, if we believe that a good reader is one who can most quickly grasp the meaning of a passage, the fast reader is necessarily the good reader. We can then dispense with any debate about rate versus comprehension.

Efficient readers differ in their rates of comprehension. It takes some good readers a little longer than others to discover the literal and implied meanings of a passage. An individual's temperament and rhythm of learning sometimes account for these differences. Standardized tests of reading are usually based on the assumption that speed of comprehension is an essential aspect of reading competence. For this reason they may frequently obscure a pupil's real reading potential. Standardized test scores should be interpreted with this fact in mind. In order to assess the reader's true capabilities we need to go behind the scores and analyze the specific nature of his performance on a test.

There are important interrelations between speed and comprehension in reading. On the one hand, improved comprehension facilitates growth in speed. On the other hand, habits of more rapid reading often aid comprehension by shifting attention from individual words to the larger word patterns that carry the meaning. The development of comprehension, which is primary, may therefore be cultivated in some children, especially in the intermediate and upper grades, by encouraging faster reading.

While the teacher's aim should be to develop maximum speed of reading within the limits of the child's comprehension, a special effort should be made to teach him how to adjust his rate to his purpose and to the type of material he is reading. When the material is difficult and a high degree of accuracy is required, a very slow rate is appropriate. Many readers, even very good ones, assume that all materials must be read at a "normal" rate. They must be taught how to "shift gears" when they attack a verbal problem in arithmetic or a difficult passage in science. Thus, although superior readers tend to excel in both speed and comprehension with ordinary narrative material, they employ slower rates when these are needed for maximum comprehension.

CAUSES OF PROBLEMS RELATED TO READING RATES

The rate at which a person reads is determined by various factors. Low intelligence, which leaves its impact on all reading skills, can have a marked effect on rate of reading. Poor health also seems to have a detrimental influence on the rate at which an individual reads, although it must be noted that some people in poor health are among the most prodigious and most rapid readers. Additional causes of unduly slow reading are lack of skill in word recognition, vocalization, or "excessive" subvocalization, pointing to words, overemphasis on oral reading, and lack of interest and purpose.

Lack of Skill in Word Recognition

The person who has difficulty in recognizing words quickly and accurately is likely to be a very slow reader. He is at a special disadvantage when he wishes to find the answer to a question. He is also handicapped when he tries to read study-type materials that contain words not easily recognized by him.

Often the methods by which an individual has been taught to recognize words play an important role in reading rate. The person who habitually analyzes all words by phonic methods will have slower habits of word recognition than one who has learned to analyze words only if he cannot quickly identify them as wholes. This fact should not be interpreted to mean that a knowledge of phonics is detrimental to speed of reading. Rather, it suggests that misuse of phonics may have an undesirable effect on rate of reading. Phonics is an important aid to word recognition only when faster methods fail to bring results. Moreover, the person who can identify a large number of words through effective use of methods of word attack other than phonics, such as recognition of a sight word or use of context clues or structural analysis, is more often the one who can more speedily accomplish his purpose in reading.

Vocalization

Early stress on speech sounds in reading instruction inevitably creates strong associations in the mind of the child between the sight of a word and its sound. The sound image is intended to serve as a bridge between visual perception and the apprehension of meaning, and normally the child becomes less and less conscious of language sounds as he seeks meaning on the printed page. Exclusive preoccupation with sounding in the initial stages of reading tends to cause lip movements and possibly excessive subvocalization in later stages. Speed of reading is then frequently restricted to the rate of oral reading. Under these conditions the child is obliged to unlearn habits deeply fixed in the beginning.

Closely related to the habit of vocalization is the feeling some readers have that they must "read" every word in order to comprehend. In many types of reading, as in skimming and scanning, the good reader finds the key words and supplies the intervening words with sufficient accuracy to derive the meaning intended by the author. In these cases the reading materials are not simply a continuity of symbols intended to correspond to the spoken language; they are, rather, a set of clues, a sort of shorthand, designed to communicate meaning without the need for vocal articulation of all the words.

Pointing to Words

Another practice likely to arrest development in rate of reading is pointing to each word as it is being read. In early reading instruction in the first grade, when it usually takes the reader longer to recognize a word than to say it, pointing with the finger may not reduce reading rate. However, the practice can have a detrimental effect later on speed of reading, for the habit may become established, with the result that the pupil persists in its use after he should be reading at faster rates than are possible when pointing at each word.

Many first-grade teachers supply the children with markers in the form of heavy strips of paper, often about the length of a line of print and about an inch in width. With these markers, which the boys and girls keep under the line being read, the children can often keep their place more easily than they otherwise could. Probably if a marker is used only for a very limited length of time it can serve as a helpful crutch. The danger is that children may get into the habit of needing some means other than their eyes and mind to keep the place. Like all other crutches, markers should be discarded as soon as they have helped a person over a difficult situation.

Overemphasis on Oral Reading

Oral reading has its proper place in reading programs, but a program dominated by oral reading practice is almost certain to produce habits of slow silent reading. Even in the initial reading period children should be encouraged to read words silently much of the time. In general, it is recommended that children be asked to read a passage silently before they are called on to read it orally. By this means silent reading habits are established, and the subsequent oral reading will be improved because of increased comprehension of the material read. The practice of children following in their books while someone is reading the same material orally to them is to be discouraged after the pupils have learned to read more rapidly silently than orally. Otherwise they may tend to reduce their silent reading rate to be more equal to their oral reading rates.

Lack of Sufficient Practice in Reading at Different Rates

An error of omission in some instructional programs is the lack of emphasis on differential rates of reading. Many boys and girls need considerable guidance in acquiring versatility or flexibility in reading rates and sufficient time to practice this skill. Unless boys and girls are supervised in time afforded for this practice, there is likely to be little positive effect from admonishing them to read slower or faster.

Lack of Interest and Purpose

The ability to read rapidly is only in part a matter of habit and skill. Perhaps even more important is the attitude of the reader. If the pupil knows what he is looking for on the printed page, he will be impatient until he finds what he wants. He will not dawdle over the passages that are only secondary to the goals he is seeking or that are irrelevant to them. Clear purposes are therefore basic to the improvement of both comprehension and rate.

The daydreaming pupil makes little progress in reading. But when his interest has been kindled, when the action in a story moves toward a climax, when the narrative brings smiles or tears, he races down the lines to learn the outcome. The scene before him will not be obscured by laborious struggles with printed words. With the well-selected story, the words, the page, even the immediate environment fade from consciousness and only the people and the places and the actions in the story remain. For many children the key to reading speed is interest. Abundant, highly motivated reading will do what no tachistoscopes or flashmeters can.

APPRAISAL OF READING RATES

In order to plan an effective program of reading instruction that will help each child learn to read at appropriate rates, careful appraisal should be made of every pupil's reading rates.

Since an effective reader has more than one reading rate, it is not a simple matter to make an appraisal. Consequently, a variety of means needs to be used. *Informal observation* is one. The classroom teacher has many opportunities to note the characteristics of a pupil's reading rates. He can observe whether the child wastes time while reading. By studying the child in reading situations he can gather evidence as to whether the pupil is able to adjust his rate of reading to his purpose and to the difficulty of the material. He can note whether he skims parts of it and reads other parts more carefully.

Sometimes important evidence about a pupil's reading habits as they affect rate of reading can be secured through *conferences*. The teacher can often discover by this means whether the pupil knows that variations in rates are necessary to good reading. Answers to questions as to the type of situations in which skimming or slow reading is required can also be illuminating to the teacher desirous of learning more about a pupil's rate of reading. Tests, too, can furnish valuable data. Some of the standardized reading tests contain subtests for determining rate, among them the following: the *Sangren-Woody Reading Test* (Harcourt Brace Jovanovich), the *Iowa Silent Reading Tests: Elementary Test* (Harcourt Brace Jovanovich), the *Gates-McGinitie Reading Tests* (Teachers College Press, Columbia University), and *Diagnostic Reading Tests* (Committee on Diagnostic Testing). However, tests in which rate is measured in only one type of situation do not give a clear index of an individual's rate of reading. For this reason tests need to be supplemented by other means of appraisal. Because of these limitations in the measurement of rate, many teachers like to make tests of their own. One type is described in Chapter 7B. Tests similar to the one described there can be used to record the pupil's reading rate in a variety of situations.

Whenever a pupil is timed while reading, whether he is taking a standardized or nonstandardized test, allowance should be made for the fact that the results may be inaccurate because the pupil knows he is being timed. No matter how hard a teacher may try to keep the testing situation free from strain, some children, as soon as they know they are being timed, show the effects of working under pressure. There are many children who cannot do their best under such conditions.

One type of record that the teacher may find it advantageous to keep is a *checklist* on which he indicates change or persistence in attitudes or habits or skills concerned with the improvement in reading rates. By means of a checklist the teacher can be spared the necessity of depending on his memory as to the reading skills of each of his pupils. Questions such as the following may be on the checklist: (1.) Does the child recognize the need of variation in rate? (2.) Is he able to adjust his rate to his purpose and to the material he is reading? (3.) Does he know when to skim?

Charts, graphs, and tables are useful in appraising growth in the ability to employ appropriate reading rates. In keeping this type of record, the teacher should be sure to compare only those data that are truly comparable. Rate in skimming an article should not be compared with rate in reading a selection of similar difficulty when more detailed examination is required. For skimming, a reading rate of 400 words per minute may be slow, while a work-type rate of 200 words per minute may be fast. Rate of reading two selections that are unlike in difficulty or type cannot be directly compared.

Another point is that if rates in reading are charted, they should be recorded over a relatively long period of time. In many situations there are too many rather insignificant variations in rate from day to day to make a short-term study of rates of reading of much value. It often takes more than a few days of successful practice to show measurable improvement, even when real progress is being made from the beginning.

Furthermore, the learner himself should be informed of his progress. If a child is old enough to try to improve his rate of reading, he is old enough to understand the simple record of his performance. The learner's concern should be the improvement of his own skill, not a desire to equal or surpass others or to attain a norm.

National norms on standardized tests are not very helpful to teachers who wish to evaluate their pupils' reading rates. Different tests show different medians for the various school grades, probably because of the wide variation in difficulty and type of content they present.

CONTROLLED READING

Various machines for regulating the speed at which the printed page is exposed to the reader are commercially available. The basic principle of most of these devices is that of an instrument known in psychological laboratories as a tachistoscope. This is a contrivance that flashes words or phrases on a screen at a controlled rate. The use of the tachistoscope and similar instruments in reading instruction is sometimes called controlled reading.

The chief purpose of these instruments is to increase the reader's ability to perceive whole words and phrases quickly in a single fixation. Through intensive and prolonged practice a child may be able to perceive—that is, recognize and identify—words and phrases with progressively greater speed. The theory is that such training will transfer to the printed page and will result not only in improved reading rate but also in better comprehension, because meaning is usually derived from whole words and words in combination rather than from individual letters.

Among the well-known pacing devices are the Harvard Reading Films developed by Walter F. Dearborn and his colleagues. These films, however, have not as yet been made in an edition usable in the elementary school. The films present reading material through bright exposures of part or all of a line of print at a time. Regressive movements of the eyes are thus discouraged, since the reader is forced to move his eyes more and more rapidly in left-to-right movements in order to comprehend the meaning. Tests are available with each film to test the reader's comprehension.

Other devices that employ "pressure methods" are the SRA Reading Rate Accelerator (Science Research Associates, Chicago), the Keystone Reading Pacer (Keystone View Division/Mast Development Company), and the Renshaw Tachistoscopic Trainer (Stereo Optical Company, Chicago), and the Shadowscope Pacer (Lafayette Instrument Company, Lafayette, Indiana). The Keystone Tachistoscope, also available through the Keystone View Division of the Mast Development Company, is a popular device for increasing rate of perception of individual letters and words. All of these and similar machines present printed matter at controlled rates of speed. Faced with a gradually increasing rate of exposure, the reader is pressed to "take in" meaningful units on the line at a pace that can be constantly accelerated. For a description of mechanical aids of this type, the reader may wish to consult the book *Improving the Teaching of Reading* by E. V. Dechant.[1]

Unquestionably, the reading machines have been effective in improving reading rate in many cases. How permanent the improvement has been is a matter of conjecture. Quite possibly the machines have an initial advantage in that they provide novelty and interest in the improvement of reading. Unfortunately, after a time the novelty may wear off, and consequently one of the chief reasons for the success reported with instruments of this type may no longer operate.

In controlled reading, emphasis is placed primarily on the improvement of rate. Programs of improvement in reading should also place stress on comprehension. Although research studies indicate either that there was no loss in comprehension or that slight gains were made, the little increase in power in comprehension has not always been commensurate with the amount of time and energy spent on attempts at improvement of reading.

The use of mechanical aids for controlling the rate of reading does not eliminate the need for an attack on the underlying causes of inappropriate

---

[1] Emerald V. Dechant, *Improving the Teaching of Reading*, 2nd ed. (Englewood Cliffs, N.J.: Prentice-Hall, Inc, 1970).

rates of reading. The machines may discourage dawdling habits of reading, but in themselves they do not eliminate the chief causes of unsatisfactory rate of comprehension, such as lack of skill in methods of word recognition, lack of skill in selecting details, difficulty in organizing what is read, failure to read material critically, and inability to locate information rapidly. In fact, controlled reading can even have a detrimental effect on some of these factors. For example, the person whose chief cause of slow reading is a difficulty in recognizing words may develop even poorer habits of word recognition because he is not given time to apply sound means of word identification. Nor can the efficient reader employ the flexible habits of reading that are needed to get meaning quickly. When he comes to a word that he must analyze, he wants to stop for a longer pause. He may find it advisable to make regressive movements if he discovers that he has just finished reading a point that he should note carefully. He will want to vary his rate in accordance with his purpose in reading, rather than follow the operation of mechanical shutters that compel him to read every line or part of a line in the same time as preceding ones.

"SPEED READING" COURSES

This chapter on reading rates would hardly be complete without mention of the "speed reading" courses presently in vogue on the adult level. The advocates of some of these courses claim that the eye can be trained "to take in" the printed page much more rapidly if the usual eye movements are discontinued and new ones adopted. Of one such method, the "Reading Dynamics" program, Robert Hermann[2] states the following:

> Basically the Wood method abandons conventional eye movements and trains the eye to move vertically down the center of the page. Some Wood readers use a swinging, zigzag, downward movement. Some literature indicates that a few Wood readers can take a whole page or even two pages in a single look, and that some of them read down one page and up the next.

It is a matter of heated controversy what interpretation should be given to assertions of phenomenal reading rates of 4,000 and more words read per minute. Since photographs of eye movements seem to indicate that such speeds are impossible in continuous line by line reading,[3] there are those who argue that when such rates are seemingly attained, the reader is skim-

[2] Robert Hermann, "The Argument over Racing through Print: Is It Speed You Need to Enjoy Reading?" (New York: Bantam Books, 1967), Ch. VII in *New Dimensions in Reading*, eds., Ralph Staiger and David A. Sohn, p. 152.
[3] Robert Karlin, *Teaching Elementary Reading: Principles and Strategies* (New York: Harcourt Brace Jovanovich, 1970), p. 270.

ming or scanning, not engaging in continuous reading. The nature of the eye movements acquired by some persons who have taken a speed reading course is also a matter of debate. According to Ehrlich,[4] the eye movements of those individuals are not vertical down the page but follow across a line of print in a series of saccadic movements and fixation points in the same manner as those of other readers.

And so the argument continues. The student interested in further reading on the topic is referred to the article quoted above by Hermann and to one entitled "An Evaluation of Forty-One Trainees Who Had Recently Completed the 'Reading Dynamics' Program," by Stanford E. Taylor, reported in the Eleventh Yearbook of the National Reading Conference (pp. 41-56). The reader may also wish to evaluate "speed reading" courses in terms of the criteria stated in the Resolution adopted by the Delegates Assembly of the Tenth Annual Convention of the International Reading Association in May 1969, which we quote on pages 523–524).

GUIDELINES FOR IMPROVING READING RATES

To assist the teacher further in helping boys and girls to read at appropriate rates, guidelines that should be kept in mind by the teacher are now discussed. Only those generalizations are presented on which there is little, if any, disagreement among specialists in the teaching of reading.

1. Growth in ability to read at appropriate rates is subject to training. Assistance can be given the person who is not reading at appropriate rates. Studies show that remarkable increases in rate have been achieved in a brief period of time in many clinical situations, supervised reading courses, and classroom situations where this phase of reading has been stressed. In fact, there is reason to think that almost all readers could make valuable increases in the speed with which they read, without loss in comprehension, if they were given appropriate help. Emphasis on increase of reading rates should usually be postponed until the intermediate grades, when pupils have ordinarily gained proficiency in reading skills basic to the development of greater speed.

2. Reading rates should vary with the purpose of the reader and the type and difficulty of the material. In fact, the desirable rate may vary even within a given selection from one part to another. Both the teacher and the learner should be aware of this fact. In the first grade the teacher will usually set the purpose for reading. He may ask a pupil to read the next page to find out what Bobby did when his mother told him what she wanted for her birthday, or he may ask the pupil to glance over the next page to find the

---

[4] Eugene Ehrlich, "Speed Reading" in *Readings in Reading: Practice, Theory, Research,* Delwyn G. Schubert and Theodore L. Torgerson, eds. (New York: Thomas Y. Crowell Company, 1963), pp. 530–532.

new word *mother*, which has been presented on the board or on a word card. The teacher may show the pupil that in the latter assignment it is not necessary for him to read every word and that consequently it should not take him as long to read that page as it would if he read the page to answer a question about it. Thus, an early beginning can be made in helping boys and girls learn to read at different rates and for different purposes.

Later in the development of skill in reading, the learner should be given increasing opportunity to decide on suitable purposes himself and to determine what rate of reading he will need in order to accomplish his objective.

A somewhat arbitrary classification of reading rates may help to clarify for boys and girls and for the teacher the ways of adapting speed to the nature of the material and the purpose for reading it. Reading rates have been divided into three categories: rapid reading, moderately rapid reading, and slow reading. Scanning and skimming can be considered two kinds of rapid reading; however, a person can be reading rapidly without engaging in either scanning or skimming. In scanning, as the term is used here, the reader rapidly searches the page of specific information. He may be scanning as he glances at the contents to see if it gives information on a given topic. Scanning is done when a person looks at a page of a table of contents to find the title of a given chapter so that he can tell on which page the chapter begins, or when he looks over the words on one or more pages of a dictionary in order to locate an entry word. A person is skimming when he reads a paragraph or longer selection rapidly to get the main idea and possibly a few supporting facts.

Rapid reading is also appropriate, as, for example, when the reader looks at a newspaper to find out what is going on in the world or reads a magazine article just for fun. Moderately fast reading is called for when the reader wishes to note some details. Slow reading is advisable in a study-type of situation or when appreciation of the beauty of style or of the unfolding of the details of a situation or the personality of the characters is desired.

3. Teachers and pupils should have clearly defined goals for the improvement of reading rates.   General objectives are not enough. The teacher should try to find out the needs of the pupils in order to help them overcome their difficulties. The aims should be specific—for example, to learn when to read at the different rates, to read study-type material more slowly so as to have an opportunity to get the thought of the selection, and to read fiction rapidly while maintaining the desired amount of comprehension.

The pupil, too, should have clearcut objectives. Results are better when the learner is consciously seeking specific goals.

4. Development of ability to read at appropriate rates should not interfere with development of other reading skills.   Rates of reading should not be increased at a sacrifice of comprehension. To be sure, when a pupil has been reading more slowly than his immediate purpose warrants, rate should be increased. Increase in rate sometimes brings about a better degree of comprehension, if teaching methods eliminate defects in rate and comprehension simultaneously. It requires insight on the part of the teacher to know when rate and when comprehension should be stressed the more.

Much of what has been said about the effect of improvement in rate on comprehension can also, in general terms, be said of the relation that should exist between increase in rate and other reading skills. In the case of skill in locating information, for example, it would be unfortunate if greater speed in finding an entry in an index caused the reader to become less accurate in doing so. The goal is to spend less time in finding an entry without sacrificing accuracy.

5. Neither haste nor undue tension should characterize the efforts to read at appropriate rates. All practices in an effective program of developmental or remedial reading should be in harmony with the principles of

Figure 7.1 Expanding horizons through the use of reference books. (© Field Enterprises Educational Corp.)

mental health. Studies of child development have shown the harmful effects of creating pressures which result in anxiety and fear of failure. However, this does not mean that at times measures should not be taken to prod a person whose poor achievement, below his expected level, is due to daw-dling habits or to lack of effort. Not only are haste and undue tension un-desirable from the point of view of maintaining an emotional equilibrium but they are also detrimental because they interfere with success in learn-ing. Consequently, the child should be encouraged to do his best without becoming frantic when he fails to achieve his goal.

6. The marked difference in children's ability to read at appropriate rates should be recognized.   Part of the variation among children results from differences in training received in school and practice outside of school. A further cause lies in the variations in innate capacity of individ-uals to master the intricacies of learning to read at the appropriate rates. Some will never become as skillful as others in reading at desirable rates.

An effective program for helping pupils to acquire skill in reading at appropriate rates recognizes these variations among individuals. The teacher needs to know what stage of learning to read each child has reached, and he must work out a program that is adapted to the needs of individual children. He should not be satisfied with averages. Some chil-dren who read with less than average speed for their grade in all types of reading situations may still be working up to capacity or even straining themselves to do good work beyond their capacity. On the other hand, some children, although surpassing norms in rate of reading, may still be read-ing below their potential.

Outline for Chapter 7B

DEVELOPING APPROPRIATE READING RATES

Methods of Developing Appropriate Rates
    Developing Skill in Reading at a Rapid Rate
    Developing Skill in Reading at a Moderately Rapid
        Rate
    Developing Skill in Reading at a Relatively Slow
        Rate
Reading Lessons and the Development of Appropriate
        Rates
    Improving Reading Rates at the Lower Primary-
        grade Reading Level
    Improving Reading Rates at the Intermediate-
        grade Reading Level
        A Suggested Teaching Plan
        Explanation of the Teaching Plan

7B
CHAPTER

Developing Appropriate Reading Rates

The purpose of this chapter is to demonstrate how the teacher can help children to develop reading rates appropriate to the various types of materials and purposes for reading.

METHODS OF DEVELOPING APPROPRIATE RATES

In this chapter reading rates are grouped for convenience into three categories: rapid reading, moderately fast reading, and slow reading. Each of these types of reading is desirable under certain circumstances and undesirable under others. The efficient reader knows not only how to use these but also when.

Some of the following suggestions are given for the improvement of rate in connection with the regular reading lessons in the basal reading textbook. Also included are recommendations that can be used in the content fields, and others that can serve as practice exercises. Samples of a few practice exercises are given. No attempt has been made, however, to designate the type of situation in which the suggestions can best be used. Nor are all the methods recommended for use with all groups or individuals. Selection should be made on the basis of the principles set forth in the preceding chapter. It is hoped that the list of recommendations will suggest to the teacher many others that are especially adapted to her pupils.

Some activities performed by pupils can be helpful for increasing rate whether fast, moderately fast, or rather slow reading is called for by the purpose of the reader and the material. The following are illustrative:

1. Discussing the importance of reading at the fastest rate possible in keeping with the aim of the reader and the nature of the material.

2. Discussing the importance of maintaining a desired level of comprehension as rate is increased.

3. Explaining that some readers read too fast to achieve the comprehension level they wish to attain.

4. Explaining the importance of purpose in reading, in order to help pupils understand the optimum speed at which the material should be read.

5. Explaining the relation between type and difficulty of material and the optimum speed at which the material should be read.

6. Estimating the speed (in terms of fast, moderately fast, and slow) at which materials of designated types and difficulty should be read.

7. Reading while being timed and later checked for comprehension.

8. Practicing reading of words, phrases, or sentences that are exposed for varying lengths of time either by a commercially produced reading machine or by a teacher-made tachistoscope. The teacher can make a tachistoscope by cutting a slit in a piece of tagboard and sliding the words or groups of words, listed in column form, through the slit, at varying intervals. If he uses a tachistoscopic device, he should, however, be fully aware of some problems connected with their use, as discussed earlier (*see* page 221).

9. Listing in one column possible speeds at which the pupils might read and in a second column topics on which they may be reading for stated purposes. Lines can then be drawn between the columns, matching the speed with the corresponding topic.

10. Listening to the teacher read in meaningful phrases.

11. Reading silently material in which the phrases have been marked or separated.

12. Matching words given in two columns which when combined make meaningful phrases.

13. Marking the meaningful phrases that occur in a selection.

14. Indicating orally the meaningful phrases in a selection.

15. Keeping a record of progress in reading at appropriate rates.

16. Reading a selection in which varying rates are appropriate and indicating where and why the variations should occur.

17. Discussing importance of freedom from interfering movements, such as vocalization in supposedly silent reading and pointing to words when reading.

18. Engaging in any activities that will help improve skill in word recognition. (For suggestions *see* Chapter 5B.)

Developing Skill in Reading at a Rapid Rate

Activities such as the following may be of value in the development of skill in skimming or scanning.

1. Discussing in what situations scanning can properly be used; for example, when the reader wishes to ascertain whether information on a given topic or an answer to a question is provided.
2. Scanning a paragraph to find out whether a named topic is discussed or to find the sentence that answers a stated question.
3. Discussing in what situations skimming can properly be used; for example, when the reader wishes to get only a general impression of what is discussed in the selection.
4. Explaining how the eyes may move on a page when scanning or skimming. It may help some of the boys and girls to know that in scanning and skimming the eyes do not need to move from the end of one line to the beginning of the next, but that often they take in only a part of each line as they move rapidly over the page.
5. Skimming a selection while consciously moving the eyes rapidly across and down a page, without stopping to note details.
6. Scanning a table of contents to find out on what page a chapter on a given topic begins.
7. Scanning parts of an article in an encyclopedia to find a desired fact.
8. Scanning a page in a book to find a given "new word" that has been presented.
9. Scanning a page to find the answer to a question based on that page.
10. Skimming a book to find out whether one would like to read it.
11. Skimming a selection after a more thorough reading to see if any points to be remembered have been forgotten.
12. Timing oneself or being timed while engaging in many of the types of activities that have been suggested.
13. Finding a word in a dictionary.
14. Scanning a telephone directory to find the name of a person whose telephone number is desired.
15. Reading a paragraph in which some words have been omitted, words without which a reader can get the general thought of the paragraph. The pupils can be told not to try to guess the missing words but to see if they can understand the paragraph as it is written while reading it rapidly.
16. Skimming a story after previous reading to determine what characters are needed for a dramatization of the story.
17. Scanning a selection to find proof for a point made.

The following are ways in which improvement may be brought about in reading at an effective rate when fast reading, but not skimming, or scanning is desired, as is often the case when reading a magazine or a book of fiction:

1. Explaining when fast reading other than skimming should be used.
2. Identifying situations in which fast reading, other than skimming, is desired.
3. Getting practice in reading rapidly easy material or material with which the reader has some familiarity.
4. Getting practice in selecting the main idea of a paragraph, without intent to note details, as rapidly as possible.
5. Timing oneself or being timed while reading rapidly.

Practice Exercises

Some pupils can be helped to acquire appropriate reading rates by means of practice exercises. Many workbooks, some accompanying basal textbooks and others independent of them, provide such exercises. However, the teacher may often find it desirable to construct exercises of his own. The teacher will find suggestions of possible practice exercises in the lists here given.

The following samples of exercises are representative of some that may encourage either skimming or rapid reading without skimming.

1   An exercise such as the following, especially if timed, is particularly helpful to pupils inclined to use too much time in locating the main thought in a paragraph or longer selection.

Directions: This exercise is to help you learn to locate rapidly a certain sentence in a paragraph. You will be timed while you are doing this exercise. Preceding each paragraph there is a sentence. You are to find the sentence in the paragraph that expresses the thought of that sentence. When you have located the sentence in the paragraph, draw a circle around the first word of it and continue with the next paragraph.

Sentence: The Indian elephant has a lighter skin than the African.

> There are many differences between the two kinds of elephants, the African and the Indian. The African elephants grow larger than the Indian elephants. As a rule, both the male and the female of the African elephant have tusks, but only the Indian male has them. The tusks of the African elephant are larger than those of the Indian. The ears of the African elephant are also larger. The elephant in Africa has two knobs at the end of its trunk, but the Indian has only one. The elephants from Africa are darker than those from Asia. Even the texture of skin of the two animals is different, for that of the Indian elephant is not as rough as that of the African.

2   An exercise such as the following, in which the child's rate during the

first two minutes is checked, is valuable in stimulating him to begin reading promptly and to read at his maximum rate. The figure at the beginning of each line indicates the cumulative number of words that the child has read by the end of the line, not including the title. It should be explained that the pupils do not need to read the figures. The teacher may wish to tell the class what the numbers represent. The beginning or all of a selection like the following may be read by the pupils. If only part of a story is included in the exercises, the teacher should tell the pupils how it ends.

Directions: The following exercise is to help you get started reading rapidly when the material is easy for you and when all you need to know is the general idea of what you are reading. When you are told to begin, read as rapidly as you can while still getting the general idea of what you are reading. At the end of two minutes you will be asked to stop. As soon as you hear the word *stop,* draw a circle around the last word you read. Then finish the story and answer the questions given at the end of the story.

Dismayed Hanna Witch[1]

6	Hanna Witch was busy polishing the
14	cobwebs on the ceiling of her dungeon. Her
21	thoughts were not on the cobwebs, however,
28	because she had more important things to
35	think about. "Halloween is just around the
44	corner, and I have no idea how I'm going
52	to scare the kids," she thought. "Last year
61	I did myself over, but instead of scaring the
67	kids they didn't even notice me."
74	Hanna climbed down from her stool and
82	walked across the dirty castle floor to her
90	iron kettle. "I must come up with something
98	different this year," she said deep in thought.
105	Then staring into the kettle, she suddenly
109	hit upon an idea. . . .

Developing Skill in Reading at a Moderately Rapid Rate

In order to develop skill in reading moderately easy material with the purpose of finding the main ideas, as well as numerous details, activities such as the following may prove helpful:

1. Discussing in what situations moderately fast reading should take place.
2. Identifying situations in which reading of this type is appropriate.
3. Getting much practice in reading this type of material.

[1] Beverly Bundy, "Dismayed Hanna Witch," *Instructor,* vol. 82, no. 2 (October 1972), p. 113.

4. Getting practice in selecting the main ideas and some supporting details rapidly.

5. Being timed or timing oneself while reading.

6. Reading a page of a book to find the words that complete sentences written on the chalkboard or on a sheet of paper.

7. Reading a paragraph in which one or two words do not fit the meaning of one or more sentences. When these words are located, the children should circle each incorrect word and write a more suitable word in the margin.

8. Telling for which of a series of listed purposes one would ordinarily engage in moderately fast reading. The list might be similar to this:
   a. Reading to get the general idea of living conditions in the South during the last year of the Civil War.
   b. Looking for a word in the dictionary.
   c. Reading a report in the society column of a newspaper to find out where a certain party was held.
   d. Studying in a science book about how heat travels in order to be able to draw a series of pictures for an accordionlike folder that would illustrate conduction, radiation, and convection.

9. Using handmade or commercially produced tachistoscopic devices that are being operated at a moderately fast speed.

10. Answering questions that the teacher asks about something read to or by the pupils that can be answered in phrases. For example, the question might be: "Why did Snipp, Snapp, and Snurr want to find work?" The pupils could choose the correct phrase from a list such as this and read it out loud: a. "to go to the show," b. "to buy a present," c. "to buy a dog."

11. Reading a list of words in which some letters have been omitted, such as: a. *Ch ist s,* b. *sc ool,* c. *t ch r.* The teacher could explain to the pupils the relation between this exercise and the fact that it is not necessary for effective readers to look at every letter of a word when reading some types of materials.

Practice Exercise

Stories are well adapted for use as exercises—for example, the following— in fairly rapid reading of rather easy material. The story should be one that the children do not already know.

Directions: Read as rapidly as you can the story of *The Shoemaker and the Elves* so as to be able to answer fairly easy questions that you will be asked on it. Your teacher will time you while you are reading the story.

Questions on the story (these questions are to be answered in as few words as possible):

1. How many pairs of shoes did the shoemaker find the morning after the night when he had cut out leather for just one pair of shoes? ———

2. Why did the shoemaker and his wife decide to sit up one night shortly before Christmas? —————————

3. Where in the room were the shoemaker and his wife hiding the evening when they sat up? —————————

4. How many elves came to do the work for the shoemaker? ———

5. What did the shoemaker and his wife do to show their gratitude to their elves? —————————

6. How did the elves like their presents? —————————

Developing Skill in Reading at a Relatively Slow Rate

Many elementary-school children, especially in the intermediate grades, need help in reading for study purposes. Often they also need to learn how to adjust their reading rate for directions which they are asked to follow. Although the rate of reading for such purposes is necessarily relatively slow, pupils should be helped to read as rapidly as possible to attain their objectives. Many can profit from taking part in activities such as the following:

1. Discussing in what situations slower reading is called for.
2. Identifying situations in which slower reading should take place.
3. Reading, under timed conditions, materials that require careful understanding of what is read.
4. Finding quickly a statement that proves or disproves a given statement.
5. Selecting all points that support a stated main topic.
6. Outlining a selection that has been read.
7. Finding a word or group of words that expresses a detail stated by the teacher.
8. Repeating directions that have been exposed for a relatively long time.
9. Reading, under timed conditions, a difficult work-type selection on which detailed questions are later to be answered.
10. Reading a selection to determine whether the writer is sympathetic or unsympathetic toward a particular cause or person.
11. Reading a selection in order to find a generalization developed in the writing.
12. Reading a selection in order to answer a thought question on it.
13. Reading a selection in order to report on it.
14. Reading literary material in order to find points particularly interesting to the reader.
15. Answering questions on the details of an arithmetic problem.
16. Arranging in correct sequence the details of a story that have been listed out of order.
17. Contrasting an editorial with an objectively written news article.
18. Memorizing a significant line or longer part of a paragraph.

READING LESSONS AND THE DEVELOPMENT OF APPROPRIATE RATES

The teacher of a class using basal textbooks has many opportunities to help pupils develop appropriate rates of reading through the use of these books. Excellent suggestions are given in the guidebooks for teachers that accompany them. A few ways in which textbook stories can be used for the improvement of reading rates are indicated below in connection with two selections, one from a reader on the low primary-grade reading level and the other on a more advanced level that is representative of a book suited chiefly for boys and girls in the upper elementary school.

Improving Reading Rates at the Lower Primary-grade Reading Level

Although much less emphasis should generally be placed on speed of reading in the primary grades than in later grades, some attention should nevertheless be paid to rates of reading even in early stages of reading instruction.

The story chosen for illustrations here is the well-known one of *The Lion and the Mouse*[2] as retold by Betty Modaressi. In connection with this story the teacher can use techniques such as those suggested below which will help pupils read some parts rapidly, some with moderate speed, and others slowly, with the rate depending on the purpose to be accomplished by the reading.

1. After the "new word" *lion* has been presented, the teacher may ask the pupils to glance at page 183 to see how quickly they can locate places where the word is found.
2. The teacher may tell the class to read pages 183 and 184 to find out what the little mouse said when the lion threatened to eat him.
3. After the boys and girls have read page 185, they may be asked to find the exact words that the mouse said which made the lion decide not to eat him.
4. The pupils can be asked to read page 186 carefully in order to be able to tell in their own words exactly what happened to the lion one day when he was looking for food.
5. Before the pupils read pages 187 to 189, as the teacher refers them to questions such as the following written on the chalkboard, he may tell them to read those pages as rapidly as they can while still reading them carefully enough to find the answers to the questions:
    + What did the lion do when night came?
    + Why did the little animals not want to help the lion?
    + Why did the little mouse help the lion?
    + How did the mouse help the lion?

[2] Leo Fay, Ramon Ross, and Margaret LaPray, *Red Rock Ranch,* The Young America Basic Reading Program, Level 6 (Chicago: Lyons & Carnahan, 1974), pp. 183–189.

The following are suggestions for additional group activities that involve reading at various rates:

1. The teacher can place on a library table other stories about animals that he thinks the boys and girls will enjoy reading. Time can then be provided for the pupils to skim these stories to decide which each would like to read.

2. If the pupils decide to dramatize the story *The Lion and the Mouse* they may choose the main events that should be included in their presentation. First they may dictate, as the teacher writes on the chalkboard, the points they remember that should be included in the play. Then they may reread the story rapidly to see if they have omitted any.

3. The group may decide to make a movie of the story. After the teacher, at the dictation of the pupils, has noted on the chalkboard the pictures the boys and girls think should be included, they can skim the story to find out whether they have omitted any that should be added.

Improving Reading Rates at the Intermediate-grade Reading Level

In order to teach intermediate grade pupils to note details, the following procedure may be helpful. One teacher who taught lessons of this type, on an average of about one a week, based them on the selections within the basal reading textbooks. The first time that the reading period was devoted to work like this the boys and girls discussed some ways in which they could read at the optimum rates materials that were fairly easy for them when they wished to note rather carefully quite a number of details. Pertinent points that could be included in such a discussion include:

1. Need for concentration.
2. Suitable posture.
3. Reading as fast as possible while maintaining or increasing in ability to comprehend at the desired level.
4. Timing oneself while reading.
5. Reading a great deal.

In later lessons reference can again be made to these points and further suggestions can be given for making effective use of them.

A Suggested Teaching Plan

In order to make clear how a lesson like this can be taught in such a way as to test the boys and girls on rate and comprehension in reading material of the type indicated for a specified purpose, a copy of a plan that could be used for teaching the story *The Eagle and the Boy*, in *Joys and Journeys*,[3]

[3] Marjorie S. Johnson, Roy A. Kress, John D. McNeil, and Pose Lamb, *Joys and Journeys, The READ Series,* Level J (New York: The American Book Company, 1972), pp. 298–305.

(pages 298–305) is described here. It is followed by further explanation of the plan.

The plan for the story *The Eagle and the Boy* for a silent reading test lesson should not be followed rigidly. Instead, whatever procedure is followed for this or any other story should be determined by the needs of the pupils. This plan is merely to serve as a sample of one way in which a story could be used to help children test themselves and improve in ability to read at an appropriate rate rather easy story material, with the aim of remembering details.

I. *Topic:* Silent reading of *The Eagle and the Boy.*

II. *Pupils' Aims:*

    A. To test our rate in reading a story such as *The Eagle and the Boy* when wanting to remember details.

    B. To get practice in improving our rate of reading easy material, while at the same time reading with understanding.

    C. To find out how an eagle returned the kindness that had been shown to him.

III. *Materials:*

    A. Materials on the chalkboard

       1. Words for pronounciation: *Waukewa, salmon, precipice*

       2. Sentences for study of meaning:

         a. He saw the young bird *quivering with pain.*

         b. With pity in his eyes, he stooped over the *exhausted* eaglet.

         c. His father, a stern *warrior,* laughed and called him "little squaw-heart."

       3. Directions:

         a. Read from the beginning of the story on page 298 to the bottom of page 302.

         b. Record the rate.

         c. Answer the questions.

         d. If you have time, finish the story.

       4. Reading rates for a 1,000-word passage. (The first figure below, *333,* is the rate per minute of an individual completing the selection in three minutes; the last figure, *83,* is the rate per minute of one finishing it in twelve minutes. The rates are recorded for checking the speed every quarter of a minute; for example, *308* is the rate of a pupil reading the selection in $3\frac{1}{4}$ minutes, while *286* is the rate of an individual reading it in $3\frac{1}{2}$ minutes. It is suggested that the teacher, beginning to erase when the class has read for three minutes, continue erasing a number every quarter of a minute.)

333	200	143	111	91
308	190	138	108	89
286	182	133	105	87
267	172	129	103	85
250	167	125	100	83
235	160	121	98	
222	154	118	95	
211	148	114	93	

B. Copies of the textbook *Joys and Journeys.*

C. Books dealing with Indian and with animal stories similar in theme to *The Eagle and the Boy.*

D. Paper and pencil.

E. Individual graphs (*see* illustration).

My Progress in Reading Tests

1. 2. 3. 4. 5. 6. 7. 8. 9. 10. 11. 12. 13. 14. 15.

10.
9.
8.
7.
6.
5.
4.
3.
2.
1.
0.

Number Right

Test Number	Number Right	Rate
1.	_____	_____
2.	_____	_____
3.	_____	_____
4.	_____	_____
5.	_____	_____
6.	_____	_____
7.	_____	_____
8.	_____	_____
9.	_____	_____
10.	_____	_____
11.	_____	_____
12.	_____	_____
13.	_____	_____
14.	_____	_____
15.	_____	_____

F. Duplicated tests questions:

Silent Reading Test on *The Eagle and the Boy.*
Directions: After you have read from page 298 to the bottom of page 302, place numbers from one to ten on the slip of paper you have been given. After each number write the letter found to the left of the word or groups of words in parentheses that will make the corresponding sentence correct.

1. One day when Waukewa went (a. fishing, b. hunting, c. out walking), he found a young eaglet.

2. The eaglet had a broken (a. wing, b. leg, c. claw).

3. Waukewa went slowly to his father's lodge, carrying the injured eaglet in (a. a basket, b. his arms, c. his jacket).

4. Waukewa's mother was (a. pleased, b. angry, c. surprised) when she saw how gently her son was treating the eaglet.

5. It was (a. two months, b. six weeks, c. one month) before the young eagle had fully recovered.

6. So that the eagle could not follow Waukewa back to the lodge on the day when he gave him his freedom, the boy hid (a. in a hollow tree, b. in the bushes, c. in a wigwam near his home).

7. The Indians fished for salmon and trout with (a. a net, b. a fish trap, c. a spear).

8. During the winter months the Indians had been eating (a. dried meats, b. fresh venison, c. fresh moose meat).

9. Very early in the morning of a clear (a. April, b. May, c. June) day, Waukewa set out to catch salmon and trout.

10. Waukewa did not notice when the canoe began to glide more swiftly among the rocks because (a. he was thinking of the eagle that he had helped, b. he was absorbed in his fishing, c. he was watching the beauty of the sunrise).

IV. *Procedure:*

A. Introduction:

1. Introduction to the story.

   Brief discussion of incidents pupils or teacher know of animals who have rewarded humans for kindness shown to them.

2. Statement by the teacher of third aim listed above under *Pupils' Aims (see II-C).*

3. Statement by the teacher of the first two aims listed above under *Pupils' Aims (see II-A* and *B).*

B. Word study:

1. Pronunciation of words *(see III-A-1 above).*

   a. Presentation through these methods: phonics, syllabication, sight-word method.

   b. Practice on pronunciation.

2. Study of meaning of the words written in italics in sentences under Materials, through study of context clues and explanations by the pupils and/or teacher *(see III-A-2)*.

C. Directions for taking the test:

1. Reference is made to the directions *(see III-A-3 above)*.

2. Pupils place a marker between pages 302 and 303 and note that they are to stop reading for the test at the bottom of page 302.

D. Taking the test:

1. Reading from page 298 to the bottom of page 302, while the teacher erases rates on the chalkboard every quarter of a minute, beginning with three minutes and ending with twelve *(see IIIA-4)*.

2. Recording the time.

3. Answering the questions.

4. Doing the additional work, namely reading the rest of the story, silently, if time permits.

E. Correcting papers. Pupils check their papers as the teacher does the following:

1. Gives the number of the sentence.

2. Gives the letter preceding the word or group of words that forms the correct answer.

3. Reads the sentence, supplying the correct answer.

F. Recording marks on individual graphs, showing rate and comprehension *(see III-E)*.

G. Report on pages 303–305 by a pupil who has finished the story or by the teacher, or provisions made for silent reading of those pages at a later time by those pupils who have not completed the story.

H. Forward look:

1. Discussion of plans for further progress in development of appropriate reading rates.

2. Reference to books on library table *(see III-C above)*.

Explanation of the Teaching Plan

Following is further explanation of the plan outlined for teaching *The Eagle and the Boy* to indicate how a similar procedure could be used with other reading selections.

1. Length of the selection tested   The test, both for rate and comprehension, is only one part of the selection chosen for the teaching plan. A reason for limiting a test to only part of a story is to make the selection for testing no longer than, hopefully, every child can read during the allotted time. The number of words that a teacher will want to include in the part tested will vary with the selection and with the length of the class period. In some instances the teacher may wish to include the whole story, if it is not very long. On the other hand, he may not want to exclude a story containing only about 800 words. If a much shorter number of words is chosen for the selection on which the class is to be tested, it may be difficult to select enough significant points for testing comprehension.

In estimating the number of words for the selection, the following procedure was used: The average number of words in the first ten lines of the story was found to be 9.9 words. If, as in this case, a selection of about 1,000 words is decided on, the number of lines on which the test should be given could be found by dividing 1,000 by 9.9 which is 101. In counting the lines, it is recommended that at times part of a line be counted and at other times a fractional part not be counted, so as to keep the estimate of words approximately correct. When the entire selection is to be used for the test, the average number of words per line can be multiplied by the number of lines to obtain the approximate number of words in the selection.

2. Computation of rate   The rates listed under *Materials* in this plan are the rates per minute for a 1,000-word selection, beginning with three minutes and extending through twelve, exact to the quarter of a minute. The count was begun with three minutes, because among pupils for whom this story is appropriate for reading in the way suggested, there are probably only a few who would read it at more than 333 words per minute. The counting was discontinued after twelve minutes because it would seem that only a very few, if any, of the pupils would be likely to read the selection for the purpose indicated at a rate slower than 83 words per minute. If it takes a pupil longer than this or if he finishes reading in less than three minutes, the teacher should take note of that fact.

In the table given under *Materials* as explained on page 239, the first entry, 333, is obtained by dividing 1,000 by 3. Thus, the rate is secured for a person who requires only three minutes to read the selection. The next entry, *308,* is the quotient when dividing 1,000 words by $3\frac{1}{4}$, and so on.

If the teacher writes on the chalkboard before class a rate index similar to the one given in the teaching plan, he would erase a figure every quarter of a minute. He would begin erasing when the pupils had read for three minutes, starting with the first entry in the column farthest to the left and continuing down that column and then proceeding similarly with the next column. The boys and girls should be given the instruction that as soon as they have completed the required reading, they should look at the chalkboard and copy the highest remaining figure as their reading rate. If anyone finishes the selection in less than three minutes, the starting time for the recording of rate, he may be asked to write on his paper a plus sign after the number of words per minute computed for three minutes. In this instance he would then write *333+.* If anyone has not completed the assigned part at the end of twelve minutes, he could be instructed to place a minus sign to the right of the figure he copies, in this case writing *83—.*

3. The test   If a test of this type is to be given more than once, and if the results are to be compared from one test to another, as suggested earlier, it is desirable to keep the questions on all the tests of the same type. Multiple-choice questions were selected for this plan because they are easier to check than completion statements and because they usually form a more reliable test than a small number of true-false statements. To be comparable, the number of choices provided in each multiple-choice statement should be kept the same. Ten was chosen for the number of questions because ten is so small a number that many significant questions can quite easily be asked on a selection. For purposes of comparison of results, it is recommended that the number be kept constant from test to test.

4. Keeping a record   Records could be kept by each pupil on a graph or table, such as those illustrated on page 239. These records should not be posted, for each pupil should be competing with himself, not with others. Frequent conferences between the teacher and each pupil should be held so that the pupil can get aid in interpreting the results of his efforts and so that he can receive suggestions for further improvement. The pupil should recognize the fact that a slight fluctuation in the score for rate is not necessarily significant, because of the inaccuracy of the tests and the fact that the rate of learning varies with circumstances.

5. Additional work   If the test is on only part of the selection, pupils should be encouraged to finish the story for themselves, or the teacher or a pupil may tell the ending.

Other types of additional work for those pupils finishing earlier may be:

1. checking, by rereading parts of the selection, on any question in the test about which the pupil was not certain,
2. reading in a "library book" that the pupil already has at his desk.

6. Supplementary reading   If the teacher wishes to encourage children to read more on a topic related to the theme of the selection studied, he should have some additional books at hand. Telling the boys and girls briefly about the books and making provisions for their withdrawal can help stimulate more reading. Sometimes reference can be made to books in the library. If the books are not at the time in the classroom, it is recommended that the titles and authors be written on the chalkboard or bulletin board so that pupils will not forget the names by the time they go to the library.

For Further Study

Barbe, Walter B., ed., *Teaching Reading: Selected Materials,* "Are Fast Readers the Best Readers?" by J. Harlan Shores (New York: Oxford University Press, 1965), pp. 249–258.

Berger, Allen, ed., *Speed Reading: An Annotated Bibliography* (Newark, Del.: International Reading Association, 1970).

Bond, Guy L., and Miles A. Tinker, *Reading Difficulties: Their Diagnosis and Correction* (New York: Appleton-Century-Crofts, 1967), Ch. 16, "Improving Rate and Comprehension."

Dechant, Emerald V., *Improving the Teaching of Reading,* 2nd ed. (Englewood Cliffs, N.J.: Prentice-Hall, Inc., 1970), Ch. 9, "Introducing the Elementary Reading Program," pp. 264–278.

Durkin, Dolores, *Teaching Them to Read* (Boston: Allyn and Bacon, Inc., 1970), Ch. 8, "Oral and Silent Reading."

Fry, Edward, *Reading Instruction for Classroom and Clinic* (New York: McGraw-Hill Book Company, 1972), Ch. 14, "Vision."

Sebesta, Sam Leaton, and Carl J. Wallen, eds., *The First R: Readings on Teaching Reading* (Chicago: Science Research Associates, 1972), "Devices to Improve Speed of Reading," by Miles A. Tinker, pp. 209–224.

Staiger, Ralph, and David A. Sohn, eds., *New Directions in Reading* (New York: Bantam Books, 1967), Ch. VII, "The Speed Reading Controversy" by Robert Hermann.

Stauffer, Russell G., *Directing Reading Maturity as a Cognitive Process* (New York: Harper & Row, 1969), Ch. 10, Versatility in Reading."

Tinker, Miles A., and Constance M. McCullough, *Teaching Elementary Reading* (New York: Appleton-Century-Crofts, 1968). Ch. 12, "Speed of Reading," pp. 237–257.

Witty, Paul A., "Rate of Reading: A Crucial Issue," *Journal of Reading,* vol. 13, (November 1969), pp. 102–106.

Questions and Comments for Thought and Discussion

1. Today there are numerous commercial devices on the market that mechanize the act of reading in some fashion or other. In advertisements of some of these materials it is implied, if not stated, that speed of reading is our primary goal in teaching reading. Is this true? What are the reasons for your stand?

2. A case is made by some people that rate and comprehension are positively related and that comprehension increases with increase of speed in reading. Do you agree? What evidence can you give to support your position?

3. Skimming is a reading technique for securing rapidly the more important information in a selection in order to get a fairly complete idea of the content. If you think that you know how to skim, how would you describe the process as you see it? If you do not skim, can you state why you do not engage in this type of reading?

4. Can you defend the following statement? How?

> The pupil who tends to read all material at approximately the same rate, as many do, is a poor reader. A goodly number of readers at all educational levels have not acquired the ability to adjust their speed of reading appropriately.

5. From a recent research study, pronounced contrasts become evident when the most rapid readers are compared with the slowest. It would

appear that a different set of abilities must be acquired in order to improve the speed of an already fast reader from those needed to improve the speed of a slow reader. Imagine you are a teacher and you have identified a very rapid reader in your class, as well as a very slow reader. How might you go about trying to help improve their rates of reading?

6. In properly conceived and executed classroom programs to speed up reading, few pupils will achieve relatively small gains, many will make moderate gains, and a few will make relatively great gains in rate of reading. An occasional pupil will achieve exceptional improvement. The degree to which the gains are maintained or to which they are transferred to reading work-type of material is not well established. What suggestions do you have for maintenance and for transfer?

7. The term *flexibility* as applied to reading rate has been interpreted in a number of ways, and there still is some ambiguity surrounding the term—what it is, how it may be measured, and how it may be developed. Writers in the field have observed that flexibility does not just "happen" but is a composite of many factors that are trained, taught, and encouraged through an individual's reading career. What are some of these factors?

8. It has been asserted that a flexible reader selects the speed best suited to his purpose and to the reading material. Sometimes teachers direct students to vary their rate, shifting to a higher or lower rate when encountering easier or more difficult ideas or when comprehension needs differ. Does saying, "speed up," "slow down," "shift gears" really accomplish much? How would you go about achieving your ends as a teacher?

Outline for Chapter 8A

LOCATING INFORMATION AND USING IT

Basic Locational Skills
    Skill in Finding Words Arranged in Alphabetical Order
    Skill in Finding a Specified Page
    Skill in Finding an Entry Word
    Skill in Deciding on Key Words
    Knowledge of Content of Reference Books
    Interpreting Information
    Making Use of Information
Ability to Find Information in Various Types of Books
    Ability to Find Information in Nonreference Books
    Ability to Use the Dictionary
      Dictionaries for the Elementary School
      Dictionary Skills
    Ability to Use Reference Books Other than the Dictionary
Ability to Locate Materials in the Library
    Using the Card Catalog
    Finding Books on Shelves
    Using Indexes to Magazines
    Locating Other Materials in the Library
Principles Underlying the Teaching of Locational Skills

CHAPTER 8A

Locating Information and Using It

The development of the ability to locate information in printed sources has become an increasingly important concern of the school. In earlier days, pupils used relatively few books and were usually directed to the exact locations of the material to be studied. In our day of abundant newspapers, magazines, encyclopedias, dictionaries, almanacs, and other kinds of printed matter, skill in finding information is becoming ever more imperative. The increasing complexity of modern life has brought this new need into focus.

Unfortunately, many children as well as adults, including college graduates, have only limited skill in locating information. For this reason, many people simply make no effort to look for information which they need or desire. Often people who have access to dictionaries and who want to know the meaning of a word do not look it up because they have difficulty in making efficient use of this indispensable reference aid.

Happily, teachers are beginning to meet the challenge presented by changing needs, by making a persistent effort to help boys and girls receive the needed information and practice in locating materials economically and efficiently and in making effective use of them. Almost all professional books on the teaching of reading stress the importance of these skills and make suggestions for their development. Basal textbook series for boys and girls provide for growth in these skills, and the teachers' guidebooks which accompany the children's books abound in excellent recommendations as to how these skills can be developed. Many of the workbooks provide helpful exercises.

BASIC LOCATIONAL SKILLS

Basic to effective use of reading materials from various sources are skill in:

1. Finding words arranged in alphabetical order.
2. Finding a specified page quickly.
3. Finding an entry word.
4. Deciding on key words.
5. Knowing the types of content found in reference books.
6. Interpreting information.
7. Making use of information.

Skill in Finding Words Arranged in Alphabetical Order

Skill in finding words arranged in alphabetical order is needed in many types of situations, as in locating information in the index of a book, in the card catalogue, in the dictionary, in an encyclopedia, and in other reference books. Unfortunately, elementary-school teachers have often wrongly assumed that the pupil has the following skills or learnings essential to locating words arranged in alphabetical order.

1. Knowledge of the sequence of letters in the alphabet.
2. Ability to tell which letter precedes and which follows another without repeating part of the alphabet either orally or silently.
3. Instant knowledge of the part of the alphabet—the first, middle, or last —in which a letter occurs.
4. Knowledge of the fact that in indexes, dictionaries, and card catalogues the words are arranged in alphabetical order.
5. Understanding of and skill in arranging words in alphabetical order when the first letter of each word is different.
6. Understanding of and skill in arranging words in alphabetical order when the first letters of the words are alike but the second different.
7. Understanding of and skill in arranging words in alphabetical order when the first two or more letters of the words are alike but subsequent letters are different.
8. Knowledge of how to arrange words in alphabetical order when problems like these and others exist:

a. words beginning with the syllable *Mc* or *Mac;*
b. titles beginning with *the, a,* or *an;*
c. words like *grand* and *grandmother,* in which all the letters of one word are given in the same sequence in the first part of a second word;
d. names of persons, if both the first and the last names are given.

Skill in Finding a Specified Page

Another skill basic to many types of reading is finding a given page in a book or magazine quickly. Many pupils need to be taught that there are quicker ways of finding a page than to start at the beginning of the book and leaf through it until they come to the page they want. They also need practice in opening a book in the vicinity of the page they want. Development of this skill should be encouraged, as a rule, early in the first grade. Much of the practice in finding a specified page can be provided in the ongoing instructional program without the use of practice exercises.

Skill in Finding an Entry Word

Skill in finding an entry word is needed in using a dictionary, an encyclopedia, and other reference books. In order to find an entry word quickly, pupils should know the following facts about guide words:

1. In dictionaries, guide words are listed on each page of the book proper, usually in the columns at the top of the page.
2. These words indicate the first and the last entry words listed on a given page or, in the case of some dictionaries, on two facing pages.
3. By glancing at the guide words in a dictionary the reader can tell whether the word for which he is looking is on that page or, in some dictionaries, on one of the two facing pages.
4. Similar provisions are made in some of the other reference books, so that the reader can quickly ascertain whether the topic for which he is looking belongs between the first and last topics discussed on a given page.

It is not enough, however, for children to know what guide words are and where they are found. They should also develop skill in using guide words to locate entries quickly.

Skill in Deciding on Key Words

Another locational skill needed is that of knowing under what word to look for the desired information. This skill is often referred to as the ability to decide on key words. Lack of it causes much waste of time and frequently is the reason why reference books are not used more. Skill can be developed step by step through a gradation of difficulties, beginning with work on finding a topic in an index or reference book when the topic is worded in the same manner as the entry in the book. Later, pupils should be given practice in deciding which one of a variety of words is the most likely entry under which the needed information would be found. Use of subtopics in indexes should also be taught as an aid in finding key words.

Knowledge of Content of Reference Books

Many pupils need guidance in learning what type of information is contained in different kinds of books and magazines. For example, a pupil will need to learn what types of information to look for in geography books, history books, science books, and health books. He will also need to learn what types of information he can expect to find in various encyclopedias for children, in the *World Almanac,* in an atlas, in a dictionary, and in other reference books. As he develops skill in the use of these books, he will continue to discover new types of information. He cannot learn about them all at once. In the case of the dictionary, for example, he will usually first learn that it yields the meanings of words. Only later will he discover that he can find the pronunciation of words and, still later, that it contains information about syllabication and other matters.

Interpreting Information

After the reader has located information, he must be able to interpret it. Sometimes interpretation is an easy process, requiring neither special effort nor skill. At other times particular alertness is needed.

Pupils need to develop skill in learning to interpret the abbreviations given in reference material. Knowledge of many abbreviations is essential to effective reading of reference books. Pupils should know where to look for a key to the abbreviations and how to apply the information given in the key.

Common to several types of reference materials are the references to additional material designated by *see* or *see also.* The boys and girls need to know before they leave the elementary school what is meant by these directions, as well as how to use them. It is also important for them to know when they should follow the *see* or *see also* direction. Speed in locating the cross reference and in deciding whether it contributes to the topic also needs to be developed.

Another problem in the use of reference materials is selecting the points that have bearing on the purpose that the reader has in mind. How to interpret charts, tables, maps, graphs, and diagrams given in reference books is only part of the task. The pupil needs to know how to find the information given in words, groups of words, sentences, and paragraphs speedily and correctly.

Making Use of Information

After the reader has found and interpreted the information he wants, he may use it for a variety of purposes. He may compare what he has learned in one reference with what he has read in another or with what he already knows. He may take notes on it, write a summary, or make an outline in order either better to remember the data himself or to assist him as he tries to impart the information to others through informal conversation, reports, panel discussions, or illustrations. Sometimes he may compile a bibliography for his own or others' use. How to take notes, make summaries and outlines, and perform some of the other activities for purposes of retention and comprehension are discussed in other parts of this book.

ABILITY TO FIND INFORMATION IN VARIOUS TYPES OF BOOKS

The types of books in which boys and girls should learn to find information with efficiency can be classified under three categories: (1.) nonreference books, (2.) the dictionary, (3.) reference books other than the dictionary.

Ability to Find Information in Nonreference Books

Elementary-school children should learn to use the following parts of books or features in books effectively in order to locate information quickly in their textbooks and in general books:

1. The preface.
2. The introduction.
3. The table of contents.
4. Lists of maps and illustrations.
5. Chapter headings, center headings, and side headings.
6. The glossary.
7. The index.

Pupils should know where each of these parts is found, what its function is, and how to make effective use of it. Furthermore, the teacher should try to develop in them the desire to make effective use of the several parts.

The Preface

The boys and girls should learn the following facts about the preface:

1. It is found in the front part of the book.
2. It is written either by the author or the editor of the book.
3. It tells the author's purpose in writing the book and often indicates any special features of the book.
4. It is useful in indicating whether a given topic or question is likely to be treated in the book.

The Introduction

If the introduction is studied, the pupils should know that the terms *introduction* and *preface* are sometimes used interchangeably. They should learn that some books contain both a preface and an introduction. As they examine these two parts of a book, they should know that, although a study of the introduction may help them to decide whether information that they want is given in the book, its primary purpose is not to serve as a locational aid.

The Table of Contents

The boys and girls can begin using the table of contents almost as soon as they start reading books. When a simple table of contents is given, as in many primers, the pupil can find the "new story" in the table of contents with the help of the teacher. Reference can also be made to the page. If the pupil cannot read the page number by himself, the teacher may say, pointing to the page: "This number *10* tells us that our story begins on page 10." Then he can help the pupils find the page.

Somewhere in the elementary school the boys and girls should learn that the table of contents, in many instances, not only indicates the contents but also the plan of organization of the book, providing it is divided into various units or sections with subheadings. They should acquire familiarity with some of the possible formats in which tables of contents can be written, through examination and explanation.

Lists of Maps and Illustrations

Pupils should acquire the following learnings about maps and illustrations:

1. A list of maps and illustrations, when included in a book, may be found either in the front or back part of the book.
2. Textbooks in social studies, science, and health are much more likely to provide a list of maps or illustrations than general books.
3. The list of maps and illustrations gives the captions used with the maps and illustrations and also the page on which they are found.

Chapter Headings, Center Headings, and Sideheadings

Pupils should be taught the value of various kinds of headings in locating material and should be given practice in their use. As soon as side and center headings are provided in the textbooks that pupils read or in the reference books they use, simple help should be given in making effective use of these aids as a means of locating information.

The Glossary

If some of the books the pupils are using contain a glossary, they should note that it is found in the back part of the book and that special terms and words used in the book are explained in this section. They should notice that the words are listed alphabetically and that usually a pronunciation key is provided.

The Index

The following are some of the points that pupils should learn about the index of a book:

1. The index is in the back part of the book.
2. The topics are arranged alphabetically, not in order of appearance in the book, as in a table of contents.
3. In many books subtopics are given under the main entries.

The following skills should be developed:

1. Deciding under what entry information on a given topic or question is likely to be given.
2. Speed in finding an entry.
3. Locating a topic when it appears as a subtopic in the index.
4. Ability to turn quickly to the pages on which the information, according to the index, is given.
5. Ability to find quickly the lines on a page that give the information on the desired topic.

Ability to Use the Dictionary

One of the outstanding developments in materials of instruction for the elementary school in recent years has been the dictionary for children. Before that, if boys and girls used dictionaries, they had to use those planned for adults. Pupils in the early part of this century often had access only to a large, unabridged dictionary or to one or two less complete ones that were also compiled for adults. In some schools children in the intermediate grades were urged or required to have their own abridged dictionary. Because of the price and the convenience of handling, many children brought to school pocket-sized dictionaries that in many respects were more difficult to understand than the unabridged dictionaries. Those who thought that these abbreviated dictionaries would be suitable for children were wrong, for often only one short line was allowed per entry. Obviously there was little chance for explanation when no more space than this was devoted to a word. At times the entry word was defined by a synonym even more difficult for the child to understand than the word he had looked up.

Dictionaries for the Elementary School

In addition to the picture dictionaries to which reference is made in Chapter 5B, "Developing Skill in Word Recognition," (*see* page 153) the following dictionaries are commonly used in the elementary school:

Giant Golden Illustrated Dictionary, Stuart A. Courtis and Garnette Watters, eds. (Golden Press, Inc.), six volumes.
The Holt Basic Dictionary of American English (Holt, Rinehart and Winston, Inc.).
The Holt Intermediate Dictionary of American English (Holt, Rinehart and Winston, Inc.).
Illustrated Golden Dictionary for Young Readers, Stuart A. Courtis and Garnett Watters, eds. (Golden Press, Inc.), rev. ed.
Thorndike-Barnhart Beginning Dictionary, Edward L. Thorndike and Clarence L. Barnhart, eds. (Scott, Foresman and Company).
Thorndike-Barnhart Junior Dictionary, Edward L. Thorndike and Clarence L. Barnhart, eds. (Scott, Foresman and Company).
Webster's A Dictionary for Boys and Girls (American Book Company).
Webster's Elementary Dictionary (American Book Company).
The Winston Dictionary for Schools, Thomas K. Brown and Wiliam D. Lewis, eds. (Holt, Rinehart and Winston, Inc.).
The World Book Dictionary, Clarence Barnhart, ed. (Field Enterprises Educational Corporation), two volumes.

Dictionary Skills

The skills to be learned in using a dictionary even in the elementary school are so complex that the teacher should have clearly in mind the subskills about which he should give information to the boys and girls and for which he should provide meaningful practice. Zintz[1] gives a helpful listing (*see* Table 8.1). A much less detailed summary, organized in a slightly different manner, is the following listing of skills:

1. Ability to locate a word quickly.
2. Ability to learn the pronunciation of a word.

[1] Miles V. Zintz, *The Reading Process: The Teacher and the Learner* (Dubuque, Iowa: Wm. C. Brown Company Publishers, 1970), p. 169.

TABLE 8.1   Location, pronunciation, and meaning skills needed by boys and girls in the elementary school in the use of the dictionary.

Location skills	Pronunciation Skills	Meaning Skills
1. Ability to arrange words in alphabetical order, by initial letter, by second letter, and by third or fourth letters. 2. Ability to find words quickly in an alphabetical list. 3. Ability to open the dictionary quickly to the section in which the word is to be found; to the proper fourth of the book. 4. Ability to use the two guide words at the top of the page. 5. Ability to think of the names of letters immediately preceding and immediately following the letter being located. 6. Ability to use special pronunciation-meaning sections of the dictionary as, for example, medical terms, slang expressions, musical terms, and foreign words and phrases.	1. Ability to use the pronunciation key at the bottom of each page. 2. Ability to use the full pronunciation key in the front of the dictionary. 3. Ability to use and interpret accent marks, both primary and secondary. 4. Ability to select the proper heteronyms, for example rec'ord or re/cord'; ob'ject or ob/ject'. 5. Ability to identify silent letters in words pronounced. 6. Ability to recognize differences between spellings and pronunciations (lack of phoneme-grapheme relationship). 7. Ability to use phonetic spelling for pronunciation. 8. Ability to discriminate vowel sounds. 9. Ability to use diacritical marks as an aid in pronunciation. 10. Understanding of the way syllables are marked in dictionaries. 11. Ability to identify unstressed syllables in words. 12. Arriving at pronunciation and recognizing it as correct.	1. Learning meanings of new words by reading simple definitions. 2. Using pictures and meanings in the dictionary to arrive at meanings. 3. Using an illustrative sentence to arrive at meanings. 4. Using two different meanings for the same word. 5. Ability to approximate real life sizes by using dictionary pictures and explanatory clues. 6. Ability to select the specific meaning for a given context. 7. Understanding special meanings: idioms, slang expressions, and other figures of speech 8. Use of the concept of *root word.* 9. Interpreting multiple meanings of words. 10. Ability to know when meaning has been satisfied through dictionary usage.

3. Ability to find the spelling of a word and related abilities.

    a. Spelling.

    b. Syllabication.

    c. Hyphenation.

    d. Abbreviations.

    e. Capitalization.

4. Ability to learn the meaning of a word.

5. Ability to use the parts of the dictionary preceding and following the main parts of the dictionary, both in the pupil's dictionary and in an unabridged dictionary.

Locating a word in the dictionary   In order to locate a word in the dictionary quickly, the pupil needs to know more than how to find a word in a list arranged alphabetically and how to make use of guide words. The difficulty in which one fifth-grade girl found herself illustrates the need for more information. This girl's teacher had told her pupils that the unabridged dictionary in their room contained every word in the English language. One day, while the teacher was busy with another group, this girl ran across the word *busied* in her reading and was puzzled as to the meaning of the word. Had the word been *busy* she would have recognized it in print, and had she heard the word *busied* pronounced, she would have had no difficulty with its meaning. However, when she saw the word *busied* in context, she thought it would be pronounced *bu si' ed,* giving the *s* an *s* instead of a *z* sound and the *i* a long sound. She therefore went to the big dictionary and looked for the entry *busied.* When she could not find *busied* listed as an entry word, she had no idea that she might find it under another form. Consequently, she could hardly wait until she could tell her teacher about her amazing discovery that the dictionary did not contain every word in the language. When the teacher asked her which word she did not find, she told her *busied,* pronouncing the word as *bu si' ed.*

Many boys and girls have difficulty in finding a word in a dictionary when it is not given as an entry word in the form in which they meet the word in their reading. However, teachers are increasingly trying to show pupils how inflected forms can be located in the dictionary. In some schools more emphasis is being placed on structural analysis, which serves as an aid in recognizing the inflected forms.

Learning the pronunciation   The elementary-school child should learn to find the pronunciation of a word by means of respellings and diacritical marks, as interpreted in the key to pronunciation at the bottom of the page in a dictionary. The significance of the syllabication of words and the markings of the accent should be clear to him. He should understand that if two pronunciations are given for the same word, each pronunciation is used, as, for example, in the word *record,* which as a noun has the accent on the first syllable but as a verb on the second. Furthermore, he should bear in mind that if no specification is given as to which of two pronunciations should be used under given circumstances, in most dictionaries the first of two indicated is usually the preferred one. However, it should also be made clear that often two pronunciations are equally acceptable, but since one must be written before the other, the pronunciation indicated first is not necessarily the preferred one.

Finding the spelling It is a difficult feat for many individuals, even adults, to find a word in the dictionary without being sure of the spelling. The pupil should therefore be given guidance and practice in this skill. Merely to say to a child: "Look up in the dictionary the word that you do not know how to spell," is inviting frustration. Pupils should learn how the plurals of nouns and other inflected forms are indicated. They need to know that some words pronounced alike—homonyms—have different meanings for different spellings. For spelling purposes it is also often necessary to know how words can be divided into syllables and whether they are hyphenated. Consequently, the pupil needs to know the key for the division into syllables and hyphenation. Some dictionaries show syllabication by means of a space left between syllables; others show it by a hyphen, which must not be interpreted as a sign that the word is a compound word. The symbols for hyphenation also vary. In some dictionaries the hyphen is used to show hyphenation, and in others the double hyphen, one line above the other, is used for that purpose. Often the pupils need help in finding out what the symbols in a given dictionary indicate.

Another problem in spelling deals with the abbreviation of a word, if it can be abbreviated. Boys and girls should know that the dictionary gives the abbreviations of words, and they should learn where they can be found.

By means of the dictionary the pupils in the elementary school should be able to find out whether a word is always written with a capital letter. They should know where and how dictionaries give information about capitalization.

Learning the meaning Pupils need to develop the following skills for understanding the meaning of words through the use of a dictionary:

1. They should, when the word is used in context, be able to select the meaning that fits into the setting in which it is used.

2. They should be able to make effective use of the pictorial illustrations given for some words.

3. They should be able to make effective use of the verbal illustrations given, knowing which meaning of a word a given illustration fits.

4. They should understand information given about inflected forms.

5. They should know the interpretations of the symbols for the parts of speech they have studied.

6. They should know how to make use of information given about idiomatic expressions in which some words are commonly used.

7. They should understand what is meant by synonyms and antonyms, and they should know how the dictionaries they use give this type of information.

Making use of information given in the parts that precede and follow the main part of the dictionary   If there is an unabridged dictionary in the schoolroom, the teacher in a fifth or sixth grade may wish to introduce pupils to some of the types of information given in the part preceding and following the main section of the dictionary. They will be interested to know that by turning to an unabridged dictionary they can find illustrations of flags of all the countries of the world, that the dictionary gives biographical data on important persons, and that it has a very helpful section dealing with geographical locations. Even some of the dictionaries designed for boys and girls in the elementary school contain materials of great value in the front and back portions. Familiarity with all the parts of one's own dictionary should be an objective that is accomplished some time during the elementary school.

Ability to Use Reference Books Other than the Dictionary

Encyclopedias and other suitable reference materials for boys and girls can serve at least two very important purposes: that of helping the child gain needed information and that of opening for him a source of information that can continue to serve his needs throughout life. More and more schools are ordering sets of encyclopedias as well as other reference material for the various rooms in their school system. If there are no adequate reference books in an intermediate-grade room, the teacher should discover whether some can be obtained for her classroom. However, even if the desired reference books are not available in the classroom, they may often be found either in school or in public libraries. Some boys and girls have sets of encyclopedias or other reference books at home which they should utilize.

The quality of reference materials for boys and girls in the elementary school has greatly improved. There are the well-known *Compton's Pictured Encylopedia, The World Book Encyclopedia, Junior Britannica,* and *Our Wonderful World.* All of these encyclopedias give information on persons, places, and things, as well as on important events. An encyclopedia limited in scope, but excellent, is the *Junior Book of Authors,* written on a level that many boys and girls in the intermediate grades can comprehend. It contains biographies and autobiographies of famous writers of books for children, illustrated with a picture of the writer. It also gives a list of the works of each author.

A fifteen-volume resource library designed especially for preschool and primary-grade children that is filling a decided need is *Childcraft.* The publishers are Field Enterprises Educational Corporation.

There are several other types of reference materials that boys and girls in the upper elementary school can learn to use effectively. One is the *World Almanac,* published yearly, which gives concise data, chiefly in the form of isolated facts, on a large variety of topics, such as government, sports, and industry. It is especially valuable for the statistics recorded in it. The child can find the answer to many questions of interest to him; for example: "What is the population of the United States?" or "Which is longer, the Mississippi River or the Congo River?" Parts of *Goode's School Atlas,* with its variety of types of maps, constitute an excellent supplement to maps given in geography books. Familiarity with the *Subject Index to Poetry,* if a copy of it is available, can also serve the needs of some boys and girls in the fifth and sixth grades. Many pupils in the intermediate grades would profit from an introduction to *Who's Who* and *Who's Who in America.*

In the first part of this chapter there is an enumeration of skills basic to the use of many types of reference material; for example, ability to find words when they are arranged in alphabetical order, ability to use cross references, and ability to utilize information found in reference books. All of these skills are needed for effective use of encyclopedias and other specialized reference books. In addition to these skills, pupils need the following in order to use materials of this type efficiently:

1. Knowledge of what is contained in the reference books.
2. Knowledge of the organization of the reference books.
3. Ability to decide in which reference book the desired information is likely to be found.
4. Skill in finding the information.

ABILITY TO LOCATE MATERIALS IN THE LIBRARY

In order to be able to locate materials effectively in a library or learning resource center the pupil needs to know how to use the card catalogue, how to locate books on the shelves (if the library has open shelves), and how to use sources like the *Reader's Guide to Periodical Literature.* The help given in learning how to locate books in a library should be in terms of the library to which children have access. If none is located in the community, a miniature classroom library can serve as substitute.

Using the Card Catalog

Almost all libraries have card catalogs that serve as indexes to their book collections. Pupils should know that the term *card catalog* is applied to the collections of drawers in which are filed three-by-five inch cards which give data on all the books in the library. They should learn that the cards are arranged alphabetically in the drawers and that the progression of the drawers is from the top toward the bottom drawer of one stack of drawers to the top drawer in the next stack.

In order to have skill in the use of a card catalog, boys and girls must be familiar with the common types of cards used. They should know at least three of the cards that the card catalog contains—namely, the author card, the title card, and the subject card. They also need to know that on an author card the alphabetical arrangement is according to the last name of the author, on a title card according to the first significant word of the title, and on a subject card according to the subject of the book. The pupils should also realize that if an individual knows the first and last name of the author of a book, it may be timesaving to look for the book under the author card. If the name of the author is not known but the exact title is known, it is often expedient to look for the title card. If neither the name of the author nor the exact title is known, it is usually best to look for the subject card. The children should also learn that by means of the subject card they can find out what other books are available in the library on a given subject. These statements will seem quite obvious to the college student and the young teacher, but they often need to be explained to elementary-school pupils.

Guidance should be given in observing the data found on all three types of cards. The terms *B* for *biography* and *J* for *juvenile,* if these are used, should also be explained. The pupils should learn the significance of the call number and the use they can make of it in locating a book in the library.

Finding Books on Shelves

If the library accessible to the child has open stacks, the pupils should learn something about the arrangement of books.

Most small libraries use an adaptation of the Dewey decimal system of classification. If the library has that system of classification, the pupil should learn to use it. While pupils should not be asked to memorize the categories, they should have general familiarity with the system and know where in a library they can find the classification chart. The Dewey decimal system employs the following number classifications:

000–099	General works, including bibliography and general periodicals
100–199	Philosophy, psychology, ethics
200–299	Religion, Bible, mythology
300–399	Sociology, economics, education, political science
400–499	Philology, dictionaries, grammars
500–599	Natural science, including mathematics, chemistry, physics
600–699	Applied science, including useful arts, medicine, agriculture, manufacturing
700–799	Fine arts, music, recreation
800–899	Literature
900–999	History, biography, travel

Increasingly, libraries—chiefly the larger ones—are changing from the Dewey decimal system to the Library of Congress Classification. It is recommended that in the elementary school boys and girls be introduced to the latter system only if they use a library that uses that method of classification. The A to Z classes, without subdivisions, of the Library of Congress Classification, are here reproduced:

A   General Works: Polygraphy
B   Philosophy and religion
C   History: Auxiliary Sciences
D   History: General and Old World
E-F History: America
G   Geography, Anthropology, Folklore, and so on
H   Social Sciences
J   Political Science
K   Law
L   Education
M   Music
N   Fine arts
P   Philology and Literature
Q   Science
R   Medicine
S   Agriculture, and so on
T   Technology
U   Military Science
V   Naval Science
Z   Bibliography and Library Science

Using Indexes to Magazines

The number of children's magazines of excellent quality is increasing. Children at all levels of the elementary school enjoy looking at, if not reading, magazines on their levels. As soon as they are ready for instruction in the use of a subject index guide to periodicals for children, they should be assisted in using it so their interest can be pursued systematically beyond simply perusing current issues.

Some boys and girls in the upper elementary school can be taught how to locate magazine articles by means of the *Reader's Guide to Periodical Literature.* The teacher, possibly with the help of the librarian, may decide to teach the child such facts as the following:

1. Where the *Reader's Guide to Periodical Literature* is located.
2. How often it is published.
3. Method of cumulation.
4. Type of information it contains.
5. How to locate information in it.

Pupils should also find out where a list of the magazines the library has is posted and where both the bound and unbound periodicals are kept.

Locating Other Materials in the Library

Increasingly, there will be an urgent need for boys and girls even in the elementary school to learn to locate materials other than books and magazines both in their classroom and in central libraries or learning centers. With the greater supply of films, filmstrips, slides, tapes, and records, those in charge of libraries are finding it imperative to store these aids according to a system that will facilitate their use. With growing individualization of work in many schools, and with libraries increasingly being used as learning centers, it is becoming all the more important that boys and girls know where to find these materials. The system of storage used will vary considerably from library to library. If time is to be saved and use of the materials encouraged, elementary-school pupils will need to be familiarized with whatever method of organization is used in libraries to which they have access.

Undoubtedly, in the near future guidance not only in locating materials in learning centers but also in making use of newer media will be an essential in an elementary-school program. If predictions concerning the library of the future come true, then skill in making use of audiovisual aids of many kinds and of operative systems such as storage banks and dial access will be a decided asset to learning.

PRINCIPLES UNDERLYING THE TEACHING OF LOCATIONAL SKILLS

An overriding principle that should be observed when determining procedures for helping boys and girls acquire skill in locating information and using it is that the need for learning these skills should arise, when possible, out of the daily lives of the pupils. Additional guidelines include:

1. Readiness for a locational skill facilitates learning. In part, readiness for this type of skill, as for other learnings, is a matter of maturation. However, to a considerable extent it is closely related to the experience background of the learner. Fortunately, the background of experience can be broadened, and the teacher is in a key position to help. No teacher needs to wait complacently for a child to become ready to learn how to locate material in print. Readiness can be achieved through a well-planned sequence of activities, preferably those that relate to problems for functional use of printed sources.

2. The optimum grade placement of a skill either for initial presentation or for practice purposes has not been ascertained. It is generally agreed, however, that although the bulk of the work in developing skill in locating information should be done in the intermediate grades, work in the primary grades can make a significant contribution in this area. In the first three grades help can be given in locating some of the information that children wish to find in books and magazines. Furthermore, in the primary grades a stable foundation can be laid for skills that can be developed in the intermediate grades.

The following are some of the skills in locating information that are developed, at least in part, in many primary grades:

a. Looking at the pictures to get an idea as to the content of a book.

b. Noting the titles of stories as they appear in the main part of the book.

c. Finding page numbers.

d. Reading the titles of stories as listed in the table of contents.

e. Looking at the titles of stories in order to see which ones are likely to deal with a given topic.

f. Knowing where, in the room or school or public library, books of interest can be found.

g. Learning alphabetical order.

h. Arranging letters and words in alphabetical order.

i. Knowing how to use a picture dictionary.

j. Using a glossary in a textbook.

k. Learning a few facts related to using a dictionary for children.

l. Finding material and looking at pictures in an encyclopedia for younger children; for example, *Childcraft.*

m. Looking at pictures and getting information through the teacher's reading from encyclopedias such as *Compton's Pictured Encyclopedia, The World Book Encyclopedia, Britannica Junior,* or *Our Wonderful World.*

n. Getting information from atlases, yearbooks, and the *World Almanac.*

3. Opportunity should be provided to make use of skills learned. Closely related to the problem of readiness for learning a skill is that of making use of what is learned. Since the pupil is, as a rule, more receptive to learning if he knows he will find it of value, only those abilities of real worth to a child before he is an adult should be developed. Fortunately, many skills that are needed by adults are also important to children. By providing the child with an opportunity to make real use of his skill, the teacher helps furnish the child with distributed practice, important in the learning of any skill.

The children should be stimulated to make use of the skills that they are acquiring and to recognize situations in which they can do so. The teacher can also lead discussions in which the group decides what use can be made of skills. In addition, as the teacher sees boys and girls make application of the recently acquired skills, he can call such activities to the attention of the class. He can also encourage pupils themselves to report ways in which their new abilities have proved helpful to them.

4. Provision should be made for evaluating skill in locating information. One way of appraising the skill of intermediate-grade boys and girls to locate information is by means of standardized tests. Unfortunately, most standardized reading tests for the elementary school do not test skill in locating information. Two tests that do devote sections to this skill are the *Iowa Silent Reading Test* and the *Iowa Every Pupil Test*.

The teacher can also appraise skill through more informal means, such as teacher-made tests, observation of pupils while doing practice exercises designed to develop skills in locating information, and observation of pupils when they look up information while not taking tests or doing practice exercises. An advantage of the teacher-made tests over standardized tests is that the locational skills not tested in the commercially produced tests can be included. A further point in favor of teacher-made tests is that the teacher has the opportunity to devise test items that apply specifically to what the pupils are or will be studying. As he observes boys and girls in nontesting situations, he can note not only their skills but also their attitudes toward finding information and utlizing it. For example, expressions showing dislike of looking up words in a dictionary tell the teacher something he ought to know for planning future strategy.

In making evaluations it is important to observe these criteria:

a. Evaluation should be made in terms of the objectives. Before a teacher begins instruction in locating information a survey test giving information on the pupil's abilities in a variety of locational skills may be given.

b. Both teacher and pupils should take part in evaluation procedures. If the pupil has a voice in planning the means of appraisal, he is more likely to try to improve in the skills that are being taught. Furthermore, his attitude toward the tests will probably be more favorable.

c. Evaluation should be a continuous process. It should not be confined to appraisal when work on a skill is begun and when the time to be spent working on it systematically is ended. Throughout the period of learning, checks should be made on how successful the teaching and learning have been.

5. Systematic instruction should be given in the development of the locational skills. While it is possible that for a small minority of the boys and girls in the elementary school no instruction beyond the incidental will be essential, in many instances even such children will profit from lessons definitely planned to help them acquire greater facility in the locational skills. For a large number of pupils, much floundering and inefficiency will result unless they are given direct help in the development of the ability to locate information. How these skills can be developed incidentally in the content subjects is discussed in part of Chapter 10. To supplement such instruction, direct assistance can, and in most cases should, be given by providing presentation lessons, in which the pupils are taught locational skills, and practice exercises, in which they can strengthen their command of the skills. In the following chapter suggestions as to types of practice desirable are given.

6. Materials of instruction should fit the needs of the individuals. Many teachers are not aware of the excellent materials that are available for the development of locational skills. Through the sensible application of the many suggestions given in the teachers' guides accompanying most of the basal textbook series in reading, the teacher can utilize many stories and articles in the reading books. Textbooks and workbooks in the language arts also frequently devote a sizable number of pages to the development of these skills. Some of the publishers of dictionaries for children are supplying exercises to help develop skill in the use of the dictionary.

Outline for Chapter 8B

DEVELOPING SKILL IN LOCATING INFORMATION AND IN USING IT

Developing Basic Locational Skills
    Finding a Given Page in a Book Quickly
    Finding Words Arranged in Alphabetical Order
    Deciding on Key Words
    Interpreting Punctuation Marks, Diacritical Marks,
       Abbreviations, and Symbols
    Selecting Points that Have Bearing on a Given
       Problem
    Utilizing Information Gained
Developing Skill in Using Nonreference Books
Developing Skill in Using the Dictionary
Developing Skill in Using Reference Books Other than
    the Dictionary
Developing Skill in Locating Material in the Library

CHAPTER

Developing Skill in Locating Information and In Using It

Anyone with ordinary intelligence and average reading ability should have no difficulty in acquiring the locational skills. Unfortunately, however, because of inadequate instruction, many persons who have graduated from high school are deficient in this area. A teacher who puts into practice the principles set forth in the preceding chapter can do much to help pupils attack their problems of finding information in printed materials. The following pages will illustrate ways of putting these principles into effect.

DEVELOPING BASIC LOCATIONAL SKILLS

Basic to the development of skill in locating information in various types of books and magazines are supportive skills in:

1. Finding a given page in a book quickly.
2. Finding words arranged in alphabetical order.
3. Deciding on key words.
4. Interpreting punctuation marks, diacritical marks, abbreviations, and symbols.
5. Selecting points that have bearing on a given problem.
6. Utilizing information gained.

Finding a Given Page in a Book Quickly

Pupils can be given help in quickly finding a given page in books of various types by means of activities such as the following:

1. Telling the pupils in the first grade where to find page numbers in a book.
2. Teaching the pupils how to turn the pages of a book.
3. Having the pupils try to open a book as near as possible to a given page before they begin turning pages.
4. Giving the pupils practice in finding a given page quickly by having them keep a record during a short period of time of how many attempts they had to make before locating the right page.
5. Having pupils estimate to which page you have opened a book.

Finding Words Arranged in Alphabetical Order

Finding words in lists arranged alphabetically is a basic skill in locating information. The following methods are illustrative of the means by which this skill may be developed:

1. Having the pupils memorize the letters in alphabetical order.
2. Writing the letters in alphabetical order on the board with some letters missing and asking the pupils to supply the missing letters.
3. Asking pupils to name or write the letter that immediately precedes or follows a given letter.
4. Having the pupils state in what part of the alphabet—first, middle, or last—given letters are found. Some teachers may prefer making the division of the alphabet into the first, second, third, and fourth quarters.
5. Having the pupils arrange letters in alphabetical order.
6. Asking the pupils to arrange in alphabetical order a series of words in which the first letters are different; in which the first and second letters are different; and in which the first three or more letters are different.
7. Helping pupils to discover that persons' names are usually listed according to the last names, and that when two or more persons have the same last name, their names are arranged according to the first names.
8. Asking the pupils to arrange in alphabetical order the names of the boys and girls in their class.
9. Explaining to the class that as the teacher shows each word card of a set, a pupil is to respond by naming a word beginning with the letter immediately preceding, in alphabetical order, the letter with which the word on the card begins. A variation of this procedure is to have a pupil give a word beginning with the letter immediately following, in alphabetical order, the letter with which the word on a given card begins.
10. Guiding pupils to note that on each page of the dictionary and in many other reference books words known as guide words are given. The pupils should learn that the first guide word, found near the upper lefthand

corner, designates the first entry word on that page and that the second guide word, usually written near the upper righthand corner, indicates the last entry word on that page. They should also learn that looking at the guide words can help the reader to determine quickly which words are found on a given page or pages.

11. Having the pupils indicate whether a given word comes between two stated guide words.

12. Asking the pupils to name words that are expected to be found as entry words on a page in the dictionary for which the guide words are stated.

13. Providing the pupils with a list of numbered sets of guide words from a dictionary, opposite which there is a list of words, arranged in a different order, each of which appears between one of the pairs of guide words. On the line to the right of each word in the second column the pupil writes the number of the matching guide words.

Practice Exercises

Below are samples of practice exercises that can be used in teaching boys and girls to find words or write words in alphabetical order.

1 *Directions:* Write the letters that come immediately before and after, in ABC order, each of the following letters:

1. ——— *t* ———   5. ——— *o* ———
2. ——— *f* ———   6. ——— *w* ———
3. ——— *d* ———   7. ——— *v* ———
4. ——— *q* ———   8. ——— *k* ———

2 *Directions:* Supply the missing letters:

1. a ——— c d ——— f ——— h i ———
2. r s ——— u ——— w ——— y z

3 *Directions:* Write *yes* on the line to the left of each number if the words in that item are arranged in alphabetical order. Otherwise write *no.*

——— 1. camel, cat, lion, fox
——— 2. bay, gulf, lake, ocean
——— 3. talk, tear, tease, take
——— 4. James, Jones, Johnson, Jacobson

4 *Directions:* Put an x through each word that is not in alphabetical order in the lists that follow:

1. apples, bananas, pears, oranges, plums
2. stone, brick, granite, marble, wood, stone

5 *Explanation:* In providing pupils with practice in arranging words in alphabetical order, the easiest type of exercise is one in which the first letters of the words are different. More difficult is an exercise in which only some of

the first letters of the words are different, so that the alphabetical order of the word needs to be determined in part by the second letter of the words; still more difficult is an exercise in which the third and fourth letters of a word help to determine the alphabetical order. (In the exercise that follows the third letter of *bluebirds* and *blackbirds* determines which word comes first.)

Directions: Write *1* to the left of the word that should come first in alphabetical order, *2* to the left of the word that should come second, and so on:

————bluebirds   ————doves
————blackbirds   ————chickadees
————bobwhites   ————cardinals
————ducks   ————cranes

6   *Directions:* Each of the following lists of names is in alphabetical order. Number the words as they should appear if the two lists were to be combined into one alphabetical list.

————Albright, Marian   ————Alexander, Marjorie
————Ayres, Harold   ————Douda, Helen
————Fleischer, Susan   ————Foster, Arthur
————Fleming, Gertrude   ————Gordon, Evelyn
————Manton, Cecil   ————Miller, John
————Meier, Roberta   ————Nelson, Nels
————Otto, Charles   ————Nelson, Samuel
————Owens, James   ————Sutton, Maria
————Spoerr, Geraldine   ————Wright, Jean
————Staples, Daniel   ————Young, Richard

7   *Directions:* On one page of a dictionary the guide words are *Nashville* and *Nature.* Write *yes* to the right of the following words that you would expect to find on that page. Write *no* to the right of the others:

1. narrow ———   6. net ———
2. nail ———   7. neck ———
3. nature ———   8. needle ———
4. nation ———   9. nurse ———
5. name ———   10. navy ———

Deciding on Key Words

One of the more difficult locational skills is to decide on the key words under which certain information can be found. Through a progression of activities from the less to the more difficult, and from the known to the unknown, this ability can be developed. Some methods that can prove helpful in developing this skill are:

1. Asking the pupils to tell under what key word in an index a reference may be found for a question such as: "In what year did George Washington become president of the United States ?"

2. Providing the boys and girls with an exercise in which they will choose the one of three or four words under which a reference is the most likely to be listed that gives information on a stated topic.

3. Asking pupils to indicate the word in a list of proper names consisting of more than one word, such as the following, which would serve as a key word when locating information on the person or place: *Thomas Edison, United Nations, West Germany, Hawaiian Islands.*

4. Providing guidance as the pupils consult an index to find out whether a given problem is discussed, and then report on the procedure they used in locating the reference giving the information desired.

Practice Exercises

These samples show several ways in which practice in deciding on key words can be provided. The value of such exercises can usually be greatly increased if the pupils are given a chance to discuss their reasons for making their selections.

1   *Directions:* Draw a line under the key word in each of the following questions that seems to you is the most likely entry word in an index of a nonreference book or in a reference book such as an encyclopedia under which you would find an answer to the question:

     1. What is one of the chief exports of the Philippines?
     2. What was the color of the uniform of the soldiers of the South during the Civil War?

2   *Directions:* Draw a line under the word or group of words in parentheses that you would choose as the most likely key word in an index to give information about the question:

     1. In what year did George Washington become president of the United States? (Washington, George, president, United States)
     2. In what year did the Mexican War, which was fought between the United States and Mexico, begin? (wars, Mexican War, United States, Mexico)
     3. What were the provisions of the Kansas-Nebraska Bill? (Kansas-Nebraska Bill, Nebraska, provisions, bill)

Interpreting Punctuation Marks, Diacritical Marks, Abbreviations, and Symbols

Since in indexes, dictionaries, and other reference books punctuation marks are used in different ways, and since the abbreviations and symbols used vary somewhat from one book to another, it is suggested that, although there are common problems, most work on this topic be taken up as each new reference book is studied. The following are ways in which these interpretative skills can be developed:

1. Helping the pupils find out how syllabication of words is indicated in their own dictionaries and how the hyphen between compound words is indicated.

2. Asking the pupils to look up in the dictionary words like *bluejay, Sunday school,* and *good-by* to find out which are hyphenated.

3. Helping the pupils to find the key to the diacritical marks, abbreviations, and symbols used in a reference book.

4. Providing practice in pronouncing words according to the respelling indicated in a dictionary.

5. After helping the pupils learn how division into syllables is shown in their dictionaries, asking them to divide words into syllables after consulting a dictionary.

6. Providing practice in interpreting accent marks by having pupils pronounce words that are not always accented in the same way, such as *pres´ent* and *pre sent´.*

7. Asking the pupils to give words illustrating the various sounds of letters and of letter combinations such as *a, e, c, th.*

8. Teaching the abbreviations for words commonly used and then testing the pupils on them.

9. Explaining to the group that when a word has two correct pronunciations, both are usually indicated in a dictionary, and that if one is preferred, that is given first. It should also be pointed out that it must not be taken for granted that if there are two pronunciations given, the second one is not as desirable as the first, for the two may be equally desirable.

10. Explaining to the boys and girls that if every letter in the alphabet stood for but one sound and every sound were represented by but one letter, there would probably be no need to have the pronunciation of a word indicated in a dictionary.

11. Helping the boys and girls discover that one and only one vowel sound is heard in each syllable. The pupils might give the vowel sound in each syllable of a group of words listed on the chalkboard.

Selecting Points that Have Bearing on a Given Problem

After the necessary reference pages have been located, skill in selecting points that have bearing on a given problem can be developed through various activities, such as:

1. Asking the class questions that are phrased in words similar to those used in the text that serve as an answer to them, and asking questions when the answers are not phrased in the same way.

2. Asking pupils to find the answer to a question or a direction such as the following, in which the answer consists of two or more sentences referred to in various parts of a paragraph: "Name three reasons why many cranberries are produced in Massachusetts."

3. Providing practice in formulating problems, so that the pupils know specifically what information they are looking for. This might be done by having the boys and girls write the question or questions that they want answered.

4. Providing practice in skimming by having pupils read as rapidly as possible, while they are being timed, a selection to spot certain words, sentences, or thoughts.

5. Asking the pupils to list items they would expect to find under a certain topic.

Practice Exercises

To provide practice in deciding which points have bearing on a given problem, the teacher might ask the pupils to write an x on the line to the left of each sentence that gives information on the topic stated.

1. Topic: How to make molds of footprints.
   ———a. Before making a mold, clean the footprints.
   ———b. Detectives often study the footprints of human beings.
   ———c. Plaster of Paris can be used to make a mold.
   ———d. The footprint should be thoroughly dry before the plaster of Paris is poured onto it.

2. Topic: Where the robin migrates in winter.
   ———a. The robin is larger than the house wren.
   ———b. Robins usually breed more than once during a season.
   ———c. In winter robins fly as far south as Mexico.
   ———d. Robins stay in the northern states till November.

Utilizing Information Gained

After the exact information needed has been located, skill in utilizing it can be acquired through activities such as the following:

1. Having the pupils judge whether a statement is reliable by considering who wrote it or in what book it appeared.

2. Giving pupils practice in deciding which of a series of statements are relevant to their problem.

3. Having pupils compile a bibliography of information helpful on a topic.

4. Providing opportunity for the pupils to give a talk or write a paper on information they have gathered.

5. Giving the pupils opportunity to explain to others what they learned, by putting on puppet shows or making friezes or "movies."

6. After the pupils have looked up a topic in an encyclopedia, giving them time to write a small number of interesting and significant facts that they learned and then having others in the class read those sentences.

7. Giving the pupils an opportunity to compare facts read in an encyclopedia with their own experiences.

8. Having pupils compare the information on a given subject gained from one encyclopedia with that on the same topic in another encyclopedia.

DEVELOPING SKILL IN USING NONREFERENCE BOOKS

Skill in using the various parts of a book for locating information can be acquired by means of the following methods:

1. Having pupils examine the various parts of a book to find out where they are located, what they contain, and how the data given in them are arranged.

2. Providing practice for the pupils in examining the preface of a book to see if the book is likely to contain information needed on a given topic.

3. Having the pupils find answers to questions about the various parts of a book; for example: "What is the purpose of the preface?"

4. Helping pupils make a chart on which they list the important points to remember about each part of a book; for example: "The index is found in the back of the book."

5. Even in the first grade, having pupils turn to the table of contents of their reader to find the page of the story they will read.

6. Helping pupils find the answer to questions such as the following as they examine the table of contents in their textbook in social studies: "How many chapters are there in the book?" Or "In which chapter would you expect to find information about the fire department?"

7. Through examination of the table of contents of several books, having pupils make a list of books in which information is given on a topic in which they are interested.

8. Helping pupils to discover the chief differences between a glossary and a dictionary.

9. Explaining to the boys and girls the meaning of the word *appendix.*

10. Having the pupils look up cross references quickly.

11. After making and distributing duplicate copies of a table of contents and an index, asking pupils questions answered in these.

12. When discussing a place of special interest, having the pupils look in the index of their social studies books to find out where, if at all, it is shown on a map in these books.

13. Having the pupils construct a table of contents and an index for a class notebook they are making—one on "Famous Modern Americans," for example.

14. Helping the boys and girls write a preface for a class notebook on a topic such as "Autobiographies of Boys and Girls in Our Fifth Grade." They could also include in it an appendix giving name, date of birth, and place of birth of each pupil.

15. Having the pupils compile a list of words that have interesting origins (*neighbor* is such a word) and letting them explain the etymology of these words to the class. An illustrated chart might be made to help the pupils remember the information.

Practice Exercises

These three samples of exercises show how practice exercises can be used to develop skill in locating information in nonreference books:

Although work on the table of contents can be begun in the first and second grades, in these lower grades, as a rule, the work should be done only if it is a help in finding an entry in the table of contents. In the intermediate grades, however, exercises such as the following can be used. Since the questions are based on the table of contents given in *Shining Hours*,[1] if this specific exercise were used, each pupil would have to have access to a copy of this reader. The exercise can be easily adapted for use with any reader.

1   Directions: This exercise is to help you learn to make good use of a table of contents in a book. Find and write the answers to these questions by using the table of contents of *Shining Hours.* Your teacher may decide to time you while you are doing this exercise.

1. Into how many parts are the stories and poems divided? (Do not count the Glossary or Little Dictionary as one part)._____
2. What is the first word of the third story listed under "The World's Children"?_____
3. Who wrote "The Legend of Betsy Ross"?_____
4. On what page does the story "The Dragon Chair" begin?_____
5. On what page does a poem by Edward Lear begin?_____

2   Directions: To help you find out what types of material are found in appendixes of books, study the appendixes of three books and fill out the following form.

1. *Name of author:*_____*Title:*_____
   *Type of materials:*_____
   _____
   _____

2. *Name of author:*_____*Title:*_____
   Type of materials: _____
   _____
   _____

3. *Name of author:*_____*Title:*_____
   *Type of materials:*_____
   _____
   _____

[1] Nila Banton Smith, Hazel Hart, and Clara B. Baker, *Shining Hours* (Indianapolis, Indiana: The Bobbs-Merrill Company, 1964).

3 After the boys and girls have studied the parts of a book, a list of questions similar to the following might be used as a means of review and evaluation.

Directions: Draw a line under the correct word or group of words in parentheses.

1. The index of a book is arranged (alphabetically, by chapters, in the order in which the points are taken up in the book).
2. The preface is found in the (front, middle, back) part of the book.
3. The glossary (tells the purpose of the author in writing the book, gives the list of chapters in the book, gives the pronunciation and meaning of some of the words used in the book).
4. The table of contents is arranged (alphabetically, by chapters, in the order in which the points are taken up in the book).

DEVELOPING SKILL IN USING THE DICTIONARY

Some procedures that can help in the development of skills essential to the effective use of the dictionary are listed under "Finding Words Arranged in Alphabetical Order," on page 268, and under "Interpreting Punctuation Marks, Diacritical Marks, Abbreviations, and Symbols," on page 271. Additional suggestions follow.

1. Providing practice in deciding which inflectional forms are likely to be treated as distinct words in a dictionary and given separate entries and which forms are likely to be treated as run-on entries.
2. Having the pupils make a list of the types of information given for an entry word.
3. Providing practice in which the pupils select from a dictionary the meaning of a word that is appropriate in a given context.
4. Providing practice in looking up the spelling of a word in the dictionary by helping the pupils decide on probable spellings of it and then looking for these in the dictionary.
5. Providing practice in pronouncing words that according to the dictionary have two correct pronunciations.
6. Providing the pupils with sentences in each of which a word is underlined and asking the boys and girls to restate each sentence without using the underlined word. An example of such a sentence is: "The boys and girls did not *anticipate* a big crowd."
7. Providing practice in using the abbreviations and arbitrary signs in the dictionary.
8. Helping pupils discover how the thumb index may aid them in locating a word.
9. Having a pupil from one of two teams into which the class is divided give two guide words from a page in a dictionary and write them on the chalk-

board, while a pupil from the other team names a word that would be expected to be found on that page of the dictionary and writes it on the board. This practice could be provided in somewhat the same way that spelldowns are sometimes conducted.

10. Providing practice in finding out through the dictionary the possible parts of speech of a word like *effect* and in using it in those ways in sentences.

11. Giving help in finding the various definitions of a word that may be used as different parts of speech; for example, *effect* as a noun or as a verb.

12. Asking the pupils to find the answers to questions like the following through using the dictionary: "Are the American robin and the European robin alike?"

13. Having the pupils make a composite list of sentences illustrating all the meanings of a word that they can think of or that they can find in a dictionary; for example: "I can *run* fast" or "He can *run* the machine."

14. Having the pupils explain with the help of the dictionary the meanings of words that are homonyms, and then having them use the words in sentences.

15. Asking the pupils to look up the meaning of the words *prefix* and *suffix,* and then draw up a list of prefixes and suffixes with meanings and examples of words of which they form a part.

16. Having pupils give words containing common prefixes and suffixes.

17. Asking the pupils to look up in the dictionary a list of words often mispronounced, like *handkerchief,* and giving them practice in pronouncing them correctly.

18. Having the pupils make their own picture dictionaries, or make one as a class project.

19. Asking pupils to look up words like the following to find out which should begin with a capital letter, whatever their use in a sentence may be: *river, history, Bible, Indian.*

20. Having the pupils find the meaning of words that are often confused; for example, *suppose* and *expect.*

21. Teaching the pupils the most frequently used rules for syllabication, and having them divide words according to these rules and check their work in the dictionary.

22. Helping the children get meaning from illustrations in a dictionary by asking them questions about a picture or by having them explain how a given picture supplements the verbal explanation.

23. Drawing the attention of pupils to aspects of an illustration that give an indication of the size of what is pictured.

Practice Exercises

The following are samples of exercises for developing skill in using the dictionary.

1   Directions: Decide in which part of the dictionary you would look for each of the following words. Write a *B* (for Beginning) if it is found near the beginning of the dictionary. Write an *M* if it is found near the middle, and an *E* if it is found near the end.

1. shoemaker———
2. memory———
3. correct———

4. theater———
5. discovery———
6. whales———

2   Directions: Look up in your dictionary the following list of words that are often mispronounced. On the line to the right of each write the respelling of the word with markings, including the accent, as given in the dictionary. Your teacher may give you an opportunity to pronounce some of the words to your classmates.

1. athletic _____
2. adult _____
3. handkerchief _____
4. little _____
5. often _____
6. library _____

3   Directions: To the right of each sentence write the spelling of the italicized (or underlined) word. If necessary, consult your dictionary to get the correct spelling.

1. I think that this trip was really necess——ry. _____
2. Did you *rec——ve* my message? _____
3. The boys and girls will leave in two *sep——rate* groups. _____

4   Directions: Some of the following compound words, which are divided into syllables, should be separated by a hyphen and others should not. Consult your dictionary before you write the words correctly on the lines left for the purpose. Study the spelling of the words so that you can write them if your teacher dictates them to you.

1. an y bod y _____
2. green house _____
3. out of date _____
4. sis ter in law _____
5. shell fish _____
6. steam ship _____
7. two edged _____
8. ex pres i dent _____

5   Directions: Here are some of the meanings and illustrations given for the word *way* in a dictionary.[2]

1. Road, or any passage: *The way was muddy after the rain.*

[2] From *The Holt Basic Dictionary of American English* (New York: Holt, Rinehart and Winston, Inc., 1966).

2. Route (from one place to another): *the way to Boston; the way home.*
3. Direction: *Everyone face this way!*
4. Distance: *She lives a long way from here.*
5. Away; far: *to be way behind in a race.*
6. Room; space for action; *Make way for the parade.*
7. Progress; advance; headway: *We pushed our way through the crowd. He made his way to work.*
8. Manner: *The child has winning ways.*
9. Means or method: *Sailors know many ways of tying a knot.*
10. Habit; customary manner: *The ways of another country are different from our own.*
11. Wish; desire; will: *Little Cyril's mother always lets him have his way.*
12. Characteristic; respect; feature: *In many ways she is like her father.*
13. Condition: *The old dog is in a bad way.*

Use the word *way* in thirteen sentences of your own to show each of the thirteen meanings given above.

6   *Directions:* Here are some of the meanings found in a dictionary for the word *head*.[3] On the line to the left of each sentence given below write the letter appearing before the meaning of the word *head* that the word has in each of the sentences.

    a. The part of the body of man and most animals that contains the brain, mouth, eyes, ears, etc., and is located at the top of the upright body or the front of a four-legged or crawling body in ordinary motion.
    b. The enlarged part of something resembling the part of the body known as head.
    c. Top or upper part.
    d. Front end.
    e. The round, firm part of a plant.
    f. Portrait.
    g. Topic or title.
    h. Mental ability.

    —— 1. Mother bought a head of lettuce.
    —— 2. Our teacher asked one of the boys to be at the head of the line.
    —— 3. Mr. Jones carved a granite head of the President.
    —— 4. The head of the hammer was securely fastened.
    —— 5. Jimmy has a good head for numbers.

7   *Directions:* Look up the answers to the following questions in your dictionary and answer them by writing *yes* or *no* on the line to the left of the questions. On the line to the right of each question write the page in your dictionary on which you found the answer.

[3] From *The Holt Basic Dictionary of American English.*

———— 1. Did the English obtain the Magna Carta from King Alfred? ————————

———— 2. Should the word *English* always begin with a capital letter? ————————

———— 3. Can the word *affect* be used as a noun? ————————

———— 4. Is *gotten* a word? ————————

———— 5. Is it correct to place the accent on the second syllable in *theater?* ————————

DEVELOPING SKILL IN USING REFERENCE BOOKS OTHER THAN THE DICTIONARY

Skills needed in order to locate material in reference books other than the dictionary can be developed through activities like the following:

1. Providing opportunity to use as many as possible of the following reference books: *Childcraft, Compton's Pictured Encyclopedia*, the *World Book Encyclopedia, Junior Britannica, Our Wonderful World*, the *Junior Book of Authors*, the *Index to Poetry*, the *World Almanac*, and a standard atlas.

2. Providing the pupils with a list of topics on which they are to check those that are likely to be found in an encyclopedia.

3. Having pupils answer a list of questions, the answers to which are to be found in one or more of the reference books listed in the first item above.

4. Having pupils give information found on one or more of the maps contained in an atlas to which they have access.

5. Asking pupils to tell in which volume of a set of encyclopedias information on a specified topic would be likely to be given. For this purpose the information on the labels on the back of the encyclopedias should be written on the board or duplicated on paper.

6. Showing pupils the filmstrip, "How to Use an Encyclopedia."[4]

7. Explaining the use of the index volume of a set of encyclopedias and providing pupils with practice in using it.

8. Giving pupils a list of questions to answer in one word or a few words after consulting an encyclopedia.

9. Having pupils make a chart to indicate in what reference books they would try to locate information on specific problems.

10. Asking pupils in what reference books they would look if they wanted stated types of information; for example, data on the life of Hans Christian Andersen.

11. Helping pupils discover and list similarities and differences between an encyclopedia and a dictionary.

12. Asking pupils when giving reports to tell from what references they received their information if reference books were consulted.

[4] "How to Use an Encyclopedia." (New York: Popular Science Publishing Company).

13. Providing pupils with an opportunity to report on any topic of interest to them on which they found information in a reference book, and to state what reference book they consulted.

14. Having a "quiz program" based on information found in reference books. It would be helpful, in some instances, to have the pupils indicate in which reference book the answer to each question was found.

15. Explaining the means used to keep a reference book up-to-date, such as supplements to encyclopedias.

16. Providing the boys and girls with the opportunity to make a bibliography of materials available in the school library on a given topic.

Practice Exercises

The following are four of the many types of practice exercises that can be used in order to develop skill with reference books.

1 Directions: Find the answers to these questions in the *World Almanac.*

1. Is the population of the village, town, or city in which you are living given in the *World Almanac?* If so, what was it according to the last edition of the *World Almanac?*
2. Where was Thomas Edison born? _____
3. What is the state flower of Minnesota? _____
4. What state leads in the production of cotton? _____
5. When was Florida admitted to the Union? _____
6. What is the state bird of Ohio? _____
7. In what building did Abraham Lincoln die? _____

2 Directions: Below each entry taken from the *Reader's Guide to Periodical Literature* are given some parts of the entry. On the lines provided, explain what each means or represents.

1. *Entry:* Another spring project: birdhouse building. S. Miller. il Audubon Mag 57:94 Mr '55
   a. Another spring project: birdhouse building _____
   b. S. Miller _____
   c. il _____
   d. Audubon Mag _____
   e. 57 _____
   f. 94 _____
   g. Mr _____
   h. '55 _____
2. *Entry:* ABC's of flower arrangement. F. Hullenlocher. il Bet Hom & Gard 24: 62-5 Je; 74-7 Jl '56
   a. F. _____
   b. 62-5 _____
   c. 74-7 _____

3 Directions: Place an x on the line to the left of each of the following topics that you would expect to be found in an encyclopedia:

———— 1. The population of your home town
———— 2. An account of the Battle of Gettysburg
———— 3. Early attempts at aviation
———— 4. The spelling of the word *necessary*

4 *Directions:* Below the question is a list of different kinds of books that are lettered from (a) through (g). On the line to the right of each question, write the letter or letters given to the books in which you would expect to find an answer to the question:

1. What was the population of Delaware, Ohio, during the past year? ——
2. What were the chief exports of France during the past year?————————

3. How often should a person clean his teeth? ——————————————

4. What causes a dental cavity? ————————————————————

5. What is the origin of the word *belfry?* ——————————————

6. What part of speech is the word *produce* when the accent is on the second syllable? ————————————————————

Books

a. *Compton's Pictured Encyclopedia*
b. *The World Almanac*
c. *Junior Book of Authors*
d. *Reader's Guide to Periodical Literature*
e. A dictionary
f. An atlas
g. A hygiene book

DEVELOPING SKILL IN LOCATING MATERIAL IN THE LIBRARY

Some procedures effective in learning to locate material in the library are:

1. Taking the children on a trip to the library.
2. Helping pupils draw a diagram showing the location of materials in their library.
3. Displaying and explaining to the children a chart giving the Dewey decimal system of classification if that method of classification is used in their library.
4. Asking the pupils to write a subject card, an author card, and a title card as you give them the necessary bibliographical data on a book.
5. Asking pupils to list the facts given in a card catalogue in addition to the author and the title of a book.

6. Asking pupils to suggest subjects under which they may be able to find on a subject card references to the answer to a given question; for example, "What was travel like in the country in 1865?"

7. Having pupils put on a skit that illustrates "do's" and "don'ts" of library behavior.

8. Having a pupil act as librarian and explain to his audience the meaning and use of a call number.

9. Explaining to the boys and girls the plan of cumulation followed in the *Reader's Guide to Periodical Literature* and having them find entries on articles included in various volumes.

10. Asking pupils to explain every part of an entry found in the *Reader's Guide to Periodical Literature.*

11. Helping pupils make a card catalogue of the books in their own room library. Guide cards should be included in the catalogue and *see also* cards.

12. Having pupils gather from reference books information needed for work on a unit in science or social studies.

13. Providing time for pupils to examine and read various magazines in the library, and then to give reports on them.

Practice Exercises

Following are suggested activities for developing skill in locating material in the library.

1 *Explanation* After the teacher or one or two pupils have drawn a diagram of a card catalogue on a chart, the pupils could be asked questions concerning it.

1. In which drawer would you look for a book by Louisa M. Alcott?
2. In which drawer would you look for the title of another book by the author of *Doctor Doolittle?*
3. What uses can you make of a card catalogue besides finding out what books are in the library?

2 *Directions:* Find the answers to the following questions by consulting the card catalogue in your library.

1. What is the call number of the book *Up a Road Slowly?*
   _____

2. What books written by the author of *The Singing Tree* are in your library? _____
3. What is the title and call number of a book in your library on early pioneer life? _____
   _____
4. What facts other than the title and author are given on the subject card for the book *Call It Courage?* _____
   _____

3 After pupils have finished the following exercises, opportunity should be provided for checking the correctness of their answers by consulting the card catalogue.

Directions: What is a broader subject under which you might find a reference listed in your card catalogue on each of the following subjects?

    1. Thomas Edison _____
    2. Description of Yellowstone National Park _____
    3. Tennis _____
    4. Recipes for cakes _____
    5. The settlers of Plymouth, Massachusetts _____

4 The pupils could be given a diagram of the library they are using that shows the location of the various stacks and tables and racks where books or magazine are kept. The various positions should be numbered so that the pupils can refer to them by number. Make certain that pupils understand the diagram.

Directions: On the diagram showing the arrangement of your library, the bookshelves and tables are numbered. Answer the following question by writing the number of the bookshelf or table used in the diagram. If you do not know the answer to a question, study the arrangement of the library before you try to write an answer.

    1. Where are the books for very young children kept? _____
    2. Where are the books on biography kept? _____
    3. On what table are some of the newest books for boys and girls placed?
    _____
    4. Where are the books on American history placed? _____
    5. Where are the encyclopedias for boys and girls kept? _____

For Further Study

Harris, Albert J., and Edward R. Sipay, eds., *Readings on Reading Instruction,* 2nd ed. (New York: David McKay Company, 1972), article #58, "The Development of Locational Skills" by Martha Dallmann.

Karlin, Robert, *Teaching Elementary Reading: Principles and Strategies* (New York: Harcourt Brace Jovanovich, 1971), Ch. 7, "Reading in the Content Fields."

Mazurkiewicz, Albert J. ed., *New Perspectives in Reading Instruction: A Book of Readings* (New York: Pitman Publishing Company, 1964), "Teaching the Reading-Study Skills" by Arthur Heilman, pp. 418–424; and "How to Teach Dictionary and Index Skills" by Mary E. Coleman, pp. 425–536.

Schubert, Delwyn G., and Theodore L. Torgerson, eds., *Readings in Reading* (New York: Thomas Y. Crowell Company, 1968), "Who's Brand of Reading Methods Is the 'Best Way'?" pp. 307–308; and "Locating, Introducing and Using Easy-to-Read, High-interest Reading Matter," pp. 316–321.

Trinker, Charles L., ed., *Teaching for Better Use of Libraries* (Hamden, Conn.: The Shoe String Press, 1970).

Questions and Comments for Thought and Discussion

1. In one classroom we have thirty pupils, each of whom has his own dictionary. Down the hall in another classroom we have six or eight copies of several different dictionaries. How do you account for these two quite differing practices at the same grade level? Which would you, as teacher, prefer? Be able to give reasons for your response.

2. What is your position on the following controversial statement? Be able to state your case.

> Dictionary skills are an inseparable part of the language arts program in general and the reading program specifically and need not, in fact, should not, be taught in isolation.

3. Some writers have urged that we pay more attention to the concept of "dictionary readiness." They name as prerequisites such matters as readiness for locating words, readiness for deriving the meaning, readiness for pronunciation. What constitutes each of these facets of readiness?

4. When children learn how to use reference books certain problems almost inevitably arise. For example, there is the problem of children copying when gathering data in a reference work. Or there is the concern that children not use the encyclopedia until they know how to outline or write material in their own words. Imagine you are a sixth-grade teacher and you have to deal with one of these problems. How would you proceed?

5. It has been contended that comprehension is the important factor to consider when selecting encyclopedias for children. Since many children have interest levels higher than their reading ability, it is claimed that definite training in use of encyclopedias is important for helping children to absorb the information given in encyclopedias. Do you agree? Be able to defend your answer.

6. In considering the role and function of the elementary-school library, certain problems of terminology arise. Should the library be called an instructional materials center, a learning resource center, an educational media center, or just a library? Be able to give reasons for your preference.

7. Several questions come to mind as we are placing more emphasis on the use of the dictionary in developing better word usage. How soon can children begin to use dictionaries other than picture dictionaries? How valuable would a thesaurus be in an intermediate-grade classroom?

Outline for Chapter 9A

ORAL READING

9A CHAPTER

Oral Reading

Sixty years ago reading instruction in most elementary schools was instruction in oral reading. Numerous educators had called attention to the sterility of the exclusively oral approach. Thus, Edmund B. Huey wrote in 1908:

> Reading as a school exercise has almost always been thought of as reading aloud, in spite of the obvious fact that reading in actual life is to be mainly silent reading. The consequent attention to reading as an exercise in speaking . . . has been heavily at the expense of reading as the art of thought-getting . . .[1]

In this statement Huey confirmed the views of earlier educational leaders such as Horace Mann and Francis W. Parker. It was not until the early 1920s, however, that a widespread shift of emphasis from oral to silent reading took place. In this period a great quantity of published materials, including a yearbook of the National Society for the Study of Education, numerous research reports, textbooks on the teaching of reading, reading manuals, and series of basal readers stressed the need for instruction in silent reading.

[1] Edmund B. Huey, *The Psychology and Pedagogy of Reading* (New York: The Macmillan Company, 1908), p. 359.

The chief arguments in favor of silent as against oral reading were based chiefly on two considerations:

1. Most reading outside of school is silent reading.
2. Silent reading emphasizes meaning rather than sound. Psychologists of many schools—behaviorist, gestalt, organismic, and others—were concerned with the ways in which communication takes place between the writer and the reader.

Experimentation with various methods of teaching reading, and the rise of the tests and measurements movement, further strengthened the trend toward silent reading instruction.

THE IMPORTANCE OF ORAL READING

As teachers began to emphasize silent reading many of them, unfortunately, began to neglect oral reading. Especially in the intermediate grades little attention was paid to oral reading. It may be true that not more than about 1 percent of out-of-school reading is oral. However, frequency of use should by no means be the sole determiner of the emphasis to be placed on the development of any ability. Such factors as the value of the skill and the relative difficulty of mastering it should also play an important part in any decision concerning what is to be included in the curriculum. Oral reading is a valuable skill, one that is not automatically learned in an effective program of silent reading instruction. Rather, in the case of a large number of boys and girls—probably the great majority of them—specific attention is required on the part of the teacher if adequate skill in oral reading is to be acquired.

Values of Oral Reading

A point being stressed, even at times overstressed, by linguists and some educators that is influencing the teaching of reading is the primacy of oral over written communication. With this emphasis has come a higher valuation on oral reading and on its accompanying skill, listening, especially in the early stages of learning to read.

One important value of oral reading that is often not given due attention is that it can produce beneficial results in the social and emotional development of children. The growth in literary appreciation that can come as boys and girls read orally to each other is in itself justification for oral reading instruction. Furthermore, sympathetic relations among members of a group may often be created or strengthened by means of the oral reading experience. A boy or girl may acquire a much-needed feeling of acceptance in his group by being able to contribute a story, a joke, or an interesting fact by reading aloud from a book, a magazine, or a newspaper. Pupils who do not excel in other activities may find recognition in superior performance in oral reading. Moreover, oral reading may help them develop self-assurance and poise.

Many additional values can be achieved through oral reading. Oral reading can help pupils:

1. To communicate ideas.
2. To provide enjoyment for others.
3. To add to the reader's understanding of what he reads.
4. To diagnose problems in silent reading.
5. To increase vocabulary.
6. To improve speech.

Functional Situations for Oral Reading

At all times when oral reading is included in the day's program it should serve a purpose that is considered worthwhile not only by the teacher but also by the pupils. Frequently the function may be in relation to the on-going activity of the classroom. Opportunities for purposeful oral reading are exemplified by the following activities, which are merely suggestive of many others:

1. Reading captions under pictures on bulletin boards and flannel boards.
2. Giving oral reports on reading stories orally, including original ones by the boys and girls, to another group, possibly within the context of a program consisting of a variety of activities.
3. Putting on a make-believe radio or television program.
4. Rereading orally short selections that have been read silently with the purpose of clarifying the meaning.
5. Reading orally to prove a point.
6. Reading orally to give one's interpretation of a selection.
7. Participating in a panel that is reading a series of short stories or a longer story in parts.
8. Giving a puppet play in which the "conversation" is read.
9. Reading reports.
10. Reading the minutes of a meeting.
11. Reading announcements.
12. Taking part in choral reading.

13. Putting on a program in which a narrator reads orally the "conversation" of "characters" made by pupils with *origami* (the Japanese art of paper folding).[2]

Sometimes the main function of oral reading practice may be to increase the pupils' skill in that activity. At such times, it is usually advisable that boys and girls recognize the objective to be served by the practice. Attention might be focused on maintaining or acquiring contact with the audience, on effective phrasing, and on skillful interpretation of the mood the writer seems to wish to portray. Exercises in the form of practice in pronunciation, enunciation, and modulation of voice are also valuable for many boys and girls. Among the suggestions listed under "Instructional Practices" (page 303), are included some that provide specific practice in attaining these and other desirable skills of oral reading.

RELATION BETWEEN ORAL AND SILENT READING

Almost all the skills that are important in silent reading are also needed in effective oral reading, because in a certain sense all oral reading is preceded by silent reading. A word in print cannot be given orally unless the reader has recognized the word and by that very act has read it silently. Consequently, skill in word recognition, possession of a suitable meaning vocabulary, and the ability to comprehend what is read are essentials of both oral and silent reading. Even rate of reading is a factor in both types, because the individual who cannot read silently as rapidly as he can say the words he is reading is handicapped in his oral reading.

The effective oral reader possesses many of the silent reading skills and, in addition, many abilities peculiar to oral reading. One of these is correct pronunciation of words. In silent reading the pupil must recognize the word and know its meaning, but it is not essential that he know how to pronounce it. Clear articulation, a pleasing and well-modulated voice, and proper contact with the audience are additional concerns of the oral reader. Furthermore, in oral reading thought getting, common to both oral and silent reading, must be followed by vocal interpretation, because it is necessary to convey to the audience the reader's grasp of the meaning of the passage. Thus, oral reading, if done well, becomes a highly complex skill.

Oral reading can serve as an aid to silent reading in many ways, some of which are illustrated later in this chapter and in the B chapter that follows. Oral reading, for example, helps in the diagnosis of difficulties in silent reading. As a pupil reads a selection orally, the teacher can fre-

---

[2] Two books helpful to the teacher who wishes to learn more about origami are Isao Honda *All about Origami* (Tokyo, Japan: 1960); Toto Bunka Company and Shari Lewis and Lillian Oppenheimer, *Folding Paper Puppets* (New York: Stein and Day, 1962); the latter is distributed by J. B. Lippincott Company, Philadelphia.

quently detect the types of errors that keep the pupil from reading well silently. Difficulties such as the following, common to both oral and silent reading, often are revealed: omission of words or phrases; insertion of words or phrases; substitution of letters, words, or phrases; skipping lines; repeating lines; and phrasing so inadequately that it interferes with thought getting and interpretation.

Learning to read well orally, then, is more difficult in some respects than learning to read well silently. Not only must the oral reader have a good grasp of the meaning of the material he reads but he must have many other abilities besides. He needs not only, as in silent reading, to get the thought but he must also interpret or convey it to his listeners. He must know his listeners—their interests and probable attitudes toward the material read as well as their capacity to understand it—and he must be sensitive to their reactions as he reads to them. He must be fluent enough to focus his mind on the thought rather than the recognition and pronunciation of individual words. He must reproduce in his reading the mood and intention of the author, recognizing irony or pathos, happiness or depression, excitement or pensiveness. To accomplish his purpose he must know how to use pauses effectively. He must have skill in using his voice. He must be free of mannerisms that might detract attention from the message he brings. He must make a poised appearance.

It is important that the person who is to read orally to a group be given, as a rule, the opportunity to read the material silently before he reads it to others. Silent reading preceding oral reading is desirable in order that the reader be given the opportunity in his first reading to solve problems of word recognition and pronunciation that he may have. Furthermore, the reader will be likely to interpret the meaning of the writer more accurately if he has the chance to get the meaning himself before he is confronted with the task of interpreting. In oral reading the reader is in the limelight in a social situation, and he may become uncomfortable unless he has the security of knowing the material he is to present to his audience. Even the adult reader usually likes to read beforehand that which he is to read to others, whether the material consists of minutes of a meeting written by someone else, a story from a magazine, or an article from the newspaper. However, there is also a legitimate place for sight reading.

The term *sight reading* is here used to refer to oral reading when the reader has not previously read the material either silently or orally; that is, when he reads it orally at first sight. As indicated in the preceding paragraph, such procedure is usually undesirable for the reasons given. However, it can be used advisedly at times, for example, when the teacher is the only listener. The purpose in having a pupil read to the teacher might be diagnostic. Through hearing the child read orally material that he has not previously read, the alert teacher can detect problems that cannot be isolated through tests on the child's silent reading, such as reversals of letters or words, omission of letters or words, or repeating lines. Sight reading, too, can be justified in a small group if the pupils are intent on helping one another practice reading stories or other material that they later will read to another group of boys and girls or to visitors.

Occasionally, too, sight reading may be justified for still another purpose. The boys and girls may be reading orally without previous practice in silent reading in order to have practice in sight reading in an audience situation. The teacher may want to explain to the pupils that sometimes people do get called on to read something orally without having had the opportunity to read it beforehand. It can be made clear to the boys and girls that practice in sight reading may help them to feel at ease if sometime someone asks them to read orally without their having the chance to precede the oral reading by silent reading.

It is important when pupils do sight reading in front of their peers that an atmosphere of understanding and good will permeate the situation. A child required to read by sight to an audience, unless the situation is one that is well controlled to eliminate problems, is in a precarious position. In an atmosphere lacking in good will and mutual understanding, he may become frustrated and otherwise emotionally upset to the extent that he develops a dislike for reading. Such an attitude may result in serious reading retardation.

ORAL READING IN THE EARLY STAGES OF LEARNING TO READ

The role of oral reading in the early stages of learning to read has been and continues to be a point of argument. The debate, however, no longer centers on whether there should be any oral reading at that time. Nor does it turn on the question of whether there should be silent reading in the first grade. The issue is primarily how oral reading, as part of the developmental program of the first grade, should be conducted. Some would argue that from the very beginning the child should not read orally without having read the material silently beforehand. Arguments of proponents who are against oral sight reading at that early stage are stated below:

1. Before a child is asked to sight read before an audience, he should have developed basic reading skills to the extent that he will not, with easy material, be confronted with problems of word recognition or of comprehension in what he may be called on to read to a group. If he lacks such skills, he will have difficulty in interpreting the written message to an audience, and when required to perform this task in front of others, may suffer emotionally.

2. When the beginning reader reads orally material he has not previously read silently, he may read it word by word and thus develop into a reader who habitually reads in that manner. It is also argued that he

may so firmly establish the habit of reading without expression that even when he ceases later to be a word-by-word reader that habit may persist.

3. When the reading material is read haltingly, as the immature reader is likely to do if his oral reading has not been preceded by silent reading, the interest of the audience will be low. In fact, listeners will frequently be bored. Anything that may cause lack of interest in any phase of reading during the initial period of reading instruction should be eyed with serious misgivings. The gravity of such a situation will be obvious as one recalls that one of the main objectives of beginning reading instruction is to interest boys and girls in reading.

An undesirable practice followed in many first grades is that of having the pupils read around the class orally while the rest of the boys and girls are supposedly following in their books. Even when boys and girls have read the selection silently beforehand, if considerable time has elapsed between the silent reading and the oral, reading is likely to be done in a halting manner and thus be harmful to the oral reader and uninteresting to the audience. Moreover, incentive for interpretation of the written message by the oral reader is not likely to be strong. The members of the audience are in danger of getting practice in half-listening and half-reading, since they lack incentive for both effective listening and significant reading. It should be noted that when boys and girls are asked to read silently while someone is reading orally to them after they have learned to read more rapidly silently than orally, even greater harm is likely to be done to them than earlier. When the learner has reached that stage, which is frequently reached during the second half of the second grade, there is danger that his silent reading will be reduced to the speed of his oral reading.

There is, however, an important place for oral reading in the first grade. It has been pointed out that probably many boys and girls in the first grade do not get the feeling that they are reading unless they are reading orally. At a stage in reading instruction when attitudes concerning reading are of the greatest significance, to deprive the child of the opportunity to do oral reading may prove disastrous as far as his future success in reading is concerned. It may even affect adversely his personality development when the importance of reading is emphasized as much as it usually and rightly is in the typical first-grade room.

How then does oral reading fit into the beginning reading program? Here are a few suggestions:

1. The boys and girls can read silently in short segments the story in a basal reader. For example, in the beginning days of reading instruction, possibly when the pupils are reading preprimers or primers, the teacher may ask them to read only one sentence at a time silently. He may ask

them, for example, to read the next sentence silently to find out what Tom then said to his mother. Then he may ask a pupil to read the sentence as he thinks Tom said it. To be sure, every sentence that is read silently should not be read orally. At times the teacher may ask questions about what was read. At other times he may ask the boys and girls to point to a word or words he names. At still other times the pupils might discuss what they have just read. Or they might predict what they think will happen next.

2. Reading a selection by parts is also, after previous silent reading of the selection, good reason for oral reading. It is advisable that pupils to whom parts have been given have the opportunity to reread the material silently after the assignment of lines has been made.

3. Even in first grade, occasionally one or more pupils might read to the class material the group has not read. The persons doing the reading should practice beforehand both silently and orally the material they will read. The teacher can do much to make such reading a real occasion, a program for the listeners.

4. The children can read orally the experience charts they have helped construct.

5. Oral reading at home by the pupils should be encouraged. For suggestions as to how parents can help in the oral reading program, the reader is referred to page 300.

PROPORTION OF TIME FOR ORAL AND SILENT READING

What should be the proportion of oral to silent reading? A precise answer to this question cannot be given for each grade, for the apportionment depends on a variety of factors. One of these is the length of the reading period in schools that set aside time daily for reading instruction. There is wide variation in the same grades in various schools, and often there are differences within the same building if there is more than one room of the same grade. Moreover, even when the reading periods in two rooms of the same grade are of equal length, the time spent in oral reading may vary greatly. In one room more time may be spent in silent reading during study periods than in the other. Furthermore, the amount of oral and silent reading done during other class periods, such as social studies or science, will influence the question of the proportion of time to be devoted to each. Reading at home, too, will affect the division of the reading period between the two types of reading. Factors like individual differences among children, their past training, the methods used by the teacher, and his skill in teaching reading will also need to be considered.

In the first grade and in the first part of the second grade, when most children cannot read more rapidly silently than orally, oral reading will not ordinarily affect the rate of silent reading unfavorably. However, even in beginning reading an undue amount of vocalization in silent reading may result from overemphasis on oral reading.

Oral reading in the lower grades is abundantly justified by the extreme pleasure that many children experience when they read to others or listen to others read to them. Although oral reading exercises can prove boring to all concerned, most children look forward to the opportunity to read aloud to the teacher or classmates when there is an atmosphere of approval. It would seem unwise to deprive children of a satisfying experience that strengthens the desire to learn to read. Every avenue to genuine reading interest should be utilized.

A teacher may ask a child to read aloud to him in order to learn the child's specific needs in reading. Children may read aloud to each other to share a pleasurable reading experience or to pass on desired information. Group exercises in oral reading, however, with all members of the group following on the page, should generally be avoided.

APPRAISING SKILL IN ORAL READING

Before the teacher attempts to appraise the oral reading skill of his pupils, he will advisedly have in mind the characteristics of the efficient oral reader.

Characteristics of the Effective Oral Reader

The teacher who undertakes to evaluate children's growth in oral reading skill will look for such familiar signs as these:

1. The pupil recognizes common words at sight.
2. He pronounces the words correctly.
3. He shows that he knows the meaning not only of the words but of the entire selection.
4. He uses variety and appropriateness of tone, pitch, force, and speed.
5. He enunciates clearly.
6. He appears at ease while he reads.
7. He is free from interfering mannerisms.
8. He is responsive to the reactions of the audience.
9. He exhibits interest and enthusiasm when he reads.
10. He gives his own interpretation of the selection through his oral reading.
11. His posture is erect and dignified without being overformal.
12. He handles his book effectively.

Comprehension is a primary requisite to efficient oral reading. As explained earlier in this chapter, this fact constitutes one important reason why pupils should not ordinarily be encouraged to read a passage aloud until they have first read it silently and understand it. Good phrasing, effective expression, and appropriate emphasis all depend on the reader's grasp of the meaning. It is sometimes possible for a skillful reader to read orally without giving full attention to the content, but for most children good comprehension is a first requirement for accurate, intelligible oral reading. Meaning will determine the correct selection of word accents, the sound values of letters, and the intonation appropriate to the purpose of the writer.

The physical behavior of the oral reader, while distinctly secondary to the problem of comprehension, requires some attention on the part of the teacher. Formal restrictions that were once imposed with respect to the position of the feet and hands are no longer observed. Children are encouraged to stand erect; to assume a natural, relaxed position; and to avoid leaning against a desk, table, or chair. The book or magazine should not shield the face of the reader. Ideally, contact with the audience is maintained by frequent upward glances toward the listeners, but such contact is the result of a feeling of ease and an eagerness to communicate, rather than conscious effort or deliberate drill.

It is recommended that pupils know what traits are considered important for effective oral reading. In the intermediate grades, and probably even in the upper primary, the boys and girls can take part in drawing up a checklist of the qualities of a good oral reader. These points may be recorded on a chart. If there is not enough display space in a classroom to keep the chart up all the time, it could be stored until it is to be used, namely, when the pupils are reading orally or are preparing for oral reading.

The points to be included in a checklist for use by the boys and girls will necessarily vary from grade to grade. In the lower grades a brief listing couched in simple language will be all that is desirable. In the intermediate grades the list of items may be similar to the one recorded on the sample on page 316.

Checking Oral Reading

Informal observation of a pupil's performance in the oral reading situation, especially with the aid of a checklist, is one of the best methods of evaluating growth in the skills peculiar to oral reading. Defects such as bad posture, finger pointing, and poor intonation are easily noted by the alert teacher who is interested in improving the oral reading performance of his pupils. A record may be kept of the diagnosis, in a manner similar to that suggested on page 316. Boys and girls can participate in the appraisals made. It is recommended that the suggestions for improvement given in class be leveled, as a rule, not at any one individual but that they serve as points for consideration by all the pupils who have read orally on a given day.

Mention is frequently made of standardized oral reading tests. Such tests, however, are in reality devices to determine a pupil's skill in silent reading. They are helpful in revealing to the teacher the specific difficulties that a pupil encounters when dealing with words and sentences. Valuable data can be obtained for use in diagnosis of reading problems from reading tests such as the following, though these tests do not measure the specific skills of *oral* reading: (1.) the Gray Oral Reading Check Tests (Bobbs-Merrill Company), (2.) the Gates Oral Reading Test (Teachers College Press, Columbia University.), (3.) the Durrell Oral Reading Test (Harcourt Brace Jovanovich), (4.) the Jenkins Oral Reading Test (The Bobbs-Merrill Company), (5.) the Slosson Oral Reading Tests (Slosson Educational Publications, East Aurora, New York), (6.) the Leavell Analytical Oral Reading Tests (American Guidance Service, Minneapolis, Minnesota), and (7.) the oral sections of the Diagnostic Reading Tests (Committee on Diagnostic Reading Tests). These tests measure points such as reversals of letters and words, substitutions of letters and words, omissions, and inadequate return sweeps of the eye as the eye moves in reading from the end of one line back to the left side of the page.

While oral reading tests can provide some insight into what is occurring as the reader reads silently, it must not be assumed that the excellences or the difficulties in oral and silent reading are exactly the same. Qualities such as shyness or nervousness or self-consciousness may interfere in oral reading but have no effect on silent reading—in fact, may not be present. Similarly, a child who reads too rapidly silently to get the meaning of what he reads may have a problem that will not show up in oral reading.

For an indication of the pupil's skill in reference to points peculiar to oral reading—such as phrasing, expressiveness, and reaction to the audience—the teacher must rely on his own careful observation of pupil performance and such cumulative anecdotal records as he may find time to keep.

CAUSES OF DEFICIENCIES IN ORAL READING

Reference was made earlier in this chapter to some of the manifestations of pupil difficulties in oral reading. These overt signs of trouble—such as omission of words, reading at too rapid a rate for effective interpretation, or nervousness while reading—are often indexes of underlying problems. Among the factors that frequently contribute adversely to oral reading are: (1.) an undesirable audience situation; (2.) unsuitable material; (3.) lack of skill in some abilities important in silent reading—

such as skill in recognizing words and power of understanding what is read; (4.) need of specific help in development of skills peculiar to oral reading—such as desirable posture, correct handling of the book, or effectiveness of interpretation; and (5.) insufficient preparation for the reading of a given selection.

An unsatisfactory eye-voice span, as mentioned on page 216, can contribute to problems in oral reading. The eyes of the effective oral reader focus ahead of the words he is reading orally. If the eyes of the oral reader were fixating on the word he speaks, there would be danger of word-by-word reading, with its accompanying lack of interestingness and clarity of interpretation. For most readers it is probably conducive to smooth oral reading if their eyes are, as a rule, a few words ahead of the voice, far enough so that the reader can read every word with proper interpretation because he knows the context in which it occurs. If the eye-voice span is too long, however, the reader may forget some of the words before he has read them orally, with resulting difficulties— such as substitutions, omissions, or additions. Problems related to the length of the eye-voice span can best be approached indirectly. For example, familiarity with the material, appropriate level of the difficulty of it, desire to communicate to the audience the meaning of the passage —all help in the establishment of a suitable length of span between the word on which the eye fixates and the one being spoken.

Another difficulty some boys and girls have in reading orally is that their rate is not suitable—either too fast or too slow. The desirable speed depends on factors such as the material to be read, the purpose in reading it, and the size of the audience. A rule-of-thumb is that the rate for oral reading should be approximately the same, under given circumstances, as it should be for talking.

GENERAL SUGGESTIONS FOR THE IMPROVEMENT OF ORAL READING

Chapter 9B presents specific suggestions for procedures planned to help boys and girls become better oral readers. In this section of the present chapter are listed and discussed some general recommendations on which the details of procedure can be based. The discussion that follows includes suggestions for alleviating the causes of deficiencies in oral reading, which are listed in the preceding section.

1. Children should be given many opportunities to do oral reading and they should be encouraged to make use of these opportunities. The fact that apparently it is possible for children to learn to read for meaning without oral reading experiences in the classroom does not justify depriving them of the chance to engage in oral reading. Children's motives for oral reading, on which the teacher can build, are of many kinds. The boys and girls may read aloud to the teacher to show their progress in mastering the printed page; they may do so to share a poem or a story with other children; they may read orally to prove a point or to raise a question. They may engage in additional activities of the type suggested on pages 289–290.

2. The skills of oral reading can be improved through instruction. Successful experiences in oral reading may give needed self-confidence to the shy child. Approval by teacher and class will help him to take further, perhaps timid, steps toward self-assured oral reading. Teachers can help boys and girls to overcome monotony of rate or pitch and to read literary materials aloud with feeling and animation.

3. Most instruction in oral reading is preferably incidental. There is a proper place for formal exercises in oral reading in rehearsal for assembly programs or for special events in the classroom, but throughout the year the instruction is likely to consist of helpful suggestions as the child undertakes to communicate with his classmates from the printed page. Such suggestions should always be made in such a way as not to embarrass the reader. Usually they are made priviately. They should be given along with praise for those good qualities the child displays.

4. The teacher's example can be a model for the oral reading of the boys and girls. Not all teachers are skillful oral readers, but all can learn to read aloud with good enunciation, appropriate volume and emphasis, and an interesting variety of pitch and rate. Teachers in all grades should cultivate this ability.

5. Ordinarily the pupils should be encouraged to listen to the reader without following him in their own books. Reasons for this generalization were given earlier in this chapter.

6. Children should have access to a wide variety of suitable materials for oral reading. Such materials should be easy and interesting and often include dialogue. They should include stories and poems, both published materials and the children's own work. Stories or articles cut out of discarded books and magazines make excellent material for oral reading. On special occasions, such as holidays or the birthdays of famous persons, stories about the exploits of national heroes and the meaning of the holidays may be used. Humorous anecdotes are especially suitable for oral reading.

7. Oral reading should take place only when there is a receptive audience. The reader must be eager to communicate, and the audience must be eager to listen. Until such conditions exist, it would be better to postpone the oral reading. The group might set up simply-worded standards of behavior that an audience should meet. They might also discuss what characteristics of the reader make it easy for an audience to be good listeners.

8. Adverse criticism by members of the audience should usually not be directed against one individual reader but should be stated as applicable to some or all of the group. Occasional favorable comment on specifics by the teacher is desirable, and certainly suggestions given privately by the teacher are in order.

9. The cooperation of the parents should be enlisted whenever possible. Although parents should not be expected to help teach the skills of oral reading, they can encourage children to read aloud to them and to other children in the home. Such experiences effectively supplement the limited opportunities the school can provide for oral reading. At meetings of the Parent-Teacher Association teachers might well suggest ways in which parents can help with reading, oral reading included. At these meetings suggestions can be given as to what standards in oral reading should be expected from boys and girls. Recommendations for a program of home reading, where the parent reads to the child and the child to the parent, can also profitably be given. Since problems in reading differ from grade to grade, home-room meetings of the PTA are especially suitable for group conferences with parents about how they can be of help. Brief bulletins to parents about their possible role in the program of oral reading can also be of value.

Outline for Chapter 9B

DEVELOPING SKILL IN ORAL READING

Instructional Practices
Oral Reading by the Teacher
Oral Reading by Children in Small Groups
Reading Poetry Orally
Choral Reading
    Values of Choral Reading
    Background for Choral Reading
    Grouping for Choral Reading
    Casting
    Selection of Material
    Additional Suggestions
Dramatization and Oral Reading
Puppetry and Oral Reading
    Values of Puppetry
    Puppets and Puppet Stages
A Prepared Oral Reading Program
    Teaching Plan
    Explanation of the Plan

CHAPTER

Developing Skills in Oral Reading

In order that the child may learn to interpret the written page effectively to others, he should be given abundant opportunity to read meaningful material aloud. Providing the boys and girls with this opportunity is one of the most important ways in which the teacher can help them become skillful oral readers. However, although experience in reading in purposeful situations is basic, some direct instruction is also usually valuable and at times necessary.

INSTRUCTIONAL PRACTICES

Following are some illustrative teaching practices which may prove helpful as direct instruction in oral reading:

1. Stressing the importance of correct pronunciation through class discussion and comments by the teacher.
2. Requiring pupils to check pronunciation before reading orally, and giving them help when necessary.
3. Teaching the interpretation of diacritical marks in the dictionary.
4. Stressing the importance of clear enunciation.

5. Practicing the enunciation of words in which the endings *ing, ed,* and *t* are often slurred.

6. Teaching pupils to note the number of syllables in a word, using a dictionary if necessary.

7. Having pupils divide assigned words into syllables.

8. Using rhyme to illustrate correct pronunciation, as: "Just rhymes with must, not with best!"

9. Having pupils make a list of words they habitually enunciate poorly.

10. Listening to records to note examples of excellent enunciation.

11. Having pupils make tape recordings of their voices to note the quality of enunciation.

12. Having pupils listen to the teacher read a sentence with good phrasing and say it back to him, (This should, as a rule, be done individually, with different sentences.)

13. Contrasting good and poor phrasing in the reading of a sentence.

14. Exposing for very short duration phrases to be read orally.

15. Having pupils read passages silently to note proper places for pausing and then read them orally.

16. Teaching the use of punctuation marks in determining where the pauses should come.

17. Reading a selection orally without pausing for punctuation marks and asking the class to supply them where they are needed.

18. Having pupils look for answers through silent reading of a passage and then read the appropriate parts aloud.

19. Having pupils summarize a selection after reading it aloud.

20. Preparing in advance questions to be answered by the pupil after reading orally.

21. Explaining to the pupils the role of the reader as interpreter.

22. Explaining some of the rules of good interpretation, such as those pertaining to (a.) reading a selection beforehand, (b.) making certain that one understands what is to be read, and (c.) reading with expression.

23. Choosing materials that pupils will be able to interpret adequately.

24. Emphasizing the importance of having a clear purpose for the oral reading.

25. Helping pupils overcome individual mannerisms that draw attention away from the message.

26. Providing pupils with sentences for oral reading that express strong emotions—such as love, fear, sadness, surprise, anxiety.

27. Demonstrating to the class the need for variety of tone, pitch, and rate in oral reading, by contrasting monotonous with varied expression.

28. Demonstrating and having pupils practice the use of different types of tone, pitch, and rate with different materials.

29. Giving practice in expressing different moods through changes in voice qualities.

30. Having pupils listen to speakers who use their voices effectively.

31. Having pupils find the words in a sentence that are especially significant in the context and then read the sentence to emphasize the important words.

32. Arranging for pupils to read in concert with others, as in choral reading.

33. Having the class formulate standards for good oral reading, including ways of holding a book or magazine.

34. Making and encouraging the pupils to help make displays that will emphasize points to observe in oral reading.

35. Getting class participation in deciding on appropriate times and materials for oral reading.

36. Listening to pupils individually read for diagnostic purposes.

37. Having pupils reread a short selection orally as an aid to comprehension.

38. Discussing with a class what a reader can do to make it easy for an audience not to be restless.

39. Encouraging pupils to prepare a sketch in which varying inflections are used to say the same expression in order to produce different meanings. For example, the sentence "What a day!" could be given so as to express more than one reaction to the day.

40. Helping the class draw up standards of the minutes of a club meeting for oral reading.

41. Encouraging boys and girls to make a study of various ways in which oral reading is used outside of school.

42. Encouraging the beginning reader to read at home to interested parents or sisters and brothers material he has read at school. Duplicating copies of an experience chart for each child to take home, after he is able to "read" it, is one way of making it possible for the child to demonstrate his newly acquired skill.

ORAL READING BY THE TEACHER

Some persons insist that a day should never pass during which the elementary-school teacher does not read something orally to the class. While this may be an extreme view, certainly frequent oral reading by the teacher is highly desirable. By means of such reading, pupils can be acquainted with literature of genuine worth that is too difficult for them to read by themselves. Moreover, the teacher is able by this means to set standards of performance to which the pupils can aspire.

Naturally, not all teachers are equally skillful in oral reading. For many, it is desirable to precede the reading with careful preparation through prior silent reading of the selections, or even rehearsal of the oral reading activity itself. Such preparation includes also a careful consideration of the material to be used. Stories read to children should be of high quality but on the level of the children. They should be of the kind that lend themselves to oral reading. For younger children, especially, stories with much conversation in them are likely to have the greatest appeal. In addition to fiction, the reading material may include selections from poetry, social studies, current events, and even science.

A procedure that the intermediate-grade teacher may find valuable is one in which the boys and girls alternate with him in reading a rather lengthy story, possibly an entire book. Fifteen or twenty minutes daily might be spent thus. The pupil or pupils, whose turn it is to read orally on a given day, should beforehand have practiced carefully reading orally the part of the selection assigned to them. Often it is advisable in reading of this type that the teacher serve as reader most of the time in order that the interest of the audience will not be lost.

Teachers sometimes ask: "When and how should the pictures be shown when a book is read to the class?" The answer must depend on the circumstances. Many picture-story books are poorly adapted to reading to a group. Such books are more suitable for individual reading or reading shared by two or three children. Most of the modern picture books for young children have more illustrations than text; indeed, the central message is in the pictures while the text is only commentary. In such cases, it is best to have the pupils grouped as closely as possible around the teacher. The teacher reads the text material on a page and holds up the book to show the picture, turning it in all directions so that everyone may see. The children should have time to see and enjoy each scene as the story progresses. To help the pupils' observation, the teacher may at times decide to point out details in some of the pictures as the story goes along. If the class is too large for convenient showing of the pictures to all pupils, the story should be read to children in smaller groups. No child should be made to feel neglected because he was unable to see the pictures. And after the reading, the book should be added to the room collection, where individual pupils can re-examine it at leisure.

ORAL READING BY CHILDREN IN SMALL GROUPS

In both primary and intermediate grades, the children can be divided into small groups of three or four or five who will meet in various parts of the room to read orally to one another. If this procedure can be carried out effectively in a room, much of the problem of finding time for everyone to get as much practice in oral reading as is desirable can be solved. Care must be taken that the material read is very easy and very interesting. Furthermore, in each group there should be at least one person who can serve as chairman and help the others with words they cannot recognize. So that an orderliness conducive to work prevails, it is usually necessary to work out rules of procedure for group reading, designating such points as order of reading, responsibilities of the chairman, responsibilities of the reader, and duties of the listeners. If possible, there should be a rotating chairmanship, but no child who is unable to perform the duties of a chairman should be appointed to the post. The teacher can spend his time going from group to group, observing points that he may wish to bring up at a later time so as to provide for improvement in routine. This plan works only when pupils can read the material they have fairly well and when the teacher is able to maintain the desired orderliness even when he is not at all times in direct contact with each group.

Practice in reading in small groups can be especially valuable when the various groups read in order later on to give information to the rest of the class on a problem that the class is studying. At times, the boys and girls, as they are working in small groups, might be practicing reading selections, possibly stories in a basal reading textbook, that later they will want to read at home to their parents.

Marguerite Goens, formerly first-grade teacher in Indianapolis, worked out an excellent plan for small-group reading through the help of the third grade in her building. In this cooperating third grade several of the best readers went to the first-grade room twice a week for twenty minutes to take charge of oral reading groups consisting of three or four pupils each. While the assistants were working with the children, the room teacher circulated from group to group giving needed assistance. In order to make certain that the reading material was of worth and on the level of the readers, and that it fulfilled the requirements of oral presentation, everything that was to be read, including material that pupils brought to school, had to be approved by the teacher before it was read orally. The group work did not take the place of the developmental reading classes, but it did serve as a very vital adjunct to it.

READING POETRY ORALLY

One of the neglected areas of oral reading in many schools is that of poetry reading by boys and girls. It is an art so filled with rich opportunities for developing appreciation that much more emphasis should be placed on it than is commonly the case. Unfortunately, when poetry is read orally, it is often done so poorly that the results actually interfere with its enjoyment.

As a rule, the child who does the reading should be well prepared. There are occasions when the boys and girls might read, without preparation beforehand, in order to be given specific help in reading poetry more effectively. But when the aim of the teacher is to have the audience get enjoyment from the reading, the pupils should be able to read the poetry so as to arouse appreciation in their listeners. At all such times the pupil should practice reading his poem orally before he appears in front of his audience. If possible, the teacher should help him while he is practicing. He can do so by assisting the reader in getting the meaning of the poem through questioning, through comments, and through reading orally part or all of the poem himself. All the other elements essential to effective oral reading of prose, such as skill in word recognition and handling the book with facility, are also requirements for reading poetry. Because pupils are more accustomed to prose than poetry and because difficulties in interpretation of poetry are often greater than those in interpretation of prose, to achieve as good a result when reading poetry as when reading prose is difficult for many boys and girls. The child must have a feeling of confidence and poise as he comes in front of his audience, a becoming self-assurance that results from knowledge of being well prepared and having a worthwhile contribution to make. Some pitfalls in reading poetry that the teacher must try to help the child avoid are "sing-song" reading, lack of discrimination between commas that represent grammatical structure and those that represent rhetorical phrasing, and over-dramatic reading.

The poetry should be well selected. Even for young children there is much poetry of superior quality. An examination of the excellent anthologies of literature for children will suggest many poems and will give the names of poets whose work, other than that quoted in the anthology, is worth investigating. At times the teacher may choose the poems to be read, but no pupil should be forced to read a poem that he himself does not enjoy, or one that he does not want to read to the group. When a girl or boy has a voice in choosing the poem, however, the selection should not be left entirely up to him. The teacher is responsible for seeing that no poem chosen is of poor quality. Furthermore, in the choice of poems the ability of the reader to interpret and of the audience to enjoy must be considered.

The reading of poetry should be done in a suitable setting. Sometimes the teacher should help create the mood needed for enjoyment even before the pupil begins reading. The teacher can at times do this by means of questions or discussion. For example, before a child reads the poem "The Swing" by Robert Louis Stevenson, the teacher may give the audience a chance to tell whether they like to be up in a swing and how they feel when they are swinging. At other times a picture may help children get into the right mood for a poem. Before a pupil reads "The Duel" by Eugene Field orally, a picture of a gingham dog and a calico cat, with a discussion as to how the two look at each other, may get the pupils interested in finding out how the gingham dog and the calico cat in the poem got along. Printed pictures that express the mood of the poem well are sometimes available. At other times the reader may wish to draw beforehand a picture that he thinks will make the audience want to hear his poem. Interest in the poem may be aroused by posting the picture on a bulletin board even as long as a few days before the poem will be read. A question written near the picture, such as: "What is happening in this picture?" might arouse curiosity.

The audience should often have more access to a poem than is afforded by one reading. Poems that are read orally may be posted on a bulletin board so that everyone can read them. Or they may be put into a booklet placed on the library table, easily accessible to all the children. Oral rereading of the poem by the person who had earlier read it to the class is often effective. When a series of poems has been read, the pupils may be asked to specify a few that they would like particularly to hear again.

CHORAL READING

Choral reading in its simplest terms, can be defined as the speaking of poetry or prose by several or many voices either in unison or by parts, with possibly some solo work included.

Values of Choral Reading

Many values may be found in choral reading at its best. One of these is the beneficial effect it can have on personality development. The shy child becomes more self-confident when he can quite inconspicuously, in group work, get the assurance that comes from knowledge of a contribution to a shared undertaking. Similarly the "show-off," even in solo parts, can learn to submerge himself for the good of the group and find satisfaction in so doing. Another value that can result from choral reading is an understanding and appreciation of poetry and poetic prose. This, obviously, can be expected only if literature of enduring quality is used for choral reading purposes.

A third value is the beneficial effect choral reading can have on the speech and the oral reading of the child. The emphasis placed in choral reading on voice quality, interpretation of meaning, enunciation, and articulation can affect oral reading favorably. Furthermore, the poise and self-assurance that it aims to develop, and under favorable conditions achieves, are essentials of effective oral reading of any type.

It is not the purpose of this chapter to give a comprehensive treatment of how to teach choral reading. The description that is given, as well as the suggestions for teaching it that are included, will serve chiefly to help make clear the relation between choral reading and other oral reading.

Background for Choral Reading

Before the teacher begins choral reading with his class, whether he teaches in the primary or intermediate grades, it is advisable that he ascertain whether or not the boys and girls have been introduced to a variety of worthwhile poems. If the field of their appreciation of poetry is narrow, his first step should probably be reading or—better yet—saying poems to the class. As he repeats a poem, pupils may wish to join him on whatever lines or parts of lines they remember. At other times he may want to precede the reading of a poem by giving a brief background for the poem, to set the mood for it or to provide valuable information that will add to the appreciation of the poem. He may accomplish this purpose by comments he makes or by class discussion. After reading a poem or saying it to the class, if the boys and girls are able to read it, they might read it orally with him. Help can be given with the rhythm of the poem so that it adds to the words, not detracts from them through sing-song. To some poems children could beat time or walk or run or skip as the poem suggests. Music that harmonizes with the theme of a poem could be played. Pictures in the room suggesting the mood of some poems, books or poetry in which the illustrations add to the significance of the words, flowers, or other objects of beauty through the sight of which the pupils may catch the spirit of a poem could be used to help interest boys and girls in good poetry. Flannel boards and bulletin boards can serve as means of displaying illustrations of some favorite poems. A poetry corner in the classroom may serve as further motivation. In the upper primary and intermediate grades pupils might bring to school poems that they find particularly enjoyable. In one class every boy and girl selected a favorite poem, which the teacher typed and then combined into a class booklet. The table of contents gave not only the title of the poem but also the name of the person who selected it. Enthusiasm for reading the booklet ran high, partly because the boys and girls wanted to read the choices of their classmates.

To succeed in laying a suitable background for the appreciation of poetry, the spirit of the classroom must be one in which thoughts of poetry are encouraged. It must be one in which creativeness and imaginativeness have a place. It must be one in which teachers and pupils work together cooperatively; one in which, to paraphrase Samuel Crothers in his book, *The Gentle Reader,* the birthright of imagination is not sacrificed for a mess of knowledge.

For further suggestions on oral poetry reading the reader is referred to the section of this chapter entitled "Reading Poetry Orally."

Grouping for Choral Reading

While a background for choral reading is being laid, it is usually advisable with beginners in the art to have pupils attain some skill in saying poems in concert before any attempt is made at grouping for choral reading. It is wise at that time for the teacher to take note of the characteristics of the voices of the various individuals as he hears them talk or read—usually, if not always, without the boys and girls being conscious of the fact that he is testing for grouping. Since the simplest grouping is a two-part division of voices, into the high and low, the teacher will want to note mentally which voices belong in each group. Sometimes he may also employ a more direct method as he tests voices by having pupils repeat a sentence or sing a tune or count to ten. He may wish to enlist the help of the boys and girls in doing the grouping. After the pupils have had some practice in two-group speaking, the teacher may wish to organize a third group, including in it the pupils whose voices are on the borderline between high and low.

Care must be taken when grouping that no misunderstandings result. Some girls may be inclined, unless caution is exercised, to think that it borders on the disgraceful to have a low voice and be in a group with many of the boys. The teacher should point out that in the elementary school in two-part grouping there are usually some boys and some girls in each of the groups. He could also point out that the blend of the voices of both boys and girls in each division contributes as much to choral reading as it does to singing. It should be made clear that the grouping done before much time has been spent on choral reading is subject to change later. Reasons for change may be that the child's voice has changed or that the testing situation produced inaccurate results. The need for more pupils in one of the groups with different poems may also result in reassignment of groups. It is important that a pupil be happy in the group to which he has been assigned. Better that the reading of a poem be poor than that one child be made unhappy by his role in an activity that should bring joy to all participants!

Casting

After grouping comes casting. By casting a poem is meant dividing the lines of a poem or prose selection into parts and assigning these parts to individuals or groups of individuals.

It should probably be pointed out that a poem can be read in unison for choral reading, with high and low or with high, intermediate, and low voices saying the same lines. Such reading is more difficult than that in which the several groups speak different lines. Reading in unison as choral reading is not to be confused with concert reading in which there is no division into types of voices. Because of the difficulty of effective reading in unison, that type of choral reading is usually not attempted in the elementary school, although, all boys and girls saying the same lines without grouping of voices is common practice.

There are several types of casting commonly used in elementary schools. The reading may be done in a solo-chorus combination, as, for example, when the teacher or other leader reads alone all parts excepting the chorus parts, in which the entire class participates. The dialogue type of choral reading can be done either by two individuals who take the parts or by two choruses saying alternate lines or groups of lines. The line-a-child casting differs from the dialogues by two persons in that lines are assigned to three or more individuals. Similarly, line-a-choir reading differs from dialogues participated in by two choruses in that three or more groups say the lines. The use of various combinations of these types in reading a single long selection makes possible considerable variation of pattern of reading. Which type should be used will be determined in part by the ability of the group, the selection itself, and the objectives to be accomplished. Frequently the children, under the guidance of the teacher, should have a voice in deciding on the type of casting to be done and the assignment of parts.

Selection of Material

The final responsibility for selecting material for choral reading lies with the teacher. While it is desirable that boys and girls, especially those somewhat experienced in choral reading, be encouraged to help in the choice, it should be clear to them that their recommendations will not necessarily be accepted. The teacher will not want to subject the class to poorly chosen verse or prose for choral reading because one or more pupils suggested it.

There are certain standards that should be observed in the selection of material. If boys and girls participate in the selection, standards should be applied by them, too. However, in a pupils' checklist the wording might be different from that in a list such as the following, which is prepared for the teacher. These points should be noted about a poem to be used for choral reading.

1. It should have literary value.
2. It should be on the pupils' level of understanding.
3. It should be one the boys and girls will enjoy.
4. It should be one that the teacher will enjoy teaching.
5. It should have a rhythm.
6. It should fill a need of the class.
7. It should be adaptable to choral reading of the type that the boys and girls are capable of doing.

Books containing poems chosen for their suitability for choral reading, with suggestions for casting, can be of value to both teachers and pupils. Some such books are *Choral Speaking Arrangements for the Lower Grades* by Louis Abney and Grace Bowe (The Expression Company), *Choral Reading for Fun and Recreation* by Helen A. Brown and Harry J. Heltman (Westminster Press), and *Let's Say Poetry Together* by Carrie Rasmussen (Burgess Publishing Company). Poems listed in such books, however, are not necessarily the most suitable for any given group of boys and girls. Wide acquaintance with poetry, access to the best anthologies of poetry for children, as well as books of poetry by single authors, will keep the teacher and, to some extent, the pupils from being limited by poems suggested in books designed specifically for choral reading.

Additional Suggestions

Following are additional points that the teacher should bear in mind as he helps boys and girls in choral reading:

Choral reading should be pleasurable. If it is not, the major reasons for doing it will probably not be accomplished. This does not mean that hard work may not be necessary in order to get the desired results but it does mean that if appreciation of good literature is to result, the pupils must enjoy the work.

Boys and girls should be helped, if help is indicated, to comprehend the meaning of the material they use for choral reading. This does not mean that the child must know every word in a selection or that he must have the depth of insight into a poem that an adult might have. However, problems in vocabulary should not be allowed to interfere with the interpretation of meaning. Nor should comprehension of the poem be limited by lack of sufficient insight to make it meaningful to the child. Fortunately there is no reason why the teacher cannot help boys and girls with problems of word meaning and of comprehension of poems which but for difficulty in these two respects might be highly suitable for choral reading. He can frankly approach the pupils with the thought that attention to some of the words will enhance their understanding and hopefully their enjoyment of a poem. On such a comment might follow a brief period of word study. Similarly, through questions and comments, the teacher can help the members of the class with the meaning of a poem as a whole.

Boys and girls should be aware of the importance of good posture in choral reading and they should be stimulated to want to assume such a posture. The teacher's posture should be exemplary. Practice in desirable posture might be valuable. Discussion of the need of good breath control and of the relation between breath control and posture might be helpful.

The teacher might well emphasize with the boys and girls the importance of good speech. He can show them, through illustration and demonstration, the difference between slovenly and clear enunciation. In fact, a group of boys and girls could put on an informal dramatization depicting both faulty and good enunciation.

A good leader is essential to effective choral reading. The leader can show the speakers or readers when the different parts should come in, when the voices of a group should be softer or louder, happier or sadder, faster or slower. Use of a baton is probably rightfully frowned on, since it seems better that the leader use his hands or his body as a whole to communicate with the group. During practice periods at times a pupil might serve as leader. When there is an audience, the teacher should be the leader so that he can deal inconspicuously and competently with any problem that may arise.

Costuming is to be discouraged in choral reading. The wearing of costumes might detract from the beauty of the interpretation as presented by children's voices. Some teachers like to have their pupils wear uniform apparel when engaging in choral reading, having the boys wear light shirts and dark trousers and the girls white blouses and dark skirts. But what could be as effective as boys and girls dressed in their better school clothes as they interpret in their unsophisticated way a worthwhile message from a poem that is of lasting value to them!

DRAMATIZATION AND ORAL READING

Dramatization can serve various important purposes in the elementary school, one of which is improvement in oral reading. It is true that oral reading is not a part of many types of dramatizations by elementary-school children. Frequently, plays planned by boys and girls are given somewhat impromptu, without any lines recorded and without, therefore, any reading to be done. However, under some circumstances oral reading has a legitimate part in dramatization. Some situations in which oral reading is used are as follows:

1. Sometimes when boys and girls make up their own plays the lines are recorded, the parts assigned to children, the lines practiced as the children read their parts orally, and finally the play is read to an audience.
2. Some reading series contain dramatic selections not designed for memorization, but planned for oral reading.
3. Some printed plays, later to be memorized by the pupils, are read by them orally in early practice periods.
4. Narrators of plays often read their parts to the audience.
5. Frequently the lines for a puppet play are read orally. Sometimes they are read by characters behind the scene. At other times they may be read by a person in view of the audience, who plays a role similar to that of the narrator.

PUPPETRY AND ORAL READING

Since puppetry affords many excellent opportunities for oral reading, it is discussed here in greater detail than the other points to which reference was made in the preceding paragraph.

Values of Puppetry

Puppetry can serve many valuable objectives, among them the following:

1. It can be used as a means of motivation for schoolwork in various areas. For example, a puppet show based on some phase of colonial life, such as the colonial school, can play a significant role in interesting the boys and girls in that period of history.

2. It can be a means of giving information. For example, a well-planned and well-executed puppet show featuring some important phases of Benjamin Franklin's life may give the members of the audience and the participants in the puppet play valuable information about Franklin.

3. It can be used when giving oral reports. In a report on *Miss Hickory,* the child giving the report may decide to have puppets tell the last part of the story, where Squirrel finally gets the hickory nut head that he had so long coveted.

4. It can serve as a means of self-expression.

5. It can provide boys and girls with the experience of making puppets, designing and making the stage, sewing or painting the backdrop, and making the furniture.

6. It can develop into a happy leisuretime activity for the child who will make of puppetry a hobby.

7. It can provide opportunity for oral reading in a functional and interesting setting.

Puppets and Puppet Stages

A few suggestions are here given as to kinds of puppets and puppet stages that can be used in puppet plays. For more suggestions on the topic the teacher is referred to books on literature for children and on the teaching of the language arts, which frequently include a section on puppetry. Additional references include *The Puppet Theater Handbook* by Marjorie Batchelder (Harper & Row), *Puppets and Plays—A Creative Approach* by Marjorie Batchelder and Virginia Comer (Harper & Row), *Puppets into Actors* by Olive Blackham (The Macmillan Company), *Shadow Puppets* by Olive Blackham (Harper & Row), *A Handbook of First Puppets* by Alexander Ficklen (J. B. Lippincott Company), *Puppet and Pantomime Plays* by Vernon Howard (Sterling Publishing Company), *First Book of Puppets* by Moritz Jagendorf (Franklin Watts), *The Puppet Book* by Shari Lewis (Citadel Press), *Easy Puppets* by Gertrude Pels (Thomas Y. Crowell Company), *The Puppet Do-It-Yourself Book* by Lois Pratt (Exposition Press), *Puppetry, Marionettes, and Shadow Plays* by Loren Taylor (Burgess Publishing Company).

Puppets should be distinguished from marionettes. It is customary to apply the term marionette to those lifelike creatures that are controlled by strings; the term *puppet* is often reserved for figures that are not manipulated by string. Because of the difficulties of handling marionettes, they are not commonly used in the elementary school. However, the same opportunities for oral reading that are pointed out here can be achieved as well through marionettes as through puppets.

Puppets can be classified in a variety of ways. One division is that of 1. stationary or table puppets, 2. rod puppets, and 3. hand puppets. Of these, the stationary puppet is the simplest. Stationary or table puppets can be placed on a table and left there, without motion, throughout a short play when the puppet is the chief actor. The parts can be read orally. The puppet can represent the entire body or the head only. Examples of stationary puppets are a puppet head made from a bottle, with features pasted or painted on; the head of a puppet made from a tin can onto which eyes, ears, mouth, nose, and hair are attached or painted; a paper doll made to stand erect by a tripod made of stiff paper attached to the back side of the base of the puppet.

A rod puppet is one that is controlled by a rod. Any two-dimensional or three-dimensional object, such as a block of wood or an apple or a balloon, with a rod attached to it for manipulation of the puppet may serve as a rod puppet. Another frequently made rod puppet is one in which a paper bag serves as head and body, to which a tongue depressor or other type of rod is attached. As one or more pupils read the parts of the play, the rod puppets can be shown either in full view of the audience or on a puppet stage.

The term *hand puppet* is applied to puppets that are controlled directly by the hand, without a rod. They are of endless variety. Paper-bag puppets, puppets made of socks, balloon puppets, tin-can puppets, light-bulb puppets, and papier-mâché puppets are examples of hand puppets. In most cases the head of such puppets is made of the material designated in the name of the puppet while the body is often represented by a "dress" made of paper or cloth. Hand puppets are usually used on a stage, but they can be shown without a stage as one or more of the pupils read or speak the lines.

A table top, a curtain supported by a rod resting on the back of two straight chairs, a box placed on a table, a doorway with a curtain across the bottom half may serve as temporary stages. Stages can also be constructed from paper cartons or from wood.

Even when the puppets are crude and the stage setting simple, boys and girls through excellence of reading can make the little dolls "come to life."

A PREPARED ORAL READING PROGRAM

In this section is presented a teaching plan that illustrates how a class period devoted to oral reading that has been prepared beforehand can be conducted. An explanation of phases of the plan follows.

Teaching Plan

This plan for a fourth-grade class, like all other teaching plans, should not be thought of as a model that should be followed exactly; rather it is hoped that it will serve as one concrete illustration of what can be done. The needs of the boys and girls should determine the procedure to be followed in any one situation.

I. Topic: Prepared oral reading of Christmas stories.

II. Pupils' aims:
    A. To see if we will like the Christmas stories that will be read to us.
    B. To try to read so that our listeners will enjoy hearing us read.
    C. To be good listeners.

III. Materials
    A. Board work:
        1. "Old Hans and the Toyshop Twins"
            Kenneth Jackson
            Betty Thurston
            Lois Roth
            Jean VanSickle
        2. "The Christmas Tree"
            Jimmie Reed
            Beverly Myers
        3. "The Snow Santa Claus"
            Doris Gale
            Ted Hershey
        4. "A Christmas Friend"
            Ted Gardner
            Norma Staley
    B. Copies of the stories listed under A above.
    C. Chart entitled "Oral Reading" with these points listed on it:
        1. Posture
        2. Voice
        3. Pronunciation
        4. Enunciation
        5. Getting the message across
        6. Remembering the audience
        7. Listening
    D. Individual cards such as the one illustrated:

Gardner, Ted		Oral Reading						
Dates:								
1. Posture								
2. Voice								
3. Pronunciation								
4. Enunciation								
5. Getting the message across								
6. Remembering the audience								
7. Listening								

IV. Procedure

A. Motivation

The teacher says: "How many of you like to hear or read Christmas stories? A committee has prepared several stories which they will read to you."

B. Noting points to watch when reading orally:

1. The teacher, referring to the chart mentioned under III-C above, states that the boys and girls have tried hard to watch those points as they practiced their reading.

2. Two pupils put on a two-minute skit in which they demonstrate good and poor posture while reading orally, and the class briefly names points of excellence and of criticism in the two types of posture demonstrated.

3. The pupils tell what "remembering the audience" means, stressing the fact that while "looking at the audience" is important, it should not be done mechanically.

4. The pupils indicate what a good listener does.

C. Statement of the procedure to be followed in reading the stories: The teacher explains to the boys and girls that after a few introductory remarks the boys and girls whose names are written on the program on the board, under III-A, will read the stories listed there.

D. Reading of the stories by the children preceded by an introductory remark or a question on each story by the teacher or by the reader.

E. Brief discussion of the content of the stories.

F. Pupils' evaluation of the reading:

1. Pupils name the points on the chart that they think were watched particularly well.

2. Pupils name the points on the chart that they think need to be improved upon.

3. Group discusses means by which they can improve on the points referred to under 2. above.

4. Teacher explains that later on he will individually discuss with those who read the quality of their reading.
At that time cards like the one illustrated can be used for making an analysis of each pupil's reading.

Explanation of the Plan

In a lesson of this type this procedure might be followed: 1. preparation before class, 2. deciding on the aims for the period, 3. reference to the points to be observed in the oral reading, 4. announcement of the plan of procedure in reading, 5. reading of the selections, 6. discussion of the story, and 7. evaluation of the reading. Each of these points is discussed here to clarify it in relation to the teaching plan presented and to indicate a few of the possible variations from it that the teacher may wish to make.

1. Preparation before class. Preparation should include choosing the readers, selecting the materials to be read, practicing reading the selections, providing for the materials needed during classtime, and making seating arrangements.

a. Choosing the readers. The teacher who helped make plans for the reading program described earlier was in the habit of choosing no pupil for a second turn at participating in an oral reading program before everyone in the room had had the opportunity to take part in one. He also made certain that pupils of varying ability appeared on each program. He took this precaution because he realized that while it would be relatively easy to keep a program interesting if all participants were good readers, it would be difficult to hold the interest of the audience if only the poorer readers performed.

The question is often asked: "Should the poor reader really be expected or allowed to take part in an audience reading program?" The answer is: "Yes, as a rule," If a pupil is not permitted to read because he has decided difficulties in reading, he may feel slighted, even though often he may act as if he were pleased that he did not have to read. Moreover, it is the poorer reader, more than the excellent one, who needs the practice. The teacher can help save the former from feelings of inadequacy in the oral reading situation by giving him shorter selections than most others in the group so that he can prepare thoroughly what he reads. It is probably good policy to give some of the better readers relatively brief selections, too, so that the one who is less able will not think of the brevity of his reading as a stigma attached to his performance. Also, the teacher can see to it that the child who cannot read as well orally as the others has very easy material to read. Help from the teacher in preparation for the reading can often preserve the ego of the reader, with a minimum of undesirable emotional reactions. At the same time, in this way the pupil can get real help in becoming a better reader. Some teachers, rather than depriving a poor reader of the opportunity to read orally, wisely help him all but memorize his selection before class so that he may perform well before his peers.

There are, however, undoubtedly some pupils in the intermediate grades who should be excused at least for a part of the year from participating in oral reading. A child who is so shy that he will be harmed rather than helped through reading orally should not be required to read. Great care should be taken in deciding when a child should not be asked to read. Some poor readers feel slighted as did Jim, a fourth-grader with approximately third-grade reading ability, who complained to his tutor that his teacher never called on him to read orally.

b. Selection of material. The material to be read orally should be selected with particular care. Sometimes the teacher will make the selection by himself, always remembering that the material should be at the level of the pupils' interest. At other times pupils should have the opportunity to select from a variety presented by the teacher.

When children make their own suggestions, the teacher, perhaps in consultation with a pupil committee, will advise as to the suitability of the selections.

The material selected should be easy for the reader to read orally and easy for the audience to comprehend. Often it is advisable to select material for audience reading that is a grade or so lower in difficulty level than the reader's silent reading level. Effective oral reading requires ability in silent reading plus the complex skill of interpreting to others what is read.

A variety of suitable materials is available. Stories, both humorous and serious, fanciful and realistic, are one source. Anecdotes make very good reading. Work-type materials of the kind that requires more than one reading or very careful attention have no legitimate place in an oral reading program. Sometimes each child on the program may have a separate, very short, selection to read. At other times a longer one may be apportioned to two or more, or even all, of the persons who will be reading. Appropriate selections are easily available in most situations because only one copy of a book or magazine article is needed. This is true even if more than one pupil is preparing material out of the same book or magazine, since they can practice at different times and since no one should be reading silently while someone is reading orally. Many teachers like to cut materials out of books that are ready to be discarded or magazines that are not being saved. Mounted material can often be handled better while it is being read and can be kept in better condition when filed for later use.

c. Preparation of the reader. Each reader should be thoroughly prepared for the reading. As a rule, silent reading of the selection beforehand is not enough. The pupil should read it orally one or more times, either to the teacher or to someone else who can help him not only with word recognition but also with problems of interpretation. If several children are to read parts of the same selection, at times they can help each other during the practice period. But the teacher is always responsible for seeing that no one comes before the class inadequately prepared. Furthermore, each pupil should know exactly where his selection is to begin and end if he is to read only part of an article or story.

d. Provision for materials and equipment. Careful provision should be made, often with the help of the boys and girls, so that supplies and equipment needed during the class period will be available. Included may be material placed on the chalkboard, as in the case of the plan reproduced in this chapter. If a plan like this one were used, the program for the period could be listed on the board, with the title of each story to be read and the names of the persons who were to read each in the order of appearance. Sometimes, boys and girls like to make duplicates of the program on paper to distribute to the audience at the beginning of the class period.

A chart similar to the one referred to in the plan, giving the points the pupils will watch in their oral reading, can be displayed. So that the pupils may wholeheartedly accept the skills for the improvement of which they will work, it is usually advisable to have the list worked out cooperatively by the pupils and teacher. The wording should be meaningful to the pupils. If the word *enunciation* is used, as it is on the list given in the plan, the teacher should make certain that the boys and girls know what it means. The list can be drawn up early in the school year and can then be reproduced on chart paper. For easy reference, it could be either kept posted in the room at all times or else exhibited whenever pupils give reading programs.

Each pupil should be provided with a card similar to the one illustrated on page 316. These cards could be kept by the teacher or the child. The record should not be kept for competitive purposes, and only the teacher and the owner of a card should have access to it. A check can be placed on the chart after each item on which the child does well and a minus sign after each item on which he needs to improve. Although provision is made for checking eight different times on the card reproduced here, the number could vary. A place is left for the date of each reading. Space for comments is on the back of the card.

Sometimes other materials may be needed. A map often adds to the value of the reading by enabling the pupil to locate places about which he reads. At times pictures help the audience to visualize what will be read. Realia, too, may profitably be exhibited, if they help accomplish the purpose set for the oral reading. For example, pupils in the fifth or sixth grades can be aided in getting into the mood of the story about Nancy Hanks, the mother of Abraham Lincoln, if a replica of a log cabin is shown as representative of the type in which Lincoln lived when he was a boy.

e. Room arrangements. Arrangements should be made before class for proper seating of the audience and of the participants in the program. Sometimes all that is needed is to reserve seats near the front of the room for those who will read. At times, if there are portable seats, they can be rearranged so as to make it as easy as possible to have a desirable audience situation. If, as in the plan that is reproduced, Christmas stories are being read and if there is a Christmas tree in the room, someone can see to it that the shades are pulled and the lights are lit on the tree before class begins.

2. Deciding on the aims for the period The aims can be suggested by the pupils who prepare the oral reading or by the teacher. No matter who states them, it is important that they are objectives that the class can wholeheartedly accept. In the teaching plan given on page 316 three aims were listed. The second aim, the aim of the readers: "To try to read so that our listeners will enjoy hearing us read," should be determined before class as the boys and girls practice reading. The first and last are suggested objectives for the members of the audience. It will be noted that the first aim, as stated, is not that each child should enjoy the story. There can be nothing mandatory about appreciation. A person does not enjoy something because he sets out to enjoy it or because he is told to enjoy it. In the plan described, the aim that deals with appreciation leaves the final choice explicitly with the audience, for all that is suggested is that they find out whether or not they will enjoy the stories. That is as far as the recommendation should be made when appreciation-type of teaching is done. The third aim is emphasized in *B-4* under "Procedure," which states: "The pupils indicate what a good listener does."

The audience is entitled to have a reason for listening. If the children have no purpose, they will often pay inadequate attention to what is read. Therefore, a suggestion as to what the purpose might be should be given either by the pupils who will read or by the teacher. At times the purpose may deal with entertainment and at other times it may be to get information. It is not necessary that in every oral reading lesson the audience specifically decide that they will try to be good listeners. After a while it should be taken for granted that this will always be an objective. Nevertheless, occasionally additional elements may well be stressed for observation as far as the conduct of the audience is concerned. It is often advisable that each person who reads have in mind a particular point that he wishes to observe especially well.

As a rule the number of expressed aims should be greatly limited, probably to three at the most. It is to be assumed that the pupil will always have certain objectives in mind in reading of this type, without mention being made of them. A large number of stated aims is likely to result in diffusion of effort. There is much to be applied to educational practice in the quotation that says: "This one thing I do." Multiplicity of aim can be decidedly disadvantageous under some circumstances.

3. Reference to the points to be observed   It is not necessary that the points to watch in oral reading should be discussed in each audience reading situation before the boys and girls begin reading. Sometimes they may be taken up after the reading only, and at other times no class mention needs to be made of them. Several factors should enter into the decision as to whether they should be discussed, either before or after the reading. One is the time available for discussion during the lesson. Another is whether the mood to be portrayed through the reading can better be created if no mention is made of the skills to be developed.

4. Announcement of the plan of procedure   Although in the plan given the teacher made the announcement, often the teacher can remain entirely in the background and a pupil, appointed as chairman of the meeting, can make the announcement. At other times, when the pupils are handed copies of the program, no mention of the order needs to be made.

5. Reading of the selections   It is essential that the atmosphere of a program should be maintained throughout the time set aside for reading. The teacher should not correct or prompt the reader unless it is absolutely necessary for the continuance of the program. Interruptions should probably be made no more often than in an assembly program. Possibly the only occasion when the teacher is justified in intervening arises when the child stops reading because he does not know the next word even though previously he had been instructed to proceed as best he could.

6. Discussion of the story   Sometimes the discussion of the story may be omitted—certainly in cases in which the mood created by the story might be destroyed by talking about it. Usually, if there is discussion, it should be brief. It might be led by the teacher or by a pupil. Occasionally, if the aim is to see how well the boys and girls have acquired the information given, they might check themselves on their ability to answer written questions on what was presented.

7. Evaluation of the reading   It is not recommended that the teacher check the individual "score" card while the child is reading. Some pupils may not be made self-conscious by such a practice, but others will surely either concentrate on technique rather than thought or become tense.

Hard and fast rules about evaluation should not interfere with occasional informal comments on the success with which a pupil has mastered specific skills of oral reading. However, usually it is most effective to discuss group progress in general terms at the end of the reading period. Individual pupils should be encouraged to keep their own scores and compare them with the teacher's judgments in private conference. No child should feel that he is going on trial when he rises to read.

For Further Study

Anderson, Verna, *Reading and Young Children,* "Oral Reading," (New York: The Macmillan Company, 1968), pp. 268–274.

Artley, Sterl, "Oral Reading as a Communication Process," *The Reading Teacher,* vol. 26 (October 1972), pp. 46–51.

Bond, Guy L., and Eva Bond Wagner, *Teaching the Child to Read,* 4th ed., "Oral Reading" (New York: The Macmillan Company, 1966), Ch. 12.

Durkin, Dolores, *Teaching Them to Read* (Boston: Allyn and Bacon, Inc. 1970), Ch. 8, "Oral and Silent Reading."

Harris, Albert J., and Edward Sipay, eds., *Readings on Reading Instruction,* 2nd ed. (New York: David McKay Company, 1972), article #69, "Characteristics of Effective Oral Reading" by William S. Gray, pp. 356–360; and article #70, "Toward More Purposeful Oral Reading" by Emery P. Bliesmer, pp. 360–364.

Possien, Wilma M., *They All Need to Talk* (New York: Appleton-Century-Crofts, 1969), Ch. IV, "Creative Dramatics," and Ch. VIII, "Poetry and Choral Reading."

Spache, George D., and Evelyn B. Spache, *Reading in the Elementary School,* 3rd ed. (Boston: Allyn and Bacon, Inc., 1973), pp. 330–344.

Tinker, Miles A., and Constance M. McCullough, *Teaching Elementary Reading* (New York: Appleton-Century-Crofts, 1968), Ch. 11, "Reading Aloud."

Questions and Comments for Thought and Discussion

1. What values do you see in choral reading?
2. Be able to name six or eight criteria for effective oral reading; that is, six or eight requirements oral reading must meet if it is to be called good

reading. How may a list of these be used to advantage in teaching? Consider their possible value to both the teacher and the pupils.

3. What is your reaction to the following statement which, in substance, is sometimes heard among reading instructors?

> Oral expression may be improved among all children in the ideal classroom of the future. Here the teacher will accept individual differences, plan for and with the children, supply quantities of interesting materials, and provide many real opportunities for speaking and reading aloud.

4. To develop all aspects of oral reading the teacher must use both systematic instruction and highly motivated practice. What are some activities that offer good opportunities for the development of oral reading skills?

5. The proficiency with which children are able to use oral language when they come to school will vary markedly from individual to individual. But no matter how capable a child is in the use of oral language when he comes to school, his skill in this area can always be improved or extended. Can you suggest some techniques that may help the school discharge its responsibilities during the child's primary years.

6. One objective of teaching listening should be to develop the ability to listen appreciatively. Many opportunities arise during the school day to use this important listening ability. Teachers should be aware of ways to cultivate and improve it. What are some effective ways?

7. Oral reading and speech have much in common. But there are also many differences. One is pointed out in this quotation:

> Whereas *talking* involves only two entities, you and your audience, [oral] *reading* involves three—the creator of the ideas (the author), the recipient of the ideas (the audience), and the translator of the ideas (you, the reader).[1]

Of what import is the thought of this quotation to the teacher of reading?

[1]E. F. Elson, Alberta Peck, George Willey, Samuel Hirsch, Theodore Moore and Earl Wynn, *The Art of Speaking* (Boston: Ginn and Company, 1966), p. 440.

PART III

The Reading Program in Action

Outline for Chapter 10

READING IN THE CONTENT AREAS

Special Problems in Reading in the Content Areas
 Problems in Vocabulary
 Problems in Comprehension
  Remembering What Is Read
  Organizing What Is Read
  Understanding Cause-effect Relations
  Making Generalizations
  Judging the Authenticity of Statements
  Interpreting Graphs, Tables, Charts, and Maps
  Problems in Reading at Appropriate Rates
  Problems in Locating Information and Using It
  Interesting Pupils in Independent Reading in the
   Content Areas
 Guiding Growth in Reading in the Content Areas
  Guidelines
  Meeting the Problems
   Problems in Vocabulary
   Problems in Comprehension
   Problems in Reading at Appropriate Rates
   Problems in Locating Information and Using It
   Independent Reading in the Content Areas
 Nonreading Experiences as Enrichment for Reading
 Use of the Textbook in the Social Studies
  Cautions in the Use of Textbooks in the Social
   Studies and Science
  Suggested Procedures for Using a Textbook in the
   Social Studies in the Intermediate Grades
  Adapting a Textbook Lesson to Individual Differences
   Suggested Procedures
   Rewriting Textbook Material on the Level of the
   Retarded Reader

CHAPTER 10

Reading in the Content Areas

In Part II we focused our attention on the development of various skills and abilities important to all types of reading situations. Now we consider how application can be made of these learnings to the reading program in action. Our first consideration is reading in the content areas.

Careful studies have indicated that reading is not a general ability but a composite of specialized skills. These specialized skills are required in various curriculum areas. The correlations between general reading ability as measured by standardized tests and ability to read materials in specialized fields have usually been low. The necessity of paying particular attention to reading in the content areas is also emphasized by the fact that many teachers in the intermediate grades believe that a major reason for failure of boys and girls in the social studies, for example, is lack of skill in reading the material. Teachers of mathematics in the elementary school have long known that inability to read the "story problems" of arithmetic constitutes a real problem for many pupils. In science, in health, in literature—in whatever area reading is expected of the pupils—a low degree of reading skill constitutes a serious handicap.

Obviously one reason for the problems some boys and girls encounter when reading in the content areas is their failure to acquire the skills essential to all reading. If a pupil has failed to develop skill in word recognition,

Figure 10.1 Reading is an important tool in acquiring knowledge in all content areas. (Bausch & Lomb.)

in comprehension, in reading at appropriate rates and in other essentials of reading of all types, he will be unable to read effectively in the content areas. However, some boys and girls who are efficient readers in their basal reading textbooks or who read many kinds of general books with ease have decided problems when reading in the content areas. The problem may be that they read all materials as they would read that given in reading textbooks or in books for recreatory reading. Their difficulty may be that they cannot effectively meet the problems in word recognition, comprehension, and other aspects of reading that are somewhat peculiar to reading in the areas of history, geography, science, or mathematics. Furthermore, often little motivation is required to interest boys and girls in the story-type reading of much of the typical material in basal readers, while incentive for reading the study-type in the content areas may frequently need to be provided.

SPECIAL PROBLEMS IN READING IN THE CONTENT AREAS

Although there are various possible problems in reading in the content areas, there is probably not a single one that is unique to any one of the areas. The problems are special only insofar as they occur often or are more crucial in a content field or that they require special attention for other reasons. Problems in word recognition, comprehension, reading at appropriate rates, reading orally, locating information, and doing independent reading in the content areas will now be considered.

Problems in Vocabulary

Often the problem in the content areas for a child who reads up to the norm for his grade in the basal reading textbook is one of vocabulary. In the social studies the pupil encounters such "new words" as *isthmus, environment, latitude, legislature, emancipation, adaptation, culture.* In elementary-school science many words occur of which the child previously has had no knowledge, such as *planetarium, solar, convection.* In mathematics words such as *equation, dividend, quotient;* and in books about music and art words such as *percussion, bas relief, perspective* frequently give difficulty. Words unfamiliar to the reader will be found in any reading material likely to help the child increase in knowledge and power with words. In fact, textbooks in reading beyond the beginning stages of reading instruction are designed to present some words that are new to the child. The special point of difficulty in vocabulary in reading in the content areas is that the child is often confronted with a large proportion of words unknown to him, a proportion larger than in the basal readers.

Frequently, too, in the content areas a word may have a different meaning from the one that the child has been accustomed to associate with it. Neither the word *range* as used in the phrase *mountain range* nor the word *mouth* in the expression *mouth of the river* has the meaning that some children have previously associated with them. The *page* of the Middle Ages, the *draft* of the Constitution, the *cradle* of civilization can be a matter of difficulty for the child who has given other meanings to those words. Homonyms, particularly, are often a source of trouble. The *steppes* of some near-polar regions are not the *steps* with which the pupil has had contact.

Another vocabulary problem lies in the number and difficulty of the concepts presented. Expressions such as *no taxation without representation* or the *consent of the governed* need to be made meaningful to many pupils before they can comprehend the material they read in the social studies. The teacher, however, cannot expect the children to comprehend the full meaning of many of the concepts all at once. *Liberty* can acquire added meaning for the child as he reads about and discusses from year to year more and more situations in which liberty or lack of it is evident. It will mean more and more to him as again and again, with increasing insight, he notes the beneficial effects of environments characterized by a spirit of liberty and the deleterious results of regimentation. The boys and girls will grow in ability to note the difference between liberty and license. They will, hopefully, in time come to realize that liberty should be sought not only for self but also for others.

The first time the children read or hear the term *scientific method,* the teacher may find it wise to explain and illustrate the meaning of the expression. Then, year after year, the children can be guided so that they will develop a more accurate understanding of its meaning and a deeper appreciation of its value when used in situations to which it is applicable. At each stage of development the pupil will probably be benefited if he is helped to increase his understanding until he finally comprehends what a mature educated adult understands when he reads or hears a term symbolizing such a concept.

Problems in Comprehension

There are problems of understanding besides those pertaining to vocabulary—including concept building—that confront many pupils when reading in the content areas and that, therefore, necessitate careful reading. To be sure, not all reading in the content areas should be of the study type. However, much of the material in these areas requires more meticulous reading than that which the pupils need in basal reading textbooks or books of fiction. This point is especially true of many of the problems presented in mathematics. Following directions for performing an experiment in science also requires attention to detail that is often unessential—in fact, even undesirable—for reading many other types of materials. In the social studies, where material often shows a bias, critical evaluation is frequently needed. Reading with the intent to remember for a long time or possibly always is also often demanded of the reader who wishes to accomplish worthwhile objectives that he may set for himself when reading in the content areas. The many references to names and places may put a tax on memory. Referrals to maps and pictures, helpful though they may be, can interfere with the sequential reading by the person unaccustomed to reading material in which many references of that type are made. Charts, graphs, maps, and diagrams often need to be studied in order to make the text meaningful.

The organization of the material in the social studies is at times more complex than that to which the pupil is accustomed in much of his other reading. In the basal reader and the story book, chronological order usually has been the simple determinant of the organization. In the social studies cause-effect relationships, inverted sequence of time, and progression from incidents to generalizations or from generalizations to incidents many times form the basis of the organization. Center heads, side headings, and other organizational clues—although helpful when their use is understood —can be a stumbling block for the reader not skilled in their use.

For the reasons stated in the preceding paragraphs, and others, the pupil may have problems in comprehension as he reads in the content areas unless he is given help in meeting difficulties as they arise.

Remembering What Is Read

The expectation that pupils should remember a good deal of what they read in the content areas, especially in textbooks, forms one of the chief problems in reading in those fields. When reading in the basal reading textbook, the child usually does not need to remember what he read long after he has read the material. When reading in the social studies, however, it is often important to remember many points. Some should be remembered for a long time; others should be remembered always. Frequently, unless a pupil can remember what he has read one day, what he reads on subsequent days may have little meaning for him.

In the social studies names of persons and events, which in the typical textbook occur in great numbers, are often a special cause of difficulty. The reader is frequently unable to determine which names are important enough to remember. Guidance in discerning that which is worth remembering is often essential.

In science, too, it is often imperative that the boys and girls be given help in determining what points should be retained. The pupil who one day reads and understands what *convection* is but does not remember what he learned will be at a loss when at a subsequent time reference is made to it, possibly in the same textbook, with the assumption by the author that the pupil remembers what is meant by the term. His problem in remembering may be caused by the fact that he never really understood what he read. Or it may be that he tries to remember every fact without relation to the generalization that can at times be drawn from facts. Lack of purpose in reading, other than possibly to answer factual questions may be the cause of much undesirable forgetting of what is read. Another cause of inability to remember what is read may be failure to do what is sometimes referred to as *associational reading*. Many boys and girls seem to make relatively few, if any, associations with past experiences, either firsthand or vicarious, as they read in the content areas.

In mathematics both immediate and long-time recall is often essential. Whenever there is a problem to be solved, the pupil must remember the conditions stated until he has solved it. Some children do not do so; they forget what they have read even before they have finished the sentence or group of sentences that give the terms of the problem. Long-time recall in solving problems in mathematics is often not necessary or desirable. As a rule, the reader does not need to remember the information presented in a problem after he has correctly solved it. However, there are many points learned in mathematics that should be remembered permanently and should be remembered with exactitude. The child who has noted that twelve inches equal one foot needs to learn that fact so that he remembers it all his life and so that he remembers exactly how many inches equal one foot.

Organizing What Is Read

Another problem that confronts many pupils when reading in the content areas is understanding the organization of a book and organizing in their own minds material they have read. Frequently in both the social studies and science the organization followed by the author is indicated through center headings, side headings, and divisions subordinate to the second order of classification. (Sometimes the major divisions of the material are indicated by center headings, with side headings as the first order of division of the center headings; at other times the major divisions of the topic are shown by side headings, with center headings as the first subdivision of side headings.) Since such organizational clues are there to help the reader, failure to make adequate use of them can greatly increase the difficulty of reading the material with comprehension.

The ability to organize what is read by means of summarizing it is often needed in reading in the content areas—more often than in basal reading textbooks, in which boys and girls often have had most of their reading instruction. One way of summarizing information is through making an outline. Outlining is usually not needed for reading books of fiction or the basic reading books. To be able to outline, however, can be a decided aid when reading for certain purposes in the content areas.

Understanding Cause-effect Relations

Reading materials in the social studies and in science abound in important references to cause-effect relations. For example, in history the understanding of the relation between slavery and secession and the Civil War may be essential to intelligent reading of material dealing with this subject. In geography the causes of erosion may constitute the theme of a selection. Understanding in science may be based on the effect of a law of motion in a situation described. Failure to recognize the relation may interfere with comprehension and later with recall.

Even though an author explicitly states that one event caused a second one, the pupil may not understand how the one caused the other. At times, too, the reader may erroneously attribute such a relation to two events that do not have a causal relation but are both the cause or the result of a third event. The wrong association is at times made because the two are discussed in proximity in an article or because they took place at the same time. Failure to comprehend a cause-effect relation or to assume one when there is none may seriously interfere with comprehending what is read in the content areas.

Making Generalizations

The reading of materials in the social studies and in science presents many occasions when the reader is in special need of the skills important in making generalizations. If he arrives at a wrong generalization or accepts one that is false, the reading can have disastrous results. In the social studies skill in reading depends to a large extent on the degree to which the reader can arrive at sound conclusions and on the extent to which he can detect errors in reasoning of which the writer may have been guilty.

There are several dangers in arriving at generalizations. The pupil may 1. make generalizations on insufficient data; 2. make overgeneralizations on data presented; 3. make undergeneralizations on data given; 4. fail to distinguish between generalizations and data given to support them, confusing a detail with a generalization and a generalization with a detail; 5. be unable to detect when a generalization made in a book is too broad for the data presented; 6. be unable to apply generalizations to situations with which he is later confronted.

Judging the Authenticity of Statements

Especially in the social studies there is much need to consider whether or not statements are authentic. A pupil needs to note, for example, when certain information was published. A statistic on the population of New York City in a book published in 1954 should indicate to the pupil that to learn how many people are presently living in New York City, he needs more recent information. When controversial issues are discussed, the reader needs to be able to take into consideration who made the claims in order to detect on the part of the writer possible prejudice, lack of information, or a reputation for accuracy or inaccuracy. When reading some types of social studies materials, he needs to be able to judge whether a fact or an opinion is being expressed. For reading historical fiction the ability to determine which points are historical and which are embellishments on actual happenings is needed.

In science, too, it is important to have or to develop skill in judging the authenticity of what is read. Who makes the claim as to the achievements of the Americans or of the Russians in space ventures may make a difference in what is recorded. Whether the person writing an article is likely to have sufficient information to speak with the authority he assumes is another point that needs to be considered in reading science materials. Surely with the vast explosion of scientific knowledge during recent decades, the date on which a report was written is of great importance in some areas of science. However, along with developing skill in judging statements through examination of the date when they were made, the pupil needs also to be aware of the fact that some information in the area of science recorded several decades ago is as authentic now as then. An illustration is the statement that many animals have protective coloring. Another example is the fact that Benjamin Franklin invented the Franklin stove. Furthermore, a report on possible next steps in the exploration of space needs to be interpreted in terms of the background of the writer, not only his possible prejudices but also his knowledge.

Interpreting Graphs, Tables, Charts, and Maps

Books on both the social studies and science, especially the former, contain many graphs, tables, charts, and maps. Frequently these are essential to full understanding of the text. They are likely to be especially valuable for the reader when the writer draws attention to certain aspects of the illustrations. For example, in connection with a map showing the Great Circle route, the reader may be asked to compare the distance between two cities when the Great Circle route is followed by a plane, with the distance between the two cities if a plane followed a parallel of latitude. It is not suggested, however, that the reader study in detail all illustrative material presented, for its value will depend in part on the purpose of the reader. If he is, for example, reading a selection to answer a certain question, he will not need to refer to a table illustrating some other point.

Many boys and girls are not aware of the value of illustrative materials and consequently do not attempt to interpret them. Others, though recognizing their worth, lack skill in interpreting them and consequently do not take time to "read" them. Still others make errors when trying to understand them. Since very little "reading" of this type is required in basal reading series and in books of fiction, the teacher should recognize the need for special instruction as pupils read in the content areas. With the increasing production of graphical and tabular materials, skill in interpreting them has become important as never before.

Problems in Reading at Appropriate Rates

Reading material in the content areas at inappropriate rates may be due to lack of comprehension skills. Or it may be due to other factors discussed in Chapter 7A, "Reading at Appropriate Rates." A special problem pertaining to the rate of reading in the content areas is that some pupils who have done most of their reading in material easy to comprehend and for purposes that could well be achieved through rapid reading try to read more difficult material for study purposes at the same rate at which they had previously been reading. The premium teachers often erroneously place on speed of reading at all times may cause the better readers to have a handicap when studying in the content areas. The problem in reading at appropriate rates in the content areas is essentially that of learning to read as rapidly as possible without tension or undue strain materials of all types in the content areas, in harmony with the difficulty of the material and the purpose of the reader.

It is wrong to assume that all reading in the content areas is study-type material. If that is the only kind of reading the pupil does, his range is too limited. For some of the materials in the content areas—such as reports in newspapers or magazines—the most desirable rate to accomplish the purpose of the reader might be skimming. At times, rapid reading but not skimming might be the rate at which the reader's purpose is best attained; for example, when he is reading an anecdote about Abraham Lincoln. Reading at a moderate rate might be desirable when the pupil is reading fairly easy material in his textbook in order to answer questions he has been given. At times, however, to find answers to questions, especially when the material is rather difficult, the slowness of careful study might be the most suitable rate. Thus, the need for flexibility of rate should be recognized. Furthermore, a pupil may need to be warned against dawdling habits when reading at any of the rates indicated. It is possible to dawdle when skimming; that is, not skim as rapidly as one could for the purpose in mind. It is possible to dawdle when doing careful study-type reading. At each of the levels of reading rates the pupil should be encouraged to read as rapidly as he can commensurate with the fulfillment of his purpose in reading.

Problems in Locating Information and Using It

When the single textbook was the vogue in social studies classes and in science classes, the need for locating information when studying was not nearly as great as it is now when a variety of reading materials are utilized in those areas. To be sure, even when only one textbook is used, pupils can often benefit from guidance in using the table of contents, the index, the appendix, and other special features of the textbook. However, in classrooms in which one textbook does not constitute the curriculum of a content subject, it is imperative that boys and girls know how to locate information from various sources and how to make use of it. The teacher who merely tells a pupil, when making an assignment for outside reading, that he should look up information on a given topic is not giving the help that many children need. For greatest effectiveness there is need of guidance in locating information and utilizing it along all the lines indicated in Chapters 8A and 8B. These skills include, among others, 1. developing the basic skills of finding words arranged in alphabetical order, deciding on key words, and discovering what types of information are given in various kinds of books; 2. interpreting punctuation marks, diacritical markings, abbreviations, and symbols; 3. selecting points that have bearing on a given problem; 4. utilizing information gained; 5. developing skill in using nonreference books; 6. developing skill in using the dictionary; 7. developing skill in using reference books other than the dictionary; and 8. locating materials in a library.

As in the case of guidance in the use of other special skills needed for reading intelligently in the content areas, the content subjects afford excellent opportunity for teaching skill in locating information. They serve three purposes. They present situations that require knowledge of how to locate information, thereby furnishing an incentive for learning needed skills. They provide practice needed for perfecting a skill that is being learned. They help the child obtain information in the content areas.

Interesting Pupils in Independent Reading in the Content Areas

Far too often in the past pupils' independent reading has been largely confined to books of fiction. With the excellent array of books for children in the areas of the social studies, science, art, and other content areas, it is, indeed, unfortunate if the pupils in an elementary school do not read them. Books on history, minority cultures, biography, far-away lands and people, health, music, and art can give boys and girls insight into themselves and the world around them. It is regrettable if a child chooses to read none or only a few of the books of this type.

The chief problem in relation to independent reading in the content areas is getting the "right book to the right child." Another is helping boys and girls develop skill in evaluating the authenticity of the material they are reading. Still another is helping pupils to differentiate between fact and fiction; between what is historical background, for example, and that which is an embellishment of the facts of history.

GUIDING GROWTH IN READING IN THE CONTENT AREAS

In Part II of this book suggestions are given for meeting the problems related to the skills of reading as they apply to reading in general. Here they are discussed insofar as they pertain in particular to the content areas.

Guidelines

The following guidelines are especially applicable for fostering growth in reading in the content areas.

1. Many reading skills are appropriately taught in the content subjects The teacher should help boys and girls develop skills in the meaningful setting provided. This principle applies not only to the so-called study skills, such as locating information, but also to other reading skills, among them skill in recognizing words, understanding what is read, and reading at appropriate rates.

2. The material to be read should be on the reader's level Readability formulas such as that by Edgar Dale and Jeanne Chall, are of value in ascertaining the level of difficulty.[1]

[1] Edgar Dale and Jeanne S. Chall, "A Formula for Predicting Reading Ability," *Educational Research Bulletin*, vol. 27 (January 21, 1948), pp. 11–20.

3. Every teacher of the content subjects should consider himself a teacher of reading In departmentalized set-ups teachers of content subjects often fear that the time they might spend on helping pupils to read better in their field is time lost to them for teaching the subject matter of their area. Their fears are groundless. Effective teaching of reading skills important to a content subject will improve the pupils' comprehension of the subject matter.

4. The teacher of the content subjects, whether or not he is the room teacher who has the pupils for all subjects, should have clearly in mind reading objectives for his area of learning These goals should include primarily those skills particularly important for reading in the area. For example, one objective might deal with guiding the child in learning the specialized vocabulary that he encounters in his subject.

5. The program for guiding boys and girls to read more effectively in the content areas should include various types of approaches Among these approaches are: (a.) presentation lessons in which the pupil is helped to understand how he can improve in some skill needed for effectiveness in reading in a given area; (b.) practice exercises in which special help is provided in the maintenance of a needed skill; and (c.) incidental means of strengthening the skills needed which could be supplied by activities in the on-going school program.

6. The readiness principle applies with special force to reading in the content subjects Before a pupil is asked to read a chapter or a part of a chapter in a textbook, he should be mentally prepared for the task. The words he encounters on the printed page are abstract symbols to him unless he can bring a body of experience to the reading. Moreover, often he should have had prior experience with words that symbolize the images and concepts he is to learn.

7. Pupils should learn to approach a reading assignment in the content areas with clearly conceived purposes They should know what they are looking for, and why. Such purposes may arise out of previous class discussions, demonstrations, or experiments.

8. Opportunity for pupil evaluation of growth in needed reading skills should be provided For evaluation to be most beneficial it is important that the pupils have goals to be achieved in mind.

9. An effective program of reading in the content subjects should stimulate boys and girls so that they will want to read in those areas during leisure time as part of their independent reading Unless the boys and girls are stimulated to read such materials outside of school and in later years, the program will not have been entirely successful.

Meeting the Problems

Below are given some suggestions for putting into practice guidelines such as those described in the preceding paragraph.

Problems in Vocabulary

It is hoped that suggestions such as the following will stimulate the teacher to think of additional ones that will be peculiarly adapted to the needs of at least some of the boys and girls in his class:

1. Before pupils begin reading a selection, the teacher might write on the chalkboard, frequently in context, the words with which he thinks his pupils will be unfamiliar. For example, he might have on the chalkboard the words *taxation without representation,* using the expression within the context of a sentence. The sentence might be: "The colonists were opposed to *taxation without representation,*" with the phrase to be studied underlined. He might then say to a fifth-grade class that he imagines everybody knows what taxes are and that consequently they will have no trouble with the word *taxation* (at which he points in the sentence on the chalkboard). He might then ask the class to read the sentence silently to see if anyone can figure out what the word *representation* means in the sentence. If no one can give an adequate explanation, he might explain the word or might tell the boys and girls that as they read a certain part of the social studies work for that day he thinks they may be able to find out what is meant by the expression *taxation without representation.* After the class has read silently the selection in which the term occurs, discussion should follow. Pupils might make up meaningful sentences of their own from which it is evident that they know the meaning of the term.

2. The teacher might help the boys and girls with variants of a word they are studying. For example, if the phrase *taxation without representation* is taught as suggested in the preceding paragraph, the class might give the root of the word *taxation* and then name variants—such as *taxed, taxes, taxing, taxable.* Similarly, they could proceed with the word *representation,* as they name the root word *represent,* and suggest variations of the word—such as *represents, representing, represented.*

3. The boys and girls might make an illustrated chart highlighting some of the words in the specialized vocabulary that they are studying in connection with a unit of work or an area of learning. For example, having completed a unit on "Neighbors around the World," the pupils might make a chart illustrating words such as *igloo, pyramid, scroll, totem pole, fiord.*

4. The class could have quiz program based at least in part on the vocabulary they have studied in connection with a unit of work.

5. Through a test containing items such as the following the boys and girls could check their knowledge of vocabulary studied while concentrating on a unit of work or area of study.

> *Directions.* Draw a line under the group of words that best explains the meaning of the word *mouth* as it is used in the illustrative sentence.
> *Illustrative sentence:* The *mouth* of the Mississippi River is in the Gulf of Mexico.
> *Test item. Mouth* means (a.) the beginning or origin of a river, (b.) the part of a river that empties into another body of water, (c.) the branch of a river, (d.) a cavelike opening through which a river flows.

Problems in Comprehension

A few recommended procedures are listed below that may help boys and girls increase in power to read with comprehension in content areas. Suggestions are given relative to (1.) remembering what is read; (2.) organizing what is read; (3.) understanding cause-effect relations; (4.) making generalizations; (5.) judging the authenticity of statements; and (6.) interpreting graphs, tables, charts, and maps.

Remembering what is read In an attempt to help boys and girls improve in ability to remember what they read in the social studies or other content areas the teacher might do the following:

1. Have the pupils list details stated in a paragraph that support the main idea of the paragraph.
2. Help the pupils construct a paragraph that includes various details supporting a stated topic sentence. For example, after reading about the hard winter at Valley Forge, the pupils could write a paragraph, either individually or as a class, that furnishes details to support this topic sentence: "The winter at Valley Forge was a discouraging period of our history."
3. Assist the pupils in determining which details are important to illustrate in a mural on a theme such as the history of transportation or life in the far West.
4. Select the details that throw light on how a character should act in a play the class is planning to give on a subject such as the first Thanksgiving in Plymouth or on the topic "Man Walks on the Moon."
5. After the pupils have read a problem in mathematics silently, have them answer questions on information given, without recourse to the problem —such as: (a.) Was the house sold at a gain or a loss? (b.) What are we *to find* in this problem?

6. For a social-studies class, make a chart listing all the people important enough for the pupils to remember always. Have the class decide on an important sentence about each, one that summarizes the work of the person. Then, from time to time, have pupils give the important sentence to be remembered about each person. So that the boys and girls can review the statements by themselves, they might be given a duplicated list of the sentences decided on or they might copy the sentences into a notebook. Illustrations of possible sentences to remember are:

> Columbus discovered America.
>
> De Soto discovered the Mississippi River.

Instead of important people, the chart might be made on important dates or on important events. Summarizing sentences such as these might be decided on for the chart on dates:

> In 1492 Columbus discovered America.
>
> In 1607 the first permanent English settlement in America was made in Jamestown, Virginia.

For the chart on important events sentences such as this one might be remembered:

> The Treaty of Paris of 1676 stated that all land in North America east of the Mississippi River excepting New Orleans would belong to England and all land west of the Mississippi River and New Orleans would belong to Spain.

Organizing what is read   In order to develop skill in organizing what is read in a content subject, some pupils might do the following:

1. State which of two or more summaries of a paragraph is the better.
2. Note the use of center headings and side headings in books in the social studies or science.
3. Predict what will be reported under a side heading in a book, after having read the account given under the preceding side heading.
4. Group questions the boys and girls have set for study of a unit. For example, in discussing with the teacher what questions they would like answered in a study of the problems: "In what ways is Mexico a land of contrasts?" at first the questions could be listed on the chalkboard in whatever order pupils give them. Next the teacher could explain that it will be easier to find answers to the questions if the class organizes them around main topics. Then pupils could decide on the groupings, with the guidance of the teacher.

5. Find the topic sentence in a paragraph and note the details supporting it.

6. Check the correspondence between (a.) the center headings and the side heading of a given selection in a social studies or science book, and (b.) the parts of an outline the teacher has made.

7. Rewrite an incorrectly made outline of subject matter in the content areas.

8. Make an outline of a selection using the center headings and the side headings of a well-organized selection as determiners of the outline.

9. Give a talk according to an outline determined by the person giving the talk with the help of the teacher.

For additional ideas on organizing what is read, the reader is referred to the part under "Developing Skill in Making Summaries and Organizing Material" in Chapter 6B (*see* page 190).

Understanding cause-effect relations   To help the boys and girls gain in proficiency in understanding cause-effect relations, as they come across them in their reading in the content areas, they might engage in activities such as the following:

1. Explaining how a given event caused another.

2. Stating what they think might have happened had a given event not occurred in the manner that it did.

3. Making a list of cause-effect relations stated in material assigned.

4. Matching a cause with its effect as given in a two-column exercise, in which in column A are given the causes of events that are listed in a different order in column B. For example, one item in column A might be *secession,* to be matched with *Civil War* in column B.

5. Indicating what would be likely to happen if a certain direction in a science experiment were not followed.

Making generalizations   The teacher might help pupils acquire skill in making generalizations when reading in the content areas by:

1. Having the pupils test stated generalizations in terms of the details given to support them.

2. Asking the pupils to select among a list of details the one that does not contribute to the generalization reached.

3. Having the pupils write a generalization that can be made from a list of facts presented.

4. Giving pupils an exercise such as the following.

Directions. Decide which of the following sentences contain generalizations about Benjamin Franklin and which contain facts that might help support a generalization. If a sentence contains a generalization, write the letter *G* (for *generalization*) on the blank to the left of it; if it contains a detail that might support a generalization, write the letter *D* (for *detail*) on the blank.

——— He invented the Franklin stove.
——— He was ambassador to France.
——— He helped draft the Constitution.
——— He did much to help his fellow men.
——— He helped frame the Declaration of Independence.

5. Asking the pupils to find details that support a given generalization.

6. Having pupils compile a list of generalizations of questionable validity in a given content area that they have heard. The pupils could be asked to give reasons for their questioning of each generalization.

For additional ideas on making generalizations the reader is referred to "Developing Ability to Arrive at Generalizations and Come to Conclusions," in Chapter 6B (*see* page 193).

Judging the authenticity of statements   Through suggestions such as those given in the preceding list under "Making generalizations," the teacher can also help boys and girls judge the authenticity of some types of statements. Following are additional ways in which he can do so:

1. Having the pupils compare two somewhat contradictory reports in newspapers on a current event, as they note points of contradiction and as they try to explain them.

2. Asking the pupils to read a report on a political issue that is controversial and have them decide what sentences would probably be deleted or changed if a person on the other side of the controversy were to report on the issue.

3. Reading the qualifications of two people writing on the schools of Russia. The background of one, as described, should be such that it would be highly probable that he could write with authority on the subject, while the background of the other would be such that his report would not bear the weight of that by the other writer.

4. Rewriting an article about American or Russian successes in the space race appearing in an American paper so as to express the point of view that might be taken in a Russian newspaper.

Additional suggestions are given, on page 197 under "The Author" and on page 198 under "Propaganda Techniques."

A warning is in order here. Critical reading of material in the social studies is not to be interpreted as calling for a "debunking" of characters in history. More harm than good is done, it would seem, by those who propose to show boys and girls that there were many flaws of character in some men who have made outstanding contributions. The opposite extreme should also be avoided. For example, the biographer who pictures heroes of history as infallible persons is missing the mark. Furthermore, the author of a history book who assumes that the United States is and has always been right is a menace to clear thinking. The boys and girls should be taught to recognize writings of such an author by the style and content.

Interpreting graphs, tables, charts, and maps   The following types of activities may prove helpful in teaching boys and girls to read graphs, tables, charts, and maps with greater understanding:

1. Making a calendar to record weather conditions.

2. Making a map of the classroom or community.

3. Studying a map and map legend and then answering questions based on them.

4. Showing information of various types—for example, surface features, population centers, political divisions—on maps that have been duplicated.

5. Making, in answer to a question, a list of important points that can be gained for a stated purpose from a given map, table, graph, or chart.

6. Studying an exhibit placed on the bulletin board of various types of graphs—including line graphs, bar graphs, circular graphs, and pictorial graphs—and answering questions also posted on the bulletin board of significance in the content areas that can be answered through a study of the illustrative material.

7. Using charts, graphs, tables, and maps as the boys and girls give special reports, if through use of them they can add to the clarity of the presentation.

8. Having a quiz program in which questions are asked about a content area that can be answered through examination of graphic or tabular aids copied on transparencies and projected so all can see.

9. Making charts that clarify some important learning the class has acquired while studying a topic in a content area—such as, for example: (a.) the proportion of persons on earth belonging to each of the races, (b.) the territorial expansion of the United States, (c.) the work of parents of the boys and girls in the class, (d.) the increase or decrease in the cost of living.

Problems in Reading at Appropriate Rates

The following suggestions illustrate how pupils can get practice in reading at appropriate rates in the content areas when working on a unit or area of study.

Developing skill in rapid reading   Some of the ways in which the boys and girls can get helpful practice in skimming or other rapid reading when working on a unit on Mexico are:

1. Glancing at books such as the following to see which ones they would like to read: *The Watchdog* by Laura Bannon (Whitman Publishing Company), *My Pet Peepolo* by Ellis Credle (Oxford University Press), and *Let's Read about Mexico* by Stella Burke May (The Fideler Company).
2. Reading one or more books on Mexico rather rapidly, merely to get the story.
3. Skimming an article in an encyclopedia to see if it contains information about the observance of September 16.
4. Skimming a page in an index of a social studies book to find out if it contains an entry on Miguel Hidalgo.
5. Glancing at the table of contents in the book *The Real Book about Explorers* by Irvin Block (Garden City Books) to see if a chapter is devoted to Hernando Cortes.

Developing skill in reading when a moderately fast rate is required   The boys and girls can get practice in reading material at the optimum rate when moderately fast reading is desirable in the following ways:

1. Reading a selection in a social studies textbook on Mexico City in order to find the answer to a set of relatively easy questions that the reader has seen before he began to read.
2. In a book that is moderately easy to read, reading about Mexican art in order to be able to tell the rest of the class a few points of interest on the subject.
3. Reading the writing under a picture of a Mexican housewife grinding corn on a huge stone to find out what the woman is doing.

Developing skill in reading when a slow rate is required   Opportunity to help pupils read at the maximum efficiency when a rather slow rate is required may be provided in situations such as the following:

1. Reading preparatory to giving a talk on the Mexican and the American sides of issues leading up to the Mexican War.

2. Studying directions in order to make a Mexican dish; tortillas, for example.

3. Studying the history of Mexico in order to be able to make a frieze portraying important events in the history of the country. Events such as these might be pictured: the arrival of Cortes in Mexico; the conquest of the country by Cortes; the attitude of European settlers who came to Mexico; the work of the missionaries; the long struggle for freedom; the war with the United States; and, finally, the progress Mexico is making in the present century.

Problems in Locating Information and Using It

In unit work carried on in the social studies or science many situations arise in which the need for locational skills becomes evident and in which practice in improving these skills can be given. As the possibilities for the development of locational skills in connection with a unit are considered, it is important for the teacher to bear in mind that only those activities dealing with locational skills should be performed in connection with the unit work that really help toward the accomplishment of the objectives set for that work. If more work on any of the skills is needed than is provided by activities that help in the attainment of the objectives for the unit study, this practice should usually be given at other times through exercises and lessons specifically designed for the development of these skills. Otherwise it is probable that the work on the problem of study will lack the unity which the very name *unit* implies.

Developing locational skills in a unit on community workers   Even in a unit planned for the primary grades, many locational skills can be developed as problems that arise in connection with the unit are being solved. The following list suggests some ways in which a unit on community workers can be instrumental in developing skill in locating information and using it.

1. The boys and girls could place in a file mounted pictures of community workers. The pictures could be arranged alphabetically by groups, with those of firemen preceding those of postmen, because the **f** of **firemen** precedes the **p** of **postmen**. Guide cards could be made similar to those used in a card catalogue.

2. The pupils could look for books on the various community workers they are studying.

3. They could examine the table of contents of some of the books on community workers to find out on what page information is given on a worker.

4. The members of a committee or one individual could look for information in a book that will give them the answer to a specific question, for example: "What does a fireman do when he hears a fire alarm?"

5. They could compile a list, arranged in alphabetical order according to the last name of the author, of books on community workers. They could use three-by-five-inch cards to be filed or sheets of paper on which they could list a number of references.

6. Before drawing pictures for a "movie" or a frieze on community workers, they could look in books for pictures that would give them some needed background information.

7. As a group project they could make a picture dictionary containing words learned while working on the unit.

8. For a booklet that the group could make, the pupils could write a table of contents, a preface, and an appendix. In the appendix they might include: (a.) a table showing the work of each of the workers studied; (b.) a picture of each community worker, showing the type of uniform or clothes he wears; (c.) a diagram showing where the workers work. This diagram could indicate, for example, the location of the post office, the fire station, bakeries, and police headquarters.

9. The more mature pupils could find information that deals with the topic in *Compton's Pictured Encyclopedia* or the *World Book Encyclopedia.* Younger ones could find information in *Childcraft.*

10. As the pupils notice how the teacher finds information in encyclopedias, they can learn some of the uses of these books.

11. Skill in learning to make use of the information that is located can be provided as the boys and girls give talks to their classmates or others about what they have read.

12. The pupils could be helped to find in their picture dictionaries the spelling of words needed for writing.

13. They could look for poems useful for the unit and make an index of poems found.

14. They could collect songs about community workers and make a file showing in which books the songs are printed.

15. They could get help in interpreting charts and graphs that are of value in connection with the unit and they could show graphically such data as: (a.) the number of milkmen, policemen, postmen, firemen, bakers, and doctors in the community; (b.) the number in each of the categories of community workers who are fathers or mothers of the boys and girls in the room; (c.) the increase in the number of firemen in the community during various intervals in the past few decades. Pictorial graphs could be made to show some of the suggested data.

Developing locational skills in a unit on the Western states   Skill in the location of information can be developed in a large variety of situations in connection with a unit on the Western states, work typically taken up in the fifth grade. The following ways in which locational skills can be learned in such a unit will, it is hoped, suggest many others.

1. A committee of boys and girls could look up material in encyclopedias and in history books other than the textbook preparatory to putting on a skit on an interesting episode in the settlement of the West. Topics might be: the work of Sacajawea, the building of the first transcontinental railroad, traveling westward by covered wagon, the discovery of gold in California. An activity of this type could provide boys and girls with practice in such locational skills as the following: (a.) clarifying the problem that they wish to investigate, (b.) deciding in what books to look for information, (c.) learning to locate the books they wish to use, (d.) using the table of contents, (e.) deciding on possible key words and looking for these words in an index or in an encyclopedia, (f.) locating the information needed on a page, (g.) making an outline of the information gathered from various sources, (h.) using the outline to prepare the skit.

2. The pupils could make a collection of pictures dealing with the Far West and file them alphabetically, using guide cards to indicate their position in a filing drawer.

3. Individuals, committees, or an entire class could make a notebook on some phase of the Western states and include in it a preface, an introduction, an appendix, and an index. Some topics that might be chosen are: beauty spots of the West, the opening of the West, the coming of missionaries, and famous men and women in the settling of the West. A few suggestions for the content of the appendix are: (a.) a list of important dates, (b.) a page giving biographical data about the famous people connected with the Far West, (c.) a sheet giving data in tabular form about the national parks of the West.

4. Many locational skills could be used in making a frieze showing the means of communication used in pioneer days of the West, such as the wagon, clipper ship, stagecoach, pony express, overland stage, railroad, and telegraph. Some of the locational skills that could be used in a project of this type are: (a.) finding pictures of the various means of communication, (b.) using encyclopedias and history and geography books for wide reading, (c.) selecting the points that have bearing on a given problem, (d.) finding the dates when a given means of communication was used so that the correct sequence of events will be known, and (e.) making use of the information found.

5. A large variety of locational skills could be used in giving a talk on topics

on the Western states; for example, any one of the states of this section of the country; famous pioneers like John C. Fremont, Kit Carson, John McLoughlin, Marcus and Narcissa Whipman, Buffalo Bill; and important events, such as the discovery of gold in California.

6. The pupils could make a card file of books of value in connection with the study of the West. They could make subject cards, title cards, and author cards. Guide cards, similar to those used in the card catalogue, could also be made.

7. When drawing pictures to show, for example, the life history of a salmon, they could consult various textbooks and reference books—encyclopedias, the *World Almanac,* an atlas, and history and geography books.

8. Making an illustrated dictionary of words and phrases learned while studying the unit could involve such locational skills as: (a.) arranging words in alphabetical order, (b.) looking words up in a dictionary or other reference books, (c.) finding illustrations of the terms, (d.) using a dictionary to determine the spelling of words.

9. If a pageant or play were given showing, as an activity, the development of the Western states, various skills named earlier in this chapter could be used, namely: (a.) finding words in alphabetical order as the pupils locate words in an index or encyclopedia; (b.) finding a given page in a book quickly; (c.) deciding on key words under which needed information might be expected to be found; (d.) deciding on the type of book in which needed information would be likely to be found; (e.) interpreting punctuation marks, diacritical markings, abbreviations, and symbols used in the various references; (f.) selecting points that have bearing on a given problem; (g.) utilizing information gained; (h.) using the parts of the usual type of book (nonreference book), such as preface, introduction, table of contents, main part, index, appendix, and glossary; (i.) using encyclopedias, dictionaries, and other reference books; and (j.) locating material in the library.

Independent Reading in the Content Areas

As stated earlier in this chapter, as far as independent reading in the content area is concerned, one of the chief responsibilities of the teacher is to interest pupils in reading in these areas and to try to get "the right book to the right child." Getting the right book to the right child involves knowing the child (his interests both in books and in nonreading situations) and knowing books.

Guidelines for deciding on the "right book" in the content areas   Books in the content areas should be equal in quality to those of other types. For example, in historical fiction, as in all fiction, there should be a worthwhile theme, a strong plot, and convincing characters. However, certain criteria pertain in particular to books in the content subjects designed for independent reading. Some of these are:

1. If the book is historical fiction, it should be historically accurate. While many of the details of this type of book will understandingly not report actual happenings, the background on which the story is based should be in harmony with what history records.

2. The story elements should not be sacrificed in historical fiction. It should tell a good story.

3. Any book on history should give the pupil improved perspective of happenings in the past.

4. Fiction based primarily on a geographical background, such as *Heidi*, should give the pupil a clearer portrayal of life in a region than he had before reading the book. The differences among people should be emphasized less than the likenesses—in needs, in longings, and in hopes. Nor should generally outmoded customs, such as the wooden shoes of Holland, be presented as typical of a country.

5. Regarding supplementary books in science, there should be an affirmative answer to these questions: (a.) Are the points presented as facts scientifically accurate? (b.) Unless the book deals primarily with the history of science, does it give up-to-date information?

6. Books dealing with minority groups should serve to help pupils from both the minority and majority groups to better living without resorting to so-called moralizing.

7. Books dealing with minority groups should present the point of view that all problems faced by minority groups are common problems of both minority and majority groups and that they require concerted effort for best solution.

8. A biography for children should be about a person who is worthy of admiration, at least in some respects.

9. A biography for children should not deal with problems beyond the understanding of the reader.

10. All books for independent reading in the content area should be such that if the "right child" reads them, he will want to read additional worthwhile books in that area.

Ways of interesting children in independent reading in the content areas   Many of the suggestions given in Chapter 11 are applicable to independent reading in the content areas. A few additional ones are listed here.

1. To interest boys and girls in books on aviation a sign written in white letters on a blue background (to simulate sky writing) with the words *All about Aviation* could be placed near a number of books on that topic. The writing could be done in cursive writing, with a flourish to resemble that of sky writing. A small airplane could be drawn on the sign to attract further attention.

2. A pupil-made model of the home of one or more animals could be placed near books on animals. The home of the beaver might, for example, be made of papier mache. One illustration could show the exterior of the home, with considerable emphasis on the unique surroundings of the beaver's habitat. A second model of the home might be a cross-section view, showing the interior. A pupil or a group of pupils might explain their production to the rest of the class and refer them to additional books about beavers and other animals.

3. To interest boys and girls after a study of various people of the world in continuing reading on the subject, a series of dioramas might serve as a powerful stimulation. Homes of dwellers of artic, temperate, and tropical regions used by primitive and modern man could be placed on exhibit; and titles of books, with the authors' names and an indication of where the books can be obtained, could be listed near the dioramas.

4. As a pupil gives a report on a book of historical fiction in order to interest his classmates in reading it, he might add to the interest of his report by showing the class a time line which he has drawn to illustrate the events of history that occurred during the time when the story took place.

5. An imitation travel bureau in the room could display travel folders along with books that will help a child "travel" in imagination to a place of interest.

6. Dramatized scenes from a book of biography by some of the pupils who have read the book might interest others in reading it. What child of fifth-grade reading ability could resist wanting to read Kate Seredy's *The Good Master* after seeing scenes such as these that are described vividly in the book: (a.) Kate's arrival at the railroad station and Jancsi's disappointment when he met the girl who had wrongly been described to him as a "delicate" person, (b.) Kate marooned on the rafters of the kitchen waiting for the stove below the rafters to become cool enough for her to use it as a ladder for her descent!

NONREADING EXPERIENCES AS ENRICHMENT FOR READING

Although this book deals primarily with means of helping boys and girls grow through reading, it is important to note that reading in various content areas can be greatly enriched through the use of nonreading procedures. The many types of audiovisual equipment can be a decided source of help in the teaching-learning situation in the content subjects. The reader is referred to several means of vitalizing the social studies that have of late received considerable publicity," namely, that of "games and simulations" as proposed and developed by Jerome Bruner and his associates and that of the "process analog" advocated by William Fiedler. Both employ dramatization, including role-playing.[2] The contention of the writers of this book is that "games and simulations" and the "process analog," if used, should be a supplement or complement to reading in the social studies, not a substitute for it.

USE OF THE TEXTBOOK IN THE SOCIAL STUDIES

In the majority of the schools of this country a textbook is used in the area of the social studies in the upper grades of the elementary school. With the many excellent textbooks on the market this practice is not to be criticized. Much of the criticism that has been hurled against textbooks in the social studies should be directed not against the use of textbooks but against the misuse of them.

Cautions in the Use of Textbooks in the Social Studies and Science

The following are some of the cautions to be observed when using a textbook in the social studies or in science:

1. One textbook should not constitute the curriculum.
2. Many books other than the basic textbook should be made available. In some rooms boys and girls have ready access to a few copies of each of several textbooks. Well-selected general books on varying levels of difficulty should also be available to the pupils, some in the home room and others in the school library or learning center.
3. Magazines and current events papers should be part of the classroom or school library.
4. An abundance of visual aids to learning should be utilized. Films, filmstrips, slides, transparencies, still pictures—these as well as many others can richly complement or supplement the reading.
5. Pupils should not, as a rule, be asked to read a textbook without help being provided in the comprehension of material presented. The material in a textbook is not to be "covered," but, as someone has said, it is to be "uncovered" with the guidance of the teacher.

[2] For a brief description of means of enriching the social studies, *see* William R. Fiedler, *"An Alternative to Reading for the Social Studies,"* Thirty-first Yearbook, Claremont Reading Conference, Malcolm F. Douglass, ed. (Claremont, Calif.: Claremont Graduate School Curriculum Laboratory, 1967) pp. 205–211.

6. Use of the study-recitation type of procedure should be avoided, as a rule.

7. Reading orally the material from the textbook by a pupil while others in the class presumably follow in their books is an undesirable procedure. It is to be criticized for various reasons, among them: (a.) The reader has little incentive for reading well orally when a true audience situation is lacking, (b.) The persons not reading are likely to half-listen and half-read, thereby getting poor practice in both those facets of the language arts, (c.) The subject matter of a textbook for a grade usually is not adapted to oral reading or to hearing it read orally.

8. Not all the material in a textbook needs necessarily to be read by the pupils, especially not if the large number of worthwhile activities other than studying the textbook make it impossible to do justice to them and to all the reading material in the textbook. It is important that some topics in the social studies be studied in much more detail than is presented in the textbook. Consequently, the teacher, to save time for those additional types of activities, might present essentials related to other topics in the textbook without requesting all to read everything given in the textbook on those topics.

Suggested Procedures for Using a Textbook in the Social Studies in the Intermediate Grades

Although the procedures suggested in the pages following are geared to teaching with the use of an intermediate-grade social studies textbook many of the ideas might also be adapted for use with primary-grade pupils. Many, too can be utilized when reading textbooks in science.

One of the points emphasized in the preceding list of cautions to observe when using a textbook in the social studies or science is that the teacher should help the boys and girls with the study of the textbook. As a rule, parts of the textbook should not be assigned for study during a period preceding a "recitation period." Rather, during class time the boys and girls should be helped with the study of the textbook. Nor is it enough, as a rule, to give the pupils some help preliminary to their reading the selection for the day and then having them discuss what they read afterward. To provide more help with textbook reading in the social studies, when most of the day's work is based on the textbook, the reading material for the day could be divided into several parts; help could then be given preceding and following reading of each of these parts. An outline that might be followed with such a lesson, when the textbook material for the day is divided into three parts, could be something like this:

1. Introduction to the work for the day. This part might include any of the following:

      a. Connecting the work for the day with that which preceded and/or which is to follow.

      b. Interesting the pupils in the work of the day.

      c. Statement of the aim(s) for the day's work.

2. Word study and/or location of places.

3. Initial study of the first part of the textbook to be studied that day.

      a. Activity or activities preceding the silent reading of the part.

      b. Silent reading of the part for a stated purpose.

      c. Activity or activities following the silent reading of the part.

4. Initial study of the second part of the textbook to be studied that day (to be studied as indicated under 3).

5. Initial study of the third part of the textbook to be studied that day (to be studied as indicated under 3).

6. Follow-up activity or activities. Possible activities are giving a report, having a panel discussion, summarizing.

Activities to Precede the Silent Reading of a Part of a Day's Work with a Textbook

Item 3a above states: "Activity or activities preceding the silent reading of the part." Below are suggestions for activities, one or more of which might precede the silent reading of one of the parts to be studied on a given day, with a part possibly from one to three paragraphs in length.

1. The pupils read silently questions on the selection placed on the chalkboard or duplicated on sheets of paper.

2. The pupils comment on what they already know on the topic about to be read. Questions are so directed by the teacher that the pupils utilize their own experiences, both firsthand and vicarious.

3. The teacher asks a question of the pupils orally. For example, he states in question form the purpose for the reading of the part without giving time for discussion of the question before the reading. He might ask: "What is the difference between winter and spring wheat? Read the next two paragraphs to find the answer."

4. The teacher distributes to some pupils questions on one or more slips of paper, which are to be answered after the reading of the part in the textbook. No pupil is given more than one question.

5. The teacher indicates to the pupils a list of points to note in the selection. These points may be written on the chalkboard before class.

6. The teacher helps the pupils with the pronunciation and/or meaning of difficult words used in the selection.

7. The teacher gives a brief resume of the part the pupils are then to read in order to obtain more ideas or a clearer concept.

8. The teacher or a pupil reads a short story or part of a story bearing on the topic of the selection. A brief discussion of it might follow in order to give purpose or background for the reading of the selection in the textbook.

9. The teacher or a pupil tells a story or anecdote to serve as purpose or background for the reading of the selection. For example, an anecdote about Lincoln might precede reading about him.

10. The teacher or a pupil gives a report to serve as purpose or background for the part to be read silently.

11. The teacher points out the relation of a selection to the major purpose of the study of the unit on which the boys and girls are working. For example, if the pupils are working on a notebook of important cities, it might be made clear by the teacher that reading a given selection will provide them with data for the project.

12. The pupils look at pictures, either in the textbook or elsewhere, in order to gain background for the reading.

13. The class studies maps in order to gain background for the reading.

14. The teacher or a pupil makes reference to an exhibit on a bulletin board that serves as background for the reading to follow.

15. The teacher or a pupil shows objects related to the topic of the part to be read. For example, if the pupils are to read about the invention of the cotton gin, a sample of raw cotton with seeds in it, followed by a little experimentation with the removal of a seed from the cotton, puts meaning into the statement in the textbook that it is difficult to separate the seeds from the cotton by hand.

16. Some pupils give a brief skit, sing a song, or play a game that serves as background for the reading. For example, before the boys and girls read about the discovery of gold in California, a few pupils might put on a skit dramatizing Sutter's discovery. Or before the pupils read about the play activities of boys and girls in some foreign country, a game popular in that country can be played, for demonstration, by a few pupils.

Activities to Follow the Silent Reading of a Part of a Day's Work with a Textbook

Item 3c in the outline on page 353 refers to "Activity or activities following the silent reading of the part." Below are possible activities that could be used following the silent reading of one of the parts of the textbook to be studied on a given day. (The part often will be only one, two, or three paragraphs in length.) Such follow-up procedures are usually desirable to assure that learning has taken place and to serve as further stimulation. It will be noted that some of the procedures already suggested for possible use before a part is read are also included in the following list for use after a part has been read.

1. The pupils answer questions that have been written on the chalkboard or duplicated on sheets of paper.

2. The pupils answer questions that the teacher or a pupil asks orally.

3. A pupil summarizes important points of a selection.

4. The pupils answer questions on the content of a selection, written on numbered slips of paper on each of which is a different question.

5. The teacher or pupils state related facts not given in the textbook.

6. A pupil lists on the board important information given in a selection.

7. The class outlines the selection, either individually or as a group, or the boys and girls complete an outline partially made by the teacher. This is an example of an incomplete outline, which the pupils could fill in:

The "Starving Time" in Virginia

    I. Causes of the "starving time."
      A.
      B.
   II. Rules John Smith made to end the "starving time."
      A.
      B.
  III. Effects of John Smith's regulations.
      A.
      B.
      C.

8. The pupils decide on illustrative material that they can bring to expand the ideas given in the selection.

9. The pupils illustrate what is described in a selection. For example, if a paragraph describes the moat around a castle, the pupils draw a diagram of one.

10. The teacher helps the pupils with word study.

11. The pupils locate places mentioned in the selection.

12. The teacher or a pupil tells an anecdote to make clearer the meaning of a selection read.

13. The teacher or a pupil gives a report to enlarge on learnings from the selection read.

14. The pupils study pictures or examine objects that make the meaning of the selection clearer.

15. The teacher or a pupil gives a demonstration pertinent to the material studied. For example, a cause of erosion might be demonstrated.

16. The teacher or a pupil make reference to a display on a bulletin board explaining a phase or all of the part read.

Adapting a Textbook Lesson to Individual Differences

In a typical intermediate-grade class there are usually one or more pupils for whom the reading of the textbook is on the frustration level. These boys and girls deserve the serious attention of the teacher. There are various ways of coping with the situation, none of them perfect.

Suggested Procedures

It is hoped that some of the procedures suggested here will help the teacher in meeting the needs of the boys and girls for whom the reading of the textbook in the social studies or science is too difficult. With each of the suggestions, one difficulty with the procedure is stated, not to discourage the reader of this book from trying to do something about the problem but to forewarn him of the shortcomings of the situation.

1. Finding parallel reading material for the retarded readers—some on their level. However, day in and day out it is difficult for the teacher to find such material.

2. Helping the poorer readers while the rest of the class reads silently. Care needs to be taken, if this procedure is followed, that the rest of the class is not deprived of some of the attention of the teacher to which they are entitled.

3. Having a better reader read the material to a retarded reader. While this practice may be all right at times, it cannot be followed repeatedly without "short-changing" the able reader, whose time should be spent primarily in self-improvement, not chiefly in tutoring.

4. Gearing the activities preceding and following the silent reading so that the retarded readers can profit from them. A difficulty lies in the fact that if the activities are geared to the child who is retarded in reading and not able to read effectively, there is danger that they are not geared to the better readers who are doing all the silent reading.

Rewriting Textbook Material on the Level of the Retarded Reader

One fifth-grade teacher was pleased with the results she obtained when she rewrote for a time the material in the textbook on the level of some of her pupils who were several years retarded in reading. They would participate in the activities preceding and following the various times for silent reading, either actively or passively. Questions asked them or words with which they were helped would be of some value in reading the rewritten selection. Then while the rest of the pupils were reading a part of the textbook, the retarded readers would be reading their adapted versions. Sometimes the teacher had guiding questions listed on the retarded readers' rewritten material. Then these pupils were asked some of these questions during the activities following silent reading.

When reporting on the venture the teacher of the fifth-grade pupils reported that soon after the plan had been put into operation, she noticed that the children who had previously been sitting listlessly and bored began to participate in answering questions on their level and were taking an active interest in the work. What pleased the teacher particularly was the response she received after she had for a time rewritten the material for these slower pupils. On a certain day she explained to the group that she did not have material for them and suggested that that day they read out of the textbook with the rest of the class. She was greatly encouraged that after the experience of success that the pupils had had with reading on their own level they not only read the assigned textbook material but also took an active part in questions and discussions that followed. The children had evidently, under the time-consuming plan the teacher had worked out in rewriting materials for them, broken their blocks of not trying to read because of frustrations in the past. Success in reading the simpler material was instrumental in giving the children confidence in taking part in more difficult assignments.

A shortcoming of the type of procedure just described is that it takes a considerable amount of the teacher's time to rewrite the material that is given in a textbook.

For Further Study

Binter, Alfred R., John J. Diabal, and Levand K. Kise, eds., *Readings on Reading* (Scranton, Pa.: Intext Educational Publishers, 1969), Part VII, "Reading in the Content Areas," containing articles by Gertrude Whipple, E. Elona Sochor, Maurice Hartung, and George G. Mallinson.

Bond, Guy L., and Eva Bond Wagner, *Teaching the Child to Read*, 4th ed. (New York: The Macmillan Company 1966), Ch. 13, "Reading Content-Subject Materials."

Harris, Albert J., and Edward R. Sipay, eds., *Readings on Reading Instruction*, 2nd ed. (New York: David McKay Company, 1972), Ch. XI, "Reading in Content Areas," containing articles by Steryl Artley, Martha Dallmann, Edith F. Miller, Martha Weber, and the Metropolitan School Study Council.

Huus, Helen, *Children's Books to Enrich the Social Studies* (Washington, D.C.: National Council for the Social Studies, 1961).

Karlin, Robert, *Teaching Elementary Reading: Principles and Strategies.* (New York: Harcourt Brace Jovanovich, 1971), Ch. 7, "Reading in the Content Fields."

Mazurkiewicz, Albert J., ed., *New Perspective in Reading Instruction: A Book of Readings* (New York: Pitman Publishing Corporation, 1964), Part Eleven, "Reading in the Content Areas," containing articles by Albert A. Gallen, Glenn O. Blough, Robert V. Duffy, John B. Clark, Leland B. Jacobs, and Alvina Treut Burrows.

Spache, George D., and Evelyn B. Spache, *Reading in the Elementary School,* 2nd ed. Boston: Allyn and Bacon, Inc. 1969, Ch. 9, "The Combined Program for Intermediate Grades."

Strang, Ruth, Constance M. McCullough, and Arthur Traxler, *The Improvement of Reading,* 4th ed. (New York: McGraw-Hill Book Company, 1967).

Questions and Comments for Thought and Discussion

1. Special problems in reading in the content areas are discussed in some detail in this chapter. Can you give illustrations of how these or others were a real problem to you or someone else? What, if anything, was done toward their solution in the case or cases to which you can refer? What might have been done if nothing actually was done?

2. Several suggestions are given in this chapter for helping boys and girls remember what they read in the social studies. Can you think of others or of ways of implementing those that are suggested in the book?

3. You may wish to examine books in the library that would serve well the needs of some boys and girls for independent reading.

4. Examine several elementary-school science or social studies textbooks. What problems might a boy or girl meet when reading them? How could the teacher help in the solution of these problems?

5. You may find it profitable to plan a lesson based in part on a textbook in elementary-school science or social studies, using some of the procedures suggested on pages 352–357.

Outline for Chapter 11

DEVELOPING CHILDREN'S INTERESTS IN READING

The Aims of Guidance in Wide Voluntary Reading
Studying the Interests of Children
    Nonreading Interests
      Hobbies
      Television
    Reading Interests
Guidelines
A Planned Literature Program
    Curriculum Designs
    Steps in Planning a Literature Curriculum
Teaching-learning Techniques
    Oral Communication
    Written Communication
    Audiovisual Presentations
    Record-keeping
    Miscellaneous Activities
Other Considerations
    Book Week Activities, Book Festivals, and Book Fairs
    The School Library or Learning Resource Center
    Book Selection
    Development of Interest in Poetry

CHAPTER 11

Developing Children's Interests in Reading

The development of keen and continuing interest in reading is not only one of the basic aims of reading instruction but also an essential condition for sturdy growth in reading ability. Successful reading depends on the drive that comes from within the learner. The use of outward compulsion achieves little in the way of reading progress and may in fact inhibit the growth of reading interest. Only as the abundant energies that are resident in all normal children are released may we expect rapid and enduring gains in reading skill and interest. We must, therefore, discover and nurture the interests that impel the child to seek meaning from the printed page.

For this reason, what is variously called "free" reading, "recreational" reading, and "personal" reading has come to occupy a place of first importance in the school program. While not long ago teachers tended to regard this kind of reading as peripheral to the instructional program—a kind of extracurricular activity—today "reading for fun" is considered a legitimate and desirable activity for school hours. The systematic study of children's interests has thus become a central part of the instructional program in reading.

THE AIMS OF GUIDANCE IN WIDE VOLUNTARY READING

How great the importance of wide voluntary reading is can be seen from an examination of some of the major purposes of this type of reading.

1. Providing leisure-time activities   Perhaps the first, though not necessarily the most important, purpose is the development of the habit of reading in leisure time. Children should have much leisure time, and they should have abundant resources for its constructive use. Certainly some of these resources should take the form of sports, hobbies, and social activities. But reading good books and magazines should also be a source of much pleasure. Developing the love for good reading is one of the greatest benefits that we can provide for children.

The leisure hour is the time for fairy tales, folk tales, fables, myths, tall stories, and the sagas of heroes. It is the time for *Winnie the Pooh*, for the stories of Dr. Seuss, for *Mary Poppins*, for *Mother Goose*, for *Alice's Adventures in Wonderland*, for the *Arabian Nights*. For some children it is the time for poetry—for the nonsense verse of Lewis Carroll and Edward Lear, the humor and pathos of Rose Fyleman and Eugene Field. The leisure hour can be an hour of magic, enchantment, relaxation, and relief. It can help the child to see the wonder and the beauty in the "commonplace" world all around him.

2. Expanding the horizons of children in space and time   Most children, like most adults, live in a circumscribed world. It is true that radio, television, and motion pictures have expanded the world measurably in our generation, but the new media have not supplanted print as a means of broadening our horizons. Each of the new media has something unique to give, but each has its limitations. Only the printed word can offer to the reader the world of the past in a mood of reflection and reminiscence and interpretation. New symbols evoke, through the various electronic media, the excitement of the possibilities of the future. But only the book can fully unfold the meaning of that future in words which supply the reader with the means to communicate to others his aspirations for the life of tomorrow.

3. Providing vicarious experience   Closely related to the objective of the widening horizon is that of the vicarious enrichment of experience. The materials and methods employed in the achievement of this objective will be substantially the same as those used in the effort to expand young people's intellectual horizons, but the direction the instruction will take will vary in essential particulars. Here the purpose will be to build a stock of impressions that the child's direct experience cannot provide. It is by means of the rapidly growing, well-organized mass of experience with people, places, things, and processes that the child or youth develops the

Figure 11.1 Reading can be fun. (DeKalb Public Schools, DeKalb, Illinois.)

ability to comprehend what he reads, to converse interestingly, to discuss intelligently, to make constructive use of his leisure, to live comfortably with himself in hours of solitude.

The peculiar advantage of children's literature is that it can offer an emotionalized approach to reality which enables the reader to identify himself personally with his subject. Carol R. Brink's *Caddie Woodlawn* and Laura Ingalls Wilder's "Little House" books do not merely list the facts about frontier life; they enable young readers actually to live it, endure its hardships, and rejoice in its simple, homely but authentic delights. Figures about exports take on meaning when young readers share in spirit in the life of the farmer or factory worker who produces them, the railroad or airplane worker who transports them, the stevedore who trucks them on the dock, the seaman who looks after their safe delivery. Children's literature is a means of seeing the world through other people's eyes for a time, and it multiplies a hundredfold the experiences and insights of each person who reads.

4. Developing esthetic sensitivity   Many complaints have been made about the general level of taste of the American people. The banality, transparency, and even venality of typical radio and television programs have been widely commented on. The public taste in motion pictures has been criticized with equal severity. The run-of-the-mill picture makes its appeal to people of limited intelligence and crude taste, and producers say that these are the only films that can profit at the box office. There is reason to believe that the case has been overstated, since the public has often responded enthusiastically on those rare occasions when a really superior picture is offered. Nevertheless, it is clear that for multitudes of people the area of esthetic sensitivity has scarcely been cultivated. Good literature for children can help in the development of discrimination among esthetic values, if the children can be introduced to it in an atmosphere conducive to such development.

Many boys and girls will at first find it difficult to obtain a deep pleasure from such a lovely but quiet, somewhat slow-moving book as Kenneth Grahame's *Wind in the Willows*. For some children, especially if it is read to them a chapter at a time, its humor, its receptiveness to the more subtle physical sensations, and its beautiful, simple style will prove irresistible. For others, it should be preceded by other stories more obvious, more dramatic. Hugh Lofting's *Dr. Doolittle*, Pamela Travers' *Mary Poppins*, Louisa May Alcott's *Little Women*, Dr. Seuss' *The 500 Hats of Bartholomew Cubbins*, or Robert Lawson's *Rabbit Hill* will for some boys and girls be worthy preliminaries. For each child, certainly each group, the "literary escalator" will be different.

The development of esthetic appreciation was the earliest of the school's stated objectives in the teaching of literature, and for a long time it was the only one. Today, although we see many other valuable uses for literature, literary judgment, enjoyment, and appreciation remain among the most important.

5. Helping children to understand themselves and others Evelyn Wenzel, in *Elementary English* (February 1952), discussed the "Little House" books of Laura Ingalls Wilder. This fine series of stories certainly possesses great literary merit, but Professor Wenzel in this article considers these books from another viewpoint. She has recognized them as being a means of helping young people meet their personal needs. She finds in Mrs. Wilder's work many situations dealing with:

1. Young people's need for security: material security, emotional security.
2. Young people's need for achievement: physical, intellectual, spiritual, and moral achievement, growing up, overcoming fears and misunderstandings, overcoming sibling troubles, meeting the problems of an expanding world, dealing with adolescent problems and the problems of courtship and marriage, and gaining insight into some of the mysteries of life.
3. Young people's need for change and escape. Professor Wenzel's is a valuable analysis — one that might be made of many other writers whose

work has hitherto been considered from the point of view of literary excellence alone.

As children grow up, they have the need to understand and accept differences in others as well as in themselves. They must learn to accept the handicapped member of the class without derision, condescension, or fear. Actually, most children can do this quite unconsciously, but often their attitudes have been poisoned by adults. Teaching good human relations, therefore, is not so much a matter of developing new attitudes as of having children unlearn acquired ones.

The problem is especially serious in the case of differences in race and national origin. Many fine books have been written for children of various ages to develop an appreciation of differences and a respect for other cultures. Lorraine and Jerrold Beim's *Two Is a Team*, for the primary level, and Jesse Jackson's *Call Me Charley*, for the intermediate-grade level, illustrate the many excellent books portraying Blacks. Laura Armer's *Waterless Mountain*, for younger children, and Florence Crannel Means' *Whispering Girl* and Sonja Bleeker's well-written anthropological studies, for older children, are examples of sympathetic portrayals of the Indian. Many of us are familiar with Mrs. Means' *Moved-outers*, about a Japanese relocation camp in California; and with Eleanor Estes' *Hundred Dresses*, a poignant story of an immigrant girl. Books about people in other countries are constantly increasing in number and improving in quality.

Fortunately for the teacher, there are now appearing many new guides to children's literature dealing with personal and human-relations problems. *Reading Ladders for Human Relations*, published by the American Council on Education (*see* page 375) provides lists of children's and young people's books dealing with four human relations themes. The Children's Book Center of the University of Chicago publishes a monthly list of the best new children's books, annotated and classified according to theme. Charlemae Rollins has written an excellent booklet called *We Build Together*, listing young people's books about Blacks and suggesting criteria for the evaluation of such books.

One means of helping children to understand themselves and others through books is what is sometimes referred to as bibliotherapy. Since the teacher is not a psychiatrist, he needs to proceed rather cautiously in this area. One book from which the teacher may get substantial help is *Facilitating Human Development through Reading* by Joseph S. Zaccaria and Harold A . Moses, a 1968 publication of the Stipes Publishing Company, Champaign, Illinois. The major part of the book is an anthology of books recommended for various possible problem situations such as peer relations, poverty and cultural deprivation, religion, self-acceptance. Books or stories recommended, for example, for development of self-acceptance include "The Ugly Duckling" by Hans Christian Andersen and *Huckleberry Finn* by Mark Twain; for insight on poverty and cultural deprivation *The Hundred Dresses* and *The Moffets* both by Eleanor Estes, *Strawberry Girl* by Lois Lenski, and *A Tree for Peter* by Kate Seredy. The reader is also referred to the pamphlet *Bibliotherapy: An Annotated Bibliography* compiled by Corinne W. Riggs, for many references to books and articles in periodicals supplying information to the teacher and other adults on topics related to problems disturbing some boys and girls. A few of the many listings in this pamphlet are here given:

> Malkiewicz, Jospeh E., "Stories Can Be Springboards" *Instructor*, vol. 79 (April 1970), pp. 133-134.
>
> National Society for the Study of Education, *Development in and through Reading*, Sixtieth Yearbook (Chicago: University of Chicago Press, 1961), Part I.
>
> Newton, Eunice S., "Bibliotherapy in the Development of Minority Group Self-concept" *Journal of Negro Education*, vol. 38 (Summer 1969), pp. 257-265.
>
> Witty, Paul A., Alma M. Freeland, and Edith H. Grotberg, *The Teaching of Reading: A Developmental Process*, (Boston: D.C. Heath and Company, 1966), Ch. 4, "The Role of Developmental Needs."

6. Helping boys and girls develop a greater sense of values   Closely related to some of the aims of the voluntary reading program that have been mentioned is that of assisting boys and girls in acquiring values by which to live a worthwhile life. In an article entitled "Developing Life Values through Reading" May Arbuthnot[1] summarizes her recommendations as to types of books children enjoy at different ages that help build life habits and values, in the three categories listed below; she gives illustrations of books for each group, a few of which are included in the listing:

> For the youngest—reassurance and achievement (*Make Way for Ducklings* by Robert McCloskey, *Peter Rabbit* by Beatrix Potter, *Snowy Day* by Ezra Jack Keats).
>
> Middle years—7-10, curiosity and zest for living (*Mr. Popper's Penguins* by Richard and Florence Atwater, *Mary Poppins* by P.L. Travers, *The Family under the Bridge* by Natalie Carlson).
>
> Preadolescents—10-12 or 14, compassion and courage (*Smoky* by Will James, *The Door in the Wall* by Marguerite de Angeli, *Tituba of Salem Village* by Ann Petty).

[1] May Hill Arbuthnot, "Developing Life Values through Reading," *Readings on Reading Instruction*, 2nd ed. Albert J. Harris and Edward H. Sipay, eds. (New York: David McKay Company, 1972), pp. 318-325. (This article first appeared in *Elementary English*, vol. 43, January 1966, pp. 10-16.)

STUDYING THE INTERESTS OF CHILDREN

In order that we may effectively guide the reading of children, we must know a great deal about their reading and their nonreading interests.

Nonreading Interests

Reading interests are the product of the general interests of children and youth. Often, therefore, the process of stimulating reading interests involves the expansion and enrichment of the child's general interests. In this section we shall examine the various interests that have been found to be characteristic of boys and girls at various age levels.

Hobbies

The teacher who discovers the hobbies of the boys and girls in his classroom will realize that often children progress through a series of hobbies and diverse intellectual interests. One talented boy, for example, was successively preoccupied with the following topics from ages five to fourteen: animals, stamps, rocks, magic, chemistry, medieval heraldry, military strategy, photography, maps, hunting and fishing, navigation, locksmithing, and science fiction. Subsequently he developed an interest in hot rods, but fortunately for his safety pursued it only in magazines. In the fishing stage his involvement was limited to the purchase of equipment with the small sums he earned as a newspaper carrier. Because no fishing waters could be found in a reasonable distance from his home, his fishing hobby was strictly an activity of the imagination. But what is important is that during this phase he read *Field & Stream* and other outdoor-life magazines. In each of these stages his hobby was enriched through the reading of weekly armloads of library books, which opened new worlds to him in his chosen field of interest. Only in his sports interests did he confine himself generally to the physical activities themselves.

Television

The mass media of communication, especially television, are extremely popular with children. Research indicates that television has maintained its popularity with elementary-school children throughout the years that it has been available on a large scale. It is the favorite leisure-time activity of young boys and girls. Richard L. Tobin[2], Communications editor of the *Saturday Review*, reported that Gerald L. Looney of the University of Arizona found that on the average the prekindergarten child in his study

[2] Richard L. Tobin, "Murder on Television and the Fourteen-year-old," *Saturday Review*, January 8, 1972, p. 39.

spends more than 3/5 of his waking hours watching television. He stated that by the time the child enters kindergarten he will have spent, on the average, more time watching television than a student spends in four years of college classes.

Complaints about the quality of many television offerings for both children and adults are numerous and vigorous. That they are, indeed, justified can be seen from a recent survey by staff members of the *Christian Science Monitor,* also quoted by Tobin. The staff recorded in seventy-four hours of viewing during one week "217 incidents and threats of violence and 125 killings and murders in full view of the video audience."

Although the conditions reported in these studies may not be representative of populations other than the one he investigated, undoubtedly the situation is serious. Teachers have a choice of encouraging boys and girls to spend much time reading worthwhile books or, by default, having them continue present-day practices in viewing television of the type and the extent that many now do. However, in our zeal for reform we must remember that there are also many highly desirable programs for boys and girls.

A much-discussed question is whether television stimulates or inhibits the development of interest in reading. The answer probably is that for some children it stimulates and for others it inhibits such interest. While many parents and teachers report that children on the whole read less today than they did before the advent of television, many librarians report an increase in the reading of children's books. Certainly the many long hours that children spend with television each week are diverted from time that in an earlier day might have been spent with good books. On the other hand, some television programs open new avenues of interest to children, who then seek books on those subjects and read them with increased interest and comprehension. The relation between television and reading appears to depend, to a considerable extent, on the nature of the program. Travelogues, science programs, and biographical and historical presentations probably serve to encourage some children to read more widely.

Reading Interests

Children differ widely in the degree to which they are interested in reading. Some read no books at all on their own, while others read several books a week. In order to discover what kinds of books will interest children, it is necessary to examine the voluntary choices of those who do like to read. Many such studies have been made.

As one might expect, pictures help a great deal to interest children in books. Children especially prefer colored pictures. However, the picture merely serves as a bridge to the content of the book. If the subject of the picture interests the reader, it will lure him to the book; if it does not, it will be ineffective.

In judging whether a book will interest a child, we must be careful not to be limited to adult standards. Children obviously do not always like books that adults consider superior. It is possible for adults to remember books they liked as children, and to assume that modern children will like them too. In some cases this is true. *Little Women, Heidi, Black Beauty, The Five Little Peppers,* and *Treasure Island* are perennially popular with children; *Robinson Crusoe, A Christmas Carol, Hans Brinker,* and *Tom Sawyer* also fall into this category. But other children's books of the past deal with topics and express attitudes that were of interest in their day but seem inappropriate or even ludicrous in our time. The same holds true for the element of literary style.

It is encouraging to note the many paperbacks of good quality for children that are flooding the market. An excellent listing of titles of paperbacks is in the *Elementary Paperback Catalog, Grades K-8* of the E & R Development Company (Vandalia Road, Jacksonville, Illinois 62650). Teachers will be pleased to note, for instance, that in the 1972-1973 catalogue a combination of twenty-six titles of the Newbery Medal Books is available for less than $28.00 and classics such as *The Good Master, All-of-a-Kind Family,* and *And Now Miguel* can be obtained for less than 75¢ each.

Magazines are popular with children eight years of age and older. They appeal to them because the selections are short and usually well illustrated, and because they are expendable, timely, and varied. Yet magazines represent a much-neglected resource of the elementary school.

One of the best-known and most reliable sources of information about children's magazines is Laura K. Martin's *Magazines for School Libraries* (The H.W. Wilson Company). Ruby E. Cundiff's *101 Magazines for Schools* is available from the Tennessee Book Company (Nashville). The National Council of Teachers of English has published a committee report entitled *Using Magazines* (Urbana, Illinois). A monthly mimeographed periodical called *Subject Index to Children's Magazines,* edited by Meribah Hazen, serves as a kind of juvenile *Reader's Guide to Periodical Literature* (301 Palomino Lake, Madison, Wisconsin).

Following an extensive review of the literature on children's interests in reading, Helen Huus makes the following summarization:[3]

Kindergarten and Grade One   Children of five and six like "pretend" stories, where animals talk and where there is rhythm to the language and where humor consists of exaggeration. Realistic stories of home, little children like themselves, play and daily activities are of interest, and "here

---

[3] Helen Huus, "Reading Interests," *Readings on Reading Instruction,* 2nd ed. Albert J. Harris and Edward R. Sipay, eds. (New York: David McKay Company, 1972), pp. 311–317. (The article appeared originally in *Problem Areas in Reading—Some Observations and Recommendations,* Coleman Morrison, ed., as part of the Rhode Island College Reading Conference Proceedings (Providence, R.I.: Oxford University Press, 1965), pp. 74–81.

and now" stories of cars, trucks, ships (including space ones), and trains are enjoyed.

Second and Third Grades   While seven-year-olds still like magic and fairies, the stories have more plot than those that interest the younger children. Eights, too, like complex fairy stories, especially if there is romance as an added attraction. Second graders are interested in all kinds of transportation, in the world and people, while third graders begin to extend their interests and obtain factual information about far away places and events of long ago, though exactly *how* far away or *how* long ago is not yet of great concern.

Fourth Grade   Fourth grade is a transition in many respects: in the amount of textbook reading required of the pupil, in the physical development of the pupil as he approaches preadolescence, and in the increasing separation of the interests of boys and girls.

Boys show interest in action and aggressiveness, in the affairs of the world, and therefore prefer adventure, science, hero stories, biography, history, and tall tales, while girls still cling to the fanciful stories, myths, stories of chivalry and romance, home life, biography, and accounts of everyday life, though not always in that order. Boys will not choose a book, ordinarily, that has the name of a girl in the title, but girls will choose a boy's book.

Grades Five and Six   Children in grades five and six continue the interests expressed, with hero worship being accentuated among the boys and romance among the girls. Science and mechanics become more interesting to boys, and girls enjoy lively adventure stories, though they prefer their excitement to be less violent than do boys; hence the popularity of Nancy Drew. Both boys and girls react unfavorably to much description and didacticism. Girls are likely to do more reading than boys, and both of them will read only a limited amount in magazines and newspapers.

Humorous stories and animal stories are liked at any age; in fact, adults, too, still enjoy reading such tales.

When we read generalizations about children's interests in reading, we must always keep in mind that each child has his own individual pattern of voluntary reading. Some average children read more than some bright children. Some boys read more than some girls. Some able readers read very little; some children of limited reading ability read a great deal. Some children continue to increase in the amount of reading as they reach adolescence. Some children read excessively, or compulsively, because of emotional maladjustment; others avoid reading for the same reason. It is the particular combination of cultural and personality factors that come together in the life of an individual child that determines his voluntary reading habits. There can be no substitute for the painstaking study of individual children to discover the extent and nature of their reading interests.

GUIDELINES

What then are some of the principles that can guide us as we help boys and girls grow in appreciation of literature and in enjoyment of other types of worthwhile reading? The importance of attention to individual differences has already been stressed. Let us now consider a few additional important guidelines.

1. Interests are acquired and, like other acquired traits, are amenable to training or teaching. They are responsive to the home and school environments and are conditioned by experience.

2. In any group of children there will be wide variations in the children's tastes and interests. It is the task of the teacher to discover, so far as possible, what these tastes and interests are.

3. Reading interests and life interests bear a reciprocal relation to each other. A child will read, or can be induced to read, about the things he is interested in; through reading he will become interested in more things.

4. In order that we may improve a child's interests and tastes in reading, we must begin at his present level. No matter how limited or immature his interests may be, they are all we have to build upon. We cannot usually advance the child from Mickey Mouse to *Robinson Crusoe* in one leap. Normally we progress by easy stages. The speed will depend on the child and the circumstances.

5. The literature program should be a balanced program. It should include many themes and areas of interest, many literary types, many media, and both factual and imaginative material. It should appeal to many different types of pupil purposes.

6. Many children who read widely will oscillate between books of high and low literary merit. All printed matter is grist for their mill. The measure of their growth is the highest literary level to which they respond with comprehension and pleasure. The reading of material of lesser quality is in itself no evidence of immaturity.

7. In the evaluation of children's reading interests, every effort should be made to ascertain the child's genuine preferences rather than his perception of what the teacher considers worthwhile.

8. The techniques of improving a child's voluntary reading habits should in general be those of enticement and persuasion rather than those of coercion.

9. The aim of the literature program should be the development of enduring worthwhile interests in reading.

10. In the development of reading interests, as in all other instruction, the teacher is the key factor. If the teacher feels affection for the

children, exhibits a sincere interest in their problems and interests, is accepting, gives encouragement, and demonstrates genuine enthusiasm for books, he can create an atmosphere that is favorable to reading. But a generalized attitude of friendliness and good rapport with children is not enough. Since the task of the teacher is to bring child and book together, he must know a great deal about the child and he must have a wide acquaintance with books.

11. An inviting setting to encourage reading should be provided. To our knowledge no studies have been made of the effect of the physical environment in the classroom on the development of reading interests in children. However, experienced teachers believe that attractive surroundings help in encouraging children to read. For many children, especially those who have little interest in reading, an attractive room provides a setting in which reading seems the natural thing to do. An inviting reading corner — with a table, comfortable chairs, and perhaps a reading lamp — may attract children who have completed their other work.

12. Home and school cooperation is of great value in the cultivation of desirable reading interests on the part of children.

A PLANNED LITERATURE PROGRAM

Let us next consider how, in harmony with the guidelines enumerated above, a planned literature program for the elementary school can function.

A proposal of a planned literature program for the elementary school should not be interpreted by the reader as negation of the voluntary reading program. While voluntary reading should be a significant part of the literature program, the acquaintance the child develops with literature should not be only incidental. A comparison of the reason for having a literature program with that for having a social studies program, for example, may make this argument clearer. Although social studies can well be taught in part incidentally, the need of a planned program, along with the incidental one, is generally accepted. So, too, it should be with the literature program. While many of the values to be gained from literature can be achieved through the voluntary reading program without much structure, a well-planned program of literature to supplement the incidental can help assure a balanced reading diet.

A literature program in the elementary school should aim to achieve the goals mentioned earlier in various parts of this chapter. In addition, it should have as objective that:

1. Every boy and girl in the elementary school become acquainted with the various types of literature for children.

2. They have an understanding of the characteristics of good literature of each type.

3. They have the ability to evaluate, on their level of appraisal, the various kinds of literature to which they have been introduced.

Nor are acquaintance and the power to evaluate sufficient. The goal should also be to help each boy and girl appreciate the various types of literature and, more important still, benefit from literature in that their lives will be made richer and more fulfilling.

Curriculum Designs

A curriculum should be set up on a school-wide basis. The dangers of rigidity need to be guarded against in planning the program. It should make allowance for individual differences among teachers, as well as among pupils. And yet it should have a design. One such pattern is reported in detail by Charlotte Huck and Doris Kuhn.[4] This reference, entitled "A Taxonomy of Literary Understandings and Skills," is well worth study by teachers interested in setting up or helping set up a program in literature. Reported below are the main divisions and first-order subdivisions of that taxonomy:

Understands Types of Literature

Differentiates fiction from nonfiction

Differentiates prose from poetry

Recognizes folk tale

Recognizes fable

Recognizes myth

Recognizes realistic fiction

Identifies historical fiction

Identifies fantasy

Understands Components of Fiction

Recognizes structure of plot

Recognizes climax of story

Recognizes character delineation and development

Recognizes theme of story

Recognizes setting—both time and place

[4] Charlotte S. Huck and Doris Young Kuhn, *Children's Literature in the Elementary School,* 2nd ed. (New York: Holt, Rinehart and Winston, Inc., 1968), pp. 688–691.

Describes author's style or use of words

Recognizes point of view

Understands Components of Poetry

Interprets meaning

Looks for imagery in poem

Can describe diction (poet's choice of words)

Recognizes sound effects of poetry

Identifies various forms of poetry

Evaluates Literature

Understands authors write to achieve purpose

Evaluates setting

Evaluates plot

Evaluates characterization

Evaluates style of writing

Evaluates point of view

Evaluates theme

Applies Knowledge of Literary Criticism

Uses criteria for type of literature

Asks appropriate questions to analyze writing technique

Sees relationships among literary selections

Recognizes similarities and differences in works of one author or illustrator

Asks appropriate questions for understanding large meanings

Recognizes that literature gives insight into human thought and action

Applies insights gained through literature to his own life

Continues to seek new understandings.

Another systematic approach to literature is reported by the editorial staff of D.O.K. Publishers, Miami, Florida, in an article entitled "Literature and Creativity—A Systems Approach."[5] In their classification, literature for the elementary-school child is divided into these categories: folk, animal, adventure, myth, fables, other lands, historical, biography. The

[5] D.O.K. Publishers, Editorial Staff, "Literature and Creativity—A Systems Approach," *Elementary English*, vol. 49 (May 1972), pp. 676–682.

levels of progression in the program are six, lettered from *A* through *F*. Three tables are included as part of the article. The first is an "Overview of Creative Behavioral Objectives," classified according to what can be accomplished with each type of literature on each of the six levels. The second, "Literary Selections by Genre," names selections suitable for the attainment of the goals of the program, listing the books according to the level of achievement on each of the categories of literature recognized in the program. The third table, "Progression of Literary Understanding," also by type and level, indicates what understandings are being emphasized. For example, the following notations are given for folk literature:

Level A—oral, repetitive features

Level B—common plot patterns

Level C—fairy tales of other lands

Level D—humor of tall tales

Level E—tall tales of America

Level F—structural motifs in longer pieces of literature.

An annotated listing of books on human relations well worth consideration for a literature program is that given in *Reading Ladders for Human Relations*.[6] The books listed in the fifth edition are arranged in four "ladders," with a theme for each ladder. These themes, with subcategories,[7] as given in the table of contents, are:

Ladder 1: Creating a Positive Self-Image

Recognizing One's Strengths and Weaknesses

Growing into Maturity and Accepting Oneself

Identifying with One's Heritage

Developing Personal Values

Ladder 2: Living with Others

Family Relationships

Friendships

Peer Relationships

Alienation and Rejection

Ladder 3: Appreciating Different Cultures

Appreciating Different Ethnic Cultures

[6] Virginia M. Reid, ed., *Reading Ladders for Human Relations*, 5th ed. (Washington, D.C.: American Council on Education, 1972).
[7] *Op. cit.*, p. XV.

Appreciating Different Religious Cultures

Appreciating Different Regional Cultures

Appreciating Different World Cultures

Ladder 4: Coping with Change

Coping with Personal Change

Coping with Social and Economic Change

Coping with Political Change.

Steps in Planning a Literature Curriculum

The steps in planning a literature curriculum are similar, in broad outline, to those that can effectively be followed in setting up any other curriculum (see pages 513–525). Probably the first step would be that of interesting the faculty in planning the curriculum. This step can be accomplished through helping them realize the importance of a program and the practicality of devising one. The groundwork is often done by the person responsible for curriculum development. But interest in the project might be triggered by a teacher or group of teachers greatly concerned about the need for the program, possibly by teachers who have attended a summer school or a workshop on the theme of curriculum development or on literature in the elementary school. Next, might come a period of general faculty orientation to the work of developing a literature program. Speakers, study groups, films—these are among the means by which this phase of the work can be carried on. Fairly near the outset a committee whose chief responsibility would be to draw up a curricular plan should be formed. A curriculum specialist or other ex-officio member of the staff might serve as chairman, or a member of the teaching staff might be so designated. Released time or summer employment is often given to particularly interested teachers capable of giving leadership in planning the curriculum. Although the major responsibility may lie with the committee, members of that group should draw heavily for suggestions on all members of the staff. After a tentative curricular plan has been developed, it is usually desirable to present it to the faculty for suggestions. Then needed changes can be made.

A trial period for the curriculum is, in many cases, of value. Either the entire elementary school can participate in this phase or only one or a few teachers can serve as directors of the pilot program. After the trial period, the curriculum can again be subjected to critical evaluation and to revision if the latter is indicated. Provisions should be made, during the planning period, for continuing improvement of the program throughout the time when it will be in operation.

Included in the curricular guide, which should be in written form, parts such as these could serve teachers well: objectives of the program, means of implementing it, titles of books and book lists, names of other materials (such as visual aids) of value in the program, means of evaluating the program, a bibliography on published reports on literature programs for the elementary school.

TEACHING-LEARNING TECHNIQUES

The suggestions for teaching-learning techniques given in the following pages can be of value both in the planned literature program and in the supplementary voluntary reading program. They are classified as they pertain to: (1.) oral communication, (2.) written communication, (3.) audio-visual presentations, (4.) record-keeping, and (5.) miscellaneous activities.

Oral Communication

Let us consider first techniques of oral communication of value in the literature program.

Oral Reading by the Teacher

Boys and girls can, in various ways, be stimulated to want to read good books and to profit from them through the use of oral communication techniques. The following experience that one fifth-grade teacher had with the book *The Flight of Pony Baker* by William Dean Howells can easily be duplicated in spirit. When she had read the first two chapters to the class, she asked who would like to borrow the copy of the book. Since every hand in the room shot up eagerly, a schedule had to be worked out so that everyone would eventually have access to the book. Later, one boy, as he returned the volume, said that he had read it but that after it had gone the rounds of the schoolroom, he would like to take it home again so that his father could finish reading it.

The teacher, who in an appropriate manner starts reading books of the universal appeal of *The Story of Dr. Dolittle* by Hugh Lofting or *Miss Hickory* by Carolyn Bailey, does not need to fear that many of the children will not be eager to finish reading such books. Maybe we should have a return of something resembling the "Opening Exercise" period that was popular in the schools of long ago — a fifteen-minute period at the beginning of the day devoted chiefly to oral reading by the teacher of a "continued story." Not only can love for good literature be acquired in this manner, providing what is read is good literature, but also a unity in the class may often be achieved.

Oral Reading by Boys and Girls

Through oral reading by peers interest in literature can be stimulated. However, it is a dangerous policy to allow a pupil to read a story to the group that he has chosen without the teacher passing on its desirability, and without the teacher having had evidence that the child can read it effectively.

Choral Reading

There is also choral reading of materials of literary value—of a psalm, of "Who Has Seen the Wind?", of "Why Do Bells for Christmas Ring?" (see page 308). Through choral reading a feeling of oneness can be created similar to that achieved through group singing. Tape recordings of pupils' choral readings can be an effective means of giving pleasure and satisfaction to an audience.

Storytelling

Storytelling by an adult is one of the most ancient of all the means by which young people have become aware of the heritage of literature. While good storytelling is an art, it is one that can be successfully cultivated by any teacher of young children. Valuable hints may be found in the pamphlet "Once Upon a Time" prepared by the Picture Book Committee of the Children's and Young People's Section of the New York Library Association. Another source is *Stories to Tell to Children* compiled by Laura E. Cathon and others (Pittsburg Carnegie Library). An excellent book, containing many examples of good stories to tell to children, has been written by Ruth Tooze.[8]

There are those who maintain that storytelling with boys and girls as an audience should be done only by adults. Excluding boys and girls from the role of the storyteller is based on the assumption that storytelling is too difficult an art for a child to engage in if the effect on the audience is to be the main consideration. Critics with this conviction would limit storytelling to such persons as the teacher, the librarian, or a college student taking a course in literature for children. The argument supporting this point of view could be that just as appreciation of music is not likely to be fostered through a poor rendition of a musical number, so love of literature will probably not be encouraged through ineffective storytelling. Many teachers, however, do not share this opinion—that storytelling should not be participated in by boys and girls.

Care must always be taken that the story to be told is worth hearing.

Dramatization

Dramatization of favorite stories can stimulate interest in reading on the part of the participants and the audience. If the full benefit is to be obtained from dramatization, the activity must arouse interest not only in the story that is being dramatized but also in other stories.

[8] Ruth Tooze, *Storytelling: How to Develop Skills in the Art of Telling Stories to Children* (Englewood Cliffs, N.J.: Prentice-Hall, Inc., 1959).

Children who have read the same book may wish to dramatize scenes from it. The dialogue may be taken directly from the book, or it may be improvised. This latter "creative" kind of dramatics is usually more fun and is less likely to be stilted and overformal. However, the nature of the story and especially the vocabulary used and the purpose for the dramatization should determine the type of dramatization selected. In either case it may be possible to record the dramatization on tape, to be replayed for other classes.

In one fifth grade the various scenes from books that the pupils dramatized were combined into one play by having the characters of each scene "come to life" as they walked out of the "pages of a book." The "book," as can be explained in a brief introduction to the play, was represented by two large screens that served as the "book" cover and some of the "pages."

There are rich opportunities for dramatization not only through the usual type of play but also through puppetry, pantomimes, and charades. Puppetry is being used increasingly in connection with literature for children, especially with interpretations of folklore (*see* page 313). Charades, representing important events in a story, a book title, or a character's name can be effective. Or a pupil or group of pupils can act out characters from a story with the aid of pantomime and simple costume, while the rest of the class guesses the identity of the characters.

Book Discussions and Informal Book Reports

When a child likes a book, he wants to talk about it with someone. He should have an opportunity to discuss it with the teacher, and he should be encouraged to tell the class about it during discussions in the story hour. Or he may give a report on the book.

Some teachers feel almost apologetic when recommending book reports. Undoubtedly many have been boring. But reports can be fun. Care needs to be taken not to allow oral book reports to become a tedious succession of routine summaries. The teacher might start by telling, now and then, of a book he has enjoyed. In time, it will perhaps be easy to get others in the group to share their reading experiences. Not infrequently, there may be a happy response to a child's review when someone in the audience speaks up promptly asking: "When are you returning the book to the library?"

When giving a report, it will be helpful for many pupils to have in mind an outline to follow—maybe one worked out by the group—such as this:

1. Telling, in a few sentences, what the book is about.
2. Describing or relating a few significant incidents.
3. Giving the reporter's evaluation of the book.

There should be no requirement that any one outline be followed rigidly.

There are many ways in which variety can be shown in oral book reports, these among them:

1. The reporter can give the review in the first person.
2. He can show an object representative of the book, such as a thimble for *Thimble Summer*, a wooden doll for *Miss Hickory*, a strawberry — probably one from a variety store, in the form of a pincushion — for *Strawberry Girl*.
3. He can, either alone or with one or a few of his classmates as helpers, put on a brief dramatization of an incident in the story.
4. He can be dressed as the main character of the book. A cap or felt hat with a feather stuck into it at a pert angle is enough to add zest to a report on Howard Pyle's *Robin Hood*.
5. He can show pictures he has drawn to illustrate his book.
6. He can record on tape his report either while giving it to the class or beforehand for playing to the class.
7. He can use a transparency he has made related to his talk.

Book Programs by Children on Radio and Television

Radio and television stations, especially in the smaller communities, welcome school groups to their programs. The opportunity to present a discussion of children's books on radio or television can serve as powerful motivation for children to read the best of the current books for young people. Both large city schools and schools in smaller towns have successfully produced children's book programs in this manner, sometimes as single projects and sometimes in a regular series during the winter months.

With younger children it is sometimes effective to have a storytelling period with a make-believe microphone. Such simulated "broadcasts" may serve to encourage the shy child who normally would hesitate to speak before a group. Programs may take the form of dramatizations, interviews, or direct storytelling. Visits to local radio studios will furnish ideas for procedures and physical settings. Later on, the children will be ready to participate in real boadcasts on radio and television. Meanwhile the focus will be on the books themselves and on the exciting activity of sharing book experiences.

Written Communication

As in the case of oral book reports, written reports have often been a means of discouraging, rather than encouraging, interest in reading. But this need not be the case. It may be desirable to work out a standard form, similar to one suggested for the oral report, but variations should be welcomed.

Here are some ideas to make written book reports functional and to make written reporting interesting to boys and girls:

1. A simple file of cards on books read by the boys and girls, including among other points the reader's reaction to the book, can be kept.

2. A class notebook can be made in which on each right-hand page are given the title and the name of the author. Below the title every child, after he has read a given book, can write a brief comment on it and sign his name to his statement (s).

3. A class or individual looseleaf notebook can be kept in which are filed alphabetically, a sheet per book, brief written reports on books read, possibly illustrated.

4. Reports may take the form of an imaginary diary of a character in a book, of an imaginary letter written by one book character to another, or of an imaginary conversation between characters in different books.

5. Each pupil may make a two-page booklet on a book he likes. It could be a large sheet of construction paper folded, with the title, name of the author, and possibly an illustration on the cover. On the second page of the inside of the folder a review written on white lined paper could be pasted, and opposite it an illustration could be drawn or quotations from the book cited. These reports could be placed on the library table for all to read.

6. So-called "category notebooks" could be made by organizing in looseleaf files the reports on books being read into categories such as mysteries, historical fiction, fables, myths. One might be called "this and that." As a child finishes reading a book he can sign his name to the page on which the title of the book he read appears.

Audiovisual Presentations

Audiovisual aids are a very effective means of awakening the children's desire to read. These aids may include phonograph records, radio and television programs, films, filmstrips, slides, and pictures.

Dramatic recordings of books that have won the Newbery Award are now available. The discs may be obtained direct from Newbery Awards Records, New York. Complete teaching aids, including background information, vocabulary lists, suggestions for prelistening and follow-up activities, and other data accompany the records. The dramatizations are expertly directed and are performed by professional actors. The famous Landmark Book Series, published by Random House, is accompanied by dramatizations based on the books. The records may be secured from Enrichment Records, Inc., New York. Other publishers produce records that dramatize children's books. Thomas Y. Crowell, for example, has issued a record of *Harriet Tubman, Conductor on the Underground Railroad* by Ann Perry, and Ginn and Company has an album of LP recordings entitled "Let's Listen." Record companies have issued recordings of many of the children's favorites, Camden (R.C.A.-Victor) has one on *The 500 Hats of Bartholomew Cubbins* by Dr. Seuss, read by Paul Wing, and another on *A Christmas Carol*. Spoken Arts Records provides unusual recordings of literature. Of particular interest to teachers of young children are the *Just So Stories* of Kipling, *You Read to Me, I'll Read to You,* by John Ciardi, and *Grimm's Fairy Tales*. A catalogue may be obtained from Spoken Arts, New Rochelle, New York. Folkways Records presents songs, folktales, and poetry. A catalogue may be secured from Folkways Records, New York. The playing of such records, both before and after reading of the books, gives the children a sense of the reality of the story and often makes the reading itself an irresistible activity.

The use of records and recordings has numerous advantages. First, it is possible for the teacher to listen in advance to a record in order to determine its suitability for a class. Second, it is possible to stop a record at any time to discuss aspects of a story or to answer children's questions. Third, it is possible to play a record over and over, as often as the teacher or the children may desire.

As the record appeals to the ear, so the slide, filmstrip, and film appeal to the eye. Like the phonograph record, however, the visual media require careful preplanning by the teacher. Especially in the case of the slide and the filmstrip, the teacher should be familiar with the content in advance. Some filmstrips come provided with a teachers' manual, which explains each frame and focuses attention on the significant ideas in the series. As a rule it is desirable to discuss with the class in advance what is to be looked for in the still or moving pictures and to follow up the presentation with questions, interpretations, and summaries.

An example of filmstrips suited to the elementary grades is the series "Our American Heritage of Folk Music," produced by the Society for Visual Education, Inc., Chicago, Illinois. This is a series of long-playing records accompanied by filmstrips on "Songs of the Sea," "Songs of the Cowboy," "Songs of the Mountains," "Songs of the Plains," "Songs of the Railroads," and "Songs of the Civil War." Each filmstrip consists of about fifty frames. The records and filmstrips together provide a pleasant stimulus to the reading of children's books dealing with these themes.

Certain radio and television programs can be recommended in connection with developing children's interest in reading. Many stations throughout the country conduct regular "book hours" to which we can call children's attention.

Although television is a relatively new medium, it has grown with unprecedented speed (*See* page 367). A large body of professional literature on the subject of children and television has come into being. Two interesting pamphlets may be recommended: *Children and TV—Making the Most of It,* a publication of the Association for Childhood Education International, Washington, D.C., and *Your Child, Radio, and TV* by Paul Witty, published by Science Research Associates, Chicago, Illinois.

Not all audiovisual aids are as formal as those described in the preceding paragraphs. Many miscellaneous aids may be used to good advantage. Bulletin boards offer almost limitless opportunities for interesting children in books. Some can be planned to interest them in reading any good books, with a caption such as "Reading Can Be Fun"; others are useful in stimulating interest in a certain type of book, such as tall tales; still others advertise only one book. Sometimes the pupil who has made an illustration for a bulletin board might inform his audience of some other episodes in the book that he thinks might be of special interest to the listeners. It is strongly recommended that a copy of the book that is illustrated be available in the classroom at the time of the exhibit so that the children can have ready access to it. Suggestions for types of displays for bulletin boards are given in this listing:

1. Children's original illustrations of favorite stories.
2. Picture strips that highlight the development of the plot of a story.
3. Posters that urge more reading or that feature particular books.
4. Simple book reports that invite others to read the books.
5. Jackets of new books.

Additional suggestions include:

1. Having a "Who Am I?" bulletin board in which pictures of main characters are to be matched with their names or with the titles of the books.
2. Making a bulletin board that will challenge the child's curiosity by posing questions which he can answer after further reading.
3. Posting poems that encourage reading.
4. Making a bulletin board with the title "Around the World in Twenty [or any other number of] Books," of which the central feature is an outline map of the world, around which are arranged book jackets connected by ribbon or lines to the points of their geographical setting. Or illustrations representative of the books can be drawn onto the map; or on a table in front of the bulletin board can be placed books connected by streamers to the appropriate spots on the map.

Many other types of exhibits can serve as motivation. In one room copies of favorite books of individuals were placed on display. The name of the child recommending a book was given; thus, it was possible for others to ask him about the book. Displays of recent acquisitions by the school are of special value if provisions are made for scheduling the loan of books. Attractive displays of good reading lists are also useful. Other worthwhile displays include:

1. Dolls dressed as book characters.
2. Clay models of book characters and settings.
3. "Peep shows" of scenes from books.
4. Diorama and panorama scenes from books.

Record-keeping

Although cumulative reading records are often regarded as devices for evaluation, they can also serve as incentive for reading. They take many forms, to some of which reference was made earlier in this chapter. Following are a few additional ideas for keeping records of books read and thus, hopefully, developing greater interest in reading:

1. A "book tree" can be made to which are attached drawings illustrating books enjoyed by one or more pupils. The "tree" can be a fairly large branch of a real tree, probably three or four feet in height, stabilized in a flowerpot by clay. The names or initials of the pupils who enjoyed a given book can be written on the back of the drawing.
2. A tree trunk and branches can be cut from brown construction paper. Individual leaves can be made from green paper or in the fall from colors suggestive of autumn leaves. As books are read, the title and author can be written on the "leaf," as well as the name of the pupil who read it.
3. Older boys and girls can make use of a four-page leaflet called *My Reading Design* (published by *The News Journal*, North Manchester, Indiana), which provides for listing of book titles and insertion of numbers in a pie graph representing different themes and types of books.

Miscellaneous Activities

The teacher who is enthusiastic about books and reading will find many other ways of interesting children in books. Teachers can cooperate with children's librarians who organize reading clubs that meet regularly in the public library. The activities of such reading groups may include film showings, book reviews by the members or by adult counselors, tours of historical sites or places of local interest, record sessions, arranging for guest speakers, parties, and discussion of reviews in magazines and newspapers.

Classroom activities may include recommending favorite books to children in lower grades, conducting imaginary conversations among well-known characters from different books, visiting the public library, writing letters of appreciation to authors of books that were especially well liked, writing brief reactions to stories that had a special impact, identifying story sites on a world map, making theme posters from books, and having each child assemble his own poetry anthology.

Other activities that have been suggested include decorating book jackets; writing a movie script for an adventure story; giving an illustrated lecture about a travel book, using postcards, slides, magazine clippings, and other pictorial matter; making a "movie" of a book by means of a series of pictures on a paper roll attached to rollers; supplying a different ending to a story; selecting the most humorous or exciting incident from a book to tell to the class; writing a letter to the librarian or a friend recommending a book; making a mural based on a story; listening to radio or television reviews of children's books; collecting pictures to illustrate a book of verse; making a scrapbook about a subject treated in a book; stretching a cord across the room and mounting on it paper-doll-like representations of characters from books; modeling soap figures illustrating characters or objects or scenes from books.

Boys and girls can also be motivated to read good literature through puzzles, riddles, and games such as these:

1. A child represents some well-known fictional character as he appears before a panel which tries to guess his identity by questions requiring direct *yes* and *no* answers. A pupil, with one or several helpers, may put on a skit in which the audience is given a clue as to the character he is representing or the book he is portraying.

2. Each pupil prepares a short description of a character in a book which he has read, and, as he gives his description to the class, the class tries to guess who the character is and the title and the author of the book in which he appears.

3. The teacher and/or pupils make a rebus of the titles of children's books or stories. These are among those on a chart of rebuses published by the Children's Book Council:

    Pinocchio: a picture of a pin, the letter *o*, a picture of a key, the letter *o*.

    Robin Hood: a picture of a robin, a picture of a hood.

    Treasure Island: a picture of a treasure box, a picture of an eye, the letter *l*, the *and* sign (&).

4. Children solve and make crossword puzzles based on books.

5. The pupils construct time lines of events within a given book. These lines are particularly adapted for use in connection with books of historical fiction or of biography.

OTHER CONSIDERATIONS

In the concluding part of this chapter these additional topics are briefly considered: 1. Book Week activities, book festivals, and book fairs; 2. the school library or learning resource center; 3. book selection; and 4. development of interest in poetry.

Book Week Activities, Book Festivals, and Book Fairs

In order to stimulate interest in children's books on a nationwide scale, the Children's Book Council each year sponsors National Children's Book Week. The Council, composed of the children's book editors of sixty leading publishing houses, is located in New York. It supplies schools with a Book Week poster, usually designed by a distinguished illustrator of children's books, streamers with children's book themes, full-color bookmarks reproducing the Book Week posters, records, picture quizzes, and other Book Week aids. Local schools throughout the country celebrate Book Week with special assemblies, open-house, plays, radio programs, and other activities.

Recognizing that fall Book Week activities often tended to result in neglect of book projects during the rest of the year, the New York *Herald Tribune* established in 1937 the Spring Book Festival. It began by awarding two prizes of $250 each, one for the best book for younger children and one for older children. The newspaper issued a special Spring Book Festival number each May corresponding to the Children's Book Week number in the fall. Spring Book Week is observed in cooperation with bookstores from coast to coast, and Book World (342 Madison Avenue, New York, New York) provides awards known as Book World Children's Spring Book Festival Awards.

Another development in the field of children's books is the book fair or book bazaar. The book fair is usually a community project involving the schools, libraries, churches, civic groups, and various organizations interested in literature and the arts. Interest in local book fairs has been stimulated by the Children's Book Council, which also publishes a volume, *The World of Children's Books*, that includes a chapter on "How to Run a Book Fair." The book fair is usually set up in cooperation with a local bookseller or jobber who supplies the books and allows a commission on direct sales and orders taken at the fair. Such proceeds from book sales are commonly applied to some educational project, often the expansion of the school library. An extensive list of books for display at the fair has been compiled by the Publisher's Liaison Committee. It may be secured without cost from the Children's Book Council.

In 1954 the first Midwest Book Fair, with 2,600 titles, was co-sponsored by the Children's Book Council, the *Chicago Tribune*, and the Chicago Public Library. Held at Chicago's Museum of Science and Industry, it attracted 44,000 visitors. Trained children's librarians were on hand to answer questions. One booth exhibited a model children's home library. Other book fairs were held that same year in New York (the *Times'* "Reading Is Fun" exhibit toured the schools in the New York area), Cleveland, Buffalo, Detroit, Washington, Minneapolis, Philadelphia, and Hampton (Virginia). Distinguished children's authors appeared at some of the fairs. Storytelling programs were held mornings and afternoons.

Book fairs need not be planned on the grand scale of those held in the great cities. In one school[9] the project is sponsored annually by two fourth-grade classes. One year library tables, usually arranged for small groups, were placed around the room for displays of new books. Book Week posters and pupil-made murals of scenes from the books lined the walls of the room. Prize-winning books, along with displays of jackets and facsimiles of the medals awarded, were featured. Original newbook illustrations loaned by the publishers were mounted on the upper shelves, and the exhibit also included photographs of authors and illustrators. A puppet show featuring characters from favorite books was shown to the children of other grades and to parents. In all these activities, the PTA cooperated closely.

The School Library or Learning Resource Center

In some schools the library has been made into a "materials center" or a "learning resource center." As such what was formerly the library serves as a central clearinghouse for all instructional materials, including audio-visual aids, pamphlets, textbooks, and the like. Since library books are only one kind of instructional material, it seems logical to many that there should be a center for all kinds of teaching aids. However, some objections have been raised to the use of the library as a materials center. It is pointed out that the work of a materials center may become chiefly a mechanical and routine activity and will add to the already great burden of the librarian. Moreover, fears are expressed that appropriations for audiovisual and other materials will be deducted from the expenditures for books. Further, the expert handling of instructional material will add to the training needed by the qualified librarian. These are valid objections.

The idea of the materials center should, therefore, not be introduced unless the school is prepared to add a specialist in audiovisual aids and sufficient clerical staff, and to provide the necessary additional space and equipment without reducing in any way the appropriation for library books and library maintenance. In the discussion in the following five paragraphs the term *library* will be used, since we are dealing with the use of materials formerly associated with libraries, rather than with the visual aids and other types of materials also found in learning resource centers.

Since the textbook has ceased to dominate instruction in modern elementary schools, greater reliance than ever is being placed on the library. The library provides an extensive and well-selected variety of recreational books, geared to many interests and levels of reading ability. It has fine reference books such as *Compton's Pictured Encyclopedia,*[10] *The World Book,*[11] and the *Britannica Junior,*[12] as well as sets such as *The Pictorial*

[9] Gladys Jacobson, "Book Fair at Daniel Webster," *Elementary English,* vol. 27 (October 1950), pp. 356–367.
[10] F. E. Compton Company, Chicago.
[11] Field Enterprises, Educational Division, Chicago.
[12] *Britannica Junior,* Chicago.

Encyclopedia of American History.[13] The library helps children to develop new interests and hobbies, and introduces them to the use of community libraries and bookstores. It serves also as a central repository for books that are loaned to teachers for classroom use.

The mere existence of a school library is no guarantee that it will be effectively used. Wherever possible, it should be administered by a full-time, trained librarian, not left to some teacher to care for after school. The librarian should have as many assistants as are necessary to take care of mechanical and routine details so that she can devote her main energies to book selection and reading guidance. A good system of classifying and cataloguing should be put into operation. The librarian should be a member of schoolwide curriculum committees in order that she can cooperate fully in carrying out educational policy. Provision should be made for all pupils to go to the library regularly. Children should feel that they are welcome in the library and that the librarian is a very useful friend and helper.

In view of the great importance of the school library in every good reading program, it is regrettable that so large a percentage of American elementary schools have inadequate libraries, or none at all. When pressures from increased enrollments call for ever more classroom space, the library room, if one has been provided, is often among the first to go. Administrators and teachers should do all in their power to convince boards of education and the public that a good library is essential to a good school. Far from being a luxury, it is a facility without which the school cannot function efficiently.

Requirements for an elementary-school library will vary with the size of the school. If the school has no library, the staff should see that a beginning, however modest, is made, and that improvement and expansion are provided for each year. The school should be provided with the statement of school library standards of the American Library Association (*Standards for School Library Programs* by the American Association of School Librarians, Chicago). This report describes standards for personnel, equipment, and materials for school libraries in schools of various enrollments.

The American Library Association recommends, for example, that schools with 200 to 1,000 pupils have a library of 6,000 to 10,000 books, and that schools with 200 to 250 pupils appropriate $1,000 to $1,500 per year to the library, exclusive of reference books, binding costs, and salaries. It recommends that six-grade elementary schools subscribe to twenty-five magazines. It advocates the employment, in schools of small enrollment, of a librarian one day per week; provision for the storage and classification of pamphlets, newspapers, films and filmstrips, pictures and slides, and realia; a professional collection for teachers, including books and magazines, supported by an annual appropriation of not less than $200; in larger schools, in addition to the reading room, it calls for one or more conference rooms and a workroom.

[13] Children's Press, Inc., Chicago.

Book Selection

With the exception of those who are experts in children's literature, few teachers are able to keep up with the great outpouring of children's books, and fewer still can judge with ease which of the new titles are suitable for children. Teachers are, therefore, dependent in great degree on the recommendations of specialists. Two excellent references that discuss and list books for children are *Children and Books* by May Arbuthnot (Scott, Foresman, and Company, 1964) and *Children's Literature in the Elementary School* by Charlotte Huck and Doris Young Kuhn (Holt, Rinehart and Winston, Inc., 1968). The numerous booklists now available will therefore be sources or valuable aids to teachers in planning their periodic requests for books. There are a few standard lists that should be part of the reference collection of every elementary school library. These include:

> *A Basic Book Collection for Elementary Grades* (Chicago: American Library Association).
>
> *Children's Books for Schools and Libraries*, Phillips B. Steckler, ed. (New York: R.R. Bowker Company).
>
> *The Elementary School Library Collection*, Mary Virginia Gaver, *et. al.* (Newark, N.J.: The Bro-Dart Foundation).
>
> *The Children's Catalog*, Ruth Giles and others, Standard Catalog Series (New York: The H.W. Wilson Company, Supplements).

In Chapter 17, "Resources for Teaching Reading," additional booklists (*see* page 560) and lists of award-winning books for children in two competitions (*see* pages 564–567) are given: these can serve as an aid to book selection.

Development of Interest in Poetry

Since poetry is often given inadequate attention in the elementary school, it is appropriate to draw attention to means of developing interest in poetry, even though many of the suggestions suitable for arousing an interest in prose are also pertinent to poetry. Following is an extensive quotation from an article "Making Poetry Live with Children," written by Leland B. Jacobs, which is filled with many helpful suggestions.[14]

> Planning for enriching children's school living through poetry involves knowing well the appeals of many poets whose work is attractive to children, he will have access to a goodly number of those poets. Undoubtedly the old established English poets—Lewis Carroll, William Blake, Kate Greenaway, Edward Lear, Christina Rossetti, and Robert Louis Stevenson

---

[14] The article appears in *Using Literature with Children*, a publication of the Association for Childhood Education International.

—will be there. So, too, will surely be found such established American poets as Eugene Field, James Whitcomb Riley and Laura E. Richards.

In addition, such well-known poets as the following certainly deserve a wide audience of children:

Dorothy Aldis	John Farrar
L. Leslie Brooke	Frances Frost
Marchette Chute	Karia Kuskin
Walter De La Mare	David McCord
Eleanor Farjeon	Elizabeth Madox Roberts
Aileen Fisher	Kay Starbird
Langston Hughes	Rosemary and Stephen V. Benét
Myra Cohn Livingston	Elizabeth Coatsworth
A. A. Milne	Ivy O. Eastwick
James Reeves	Rachel Field
James S. Tippett	Rose Fyleman
Harry Behn	Vachel Lindsay
Gwendolyn Brooks	Eve Merriam
John Ciardi	Mary O'Neill
Paul Lawrence Dunbar	William Jay Smith

Of course, there are many other poets whose one or two or handful of poems are appealing and should be at one's fingertips for use at the right time. And some poets, such as Robert Frost, Edna St. Vincent Millay, Carl Sandburg, Emily Dickinson and John Masefield have poems that children thoroughly enjoy, though they are most frequently thought of as writing for adults.

Any one well-read in poetry for children soon discovers that there never can be graded poetry lists that are successful. To say that there are "first-grade" or fifth-grade" poems is unfair to children and to poetry. Rather, the teacher selects poetry, whether it is primarily written for children or adults, which meets the children's minds and spirits whom he is currently teaching. Then, as possessors of "educated imaginations" and as consumers of the arts, poetry and children can get together quite naturally.

What Children Enjoy in Poetry

A perceptive teacher knows that children develop in poetry only as the adults in their lives guide that development. The teacher capitalizes on what children like in poetry but at the same time whets their taste with good poetry which is the work of the sensitive, original writers. Children enjoy good poetry that:

Give them an exhilarating sense of melodious movement.

Tells wonderful stories.

Releases health-giving laughter.

Carries them into extravagant or fanciful situations.

Extends their appreciation of their natural world.

Creates memorable personages or characters.

Sings its way into their minds and memories.

Pleasurable responses to poetry are evoked when poetry selections are neatly gauged to the maturity and interests of the youngsters. In the poetry of their workaday world, children respond well to poems about pets, play activities, occupations, transportation, and interesting people. In their natural world they enjoy poems about seasons, weather, animals, flowers and trees. In humorous poetry they respond to ludicrous situations, peculiar people, tongue-tickling words, absurdities, oddities and nonsense. In narrative poetry they listen enthusiastically to adventures on sea and land, patriotic achievements, courageous deeds, historical personages and events and rousing heroism. In the fanciful, they enjoy fine make-believe, the poetic interpretation of preternatural creatures and, at times, the grotesque. In general children feel akin to poetry that is rich in sensory imagery, creates moods, calls forth pictures in the mind, makes the commonplace distinctively uncommon.

Poems Must Be Read Well

The teacher is always aware that poems do not necessarily look inviting on the printed page. The printed page of poetry becomes inviting when, somehow, the child hears, back of the printed word, the poem's melody, its vibrance, its feeling tone, its movement—all those unique poetic qualities that let the print leap to life. So the teacher learns to read poetry well, and teaches children how to interpret poetry orally. A good reader is likely to be one who:

Appreciatvely comprehends the content and the poet's stance with regard to the content of the poem.

Knows that as he reads a poem to children he must both reveal what seem to be the poet's thoughts and communicate the poet's moods and nuances of meaning to the listeners.

Helps the listener to think, sense and feel with the poet.

Sympathetically interprets the full esthetic appeal and quality of mood which the poem possesses.

Takes his clues for the actual oralization from the patterning of the poem: its variety, its images, its symbols, its rhythms, its rhymes, its symmetry.

Employs effective variety in timing in his reading and utilizes the eloquence of appropriate pauses.

So utilizes tonal quality in volume, pitch and force that, through cadenced reading, enjoyment is enhanced.

Avoids elocutionary, declamatory or other forms of artificial oral interpretation in favor of wholesome naturalness.

Acts as a medium through which the ideas and feelings of the poet touch deeply the ideas and feelings of the listener.[15]

For Further Study

Arbuthnot, May Hill, *Children and Books,* 4th ed. (Chicago: Scott, Foresman and Company, 1972).

Burrows, Alvina Treut, Diane L. Monson, and Russell G. Stauffer, *New Horizons in the Language Arts* (New York: Harper & Row, 1972), Ch. 6, "Literature for Teachers," and Ch. 8, "Children's Literature in the Classroom."

Bush, Clifford L., and Mildren H. Huebner, *Strategies for Reading in the Elementary School* (New York: The Macmillan Company, 1970), Ch. 9, "Children's Interests."

Gans, Roma, *Common Sense in Reading* (Indianapolis, Ind.: The Bobbs-Merrill Company, 1963), Ch. 12, "Motivation in Reading — And Conflicting Pressures," and Ch. 13, "Satisfying Whetted Reading Appetites."

Harris, Albert J., and Edward R. Sipay, eds., *Readings on Reading Instruction,* 2nd ed. (New York: David McKay Company, 1972), Ch. XII, "Recreational Reading," containing articles by Helen Huus, May Hill Arbuthnot, Nancy Larrick, and Olivia R. Way.

Huck, Charlotte, and Doris Kuhn, *Children's Literature in the Elementary School* (New York: Holt, Rinehart and Winston, Inc., 1968).

Jacobs, Leland B., *Literature with Young Children* (New York: Teachers College Press, 1965).

Larrick, Nancy, *A Teacher's Guide to Children's Books* (Columbus, Ohio: Charles E. Merrill Books, 1964).

Reid, Virginia M., ed., *Reading Ladders for Human Relations,* 5th ed. (Washington, D.C.: American Council on Education, 1972).

Smith, Dora V., *Fifty Years of Children's Books* (Urbana, Ill.: The National Council of Teachers of English, 1963).

Tinker, Miles A., and Constance M. McCullough, *Teaching Elementary Reading* (New York: Appleton-Century-Crofts, 1968), Ch. 15, "Interests and Tastes."

[15] Reprinted by permission of the Association for Childhood Education International, 3615 Wisconsin Avenue, N.W., Washington, D.C. From the bulletin, *Using Literature with Children,* copyright 1972, "Making Literature Live with Children," by Leland B. Jacobs. The student is urged to read this entire excellent pamphlet.

Questions and Comments for Thought and Discussion

1. How can the teacher help a child, through books, to grow in understanding of himself as an individual and as a member of society?

2. There are children's book prizes which authors, artists, and publishers would like to win. The Newbery Medal is given to the most distinguished contribution to children's literature during a given year. The Caldecott Medal is awarded for the most distinguished American picture book in a given year. The range continues downward to the point where on the local level the system of awards continues, and it is not unusual to see children being singled out for having read many books over a given period such as the summer vacation. Is this a good thing at any level? Be able to comment on the practice at the local level.

3. Certain book publishers employ children to act as junior reviewers. Very frequently, armed with sets of questions and governed by certain rules, these youngsters can perform a type of service otherwise unavailable. Can you envision ways in which you could utilize junior reviewers in your classroom? What ground rules would you set up? What questions might be used as guides?

4. Some research seems to suggest that improved reading interests and habits result from a careful study of children's present interests and a varied school program for developing more desirable reading habits and tastes. Do you know of such a program? If so, what are some of its salient features?

5. For enjoyment boys and girls as well as adults will read that in which they are interested. Consequently, in order to encourage a child to read as a leasuretime activity, it is important that the teacher know his interests. How can the teacher discover these interests and then apply this knowledge as he guides the child in forming a lifelong habit of reading worthwhile materials for enjoyment?

6. What are the implications for classroom practices of the following point of view?

> Picture reading consists of gazing at the pictures of a book or an over-illustrated text or supplementary reading book with a minimum of printed matter. Picture reading is not actually a form of reading, nor is it sensibly viewed as a pre-stage of real reading. It is an evasion of reading and almost its opposite. Habitual picture readers are severely handicapped in the task of becoming readers of books later, for the habit of picture reading interferes with the acquisition of well-developed reading habits.

7. What are the sources to which a teacher can turn to become acquainted with the realm of children's literature? Where can the teacher find lists

of selected children's books? Of poems for children? How can the teacher keep informed about children's books?

8. Why is it preferable for an elementary school to have both a school library and a library in each classroom? What points do you think should be kept in mind about a classroom library?

9. During recent years the value of the book report has been questioned by many teachers. What does it mean now? Has this concept really changed? Can book reports be effective means of interesting children in books?

Outline For Chapter 12

CLASSROOM DIAGNOSIS OF READING ABILITY

Guidelines for Diagnosis
Determining the Expectancy Level
Assessment of Reading Ability through Standardized
      Reading Instruments
  Survey Tests
  Diagnostic Tests
  Criterion Referenced Tests
Assessment of Reading Ability Through Nonstandardized
  Procedures
  Informal Observation
  The Informal Reading Inventory
    Construction of the Testing Materials
    Administration of the Test
    Interpretation of the Test Results
    Additional Information
  Other Non-standardized Techniques
    Assessment of Word Attack Skills
    Use of Teacher-Made Criterion Referenced Tests
    Use of the Cloze Technique

CHAPTER 12

Classroom Diagnosis of Reading Ability

One of the fundamental themes we have been emphasizing is the importance of trying to fit the program of instruction in reading to the needs of the learner. If we are to be successful in adapting instruction to individual differences, we must necessarily have clearly in mind what the needs of the various individuals are. To locate and define them is the purpose of diagnosis, if we think of diagnosis as the means of ascertaining not only a weakness in reading but also the strengths of each pupil. Unless we have identified these needs our teaching will be lacking in effectiveness.

The extent of a person's acquisition of the ability to read is determined to a large degree by the level of his mastery of the various skills essential to excellence in reading. Thus, it becomes the task of the teacher to ascertain how far each child has progressed in the development of these skills and to provide for him instruction that gives the most promise of helping him make further progress. The teacher who, after having made a diagnosis of the learner's reading ability, bases his teaching on the pupil's requirements, is providing him with what various writers refer to as *diagnostic instruction.*

The almost exclusive emphasis placed in this chapter on the diagnosis of reading skills should not be interpreted as indicating that the skills of reading should constitute the total of the teacher's concern in diagnosis.

That assumption would, indeed, be an erroneous one. The child's interests and tastes in reading, in fact the level of his recreational reading, should, as discussed earlier, be a matter for diligent investigation by the teacher. Furthermore, the teacher who views as an objective of the reading program the development of the individual, who believes that reading should lead to desirable action will also want to search for signs that indicate whether reading has really carried over into action that is socially useful and individually satisfying. Appraisals of such goals must not be overlooked. If they are, some of the primary reasons for teaching reading are lacking in the diagnoses. Outcomes such as these are difficult to measure. However, through procedures such as informal observation, pupil conferences, and at times pupils' writing, insight can be gained that might give trustworthy evidence as to whether an individual is making constructive use of his ability to read. Important though such study is, it is not the subject of this chapter, which deals with the diagnosis of reading skills.

GUIDELINES FOR DIAGNOSIS

Several guidelines that the teacher should keep in mind when making or interpreting diagnoses of reading ability are indicated in the preceding paragraphs. Additional points of general applicability to classroom diagnosis are given below:

1. **Diagnosis of reading ability should not be confined to the poor reader** Each child has the right to instruction based on a knowledge of his strengths and weaknesses of the level of his reading ability. However, in many instances it would not be practical, with limited time and personnel, to make detailed analyses of the reading ability of all boys and girls in a room. They are an essential for those pupils who seemingly are not profiting to the extent of their capacity from the reading program as it is being conducted.

2. **The teacher should try to discover the causes of any difficulties in reading that the learner may have** Since understanding the reasons for the existence of a problem can give insight into the course of action to be followed in remedying an unsatisfactory situation, the teacher will want to search for factors that contribute to the problem. For example, background data on the level of the child's intelligence, his physical welfare, his mental health, his motivation for reading (or lack of it) can provide valuable information on which to base diagnostic instruction. Nor should the search for causes cease when the teacher has discovered one cause, for usually causation of difficulties in reading is multiple.

3. Diagnosis should be made in terms of the objectives for the reading program   The teacher who makes his diagnosis in terms of his goals will be more likely to establish a comprehensive plan for diagnosis than the teacher who knows but vaguely what he wants to accomplish.

4. Diagnosis should be a continuous process   Obviously the teacher should not be giving tests nor using checklists daily. But every day, during reading class and at other times, the teacher should be aware of clues that provide insight into the child's reading strengths and weaknesses.

5. Boys and girls should be helped to recognize the purposes of diagnosis that are being made of their reading ability   The extent to which the pupils should be informed will depend on various factors, such as the intelligence of the learner, his age, his interest in reading and in reading improvement. Even the beginning reader, when being checked, for example, on words on a list, can be told simply: "Let's see which of these words you know. I want to help you with those you don't know."

6. Boys and girls should be given an opportunity to engage in self-evaluation   With the help of the teacher the child might keep a record of "new words" mastered in a primer or first reader, of the number of days on which he did not move his lips (while the teacher observed him) when reading silently, of the number of questions answered correctly on comprehension tests set up uniformly to make comparability from one testing to another easily possible.

7. The depth of diagnosis to be made should be determined, in part, by the nature of the problem   The seriousness of the problem should be one determining factor. Another should be the ease with which a problem can be analyzed. By far the large majority of boys and girls will require only the depth of diagnosis that the classroom teacher is capable of making through formal and informal testing and through use of techniques, such as individual conferences, observation, group inventories. However, others should, ideally, be referred to a clinician or other reading specialist for further diagnosis.

8. The teacher should recognize that diagnostic procedures even at best are imperfect   Research has not established the most propitious means of arriving at a knowledge of the status of a child's reading ability. It is generally agreed that a combination of various types of diagnostic techniques brings better results than the use of only one. All of them have shortcomings, but since not all techniques have the same weaknesses or defects, hopefully when more than one is used, the disadvantages of one may be offset somewhat by the strengths of others.

9. Diagnosis should result in action   We are reminded of the school administrator—probably a fictitious character—who reportedly complained that though he had given standardized tests repeatedly to the boys and girls in his school, they were no better achievers than previously. Though none of us would be as naive about the purpose of testing as this individual, there are schools in which the results of diagnosis are not used adequately as determiners of future teaching. Diagnosis beyond the level that will be used in the improvement of instruction is a waste of time and energy and money.

DETERMINING THE EXPECTANCY LEVEL

As the teacher diagnoses the strengths and weaknesses of a child, he will want to determine the teaching procedures he will employ in the light of what can be expected of the learner. He can obtain a rough indication of reasonable expectations by means of informal methods, such as those to which reference is made in Chapter 4A under "Subjective Data on Mental Maturity" (*see* page 60). The intelligence quotient (mental age divided by chronological age) can be used as a rough index for computing what is known as the *expectancy level.* A ten-year-old with an intelligence quotient of 100 can be expected to read on the level of a ten-year-old; if he has an intelligence quotient of 80, his expectancy level can be thought of as eight years (80% of 10). However, the index of expectancy level will be no more accurate than the intelligence quotient upon which it is based. Various ways of figuring the expectancy level have been suggested. Bond and Clymer, as reported by Bond and Tinker,[1] have devised this formula for obtaining the estimated expected reading level: number of years in school $\times$ IQ/100 + 1.0. Using this formula, a pupil with an intelligence quotient of 90, who is beginning his third year of school, would have a reading expectancy of 2.8 ($2 \times .90 + 1.0$). In other words, according to this formula, the teacher can expect him to read as well as the average child in the eighth month of the second grade. A child with an intelligence quotient of 120, who is in the third month of the fifth year of his schooling, would have a reading expectancy of 6.2 ($4.3 \times 1.20 + 1.0$, or 6.16).

Durkin[2] suggests still another formula for computing what she and some other writers refer to as the *reading achievement expectancy:* namely: Mental age (M.A.) — 5. It is based on the assumption that the average child in the first grade has a mental age of about six, in the second grade of seven, and so on. According to this method of computing reading expectancy, with a mental age of eight, a child, regardless of his grade placement, could be expected to read on the third-grade level. One with a mental age of

---

[1] Guy L. Bond and Miles A. Tinker, *Reading Difficulties: Their Diagnosis and Correction* (New York: Appleton-Century-Crofts, 1967), pp. 91–95.
[2] Durkin, *ibid.,* p. 407.

ten would have a reading achievement expectancy at the fifth-grade level. In explaining the formula Durkin rightly points out that to the extent that factors other than mental age affect reading ability, the reading achievement age calculated according to her formula becomes inaccurate. She also draws attention to the fact that the concept of *grade level* is lacking in precision. However, use of any of the formulas for computing expectancy levels, when other factors are taken into consideration, can help point out to the teacher the differences in learning ability and rate which exist in every classroom, and can serve as index to him of the expectations on which he should plan the program of instruction.

ASSESSMENT OF READING ABILITY THROUGH STANDARDIZED READING INSTRUMENTS

Since, in the chapters on readiness for beginning reading instruction, we have discussed standardized and nonstandardized procedures for assessing readiness for reading, we will now limit our considerations to only those instruments that test beyond that level.

Standardized reading tests can be classified as survey tests and diagnostic tests. The former provide an average score; the latter undertake to break down the average into specific strengths and weaknesses.

While standardized reading tests, when used with great caution, can be of decided value, they must be interpreted with a clear recognition of their shortcomings.[3] At best they test only a limited number of factors important in reading. Another serious limitation lies in timed comprehension tests. The scores obtained from them give erroneous impressions to the interpreter of the test who is not cognizant of the fact that many such tests give scores that are a mixture of rate of reading and comprehension. An additional fact to note is that the grade-equivalent scores provided by the publishers of tests often are not reliable indexes.

Survey Tests

The scores on a survey test purport to tell the teacher how well a pupil can perform on a given test in comparison with other pupils of the same age or grade to whom the test was given in the process of standardizing it. Some survey tests are divided into subtests dealing with various reading skills — such as rate of reading, word recognition and word meaning, comprehension of sentences and of longer selections, skill in locating materials — while other survey tests have but one part. Neither kind provides specific information as to the needs of a person examined, although unfortunately

[3] Paul A. Witty, "Rate of Reading: A Crucial Issue," *Journal of Reading*, vol. 13, No. 2 (November 1969), pp. 102–106.

some teachers group pupils for instruction according to scores obtainable from these tests. In reading groups formed on the basis of the limited information available from survey tests, since the exact needs of the pupils as far as reading skills are concerned are unknown, the instruction cannot be specific enough to meet the requirements of each individual.

In some survey tests reading is only one of the skills checked, as for example, in the *Iowa Every-Pupil Test of Basic Skills* (Houghton Mifflin) and in the *California Achievement Tests* (California Test Bureau). In other survey tests, such as the *Gates-McGinitie Reading Test* (Teachers College Press), only reading is tested.

From a survey test the teacher can get an indication of whether a class or an individual is below, at, or above the average of the norm group (the group on which the test was standardized). The comparison is usually made in terms of the percentile rank (P.R.) or the grade equivalent score. By means of the percentile rank a comparison of the score of a pupil is made with the norm group by indicating what percent of the individuals in that group he surpasses.

The grade-equivalent score is also found by consulting tabular data furnished by the publishers of a test. If a pupil has a score on the test representing the average received by pupils at the beginning of the fourth grade in the norm group, his grade-equivalent score is 4.0. If he has the score that represents the average made by a pupil in the fifth month of the sixth grade, his grade equivalence is 6.5. Stauffer[4] wisely voices a concern about the frequent misinterpretation of the grade-equivalent score when he points out that some teachers are under the erroneous impression that a child in fourth grade, for example, who receieved a grade-equivalent score of 6.8 reads as well as a high sixth-grade child. All such a score indicates is that the child on that reading test scored higher than the average sixth-grade child taking the test.

In recent years publishers have frequently been using the *stanine* as a test norm. When this comparison of scores is used, the distribution of scores on a test is divided into nine parts, with points on the scale falling between 1 and 9. A score of 5 (the midpoint) indicates average performance; of 9, very high; and of 1 very low. A stanine of 8 is high; 7, well above average; 6, slightly above average; 4, slightly below average; 2, low.[5]

In making a selection of standardized reading tests, either survey or diagnostic, the teacher should study carefully the teachers' manuals supplied with them. Manuals will tell the *validity* of a test, which indicates the degree of accuracy with which the test measures what it is intended to measure, and the *reliability* of a test, which indicates the degree to which a test yields consistent results. The teacher should keep in mind also the purpose for which he intends to use the test. For example, tests that consist chiefly of vocabulary items may not adequately measure the degree to

[4] Stauffer, *op. cit.*, p. 427.
[5] Caroline E. Massad, "Interpreting and Using Test Norms," *The Reading Teacher*, vol. 26, no. 3 (December 1972), p. 291.

which a pupil is able to deal with words in context. The length of the test and the time available to teachers and pupils may also be important factors. Finally, the relative recency of the test may have a bearing on the selection.

Diagnostic Tests

We have already discussed one type of diagnostic test, the so-called oral reading test, which is designed to test primarily, through oral reading, the silent reading of a pupil (see page 296). For a list of widely used standardized oral reading tests and for a list of other diagnostic tests, the reader is referred to Chapter 17, "Resources for Teaching Reading." In the next two paragraphs are described two of the many diagnostic tests that assess growth in word recognition, namely the *Silent Reading Diagnostic Tests* by Guy L. Bond, Bruce Balow, and Cyril Hoyt (Lyons & Carnahan) and the *Doren Diagnostic Reading Tests of Word Recognition Skills* by Margaret Doren (American Guidance Service, Circle Pines, Minnesota). It is hoped that a description of these tests will give the reader insight into the purpose and nature of diagnostic tests.

The *Silent Reading Diagnostic Tests* can be administered either to an individual or a group. They are designed for use with boys and girls between second- and sixth-grade reading levels. Included are subtests on: (1.) words in isolation, (2.) words in context, (3.) visual-structural analysis, (4.) syllabication, (5.) word synthesis, (6.) beginning sounds, (7.) ending sounds, (8.) vowel and consonant sounds. After the scores obtained from the subtests have been transferred to a graphic profile, for ease in interpretation, "lines of importance" are drawn according to directions on the profile. Scores falling to the left of these lines indicate areas of weakness.

The *Doren Diagnostic Reading Tests of Word Recognition Skills* is a group test measuring decoding skills normally associated with primary reading levels. The subtests are on: (1.) letter recognition, (2.) beginning sounds, (3.) whole word recognition, (4.) words within words, (5.) speech consonants, (6.) ending sounds, (7.) blending, (8.) rhyming, (9.) vowels, (10.) sight words, (11.) discriminate guessing. Like the *Silent Reading Diagnostic Tests* this one by Margaret Doren provides a profile which can be helpful in assessing areas of weakness in the use of word attack skills. Although it is a very useful instrument, the length of time needed for administering it—nearly three hours—will deter some teachers from giving it.

Criterion Referenced Tests

Lately a type of test, frequently referred to as a *criterion referenced test*, has become increasingly popular. Not all persons in the field of education will agree as to how the term *criterion referenced test* should be used, but there is fairly general agreement among educators that such a test sets out to ascertain what the person tested knows or can do relative to the specific area of the subject matter checked by the test. For example, a criterion referenced test could be designed to check the learner's knowledge of and skill in finding quickly words arranged alphabetically. Such a test would ideally contain items testing skills such as: (1.) knowledge of the sequence of letters of the alphabet; (2.) ability to arrange letters alphabetically; (3.) ability to arrange words alphabetically when the first letters of the words are different, when the first letters are alike but the second letters are different, and so on; (4.) knowledge of which word of a compound proper noun (such as the name of a person, place, society) is the one that determines the alphabetical order of the name. Or a criterion referenced test could check the number of words and which words on a word list the learner knows. Or the learner's knowledge and application of the knowledge of some generalizations in phonics could be tested by an item-by-item sampling of the various specific points of information and skills sought when teaching the generalizations being tested.

Unlike the survey test, the criterion referenced test is not given to compare a pupil's level of learning with that of others. Like the usual diagnostic test it is administered to find out what the person tested knows or can do in a specified, quite circumscribed area of learning. While diagnostic tests are given primarily to discover the weaknesses of a learner, the criterion referenced test is used to find which knowledge or skills in the area being tested the learner has acquired and which he has not learned. In a sense we could think of the criterion referenced test as one type of diagnostic test, since it makes a diagnosis by showing mastery or lack of it of points considered significant in the area under study.

A successfully constructed criterion referenced test should clearly define the area of learning being investigated. It should be based on a reliable analysis of the types of information or skill that constitutes the components of needed learnings in that area. The omission of some essential points in the test might give the interpreter of the test the erroneous impression that the child is in possession of information or skill in a given area that has not been tested.

Criterion referenced tests can be designed by the teacher. However, they are also available in print. Some commercially constructed materials include such tests in their programs, as is the case with the *SRA Reading Laboratory*.[6] The Educational Testing Service[7] is also constructing criterion referenced test items. Jason Millman[8] reports that the "Instructional Objectives Exchange (P.O. Box 24095, Los Angeles, Cal., 90024) is now developing an extensive set of CR [criterion referenced] tests in reading from which a school can select those which match its instructional objectives."

[6] Jason Millman, "Criterion Referenced Measurement: An Alternative," *The Reading Teacher*, vol. 26, no. 3 (December 1972), p. 280.
[7] Educational Testing Service, "ETS Takes Part in Nation Right to Read Effort," ETS developments, vol. 18 (Spring 1971), p. 2. (This reference was found in the article by Jason Millman, referred to in footnote 6.)
[8] Millman, *op. cit.*, p. 280.

ASSESSMENT OF READING ABILITY THROUGH NONSTANDARDIZED PROCEDURES

Standardized tests, in spite of their value, have their shortcomings, some of which can be counterbalanced in part by informal diagnosis.

Informal Observation

A method that the alert, sympathetic teacher has always used is that of informal observation of the child's overall performance, his attitude toward books and reading, his play interests, his hobbies, and his reading interests. The observation may take place in nonreading as well as in reading situations. For example, a child may unintentionally reveal a dislike for reading while working with classmates on a model airplane or while discussing what he would like for Christmas. The teacher may note the kinds of book choices a child makes during the free reading period. He may observe the child's behavior as he reads a book—whether he squints, whether he stops often in his reading, whether he assumes good or poor posture as he reads.

Since few teachers are able to keep in mind the developing characteristics of many children over a period of time, it is helpful to keep an informal record of the day-by-day observations. A file folder should be kept for each pupil suspected of having difficulty in reading; in fact, teachers will find it helpful to keep such a folder for every pupil in the class. In this folder the teacher should insert, from time to time, any material that may throw light on the child's reading problems. The folder should include samples of the child's writing and drawing as well as reading exercises he may have performed. But perhaps the most important material is the teacher's report of the child's observed behavior. This may be in the form of a sentence or two for a given day (the date should be noted), such as: "Today Axel spent 15 minutes in uninterrupted reading of *The Little House in the Big Woods*. He has never concentrated before for so long on his reading, as far as I know." The notations should usually not be of a general nature, as: "I think Axel is improving." The anecdotal record should essentially be a behavioral record. In the course of six months it should be possible to discover from the record in what direction the child is moving with respect to significant aspects of reading growth. The type of information described in this paragraph cannot be secured from even the best of the standardized reading tests.

The Informal Reading Inventory (IRI)

Informal reading inventories have been designed in various ways and for a variety of purposes. The one described here, like most that are used by classroom teachers, is an instrument for finding a pupil's independent, instructional, and frustration reading levels. The *independent reading level* is determined by the highest level of reading material that the child can read effectively without assistance from the teacher or others. The *instructional reading level* is indicated by the highest level of reading material that he can handle with effectiveness when he receives help. The *frustration reading level*, the level immediately below the instructional level, is established by the level of reading material at which the reader is unable to proceed effectively even with assistance.

Because giving an informal reading inventory is rather time-consuming, the teacher may not wish to give one of the type here described to all of his pupils; he may decide to use it only with pupils who are showing undue difficulties in reading. If a teacher does use an informal reading inventory with all his pupils, he may find that he needs to interpret with special caution the scores obtained when checking the average or the better-than-average reader, for scores made by such readers on these inventories are often erratic and therefore questionable.

Construction of the Testing Materials

Typically, an informal reading inventory consists of a number of reading passages taken from a basal reader series or other graded material. Some reading inventories also include a word list for testing word recognition.

The reading passages are usually arranged in order, two at a level, ranging from the preprimer through at least the sixth-reader level; some extend as high as the ninth-reader level. While no exact specifications as to the length of each selection can be given, it is probably advisable to include in each passage on the preprimer level between 30 and 40 words and to increase the number at each succeeding level until at the sixth-reader level the passages contain between 150 and 175 words. Since the difficulty of materials in basal reading series varies, it is recommended that the readability level of each passage be checked. The Spache readability formula is recommended for the primary levels and the Dale-Chall may be used for upper-level checking (*see* page 336). About five questions (Stauffer suggests seven) are recommended for the preprimer- and primer-level passages. The number should be increased for subsequent levels. Some teachers like to use ten questions for all levels beyond the primer because of the ease of figuring percentages on a base of ten. Questions should check factual comprehension, interpretative skills, and critical reading.

Each passage selected for the testing, with accompanying questions, should be placed on a separate sheet. The pages can then be compiled into a booklet for use by the examiner, arranged in a progression from preprimer to the highest level used (sixth-reader level or beyond). A summary sheet for recording test results can serve as cover for the booklet. It is recommended that if possible the examinee read directly from the book from which the passages for the teacher's booklet are taken. When, however, a copy of the book is not easily available for use by the child, separate booklets containing only the reading passages—not the questions nor the answer sheet nor the record sheet included in the teacher's booklet—can be used by the pupil.

Administration of the Test

Obviously it would be a waste of time to start each child being examined with the passages on the preprimer level. The examiner can have him begin with the level which the teacher thinks would be only a little below the child's independent reading level. If the teacher's estimate is found to be too high, he then can ask the child to read at a lower level till he finds the passage representing the child's independent reading level. Then the child continues reading on various levels till his instructional reading level is also located.

The child reads both passages on a level, one orally and the other silently. As the child reads a passage orally, the teacher records the errors made in the teacher's booklet. It is recommended that an error be counted even though the child corrects it immediately. After a child has read a selection, either orally or silently, the teacher asks the questions on the passage and keeps a record of the number answered correctly.

There is no one system of recording errors that is superior to all others. What is important is that a given type of error be marked consistently in the same manner. When this requirement is followed, it becomes readily apparent, by looking at the recording the teacher has done, what types of errors the child made and with what frequency he made each type. The record can then be very useful in developing an instructional program based on the child's needs. Below is suggested one listing of types of errors to which attention may be given, along with a possible code for indicating them:

Error	Marking System	Explanation of Marking System
1. Substitution	horse ~~house~~	Mark out the word which is not pronounced correctly and write the substitute word above it.
2. Addition	had	Write in the added word.
3. Omission	⬭	Circle the omitted word.
4. Repetition	⎯⎯⎯	Draw a line over a repetition of two or more successive words.
5. Reversal	⌒	Draw a half-moon mark over reversed words.
6. Unknown word(s)	✗	Cross out unknown word(s).

Interpretation of the Test Results

After the IRI has been administered, the word-recognition and comprehension scores are determined for each passage. The word recognition percentages are computed by dividing the number of words in the oral reading selection into the number obtained when the number of errors are subtracted from the total number of words in the selection:

Example: 40 (words in the oral passage)
  −6 (errors)
  34 (words minus errors)

$$40 \overline{)34.00} = .85 = 85\% \text{ (word recognition)}$$
  32 0
  2 00
  2 00

Obviously no word recognition scores are obtained from silent reading passages. Comprehension scores are found for both oral and silent reading passages, as illustrated in the following example:

Example: If ten questions are used for a passage, each is valued 10 points. If one question out of ten is answered incorrectly the comprehension score is 90. (In other words, dividing the number of correct responses by the total number of questions gives the percentage correct.) Oral and silent reading comprehension scores are then averaged. Both the word recognition and comprehension scores are next transferred to a summary sheet. A sample of a summary for a third-grade pupil is given here.

Level	Word Recognition	Oral Comprehension	Silent Comprehension	Average Comprehension
PP	100	100	100	100
P	100	100	80	90
1	95	90	90	90
2	97	80	80	80
3	91	80	70	75
4	88	70	60	65
5	80	60	40	50
6	68	30	30	30

Independent Reading Level: P
Instructional Reading Level: 2
Frustration Reading Level: 3

From this table it is possible to identify the independent, instructional, and frustration reading levels of the pupil being tested, as shown below the table. Specialists in reading differ somewhat in the percentages correct that should be required for some of the levels. Those recommended here and used in arriving at the levels indicated above are:

The *independent reading level,* sometimes referred to as the recreational reading level, is the highest level of passages read with a rating of at least 99 percent in word recognition and at least 90 percent for the average of the two comprehension scores. This is the level of material the learner can handle for pleasure reading.

The *instructional reading level,* the level of material which should be used for instruction in reading, is the highest level of passages read with 95 percent word recognition and 75 percent comprehension (average of the oral and silent reading comprehension scores).

The *frustration reading level* is reached when the pupil's scores fall below either 95 percent word recognition or 75 percent comprehension (average score) and do not again reach a point beyond that level in testing on later levels. In materials of this degree of difficulty the learner is likely to be frustrated because of the numerous errors he makes.

Now let us look again at the example of the IRI summary sheet. According to the percentages given in the preceding paragraph for each of the three levels, it will be noted that the independent reading level of the individual whose scores are recorded is the primer level, because at the first-reader level recorded in the table the word recognition score is below 99 percent. The instructional reading level of the pupil is second-reader, since beyond that point his word recognition scores fall below 95 percent. The frustration level is automatically the next level below the instructional level.

When selecting reading material for a pupil whose reading levels have been ascertained, we should not, if he is reading below his grade level, ask him to read a basal reader on the level indicated; we should give him other materials on that level. Imagine the chagrin of a sixth-grade boy whose instructional level is found to be second-reader, if he were given a second-grade reader for study! What he needs is other material written on second-reader level.

Additional Information

These additional points may be of value to the reader:

1. A rough index of a child's instructional level can be ascertained from his grade-equivalent score as found through a survey test. To find it, one year should be subtracted from the grade-equivalent rating suggested by the publisher of the test. For example, a pupil with a grade-equivalent score of 6.0 has an estimated instructional level of 5.0.

2. Standardized reading inventories are also available commercially. Recommended are the *Botel Reading Inventory* (Follett Publishing Company), the *Classroom Reading Inventory* (Wm. C. Brown Company), and the *Standard Reading Inventory* (Pioneer Printing Company, Bellingham, Washington.)

3. For variations of procedure in constructing test materials for an informal reading inventory, for administering it, and for interpreting it, the reader interested in pursuing the topic is referred to the following books:

Betts, Emmett A., *Foundations of Reading Instruction*. Second edition. New York: American Book Company, 1957, pp. 438–485.

Bond, Guy L., and Miles Tinker, *Reading Difficulties: Their Diagnosis and Correction* (New York: Appleton-Century-Crofts, 1968).

Dechant, Emerald V., *Improving the Teaching of Reading*, 2nd ed. (Englewood Cliffs, N.J.: Prentice-Hall, Inc., 1970), pp. 462–465.

Durkin, Dolores, *Teaching Them to Read* (Boston: Allyn and Bacon, Inc., 1970), pp. 419–430.

Sebesta, Sam L., and Carl J. Wallen, eds., *Readings on Teaching Reading,* (Chicago: Science Research Associates, 1972), for "The Informal Reading Inventory: How to Construct It, How to Use It," by Frazier Cheyney, pp. 225–228.

Spache, George D., and Evelyn B. Spache, *Reading in the Elementary School*, 3rd ed. (Boston: Allyn and Bacon, Inc., 1973).

Stauffer, Russell G., *Directing Reading Maturity as a Cognitive Process* (New York: Harper & Row, 1969), pp. 409–416.

Witty, Paul A., Alma M. Freeland, and Edith H. Grotberg, *The Teaching of Reading: A Developmental Process* (Boston: D.C. Heath and Company, 1966), pp. 302–310.

Zintz, Miles V., *The Reading Process* (Dubuque, Iowa: Wm. C. Brown Company, 1970), Ch. 3.

Other Nonstandardized Techniques

Among other nonstandardized techniques that can be used for purposes of diagnosis are: (1.) assessment of word attack skills, (2.) teacher-made criterion referenced tests, and (3.) the cloze technique.

Assessment of Word Attack Skills

It is possible, and in many instances advisable, for the teacher to construct his own evaluative instruments to assess growth in any of the skills of reading. The following, for example, are points that might be included in a teacher-made test on the use of word attack skills: (1.) visual discrimination, (2.) auditory discrimination, (3.) letter names, (4.) consonant sounds, (5.) consonant blends, (6.) consonant digraphs, (7.) short vowel sounds, (8.) long vowel sounds, (9.) vowel digraphs, (10.) compound words, (11.) inflectional endings, (12.) prefixes and suffixes, (13.) syllabication.

Suggestions that can be applied to testing on some of the points named above are given in the chapters on readiness for reading and on word recognition.

Use of Teacher-made Criterion Referenced Tests

Teachers can construct their own criterion referenced tests in accordance with points included in the discussion on such tests available commercially (*see* page 403). When devising items for these tests care needs to be taken that:

1. The area (or "domain," as it is sometimes called,) to be tested is clearly defined.
2. The items test all phases of the "domain" being tested.
3. The items are so stated, along with the directions, that they test what they purport to test, not ability to interpret directions or comprehend the meaning of the items.

Use of the Cloze Technique

The cloze technique, described earlier as a teaching device (*see* page 180) is increasingly used also as an instrument for testing comprehension. The form of the cloze items when used for testing is the same as that which can be used for teaching purposes. Every *n*th word of a passage can be omitted, as in the following paragraph in which a blank has been left for every tenth word. Or every noun or verb or other part of speech can be deleted.

> Did you know that the flag of Alaska shows _____ seven major stars of the Big Dipper and the _____ Star on a field of blue? When Alaska was _____ a territory, before it became a state, a contest _____ held to design a flag. It was open only _____ school children. An Indian orphan boy won the contest. _____ design is still used for the state flag of _____

Use of a cloze exercise to test comprehension is based on the theory that the pupil who can the better anticipate the missing words from the remaining context is reading with the greater understanding. Various studies[9] have indicated the validity of this hypothesis, though research to date has not established the extent to which reliance can be placed on this technique either as a teaching procedure or as a testing tool. So far its value has not been demonstrated for use in the development or testing of some comprehension skills, such as judging the qualifications of an author or noting propaganda techniques. Its value in the development or testing of skills—

---

[9] Wesley J. Schneyer, "The Cloze Procedure for Improving Reading Comprehension," *The Reading Teacher*, vol. 19 (December 1965), p. 174.

such as noting details, getting the main idea, or predicting outcomes—is, however, recognizable.

The percent of correct responses in a cloze exercise is also being used for ascertaining readability (difficulty) of passages and for subsequent use in determining the independent, instructional, and frustration levels. Zintz[10] suggests the following range of correct responses for each of these levels:

Level	Percent of Correct Responses
Independent	Above 50
Instructional	Between 40 and 50
Frustration	40 or below

How the teacher can make use of information he gathers through diagnosis is, in part, the subject of the chapter that follows, "Adapting Instruction to the Needs of the Learner." Of special relevance in that chapter is the part on "Diagnostic Grouping" (*see* page 422).

For Further Study

Bond, Guy L., and Miles A. Tinker, *Reading Difficulties: Their Diagnosis and Correction* (New York: Appleton-Century-Crofts, 1967).

Bormuth, John R., "Comparable Cloze and Multiple-choice Comprehension Test Scores," *Journal of Reading*, vol. 10 (February 1967), pp. 291–299.

DeBoer, Dorothy L., ed., *Reading Diagnosis and Evaluation* (Newark, Del.: International Reading Association, 1971), Proceedings of the Thirteenth Annual Convention of the International Reading Association, vol. 13, Part 4, "Using the Cloze Procedure as a Testing Technique" by Clara L. Kirby, pp. 68–71; "Making the Most of Informal Inventories" by Dorothy McGinnis, pp. 93–99; and "Diagnostic Teaching in the Classroom" by Guy L. Bond, pp. 126–130.

Dechant, Emerald V., *Improving the Teaching of Reading*, 2nd ed. (Englewood Cliffs, N.J.: Prentice-Hall, 1970), Ch. 14, "Diagnosis and Remediation."

Durr, William E., ed., *Reading Difficulties: Diagnosis, Correction and Remediation* (Newark, Del.: International Reading Association, 1970).

Durrell, Donald D., *Improving Reading Instruction* (New York: Harcourt Brace Jovanovich, 1956), Ch. 5, "Classroom Analysis of Reading Needs."

[10] Miles V. Zintz, *Corrective Reading*, 2nd ed. (Dubuque, Iowa: Wm. C. Brown Company, 1972), p. 50.

Ekwell, Eldon E., Locating and Correcting Reading Difficulties (Columbus, Ohio; Charles E. Merrill Publishing Company, 1970).

Fry, Edward, *Reading Instruction for Classroom and Clinic* (New York: McGraw-Hill Book Company, 1972).

Harris, Albert J., *How to Increase Reading Ability,* 5th ed. (New York: David McKay Company, 1970).

Harris, Albert J., and Edward R. Sipay, eds., *Readings on Reading Instruction,* 2nd ed. (New York: David McKay Company, 1972), Part V, "Measuring Reading Outcomes and Determining Needs," containing articles by Albert J. Harris, Alden W. Badal and Edwin P. Larsen, Margaret LaPray and Ramon Ross, Emmett A. Betts, Robert McCracken, and Joseph P. Kender.

Karlin, Robert, *Teaching Elementary Reading: Principles and Strategies* (New York: Harcourt Brace Jovanovich, 1971), Ch. 2, "Diagnostic Teaching of Reading."

Maginnis, George H., "Measuring Underachievement in Reading," *The Reading Teacher,* vol. 25, no. 8 (May 1972), pp. 750–753.

Massad, Carolyn Emrick, "Interpreting and Using Test Norms," *The Reading Teacher,* vol. 26, no. 3 (December 1972), pp. 286–298.

Mazurkiewicz, Albert J., ed., *New Perspectives in Reading Instruction: A Book of Readings* (New York: Pitman Publishing Company 1964), Part Eight, "Evaluation and Diagnosis in Reading Instruction," containing articles by Mary Austin, Arthur Traxler, Albert Mazurkiewicz, Josephine Wolfe, Morton Botel, and George Murphy.

Millman, Jason, "Criterion Referenced Measurement: An Alternative," *The Reading Teacher,* vol. 26, no. 3 (December 1972), pp. 278–281.

Ransom, Grayce A., "Criterion Referenced Tests — Let the Buyer Beware!", *The Reading Teacher,* vol. 26, no. 3 (December 1972), pp. 282–285.

Strang, Ruth, *Diagnostic Teaching of Reading,* 2nd ed. (New York: McGraw-Hill Book Company, 1969).

Stauffer, Russell G., *Directing Reading Maturity as a Cognitive Process* (New York: Harper & Row, 1969), Ch. 9, "Evaluation."

Valmont, William J., "Creative Questions for Informal Reading Inventories," *The Reading Teacher,* vol. 25, no. 6 (March 1972), pp. 509–512.

Witty, Paul A., Alma M. Freeland, and Edith H. Grotberg, *The Teaching of Reading: A Developmental Process* (Boston: D. C. Heath and Company, 1966), Ch. 13, "Remedial Reading."

Zintz, Miles V., *Corrective Reading* (Dubuque, Iowa: Wm. C. Brown Company, 1972).

Questions and Comments for Thought and Discussion

1. We have noted that standardized reading tests are sometimes classified as survey tests and diagnostic tests. How can the scores of reading survey tests be of value to the teacher who is making a diagnosis of a child's reading? What cautions should the teacher have in mind when interpreting scores on a survey test?

2. Why is it important for classroom teachers of reading to be proficient in the administration of group psychological, physiological, and skill assessment tests?

3. Both an informal reading inventory and a standardized reading achievement test can be used to find a pupil's instructional reading level. How can the two instruments supplement one another?

4. You may wish to construct part of an informal reading inventory according to suggestions given in this chapter. Unless you are competent to check the readability of passages you use by means of one of the recommended formulas, it is suggested that you take the passages for your inventory from a basal reader series. Or you and other students may wish to construct all the materials for an informal reading inventory and each of you test a child with it, write a summary sheet on your findings, and give your interpretation of the results orally to your class.

5. After studying again the part of Chapter 6A, "Comprehension," that deals with the cloze technique as a teaching procedure (*see* page 180), and after reviewing the comments made in this chapter on that technique as a diagnostic tool, you may wish to construct an exercise using this procedure.

6. An oft-repeated comment emphasizes that all teaching should be diagnostic. What implications do you see in this claim for the classroom teacher?

Outline for Chapter 13

ADAPTING INSTRUCTION TO THE NEEDS OF THE LEARNER

Methods of Dealing with Individual Differences
> Grouping
>> Grouping within a Classroom
>> Division into Classrooms according to Abilities of Pupils
>> Homogeneous Grouping for Reading on a Multiage or Multigrade Basis
>> Diagnostic Grouping
>> Other Grouping Practices
> Individualizing Instruction without Grouping
>> "Reading Laboratories"
>> Programed Reading Instruction
>> Automated Reading

Reading and the Exceptional Child
> Reading and the Gifted
>> Need of Special Attention to the Gifted Child
>> Identifying the Gifted Child
>> Creating the Conditions for Maximum Learning
>> Planning Reading Programs for Gifted Children
> Reading and the Slow Learner

Reading and the Underachiever
> Causes of Underachieving in Reading
> Teaching the Underachiever Who Reads Below His Age Level
> Helping the Bright Underachiever

13
CHAPTER

Adapting Instruction to the Needs of the Learner

Much research has been done on the extent of human variability and on the effect of various methods of dealing with it. Even without the research, experienced teachers are aware that a third-grade class will usually consist of some children reading at the first-grade level and of others at the fifth-grade level. Moreover, the children differ in their *rate* of learning, so that a second-grade child placed with a third-grade child of equal reading achievement will probably soon outstrip him.

Children differ not only in their achievement levels and their rates of learning but also in almost every identifiable human characteristic. They differ when they come into the world; they differ in their early home environments, in their physical, emotional, and temperamental characteristics, in their mental potential, in their social attitudes, in their interests and special talents. They differ also in their ways of "unlocking" words. No system of instruction could possibly do full justice to all these differences in all their aspects. The important principle to remember is that differences are normal, that in many respects they contribute to the appeal as well as the difficulty of teaching.

METHODS OF DEALING WITH INDIVIDUAL DIFFERENCES

The methods used in dealing with individual differences are concerned primarily with (1.) grouping and classification and (2.) teaching technique.

Grouping

Various methods of grouping to lessen heterogeneity are used. Four of these, with some overlapping between groups, are described here.

Grouping within a Classroom

A widespread method of dealing with individual differences within a single class is to subgroup children according to ability, often on three levels. The effort to reduce the range in instructional groups is justified by facts such as these supported by many studies:

At the first-grade level, the range of achievement can be expected to be two or more years.

At the fourth-grade level, the range of achievement in a class may be four years or more.

At the sixth-grade level, the range of achievement in a class may be six years or more.

Grouping within a room is not without its limitations. The three-group plan, commonly used, or any other plan for homogeneous grouping may make the children and their parents conscious of differences in achievement and create pressure on a child to measure up to others in reading. Individual differences remain within the groups, and there is some danger that the teacher will assume that the differences have been cared for by the mere fact that the three-level plan is in operation. Certainly the problem is not solved if the teacher uses the same material with all pupils, allowing only for a difference in the speed with which the groups are expected to read them. However, when he uses different material for the groups, his needed daily preparation of work is increased decidedly; and there is a limit to the amount of work that can be expected even of an excellent teacher.

Much of the effectiveness of subgrouping within the class will depend on the teacher's understanding of the purpose for which the children are assigned to the groups. Great importance should be attached to how the teacher and the children feel about the group. Many writers emphasize the need to keep the groups flexible. Classification of children in groups should frequently be determined by specific purposes. For example, groups may be organized for the express purpose of providing instruction in developmental reading, and individual children should be regrouped as their performance requires. In other cases, a group may be devoted to the study of specific skills, regardless of the general proficiency of the members. Research groups may be formed for pupils who wish to investigate a similar problem. Other groups, interested in the same theme—such as pets, airplanes, plants, farm life, railroads—may plan presentations to the whole class. In some instances, a group may be formed in which the better readers help the slower ones—all, of course, under the supervision of the teacher.

Especially in the case of the beginning teacher, there is the problem of what to do with groups not under the immediate direction of the teacher. No group should be left to itself without some specific task. If a group is asked to spend a period in silent reading, the teacher should make sure that each child has found a suitable book to read or is in the process of finding one at the book table. If a group is planning a display or a report to the class, the nature of the task should be clear to everyone, and any questions to be asked and answered should be well formulated in advance. In no case should a group be left with mere busywork. Games and seatwork should be carefully planned to provide needed reinforcement in skills previously taught.

Teachers who follow the practice of subgroupings within the class should be keenly aware of the limitations and dangers of the method. First, it has been estimated that dividing pupils into three groups reduces variability in achievement only to about 83 percent of that in normally organized groups. Second, the tests commonly employed in the classification of pupils measure only a small, although significant number of the desired competencies. Third, the relative performance of individuals within the groups will change as the instruction proceeds. Fourth, studies have shown that academic progress under a system of ability grouping is only slightly greater than under a system of heterogeneous groupings.

More important, perhaps, than any of the foregoing caveats is a concern for the overall psychological effect of groupings on the child. If the grouping is flexible and if the child understands why he is a member of a certain group at any specified time, grouping may be quite harmless, even helpful. If the grouping stigmatizes a child with himself or others, the effect may be more serious than any loss in reading progress. Speed in learning to read is certainly no more important than growth in social maturity. Reading ability is valuable only insofar as it contributes to the general happiness and well-being of the individual and his functioning in society. We must not sacrifice the child to our desire to exhibit favorable reports of reading scores.

Division into Classrooms according to Abilities of Pupils

In schools in which there are more children in a grade than can be taught in one classroom, it is not uncommon to organize for greater homogeneity through division of the pupils into rooms of relatively equal ability. The pupils who are considered better equipped intellectually or academically are placed in one classroom and, if there are only two rooms to the grade, the others are placed in another room. In larger schools there may be one or more rooms with intermediate groups. In this plan of organization the better group, for example, would be assigned to one teacher and the other groups to other teachers throughout all or most of the school day.

Fortunately, usually the rooms are not designated as the A and B rooms. However, though the rooms may not be labeled so as to indicate the superiority of one group over others, even the children in the slower group are quick enough to discover before long what their classification is. And should they not rapidly make the discovery by themselves, associates from the brighter group are quite certain to let them know. Herein lies one of the serious objections raised to homogeneous grouping, as explained earlier in this chapter. When the division is into rooms rather than into homogeneous subgroups within a room, the effect on a child in a lower group may be especially disastrous. After all, a child in a low group only in reading may find the stigma less humiliating than if he were in a low classification in all activities he performs. To be sure, it can be argued that a teacher can tactfully explain to his class that groupings should not cause anyone in a lower group to feel unhappy. Cases of lack of success in such an effort on the part of even very understanding teachers are too numerous for school personnel to overlook this very serious problem.

As in the case of grouping within a room through use of subgroups, even the best efforts at homogeneity when grouping is among rooms still leaves a group hetereogeneous, though, to be sure, homogeneity can be increased through grouping. No criterion used for grouping—whether intelligence quotient, mental age, general school achievement, reading achievement—will equally affect the range according to other bases of classification that could well be used. For example, if intelligence of boys and girls in a fourth grade is the criterion for assignment to different rooms, the diversity in intelligence will still show considerable range; maybe the difference of the group in, let us say, reading achievement will be even greater. If reading achievement forms the basis for assignment to a given room, while there will still be great differences in reading achievement, there may be even a more marked variation in average of school marks, in intelligence quotients, in mental age, and in various other significant characteristics of the boys and girls in the room.

When subgrouping within a room is the means through which greater homogeneity is sought, it is relatively easy to keep the grouping flexible. When the grouping is achieved through division of the children into different rooms, much greater rigidity in classification is likely to result. Administratively, schools seem to find it inadvisable to make changes between rooms frequently. Consequently, a person beginning in a slow group, because of unevenness in rates of learning among pupils, may before long read so well that he equals in achievement those in a room of superior rating. Yet usually such progress is not a cause for change in room assignment. Thus, homogeneity within a room is likely to decrease as the year progresses.

Homogeneous Grouping for Reading on a Multiage or Multigrade Basis

Some schools are organized so that boys and girls are assigned to reading groups without regard to their exact grade. Frequently this type of organization in the elementary school is limited to the intermediate grades. The plan can be followed even if there is only one fourth-grade, one fifth-grade, and one sixth-grade room within a building. During most of the school day the boys and girls are in their own grade room, but for reading class they are assigned to a room of their approximate reading level. For reading instruction pupils lowest in achievement in reading among the intermediate-grade pupils will be with one teacher, regardless of their regular grade placement. Thus, a sixth-grade pupil might be reading in the lowest of the three groups. Similarly, the pupils among the highest in reading achievement will be taught by another teacher regardless of whether regularly they are in the fourth, fifth, or sixth grade. Obviously, if there are more than three intermediate-grade teachers within a building, the children can be divided into four or more ability groups for reading instruction.

It is not difficult to recognize some advantages of homogeneous grouping on a multiage or multigrade basis. The superiority of this system over that of grouping for all activities by rooms is that the stigma of assignment to a lower-level group is likely to be less if a child is in a lower section for reading only but is with classmates of a variety of abilities in all other areas of the curriculum. There are, however, significant shortcomings to this system of classification, some of which are listed for other types of homogeneous grouping earlier in this chapter. Even when ability in reading is the basis for classification, there will be considerable variation within a group. The children may be fairly alike in ability to read at appropriate rates, but greatly different in ability to comprehend what they read or in doing critical reading. Furthermore, when boys and girls are assigned to different teachers for reading, there is danger of divorcing reading instruction from reading activities other than those in reading classes, as, for example, from reading in the social studies. Lack of correlation of activities during the reading class with nonreading activities during other times of the school day constitutes another shortcoming. Other arguments frequently advanced against departmentalization in the elementary school also hold for multiage or multigrade grouping. The danger is that the teacher who teaches only reading to a child, and therefore does not know him as well as he could if he were his regular classroom teacher, may be more interested in the learning acquired than in the learner.

Diagnostic Grouping

Increasing attention is being paid to a promising technique, that of diagnostic grouping, as an organizational basis for diagnostic instruction. Grouping is determined by the specific needs of the pupils, as revealed by careful diagnosis of each child's level of achievement in reading, including both strengths and weaknesses. Through this kind of grouping some of the major criticisms rightfully made of many other grouping practices can be met. Since the groups focus on the specific needs of the learner, when a child no longer requires special help in the skill that forms the differentiating concern of the group, he is dismissed from it. When none of the boys and girls in the group are in need of additional help of the type for which the group was organized, it is disbanded. Thus, flexibility in grouping is one of the major assets of the plan. It is possible when using this grouping technique to meet the needs of the more capable, as well as the less able, reader during the same reading period. It can then be of help in the solution of a problem that has long frustrated teachers.

Let us illustrate how the theory of diagnostic grouping can be implemented in a classroom setting. We will assume that the pupils in a classroom have been tested with instruments designed to find their independent, instructional, and frustration levels in reading and their problems in word recognition. That information can be tabulated on a class summary sheet similar to the one illustrated here, where data for part of a class are re-

Figure 13.1 Visual aids as tools for diagnostic teaching can be used well in small group learning situations. (Bell & Howell Company.)

corded. On the basis of information, such as that presented in the table, groups for both the development of comprehension and word recognition skills can be formed. In the illustration given, Sally, Fred, Norma, and Steve could constitute a group in which material at their instructional level of fourth reader would be used for purposes of increasing comprehension skills. Tom and Mary could form another group organized for the same purpose, but using material on the second-reader level; while Elaine and Ralph could be in a group reading on the fifth-reader level. Similarly, groups could be formed for the development of word attack skills. Sally, Fred, Mary, Elaine, and Norma could, for example, be in a group to learn more about affixes.

	Independent Level	Instructional Level	Auditory Discrimination*	Letter Names	Letter Sounds	Short Vowels	Silent "e"	Long Vowel (open syllable)	Inflectional Endings	Affixes	Syllabication	Silent Letters
Tom	1	2	✔	✔	✔				✔			
Sally	3	4	✔	✔	✔	✔	✔	✔	✔			✔
Fred	2	4	✔	✔	✔	✔	✔	✔	✔		✔	✔
Mary	P	2	✔	✔	✔							
Elaine	4	5	✔	✔	✔	✔	✔	✔	✔		✔	✔
Ralph	3	5	✔	✔	✔	✔	✔	✔	✔	✔	✔	✔
Norma	3	4	✔	✔	✔	✔	✔	✔	✔		✔	
Steve	2	4	✔	✔	✔	✔	✔	✔	✔	✔		

*Check indicates no need of special attention.

Other Grouping Practices

Some teachers successfully employ several types of grouping within the same classroom, so that for some purposes an individual is a member of one reading group and for other purposes of other groups. A child may be in one group based on the diagnosis of his needs for skill development, and in another organized according to his interests in reading. For example, he may be in a group wanting to read tall tales or biography. Or the grouping can be in connection with a subject taken up in a content area. For instance, when the class is studying about the homes of children around the world, the group investigating homes in cold countries might include above-average, average, and below-average readers. Care needs to be taken that each child has ready access to material on his level of reading, even when he is in a group not based on his diagnosed needs.

Individualizing Instruction without Grouping

With the growing dissatisfaction with the lock-step system of instruction prevalent in many schools during the first few decades of the century and in earlier times, educators sought to devise means by which reading and other skills could be taught to better meet the needs of individuals. Some turned to grouping; others put their faith in individualization without grouping; still others saw the benefits that could be derived from use of both plans, realizing that instruction can be individualized both in group and in nongroup situations.

Among the more famous plans of individualization of past years are those of William T. Harris of St. Louis; Preston W. Search of Pueblo, Colorado; Frederic Burk of Santa Barbara; William Wirt of Gary, Indiana (the platoon school); Helen Parkhurst of Dalton, Massachusetts (the

Figure 13.2 Instruction can be adapted to the needs of the individual. (Federal Project, Minneapolis Public Schools.)

contract plan); Carleton W. Washburne of Winnetka, Illinois; and James E. McDade of Chicago. Although such research as we have has favored the individualized plans, most of these plans were discontinued after a time, and none has enjoyed widespread acceptance in American schools. Distinguishing features of all of these plans have been the use of the classroom as a laboratory instead of a lecture and recitation room; the use of diagnostic and achievement tests, practice materials, and record forms; the adaptation of learning tasks to the achievement levels of the pupils; and pupil participation in the management of the system. All of them, while making effective use of the teacher, stressed the idea of self-teaching, suggestive of the modern vogue of programed instruction. All of them provided for a rich program of socializing activities in addition to the individualized work.

The vigor and diversity of the plans enumerated in the preceding paragraph probably explain why the idea underlying them has not died. We are witnessing today a widespread resurgence of interest in programs of individualized instruction in reading. Scores of articles describing such programs have appeared in recent years. Hardly a single reading conference is held without one or more papers dealing with the subject.

In the pages that follow we will give consideration to three means of individualizing instruction, namely: (1.) "reading laboratories," (2.) programed reading instruction, and (3.) automated reading. In Chapter 15, "Approaches to Reading Instruction," along with other approaches, we will discuss these additional ways in which reading can be individualized without grouping, Individualized Reading: Seeking, Self-selection, and Pacing and "Individually Prescribed Instruction" (IPI).

"Reading Laboratories"

One example of the current interest in individualized instruction in reading is the popularity of "reading laboratories," an example of which is the Science Research Associates Reading Laboratories. These "laboratories" consist of cases of practice materials for each of the elementary-school levels. They contain, in addition to the reading selections, answer keys, check test pads, student record books, and a teacher's handbook. Materials in each grade vary in difficulty from easy to hard. Phonics surveys, word games, and colored pencils are included. Pupils are expected to move ahead as far and as fast as their learning rates and capacities will permit. The plan is essentially a variation and refinement of the one used in Washburne's school system. Emphasis is placed on the successful response and the use of intrinsically interesting materials.

Programed Reading Instruction

Programed instruction, while not a new idea in education, has been receiving extraordinary attention in recent years. Often erroneously referred to by the term *teaching machines*, it is considered by many to be the appli-

Figure 13.3 Programed instruction is a means of adapting instruction to the needs of the learner. (Keystone View Division, Mast Development Company.)

cation of the industrial use of automation to the teaching-learning process. Actually the idea, so far as reading instruction is concerned, does not differ fundamentally from the plans of individualization described in the preceding paragraph. The machines that are being perfected are by no means essential or, at the present stage, always appropriate to the plan. For many programed materials no teaching machines are used; many programs are written in workbook-type of booklets.

In programed instruction the pupil is presented with instructional materials that enable him to learn on his own. The exercises, prepared after careful editing and experimentation, are graduated in very small steps, so that even the slow learner can, at his own rate, arrive at the desired generalization. An exercise, or "frame," usually presents an explanation followed by a sentence containing a blank to be filled in, or, if a machine is used, by a button to be punched or a lever to be moved. The correct answer, given immediately below or on a page to which the pupil is referred, enables the pupil to compare his own answer with the correct one, so that he is "reinforced" if the answer is right or corrected if it is wrong. A program, or sequence of frames, is selected for the individual in terms of his specific stage of learning. The method is one of self-teaching. In the case of reading, the programs may deal with the basic skills of word recognition—such as phonetic analysis, context clues, and structural analysis—or with comprehension and location of information.

Following are examples of "frames":

The *gh* in the word *rough* has the sound of the letter _____   *f*

The *ou* in the word *rough* has the short sound of the letter _____   *u*

One company, Behavioral Research Laboratories,[1] in marketing its product provides an extensive explanation of its program by defining what programed instruction is, by indicating why it does not replace the teacher, by explaining how the program would work in the classroom, and by pointing out the advantages for the teacher in the use of programed instruction. It is reproduced here, since it is applicable to a large extent to many programs on the market.

> The program may be offered to the learner through a teaching machine, on a deck of printed cards, in a book, through a motion picture or a series of still pictures, or in a variety of ways. The information which the learner sees or reads is generally broken down into fairly short units, referred to as "frames." Each frame may be a picture, a paragraph or two of information, a mathematical equation, or some similar unit which illustrates a single idea. After the student has observed each frame in turn, the program requires that he respond by answering a question, filling in a blank, solving a problem, or some similar action which indicates that he understands what he has seen and read.

> The answers to the question asked in each frame are readily available to the student. In BRL's (Behavioral Research Laboratories) programmed textbooks, they are printed on the same page. The student covers them with a narrow cardboard "slider" and moves this slider down the page as he proceeds through the frames, thus revealing the correct answers. He may then review his work if he has answered incorrectly and will have knowledge of the correct answer before he proceeds further into the material. This assures his success. This feeling of success can completely change the classroom attitude of a student who has known only failure in his school work.

> The early frames of the program offer simple, basic ideas in the subject. As the student proceeds, each frame introduces some new idea based on the previous information, or reviews previous information from a different point of view to reinforce the ideas that have been presented. Thus the

---

[1] Behavioral Research Laboratories, *The How and Why of Effective Teaching through Programmed Instruction: A Practical Guide for Teachers and Administrators* (Palto Alto, Cal.: Behavioral Research Laboratories, undated), pp. 2–3.

student gains an ever-expanding understanding of the subject based on a gradual, orderly development of the content of the frames.

Through his regular responses, the learner is *involved* in the program and actively participates in the learning process. He is not a passive learner or reader, but must act upon the program. Because of the format and presentation of most programs, especially programmed texts, the learner may involve himself in a new material at his own pace. He may move more quickly through material that he understands easily and work more thoroughly and precisely through material of which he is unsure (all the while reinforced by immediate knowledge of the correctness of his response).

In order for a program to be successful, its developer must first decide what the student is to learn. What knowledge and concepts, skills and attitudes should the learner comprehend and understand as he proceeds through the program and how should he be able to demonstrate these effectively when he has completed the study? In other words, *what* is to be taught and how will the teacher determine, at the completion of the program by the learner, that it has been taught successfully?

So, before the program is written, the programmer might develop the tests that will be used upon completion of the program. This is a good place to start in the development of any instructional materials.

The programmer will then undertake the not-so-easy task of starting with very basic and simple ideas and information, building step by step and response by response upon these, and proceeding through a logical and ordered sequence to introduce the new ideas, concepts and skills to the learner. This entire procedure will lead up to the desired behavior of the student upon his completion of the program.

As mentioned above, many devices may be used to communicate the program to the learner. However, research substantially supports the fact that the device will teach no better than the program provided through it, and the quantity and quality of the learning are rarely affected by the format of presentation. Since books can be more easily and economically developed and produced than most of the alternatives, Behavioral Research Laboratories produces its programs in book form.

Without doubt programed learning will continue to be the subject of debate among educators. It will be examined not only from the point of view of its efficiency in achieving academic objectives, but especially from the point of view of its total effect on the pupil. Certainly in theory it has much to commend it, particularly in its stress on the principle of success in learning and on self-activity. In any case, teachers and administrators should acquaint themselves with programed materials as they appear.

Automated Reading

In 1959 attention was directed to research conducted at Yale University by Moore and Anderson, in which four young children ranging in age from two to four were taught to "read."[2] Moore later reported on progress made in the study, which then used 35 children, only two of whom would be ranked as gifted, with the remainder being within so-called normal ranges. All the children learned to type, to read, and to write. By May 1961, over 100 children had developed skills in these areas, and large-scale application of the method was made that year at Hamden Hall Country Day School in Hamden, Connecticut. Called somewhat facetiously "supervised play with a typewriter," because the basic instructional tool was the electric portable typewriter, children were permitted to "play" as they wished with the machine, which in time came to involve the striking of the keys. As the child struck a key, the teacher repeated the name of the letter or numeral. Thus, the child rapidly learned that his striking of a key triggered a response from his teacher, that different characters appeared on the sheet of paper in the machine, and that he ought to reinforce his own activity by naming the symbol before his teacher had to do this for him.

A chalkboard and chalk were likewise utilized, and the child was encouraged to "draw" the letters and symbols on the board which he had seen in typewritten form.

> Once the child knows the letters, a simple projector is fastened to the typewriter, and the child reads and types out simple sentences. Finally he reaches the stage where he reads the projected sentences into a recording machine and types out stories from his own dictation, complete with punctuation.[3]

Moore has made various changes from the early procedures advocated. The following description by Mildred Wittick indicates some of the points of variation:

> The "talking typewriters" . . . can flash a picture on a screen, identify it by saying the word aloud, and guide the child into spelling the word on a typewriter keyboard. A transparent partition separates the picture, the typing mechanism, and the typed copy from the curious hands of the child who has produced it. When the machine shows the picture of a dog and spells D-O-G, all the letters on the keyboard lock except the D. When the child hits the D, the letter appears on the paper in the typewriter. The keyboard continues to lock in proper sequences until the child has spelled out the word *dog*.[4]

[2] O. K. Moore, "Orthographic Symbols and the Pre-School Child — A New Approach," paper presented at the Third Minnesota Conference on Gifted Children, (Minneapolis: October 1960).

[3] *Carnegie Corporation of New York Quarterly*, vol. IX (April 1961), p. 2.

[4] Mildred Wittick, "Innovations in Reading Instruction: For Beginners," *Innovation and Change in Reading Instruction*, Sixty-seventh Yearbook of the National Society for the Study of Education, Part II (Chicago: University of Chicago Press, 1968), pp. 95–96.

Moore believes that the activity has to be "autotelic," performed solely for its own sake and not because of extrinsic rewards or punishments. He maintains that the curiosity or "competence" drive is all-important, and that the sooner the child is put in a position to fulfill this drive the greater, wider, and more lasting the effects will be on him as an individual. He claims that a child will learn best if he acquires skills or information in a "responsive environment," a term often used to refer to Moore's work.

Aukerman[5] describes Moore's concept of responsive environment in this manner:

1. It permits the learner to explore freely.
2. It informs the learner immediately about the consequences of the actions.
3. It is self-pacing; that is, events happen within the environment at a rate determined by the learner.
4. It permits the learner to make full use of his capacity for discovering relations of various kinds.

[5] Robert C. Aukerman, *Approaches to Beginning Reading* (New York: John Wiley & Sons, Inc., 1971), pp. 424–425.

Figure 13.4 The "non-talking" typewriter, too, can be interest-stimulating. (Federal Project, Minneapolis Public Schools.)

5. Its structure is such that the learner is likely to make a series of inter-connected discoveries about the physical, cultural, and social world.

Dorothy K. Johnson[6] reports on an experiment with the "talking type-writer" that she carried on in the Freeport, Long Island, public schools. In her experimental group were 22 children, 18 in kindergarten classes and 4 in an elementary school special class. Boys and girls in the control group were matched for age, sex, race, handedness, language maturity, and work of parents. When comparing the reading achievement of the boys and girls in the two groups she found the experimental group superior. The electric typewriter used, known as the Edison Responsive Environment instrument, is obtainable from the Responsive Environments Corporation of New York City.

READING AND THE EXCEPTIONAL CHILD

So far we have dealt with methods of organization and teaching strategies for adapting instruction to individual differences as they may apply to children in general. By and large, many grouping practices and methods of value to the average or near-average child are also applicable to the ex-ceptional child, namely the gifted and the slow learners. Their needs, too, should be diagnosed—possibly more in depth than those of the average child—and suitable instruction supplied. Moreover, special consideration should also be given to some of the concerns related primarily to teaching reading to the exceptional child.

Reading and the Gifted

The neglect of the gifted child in terms of special provisions to accommo-date his needs is one of the acute problems of the day. Results of surveys cited by Bryan and Lewis[7] indicate that avowed interest in individualizing instruction to provide for different needs is not followed up by establish-ment of a large number of programs to implement specialized instruction for the gifted.

Need of Special Attention to the Gifted Child

Since the school in a democratic society regards all children as of equal moral worth; it does not in its distribution of effort deliberately discrimin-ate against any group because of low, average, or high academic aptitude

---

[6] Dorothy K. Johnson, "Experimenting with the Talking Typewriter," *New Directions in Reading*, Ralph Staiger and David A. Sohn, eds. (New York: Bantam Books, 1967), pp. 32–36.
[7] J. Ned Bryan and Lenora G. Lewis, "Are State Departments Failing to Provide Leadership for the Gifted?", *Accent on Talent—An NEA Service to Schools of the Nation*, vol. 2 (May 1968), pp. 7–8.

and achievement. There are compelling reasons why all should learn to read as well as their capacities permit. Nevertheless, because teachers are human and fallible and because time and resources are not unlimited, they cannot always do complete justice to all the children in their classes. Many teachers find that work with retarded and average pupils is so time-consuming and the needs of these children so apparent that they tend to neglect those who obviously are superior in academic ability. The growing concern about the gifted child is therefore justified.

The type of instruction required by the bright child does not differ greatly from that given to other children. The physical, sensory, emotional, and other factors essential to good reading, as well as the specific skills of reading, are important to all. The difference is to be found in the range and level of difficulty of the materials and in special problems peculiar to the bright child.

One difference, for example, is the fact that bright children often acquire many of the reading skills independently and almost unconsciously in the course of extensive, highly motivated reading. Special lessons and exercises in these reading skills can and should be bypassed for them. All that the teacher needs to do in such situations is to be sure that these skills have been mastered.

Specialists in the education of the gifted child recognize that social maturity does not necessarily go hand in hand with academic achievement. There is no evidence that bright children as a group are less mature socially than other children. In fact, intellectual maturity is commonly accompanied by social maturity. It would not be surprising, however, if we found that some very bright children were less conforming, that they demanded reasons for rules of behavior and exhibited some impatience with other pupils less well endowed.

A degree of nonconformity is a desirable personality trait. Independence of mind is essential to social and scientific progress and to artistic creation. But it is of the greatest importance that our ablest individuals learn early in life to act responsibly and to be concerned about the well being and happiness of others. The codes of the physician, who places the well being of his patient first, and of the scientist who weighs the effect of his discoveries on society has its origin in the early face-to-face experiences of childhood. In our fascination with a child's brilliance we cannot afford to forget the great influence for good or evil that he can have upon society. Reading is one of the potent means at our disposal to lead the child on the road to responsible and constructive effort.

The present-day drive toward "academic excellence" is overdue, but it must not be permitted to distort the humanistic goals of education. The child who reads about people in other cultures and other lands should be doing more than adding to his knowledge and understanding. He should be cultivating the art of unlimited kinship with people.

Unfortunately, discussions of the problems of educating the gifted child rarely concern themselves with questions relating to emotional growth and attitude formation. They are concerned chiefly with the conservation of intellectual talent now so often going to waste because of unfavorable home and community environments and school programs not sufficiently adapted to the needs of the gifted child. One difficulty is that emotions are hard to discover and measure; it is almost impossible to formulate defensible educational objectives with regard to them, except as they result in serious and persistent antisocial behavior. Nevertheless, any consideration of the teaching of reading and literature which does not embrace the emotional dimension is necessarily incomplete and distorts any valid conception of the teacher's task.

The bright child usually has little difficulty in learning to interpret the literal and figurative meaning of a selection appropriate to his general maturity. What we cannot be so sure of is that the child will know how to identify with situations he reads about or utilize what he reads in building a mental image of the social and human consequences of conditions and events. Speed and comprehension in the reading of a poem, for example, are not enough. There must be moments of contemplation in which the reader visualizes a scene, laughs or weeps with a character in a story, and thinks with wonder about a deed of heroism. Speed tests in reading do not measure these capacities for feeling. Social sensitivity and human understanding should occupy a high place among our objectives in reading instruction.

Identifying the Gifted Child

What shall we call those whose gifts are many and great? Many terms have been used. These children have been called "able," "bright," "talented," "academically superior," "children of high academic aptitude," "intellectually gifted," "academically talented," among other expressions. These terms sometimes have special meanings; in other cases they are applied to children with special aptitudes in art, music, or mechanical activity, and in other cases to children whose intellectual potential amounts to genius. In Terman's famous study of gifted children, those with IQ's of 130 and higher were included. Havighurst speaks of children gifted with qualities of social leadership and of children who possess "creative intelligence." Gallagher divides the gifted into three categories: those with IQ's of 116 and over 15-20 percent of the school population); those with IQ's of 132 and over (2-4 percent of the school population); and those with IQ's of 148 and over (0.1 percent of the school population). These are the academically talented, the gifted, and the highly gifted.

There are in fact no sharply defined boundaries among these groups, although the problems of instruction may differ as we go up on the scale. Any dividing lines must be arbitrary. In our discussion we shall deal with the largest group of superior learners, and for convenience draw the line at approximately 120 IQ. We shall use most of the terms mentioned above interchangeably.

The usual methods of identifying bright children involve the use of individual and group tests of intelligence, achievement tests, and teacher observation. Individual intelligence tests are probably the most accurate of the methods, but they are time-consuming and require trained examiners. Group intelligence tests and achievement tests are useful as screening devices, but they may be quite inaccurate in assessing an individual's true capabilities. Errors in these tests more often result in underestimation than in overestimation of a child's potential. Teacher observation is an essential part of the evelation process because it may reveal aspects of a child's mental powers not reflected in any test. It is not unusual for a group test to rate as many as 25 percent of the gifted children below their true intelligence level.

Often in the past the description of the gifted child has been limited to the one with a high intelligence quotient, but fortunately, current definitions are more inclusive. There has been growing evidence to support the contention that if the only criterion used for designating giftedness were an intelligence quotient of 130 or above, some of the most creative pupils would not be detected. Investigators supporting this view claim that items on intelligence tests do not help identify some of the differentiating characteristics of the gifted, such as originality, imagination, or divergent thinking channeled toward constructive outcomes. In harmony with this point of view Paul Witty,[8] who has through the decades made extensive study of the gifted, proposes that "any child whose performance is consistently or repeatedly remarkable in a worthwhile line of human endeavor might be considered gifted." Such a broadened definition allows for the inclusion of pupils not only with verbal facility but also those whose talent could be fostered in the arts, the sciences, mechanics, and social leadership.

Gifted children with high intelligence quotients are generally accelerated in academic attainment. They often read early and are verbally gifted. Contrary to a stereotypical view, the intellectual giftedness of these pupils does not restrict them, as a group, from being socially as well as emotionally more mature than their peers. Moreover, the gifted child has been found to be physically better developed than the average child of his age group. Other observable characteristics, which help to distinguish the intellectually gifted from the average or below average, include these: rapidity of learning, good memory, marked reasoning ability, wide scope of information, large vocabulary, superior reading ability, keen power of comprehension.

It is interesting to note that characteristics descriptive of pupils whose giftedness is identified through their verbal ability differ considerably in some respect from those of the gifted creative children. The latter are de-

[8] Paul Witty, Alma Freeland, and Edith Grotberg, *The Teaching of Reading: A Developmental Process* (Boston: D. C. Heath, 1966), p. 340.

scribed more often as encountering problems in social adjustment, as being original in their thinking but highly impatient with routine, and as frequently being disruptive in classrooms. But, like the verbally gifted, they are often early readers. Because of their interest in reading it is frequently possible to assist them in wide reading so as to extend their interests and to enable them to identify with persons similar to those whose biographies are part of the literary heritage.

Creating the Conditions for Maximum Learning

The key to good teaching is the teacher himself. Materials and methods are important, but no amount of pedagogical theory, library resources, audio-visual aids, laboratories, auditoriums, or testing programs can compensate for the lack of the competent, resourceful teacher. This fact is doubly significant in the case of the academically superior pupil.

The bright child needs a bright teacher. All children need teachers who are above average in intelligence, devoted to teaching, and sympathetic to children's educational needs. But the bright child needs a teacher who is distinctly superior in mental ability. His IQ need not be as high as that of the brightest child in his class, but he should be bright enough to feel secure in his relations with the child and to command his respect. He should be willing to learn from the bright child, and sometimes to let the child teach the things the teacher does not know as well.

Statements by gifted children describing teachers they like reveal that they want teachers who know their subjects, related fields, and current events; who use humor and illustrative material to add interest to the subject; and who are skillful in relating the subject to other fields and to the pupil's lives. They want teachers who require them to learn, to work together on class projects, to discuss problems together, and to assume initiative and responsibility. They like teachers who are versatile, fair, even-tempered, and patient.

The teacher of the gifted can and should be more permissive in his assignments to gifted children than to those of more limited abilities, who usually desire and need definite and detailed instructions for a task. Gifted children are more likely to ask questions about the *why* of the methods employed by the teacher; and the teacher should freely discuss his reasons and objectives with them. If the pupil is egotistic or immature because of coddling at home, the teacher should set challenges and require performance that will result in the development of a more accurate self-image on the part of the child. In short, the teacher of the academically superior child should have all the qualities of any good teacher, but he should have them to a high degree.

Next to a good teacher in importance is the provision of abundant reading materials difficult enough and diversified enough to provide a genuine challenge and to appeal to the wide range of interests so characteristic of the bright child. For truly gifted children the book and magazine resources of most elementary schools are inadequate. Public libraries, state traveling book collections, and even the paperback selection in supermarkets and elsewhere need to be utilized to meet this child's interests. Academically superior pupils tend to be omnivorous readers, particularly when suitable reading materials are readily accessible. They are attracted, also, to encyclopedias, atlases, dictionaries, and all types of reference materials. As a consequence, the school library assumes great importance in the reading guidance of gifted children. Failure to provide proper library facilities in elementary schools must necessarily result in great waste of the precious resources represented by the learning potential of these children.

The need for more and better reading materials implies also the necessity of a wide knowledge of children's literature on the part of the teacher. No teacher can possibly have read all the books that gifted children are likely to read or should read, but fortunately there are excellent guides and booklists which should be available to the teacher in the school library. Aids of this type are listed in the final chapter of this book (*see* page 559).

In providing books for individual reading, teachers should make certain that they include titles that will challenge the able reader. Many superior readers in the upper elementary grades enjoy reading books generally considered adult fare. They should be encouraged to read suitable books on that level.

Planning Reading Programs for Gifted Children

Studies of the reading habits of verbally gifted children reveal that they spend many hours a day reading, that they have wider interests and do more voluntary reading than the average child, and that about half of the highly gifted read before they enter school. Significantly, they learn to read by a great variety of methods, and it may be assumed that in their cases the method employed is far less important than the versatility and skill of the teacher and the availability of suitable reading materials.

Plans employed for meeting the needs of gifted children in general fall into three main categories: (1.) enrichment, (2.) acceleration, and (3.) special grouping. Of these, perhaps the most popular plan is that of enrichment. In an enrichment program provision is made for individual differences in ability within the setting of the regular classroom. The gifted child remains with his age-mates, but is encouraged to take on more complex tasks. More emphasis is placed on original thinking and problem solving. In the case of reading, the academically superior child is expected to choose books calling for higher levels of comprehension than those possessed by other members of the class.

A promising form of enrichment is the unit organization of instruction, especially in the middle grades. In this plan the teacher may propose a number of topics for study from which all the pupils make a choice. With the aid of the teacher, the class assembles a bibliography for the chosen topic, using the various reference aids in the classroom and library. The teacher then assists the pupils in developing the topic. Some of the reading selections may be read and enjoyed by all the pupils, but the abler members of the class will also select reading materials commensurate with their abilities. The task of the teacher in the content areas is to assist all pupils, regardless of ability, to grow toward increased maturity in reading.

The policy of acceleration may take different forms. One of these is early admittance to school of the bright child. Certainly there is nothing sacred about age six as the earliest entering age, particularly since the differences among children of the same chronological age are so wide. In schools with a nongraded primary division it is possible to permit bright children to complete the three-year period in less time, especially if they are socially and emotionally well adjusted. Double promotion is another plan of acceleration, but one to be used with great caution to avoid the danger that the child will miss basic steps in skill development or the building of background information.

Many parents and school officials are reluctant to adopt a policy of acceleration because of the fear that the accelerated child will have difficulty in making a good adjustment in a group of older children. Research studies have indicated that, in general, pupils have benefited from programs of acceleration and that the fear of social maladjustment because of acceleration is usually unfounded. Nevertheless, the needs and social maturity of each child should be carefully studied before he is advanced to a group of older children.

Special classes for gifted children have been organized in a sizable number of elementary schools. An alleged advantage of such classes is that they enable gifted children to enjoy the opportunity of working with their intellectual peers and so to benefit from the give-and-take of planning and discussing with other children equally alert and eager to think and to explore. But in this kind of segregation they miss early associations with children less gifted, with whom they will be living as adults. Better than total division of the gifted from other boys and girls, in the opinion of many educators, is the practice engaged in at some schools in which the gifted are in special classes only part of the school day and are kept with their age-mates for the remainder of the day, usually for such activities as music, art, and physical education.

Reading and the Slow Learner

The slow learner, as the term is used here, is not to be confused with the underachiever in reading, to whom attention is given in the last part of this chapter. When we speak of the slow learner we are referring to the individual who has below-average mental ability for performance in academic areas. We designate him as an underachiever in reading only if he is not reading up to the level at which, with his intelligence, he could be expected to read. Although, on the very basis from which intelligence quotients are derived, the average IQ is 100, usually a range of ten points above and below that figure is considered within the area of normalcy. Thus, in terms of intelligence quotients, we are categorizing as slow learners those boys and girls with IQs of less than 90. The lower limit of intelligence with which we are here concerned is less definitive, as we are referring only to those individuals below average in mental capacity who are members of the regular classroom, not to those who are in special-education rooms. This delimitation gives us those slow learners, as a rule, who are able to learn to read with considerable profit, for usually children with IQs of less than 65 or 70 are not found in the regular classroom beyond the primary division.

Probably the greatest impediment to successful performance, to the limit of the capacity of the slow learner, is the attitude toward him of those with whom he comes into contact—his parents, his teachers, other adults, his peers. Many parents, especially those with average and above-average intelligence, find it difficult to accept the slow learner at full worth, as an individual entitled to the same rights to the pursuit of happiness as the brightest among us. Some are ashamed that they are the parents of a child below average in learning capacity. Often this attitude is perceived even by the slowest among the slow. Some parents even use epitaphs such as *stupid* to the child's face!

Teachers have not been innocent of maltreatment of the slow learner on the affective level. Many prefer having the bright child in their classrooms. Often unintentionally on the part of the teacher, yet insidiously, that attitude carries over into their actions, and the boys and girls who are slow learners sense it. Teachers who frequently praise high academic performance of the average and above-average child may not realize what a depressing, discouraging effect such references must have on the one who never can achieve academically up to the level that the teacher deems praiseworthy. Another example of inhuman treatment is urging the slow learner to reach levels impossible for him to attain. Nor has homogeneous grouping in spite of the best of intentions on the teacher's part, had a salutary effect on the ego of the children in the lowest group.

Teachers of reading are, at times, too eager to get a child to become a good reader, regardless of other consequences. At various points throughout this book we have stressed that it is less important that a child develop into an effective reader than that he become a well-balanced individual who can lead a socially useful and personally satisfying life. To the extent that reading contributes to this objective it is important; when it begins interfering with it, its value is less than questionable. While the teacher will, indeed, want to strive to help the slow learner read up to his capacity, he should not have that as his highest aim. Usually there need be no conflict between means of accomplishing both of these objectives.

The teacher who accepts the slow learner along with his problems with understanding and respect and appreciation is in a key position to make a better world for the child. His influence on parents can be of great moment, as he points out to them the need of accepting the child as he is, of not expecting too much from him academically, of noting his achievements both in academic and nonacademic areas, of letting him know that his accomplishments are recognized. The teacher can affect the attitude of other adults through casual conversation, through parent-teacher conferences, through group meetings with parents. He can favorably influence the peer group through day-in, day-out classroom actions as they observe the teacher in his treatment of the slow learner, as they hear him emphasize the contributions of each child, as they realize they are in a classroom in which an atmosphere of friendliness and of respect for one another prevails.

As important as the attitude that others show toward the slow learner is that with which he regards himself—his self-concept. The latter can be determined by the former. The child who is treated as if he were inferior is usually quick to develop the belief that he is of lesser value, that he is tolerated rather than accepted in a group, that there is no use trying to do anything well since he considers any attempts he might make as doomed to failure. No wonder that the slow learners are often an unhappy group of human beings, robbed by their fellow men of the satisfaction of many of their innate needs—of a feeling of accomplishment, of a knowledge that they are wanted in the groups to which they belong, of the blessing of loving and being loved. And yet we as teachers have wondered why the slow learner has not been quicker to respond to our teaching, forgetting that we, in a state of even temporary discouragement, find it difficult to develop incentive for achievement or stamina for work!

When we refer to the matter of self-concept in its relation to success in reading, we are referring to a healthy self-concept, which enables the child to accept himself realistically, without undue concentration on himself. With such an attitude he will view his limitations with understanding. It will also help make it possible for him to attribute to himself the dignity deserved by every human being. He will pay due attention to his accomplishments and will focus on his possible future attainments. He will be sensibly competitive with his own past record of achievement rather than with those of others. What the teacher will do to assist the child with inferior ability—or any other child, for that matter—in achieving such a perspective can be of value to the child not only as he faces the developmental task of learning to read but also as he approaches other situations confronting him.

READING AND THE UNDERACHIEVER

There is, in professional literature, a variety of terms used to designate the pupil who is behind in reading. The expressions *retarded reader, problem reader, underachiever in reading* are all in vogue, each with a somewhat different meaning than the others. We have chosen to use, as a rule, the term *underachiever,* as we refer to the child who is not reading up to capacity. Thus, the gifted child as well as the slow learner can be an underachiever. So can the great number of boys and girls with average mental ability who likewise are reading below expectation.

We recognize at least three types of underachievers. One is the youngster who is not reading as well as he can, but who is able to improve his performance under the guidance of his regular classroom teacher. Another has difficulties that are serious enough so that he requires the assistance of a special reading teacher. A third type, fortunately an exception, has problems which call for intensive study by the staff of a reading clinic. When a child fails to make progress in reading in spite of persistent efforts by the school to help him, he needs the attention of specialists who are skilled in the investigation of causes that interfere with learning to read. It is with the children who can be given special help by the classroom teacher that we are here chiefly concerned.

Causes of Underachieving in Reading

Knowledge of the causes of unsatisfactory progress in reading is valuable from two standpoints. Such understanding can help the teacher (1.) to prevent retardation and (2.) to deal intelligently with difficulties as they arise. The task is to look behind the symptoms and find the causes. These will usually be a combination of several elements; indeed, multiple causation is a basic principle of remedial reading. The causes of reading difficulty are usually numerous, complex, and interrelated.

Because of their interrelatedness, the search for causes should not end when one apparent cause has been found. Frequently, a primary cause of retardation in reading, especially if the difficulty is one of long duration, results in one or more secondary causes, which may in turn greatly influence the effectiveness of the reading. Thus, for example, illness, with consequent irregularity of school attendance, may be at the root of a child's reading difficulty. It may result in lack of interest in learning, which by itself is significant enough to bring about serious problems in learning to read.

Reading Deficiency and Personality

Reading problems are often associated with personality problems. Since reading is so important in the life of every child, failure in this activity may be expected to cause anxieties, feelings of insecurity, and even aggressive behavior. On the other hand, children who come to school with a sense of inadequacy, a feeling of being unloved, or an unconscious hostility against the adult world may lack the necessary incentive to learn to read or may be prepared to resist efforts on the part of the teacher to teach them. The factors of personality problems and reading problems are no doubt frequently reciprocal. For this reason, it is commonly necessary to provide personal guidance along with corrective instruction in reading. Certainly the teacher needs at all times to consider the total development of the child, not merely his reading needs.

Reading Deficiency and the Home Situation

Various investigations show that situations in homes or poor family relations are contributing causes to poor progress in reading. However, the emotional stresses resulting from conflict or deprivation in the home are only one source of reading retardation in school. Indifference on the part of parents toward a child's reading may be responsible for a lack of incentive to learn to read. Paradoxically, oversolicitude on the part of parents may also create tensions that impede reading progress. If there is hostility between child and parent, the very eagerness of the mother and father to note reading progress may serve as a motive for holding back. More typically, the desire of the child to gain parental approval results in fears that inhibit normal and felicitous growth in reading.

The reading background provided by the home is a potent factor in determining how well the child will succeed in school. When parents show an enthusiastic interest in their children's reading, when they read stories to them and show them the pictures, when they discuss the contents of the books with them, they are laying strong foundations for pleasurable, independent reading. Especially important is the presence in the home of a variety of attractive, appealing books for children. Time for quiet reading provided at home and a reasonably comfortable place for reading also help to start the child on the road to the enjoyment of books.

Fortunately, many children who come from impoverished or otherwise unpromising home environments nevertheless become excellent readers. Perhaps in a few instances the very lack of favorable home surroundings may serve as an incentive for greater effort in learning to read. The example of Abraham Lincoln comes to mind. Such cases, however, are exceptional. As a rule, when children from unfavorable home environments become good readers, as they often do, it is in spite of, not because of, their early deprivation.

Reading Deficiency and Early Experiences with Reading

Children's first experiences with reading will in great measure determine their later progress. If they are faced with reading tasks for which they are not ready, they may build antagonistic attitudes toward reading which interfere with normal growth. Moreover, they may develop inappropriate habits of word attack or sentence reading which will cause trouble throughout the formative years.

Examples of such habits are many. The child may develop the habit of sounding the words without giving attention to the meaning. Or he may feel that partial recognition of words is satisfactory. Word pointing and its companion, line pointing, may serve too long as a crutch in silent or oral reading. These devices may be harmless or even helpful at the very beginning, but children should soon learn to do without them if they are to read for meaning and develop appropriate speed. The same may be said about the use of markers (strips of paper moved from line to line during reading). The child should be encouraged as early as possible to develop independence in making accurate return sweeps from line to line. Extremely slow rate of reading, word-by-word reading, and overanalytical methods of word attack may also be responsible for unsatisfactory growth in reading.

Reading Deficiency and the School Climate

The general atmosphere of the school can be an important factor in children's success in reading. If there is a feeling of tension or pressure, if the child senses that the school authorities are anxious about his reading, he may develop harmful attitudes toward the reading process. On the other hand, if there is a bright, relaxed atmosphere, reading tends to take on the aspect of a delightful challenge. Such an atmosphere is created primarily by the ways in which teachers talk about reading, by their reactions to children's successes and failures, and by the variety of stimulating activities going on in the school. Physical surroundings, too, play a part in forming children's attitudes toward reading. Dreary, unstimulating classrooms lacking in suitable reading materials may inhibit the reading growth of pupils who might burgeon in a more evocative environment. Overcrowded classrooms, regimented instruction, antiquated textbooks, and lack of good school libraries may be responsible to a degree for much of the reading retardation found in our schools.

Reading Deficiency and the Quality of Instruction

It is not pleasant for those of us who are teachers of reading to be reminded of the fact that reading deficiency is frequently due to the quality of the instructional program. However, if much is to be done to improve on the present situation in reading, that point must be faced squarely and procedures for altering it introduced.

Reading Deficiency and Other Factors

Basically, the causes of reading deficiency must be sought in the presence or absence of the elements important to growth in reading, discussed in Chapter 2. Physical well-being, visual and auditory acuity, intelligence, experience background, mental health, and interest and purpose in reading are essential factors to be investigated when the child fails to make expected progress in reading. The process of exploring causes of reading retardation is essentially one of finding out which of these essential elements are lacking in a significant degree.

Teaching the Underachiever Who Reads Below His Age Level

We have noted that many slow learners are not reading below their expectancy level (*see* page 437). We would not call them underachievers since we use that term to designate those who read below their intellectual capacity. Some gifted children, though they may be reading above the average of their age or grade, may thus still be underachievers. Bearing these points in mind, let us next consider ways of guiding, first, the underachiever who is reading below his age level and, second, the one who is reading at or above it. The former is often referred to as the *retarded reader* or the *disabled reader,* and the latter as the *bright underachiever.* It is with this interpretation that we are using these terms.

Perhaps the first thing a teacher should keep in mind in teaching the disabled reader is the need to enlist his enthusiastic effort in the process of improvement. Most pupils who have had severe and persistent difficulty in learning to read have developed negative attitudes toward reading. They have, for one reason or another, experienced repeated frustration in a task that they recognize as the most important challenge facing them day after day. The result may be fear or hostility or indifference. Sometimes the awareness of parents' concern or annoyance pursues them to the school door. They may feel that the good opinion of the teacher or classmates depends on their performance.

Such children are in great need of "success experiences." The school day must be a day of achievement. The teacher should patiently seek out opportunities to enable the retarded reader to excel in some activity, whether in singing or dancing, in making something, or reporting an everyday experience. Sometimes a disabled reader may do very well in taking part in a dramatic activity. The child must feel that he belongs, that he is respected. He should have something good to report when he returns home.

The experience of success is of greatest consequence in his work in reading. If the materials he is called upon to read, or the phonics and other reading exercises are chosen with a view to his abilities, he will be emotionally prepared to take the next step. He need not be praised for every correct response, but he must know when he has done well.

Every effort should be made to stimulate the child's desire to read independently in books of his own choosing. It is quite possible to cultivate in disabled readers an interest that will lead to lifetime habits of reading. The use of pictures, dramatizations, conversations about books, and other devices for arousing interest are doubly important in the case of the retarded reader. Easy, well-illustrated books and magazines should be attractively displayed on the book table and the magazine rack.

Too often the physical environment and the program for the special class in remedial reading are barren and forbidding. The overconscientious teacher feels that every moment must be spent with reading workbooks, objective tests, and laborious oral reading. The remedial reading room should be one of the most inviting rooms in the school. The program should include the showing of films, group discussions, "creative writing," the exchange of jokes and riddles, and oral reports of personal experiences. Reading then becomes what it ought to be—a part of the communication process and the outgrowth of real-life experiences. Under circumstances such as these, teachers who dreaded that "period with the slowpokes" may find teaching them the most rewarding experience of the school day. If remedial reading instruction is to be successful, both pupil and teacher must find pleasure in it.

A word should be said at this point about the relationship between pleasure and learning. The commonly used expression "reading for fun" refers not to a marginal or frivolous use of reading ability but to an essential condition for learning to read. Only when the learner finds satisfaction in the activity may we look for the free and unrestrained flow of childhood energies into the task of converting visual symbols into sound and meaning. Even very difficult reading material affords satisfaction when the reader feels that he is achieving a clearly understood purpose. For the young child the appearance of too many unfamiliar words or concepts in the reading material is a distraction and a hindrance to enjoyment. For the retarded reader, especially, the prescription must be easy, abundant, interest-charged reading material.

Another consideration in the planning of work with the disabled reader is the role of the parent. Teachers who have responsibility for large numbers of children cannot be in frequent communication with all the parents, but in the case of the severely retarded reader such communication is essential. The personal interview is the most effective form, but in the absence of opportunity for face-to-face discussions the letter-report can be most useful. Parent and teacher have much to learn from each other about the child. The teacher needs to know as much as possible about the child's home situation and his behavior with respect to play, TV habits, sleeping habits, and especially his reading at home. On the other hand, the parent needs to have advice as to methods of reinforcing the efforts of the teacher in providing appropriate reading guidance.

In some instances the parents are indifferent to the child's school problems. In others, they are overconcerned and competitive and place undue pressure on the child. Sometimes the parent adopts a punitive attitude toward the child who is not doing well in reading. The parent should be informed early about any important difficulty a child is having, so that he or she will not be shocked or agitated to discover that the child needs special help. As a rule, parents should be discouraged from attempting to give reading instruction at home; they should be encouraged to provide the environment, the stimulation, and the good example that will strengthen the teacher's efforts to build constructive attitudes toward reading on the part of the child.

Finally, appropriate guidance for the underachiever should extend to the work in the content subjects. Gains achieved in the reading period can be quickly canceled out if the child is confronted in science, social studies, hygiene, and other subjects with regimented textbook materials that yield little meaning for him. Habits of partial comprehension acquired in the course of the school day may nullify whatever has been learned in remedial reading sessions. Careful preparation in the way of concept formation, explanation of new terms and old terms with specialized meanings, and the use of diversified reading materials at many different levels of difficulty are some of the procedures required by all pupils but particularly by those who are seriously deficient in reading ability.

Guidelines

The following are some additional suggestions for working with the underachiever who is reading below his age level. Many of them can be applied, with or without modification, to teaching the slow learner regardless of whether he is also an underachiever.

1. Be encouraging, but not beyond the point of truthfulness   While every good teacher tries to encourage all children, optimism is especially important in the case of the backward reader. Frequently, the retarded reader is a discouraged person. Again and again, without success, he has tried to learn to read. Often he has come to think of himself as a failure not only in reading but in almost everything. Consequently, primary emphasis sometimes needs to be placed on providing an activity in which the child can perform with superior results.

The teacher must, however, guard against encouragement that belies facts. A child should not be given the impression that it is going to be easy for him to become a good reader, for, unfortunately, such is usually not the case. As a rule, learning to overcome ineffective habits of reading is a slow and laborious task. The child who has been promised an easy path to learning to read will be discouraged when he later discovers that it is difficult.

The extent to which the teacher can be encouraging as he begins to give help in remedial reading will vary greatly with the situation. In some instances it is fairly easy to predict that the task will not be an unduly arduous one. In other instances it may be a long time before the child acquires the basic skills of reading. The teacher's remarks and his attitude toward teaching a retarded reader must be greatly influenced by a large variety of facts. The more background data the teacher has, the more readily he will be able to make accurate predictions of success.

In most instances there are some points that the teacher should make clear to a pupil at or near the beginning of the work on remedial reading. He can tell the child that there is reason for believing that he can learn to read. The teacher may wish to tell the pupil, too, that many boys and girls who have problems like his have learned to read when taught by methods that will be followed in his case. Early in the period of giving special help it is sometimes desirable to point out to the child that much depends on his own willingness to work hard to learn to read. Many of the children are old enough to profit from being told that they themselves need to put forth real effort if they want to become better readers.

2. Interest the pupil in reading   Frequently the underachiever lacks interest in reading; repeated failure or inability to read as well as his peers is not conducive to the development of such interest. Consequently, one of the first problems, and one of the most difficult, is to inspire the reader to want to read. Sometimes an interest in reading is stimulated through assurance to the child that he can most likely learn to read. Another means is surrounding him with books that contain many pictures on topics in which he is interested. Since often he cannot read these books, the teacher should devote some time daily in telling him points of significance about one or more of them. Another device often used is having some of the pupils tell about points of special interest they have learned from books as they are showing them to their classmates.

Everything that has been recommended earlier in this book as a means of interesting boys and girls in reading also holds, at least to some extent, in the case of the retarded reader. It should be remembered, however, that it is usually much harder to develop reading interest in the retarded reader than in the average or superior reader.

3. Select carefully the time of day when the special help is given   It is unwise to ask the child to do special work in reading at a time of day when he is tired. It is usually undesirable to schedule remedial work for a recess period, for the disabled reader is even more likely than the others to require the relaxation of the play period. Moreover, a child who is deprived of the activities of the recess period may become resentful toward the remedial-reading program. The same principle applies to other parts of the school day in which he would be deprived of the opportunity to take part in some activity that he likes particularly well. Usually it is not conducive to maximum achievement to keep the child, because of the special help, from participating in music, art, or other activities that particularly attract him. Special help in reading should, if possible, be given during a period regularly set aside for reading instruction.

4. Use appropriate materials of instruction   Teachers of retarded readers often point out that not enough suitable material is available on the child's level of development and at the same time on his reading level. The complaint is justified. A fourteen-year-old boy with a reading ability of a typical second-grade child is not going to care much about reading a second-grade reader. However, the problem is no longer quite as acute as it used to be. A large number of general books, on subjects of great interest to children throughout the intermediate grades, are written so simply that even a retarded reader can enjoy them, especially with a little help. Some sets of readers, too, are especially designed for the retarded reader.

A number of reading lists have been prepared to aid the teacher in locating suitable books for slow readers or underachievers in the elementary school. Some of these are named in Chapter 17, "Resources for Teaching Reading" (*see* page 569). The problem of finding appropriate materials is more serious with the child who has so small a reading vocabulary that he cannot even recognize the words in a preprimer. Books that are challenging in thought to a nine-year-old child who cannot read on the preprimer level are not available. Sometimes, with the intelligent child who cannot read, the teacher can explain that at first he will find the books decidely below his level of interest. He should also then be made to feel that his chief interest should be in the results he accomplishes on his road to becoming a good reader, rather than in the subject matter. One teacher showed a child some books in a series that he had selected for the pupil's reading, explaining that while the earlier books lacked subject matter that would be challenging to him, the later ones contained many selections of real interest. The teacher might also tell the child that he may find, as many adults do, that sometimes it is fun to read subject matter that is chiefly designed for younger readers.

Teacher-made materials sometimes contribute to the solution of the problem of what to have the retarded child read, particularly in the early stages of learning to read. The teacher can often write material, either dictated by the pupil or written by the teacher without contributions from the child. It is too time-consuming, however, for the teacher to continue to write all the material that a child will be reading.

5. Decide on the methods to be used on the basis of a careful diagnosis The teacher who uses the same methods of procedure with all retarded readers will usually not get satisfactory results. Considerable time spent on diagnosis can be very valuable if the results are utilized in planning the program.

6. If a method does not seem to work well with a pupil, change your procedure after you have given the method a fair trial No one method has been proven to be so much superior to all others that the teacher should persist, in spite of lack of results, in using it with any child. Even if the teacher has used a given procedure effectively with many other children whose needs seem to be similar, he should change his plans with a specific pupil if they are not productive of results with the child. However, he should not shift from one method to another without persisting long enough with the first to be sure that it will not be successful. Some children take a long time to learn by any method. Too much change in method, here as in other learning situations, is likely to result in confusion.

7. Use a variety of methods   The use of one method, no matter how good, to the exclusion of others usually does not produce the best results. No one method alone is likely to be best fitted to the needs of any individual, for reading is so complex a process and retardation in reading is ordinarily caused by such a multiplicity of factors that various types of approaches are needed. It is especially important that a variety of methods be used when several persons are being taught as a group. Frequently one method, although helpful for all, is not the most felicitous one for every individual in the group.

There is, however, also danger in too much variety of method. The number should be limited somewhat so that it will not be necessary for the child to expend an unwarranted amount of time and energy in becoming accustomed to various ways of learning to read. Best results are usually attained only after a person has had considerable experience with a particular method.

8. Make continuous appraisal of the pupil's progress and encourage him to do likewise   Charts or graphs, kept by either the teacher or pupil, can serve as an incentive to learning. However, because of the complexity of the reading act, these records often can show but one segment of the total activity. The pupil should be aware of this fact. The records should deal with some aspect of reading on which fairly objective data can be obtained. A record may be kept of the number of words a child has learned during intervals of time—a week or ten days, for example. A chart may be kept showing the number of pages in general books that a pupil has read. Other accomplishments that may be recorded are: the number of questions a pupil answers correctly on teacher-made tests; the rate of reading for stated purposes; the number of words missed when reading orally from a designated book; the number of words recognized from a standardized word list.

The child should be helped to realize that if he fails at times to show progress on a record, it may not necessarily indicate that he is not learning. The nature of learning curves, including plateaus, may need to be explained to the child, in language that he can comprehend.

9. If instruction is given in group situations, make certain that it is provided under the best circumstances possible   Some work with retarded readers can be done satisfactorily only if help is given on an individual basis. At other times, however, work in small-group situations seems advisable. Furthermore, there are instances when sheer lack of time on the part of the teacher makes it necessary to give help to two or more persons at one time.

The following suggestions may prove helpful when grouping seems desirable: (a.) *Group the pupils according to their needs.* For skill development the grouping should be according to the type of skill in which they are deficient. All those of approximately the same level of reading ability who need help in word recognition of a given type may be taught together, while those whose major difficulty is a specific phase of comprehension may form another group. However, boys and girls of widely different ages should not be placed in the same group because of the unhappiness it might cause the older children. (b.) *Keep the groups flexible so that changes can quite readily be made as needs change.* The administration of any program for helping the disabled reader should allow for the maximum of change from one group to another, whenever such a shift would be to the best advantage of the learner. (c.) *In group work, pay special attention to the needs of each person.* Even when the teacher is helping several children at the same time, much can be done to individualize the work. A child who has more skill than the others in his group in oral reading could be asked to read orally the more difficult parts of a selection. A child who has particular trouble with a certain word should be given the appropriate help in deciphering it. (d.) *Help each individual to realize that he is an important member of the group.* The attitude of the teacher has much to do with whether a child feels important. The teacher can find many ways to show each child that he considers him of real value as a contributing member of the group. Even the boy or girl who cannot read can be helped to feel his worth if he can show pictures of interest to others or tell of experiences that his age-mates recognize as valuable contributions.

Special Methods for Remedial Reading

In general, the procedures that are most effective for the child retarded in reading are the same as those that can be recommended for other boys and girls. Remedial reading at its best is essentially an adaptation of the same procedures effectively used with normal readers to the individual needs of retarded readers. A child with difficulty in word recognition can, as a rule, be helped most to acquire power in this respect by the same means used with other readers. Similarly, a child retarded in skill in selecting significant details can usually progress to the best advantage if he is helped to develop this comprehension skill by means of the same general procedures used with other children, if special attention is paid to his level and his responses in learning situations.

There is no bag of tricks nor list of teaching devices that can be presented with the guarantee that these will change pupils retarded in reading to average or above-average readers. There are, however, several methods of teaching reading that are often associated primarily with remedial reading. These are briefly described here.

1. The Fernald Kinesthetic Method[9] Although Dr. Fernald recommends her method for use with any child, it is more often used with seriously retarded readers who do not respond to other methods. Important as-

[9] Grace M. Fernald, *Remedial Techniques in Basic School Subjects* (New York: McGraw-Hill Book Company, 1943).

pects of the method are these: (a.) In the earliest stage of instruction the teacher writes the word to be learned in large letters as the child watches her. Then the child traces the word with his finger as he says it part by part. He tries to write it from memory. As he writes the word, he again says it. He then compares his copy with the original and, if he finds an error, tries again to learn the word by the same method he has employed so far. Emphasis is placed on reading words that the pupils use as they describe experiences they have. Consequently, experience charts are often used with this method. (b.) When the child has learned quite a number of words, he is no longer asked to trace each new word. He is instructed to write words that he learns on cards and to file them in an individual word box. When he writes stories he is encouraged to use this file if necessary. (c.) When the pupil has made considerable progress in learning a word by this method without tracing it, new words are presented to him in print, not in writing. It is then that the pupil advances to the stage at which he is able to recognize a new word through its resemblance to a known word and through the aid of context clues.

Many teachers consider this method too slow and laborious and mechanical to use in a developmental reading program. Some object to emphasis on this method even in remedial reading. There are, however, pupils who have learned to read by the Fernald method who have encountered only failure in the use of others. It is for this reason that some teachers, who do not favor its use even with all retarded readers, try it with some of them when little, if any, progress has been made with other methods. Many adaptations of the Fernald method have been made. Use of the typewriter by the pupil is part of one of the modifications.

2. Use of experience charts   Some teachers rely heavily on individual work with retarded readers on experience charts, of which a detailed description and evaluation are given in Chapter 4B. Modifications of the typical procedures followed in group situations are required. As in the experience charts for groups of children, the teacher records in writing the sentences that are dictated to him. Then the child "reads" the sentences, often in part from memory. Sometimes these sentences are in the form of book reports on picture books or simple stories that the child has read or on books the teacher or others have read to him. Autobiographical sketches are frequently dictated and also illustrated by the child. Since these materials are ordinarily for individual use, they are usually recorded on sheets of paper rather than on tagboard.

3. Use of games and other drills   Special mention is made of games and drills in connection with teaching the disabled reader because with such readers it is often more necessary than with others to use these activities to a considerable degree. This is true because frequently these children need more repetitive practice than those not retarded. The same criteria for drill should be observed in connection with work in remedial reading as are valid at other times.

Organizational Plans

Help can be given to the disabled reader under a variety of plans. Much of it can undoubtedly be provided most effectively by the teacher from day to day as he adapts all his instruction to the needs of his class. Individual help given by the teacher during or just after a class period will frequently clear up the difficulties of a child who is falling behind in acquiring a reading skill. Prevention of further retardation through early attention to problems is the keynote of this informal plan. Those boys and girls who have some special difficulty in reading can sometimes be put, for a day or a week or longer, in a group by themselves for special help. Such instruction at times may be a substitute for work with the child's usual group; in other instances it may be in addition to the regular classwork in reading. Groups can be formed for longer duration, possibly for the whole year. Thus, much of the problem of remedial reading can be dealt with informally in the regular classroom.

There are instances, however, when a more formal plan for remedial reading may be warranted. In some schools children seriously retarded in reading are assigned to a classroom by themselves, preferably with a teacher qualified to deal with problems in this area. Ideally such a class is kept considerably smaller in enrollment than the average. If more than fifteen pupils are placed in it, the effectiveness of the program of instruction is likely to be greatly reduced. A criticism of this organization is that all the school associations of a pupil in a class for retarded readers are with boys and girls with the same limitations. The stigma that is likely to become attached to such a class is another factor frequently raised as objection to this plan. Further objection lies in the expense of any program where classroom size is necessarily limited to the extent that it ideally ought to be in a room reserved for retarded readers. Furthermore, unless the special class serves a fairly large district, there are not likely to be enough retarded readers of similar age and intelligence to constitute even the small number of pupils desirable for the class. Often the plan followed is that of having a specialist in reading meet with pupils from various rooms for limited parts of the school day. Under such a plan, the reading teacher ordinarily has a room of his own, often designated as the reading room. During the first half of the forenoon he may help one group of children who have been excused from their homeroom for that length of time. At the middle of the forenoon these boys and girls go back to their own rooms where they resume work with their classmates. At that time another group begins its half-forenoon session with the reading teacher. The afternoon can be divided similarly. The school day can be divided into more than four parts, possibly periods of sixty minutes' duration, to allow for more shifts of pupils during the day.

One of two plans is typically used to determine which pupils needing extra help in reading should be in the reading room at the same time. For purposes of administration it is usually easier to assemble at one time in the reading room all the children from a given classroom who need extra help in reading work. To facilitate matters of programing, many of the homeroom teachers concurrently conduct reading classes for those of their children who are not in the reading room; thus, the retarded readers do not miss work in social studies or other areas of study. Such a plan usually interferes less with the other activities of the boys and girls than one in which the reading teacher has, at the same time, those pupils from all rooms who have the same or similar reading problems. According to this latter plan children reading on a preprimer level, for example, regardless of their home room or grade, would meet with the reading teacher at the same time. Not only does such a plan often create many disrupting influences in the other learning activities of the children, but frequently, too, the resulting grouping is undesirable from the point of view of the socialization of the child. Under such a plan a sixth-grade pupil may be grouped for reading with a second-grade child.

Assignment of pupils to special classes will present additional problems. Who should be assigned to these classes? Should superior pupils who are not reading up to their potential be enrolled in them. What types of tests should be used for screening pupils? How long should the class periods for reading be? Who should determine what pupils are to be assigned to the special classes and when they are to be returned to regular instruction? How large should the classes be?

These and many other questions will occur to the administrator and the teacher who are concerned with the reading problem. The solution of most of them will depend to a considerable extent upon local conditions. The point at which pupils should be assigned to special classes will usually be determined in part by the number of teachers and classrooms available for remedial work. Quite probably the pupils who fall in the lowest tenth percentile will require the skilled help of the special teacher. Generally speaking, however, the superior pupil who is not reading up to his capacity, but up to his grade level, should not be assigned to a special class. He should be given individual attention in regular instruction and provided with new challenges in the form of more difficult reading materials and more demanding classroom tasks. Screening tests should be of the survey type because the diagnostic test is expensive and time-consuming. However, diagnostic tests, including one such as the Gray Oral Reading Paragraphs, should be given in the remedial classes to determine specific instructional needs, and in regular classes when reading instruction is planned. Most survey tests include some diagnostic features which will be useful in any reading instruction. In general, remedial class periods should not extend much beyond forty-five minutes in length, and the class size should not exceed fifteen. The exact size of the class should depend on the nature and extent of the disabilities of the boys and girls enrolled in it.

Assignment to remedial sections should be based on consultation between the classroom teacher and the remedial teacher or principal.

In every large school system there will be some pupils who do not respond to instructional guidance, either in regular or special classes. In a few cases such lack of progress may be due to extremely low mental ability, but pupils so deficient are rare and will normally be entered in special schools. More commonly, the difficulty will stem from some physical, emotional, or other handicap which can be at least partially overcome through expert diagnosis and guidance. The problem is chiefly one of intensive and patient study.

Because most teachers have neither the time nor the specialized training to make such diagnoses or to plan such guidance, expert help is needed. Unfortunately, however, the supply of highly trained personnel is as yet severely limited. Many universities and some hospitals conduct psycho-educational clinics in which help in reading is given. Some governmental agencies, such as the Institute for Juvenile Research in Illinois, provide diagnostic service, but they usually have long waiting lists and are seriously understaffed. Most clinics are obliged to charge a fee. Large school systems generally operate reading centers, but small town and rural schools are lacking in clinical facilities. There is great need for county units to provide the service that the small school cannot give.

One of the values of the reading center is the opportunity it provides for in-service education of teachers. Although the nucleus of the center must necessarily be the technically trained clinic staff, the great amount of individual instruction required by children referred to the clinic will call for the aid of a number of qualified teachers.

In some cities teachers are relieved of regular teaching duties in the classroom for a year or two to serve as teaching assistants in the reading center. After their work with severely retarded readers in the center, they return to their classrooms with a better understanding of the problems of retarded readers and with more skill in dealing with reading problems in the classroom. Teachers who have served in reading centers are often qualified to act as reading supervisors and to aid in developing remedial programs in elementary schools.

Helping the Bright Underachiever

In a sense almost everyone is an underachiever. We tend to perform up to full capacity only under pressure. The pressure may consist of a drive or ambition, a keen but perhaps transitory interest, circumstances that demand the full exercise of our powers, or a strong desire to win the approval of others in certain situations. Some children are driven to high achievement in school subjects by a desire to compensate for a real or fancied deficiency in physical skill or in general social adjustment.

What concerns the teacher of reading, however, is persistent failure of a bright child to perform up to his full potential in reading and to achieve the kind of growth that may reasonably be expected of him. It is of great importance that the causes of his inadequate performance be discovered as early as possible.

The possible causes of underachievement in some bright children are numerous, and for the most part they do not differ in kind from the causes of underachievement among average and below-average children. Among these causes is the familiar one of a lack of a strong foundation of reading skills—such as methods of attack on unfamiliar words, getting the main idea of a passage, reading at appropriate rates. Although many able learners acquire these skills on their own, others do not. Like most children who fail to learn the basic skills early, the bright child may develop negative attitudes toward reading which persist throughout the elementary grades and beyond. Indeed, the bright child tends to be more sensitive than others to his unsuccessful efforts in reading during the initial stages.

In some instances conditions in a bright child's home may be responsible for underachievement in reading. If parents do not place a high value on academic excellence, if the home has few books or magazines of quality, if the child is not given encouragement or opportunity to read at home, he may never realize his own potential or set himself goals commensurate with his abilities. It then becomes necessary for the school to compensate for the impoverished cultural environment at home by providing intellectual and cultural stimulation through an abundance of direct and vicarious experiences.

Some bright children, perhaps *because* they are bright, enter school before they are matured sufficiently to cope with the adjustments and the tasks required by the school situation. Others are handicapped by being transported from one school situation in which they felt secure to another in which the surroundings are strange, the methods different, and a teacher's personality in contrast to the one he had before. Frequent absence from school because of illness or other factors is detrimental to the educational progress of most able pupils, as it is to that of average or slow learners.

Emotional problems, often stemming from discordant family relations, may interfere with satisfactory growth in reading. Children who experience continued anxiety, feel rejected, or show hostility toward the adult world frequently suffer a lack of self-confidence that is necessary for learning; they are emotionally distracted when they should be concentrating on their reading. This is not to say that all bright underachievers are emotionally disturbed or that emotional difficulties always result in underachievement. The teacher should, however, be alert to the possible presence of emotional factors as a possible block to the full realization of the bright child's reading potential.

It has been estimated that as many as 25 percent of the gifted children in a typical class are underachievers. Whatever the true proportion may be, we cannot afford the waste of talent arising from any child's failure to reach attainable goals in reading. We must do all we can to discover the obstacles to maximum growth and, so far as possible, to remove them.

For Further Study

Binter, Alfred R., John J. Diabal, Jr., and Leonard K. Kise, *Readings on Reading,* (Scranton, Pa.: Intext Educational Publishers, 1969), Part IV, "Human Variation in Reading Performance," containing articles by Emery P. Bliesmer, Arthur I. Gates, J. Harlan Shores, Paul Witty, C. P. Goetzinger, D. Dirks, and C. J. Baer; and Part VII, "Reading Disabilities," containing articles by Morton Wiemer and Ward Cromer, Jack A. Holmes, W. Dale Bryant, and Walter B. Barbe.

Bond, Guy L., and Eva Wagner, *Teaching the Child to Read,* 4th ed. (New York: The Macmillan Company, 1966), Ch. 16, "Adjusting to Individual Needs."

Della-Piana, Gabriel M., *Reading Diagnosis and Prescription: An Introduction* (New York: Holt, Rinehart and Winston, Inc., 1968).

Frost, Joe L., ed., *Issues and Innovations in the Teaching of Reading* (Chicago: Scott, Foresman and Company, 1967), Part VII, "Reading for the Gifted," containing articles by Irving H. Anderson, Ruth Strang, and C. F. Lehmann; and Part IX, "Diagnosis and Remediation of Reading Difficulties," containing articles by Robert Karlin, Jeannette Veatch, N. Dale Bryant, and Patricia M. Carrigan.

Gans, Roma, *Common Sense in Teaching Reading* (Indianapolis, Ind.: The Bobbs-Merrill Company, 1963), Ch. 19, "Readers in Low Gear."

Spache, George D., and Evelyn B. Spache, *Reading in the Elementary School,* 2nd ed. (Boston: Allyn and Bacon, Inc., 1973. Ch. 10, "Steps toward Individualized Reading."

Stauffer, Russell, *Directing Reading Maturity as a Cognitive Process* (New York: Harper & Row, 1969), Ch. 3, "Individualized Reading Programs."

Tinker, Miles A., and Constance M. McCullough, *Teaching Elementary Reading* (New York: Appleton-Century-Crofts, 1968), Ch. 16, "Materials"; and Ch. 26, "Remedial Reading in the Classroom."

Veatch, Jeannette, *Reading in the Elementary School* (New York: The Ronald Press, 1966), Ch. 5, "The Independent Work Period," Ch. 6, "The Individual Conference," and Ch. 7, "Grouping."

Witty, Paul A., ed., *Reading for the Gifted and the Creative Student* (Newark, Del.: International Reading Association, 1971).

Witty, Paul A., Anne Moore Freeland, and Edith H. Grotberg, *The Teaching of Reading: A Developmental Process* (Boston: D. C. Heath and Company, 1966), Ch. 13, "Remedial Reading"; Ch. 14, "Reading Instruction for the Slow-Learning Pupil"; and Ch. 15, "Reading Programs for the Gifted."

Questions and Comments for Thought and Discussion

1. With what kinds of grouping practices in the elementary school are you familiar? Evaluate each in terms of the discussion on grouping in this chapter. What is your own appraisal of each?

2. What do you see as the main strengths of diagnostic grouping? Do you notice any weaknesses in the procedure? If so, what are they?

3. How can reading be individualized in group situations?

4. If you have an opportunity to see a teacher teach reading in an elementary-school classroom in which the pupils are grouped, try to determine the basis for the grouping, ways in which the instruction seems to be adapted to individual differences, and the effectiveness of the teaching.

5. Have you observed instances in which the teacher in the elementary school neglected the gifted? If so, suggest ways in which the teacher might have been more helpful to them.

6. Teachers frequently ask gifted pupils to help the less-able readers. At the present time what is your reaction to such a practice?

7. Have you known of instances in which the gifted child tried not to let his peers know that he liked school work and that he was doing well in it? What suggestions do you have for the teacher of such a child to help prevent such an unfortunate situation?

Outline for Chapter 14

READING AND THE CHILD FROM THE CULTURALLY DIFFERENT HOME

Basic Considerations
    Terminology
    Differentiation between Children from Disadvantaged
        Backgrounds and Those from Non-English-Speaking
        Homes
    Extent of the Difficulties
Problems in Teaching Reading
    Nature of the Experience Background
    Lack of Motivation
    The Divergent Language
Large-scale Attempts to Help the Culturally Different
    Description of Some Programs
        Operation Head Start, Project Follow Through, and
          Project Upward Bound
    The Work of the Task Force
    Evaluation of Programs
The Role of the School
    Focus on Fundamentals
    Guidelines for the Teacher
    Instructional Procedures
    Beginning Reading Instruction for Children from Non-
        English-Speaking Homes
    Materials of Instruction
    Volunteer Workers

CHAPTER 14

Reading and the Child from the Culturally Different Home[1]

We noted in earlier chapters of this book that the home background and the general experience background of a child can greatly affect his ability to profit from instruction in reading. Because of this fact, much of this chapter is devoted to problems of teaching reading to children from culturally disadvantaged homes. We have also noted the close interrelation between oral language and reading. Consequently, this chapter also deals with special problems in learning to read English for children from homes in which English is not spoken.

Problems of teaching reading to children from culturally different homes are many and complex. Definitive answers to these problems have not been found. Fortunately, there are in print a growing number of helpful magazine articles and books on the subject, to some of which reference is made at the end of this chapter and in Chapter 17, "Resources for Teaching Reading" (see page 543). To these and others we refer the reader who is especially concerned about the problem of teaching the culturally different. Necessarily the treatment given the topic in this chapter can merely highlight some of the perplexities and suggest a few general procedures that can serve, it is hoped, as guidelines in teaching.

[1] This chapter is based in part on the one entitled "Teaching Reading to Children from Culturally Disadvantaged and Non-English-Speaking Homes" that Walter J. Moore contributed to the third edition of this book.

BASIC CONSIDERATIONS

Before we discuss some of the problems in learning to read faced by children from culturally different homes, let us clarify the use of some terms.

Terminology

Terms such as *culturally deprived* and *culturally disadvantaged* have been criticized as being insulting to those described. Reasons for such objection are not difficult to understand. Various other terms, to each of which objection can be raised, are also used, including *culturally underprivileged, culturally different, economically disadvantaged, denied, undereducated.*

While there is need for more desirable nomenclature, we cannot bypass the acute problem that exists while we search for the words that satisfactorily designate the persons whom we are attempting to assist. We cannot postpone providing an improved program of learning experiences for the boys and girls in the groups to which we refer while we attempt to find appropriate terms. In this book we frequently use the terms *culturally different, culturally disadvantaged,* and *culturally deprived.* We are thinking of the *culturally different* boys and girls as coming either from culturally disadvantaged homes or from those in which English is not spoken or is spoken as a second language. The pupils to whom we refer as *culturally disadvantaged* or *culturally deprived* are those who come from homes in which there is a decided lack of loving parental concern, of idealism, of positive attitudes toward education and schooling, and of conversational or intellectual communication that would aid children in the present reading programs in our schools. Poverty, to be sure, is often, but not necessarily, associated with cultural deprivation; but not all culturally deprived pupils are poor. *Economically deprived* and *culturally deprived* are not synonymous terms.

Differentiation between Children from Culturally Disadvantaged Backgrounds and Those from Non-English-Speaking Homes

The reader is warned against assuming that the problems—including the reading problems—of children from culturally disadvantaged homes and homes in which English is not the main language are necessarily identical. Some of the least culturally deprived homes in this country are those in which English is not spoken. Undoubtedly, too, for a child raised in such a home many advantages can accrue from the fact that he is familiar with another culture, including the language. The zeal with which in many elementary schools foreign languages are taught attests to the fact that many educators think it highly worthwhile for the young child to learn a language in addition to English. However, we are here not concerned primarily with the advantages resulting from a home in which from early childhood a boy or girl learns what will later serve for him as a second language, even though we must not overlook the benefits that may result from being bilingual. We are here concerned with the fact that special problems in learning to read English confront the child to whom on entering school English is an unknown or almost unknown language. When learning to read English such a pupil is confronted with a difficult situation and thus is at an initial disadvantage. The problem is especially complex when the teacher assumes that the same procedures can effectively be used with children from homes in which English is not spoken or is the second language as with those who are familiar with English.

Even though unfamiliarity with the English language is not a sign of being culturally deprived, at the present time in our country a large number of homes in which English is not spoken fall into that category. One needs only to consider the situation of the Puerto Rican in our big cities to understand this fact.

Extent of the Difficulties

Frequently, as educators refer to the disadvantaged, they have in mind only the Puerto Ricans and the Blacks in the ghetto regions of our big cities. To be sure, they constitute highly underprivileged groups. But they are not the only ones who are in desperate straits. Included in that category are the whites in Appalachia, the Spanish-Americans in Texas and the Southwest, the Indians on reservations. In fact, scattered throughout the country, in rural and in urban areas, we find the disadvantaged. It is a rare community in which a teacher may be teaching where there is not at least one underprivileged child, not even in many of the most affluent suburban centers. Whether the number is large or small in any given classroom, every disadvantaged child deserves the understanding and thoughtful and sympathetic treatment of the teacher.

While many a child who is not underprivileged is retarded in reading, the incidence of retardation among culturally deprived children is much greater than it is among other children. Josephine Benson[2] reports that while in schools located in middle-class communities we can expect 10 to 20 percent of the children to be retarded in reading, the incidence of retardation in disadvantaged areas is at times as high as 80 percent.

PROBLEMS IN TEACHING READING

The problems faced in teaching reading to the culturally different are multidimensional. Moreover, as noted earlier, they are not necessarily the same

[2] Josephine T. Benson, "Teaching Reading to the Culturally Different Child," no. 27 in *Readings on Reading* Alfred R. Binter, John J. Diabal, Jr., and Leonard K. Kise, eds. (Scranton: Pa: Intext Educational Publishers, 1969), p. 266. (This article originally appeared in *Progress and Promise in Reading Instruction* of a Report of the 22nd Annual Conference and Course on Reading, Pittsburgh, 1966, pp. 140–151.)

for the culturally disadvantaged and the children from non-English-speaking homes. When considering the problems of the latter group we must be clear whether we are referring to children from such homes who are culturally deprived or to those who are not. Both groups will have special problems in beginning reading, but many of the difficulties and their solutions will differ vastly for children from these two kinds of non-English-speaking homes.

As we ponder the problems of teaching reading to children from culturally disadvantaged homes, one cannot escape the more general questions relating to the physical and psychological needs of these pupils. Many of the boys and girls from deprived areas come to school hungry. Often, because of home conditions, they are also sleepy. Disease and malnutrition may interfere with academic learning of any kind. Unless the school takes into consideration the handicaps under which these boys and girls may be living, and unless it makes a strong effort to reduce or eliminate these factors, other strategies to improve the reading program for these children are doomed to fall short of the success desired. The first prerequisite to effective teaching of reading to underprivileged children is to know these boys and girls as human beings and to identify the problems arising from their background that are likely to interfere with effective learning to read unless provision is made for meeting them. Three of these major problems are considered here, namely: (1.) nature of the experience background, (2.) lack of motivation, and (3.) the divergent language.

Nature of the Experience Background

It would be presumptuous to claim that the child coming from a disadvantaged home lacks in experience background. He may have a background quite sufficient for what is required of him in the type of home from which he comes. He may be in possession of much information essential to him for survival in his culture, information often quite remote from the teacher's stock of knowledge. However, his background is often one radically different from the one on which the usual school program is seemingly based. The seriousness of this problem is increased by the fact that many middle-class teachers assume that such a child has certain types of information that children from the inner city or from a disadvantaged section of a rural area do not have. If he talks of a violin, he may discover that some of the children in his room have neither seen nor heard one. Some of the youngsters may not know the difference between a knife and a fork.

At times the teacher assumes that a culturally disadvantaged child with a broad background, for example, of travel, if he is the child of a migrant worker, would have much to build on that would be of value to him in school. Frequently, however, the disadvantaged child has not adequately experienced what he has seen and heard. With no one in his family interested in drawing his attention to much of what he sees on an extensive journey from one part of the country to another, he may lose much of the benefit that might accrue to a child whose parents are helpful in pointing out to him, through question or comment, points of significance and interest. This failure to utilize the background experiences constitutes an additional problem.

Lack of Motivation

Teachers too often assume that almost all children want to learn to read. They are frequently wrong in this assumption when teaching the disadvantaged child. Lack of parental interest in reading—possibly because of lack of skill in reading—may bring the culturally deprived child to school without motivation to learn to read.

Some boys and girls may even have a decided antipathy toward learning to read. They may have seen a child in their neighborhood ridiculed because he enjoyed reading or because he received good marks. They may have as hero the member of a gang who scoffs at reading and at anything associated with school. They may have heard brothers and sisters and other children tell tales about school—some of which may be true—that have prejudiced them against all school learning before they even step inside a school building. To such children no teacher needs try to make advances by telling them that they are about to start on a wonderful adventure, that of learning to read. They know more exciting adventures.

The Divergent Language

That there is a language difficulty in learning to read English for the child from a non-English-speaking home, even when the home is not culturally deprived, is easily recognized. The problem may be more acute and frequently much more persistent in the case of the child from an English-speaking culturally deprived home. In either case it is important that the school be cognizant of the extent of the situation faced by the child whose language differs greatly from standard English.

While we are told that the language of the child from a culturally deprived area may be as adequate for his needs at home and in his social setting as is that of the middle-class child for his environment, it has long been claimed that it is less helpful to him at school because most basal readers portray the life of middle-class boys and girls. It has been generally accepted that the textbooks use words and present concepts frequently foreign to the child from a deprived neighborhood. With the emphasis in many systems of teaching beginning reading on keeping the reading vocabulary within the realm of the understanding and speaking vocabulary of the learner, it is little wonder, according to many educators, that the child unfamiliar with the vocabulary of the reading book has a double burden—that of learning the meaning vocabulary and the reading vocabulary, especially when reading is taught by a teacher who does not realize the difficulty or ignores it or does not know how to deal with it.

There is, however, contradictory research on the effect on learning to read of the divergence between the child's speaking vocabulary and that which is used in reading textbooks. Two eminent researchers in the field of the disadvantaged and his language, J. Allen Figurel and S. Alan Cohen, the latter with Thelma Cooper, arrive at opposite conclusions on the basis of research conducted.

Figurel[3] reported on a study of the vocabulary of underprivileged children and concluded, on the basis of a comparison of the words in the vocabulary of underprivileged children with the words in controlled vocabularies for grades two through six, that very little effective reading can be expected to be done in the textbooks in use in these grades. He found a large number of the words in the controlled vocabularies unknown to underprivileged children in the various grades. He also observed:

> If reading competency is commensurate with one's experience, and much evidence seems to prove that this is true, underprivileged children, with their limited experiences, can be expected to do very little effective reading in textbooks they now use.

Figurel reported his conclusion in 1949. Some fifteen years later he was still reiterating the observations he made and the conclusions he drew from his earlier study. In his 1964 report he pointed out that despite our knowledge of the limited vocabularies of underprivileged children, very little progress has been made with the passage of the years.[4]

The conclusion that the vocabulary of the usual beginning basal reader is too difficult for the underprivileged child who speaks an English divergent from standard American English is challenged by S. Alan Cohen and Thelma Cooper.[5] On the basis of research conducted at the Reading and Language Arts Center at Yeshiva University and elsewhere, they label as a fallacy the assumption that the "disadvantaged urban child's deficient conceptual and usable vocabulary interferes with his learning to read in the beginning grades." They conclude that, in spite of the deficiency of the underprivileged child's vocabulary when compared with that of the middle class child, "a vocabulary of the most widely used beginning reading books showed that urban Black disadvantaged children had sufficient vocabulary to handle those materials."[6] However, they did not report

[3] J. Allen Figurel, "The Vocabulary of Underprivileged Children," *University of Pittsburgh Bulletin,* vol. 45 (June 1949), p. 389.
[4] J. Allen Figurel, "Limitations in the Vocabulary of Disadvantaged Children: A Cause of Poor Reading," *Improvement of Reading through Classroom Practice,* vol. 9 (1964), p. 164, Proceedings of the Annual Convention (Newark, Del.: International Reading Association).
[5] S. Alan Cohen and Thelma Cooper, "Seven Fallacies: Reading Retardation and the Urban Disadvantaged Beginning Reader," *The Reading Teacher,* vol. 26, no. 1 (October 1972), p. 42.
[6] *Ibid.,* p. 42.

whether reading material geared to the vocabulary of the disadvantaged child would increase his chance of successfully coping with the demands of beginning reading instruction. Furthermore, the study by Cohen and Cooper dealt only with the disadvantaged urban Black child. It might be that a similar study of non-urban Blacks, of Puerto Ricans, or of other disadvantaged groups would not be supportive of their findings.

Undoubtedly the question of the relationship between the oral language of the disadvantaged and the vocabulary used in materials for the beginning reader needs further investigation before curriculum makers and teachers can deal with confidence with the problem posed by contradictory research. They may find that not so much the vocabulary but the syntax of the language and the preschool experiences of boys and girls cause the difficulty in teaching reading to the children from disadvantaged backgrounds.

Whatever may be found to be the relationship between the speaking and the listening vocabularies of the disadvantaged child and the vocabulary of the beginning basal reading series, there is a language difficulty confronting him highlighted in various phases of his development toward maturity in communicative skills. It is probably often a less tangible but more pervasive problem. The language a person hears in his preschool years and that which in turn he then speaks becomes an integral part of him. As inadequate as that language may be, it cannot be taken away from a person, intentionally or unintentionally, without something resembling a shock to the system. (Most of us have experienced nostalgia when we hear an expression somewhat restricted to our family circle when we were youngsters; we can, therefore, have an idea of the emotional involvement with the language of one's home.) Furthermore, the language of the basal reader may seem so lacking in emotional content and so stilted to the child from the home in which a dialect divergent from that of his textbooks is spoken that to him the reading material is cold, uninteresting, and boring. The dilemma in which the child thus finds himself is difficult to solve. However, teachers interested in all the pupils whom they are privileged to teach will not refuse to do something about the situation merely because no final solution is readily apparent.

LARGE-SCALE ATTEMPTS TO HELP
THE CULTURALLY DIFFERENT

Many people and many agencies are deeply concerned with the problems faced by boys and girls from underprivileged and/or from non-English-speaking homes. Individuals, private organizations, foundations, and city and federal agencies have studied or are studying the problems in the hope of coming up with recommendations for improvement. Some have devised means by which they are attempting to eradicate some of the present ills.

Description of Some Programs

We will briefly summarize a few of the programs which have been designed, in entirety or in part, to improve the reading ability of the disadvantaged, namely: (1.) Operation Head Start, Project Follow Through, and Project Upward Bound; and (2.) the work by the Task Force of the National Council of Teachers of English.

Operation Head Start, Project Follow Through,
and Project Upward Bound

Operation Head Start, the most popular of the antipoverty educational programs, was designed to give children, before entering first grade, a "head start" in schooling planned for their needs. It was begun in 1965. In late 1967 it was followed by a pilot program, *Project Follow Through. Follow Through* came into existence because many studies convinced educational and government experts that *Head Start* "graduates" seemed to benefit from early education. It was found that these pupils begin regular school only slightly behind their middle-class schoolmates and well ahead of other impoverished children who have not had preschool experience. Unfortunately, however, it seems that the educational advantage of *Head Start* youngsters fades after six or eight months in the public schools. A somewhat related type of endeavor, *Project Upward Bound,* provides special services for economically deprived youth with considerable potential who have completed the junior or senior years of high school. Statistics seem to indicate that the great majority of those who have been enrolled in *Upward Bound* programs have gone on to further study at higher levels.

The recent experience with *Operation Head Start* and *Project Follow Through* seems to endorse earlier findings that a special feature of the learning difficulty of the educationally deprived child lies in the difference between his language and that used in school. Since verbal ability or disability unquestionably permeates all areas of academic learning, a closer examination of this condition is imperative. It is not enough simply to assume that a child is "nonverbal" or "less verbal."

The Work of the Task Force

A large-scale attempt to seek solutions to the problems of culturally deprived and non-English–speaking students was undertaken by the National Council of Teachers of English, which established a *Task Force* in order to survey and report on individual programs in language and reading for disadvantaged students throughout the country.[7] The *Task Force* was concerned with the teaching of language in all aspects — reading, literature,

[7] Richard Corbin and Muriel Crosby, *Language Programs for the Disadvantaged: Report of the NCTE Task Force on Teaching English to the Disadvantaged* (Champaign, Ill.: The National Council of Teachers of English, 1965), pp. 65–69.

spelling, writing, and speaking—from preschool language programs through those that provide postschool opportunities for adults.

The *Task Force* and other agencies that have directed their attention to the problems of the disadvantaged child are in general agreement in respect to the so-called deficits that have accrued by the time such a pupil enters school. The *Task Force* sees the deficiencies as falling into three general areas: (1.) conceptual development, (2.) language facility, and (3.) self-concept. In confronting these deficiencies, the school can take two possible approaches. The school can either attempt to change the child before he enters (through the preschool program) or to meet the needs of the child after he has started school. A combination of these two approaches seems to be the most effective. An attempt should be made to prepare a child and to overcome his areas of deprivation as much as possible before he enters school; yet, once he is in school, the school must adapt itself to the child's needs and provide help in areas in which he requires attention.

Emphasized in the recommendations of the *Task Force* is the need for parental cooperation. Any consideration of a school-wide plan to help culturally deprived or language-handicapped children learn to read would be incomplete without reference to the importance of gaining the cooperation of parents. Sometimes it is erroneously assumed that culturally deprived parents are not interested in their children. Actually, many are deeply concerned about their children's welfare. If the school can convince them that it is really trying to help the boys and girls, many parents will cooperate even at considerable sacrifice to themselves.

The first step in getting the assistance of parents, then, is to convince them that the teachers' interest in their children is sincere. Another step is to explain in understandable terms what the school is trying to do. Along with this explanation should come, from time to time, suggestions as to how parents can help—through providing needed quiet (if possible) in the home for reading, through giving the child time to read, through listening to a child read or tell about what he has read, through encouraging him to go to the library. It will take resourcefulness, ingenuity, and hard work to enlist the cooperation of the home to the fullest extent possible, but the results may well be worth the cost.

Evaluation of Programs

Unfortunately, it cannot be said that all the programs for helping children from underprivileged backgrounds have been successful. They have not. After years of federal subsidy to upgrade educational achievement of disadvantaged pupils, there is still little evidence that the problem is being overcome. In fact, pupils in the inner cities are falling farther below the national averages. Joseph Froomkin, formerly assistant commissioner for program planning and evaluation, U.S. Office of Education, has stated that most of the programs are not strong enough to insulate the child from detrimental effects of an unfortunate early home environment. He has observed:

> Our approach to the poor has been irrational: We have classified children according to their ability level and have provided each group with the same resources and services, and then we act puzzled—if not indignant—when we continue to get unequal results. A child who has not learned to read by the fourth grade requires massive effort to help him catch up. We need to apply the best of the newest methods we know to make him learn, yet we don't know too much about what those methods are. In the few instances when we do know, very often nothing is done to apply them. For instance, 50 per cent of the local educational authorities still use basal readers in their remedial reading programs. I do not share the optimism of teachers who failed to teach deprived children how to read English—yet believe that they can succeed with the same method simply by putting the children into smaller groups and drilling them just a share harder. Different approaches—be they phonic or linguistic—are probably more appropriate for remediation than the basal reading approach. Yet we use them far too seldom.[8]

Jerome S. Bruner voices the opinion of many students of the problem of poverty when he states:

> The issue is certainly not cultural deprivation, to be handled with a massive dose of compensatory enrichment.
> Rather the issue is to make it possible for the poor to gain a sense of their own power through jobs, through community activation, through creating a sense of projection into the future.[9]

However, no matter what overall changes need to be made in our socio-economic structure to help the underprivileged, we teachers cannot wait for those changes to be made. We need, without delaying our attack on the existing problem, to look to reading instruction as one of the avenues toward helping the underprivileged attain desired mobility in our society. With the mingled failure and success of various programs for helping the underprivileged in learning to read and in other areas, the challenge to teachers remains, greater than ever.

THE ROLE OF THE SCHOOL

No matter how many agencies assist in the program of providing for equalizing opportunities for the underprivileged or the handicapped, the final

---

[8] Joseph Froomkin, *Washington Monitor*, Supplement to *Education U.S.A.*, March 18, 1968.
[9] Jerome S. Bruner, "Poverty and Childhood," in *The Conditions of Educational Equality* published by the Committee for Economic Development (477 Madison Ave., New York, N.Y. 10022, 1971), Supplementary Paper Number 34, Sterling M. McMurrin, ed., pp. 34–65.

responsibility for teaching reading lies with the school. It is a responsibility that the school cannot escape, though it welcomes help from the outside. In this final section of this chapter these topics relevant to the role of the school are discussed: (1.) the project *Focus on Fundamentals*, (2.) guidelines for the teacher, (3.) instructional procedures, (4.) beginning reading instruction for children from non-English-speaking homes, (5.) materials of instruction, and (6.) volunteer workers.

Focus on Fundamentals

Many cities have been waging intensive "warfare" on backwardness in reading. The program entitled *Focus on Fundamentals*, sponsored by the New York City Schools, is reported on here because of its similarity in many respects to ventures in other places.

In 1967 it was found that in the schools of New York City pupils were continuing to lose ground in reading despite efforts to remedy the situation. The gaps between achievement and the national norms showed up in the second grade, the lowest level tested, and became more pronounced, as would be expected, in the upper grades. By the time the boys and girls were in the seventh or eighth grades, those in predominantly Black and Puerto Rican neighborhoods were generally one or more years behind the average for the city school system.

In the fall of 1967 the New York City schools launched a massive program called *Focus on Fundamentals*. It was begun in early childhood classes in 267 poverty areas. The program from the outset provided for smaller classes, more books and other supplies, parental involvement, and a diagnostic program for second graders in many districts. A year later, as reported in the *New York Times* of November 3, 1967, although in all grades of the elementary school the averages for reading were still below national norms, progress had been made. In 1968, as before the launching of the *Focus on Fundamentals* program, areas populated primarily by Blacks and Puerto Ricans continued to show the most serious deficiencies.

Guidelines for the Teacher

Below are points for the teacher to keep in mind when planning and putting into practice a program for working with the culturally different child.

1. Seek to understand the child.
2. Consider the child's assets, not only his deficits.
3. Guard against an attitude of expecting but little from the culturally different.
4. Start where the child is and build on what he knows.

5. Be more interested in the learner than in what he is learning; in other words, be more interested in the whole child than in his achievement in reading.

6. Help the child realize that to be different does not mean to be inferior.

7. Zealously guard the right of the child to love his home, no matter how culturally deprived or how different it may be.

8. Read widely about work with underprivileged children.

Instructional Procedures

Research on methods of teaching reading to the disadvantaged has not been lacking. For example, Harris and Serwer[10] conducted a study (known as CRAFT) comparing the effectiveness of two language-experience approaches and two skills-centered approaches. The four methods compared were: (1.) the language-experience approach based on the oral language of the children, (2.) the language-experience approach supplemented by extensive use of audiovisual materials, (3.) the skills approach using a basal textbook with close adherence to the suggestions in the teacher's manual, and (4.) the skills approach with the use of the Phonovisual Method of attacking words substituted for the word attack procedures recommended in the teacher's manual of the basal reader. The researchers found that, with the children in the experiment, the third method produced the best results.

Harris and Morrison[11] tested the same four methods in a three-year study of the CRAFT Project (Comparing Reading Approaches in First-Grade Teaching). The following were the conclusions reached, pertaining to the relative effectiveness of approaches used.

> The main finding was that the difference in the class mean in reading scores within the method was greater than the difference between the means for the approaches and methods. This leads us to conclude that there is no significant difference between the Skills-centered Approach and the Language-experience Approach.
>
> The two skills-centered methods showed slightly higher but this was reversed at the end of the third grade.
>
> The difference between first and second methods in both skills and language-experience approaches was not significant.
>
> In the first CRAFT year the basal, language-experience and audio-

[10] Harris, Albert J., and Blanche L. Serwer, "Comparing Reading Approaches in First Grade Teaching with Disadvantaged Children," *The Reading Teacher*, vol. 19, no. 8 (May 1966), pp. 631–635.

[11] Harris, Albert J., and Coleman Morrison, "The CRAFT Project: Final Report on Teaching Reading to Disadvantaged Urban Negro Children," *IRA Convention Proceedings* (Newark, Del.: International Reading Association, 1968).

visual showed good results. The Phonovisual method took too much class time.

The girls favored over the boys through third grade, mostly in the language-experience and Phonovisual approaches.

Variables like pupil age, teacher age and experience, etc. did not seem to affect the results.

Pupil attitude toward reading was the same in all four methods.

Positive discipline was more successful in the Language-Experience approach than in the Skills approach.

The replication study added a combined Phonovisual phonics with the Language-experience Audiovisual methods. The teachers did no better than with each method used alone.

A study dealing with reading instruction of the child from a non-English-speaking home is that by Roy McCanne[12] who compared the effectiveness of these three methods in beginning reading instruction for children in Colorado from Spanish-speaking homes: (1.) the conventional readiness and basal reader approach, (2.) a modified Teaching English as a Second Language approach, and (3.) a language-experience approach. The first of these methods showed up as superior to the others provided the children were ready to learn to read when reading instruction was begun. However, McCanne points out that the seeming superiority of that method might be due to lack of experience on the part of the teachers with the other two methods.

So far no one method of teaching reading to the disadvantaged has been established as unquestionably more effective than all or any others. The most reliable generalization based on the findings of various types of research is that an eclectic approach to the problem of guiding growth toward maturity in reading is more desirable than any one single method. What combination of methods is the most felicitous for each child, the teacher will need to conclude on the basis of his professional knowledge. Here are a few suggestions that may be of value to the teacher in deciding on methods of procedure:

1. The child whose dialect differs greatly from what is considered standard speech in a given area should be helped in his language development before he is confronted with the task of learning to read. Meaningful so-called reading-readiness activities that extend his background of experience, that help increase his auditory perception and discrimination, that increase his power over language should be richly provided. However, reading should not be postponed for a child until he has be-

[12] Roy McCanne, "Approaches to First Grade English Reading Instruction for Children from Spanish-Speaking Homes," *The Reading Teacher*, vol. 19, no. 8 (May 1966), pp. 670–675.

come proficient in the use of the so-called *standard* American dialect, for one way in which he can acquire facility in the use of oral language is through reading. Furthermore, to deprive a child of the experience of learning to read for an indefinite number of months or even a year or longer is a highly questionable procedure.

2. Since it is difficult for a child to change his divergent dialect at the same time that he is beginning to learn to read, the teacher should allow him, when reading orally, to read in his dialect the material written in standard English. Later when the learning-to-read process is well underway, he can acquire, at his learning pace, the "second language"—standard English.

3. If pupils have difficulty in understanding the English the teacher uses, it is advisable for the teacher to familiarize himself with some of the expressions of the children's dialect so that he can understand them better and so that he can interpret words and other meanings to them. Fortunately children (and teachers, too) have much less difficulty in understanding a divergent dialect than in speaking it. Knowledge by the pupil that the teacher knows some of the characteristic vocabulary of the child's culture and respects it may also serve as ego-inflating to the child.

4. Relatively wide reading, rather than initial intensive concentration on the development of word-attack skills, not only seems to bring better results in the skills of reading but also to encourage reading for enjoyment.

5. It may be of value, at times, to have children with similar dialects help one another with phonics and other word recognition skills.

6. Since disadvantaged children are often more accelerated in motor than in intellectual development, opportunities to dramatize stories, put on puppet plays, and give simulations of TV programs may encourage reading.

Beginning Reading Instruction for Children from Non-English-Speaking Homes

The child from an underprivileged home who cannot speak English when he enters school has a problem with which educators have found it most difficult to cope. In addition to the disadvantages of the boy or girl from an underprivileged home where English is spoken, he comes to school ignorant even of the language used exclusively in most schools as a means of communication. Then, when he is expected to learn to read in a language he cannot even speak, he is often confronted with a task beyond his power to handle effectively. The problems of the non-English-speaking child from a cultured home are not nearly as acute as those of the one from an underprivileged home who does not know English. But, he, too, needs special attention.

Commonly accepted in the past by teachers has been the theory that the most effective procedure for teaching the child from a non-English-speaking home is to provide him with a rather wide background of oral English before beginning reading instruction. But results when following that plan have been so far from efficacious that educators are searching for better ways. Some schools are experimenting by having the child learn to read in his own language before he receives instruction in reading English. During the period that he is learning to read in his first language, the medium of instruction for most class hours, other than the reading period, is usually English. In the San Antonio (Texas) Language-Bilingual Research Project[13,14] experimentation has gone on to ascertain the effect, on Mexican-American beginners at school, of different language approaches (involving Spanish and English), on reading and on other abilities. Improvement in some nonreading abilities (including oral language) was greater with one or more of the experimental groups than with the control group, which was taught according to the usual program of instruction of the San Antonio public schools. However, the pupils in the control group showed up as well in the learning-to-read process as did the boys and girls in the experimental groups.

In spite of various experimental programs, to date no convincing answer has been found to the question as to how reading can best be taught to the large numbers of children from non-English-speaking homes. With the unprecedented interest in our time in that problem, hopefully greater insight into procedures to be followed will be gained in the foreseeable future.

Materials of Instruction

Earlier in this chapter (*see* page 464) we referred to the controversy as to whether the divergence in the vocabulary of the disadvantaged from that used in most beginning reading books is in part the cause for the high incidence of failure in reading found among the underprivileged. Though there is lack of agreement on this point, there is a consensus of opinion that the inner-city child, like the child of all other economic and cultural levels, when beginning to learn to read, should be given material based on his background of understanding. It is also generally conceded that the content of most reading books fails to meet this criterion for the disadvantaged child. Usually the life style portrayed in the readers is not that with which the underprivileged child is familiar. The difference may make him resentful

[13] Joe L. Frost, "Developing Literacy in Disadvantaged Children," *Issues and Innovations in the Teaching of Reading*, Joe L. Frost, ed. (Chicago: Scott, Foresman and Company, 1967), pp. 264–275.
[14] Richard L. Venezky, "Nonstandard Language and Reading," *Elementary English*, vol. 47, no. 3 (March 1970), pp. 334–345.

that he is shut out of the happy world frequently pictured as representative of the family life of the boys and girls filling the pages of such books. At best he may feel he is reading about a life totally alien to him, possibly one about which he does not even care to read because of its remoteness from reality, as far as he is concerned.

The question of what phase of life familiar to the disadvantaged child should be a part of the material of the basal reader is still largely a matter of conjecture. A start toward a possible solution of the problem was made by Robert Emans,[15] who investigated the preference of boys and girls before they had begun to learn to read. The children in his study showed a decided preference for those stories from a multi-ethnic reader, which were read to then individually, that deal with a city-life theme over those that focused on a family-friends-pet theme.

Another question in urgent need of investigation is "How long after the learner has passed the stage of initial reading instruction should the content of reading textbooks be chiefly confined to subjects dealing with an environment familiar to the child?" A study, also based on pupil interest, by Jerry L. Johns[16] indicated the preferences of the inner-city child in the intermediate grades. The boys and girls in this investigation preferred stories depicting middle-class settings to those showing life in the inner city. While, to be sure, interests of boys and girls should not constitute the sole criterion for decisions on content of readers, they should be given serious consideration. From a sociological point of view the desirability of expanding horizons for children on all levels of society, beyond those circumscribed by their own culture, can be used as a strong argument for not limiting the content of readers throughout the elementary school primarily to the background into which boys and girls are born.

Teachers and publishers have reacted constructively to the criticisms of the content of reading textbooks for the disadvantaged child. The Detroit Public Schools in their City Schools Reading Series paved the way for other schools. Josephine Benson[17] described the books on the preprimer level in these words:

> The books show children of multi-racial groups in urban settings to give the children an opportunity to identify themselves with characters that are familiar. The environment shown in these books is not that of the tenement or housing development type, but is one to which culturally different children might reasonably aspire. . . . The vocabulary was carefully chosen to meet the needs of these children and much repetition of words

15 Robei. .ans, "What Do Children in the Inner City Like to Read?", *Elementary School Journal*, vol. 69 (October 1968), pp. 119–122.

16 Jerry L. Johns, "What Do Inner City Children Prefer to Read?", *The Reading Teacher*, vol. 26, no. 5 (February 1973), pp. 462–467.

17 Josephine Benson, "Teaching Reading to the Culturally Different Child," *Readings on Reading*, no. 25, Alfred R. Biner, John J. Diabal, Jr., and Leonard K. Kise, eds. (Scranton, Pa.: Intext Educational Publishers, 1969), pp. 259–269.

has been provided. An evaluation of the first three pre-primers showed the City Schools Series to be significantly more effective in stimulating interest in reading and word recognition than the regular basal series.

Various other cities have been producing reading programs designed for the disadvantaged. For example, the St. Louis schools have prepared the *Skyline Series* (published by McGraw-Hill Book Company) and San Francisco has developed the *Chandler Language-Experience Readers* (published by the Chandler Publishing Company).

The Bank Street Readers, produced by staff members of the Bank Street College and published by the Macmillan Company, were also developed to give underprivileged boys and girls an easier chance to learn to read than by using the regular school readers as basal readers. These books emphasize life in the big cities, on various economic levels. They are recommended not only for the underprivileged. The publishers suggest that they would also be valuable as readers for all children, probably to supplement other readers, so that those who are privileged can better understand those who are not. Similarly, it has also been recommended that underprivileged children read the regular readers as supplementary to the Bank Street series. These recommendations seem to be in the right direction.

Rather recently, in increasing numbers, the multi-ethnic and multi-cultural reader has been appearing on the market. The selections in these readers deal with life situations typical of those in which boys and girls of various cultures and races living in our country find themselves. The pictorial illustrations give a sympathetic portrayal of the characters and the ways of living described in the text. These readers are designed for children of all socioeconomic and racial levels portraying rural and urban life, in the hope that the boys and girls reading these books will not only develop a better understanding of themselves and their own way of life but also of boys and girls unlike themselves in background.

Volunteer Workers

The key person in an educational program for helping the disadvantaged child undoubtedly is the classroom teacher. However, with the shortage of funds available in many school districts, it has been necessary for many to look beyond the classroom to find people to work with underprivileged boys and girls. In large urban centers it has frequently been customary to depend on volunteers for the full implementation of a program. The possibility of using them much more extensively than is currently the practice in smaller communities warrants exploration. Many agencies in communities of varying populations have turned to volunteers to supplement teaching of underprivileged boys and girls and have found in them an excellent source of help.

The goals of tutoring programs and after-school study centers are many.

Volunteer workers seek to uncover new interests in underachieving young-sters, to establish meaningful relations with them out of which new at-titudes and stronger motives for learning can emerge, and to help them master basic academic skills. The volunteer workers have worked hard and with considerable success to attain these goals. Probably one reason why tutoring projects, manned chiefly by volunteers, achieve the success they have is that they bring to the program the power that frequently charac-terizes what Eunice Newton refers to as "grass-root" movements of inter-ested citizens.

We have taken the first steps on the long road ahead leading to effec-tive reading programs for the culturally different child. May nothing deter us in realizing our dream of equal opportunity for all boys and girls in learning to read up to the level of their capabilities!

For Further Study

Bereiter, Carl, and Siegfried Englemann, *Teaching Disadvantaged Children in the Pre-School* (Englewood Cliffs, N.J.: Prentice-Hall, Inc., 1966).

Binter, Alfred R. and John J. Diabal, Jr. and Leonard K. Kise, eds., *Read-ings on Reading* (Scranton, Pa: Intext Educational Publishers, 1969), Part V, "Reading for the Culturally Deprived," containing articles by Kenneth S. Goodman, Mildren B. Smith, and Josephine T. Benson.

Bloom, Benjamin S., *Compensatory Education for Cultural Deprivation* (New York: Holt, Rinehart and Winston, Inc., 1965).

Braun, Carl, "Johnny Reads the Cues: Teacher Expectation," *The Reading Teacher*, vol. 26, no. 7 (April 1973), pp. 704–712.

Charnofsky, Stanley, *Educating the Powerless* (Belmont, Cal.: Wadsworth Publishing Company, 1971).

Cohen, S. Alan, *Teach Them All to Read: Theory, Methods and Materials for Teaching the Disadvantaged* (New York: Random House, Inc. 1969).

Cohen, S. Alan, and Gita S. Kornfeld, "Oral Vocabulary and Beginning Reading in Disadvantaged Black Children," *The Reading Teacher*, vol. 24 (October 1970) pp. 33–38.

Emans, Robert, "What Do Children in the Inner City Like to Read?", *Ele-mentary School Journal*, vol. 69 (October 1968), pp. 119–122.

Figurel, J. Allen, ed., *Better Reading in Urban Schools*, Annual Conference Volume (Newark, Del.: International Reading Association, 1971).

Figurel, J. Allen, ed., *Reading Goals for the Disadvantaged* (Newark, Del.: International Reading Association, 1970), "Some Reservations on the Significance of Dialect in the Acquisition of Reading" by Rose-Marie Weber (pp. 124–131); and "Problems in Teaching Reading to Bilingual Children" by Ethel L. Clapp (pp. 249–261).

Frost, Joe L., ed., *Issues and Innovations in the Teaching of Reading* (Chicago: Scott, Foresman and Company, 1967), "Developing Literacy in Disadvantaged Children," by Joe L. Frost, pp. 262–273.

Hall, Mary Anne, *Language Experience Approach for the Culturally Disadvantaged*, Reading Information Series: Where Do We Go from Here? (Newark, Del.: International Reading Association, 1972).

Harris, Albert J., and Coleman Morrison, "The CRAFT Project: Final Report on Teaching Reading to Disadvantaged Urban Negro Children," *IRA Convention Proceedings, Research Session* (Newark, Del.: International Reading Association, 1968).

Harris, Albert J., and Blanche L. Serwer, "Comparing Reading Approaches in First Grade Teaching with Disadvantaged Children," *The Reading Teacher*, vol. 19, no. 8 (May 1966), pp. 631–635.

Horn, Thomas D., ed., *Reading for the Disadvantaged: Problems of Linguistically Different Learners* (Newark, Del.: International Reading Association, 1970).

Jenkins, Esther, C., "Multi-Ethnic Literature: Promise and Problems," *Elementary English*, vol. 50, no. 5 (May 1973), pp. 694–699.

Johnson, Kenneth R., and Herbert D. Simons, "Black Children and Reading," *The Education Digest*, vol. 37, no. 7 (March 1972), pp. 41–44.

Johnson, Kenneth R., and Herbert D. Simons, "Black Children and Reading: What Teachers Need to Know," *Phi Delta Kappan* (January 1971), 288–290.

Koblitz, Minnie, *The Negro in School Literature: Resource Materials for the Teacher of Kindergarten through the Sixth Grade: A Bibliography* (New York: Center for Urban Education, 1968).

Kvaraceus, William C., *Poverty, Education and Race Relations* (Boston: Allyn and Bacon, Inc., 1967).

McCullough, Constance M., *Preparation of Textbooks in the Mother Tongue* (Newark, Del.: International Reading Association, 1968).

Noar, Gertrude, *Teaching the Disadvantaged: What Research Says to the Teacher* (Washington, D.C.: National Education Association, 1967).

Packer, Athol B., "Ashton-Warner's Key Vocabulary for the Disadvantaged," *The Reading Teacher*, vol. 23 (March 1970), pp. 559–564.

Payne, Joseph T., "Race, Reading and Poverty in Los Angeles, " *Integrated Education*, vol. 9 (November 1971), pp. 15–21.

Rauch, Sidney J., compiler, *Handbook for the Volunteer Tutor* (Newark, Del.: International Reading Association, 1969).

Shuy, Roger W., ed., *Teaching Black Children to Read*, (Washington, D.C., Center for Applied Linguistics, 1969), "Teaching Reading in an Urban Negro School System" by John C. Baratz, pp. 92–114.

Spache, George D., *Good Reading for the Disadvantaged Reader: Multi-Ethnic Resources* (Champaign, Ill.: The Garrard Publishing Company, 1970).

Strickland, Stephen P., "Can Slum Children Learn?", *American Education,* (July 1971), pp. 3–7.

Walberg, Herbert J., and Andrew T. Kopan, eds., *Rethinking Urban Education: A Sourcebook of Contemporary Issues* (San Francisco, 615 Montgomery Street: Jossey Bass, Publishers, 1972).

Wienewski, Richard, ed., *Teaching about Life in the City,* Forty-Second Yearbook of the National Council for the Social Studies (Washington, D.C.: National Council for the Social Studies, 1972).

Zintz, Miles V., *The Reading Process: The Teacher and the Learner* (Dubuque, Iowa: Wm. C. Brown, 1970), Ch. 15, "Teaching Reading to the Children of the Inner City Poor."

Zuck, Louis, and Yetta Goodman, compilers, *Social Class and Regional Districts: Their Relation to Reading* (Newark, Del.: International Reading Association, 1971).

Questions and Comments for Thought and Discussion

1. Of the following terms which do you think are among the least objectionable: *culturally different, culturally disadvantaged, culturally deprived, economically disadvantaged?* Can you suggest better terms?

2. Even if you become a teacher in a suburban community you may well find that you have one or more children in your room who are culturally different from the others. What plans could you make to help them learn to read if you are a first-grade teacher? If you are teaching in the later years of the elementary school?

3. Have you observed teachers who have a healthy attitude toward the disadvantaged child? If so, what were some of the characteristics they possessed and techniques they used?

4. What implications for teaching reading to the disadvantaged do you find in Chapter 3, "Language Development and Reading"?

5. Sometimes people apply the term *disadvantaged* to boys and girls from non-English speaking homes even though the cultural level of the home shows no deprivation. It has been pointed out that such boys and girls do not belong to the group called *disadvantaged* any more than you should be labeled as a *disadvantaged* person if you were going to school in a country in which you did not know well the language spoken in the school. You would be at a *disadvantage,* but you should hardly be called a *disadvantaged* individual. What difference do you see between the two terms?

6. What advantages and/or disadvantages do you anticipate in a reading program that calls for volunteer help in achieving its objective?

Outline for Chapter 15

APPROACHES TO READING INSTRUCTION

Studies on Approaches to Reading Instruction
    Durrell's Studies on First-grade Reading
    Studies Sponsored by the U.S. Office of Education
    Learning to Read: The Great Debate
Description of Approaches
    The Initial Teaching Alphabet
    Words-in-Color
    Diacritical Marking System (DMS)
    Individualized Reading: Seeking, Self-Selection, and
        Pacing
    "Individually Prescribed Instruction" (IPI)
    Linguistic Approaches to Reading Instruction
    The Montessori Method

15
CHAPTER

Approaches to Reading Instruction

One of the problems confronting teachers of reading in the elementary school deals with the approach to reading instruction—the organizational pattern in which reading is taught. On this question decision needs to be reached not only for beginning reading but also for later stages in the learning-to-read process. It should be noted, however, that much of the literature on approaches to reading deals with the approach to initial reading instruction.

We have already discussed some of the approaches in preceding chapters. On others we have deferred systematic discussion so that the reader will have knowledge of topics, as background for understanding, summarized in previous pages of this book.

Though claims of proponents of some approaches to reading instruction are to the contrary, no system has been unequivocally established by research to be the most propitious one. Furthermore, it is doubtful that research will ever be able to give an unqualified endorsement to any approach, as the best method, that is now in use or that may be employed at any time in the future. What constitutes the "best approach" will vary from teacher to teacher and from learner to learner. There are many persons in the field of the teaching of reading who advocate an "eclectic" approach, one that combines features of two or more approaches. Even in such a combined approach undoubtedly the combination of features, for best results, also varies from one teaching-learning situation to another because of differences among teachers and among pupils.

STUDIES ON APPROACHES TO READING INSTRUCTION

Although an exceedingly large amount of research has been done in the reading field, with much of it dealing with approaches to reading instruction, most of these studies have been rather piecemeal. The studies have typically been isolated ones made by individuals working independently without the financial backing for authoritative investigations in the field. Three of the studies among those that are an exception to this rule, are here discussed, namely: (1.) Durrell's studies on first-grade reading; (2.) the Cooperative Research Program on First-grade Reading Instruction, sponsored by the U.S. Office of Education; and (3.) the study of Jeanne Chall reported in the book *Learning to Read: The Great Debate.*[1] All three of these studies pertain to approaches to beginning reading instruction, with emphasis on the question of whether in beginning reading a code or meaning approach or a combination of the two should be used.

Durrell's Studies on First-grade Reading

One series of significant investigations of reading on the first-grade level was made by Donald D. Durell and his associates. The instructional program for the more than 2,000 first-grade children involved in the studies under Durrell's direction was aimed at three objectives: to assure reading success among first-grade children, to evaluate reading readiness practices and concepts, and to study relations among the various aspects of growth in reading. Durrell stated:

> Clinical services have indicated that reading failures at first-grade level were usually overcome when the following abilities were established through effective teaching: knowledge of letter names, ability to identify sounds in spoken words, knowledge of applied phonics. Additional services commonly needed were meaningful word recognition practice and special help in beginning silent reading. It appeared that if these needs were identified and served in initial classroom instruction, much reading difficulty might be prevented. In addition, it was hoped that rapid learners might make higher achievement if unnecessary instruction were eliminated from the reading program.[2]

---

[1] Jeanne S. Chall, *Learning to Read: The Great Debate* (New York McGraw-Hill Book Company, 1967).
[2] Donald D. Durrell, "First-grade Reading Success Study: A Summary," *Journal of Education* (February 1958), p. 2.

Ninety-one teachers in four communities and 2,300 first-grade pupils were involved in the study. Tests measured several levels of letter knowledge, the ability to identify separate sounds in spoken words, visual discrimination of words, learning rate in word recognition, and a group measure of intelligence. The following program — tested in September, November, February, and June — is described by Durrell thus:

1. Children high in learning rate, in letter names, and in hearing sounds in words were grouped together. For them, reading instruction was started at once; both word recognition and applied phonics were presented immediately. The reading readiness program of the basal reading system was skipped.

2. Children lower in learning rate and with gaps in letter and sounds-in-words knowledge were grouped together. Although some sight vocabulary was taught, the main emphasis was upon systematic instruction in letter names and on the ability to indentify sounds in words. This was followed later by instruction in applied phonics.

3. Children who were low in learning rate and in letter and sounds-in-words knowledge were grouped together. These, too, started some sight vocabulary learning, but the major emphasis was on letter names and identifying separate sounds in spoken words.[3]

Help with word recognition in the stories in the basal readers was provided from the beginning, but at a slower pace for the slower learners. Systematic review of sight vocabulary emphasized response to word meaning rather than to the name of the word; special practice in silent reading was given through the use of sentence cards.

Some of the major findings and their implications, according to Durrell, follow:

1. Most reading difficulties can be prevented by an instructional program which provides early instruction in letter names and sounds, followed by applied phonics and accompanied by suitable practice in meaningful sight vocabulary and aids to attentive silent reading. Among the 1,500 children measured in June, only 18 had a sight vocabulary of less than 50 words; this is slightly more than 1 percent of the population. Four percent, or 62 children, had a sight vocabulary of less than 100 words.

2. Early instruction in letter names and sounds produces a higher June reading achievement level than does such instruction given incidentally during the year.

3. Children with high learning rates and superior background skills make greater progress when conventional reading readiness materials are omitted from their reading programs.

4. Children entering first grade present wide differences in levels of letter knowledge:

[3] Durrell, *ibid.*, pp. 5–6.

a. All children were able to match capital letters as well as lower-case letters. Exercises in this ability should be omitted from reading readiness materials. It appears to follow that matching of nonword forms and pictures as preliminary instruction for letter and word perception is relatively useless.

b. The average child in this population could, in September, give the names of 12 capital letters and 9 lower-case letters; identify 17 capitals named and 12 lower-case letters named; write 10 letters from dictation.

5. Tests of knowledge of letter names at school entrance are the best predictors of February and June reading achievement.

6. Chronological age shows little relationship to any of the factors measured at any testing period. It correlates negatively with reading achievement. Apparently no solution to reading difficulties is to be found by raising the entrance age to first grade.

7. Mental age, as measured by the Otis Quick-scoring Tests of Mental Ability, has a low relationship to reading achievement and to letter and word perception skills.

8. There appears to be no basis for the assumption that a sight vocabulary of 75 words should be taught before word analysis skills are presented. Of the 1,170 children tested in February, only 9 achieved a sight vocabulary of more than 70 words when they knew fewer than 20 letters. Of the children who knew more than 20 letters, 675 had a sight vocabulary of more than 70 words. While a knowledge of letter names and sounds does not assure success in acquiring a sight vocabulary, lack of that knowledge produces failure.[4]

Studies Sponsored by the U.S. Office of Education

Final Report Project No. X-001[5] on The Cooperative Research Program in First-Grade Reading Instruction, is the summary of the findings, with recommendations, of what is commonly known as the *First-grade Reading Studies,* sponsored by the Office of Education, U.S. Department of Health, Education and Welfare. It is a coordinated study utilizing the findings of 27 projects supported by the government, with the understanding on the part of the directors of the projects that the studies would constitute an integral part of the Cooperative Research Program with Guy L. Bond as coordinator.

The 27 studies, conducted during the 1964-1965 school year, were made in different localities and represented a desirable geographic distribution. They were, in effect, 27 independent studies so well coordinated in research

---

[4] Durrell, *ibid.*, pp. 5–6.
[5] Guy L. Bond and Robert Dykstra, *Final Report, Project No. X-001* (Washington, D.C.: Bureau of Research, Office of Education, U.S. Department of Health, Education and Welfare, 1967).

design, instruments of measurement, information gathered, and comparability of data collected that comparisons among the studies, which involved nearly 30,000 children and 1,000 teachers, were possible in ways that had not previously existed. The major questions that the program staff investigated were:

> To what extent are various pupil, teacher, class, school, and community characteristics related to pupil achievement in first-grade reading and spelling?
>
> Which of the many approaches to initial reading instruction produces superior reading and spelling achievement at the end of the first grade?
>
> Is any program uniquely effective or ineffective for pupils with high or low readiness for reading?[6]

A wide variety of teaching approaches were investigated in the studies. Included among these were basal reader, language experience, phonic emphasis, linguistic emphasis, new alphabet, early letter, individualized reading, reading readiness, audiovisual, teacher supervisor, and approaches that for want of a better term were grouped under the heading of approaches for culturally different pupils.

Basic conclusions from the *Final Report* relevant to the question of whether the initial approach in reading instruction should be a code-deciphering process, in which letters of the alphabet are matched by the learner with the sounds they represent, are indicated in the following quotations from that report:

> From the evidence reported concerning the use of phonics in teaching children to read earlier there can be little doubt that phonics should be an important part of the reading program. However, there is disagreement on the type of phonic approach which should be used and on the amount of phonics which should be included in the reading program. It seems apparent, from the studies reviewed, that phonics does not contribute much to children's comprehension of what is read.
>
> Indications are that the initial reading vocabulary should be selected with a greater balance between phonetically regular words and high utility words. It is likely that introducing words solely on the basis of frequency of use presents an unusually complex decoding task for the beginning reader.
>
> Word study skills must be emphasized and taught systematically regardless of what approach to initial reading instruction is utilized.
>
> Combinations of programs, such as basal program with supplementary phonics materials, often are superior to single approaches.[7]

[6] Bond and Dykstra, *ibid.*, p. 41.
[7] Bond and Dykstra, *ibid.*, pp. 19, 212, 210, 210, respectively.

Reports of these studies appeared in *The Reading Teacher*.[8] The International Reading Association also placed on the market a publication entitled *First Grade Reading Programs*.[9]

The Office of Education[10] extended fourteen of the studies through the second and third grades, thus permitting for inter- and intracomparisons of studies. In the January 1969 issue of *The Reading Teacher* various investigators reported on their studies extended into third grade. The titles and main direction of a few of these included "Reading Achievement of First Grade Children Taught by a Linguistic Approach and a Basal Reader Approach—Extended into Third Grade" by J. Wesley Schneyer; "The CRAFT Project: A Final Report" (Comparing Reading Approaches in First-Grade Teaching with Disadvantaged Children) by Albert J. Harris and Coleman Morrison; "Comparison of Beginning Reading with i.t.a., DMS, and t.o. after Three Years" (initial teaching alphabet, Diacritical Marking System, and traditional orthography) by Edward Fry; and "A Three Year Look at i.t.a., Lippincott, Phonics and Word Power, and Scott, Foresman" by Robert B. Hayes and Richard C. Wuest.[11]

Speaking editorially, Russell Stauffer observed that "any attempt to compare method with method or study with study could easily produce misunderstandings and false conclusions. Each study must be examined on its own premises and results, and the reader must be careful that the conclusions he draws do not trespass on the premises and results.[12]

Later, commenting on the first-grade reading studies of the Office of Education, Stauffer pointed out:

> Regardless of the criterion used there is no one method and this is so in spite of the tragic consequences of the internal dynamism that some so-called methods have sought to advance—tragically, eccentrically, and captivatingly. Every method described used words, and phonics, and pictures, and comprehension, and teachers. True, they frequently use them differently, but they used them. There was no one phonics method that was pure or uncontaminated, if you wish, by other methods. There was no one linguistic method. ITA is not a method but a medium. Basic readers claim everything.
>
> And where does all this leave us? All the malingering that reading instruction has endured for the past decade has not led to the golden era. No approach has overcome individual differences or eliminated reading

[8] *The Reading Teacher*, vol. 19, no. 8 (May 1966); vol. 20, no. 1 (October 1966).

[9] James F. Kerfoot, ed., *First Grade Reading Programs*, Perspective in Reading Series, no. 5 (Newark, Del.: International Reading Association, 1965).

[10] Robert Dykstra, *Final Report Project No. 6-1651* (Washington, D.C.: Bureau of Research, Office of Education, U.S. Department of Health, Education and Welfare, 1967).

[11] *The Reading Teacher*, vol. 22, no. 4 (January 1969), pp. 315–319; 335–340; 357–362; 363–370, respectively.

[12] Russel G. Stauffer, "The Verdict: Speculative Controversy" (editorial), *The Reading Teacher*, vol. 19, no. 8 (May 1966), p. 564. Reprinted with the permission of the author and the International Reading Assocation.

disability. As I have said before, now that we have slashed around wildly in the mire of accusations let us remember that reading without comprehension is not reading. Let us focus our efforts on the eleven other years in school and make critical and creative reading our goal. Maturity in reading — that is the objective each child must seek and every teacher must help each child to attain. The thin crust we have punctured was just that and no more![13]

Learning to Read: The Great Debate

In the book *Learning to Read: The Great Debate,* Jeanne Chall reports on the results of her extensive investigation made under a grant from the Carnegie Foundation for the Advancement of Teaching. To gather data as bases for her report, the author (1.) read the literature in the field that deals with descriptions of various methods of beginning reading instruction and that reports on relevent research; (2.) visited classrooms in widely scattered areas in different types of school situations in this country and in England to acquire firsthand information as to how beginning reading instruction is being provided and to discuss methods with the teaching and/or supervisory staffs of the schools visited; (3.) studied books used as basal reading textbooks; and (4.) consulted with advocates of various methods of teaching beginning reading so as to obtain a clearer interpretation of each method.

Jeanne Chall's findings were revolutionary in that they are in rather direct opposition to many of the points of view about beginning reading instruction commonly held by specialists in the reading field. She throws a bombshell among those who believe that a code-deciphering approach, one in which the grapheme-phoneme relation is emphasized from the very beginning, is undesirable. In fact, the author even makes it seem rather professionally embarrassing that, according to her claims, her investigation indicates that Rudolph Flesch as well as the many laymen — often irate parents — urging a phonic approach to reading instruction are probably right, and that many professional writers on the teaching of reading are, for the most part, wrong in their premise that learning to read in the initial stage of reading instruction through a code approach is undesirable.

The following quotation from *Learning to Read: The Great Debate* gives Jeanne Chall's point of view:

> My review of the research from the laboratory, the classroom, and the clinic points to the need for a correction in beginning reading instructional methods. Most schoolchildren in the United States are taught to read by what I have termed a meaning-emphasis method. Yet the research from

---

[13] Russell G. Stauffer, "Some Tidy Generalizations" (editorial), *The Reading Teacher,* vol. 20, no. 1 (October 1966), p. 4. Reprinted with the permission of the author and the International Reading Association.

1912 to 1965 indicates that a code-emphasis method—i.e., one that views beginning reading as essentially different from mature reading and emphasizes learning of the printed code for the spoken language—produces better results, at least up to the point where sufficient evidence seems to be available, the end of the third grade.

The results are better, not only in terms of the mechanical aspects of literacy alone, as was once supposed, but also in terms of the ultimate goals of reading instruction—comprehension and possibly even speed of reading. The long-existing fear that an intial code emphasis produces readers who do not read for meaning or with enjoyment is unfounded. On the contrary, the evidence indicates that better results in terms of reading for meaning are achieved with the programs that emphasize code at the start than with the programs that stress meaning at the beginning.[14]

In spite of the author's strong statements, such as the above, setting forth the alleged superiority of a code approach over a meaning approach, she tempers her report by such statements as the following:

> My recommendation for a methods change does not apply to all pupils. Some pupils may have a unique or uncommon way of learning. Insisting on one method for all may complicate things further.
>
> My recommendation for a change in beginning reading methods does not apply to school systems that have been getting excellent results with their present methods and materials that the teachers use with confidence. Many factors may make existing methods and materials better suited to these schools than new ones. What is effective for a class of thirty-five may be too slow-moving for a class of ten or fifteen. The functional type of learning that leaves the programming pretty much up to the individual pupil may work perfectly for a small class of able children with a creative teacher who already knows what to teach and when. Imposing a set, systematic program on a teacher who is knowledgeable about reading and keenly attuned to the strengths and weaknesses of her pupils may very well destroy the beauty of what she has already achieved.
>
> A beginning code-emphasis program will *not* cure all reading ills. It cannot guarantee that *all* children will learn to read easily. Nor have the results of meaning-emphasis programs been so disastrous that all academic and emotional failures can be blamed on them, as some proponents and publishers of new code-emphasis programs claim. But the evidence does show that a changeover to code-emphasis programs for the beginner can improve the situation somewhat, and in this all too imperfect world even a small improvement is worth working for. I believe that method changes, if made in the right spirit, will lead to improved reading standards.[15]

[14] Jeanne S. Chall, *Learning to Read: The Great Debate* (New York: McGraw-Hill Book Company, 1967), p. 307.
[15] Chall, *ibid.*, p. 309.

To be sure, Jeanne Chall has not been without critics. However, her study has had a great impact on the teaching of reading in that many enthusiasts for the code approach cite her research as justification for that approach.

DESCRIPTION OF APPROACHES

As is to be expected in an era in which there is sharp controversy as to how reading can be taught most effectively, various programs, some new, have been advocated for teaching reading. In some of the programs the aim is to decrease the difficulties involved in learning to read by providing a code with a single symbol-sound relation. In others the problem of word recognition has been attacked by means other than an attempt to provide an invariable grapheme-phoneme equivalence.

Some of the approaches discussed in this book are currently enjoying popularity, while others are decreasing in popularity. It is hoped that an understanding of all here described will give the reader increased perspective on possible approaches to reading instruction even though he may not be using some of them in his own teaching. Approaches discussed elsewhere in this book under "Structure of the Reading Program" and under "Instructional Materials, Equipment and Special Facilities" as well as in other parts are: (1.) the language-experience approach (*see* page 425), (2.) programed instruction (*see* page 95), (3.) automated reading (*see* page 428), and (4.) the basal reading textbook approach (*see* page 521). In the remainder of this chapter attention is given to the following: (1.) the Initial Teaching Alphabet (i/t/a), (2.) the Words-in-color approach, (3.) the Diacritical Marking System (DMS), (4.) Individualized Reading (Seeking, Self-selection, and Pacing), (5.) Individualized Prescribed Instruction (IPI), (6.) the linguistic approach, and (7.) the Montessori method.

The number of approaches discussed in this book is necessarily greatly limited. For a discussion of other approaches the reader is referred to these books: *Approaches to Beginning Reading* by Robert C. Aukerman (John Wiley & Sons, Inc., 1971), and *A Decade of Innovations: Approaches to Beginning Reading* Elaine C. Vilscek, ed. (International Reading Association, Newark, Del., 1968), in vol. 12, Part 3, Proceedings of the Twelfth Annual Convention.

As indicated earlier (*see* page 481), the advocates of some of the programs have perhaps reported on them with undue enthusiasm. It is well, therefore, in making evaluations to keep in mind the following statements by Robert Dykstra:

> . . .the superiority of a single method of reading instruction is yet to be determined. It appears that a composite of methods would produce the

best results and that an effort should be made to determine what each method would contribute to the reading program.[16]

The Initial Teaching Alphabet

The Initial Teaching Alphabet, commonly referred to as *i/t/a*, came into prominence in England in 1961. It was introduced into this country by John Downing from England in 1963. Advocates of *i/t/a* propose to simplify the process of learning to read by circumventing a serious difficulty of written English, namely, that some letters or combinations of letters represent more than one sound and that some sounds are symbolized by more than one letter or combination of letters. I/t/a provides a forty-four letter alphabet in which each character allegedly represents only one sound and in which each sound is represented by only one character.

Of the forty-four-letter alphabet of i/t/a, twenty-four letters are found in the alphabet commonly used in writing English, which is referred to as traditional orthography. The remaining characters are either combinations of letters in the traditional alphabet or new symbols.

Proponents of i/t/a stress that they do not consider the system a method of teaching but a way of writing and therefore a means of reading. They claim that with this alphabet a code or a meaning approach can be used. However, it would seem that if a code approach is not used, there would be little if any reason for having a variation from the traditional orthography. After all, the advantage claimed by adherents of any symbol-sound equivalence system is that such a system provides a simplified code with a consistent grapheme-phoneme relation.

It should be noted that leaders of i/t/a advocate the use of their alphabet only for beginning reading. They suggest that as soon as the child has considerable proficiency in reading materials written in i/t/a he should begin making the transition to material in traditional orthography. The time when this stage of readiness occurs varies, it is claimed. Some children may be ready to make the transition fairly early in the first grade while others may not reach that point until varying times during the second and third grades.

Boys and girls using i/t/a are early encouraged to write in that orthography. Reputably they write more prolifically than their peers who from the beginning use the traditional orthography. In fact, early proficiency in creative writing is one of the chief reasons given by some advocates of i/t/a for use of that alphabet. However, since the child using i/t/a writes words as they sound, when recording his thoughts in i/t/a, though this practice may lead to greater ease in writing while that alphabet is being used, when the transition is made to traditional orthography the child has not learned how to spell correctly the English words which have

[16] Dykstra, *Final Report, Project No. 6-1653*, p. 20.

irregular spellings. Even strong proponents of i/t/a admit that in the transition stage special problems in spelling may arise, as the writer makes the transfer from a system with a consistent phoneme-grapheme relationship to one with many irregularities between sound and written symbol.

Enthusiasts of i/t/a claim such advantages as the following:

1. It is much simpler for the child to learn to read by means of a symbol-sound code in which every character has but one sound and in which every sound is represented by but one symbol.

2. Children learn to read much more rapidly with i/t/a than with traditional orthography.

3. Making the transition from reading i/t/a to reading traditional orthography is relatively easy, so that soon after making the changeover the learner can read even in traditional orthography more effectively than one who started reading in that orthography.

4. Pupils being taught with i/t/a have greater skill in written self-expression than boys and girls using traditional orthography.

5. Children with speech defects who are taught with i/t/a as a beginning method of reading instruction are likely to be helped more than other children toward lessening or overcoming their speech difficulties.

There are also critics of i/t/a. A contention of those who are unconvinced that it is the most effective means of beginning reading instruction is that it has not been used long enough in this country to justify the claims for superiority made by its proponents. Since there is lacking the completion of longitudinal studies through which children are observed from the time of beginning instruction in reading through the grades of the elementary school and beyond, they argue that the long-time comparative effect of reading with initial use of this alphabet versus other approaches to reading instruction has not been established. Furthermore, critics of the system point out that the number of pupils participating in often-quoted experimental set-ups involving use of i/t/a has been too small to establish the validity claimed for the studies. Other arguments advanced by the critics of i/t/a are:

1. In addition to disadvantages resulting from the small number of children used in experiments, these experiments have not been set up with adequate attention to other factors essential for obtaining valid generalizations of worth. Critics of the system have pointed out shortcomings in the experimental pattern of the most quoted i/t/a experiment in this country, that of Albert J. Mazurkiewicz in the Lehigh-Bethlehem study. Alledged lack of control of variables in the experiment and control groups constitutes a major source of criticism. Lack of comparable phonics instruction, included in both control and experimental groups on which major studies have been made, has been one of the uncontrolled variables.[17]

2. Some of the superiority claimed by experiments with i/t/a may be due to the so-called Hawthrone effect, which operates to the advantage of an experimental group in that attention given to individuals as participants in a new experimental program tends to increase the learning that takes place.

[17] Arthur W. Heilman, "Research Findings Concerning Phonics in Beginning Reading," *A Decade of Innovations: Approaches to Beginning Reading*, Elaine C. Vilscek, ed. (Newark, Del.: International Reading Association, 1971), vol. 12, Part 3, Proceedings of the Twelfth Annual Convention, pp. 100–107.

3. It has not been established that the problems involved in making a transition from i/t/a to traditional orthography is not so great that it might more than counterbalance the advantages in other respects that are claimed for the system.

4. The spelling of children taught to read with i/t/a is, according to some studies, poorer than that of other children.

In summarizing research in England, including the University of London study,[18] and in the United States, Robert Aukerman states:

> Since much of the statistical evidence is reported on a variety of bases, comparisons are difficult to make. It is understood that attempts are now being made to obtain reports that provide compatible information.[19]

Words-in-Color

The words-in-color program, like i/t/a, aims to decrease reading frustrations and increase reading power by providing a reliable symbol-sound code. The following explanation of the words-in-color program is given in one of the brochures of the company that publishes the materials.[20]

> Each of the 52 sounds of English is printed in a distinctive color on wall charts. Alphabet letters or groups of letters (350 signs of English) are colored according to how they sound in a given word. Thus color is used to make English phonetic without in any way changing traditional spellings.
> A sound is always represented by *one* color—regardless of its spelling. If it is the short sound of *a,* it is white whether it is in *pat* or *laugh.* Children use these color clues to help them fix the image in their minds.
> From the beginning, the pupil writes and reads in *black and white* each colored sign that he is introduced to so that there is immediate and constant transfer. Since he carries the images of these signs in color in his mind, the pupil can evoke and re-evoke the images if he needs them for reading or writing. Thus he is not dependent on printing in color.

Essential to the words-in-color program are the 21 colored charts of letter sounds and word families. These charts present the 52 sounds of English that the originator of the program identified. In addition to the 52 colors to represent these 52 sounds are 52 shades of colors—one for each of the 52 colors. The shades indicate slight variations from the basic sounds. Words-in-color materials include series of books, as well as word

---

[18] John Downing, "The i/t/a (Initial Teaching Alphabet) Reading Experiment," *The Reading Teacher,* vol. 18 (November 1964), pp. 105–110.

[19] Robert C. Aukerman, *Approaches to Beginning Reading* (New York: John Wiley & Sons, Inc., 1971), p. 343.

[20] Educational Solutions, Inc., Box 190, Cooper Station, New York, New York 10003, now distributes the words-in-color materials.

cards and worksheets, that each learner should have if the greatly detailed guide for the teacher is being followed.[21]

Like i/t/a, the method is recommended for use only in beginning reading instruction. Also like i/t/a, it has not been used long enough in this country to give validity to the claims for superiority over other systems, for it was not until 1959 that Caleb Gattegno, who originated the system, made application to the English language of his studies with it in Amharic (in his literacy program in Ethiopia) and in Spanish. The first copyright for the words-in-color materials in this country was obtained as late as 1963. However, a number of studies on the value of the method have been made, among them the "Right-to-Learn" program for teaching adults to read, carried on in Cleveland, Ohio[22] and the study under the directorship of Mary Austin[23] in the first-grade rooms of the Willoughby-Eastlake (Cleveland suburbs) schools. For a summary of other studies on words-in-color the reader is referred to *Approaches to Beginning Reading.*[24]

Diacritical Marking System (DMS)

The diacritical marking system (DMS) that is here described, like words-in-color and i/t/a, is planned for use in beginning reading only. Also like words-in-color and i/t/a, it is based on the principle that a single grapheme-phoneme (written symbol-sound) relation greatly simplifies the problems of beginning reading instruction. The near-equivalence is secured by adding diacritical marks to the letters in the traditional alphabet. Basic rules for markings in this system are listed below, as given in the article by Edward Fry.

Basic Rules

1. Regular consonants and short vowels are unchanged.
2. Silent letters have a slash mark.   (write right)
3. Long vowels have a bar over mark.   (mādé māíd)
4. Schwa vowels have a dot over mark.   (ȧgo lemȯn)
5. Other consistent sounds than those above are indicated by the bar.   (i̱s a̱u̱tō)
6. Digraphs have a bar under both letters.   (s̲h̲ut c̲h̲at)
7. Exceptions to the above stated basic rules have an asterisk above the letter.   (ȯ̈f ȯ̈ncé)[25]

[21] Aukerman, *ibid.*, pp. 358–363.

[22] *Right-to-Learn,* PACE Project (Cleveland: Cleveland Public Schools, 1965).

[23] William G. Dodds, "A Longitudinal Study of Two Beginning Reading Programs: Words-in-Color and a Traditional Reader," unpublished doctoral dissertation (Cleveland: Western Reserve University, 1966). The footnote giving this reference in *Approaches to Beginning Reading* by Robert C. Aukerman (John Wiley & Sons, Inc., 1971), p. 364 refers the reader to the October 1968 *Ohio Reading Teacher*, pp. 8–11.

[24] Aukerman, *ibid.*, p. 367.

[25] Edward Fry, "A Diacritical Marking System to Aid Beginning Reading Instruction." *Elementary English*, vol. 41 (May 1964), pp. 527–528.

A specimen of DMS writing is given below.

The Little Red Hen

Once upon à tīmė Littlė Red Hen livėd in à barn with hėr fīvė chiċks. À pig, à cat, and à duċk madė thėįr hōmė in thė sāmė barn. Eàch dāy thė littlė red hen led hėr chiċks out to look for food. But thė pig, thė cat, and thė duċk woŭld not look for food.[26]

Edward Fry claims superiority for the DMS over other systems devised to simplify the grapheme-phoneme relation for beginning reading. He asserts: (1.) other systems have devised alphabets too unlike the traditional alphabet to assure maximum ease in making the transition from the new forms to the regular alphabet, and (2.) the grapheme-phoneme relation in other alphabets is less nearly constant than in DMS.

Individualized Reading: Seeking, Self-selection, and Pacing

The term *individualized reading* has many·meanings. In the following paragraphs the words are capitalized—*Individualized Reading*—to indicate that the method described is a program of reading in which the total program is on an individualized basis. This is essentially one worked out by Jeannette Veatch.[27]

The common elements that underlie Individualized Reading as practiced in numerous schools and school systems are: (1.) the use of many books, diversified as to interest appeal and ability level; (2.) little or no reliance on basal readers as instructional tools; and (3.) major emphasis on children's preferences in the selection of reading materials. In general, the skills of reading are taught in connection with problems the child actually encounters in his reading. Isolated exercises and drills for a whole group, and even for individual pupils, are rarely, if ever, used. However, Individualized Reading follows no rigid formula.

Though the procedure is varied and supplemented in numerous ways according to the needs of the learner and the creativity and the philosophy of the teacher, typically an Individualized Reading program can be described as follows. In a classroom well equipped with books on a large variety of subjects and on different levels of difficulty, most of the boys and girls during the reading period are reading independently in books of their choice, while the teacher confers with one pupil at a time. During the conference the teacher may listen to the child read orally and ask questions about his silent reading as he tries to determine the child's level of achievement and to ascertain his strengths and his weaknesses. The teacher gives help as needed and may provide guidance—but guidance only, without con-

[26] *Op. cit.*, p. 529.
[27] Jeannette Veatch, *How to Teach Reading with Children's Books* (New York: Teachers College Press, Columbia University, 1964); *Individualizing Your Reading* (New York: G.P. Putnam's Sons, 1959); *Reading in the Elementary School* (New York: The Ronald Press, 1966).

Figure 15.1 Self-selection is an aspect of individualized reading. (New Haven Redevelopment Agency, Wooster Square Project, Al Gregory, Photographer.)

trol—for the child's future reading. Most of the reading is in general books, though if the child chooses to read selections in basal readers he may do so, depending on their availability in the classroom. At times, flexible groups will be organized temporarily, for work on a common problem—usually a skill development problem. At times, also, two or more pupils may work together to plan a presentation they will give for the entire class—possibly a play on a book they have enjoyed or a choral reading program of poems they like. In many Individualized Reading programs the pupils are encouraged to keep a record of books read. Some also keep a written account of acquired learnings, such as additions to vocabulary, generalizations related to reading skills of which they have learned to make application, difficulties encountered. The teacher, too, keeps a record. He makes notations on each child's strengths and weaknesses, taking his notes during or after individual conferences.

Willard C. Olson,[28] one of the early proponents of Individualized Reading, used the expressions *seeking, self-selection, pacing* to describe the process. By *pacing* he meant the adjustment of teaching materials and experiences to the learner's growth. He thought of pacing as an activity that essentially the child, rather than the teacher, performs.

Many teachers seriously doubt the young child's ability to select reading material best suited to his needs. Another point of criticism of the plan, as voiced by some of its critics, is the limited length and the infrequency of

[28] Willard C. Olson, *Child Development* (Boston: D.C. Heath and Company, 1949).

the individual conferences with each child. It is doubtful whether in a classroom of thirty pupils, with an hour devoted daily to reading, a teacher could, during the course of a week, hold more than one or two five- or six-minute conferences with each child. To some critics it seems impossible to accomplish effectively the multiplicity of tasks that are named as concerns of the conference period. It is also claimed that a teacher, who has many responsibilities in addition to teaching reading, cannot spend as much time in preparation for Individualized Reading as is necessary, without neglecting other areas of study. Critics of the plan as described here usually favor individualized reading as a supplement to a basal reading program rather than as *the* program of reading instruction. They assert that the advantages claimed for Individualized Reading can be achieved when a combination of the two programs, a basal reading program and an Individualized Reading program, is followed. This is also the point of view of the authors.

What are the alleged advantages as set forth by the proponents of Individualized Reading? Foremost among them is the claim that the method is instrumental in developing in more children a love for reading and habits of extensive independent reading. They state that it contributes to a happy, carefree climate in the classroom, builds self-confidence in children, and removes insidious distinctions between "slow" and "fast" readers.

At the present time we turn in vain to research for a settlement of the argument for and against Individualized Reading. Such studies as have been made do not reveal dramatic gains nor significant losses in the pupils' performance as measured by standardized tests of reading. It is argued by some persons that, with teachers of comparable ability and creativity and with equally suitable instructional materials, there is no superiority of Individualized Reading over basal reading programs stressing the sequential development of reading skills.

In any case, the inexperienced teacher not trained in the techniques of Individualized Reading and lacking the advantage of a sympathetic, able supervisor is well advised not to plunge into the program. It is best to study the plan first, examine the books, articles, and manuals on the subject carefully, and then to make tentative beginnings. Of supreme importance, also, is a wide knowledge of and love for children's books. The young teacher who has not had a good course in children's literature should probably spend at least a year in reading books for children and consulting the numerous guides, commentaries, and lists now available.

As we consider the Individualized Reading program as advocated by Jeannette Veatch, which is described here, let us also bear in mind that long before that program attracted national attention teachers had been experimenting with programs for teaching reading skills that give the individual child the time and attention he may require if he is to attain the effectiveness and efficiency of the mature reader. These teachers have tried to assess the strengths and weaknesses of pupils so that they—and the child—will know more precisely in what areas he is succeeding and those in which he needs to improve. They have tried to encourage children to make their own choices of reading material, and both teachers and children have concentrated their efforts on adequate record-keeping in order to indicate the quality of the materials read, the specific skills and abilities worked on, and developing interests as these unfold. Teachers who have experimented with individualuzed reading techniques believe that such approaches allow the child to *seek* that which stimulates him, *choose* that which helps him develop most, and *work at his own rate* with what he has chosen. These are, indeed, the factors deemed important by Willard Olson, who identified the *seeking, self-selection,* and *pacing* patterns of children in their use of books.[29]

"Individually Prescribed Instruction" (IPI)

While "Individually Prescribed Instruction," as the term indicates, is a program in which reading instruction is individualized, it differs drastically in many respects from the procedures of Individualized Reading as recommended by Jeannette Veatch.

IPI was introduced by Robert Glaser and John O. Bolvin of the School of Education of the University of Pittsburgh in collaboration with the Learning Research and Development Center of the Baldwin-Whitehall school district in the Oak Leaf School in Pittsburgh. In the middle 1960s administrators and teachers from various parts of the United States began visiting the school for observation and participation in the IPI program of instruction. The program appeared to work well, particularly in those schools that had installed nongraded primary programs.

Beginning in kindergarten, children receive a complex battery of general aptitude and intelligence tests and a series of reading readiness tests, which determine ability and competence in particular areas of the curriculum. Children who are mature enough to begin reading instruction undertake this task at the kindergarten level. Some are moved immediately into a primary reading program because they have achieved a certain degree of competence in basic skills.

When pupils have successfully accomplished a designated set of skills at a particular level, they progress to a more difficult level for reading instruction. Currently, many school systems are moving their pupils through the ten levels of learning that were identified by the Oak Leaf School in Pittsburgh. Emphasis has been placed on the use of comprehensive diagnostic tests to assess the learning abilities of each child at every level of instruction. As soon as the child demonstrates that he has a high degree of competency in a particular skill—such as reading, spelling, listening, speaking, writing, or grammar—he is moved into a more difficult instructional program which is designed to challenge his innate abilities.

Using materials collected from commercially prepared sources, teachers'

[29] Willard C. Olson, "Seeking, Self-Selection, and Pacing in the Use of Books by Children," *The Packet,* vol. VII, no. 1 (Spring 1952) (Boston: D.C. Heath and Company, 1952).

files, and newly innovated materials, master files are set up which are the core material for the entire program. "Prescriptions" are written for each child and IPI clerks fill these prescriptions, which may entail transparencies, filmstrips, records, supplementary readers, and the like. Many school systems have been successful in developing their own variations of the Oak Leaf model.

Linguistic Approaches to Reading Instruction[30]

Linguistics is not a new field of inquiry and research. Interest in the nature of language dates back to ancient history. It is only of late years, however, that the question of the application of the findings of linguists to teaching elementary-school subjects has been given much consideration. Understandably the point of inquiry is focused primarily on the bearing that the view of linguists can or should have on the language-arts program. In this connection questions such as these are of concern to the teacher of reading:

Should the reading program be linguistically oriented?

How can effective application of linguistics be made to the teaching of reading?

These questions are particularly relevant as they apply to the teaching of word recognition and comprehension.

No attempt is made in these pages to present to the reader enough data to answer intelligently the puzzling questions concerning the teachings of linguists in their application to reading instruction. What is attempted is to provide him with some basic information on the topic, of use in further reading and study.

Definition of Terms

Linguistics has been defined in various ways. It has been referred to as the study of language. LeFevre[31] calls it "a scientific method of studying language." Fries defines linguistics as:

> . . . the body of knowledge and understanding concerning the nature and functioning of human language achieved by the scientific study of the structure, the operation, and the history of a wide range of very diverse human languages.[32]

[30] This discussion of linguistics is, in part, an adaptation of information given in *Teaching the Language Arts in the Elementary School,* 2nd ed. (Wm. C. Brown Company, 1971), by one of the authors of this book, Martha Dallmann.
[31] Carl A. LeFevre, "The Contribution of Linguistics," *Issues and Innovations in the Teaching of Reading"* (Chicago: Scott, Foresman and Company, 1967), pp. 199–205.
[32] Charles C. Fries, "Linguistic Approaches to First Grade Reading Programs," *Reading Instruction: Selected Materials,* Althea Beery, Thomas C. Barrett, and William R. Powell, eds. (Boston: Allyn and Bacon, Inc., 1969) pp. 372–382. The article is a reprint from *First Grade Reading Programs, Perspectives 5,* (Newark, Del.: International Reading Association, 1965), pp. 45–53.

Reference is made earlier in this book to some of the terms used by linguists that frequently occur in educational literature: namely *phoneme, grapheme,* and *decoding.* Further clarification of these words, as well as explanation of other commonly used ones is given here.

+ *Phoneme.* A phoneme is the smallest significant (sound) unit of speech.

+ *Grapheme.* A grapheme is the written symbol of a sound. It may be a letter of the alphabet or it may be a word.

+ *Morpheme.* A morpheme is the smallest meaning-bearing unit. The word *work* consists of one morpheme, but the word *worker* of two, *work* and *er.* The latter is called a bound-form morpheme for it is not a meaning unit when standing alone, without being "bound" to a free-form morpheme, such as *work,* which has meaning without being "bound" to another morpheme.

+ *Grapheme-phoneme relationship and phoneme-grapheme relationship.* The term *grapheme-phoneme relationship* refers to the written symbol-speech sound relationship. That term and the term *phoneme-grapheme relationship* are often used interchangeably. However, more discriminatingly, the former can be thought of as the relationship when the written symbol is equated with the oral symbol (as in reading); conversely, the latter designates that relationship when the oral symbol is equated with the written (as in writing).

+ *Decoding and encoding.* The term *decoding* designates the process used when a person substitutes the phoneme for the grapheme (as in reading). The term *encoding* refers to translating the oral symbol (the spoken word) into its written symbol.

+ *Breaking the code.* The expression *breaking the code* is used to refer to the process by which an individual learns what the language codified into written form means when translated into oral terms. Roughly speaking, it designates learning to read by acquiring familiarity with the grapheme-phoneme relationship.

Application of Linguistics to Teaching Reading

Suggestions for the application of phonetic principles to the teaching of reading have, during the past few decades, been made by a number of eminent linguists. They emphasize the point that reading and writing are relatively recent inventions and that they are derived from spoken language. They regard the study of speech sounds as central to any defensible theory of reading instruction.

1. Work of Bloomfield, Barnhart, and Fries   Of historical interest in the development of linguistic approaches to reading is the work of Bloomfield, Barnhart, and Fries. It is briefly described here even though a number of present-day writers, interested in making application of linguistics to reading, do not accept all their theories.

The late Leonard Bloomfield worked out a plan for initial reading instruction which is based on the reproduction of speech sounds through the use of visual symbols.[33] In Bloomfield's theory, the early stages of reading instruction should be concerned exclusively with mastery of the mechanics of reading. Nonsense words may serve very well in fixing the skills required for later meaningful reading. He suggests the following four stages in a sequence designed to promote the development of the essential mechanical skills that will lead eventually to fluent, effective reading:

a. The recognition of the letters of the alphabet. These are to be presented in two-letter and three-letter words, in groups arranged according to the five vowel letters. Each letter in a group should represent a single phonetic value. Thus, only the short *a* or only the hard *g* should be included in a word group. Work in this stage should be continued until the pupils are thoroughly trained.

b. Learning regular spellings in which double consonants and other digraphs appear in consistent uses.

c. Learning words whose spellings may be called *semi-irregular,* as in the word groups *line, shine, mile,* and *while,* or *bone, stone, hole, pole.*

d. Learning irregularly spelled words, such as *father, mother, night, all, rough, cough,* and *through.* Unfamiliar words may be used. At this stage, however, each word is a separate item to be memorized so that it may be available for reading.

Bloomfield's ideas have recently been more fully developed in a book by Barnhart,[34] who has carried on Bloomfield's work with the intention of facilitating the experimental use of his method. However, the one classroom experiment in which the Bloomfield approach was compared with a conventional phonic approach revealed no significant differences in pupil achievement. Clearly, further experimentation would be desirable.

Another well-known linguist, the late C. C. Fries, advocated a procedure not unlike that of Bloomfield's. Reviewing the history of linguistic science over a long period and of changes in theories of reading instruction, Fries outlines the implications of modern linguistics for the teaching of reading.[35]

[33] Leonard Bloomfield, "Linguistics and Reading," *The Elementary English Review,* vol. 18 (April, May 1942), pp. 125–130, 183–186.
[34] Leonard Bloomfield and Clarence Barnhart, *Let's Read: A Linguistic Approach* (Detroit: Wayne State University Press, 1961).
[35] Charles C. Fries, *Linguistics and Reading* (New York: Holt, Rinehart and Winston, Inc., 1963).

Although he recognizes that the ultimate purpose of reading instruction is reading for meaning, Fries believes that the child's introduction to reading should not be complicated by the search for meaning in words. The child's primary task is to make a transfer from auditory language signs in speech to a set of corresponding visual signs in reading. The ability to identify and distinguish the graphic shapes that supply the visual symbols must first be brought to the level of instant and automatic response to the visual signals. Substituting visual for auditory signals implies clearly that the early reading experiences should be confined to words and meanings already a part of the child's speaking repertory.

2. Likenesses and differences among linguists Linguists interested in making application of the knowledge in their field to the teaching of reading have many points of agreement. As a rule they place much emphasis during the initial period of reading instruction on the importance of selecting words for mastery on the basis of the spelling pattern, not on frequency of use. An example of a spelling pattern is the consonant-vowel-consonant arrangement occurring in words such as *hut, bat, can*. Another illustration is the consonant-vowel-consonant-final *e* arrangement, as in *date, fame, line*. In general, they agree that the aim of beginning reading instruction should be word recognition through the study of words with like spelling patterns, in series such as *can, fan, ran, ban, man, tan, van*. Some even advocate the inclusion in such lists of "nonsense words" to provide added practice.

Many linguists are united in their highly critical attitude toward phonics teaching. They condemn it on the allegation that the study in our schools typically proceeds from the sound to the word (synthetic approach) rather than from the word to the sound (analytic approach). They believe that in the synthetic approach untrue sounds are produced as, for example, when the child sounds the *h* in *hat* as *huh*. So they propose that the learner be introduced, for example, to the grapheme *h*, with its corresponding phoneme, by his attention being drawn to the *h* in a large number of words of the same spelling pattern beginning with the letter *h*, such as *hat, ham, had, has*. However, Emans[36] points out that linguists when criticising the teaching of phonics are unaware of the fact that phonics is typically taught in the schools of today by analysis of the sounds in words rather than by a synthesis of them. Emans also draws attention to the fact that while linguists in general are highly critical of a phonics approach they seem to be unaware of his contention that a linguistic approach to reading instruction is a phonics (sound) approach, since emphasis is placed on the identification of sounds, though it is in spelling patterns.

Another criticism by linguists is that the teaching of phonics, as it is

---

[36] Robert Emans, "Linguistics and Phonics," *The Reading Teacher*, vol. 26, no. 5 (February 1973), pp. 477–482.

done in many of our schools, is poorly organized, with gaps in learnings to be acquired and with a defective sequence in the development of the desired learnings. They are also in general agreement in their opposition to much use of the sight method (the whole-word method). They claim that the method encourages guessing, requires every word learned by that method to be memorized, and may result in word-by-word reading. It is interesting, in the light of this objection, to note that the child is, after all, learning by the whole-word method, even when he learns words, as recommended by linguists, consistent in spelling patterns, as he names words such as *hen, den, men, ten,* and possibly including nonsense words such as *gen, ren, jen.* Fries' explanation pertinent to this claim is that "in the spelling-pattern approach it is the pattern itself [not the particular word] that is repeated frequently using a variety of words and matrixes."[37]

We have noted some of the points on which many linguists interested in the field of the teaching of reading are in agreement. Let us next consider some points of disagreement.

a. *Not all linguists believe that the very first "lessons" should consist of study of lists of words with the same spelling pattern.* While Bloomfield and many other linguists are of that opinion, Henry Lee Smith, Jr., for example, advocates that the child's first reading instruction, before he turns his attention to lists of words arranged in spelling patterns, should be given through the use of experience charts.

b. *Linguists differ in their lists of recommended words arranged according to spelling patterns.* There are wide differences in this respect from one series of linguistically-oriented readers to another.

c. *There is variation among linguists as to their recommendation concerning how long and how many lists of words should be presented to the beginning reader, according to spelling pattern, before he should be supplied with material using words in sentences.* In fact, some linguists recommend that sentences should be the unit of instruction even in the initial stages.

d. *Some linguists are opposed to the use of pictures to accompany the text in beginning reading instruction; others favor that practice.* Those against their use fear that the child might be reading pictures rather than mastering the grapheme-phoneme equivalence.

3. The role of the linguist in reading instruction   Although the teacher of reading can and should learn much from linguists about the science of

[37] Charles C. Fries, "Linguistic Approaches to First Grade Reading Programs," *Reading Instruction: Selected Materials,* Althea Beery, Thomas C. Barrett, and William R. Powell, eds. (Boston: Allyn and Bacon, Inc., 1969), pp. 373–382. The article is a reprint from *First Grade Reading Programs, Perspectives 5* (Newark, Del.: International Reading Association, 1965), pp. 45–53.

the language he teaches, the responsibility for the program in reading instruction must remain with the educator. The teacher should obtain as much pertinent information as he can or as is practical from the various fields that can throw light on reading instruction—such as psychology, child growth and development, sociology, as well as linguistics. It is the educator who, with his professional knowledge of the teaching of reading, must determine the program as he considers, in wide perspective, possible contributions from supportive areas. The province of the linguist should be to criticize current reading programs in the light of any violation of linguistic principles inherent in them and suggest principles that should be followed as may be indicated by his field of specialization.[38]

4. **Evaluation of linguistic programs**   As the teacher evaluates the many linguistically-oriented reading programs and the so-called "linguistic programs," he "should try to determine:

a. The linguistic theories on which the material or program claims to be based.
b. The correctness of the claims made in terms of whether they are actually a significant part of the program or materials.
c. The desirability of the theories on which the system or the materials are based.
d. The ways in which application of the theories is made.
e. The teacher's judgment of these methods [and materials] in terms of acceptability in general and in terms of practicality for his teaching [situation]."[39]

When making an evaluation of programs the reader may wish to study Part 5, "Linguistics-Phonemics Approaches" in *Approaches to Beginning Reading*,[40] where Aukerman describes various programs with linguistic orientation.

The Montessori Method

The recent resurgence of interest in this country in the teachings of Maria Montessori (*see* page 52) warrants our attention to her methods and materials. Reading, according to this Italian educator (1870–1952), does not come as readily as writing and thus it requires a longer course of instruction. Likewise, she claimed, it calls for superior prowess, since it deals

[38] Kenneth S. Goodman, "The Linguistics of Reading," *Elementary School Journal*, vol. 64 (April 1964), pp. 355–361.
[39] Martha Dallmann, *Teaching the Language Arts in the Elementary School*, 2nd ed. (Dubuque, Iowa: Wm. C. Brown Company, 1971), p. 48.
[40] Aukerman, *ibid.*, pp. 141–227.

with the "interpretation of signs" and with the "modulation of accents of the voice" in order that the word may be understood.[41]

The original development of the Montessori reading method began with the impression of letters, through the novel use of touch, enabling the child to learn the whole alphabet before his interest diminished. Fundamentally the original approach was a phonetic one. Because the Italian language is phonetically oriented, the teaching of reading proceeded without undue difficulties. It was the unphonetic character of English (American) spelling that largely influenced educators—not Montessori—to give up the alphabet method of teaching reading to children, for it was here that teachers were confronted by a serious obstacle.

Some American educators have considered it more effective to teach children whole words, sentences, or rhymes by sight, adding to sense impressions the interest aroused by a wide range of associations, and then analyzing the words thus acquired into their phonetic elements to give the child independent power in grasping new words. It occurred to some that a proper approach to teaching reading could systematically employ both phonetic analysis and the Montessori method for teaching the letters, with the exact adjustment depending to a large extent on the individual system.

The didactic materials that Montessori used as aids in the teaching of reading were a collection of cards on which the single letters of the alphabet were mounted on sandpaper and a set of larger cards containing groups of the same letters. The cards on which the sandpaper letters were mounted were adapted in size and shape to each letter. The vowels were cut in light-colored sandpaper and mounted on dark cards; the consonants and the groups of letters were in black sandpaper mounted on white cards. The grouping was so arranged as to call attention to contrasted or analogous forms. The letters were cut in clear script form, with the shaded parts made broader. Montessori chose to reproduce the vertical script in use in the elementary schools during her time.

In teaching the alphabet she taught the sounds, not the names, first of the vowels alone and then of the consonants used in combination with vowels. Once the child had an essential mastery of the alphabet, he could proceed with the following steps.

First a number of little cards were made from writing paper. On each card was written in large script some well-known word, one that had already been pronounced many times by the children and that represented an object actually present or well known to them; for example, dolls, balls, doll furnishing, and simple figures. If the word referred to an object that was before them, the object was placed before their eyes, in order to facilitate their interpretation of the word.

Montessori believed that there was no question of beginning with a

---

[41] Maria Montessori, *The Montessori Method* (New York: Frederick A. Stokes, 1912), pp. 266, 267.

word that was too easy or too difficult, since the child already knew how to read the sounds that composed the word. As part of this step the child would try to translate the written word slowly into sounds. With each vocal response he would speed up the sounds, until the word would finally burst on his consciousness. He would assume an air of self-satisfaction when reading the word and then place the explanatory card under the correct object. Thus, the exercise progressed until completed.

A second step consisted of a "game" in which there were a basket of words and a large variety of toys on a table. The child (who could read) took a folded paper to his desk and later read it to the directress. If he could pronounce the word clearly and indicated the correct object, the directress allowed him to take the toy and play with it as long as he wished. After all the children had a turn, the first drew from another basket which contained the names of children in the class who could not read. The child who could read the name correctly offered the person named his toy to play with until he tired of it. It was hoped that this would eliminate class distinction and make for a congenial atmosphere. (Later the children refused to play with the games and wanted only to draw out the cards and read, word after word. Montessori interpreted this preference as meaning that it was knowledge the children were seeking and not the game.)

The third step resorted to cards naming hundreds of objects — names of children, colors, cities, and qualities known through the senses. Again each child finished a box before passing it to another, being virtually insatiable in the desire to read, according to Montessori.

Changing the written word to print was part of the fourth step. This was not a very difficult task. Now, it would seem, there remained only the presentation of a book. Yet Montessori thought that those available were not suited to her method, which emphasized meaning rather than mechanical skill. Consequently, children were not allowed to use books at this time.

Step five was the presentation of phrases and sentences until the children were ready for composing. It was at this time that Montessori actually came upon her "discovery of reading," for the children were able to interpret the meaning of whole sentences as she wrote them on the chalkboard.

Finally came the "game" wherein the child would select one card from a basket of cards with sentences describing certain actions; for example, "Close the window blinds" or "Open the door." Silence prevailed as the children read the words and proceeded to act them out.

In summarizing the original development of the Montessori approach to reading, it can be said that Montessori believed that composition precedes logical reading. Her approach, she believed, if it is to teach the child to receive an idea, should be on the mental and not on the vocal level. Such a system seemed to call for an individualized reading program so that the children could be free to work at their own pace. The entire process described could be given, under proper direction, to a child over a period of a fortnight, excluding the time necessary for teaching the letters, which was probably rather long. However, it was not expected that in this time the child would gain mastery of the skill. The materials were present for those who showed an interest; others were left to do the tasks that attracted them. Montessori believed that "the idea that through the reading of a series of words the complex thoughts of others might be communicated to us, was to be for my children one of the beautiful conquests of the future, a new source of surprise and joy."[42]

Present-day advocates of the Montessori method have employed, along with the foregoing steps, or modifications of them, additional "reading games," more individualized work, and the teaching of reading skills in relation to history, science, and other content areas. It is interesting to note that originally Montessori did not intend to teach reading and the other skills to preschool children. Originally she was of the opinion that formal teaching of the skills should not begin until the child was six. But this view changed.

The hours that many of the children in a Montessori classroom spend in fingering sandpaper letters may result in learning the shape and direction of line through the sense of touch. And when there is visual and auditory imagery with this learning, there is the resulting impression that a given letter is, indeed, that letter. However, it cannot be agreed that this process of teaching reading will necessarily work for all children exposed to the system. Perhaps a better approach to teaching reading would be a system that would incorporate Montessori techniques with some of the old and new ideas that already exist in present systems.

Although there is no perfect device for determining what is the best approach to teaching reading, there are ways in which the teacher can get help with this question. The thoughtful reading of reports on experimental set-ups and of research on innovative programs can be of aid in determining which approaches to the teaching of reading should be followed. Study of the literature on the teaching of reading—as found in books on methods of teaching, in periodicals, and in other publications—can form a background against which to make appraisals. In this book, chapter after chapter, there are suggested, directly or indirectly, those theories and practices for teaching reading that the authors consider valid.

Engaging in what used to be commonly called action research can also be of value to the teacher who desires to follow a program in the teaching of reading that will bring the best possible results. In other words, the teacher can try out in his own classroom some of the methods and techniques that seem to him to be promising.

Finally, even after the teacher has attempted to the best of his ability to evaluate various approaches to teaching reading, he will still find that his appraisal is lacking in objectivity. But he cannot wait idly for a better day to come when evaluation techniques will give him more specific direc-

---

[42] Montessori, *ibid.*, p. 304.

tions. The teacher in the classroom cannot postpone teaching reading until research has discovered without a doubt the most successful approach. As day after day he attempts to do his work as effectively as he can, he must ever make use of the means of evaluation at his disposal, imperfect though they are. If he follows this suggestion, he will not be without a guide.

For Further Study

Auckerman, Robert C., *Approaches to Beginning Reading* (New York: John Wiley & Sons, Inc., 1971).

Bond, Guy L., and Robert Dykstra, coordinators, *Final Report Project No. X-001* (Washington, D.C.: Bureau of Research, Office of Education, U.S. Department of Health, Education and Welfare, 1967).

Chall, Jeanne, *Learning to Read: The Great Debate* (New York: McGraw-Hill Book Company, 1967).

Darrow, Helen F., and Virgil M. Howes, *Approaches to Individualized Reading* (New York: Appleton-Century-Crofts, 1969).

Dechant, Emerald, *Linguistics, Phonics and the Teaching of Reading* (Springfield, Ill.: Charles C. Thomas, Publishers, 1969).

Downing, John, *Evaluating the Initial Teaching Alphabet* (London: Cassell and Company, 1967).

Downing, John, *The Initial Teaching Alphabet* (New York: The Macmillan Company, 1964).

Durkin, Dolores, *Phonics, Linguistics and Reading* (New York: Teachers College Press, Columbia University, 1972).

Fries, Charles C., *Linguistics and Reading* (New York: Holt, Rinehart and Winston, Inc., 1963).

Gattegno, Caleb, *Words in Color* (New York: Educational Solutions, Inc., 1973).

Goodman, Kenneth S., and J. T. Fleming, eds., *Psycholinguistics and the Teaching of Reading* (Newark, Del.: International Reading Association, 1969).

Harris, Larry A., and Carl B. Smith, eds., *Individualizing Reading Instruction: A Reader* (New York: Holt, Rinehart and Winston, Inc., 1972).

Hunt, Lyman C., ed., *The Individualized Reading Program: A Guide for Classroom Teaching* (Newark, Del.: International Reading Association, 1967).

Lamb, Pose, *Linguistics in Proper Perspective* (Columbus, Ohio: Charles E. Merrill Publishing Company, 1967).

Lillard, Paula Polk, *Montessori: A Modern Approach* (New York: Schocken Books, 1972).

Mackintosh, Helen K., ed., *Current Approaches to Teaching Reading,* Elementary Instruction Service Leaflet (Washington, D.C.: National Education Association, 1965).

Savage, John F., ed., *Linguistics for Teachers: Selected Readings* (Chicago: Science Research Associates, 1973).

Sebesta, Sam Leaton, and Carl J. Wallen, eds., *The First R: Readings on Teaching Reading* (Chicago: Science Research Associates, 1972), "Reading: Psychological and Linguistic Bases," by Emmett A. Betts, pp. 86–92; and "Linguistic Insights into the Reading Process" by Ronald Wardbaugh, pp. 93–112.

Veatch, Jeannette, *How to Teach Reading with Children's Books* (New York: Teachers College Press, Columbia University, 1964).

Veatch, Jeannette, *Reading in the Elementary School* (New York: The Ronald Press, 1966).

Vilscek, Elaine C., ed., *A Decade of Innovative Approaches to Beginning Reading* (Newark, Del.: International Reading Association, 1968), vol. 12, Part 3, Proceedings of the Twelfth Annual Convention of the International Reading Association.

Questions and Comments for Thought and Discussion

1. If you were employed for your first year of teaching in a first-grade room in which i/t/a is used, how could you prepare yourself before school opens in fall for teaching with that orthography?

2. You may wish to examine one or more of the approaches to reading. Two helpful sources of information are the book by Robert Aukerman, *Approaches to Beginning Reading,* and the book edited by Elaine Vilscek, *A Decade of Innovations: Approaches to Beginning Reading.*

3. When Jeanne Chall's book, *Learning to Read: The Great Debate,* was first published, one writer referred to it as a "bomb" that had been hurled into the field of the teaching of reading. In what respects might it have been thought of as a "bomb"?

4. You may wish to consult with your teacher about the possibility of a book report on Jeanne Chall's *Learning to Read: The Great Debate,* which has, indeed, caused much debate among educators and others.

5. If you have an opportunity to observe in a Montessori school you might find it very profitable to note the approach to reading instruction used in the school.

6. You may find copies of some linguistic or so-called linguistic readers in your school library. How do they compare with the more traditional readers?

7. Why is it important that teachers, not linguists, make the final decision as to how reading should be taught?

Outline for Chapter 16

IMPLEMENTATION OF THE READING PROGRAM

CHAPTER

Implementation of the Reading Program

An effective program of reading instruction in the school calls for aggressive leadership and careful overall planning. In this section we shall consider: (1.) what conditions are essential to a strong reading program, (2.) what steps are needed for the development of the schoolwide program, (3.) in what ways the program can be interpreted to parents, and (4.) how the program can be evaluated. Part of what we consider here is a summary or an application of principles discussed earlier in this book.

CONDITIONS ESSENTIAL FOR AN EFFECTIVE PROGRAM

The teaching of reading is not carried on in a vacuum. Effective reading instruction calls for a school environment favorable to learning, to growth, to solid achievement. Teachers can do much to create the conditions that are needed for helping children to read. The following are some of these conditions:

1. The physical surroundings should be suitable While it is true that some children learn to read under the most unfavorable physical conditions, if we are to get the best results with the huge numbers of children who come to us for reading instruction, we must provide schoolrooms that are well lit, comfortable, colorful. The furniture should include comfortable seats, movable desks adjustable to the physical requirements of the children, a display table for books, many open shelves along the walls, and a reading corner with a table, a lamp, and an easy chair or two. Colors in the room should be bright and cheerful. Plants in the windows; bulletin boards with constantly changing exhibits of pictures, announcements, information about the date, recent incidents affecting children in the room, and other subjects of interest to pupils; objects brought by teacher or pupils for reading and discussion—all these, and many other "conversation pieces" that may stimulate reading and discussion, should be a part of the elementary-school classroom. Records, films, filmstrips, and other audio-visual aids should be readily available when the occasion calls for them.

2. The children should be surrounded by an abundance of attractive reading materials   Children's books, tastefully arranged, representing a wide range of reading difficulty and a great diversity of interests should be found on the shelves and on the tables in all classrooms. Suitable magazines, pamphlets, and pictorial matter should be displayed on racks or deposited in files to which teacher and pupils have easy access.

3. A well-equipped and well-managed central library is essential to the schoolwide reading program   The library should have the latest reference books; an up-to-date card index; vertical files; a wide variety of children's magazines; and an abundance of books, including the great children's classics and books on hobbies, adventure, humor, science, history, biography, and fiction. The library should be the center of the "cultural" activities of the school. It should display paintings, sculpture, and other art objects that may be acquired by the school through loan or purchase. Science materials of various kinds may be exhibited here. It should, if possible, have two or more small conference rooms for pupils' committee work. It should have a librarian's office and workroom, and a storage room for back issues of magazines and other materials. It should be the repository for the visual aids to be made available to all classes in the school. Moreover, the library should be large enough to accommodate not only a whole class which may come for one or more periods during the week for browsing or for special assignments but also small groups and individual pupils who are doing research in connection with classroom projects. Arrangements should be made for systematic use of library facilities by whole classes, and individual pupils should be encouraged to make frequent use of the library. Its use should not be reserved as a "privilege" for the bright or the "best-behaved" pupils.

4. The classroom climate should be conducive to pleasant learning experiences   Many of the factors that contribute to good school morale are also needed in the creation of a classroom climate favorable to efficient learning. Strong teacher leadership combined with a high degree of pupil participation in decision-making, a sympathetic interest in the individual needs of pupils, and an atmosphere of encouragement to explore, question, and discuss are needed to stimulate maximum effort on the part of pupils. In such a climate children feel accepted. Rivalry and competition are kept on a friendly basis. Humor and spontaneous laughter are familiar experiences in each day's activities.

STEPS IN PLANNING A SCHOOLWIDE PROGRAM

The initiative in undertaking a schoolwide program of reading instruction may come from any one or more of many sources. Sometimes a series of newspaper articles or a critical book may focus attention on the problem and hence lead to thoughtful re-examination of current practices in reading instruction. Sometimes an enthusiastic administrator, or a teacher freshly returned from a leave for professional study, sparks the program. Frequently a study will emerge from faculty discussions of a commonly felt need. Whatever its impetus, the program can be successfully undertaken only if a large proportion of the teaching staff sees the need for it and volunteers to participate in it.

Determining the Reading Status of Pupils

"How are we doing?" is the first question to ask when we plan the schoolwide program. We need to know whether our present program is getting results, whether our achievements are above or below national norms, and, especially, what our special strengths and weaknesses are. Teachers know that many of their pupils do not read as well as they should, but they will find it helpful to have specific information as to the range of pupils' reading abilities and the degree of reading retardation that exists in their schools. The first step in a general reading program, therefore, is a careful study of the existing situation with respect to pupils' reading.

Although standardized reading tests have definite limitations and should never be regarded as infallible barometers of reading ability, they are useful indicators of the presence or absence of important reading skills. They are especially valuable as general screening and classification devices and as measures of the overall effectiveness of the reading program. They are one important means of determining the reading status of large groups of pupils.

The standardized tests reveal what pupils can do in a test situation. Of equal importance are the extent and quality of the voluntary reading activities of the pupils. Reading ability is of no value unless it is used. For this reason, a survey of reading attainments in a school or school system should include a study of the cumulative reading records kept by pupils of their personal, voluntary reading. Such a study does not lend itself so readily to statistical summary and analysis as data from standardized tests do, but it is no less important. In the interpretation of the records, the *nature* of pupils' choices should be given as much consideration as the number of books read.

Since so much of contemporary reading is done in the mass media, the preliminary survey should include an inquiry into the newspaper and magazine reading habits of children; indeed, perhaps the best index of the success of the reading program is the extent and quality of young people's reading in these two sources. The inquiry should deal not only with the amount of time spent in a day or week in the reading of newspapers and magazines but especially with the pupils' preferences among the various features and the range of their interests.

For a somewhat detailed discussion on evaluation the reader is referred to Chapter 12, "Classroom Diagnosis of Reading Ability." The section, "Assessment of Degree of Readiness" (pages 58–69), in Chapter 4A also gives information on evaluation.

Deciding on General Procedure for the Study

The staff will need to consider the general organizational procedure to be followed when planning the program and on guidelines to determine their study, and deliberations (*see also* suggestions for developing a literature program, pages 372–377).

Organizational Plan

In line with customary procedures when curricular programs are being planned, the faculty may decide that in some of the work the entire staff will take part, while other work will be done by committees or individuals. The entire faculty can meet in order to listen to lectures on the teaching of reading, view movies, observe demonstration lessons, hear reports from committees or from one or more staff members, express opinions, make recommendations or decisions. The group may also endorse the acceptance of responsibility by the entire staff for participating in any way in which committees may solicit their help—such as participating in short-range action research, filling out questionnaires, and making other reports. Committees can explore various areas of professional information needed for intelligent decision-making during the process of setting up the program. Topics such as these may be recommended by the staff for thorough investigation by committees: the objectives of the reading program, instructional procedures and practices, materials of instruction, plans for evaluation of the program. Additional study by individuals, usually reporting to committees, can involve reading, school visitation, attendance at conferences and workshops, writing the curriculum for reading that was accepted in principle by the faculty.

Guidelines for the Planning Period

Though the most desirable structure for work on planning a program will vary from one school system to another, the following suggestions, of rather general applicability, are some a staff may wish to accept as guidelines:

1. Since an excellent reading program in any school requires the co-operation of all teachers, every teacher should have the opportunity and the responsibility to participate in the planning Special teachers in fields such as music, art, physical education, have a stake in any schoolwide program. While they should not be expected to carry as much of the load as the teachers of classes that deal to a great extent with reading activities, their participation should be of value to them as teachers of their specialties. They can also make a contribution to the total program through suggestions they may offer, especially following study of problems involved.

Because the planning of the program can advisedly be the in-service project for the school year, participation in the orientation and planning period can justifiably be a requirement for all teachers. This statement is made with the assumption that a program of this magnitude and far-reaching effect will not be undertaken unless it has the enthusiastic support of the great majority of the teachers.

2. The plan for reorganization of a schoolwide reading program should be in harmony with what can reasonably be expected the school will be able to carry out with success A too-ambitious program may spell failure from the outset. A technique frequently employed in curriculum revision, which makes feasible some programs that otherwise might be too far-reaching for practical purposes, is that of not putting all phases of the program into operation simultaneously. Sometimes the first stage is a pilot program, carried on by only a few teachers, usually by those particularly interested in it. At other times during the first phase all teachers will concentrate in particular on only one part of the planned program, such as means of vitalizing the teaching of reading or use of audiovisual aids to teaching reading or strategies for teaching word recognition and identification.

3. Change for the sake of change should not be advocated Change can mark progression or retrogression; it can be beneficial or harmful. Only those changes should be recommended which give substantial promise of being advantageous over practices followed at the time by a school.

4. Care should be taken when planning a program for reading instruction that it will not interfere with the fulfillment of other important goals of the school A program in no area of the curriculum can be justified if it curtails the accomplishment of equally justifiable objectives in other areas of study. Nor should it affect adversely, to the best of our knowledge of child development, the harmonious growth of the learner in all aspects — physical, emotional, social, spiritual. A primary principle on which this entire book is based—that the learner is more important than the learning —should unquestionably be adhered to during the planning of any educational program.

5. Compensatory provisions should be made for those teachers who are delegated to spend a great amount of time in planning the schoolwide program   While part of the responsibility of every teacher is to grow professionally and to assist in the improvement of the instructional program, no teaching member of the staff should be expected, without compensatory arrangements, to give an excessive amount of time to a schoolwide project. Principals and supervisors, who often carry major responsibility and devote much time to the instigation of a program, can consider their contributions as part of their regular workload. Various plans are used to assure that, for some classroom teachers, their work on program revision will not constitute an unreasonable task. In some cases they are given a reduced load during part of the school year. A substitute teacher may be engaged to free the regular teacher one or more days a week or one or more forenoons or afternoons during a week. Some school systems engage a limited number of classroom teachers to devote six weeks or so of the summer months for work on the curriculum. Such provisions, whether in terms of released time from regular classroom duties or additional remuneration during vacation months, seem appropriate. However, it would, indeed, be unfortunate if any group of teachers, because such or similar provisions could not be made, would refrain from undertaking curriculum revision. As a member of a profession the teacher has the responsibility not to work by the time clock. Happily, most teachers do not even need to be reminded of this point.

6. When planning a schoolwide program, the staff should recognize that some of the plans will necessarily involve all the teachers while others could be followed by one or more teachers, but not by others   For example, if Individualized Instruction is to be engaged in, it will not be necessary to involve the total staff. One or two or more teachers could adopt a plan similar to that recommended by Jeannette Veatch (*see* page 495), while others would structure their program in other ways.

7. Even as early as the planning stage, means of evaluating the program after it is in progress, should be considered   Criteria should be established for evaluating the program in line with the objectives agreed on. Means of making application of these standards should also be a point of deliberation and decision-making during the general planning period.

8. Time should be devoted during the planning period for deciding on the general procedures for making changes, if necessary, in a program after it is in operation   Provisions should be made for needed additions or alterations or deletions following evaluations made after the program is in progress. Sometimes it may be advisable to lay alternative plans from the beginning in case the ones decided on for the program later appear not to be the best possible. Or supplementary plans that might possibly be incorporated in later stages of the program can be considered.

9. Plans should be laid for continuing study by the staff of problems related to the teaching of reading   If some of the plans require administrative approval, the possibility of obtaining such approval could be investigated and the ground work laid for later incorporating the plans as part of the in-service program.

Acquiring Background for Decision-making

To be qualified to make recommendations for a schoolwide reading program and to put them into operation, the teachers must be knowledgeable in the area of the teaching of reading. Such understanding must include familiarity with the nature of the reading process, means of fostering growth toward maturity in reading through emphasis on needed skills and on reading for enjoyment, strategies for diagnosing and making provisions for the needs of individuals. There is no substitute for such knowledge. Without it no program can be successful. In addition, it is desirable that teachers be informed on topics such as the following, some of which are primarily organizational and others chiefly instructional in nature: behavioral objectives; reading stations; services of auxiliary personnel; the structure of the reading program; individualized reading; grouping practices; programed reading instruction; instructional materials, equipment, and special facilities. Since programing, individualized reading, and grouping practices have been discussed earlier in this book, they will not be included in the discussion that follows.

Behavioral Objectives

Objectives for any instructional program should be clearly stated as guides to action. While general objectives can serve as basic guidelines, they need to be translated into specific goals of significance in day-by-day teaching. Furthermore, they should (1.) reflect a broad and comprehensive view of the reading process and of the values that can accrue from learning to read, and (2.) should be worded so that they can be the basic structure for both teaching and evaluation.

Based on the philosophy of education that emphasizes that learning implies a change in the behavior of the learner, attempts have of late been made by teachers in many subject fields and at all levels of instruction to formulate objectives, not as topics to be studied, as has been common practice, but in terms of observable effects of learning on the learner. These objectives are worded so that the attainment of an objective is revealed if the learner can show competence through satisfactory performance of the given tasks. They are referred to as behavioral objectives because the emphasis is on what the pupil can do—on the behavior he can exhibit—not primarily on what he knows. A behavioral objective might be stated as: "The pupils can arrange the following words alphabetically: . . ." rather than "To know how to arrange words alphabetically."

One problem in stating objectives behaviorally for the total reading program is that as yet there is no known way of identifying as observable objective behavior all the desired goals of a comprehensive reading program. The inclusion of some objectives but not others may result in serious omissions of very important components of reading. Another problem lies in the laboriousness of even attempting to identify behaviorally all known goals for teaching reading. And yet another shortcoming is that as the child becomes more and more conscious of the points on which he is being evaluated through behavioral objectives set by the school, he may degenerate or, at least, not develop adequately in power to establish his own objectives for reading.

If a teaching staff decides to state the objectives for a schoolwide reading program behaviorally, they should clearly recognize that an arduous task confronts them. Unless the staff is willing to spend the vast amount of time required, and unless it considers itself competent to make such a listing after much study, it should, providing it wishes to state objectives behaviorally, confine such a statement of objectives to only a few phases of the total reading program and word the objectives for other phases topically. In fact, there are sound reasons why a staff should not spend a large amount of time in working out the objectives for a program as preliminary to other work toward launching a reading program.

Many a proposed program of schoolwide dimensions has failed to come to successful fruition because the group spent so exorbitant an amount of time working on objectives that interest in the total project waned because of long postponement of work beyond the somewhat theoretical. While at the beginning of the planning period it may be beneficial to have a group meeting or two devoted to a consideration of objectives, it is recommended that a committee be established with the charge to draw up a taxonomy (organized listing) of objectives for consideration by the staff. The committee should acquaint itself with practices in setting objectives, preliminary to making its first report to the staff. While this committee is engaged in formulating objectives, other committees should be concentrating on other topics—such as materials of instruction, teaching techniques, organizational plans, to name only a few.

Reading Stations

Much attention is currently being given to the establishment and use of what are called reading stations. Typically, a reading station is a small area in a classroom or open-space area, sometimes in the form of a study carrel, equipped for independent or semi-independent study by the pupils, for one phase of the learning-to-read curriculum. A station may be designated by a number, a letter, or by a word or group of words indicative of the learning activity for which it provides, such as *phonic station* or, more specifically, *vowel station*. Typically, a station is equipped with one or more chairs, a table or desk, books, self-teaching or learning-reinforcement materials with directions to the pupil for their use and keys for self-checking or evaluation, a large piece of paper or chart on which the pupil keeps a record of his activities. In many reading stations there will also be found tapes and tape recorders, along with earphones. Tapes may give directions to the learner, provide instruction, or read stories or poems to him which he reads silently from a book or paper at the same time that he listens to a tape. At a reading-rates station there may be a reading accelerator or some other type of tachistoscope, home-made or commercially procured, through the use of which a pupil can attempt to increase his reading rates. Phonograph records may be found in a station to interest the child through music and words in, for example, folk tales of long ago or modern contributions of high literary merit to the speedily expanding wealth of books for children. Filmstrips, films, video tapes are available in some stations to serve similar purposes. Care should be taken to make the stations attractive through means such as placing a plant on a table; displaying eye-catching, well-constructed posters with appropriate captions; arranging books and other materials interestingly. While the planning, construction, and use of reading stations of merit requires much time and insight into the teaching of reading, well-planned stations can provide an excellent substitute for some of the seatwork activities that are best designated as "busy work."

Aspects of stations that appeal in particular to boys and girls are: freedom of choice often possible (though limited and guided), instructional requirements that they can meet with success, provision for self-evaluation made possible through the set-up.

As in the case of various other instructional or organizational patterns we have been discussing, when planning a schoolwide program in reading, it is not necessary for every teacher to provide learning stations for his pupils because some decide to do so. It should probably be left up to each teacher whether he wishes to use them in his teaching.

A novel and effective method can be used by a committee when reporting on reading stations to the staff. The committee might make its report by setting up stations with learning materials for teachers about reading stations, with directions for their use and with aids for teacher self-evaluation on what is explained in the reading stations equipped for their information. Through such an experience teachers may get a clearer understanding, than through oral reports, of what reading stations are and of how they can be set up and used as an effective teaching device.

Services of Auxiliary Personnel

At the time of the great shortage of teachers for the elementary schools, during the 50s and 60s, noncertificated persons, referred to by various terms—such as *teacher aides, teacher assistants, volunteer tutors, paraprofessionals*—came into the classrooms of the country in vast numbers, some as paid personnel, others as volunteers. Undoubtedly in some school districts the inability to obtain enough teachers to staff the school program was not the only reason for engaging many paraprofessionals and for eagerly accepting help from volunteers. The lower compensation of those who were paid, as compared with that of teachers, and the lack of any expense in using volunteers were also factors. The former of the two reasons, shortage of teachers, is no longer operative; but the second, the financial one, is increasingly powerful, with the tightening of financial support of schools.

There is no question but that paraprofessionals have rendered a valuable service. Their help has seldom been challenged as they assist teachers in work such as correcting papers, making charts and graphs and other visual aids, keeping record of attendance, supervising (under teacher guidance) some of the work on individual group projects. However, there is much legitimate concern where these people are given teaching responsibilities which, in the opinion of many, should be reserved for fully-qualified teachers. Since many paraprofessionals are helping with reading programs, the debate on the use of teacher aides of all types is one to be seriously considered in some school districts in relation to the planning of the total reading program.

The Structure of the Reading Program

The staff must decide whether special classes in basal reading instruction will be set up. While some teachers believe that reading instruction can best be carried on in connection with other learning experiences, chiefly on an incidental basis, the great majority of American schools provide for systematic reading instruction in scheduled periods for the development of basic skills. Systematic instruction in these skills does not preclude incidental instruction at various times throughout the school day. Nor does it take away the need of a strong literature program nor of the importance of teaching boys and girls to read in the content areas.

While it is true that some children learn to read well without any systematic instruction, acquiring all needed skills through abundant and highly motivated reading, the vast majority of children need instructional assistance if they are to learn to read at their best. The regularly scheduled reading period will continue to be indispensable for most teachers and with most children if essential skills are to be developed.

In schools in which a period is set aside in the school program for systematic reading instruction, usually a reading series is used, either as in the manner described under "Diagnostic Grouping" Chapter 13 (*see* page 422) or as indicated, with variations, in the guidebooks for the teacher accompanying the series. If the latter forms the basis for organization of the basal reading program, certain general cautions should be observed in the planning of the program. These cautions grow out of facts and principles developed earlier in this book. For example, reliance should not be placed on a single basal reader for the whole class; indeed, it should not be placed on an entire single series. In any given class basal readers designed for many levels of reading ability and containing many different kinds of material should be provided. It is fortunate that, increasingly, newer reading textbook series have, as their basic plan of organization, levels of reading which cut across grade designations. If a series is organized by grade levels, with arrangements for variations in needs of boys and girls, the reader should not be labeled according to grade level of difficulty, although the publisher's estimate of difficulty level may be indicated by some code device. All basal readers should be amply supplemented with general reading materials on many subjects and representing many levels of reading difficulty. In the primary grades every effort should be put forth to make the initial experiences with books pleasurable and rewarding. In the intermediate grades the teacher should try to relate specific reading skills to the reading situations arising in the various curricular areas. The reading in basal readers should be accompanied by reading activities in other textbooks calling for similar skills, such as locating information, summarizing a paragraph, or using the dictionary. Basal readers should not be used for mere oral drill, in smaller or larger groups, in which everyone marks time while one pupil struggles through a passage. Pupils who are able to complete the material in the basal reader rapidly and without instructional assistance should be permitted to go on to more difficult materials.

Instructional Materials, Equipment, and Special Facilities

In the preceding paragraphs and at various other places in this book we have referred to the most popular of all reading materials, the basal textbook. When planning a reading program teachers should be well acquainted with various reading series, with the many materials accompanying them, and with many other materials on the market. Study of these materials can well be the focus of concentration for one or more committees.

Guidebooks for the teacher are published with all extensively used reading series. At times these are published as separate paperbacks; at other times the suggestions to the teacher are given in a teacher's edition of the book, in which a part of the book is the same as the pupil's edition and another part is designed only for the teacher's use. Often, even in the part reproducing what is given in the pupil's edition, suggestions for the teacher are included in the margins of the pages and/or as notations written along with the lines of the text. The guidebooks can be of great help to the teacher if they are used, as most of them are intended to be used, as suggestive of possible procedures to be followed, not as prescriptive.

With almost all the basal reading series there are also consumable books for boys and girls, often referred to as workbooks. Workbooks of various types, when not used as "busy work," can be of real service. The better series have a well-developed sequence of workbooks designed to be used in conjunction with the hardback books, the regular readers. Most of these are written to give the boys and girls practice after the material in the textbook has been read. An examination of any workbook accompanying a reader will reveal a variety of ways in which it provides practice for work on word recognition and other reading skills.

But not all workbooks published as part of a reading series are planned to be studied by the child after he has read a corresponding section in the textbook. Some are designed so that a child studies a number of pages in the workbook before he reads the material that corresponds to it in the reader. In that case the new words for the selection in the reader are presented in the workbook and practice on their recognition is provided. In this type of arrangement the child thus meets in the workbook, before he even starts the regular book, all the new words in the story.

Some teachers prefer making material of the workbook type themselves, believing that it is better suited to the needs of the particular boys and girls than that given in the workbooks. Although this practice has merit, it is time-consuming and not really necessary today. It is true, however, that when workbook materials were sterile in content and poor in selection of objectives to be accomplished, it was not difficult to justify the large amount of time that many teachers, especially in the lower grades, spent in devising and duplicating materials to provide practice beyond that given in the reader on various reading skills.

In using workbooks that are not made to accompany any one series readers, there is the danger of lack of unity in objectives and procedures between reader and workbook. If the authors of the textbook series have in mind one program for the development of word recognition and the writers of the workbook follow a different sequence and observe other criteria, the articulation when using these two types of materials is often poor. This difficulty is especially likely to exist if the teacher is under pressure to require every pupil to do every page in a workbook, regardless of the appropriateness of the material to the rest of the program and to the needs of the boys and girls. Nevertheless, judicious use of workbooks that are made independently of any one series of readers can be helpful if the workbooks are based on sound principles of teaching reading.

Figure 16.1 Tapes can be an aid in the learning-to-read adventure. (Dubuque Public Schools, Iowa.)

In addition to basal readers, guidebooks, and workbooks a flood of materials for reading instruction has appeared on the market, some of which accompanies reading series, but much of which is produced without any single series in mind. They include word cards and phrase cards, films and film strips, slides, tapes and video tapes, cassettes, charts, instructional kits (often with multimedia materials), programed materials, records and recordings, among other materials. Machines for use with or without some of these materials include filmstrip viewers, filmstrip projectors, cassette players, reading rate accelerators of various kinds, motion picture machines, equipment for producing and showing video tapes, and much other equipment.

It is, indeed, difficult for the classroom teacher to evaluate the great variety of materials on the market. Of help should be the following resolution, entitled "Buyer Be Wary" and adopted by the Delegates Assembly of the Tenth Annual Convention of the International Reading Association in May 1969:

> A wide variety of services, devices, and training materials which purport to produce the improvement of reading skills is currently being offered to the general public. In some instances, the advertising accompanying these materials approaches sensationalism, exaggeration and even

misrepresentation, when judged with regard to the limits of present professional knowledge.

To aid the prospective user of reading improvement devices and services, the International Reading Association offers the following cautions:

1. Statements of possible benefits from reading improvement services should be characterized by modesty and due caution for the limits of professional skill, which does not encompass cure-all powers.

2. The possible causes of inadequate or poor reading skills are many. There is no single treatment or approach known which will effectively correct all possible causes of difficulty.

3. No ethical person who is a professional in the area of reading improvement can or should guarantee marked improvement of skills for all users of his services.

4. Distributors of reading devices or materials have an ethical obligation to submit their products to fair scientific trials before marketing, and to make the data of these evaluations available to all prospective purchasers."

WHEREAS
the members of the International Reading Association also view with grave concern the advertised claims of certain reading programs designed to enable children to teach themselves to read and to achieve considerably above normal reading levels

BE IT THEREFORE RESOLVED
that the Fourteenth Annual Convention of the International Reading Association condemn such advertising and declare it in violation of the reading profession's ethics unless (1) the claims are documented by independent replicable research, and (2) the measuring instruments used to supply the evidence upon which the claims are based are named upon request and, if not for sale by a publisher, be made available to reading specialists.

BE IT FURTHER RESOLVED
that the Fourteenth Annual Convention of the International Reading Association declares that failure of an advertised reading program to meet the above standards and procedures places its sponsors outside the bounds of ethical professional behavior and entitles them to receive professional and scientific censure.

As evaluation is being made of instructional materials and equipment, consideration should also be given to physical facilities that might be provided for a reading program. The checklist, drawn up by an ad hoc committee[1] of the International Reading Association, which is reproduced here, suggests some of the facilities that might be considered for purchase or

[1] John H. Martin, "Guidelines for Planning Special Reading Facilities," *The Reading Teacher*, vol. 24, vol. 3 (December 1970), p. 206.

construction. It is given in full even though some items included duplicate some that have already been mentioned in the preceding paragraphs, and some refer only to clinical set-ups.

1. File space
2. Storage space, both locked and open, for machines, tests, charts, kits, and so forth
3. Shelving for storing books, magazines, workbooks, games
4. Desk and table space
5. Display area for books, student work, progress charts, and so on
6. Space for materials preparation
7. Wheeled carts
8. Electrical outlets
9. Testing and tutoring rooms
10. Space for semi-independent small group work
11. Darkening and dimming equipment
12. Professional reference shelf
13. Carpeted reading corner in classrooms
14. Movable room dividers, movable walls
15. Projection screen
16. Provision for hanging charts
17. Acoustical panels on walls and ceiling
18. Full-length mirror in clinic
19. Typewriter stands
20. Toilet and sink
21. Carrels
22. Attractive color scheme.

INTERPRETING THE READING PROGRAM TO PARENTS

In any school, regardless of whether a new reading program is being proposed, careful thought needs to be given to the role of the parent. In the first place, parents have a right to know what the school's objectives in reading are and why it is using the particular procedures it has adopted in reading instruction. The intelligence and good judgment of parents should be respected. Most parents who are interested in their children's schooling are perfectly able to understand the principles on which the school's policies are based when these are clearly explained to them. The school should make clear that it regards the education of children as a team project in

Figure 16.2 Interest in reading begins at home. (Roger Rouch.)

which the home and the school have a common interest. It is no accident that in those communities where there has been friendly cooperation and good communication between home and school, the recent unreasonable criticisms of modern reading practices have had least effect.

Moreover, the school very much needs the help of the home in teaching the child to read. Parents can do much in creating a home atmosphere favorable to the development of reading ability. They are often in a better position than teachers to discover children's interests and to perceive the emotional reactions that children have toward the reading situation. By surrounding the young child with good books adapted to his level of ability, by setting the example of silent reading, by reading aloud to him and talking with him about stories and pictures, and in general by making reading an enjoyable experience for him from the earliest years, parents can lay the indispensable foundation for later success in reading.

Most parents, however, do not have the needed training for developing specific reading skills. While they should be kept informed about the changing trends in reading instruction, they should normally leave the formal instruction to the classroom teacher. When children ask questions about words or ideas encountered in the reading, they should not hesitate to give needed help. Reading drills, except perhaps occasionally at the request of the teacher, have no place in the home. Reading "games," yes; easy, attractive books for pleasurable reading, yes; but word drills and phonics (except in play) at home, no. The best contribution parents can make to the reading progress of their children is to provide them with a secure and happy home, an abundance of love and encouragement, a great variety of play, creative and constructive experiences, and unlimited opportunity for free reading in good books and magazines. Time to read, encouragement to read, and materials to read are necessary; pressure and a sense of urgency may be dangerous.

Concepts of Special Interest to Parents

Parents can be helped to understand a number of important concepts of modern reading instruction. One of these is the concept of readiness, which has been discussed earlier in this book. We know that not all children are ready to begin learning to read at the same chronological age. Since most parents assume that first grade is the time for all children to learn to read, it becomes necessary to explain to them that children vary in their readiness for initial reading instruction. Delay in any of these processes is by no means evidence of backwardness. The important thing to remember is that the first experiences with reading should be happy, successful ones. If for any reason a child is not ready to read with fluency and satisfaction, he should be given the opportunity to develop the needed maturity.

A second concept that frequently needs to be explained to parents is the policy of the school in beginning reading instruction, regardless of whether the code approach, the meaning approach, or a combination of the two is used. Parents will want to be informed about the role of phonics in the instructional program. A great many parents believe, or have recently been convinced by popular publications, that the chief weakness of modern reading instruction is the neglect of phonics. Such complaints have been heard for a long time. They were especially vigorous in the decade of the twenties, when the importance of silent reading began to be stressed in many quarters. Parents should be assured that phonics instruction is still given in school; that in many schools it relies less on mechanical and memorization methods and more on natural analytic methods; that in these schools it is given at strategic times and to pupils who need it; and that it occupies an important place in the total reading program, in the basal readers, and in the teachers' manuals. They should also be helped to realize, however, that phonics is only one of many helps to the recognition of words. The use of additional methods, involving context clues, general configuration, and structural analysis, has strengthened pupils' ability to recognize new words. If reading programs involving i/t/a, words-in-color, a linguistic approach, or other innovations are in operation or are being planned, they should be discussed with the parents. Parents will be pleased to know that the schools are not standing still in their efforts to teach children the diverse skills of word recognition.

Finally, parents should be informed about the role of oral reading. Modern schools teach children to read orally, and most of them use a certain amount of oral reading in the initial stages of reading instruction. However, they recognize that most reading outside of school is silent, that adult silent reading should usually be at least twice as rapid as oral reading, and that the skills of silent reading differ in important respects from those of oral reading. Schools, therefore, stress silent reading throughout the grades, giving attention to oral reading as a significant separate skill or using it as an aid in the improvement of silent reading. Parents whose own recollections of school reading are associated with oral communication or sounding of words may be interested in the reasons for the new emphasis. Most of them will be pleased to note the increased use of purposeful oral reading and the decline of oral reading exercises which required the class to mark time while one pupil recited.

Methods of Communicating with Parents

The best of all the methods of promoting home-school cooperation is the personal interview. In one elementary school, for example, the principal systematically interviews one or both parents of every child entering school for the first time. In the course of his conferences he tries to discover the viewpoints of the parents and their assessments of their children's needs and capacities, for he believes he has much to learn from parents. At the same time he explains to the parents the plan of reading instruction fol-

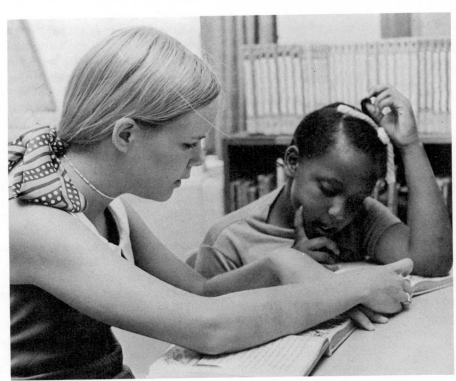

Figure 16.3 Parent involvement in tutoring projects pays dividends. (Oklahoma City Public Schools.)

lowed in the school and the major considerations that led to the adoption of the plan. Since he is able to show that the plan is getting good results in terms of national averages, the great majority of parents are enthusiastic, in spite of the fact that the reading program in this particular school is un-conventional.

In other schools certain days are set aside each year for teacher-parent conferences. On these days all teachers meet individually with parents of pupils in their classes. In these conferences teachers report the progress that the children are making in school and answer parents' questions about the instructional procedures employed. While the method is time-con-suming, it recognizes the important fact that parents are most intimately concerned with the progress of their children and hence should be both consulted and informed.

Some school systems—such as that in Seattle, Washington—publish attractively illustrated leaflets addressed to parents, setting forth in some of them the rationale of the reading program in the schools. Parents in many communities are invited, even urged, to visit the schools and to ob-serve the reading program in action. In some schools colored slides il-lustrating the use of modern reading techniques are shown at PTA meetings and to civic groups. Tape recordings made in the classroom are played at such meetings to demonstrate progress that has been achieved in certain aspects of reading.

Another valuable device for involving parents in the work of the school is the occasional chatty newsletter, written by the teacher especially for the parents of his pupils. Such a newsletter can include the names of the children; some information about the teacher himself; references to the principal, clerk, nurse, custodians, and their duties; notes of appreciation for things parents have done for the school; and announcements of PTA meetings. Succeeding newsletters can report plans for various class activi-ties; invite parents to visit the class; request materials for baking, construc-tion, nature study, and the like; and, particularly, explain the educational significance and purpose of the activities.

EVALUATION OF THE READING PROGRAM

Appraisal of a schoolwide reading program is a difficult task, made espe-cially puzzling by the fact that in spite of much research in the area of the teaching of reading, to very few issues has an unqualified solution been found. No one clear answer has been given to many questions of great im-port to those who are eager to teach boys and girls to read as effectively as possible. As one surveys, for example, the accounts of approaches to reading instruction and the investigations in that area, one looks in vain for a convincing answer. Enthusiasts of specific methods of procedure in teaching reading make contradictory claims. Interpreters of the same research present different conclusions. The teacher as well as the parent may well ask: "What is the truth about the teaching of reading?"

In spite of lack of final answers to the question and in spite of the fact that any evaluative process necessarily involves many value judgments on matters for which research has thus far not been clearcut, all schools, whether venturing on a new program of reading instruction or continuing with one established earlier, should have as a priority concern the evaluation of the program. Though evaluation should be continuous, at intervals a rather comprehensive appraisal should be made either by the staff alone or with the help of one or more outside consultants expert in making evaluations and making recommendations on the basis of their findings. The evaluation should include more than a study of how well the boys and girls are reading, as described earlier (*see* Chapter 12), though that should certainly be an important phase of it. All factors that influence the success of the reading program should be considered.

Use of Checklists

One device for evaluating reading programs is the checklist. The questions on one devised by Sidney J. Rauch[2] are reproduced here. Each question in the checklist that can be answered by a *yes* response constitutes a *plus* for the program being evaluated.

The Reading Program

1. Is it a K-12 sequential program where the skills of one level are built upon the skills of previous levels?
2. Are the following components of a good reading program emphasized?
    1. Word recognition skills
    2. Comprehension skills
    3. Study skills
    4. Planned literature program
    5. Recreational reading
3. What materials are being used to supplement basic instructional texts?
    1. Workbooks
    2. Programmed materials
    3. Instructional kits
    4. Trade books
    5. Audio-visual materials
    6. Others
4. Is a love for reading being instilled?
5. Are the following three types of reading programs being emphasized?

[2] Sidney J. Rauch, "A Checklist for the Evaluation of Reading Programs," *The Reading Teacher*, vol. 21, no. 6 (March 1968), pp. 520–522.

1. Developmental (i.e., basically the type of program for "able" readers doing grade level reading and above).
2. Corrective (i.e., basically the type of program for those pupils who are slightly below grade level and whose instructional needs can be met in the regular classroom).
3. Remedial (i.e., basically the type of program for those pupils who are seriously below grade level, and who require specialized instruction in an individual or small-group situation).

6. Is the program being continually evaluated?
7. Is reading regarded as a process rather than a subject?

Comments

The Administrative and Supervisory Staff

1. Are school leaders knowledgeable about the reading process?
2. Do they provide an atmosphere conducive to learning?
3. Do they provide time and personnel for in-service training?
4. Are the necessary basic instructional materials furnished?
5. Are the supplementary materials furnished?
6. Do they encourage educational experimentation and innovations?
7. Do they fully support the work of the reading supervisor, consultant, or specialist?
8. Are teachers consulted or advised before new programs are instituted, or changes made?
   a. Programmed instruction
   b. Initial teaching alphabet
   c. Linguistically-oriented texts
   d. Color coding
   e. Nongraded grouping
   f. Others
9. Is creativity on the part of teachers encouraged?
10. Is time provided for teacher observations and intervisitations?

Comments

The Teaching Staff

1. Are they experienced?
2. Are they receptive to change?
3. Are they receptive to offers of professional help?
4. Are efforts being made to improve their instruction?
   a. In-service programs
   b. Conferences
   c. Recommended readings
   d. Demonstrations
   e. Intervisitations

5. Are efforts made to individualize instructions?
6. Are they flexible in their grouping procedures?
7. Does the teacher consider the basal reader as a tool for teaching reading skills, rather than as a complete reading program?
8. Is the library made an important part of the reading program?
9. Are teacher-aides and/or clerical assistance available?
10. Do teachers take advantage of community resources to enrich their teaching?

Comments

The Pupils

1. Are they reading on their own?
2. Is application of reading skills made to the content areas?
3. Do they recognize reading as a four-step process (Wm. S. Gray's definition in *On Their Own in Reading*)?
   a. Word perception
   b. Comprehension
   c. Reaction or evaluation
   d. Integration of ideas
4. Is evaluation of reading skills an on-going process?
   a. Teacher observation
   b. Standardized reading tests
   c. Informal reading tests
5. Are they given opportunities to report on books?
   a. Written reports
   b. Oral reports
   c. Dramatization
6. Do pupils have a positive attitude towards the reading teacher or specialist?
7. Do they handle books and supplementary materials with respect?

Comments

The Parents

1. Are they familiar with the school's philosophy of reading instruction?
2. Has the program been adequately presented to them?
3. Are they given an opportunity to participate in various phases of the reading program (e.g., book fairs, volunteer tutoring, etc.)?
4. Are they satisfied with the reading program?
5. Are contemplated changes or new programs presented to them?
6. Are parents contributing to readiness for beginning reading?
7. Are they given opportunities to express their opinions and make recommendations?
8. Do they feel that all pupils are involved in the reading program?

9. Are the majority of parents readers themselves?
10. Do parents take advantage of community resources in enriching their children's experiential background?

Comments

Other Means of Evaluation

Just as there is no one known method of teaching reading that is accepted as *the* method, so there is no perfect device for determining what is the best currently used approach. However, there are various ways of helping the teacher with this question in addition to those already described. The thoughtful reading of reports on experimental set-ups and of research on innovative programs can be of aid in determining which approaches to the teaching of reading should be followed. Study of the literature on the teaching of reading—as found in books on methods of teaching, in periodicals, and in other publications—can form a background against which to make appraisals. In this book, chapter after chapter, there are suggested, directly or indirectly, those theories and practices for teaching reading that the authors consider valid.

Engaging in what used to be commonly called action research can also be of value to the teacher who desires to follow a program in the teaching of reading that will bring the best possible results. In other words, the teacher can try out in his own classroom some of the methods and techniques that seem to him to be of promise.

Finally, even after the teacher has attempted to the best of his ability to evaluate various approaches to teaching reading, he will still find that his appraisal is lacking in objectivity. But he cannot wait idly for a better day to come when evaluation techniques will give him more specific directions. The teacher in the classroom cannot postpone teaching reading until research has discovered without a doubt the most successful approach. As day after day he attempts to do his work as effectively as he can, he must ever make use of the means of evaluation at his disposal, imperfect though they are. If he follows this suggestion, he will not be without a guide. If with such a spirit teachers face the reading problems of the 1970s and the 1980s, the trend in the teaching of reading in those decades will continue to be upward.

Related Issues

Our discussion of the evaluation of reading programs would hardly be complete without attention to three terms that are increasingly being used when referring to the appraisal of the success with which elementary school subjects, including reading, are being taught. They are *accountability, performance contracting,* and *national assessment.*

Accountability

Accountability is not a new concept even though the term has not, until lately, been used often in professional writing. Good teachers have always considered themselves accountable for their teaching, and poor teachers have been held accountable whether they have liked it or not. Teachers are accountable to the boys and girls they teach, to the parents of those children, to the school administration, and to the public that supports the schools. All evaluation of teachers—whether by boys and girls, parents, school administrators, or the general public—has always been an indication of accountability. School administrators and supervisors have exercised their responsibility for evaluation of teachers by means such as classroom visitation, examination of the academic achievements of boys and girls, consideration of reports about teachers, and conferences with them. Through formal and informal evaluative means they have made decisions on retention, salary increments, and promotions.

The public, too, has never been slow to express its opinion of teachers. It is only right and proper that teachers should be judged by the society which engages them to teach. Of late the voices raised in protest over what schools are doing are being heard increasingly. Nor is such increased criticism necessarily undesirable. It can bespeak more interest of the public in its schools—a plea for which schools have long made. That the evaluation has become less passive in nature we realize as we note the favorable reaction of the public to books highly critical of the schools and as we think of the fact that suit was filed by an eighteen-year-old graduate of the San Francisco Unified School District against the school district and the state department of education because of alleged failure to teach him to read up to his capacity.[3]

Undoubtedly the teaching profession needs to be reminded from time to time that it is accountable. Thus, benefit can be derived from an insistence on accountability. However, there are also dangers involved in the concept of accountability as it is advocated by some of its chief proponents. An underlying difficulty stems from the fact that many advocates of accountability, as the term is now used, are seemingly unaware of the problems involved in obtaining a fair indication of the quality of a teacher's performance. Frequently they place their confidence in pre- and post-tests given the boys and girls near the beginning and toward the end of the school year. Specialists in the area of tests and measurements have long warned us that no test or combination of tests gives a perfect index of the achievement of the learner. Thus, through too much faith in test results an erroneous impression of the performance of a boy or girl can be obtained. Some of the other factors that complicate and hinder the search for adequate means of holding teachers accountable are:

[3] Gary Saretzky, "The Strangely Significant Case of Peter Doe," *Phi Delta Kappan*, vol. LIV, no. 9 (May 1973), pp. 589–592.

1. No perfect means of determining a child's potential—his learning capacity—have been devised. It is generally agreed that intelligence tests, as a rule, are the best indicator that we have. However, they are so far from reliable and valid instruments for measuring mental ability that great caution must be observed before a teacher is considered lacking because, according to test data, a child has not made progress commensurate with his ability.

2. The teacher cannot be given sole credit for the progress or lack of it made by a child. Home conditions may be favorable or unfavorable to learning. On the one hand, if all progress a child makes, let us say in reading, is attributed to the teaching, the teacher can be overrated; on the other hand, if all lack of progress is blamed on the teacher, the teacher can be sorely underrated. What complicates the appraisal is that during some periods of time home conditions can be a positive influence toward learning and at other times in the same home the environment may be devastating to intellectual development. Examples of other factors beyond the control of the teacher are: the opportunity the child has to read outside of school, the incentive for reading that he may get as he finds books in the public library that serve as reason for further exploration of the field of a newly acquired interest, the effect that a friend who enjoys reading may have on a pupil.

3. Psychologists who have specialized in the study of how learning takes place emphasize the point that learning often does not progress at an even rate, but that frequently it seemingly goes by spurts. A child may reach a plateau in his learning and remain on it, through no fault of his teacher, for much or all of a school year. Or, again, without credit to the teacher, he may be having a spurt in learning. Any system of accountability, to be fair, must take cognizance of knowledge such as this available from the field of the psychology of learning.

4. Care needs to be taken that more than academic achievement is taken into consideration as teachers are being held accountable. A teacher's influence on the whole child is of greater importance than his skill in teaching reading. Because of the difficulty of measuring even fairly accurately the effect a teacher may have on the total growing personality of the child, great caution needs to be exercised when putting into practice the concept of accountability.

5. If teachers are to be held increasingly accountable for their product, they must be provided with teaching situations in which excellent results can reasonably be expected. Overcrowded classrooms; poorly equipped libraries; lack of adequate supervision; little, if any, attention to in-service education of teachers—all these can seriously affect the results a teacher can produce.

6. One of the grave dangers of misuses of accountability is that some teachers may consider it advantageous to their rating to teach so that

their pupils will make high scores on tests. Since no combination of tests can measure adequately all the variables we consider important for child growth and development, there is imminent danger that some of the more intangible but highly important results of teaching will not be emphasized.

Performance Contracting

Performance contracting has within recent years entered the educational scene as what may be thought of as "guaranteed achievement" in learning. Under this plan school districts contract with certain educational publishers with the understanding that the publishers will provide for the school the materials of instruction and supervisory staff for work with the materials. Included in the contract is the guarantee that a certain designated level of achievement will be attained by the pupils by a specified time. The agreement usually is that if that standard is not reached, there will be forfeiture of remuneration to the company for materials used during the "trial period" and, incidentally, for the services of the supervisory personnel provided by the company. That such a plan would be the subject of much controversy can readily be understood. One of the major criticisms is that many educators are opposed to the exclusive use of materials of instruction of only one company for any school subject. Another is that there is danger of high-pressure methods of instruction developing or becoming popular with the determination that at any cost the results guaranteed by the contract must be achieved. Certainly no school district should accept performance contracting with any publisher without careful study of the implications of the contract. Since reading and mathematics are the two areas for which contracts have been most frequently issued, a study of the plan is of vital concern to teachers of reading.

A description of performance contracting with the Behavioral Research Laboratories in one of the schools of Gary, Indiana, in which the contract was cancelled before the expiration of the planned three-year term is reported in *Phi Delta Kappan.*[4] The article indicates both advantages of the contracting and problems connected with it.

National Assessment of Educational Progress (NAEP)

National Assessment of Educational Progress, ever since its beginning in 1964, has been a much discussed and often bitterly opposed issue. It was originally funded by the Carnegie Corporation, but now it receives its budget from the U.S. Office of Education. Dale Foreman,[5] formerly assistant director of research and analysis for the NAEP, states the purpose of the venture in these words:

[4] James A. Mecklenburger, "Epilogue: The Performance Contract in Gary," *Phi Delta Kappan,* vol. LIV, no. 8 (April 1973), pp. 582–586.

[5] Dale J. Foreman, "National Assessment of Elementary Reading," *The Reading Teacher,* vol. 26, no. 3 (December 1972), p. 293.

. . . to make available baseline, censuslike data on the educational attainment of young Americans relative to certain evidence and periodically to obtain evidence concerning progress in meeting these objectives.

Reading is among the ten subject areas included in the project. After the objectives for reading had been drawn up, exercises were devised for testing the attainment of these objectives. The reading tests were given to individuals from four age groups, namely persons 9 years of age, 13 years, 17 years, and to young adults varying in age between 26 and 33. Test results were secured from about 29,500 in the 9-year-old category. They were tabulated to show the percentage of that population which could perform stated reading tasks. The intention is to make assessments every five years so that comparisons can be shown between the results obtained from successive assessments.

While there are objections to the methods and procedures employed in the project, the heated opposition to it from professional teacher organizations and individuals stems from the fact that it is strongly suspected by some of involving more than a measurement of the level of reading achievement on a national scale. It is feared by them that it may lead to a national curriculum and ultimately to an evaluation of the teacher, based on how well his students perform on national tests. Whether these fears are well grounded is a matter of conjecture. The need for such fears is denied by those favoring the project.

Regardless of what method of evaluation or assessment is used by local, state, or national groups, the dedicated teacher will continue to view reading in a broad setting. He will not make the mistake of assuming that the sole task of the teacher of reading is to develop proficiency in reading. Though both our experience and our observation lead us to a strong belief that reading makes a difference in how people think, feel, and act, we hold firmly to the conviction that schools must be deeply concerned about the total impact of the reading program on the child as a person and on his outlook on life. Therein lies the great challenge in the teaching of reading.

For Further Study

Blanton, William. "ERIC/CRIER Report: Performance-Based Teacher Education: Training Teachers of Reading," *Reading World*, vol. 11, no. 3 (March 1972), pp. 232–239.

Bratten, Dale, "Performance Contracting: How It Works in Texarkana," *School Management*, vol. 14 (August 1970), pp. 8–10.

Cass, James, "Profit and Loss in Education: Texarkana and Gary, Indiana," *Saturday Review*, vol. 53 (August 15, 1970), pp. 39–40.

Criscuolo, Nicholas P., "Approaches to In-service Reading Programs," *The Reading Teacher*, vol. 24, no. 5 (February 1971), pp. 422–424.

Durost, Walter N., "Accountability: The Task, the Tools, and the Pitfalls," *The Reading Teacher*, vol. 24, no. 4 (January 1971), pp. 595–602.

Foreman, Dale I., "National Assessment of Elementary Reading," *The Reading Teacher*, vol. 26, no. 3 (December 1972), pp. 293–298.

Freshour, Frank W., "Beginning Reading: Parents Can Help," *The Reading Teacher*, vol. 24, no. 4 (January 1971), pp. 511–516.

Harris, Albert J. "New Dimensions in Basal Readers," *The Reading Teacher*, vol. 25, no. 4 (January 1972), pp. 310–315.

Harris, Albert J., and Edward R. Sipay, eds., *Readings on Reading Instruction*, 2nd ed. (New York: David McKay Company, 1972), Article #2, "Key Factors in a Successful Reading Program" by Albert J. Harris, pp. 7–14.

Hobson, Eve, "Learning and Teaching to Become a 'Real Person' through 'Educational Accountability,'" *The Delta Kappa Gamma Bulletin*, vol. 39, no. 2 (Winter 1973), pp. 24–30.

Houston, W. Robert, and Robert B. Howsam, *Competency-Based Teacher Education: Progress, Problems, and Prospects* (Chicago: Science Research Associates, 1972).

Krull, R. Pratt, Jr., "Performance Contracting," *Instructor*, vol. 80 (January 1971), p. 22.

Landers, Jacob, "Accountability and Progress by Nomenclature: Old Ideas in New Bottles," *Phi Delta Kappan* vol. LIV, no. 8 (April 1973), pp. 539–541.

Lapp, Diane, *Use of Behavioral Objectives in Education*, Reading Information Series (Newark, Del.: International Reading Association, 1972).

McDonald, James B., and Bernice Wolfson, "A Case against Behavioral Objectives," *Elementary School Journal*, vol. 71 (December 1970), pp. 119–128.

McNeil, John D., "Performance Tests: Assessing Teachers of Reading: A Proposal," *The Reading Teacher*, vol. 27, no. 7 (April 1972), p. 622.

Nephew, Eve, "Behavioral Objectives and Program Reorganization," *The Reading Teacher*, vol. 25, no. 7 (April 1972), pp. 618–621.

Otto, Wayne, and Richard J. Smith, *Administering the School Reading Program* (Boston: Houghton Mifflin Company, 1970), Ch. 8, "In-service Education and the Reading Program."

Rapport, Virginia, ed., *Learning Centers: Children on Their Own* (Washington, D.C.: The Association for Childhood Education International, 1970).

Rauch, Sidney J., "A Checklist for the Evaluation of the Reading Program," *The Reading Teacher*, vol. 21, no. 6 (March 1968), pp. 519–522.

Rauch, Sidney J., "How to Evaluate a Reading Program," *The Reading Teacher*, vol. 24, no. 3 (December 1970), pp. 244–250.

Smith, Carl B., ed., *Parents and Reading* (Newark, Del.: International Reading Association, 1971).

Sutton, Marjorie Hunt, "Accountability and Teaching Reading," *The Reading Teacher*, vol. 25, no. 6 (March 1972), pp. 526–530.

Sartain, Harry W., and Paul E. Stanton, eds., *Professional Preparation for Teaching Reading* (Newark, Del.: International Reading Association, 1973).

Strang, Ruth, *Diagnostic Teaching of Reading* (New York: McGraw-Hill Book Company, 1969), Ch. 1, "Introduction."

Tanner, Daniel, *Using Behavioral Objectives in the Classroom* (New York: The Macmillan Company, 1972).

Walker, Jerry L., "National Assessment of Reading," *The Reading Teacher*, vol. 24, no. 8 (May 1971), pp. 711–714.

Wallen, Carl J., and Sam Leaton Sebesta, *Readings on Teaching Reading* (Chicago: Science Research Associates, 1972), "Parents and School Should Share" by Elizabeth Davis, pp. 284–288.

Wanat, Stanley F., "Performance Tests: Assessing Teachers of Reading: A Response," *The Reading Teacher*, vol. 25, no. 7 (April 1972), p. 628.

Questions and Comments for Thought and Discussion

1. In the first part of this chapter several conditions essential to an effective reading program are named and discussed. Can you think of others?

2. Why is it important that no new schoolwide program in reading be planned that does not have the enthusiastic support of most teachers?

3. You will find it profitable to examine with care a number of the more recent basal reading series, as you look for evidence of some of the trends in the production of basal textbooks discussed in this chapter.

4. To most readers of this book there are undoubtedly available for examination many different types of supplementary materials for reading—materials other than the basal reading textbook. Examination and evaluation of a variety of them is recommended as a helpful activity.

5. You may wish to read more about the highly controversial project, *National Assessment of Educational Progress,* so that you will be more familiar with its advantages and/or limitations.

6. To what extent do you think a teacher of reading should be held accountable for his work? What dangers do you note in ways in which the concept of teacher accountability might be applied to school practices? Have you any suggestions as to how teachers should be held accountable for their work?

7. You may be interested in reading the article by Jacob Landers, "Accountability and Progress of Nomenclature: Old Ideas in New Bottles,"

in the April 1973 issue of *Phi Delta Kappan*. You may wish to discuss your reactions with your classmates.

8. As you continue your reading in professional books and magazines, as you attend conferences, and as you talk with others you may find rather frequent reference to teacher accountability, performance contracting, and the *National Assessment of Educational Progress*. All these are topics on which there is much current argument. You will find it profitable to note with care the alleged strengths and weaknesses of these three evaluative procedures.

Outline for Chapter 17

RESOURCES FOR TEACHING READING

Books
    Books for Teachers
        Books on the Teaching of Reading: A General
           Bibliography
        Books on Literature for Children
        Books on Creative Expression
        Books Dealing with Linguistics
        Books Dealing with Diagnosis and Remediation
        Books on the Culturally Different
    Books for Parents
    General Books for Boys and Girls
        Sources for Book Selection
        Book Awards
        Book Club Selections
        "Easy-to-read" Books
        Books for Retarded Readers
    Textbooks for Boys and Girls
    Reference Books for Boys and Girls
Periodicals
    Periodicals for Teachers
    Periodicals for Boys and Girls
Other Reading Materials
    Evaluation
    Sources of Materials
    Reading Laboratories
Tests
    Mental Tests
      Individual Tests
      Group Tests
    Reading Readiness Tests
    Reading Tests
Audiovisual Aids
    Films
      Films for Teachers
      Films for Boys and Girls
    Filmstrips
    Records
    Guides to Selection
    Producers and Distributors
Addresses of Publishing and Distributing Companies

17
CHAPTER

Resources for Teaching Reading[1]

There is available commercially a bewilderingly large number of materials for teaching reading. In spite of the great abundance of materials—in fact, in part because of it—teachers often do not know where to turn to find that which will prove to be helpful to them. With this problem in mind, many types of resources for teaching reading are listed in this chapter, with an indication as to where they can be obtained. The listing in all the categories is far from complete. It is intentionally kept brief enough so that, when making use of it, the reader will not find himself lost in a myriad of listings.

No attempt has been made to evaluate the resources to which reference is made in these pages. The worth of many materials depends on the needs of the teacher or his pupils and on the use to be made of them.

BOOKS

The first part of this section on books lists some for the teacher of reading; the second names books of value to parents; and the last deals with books for boys and girls—with general books, textbooks, and reference books.

[1] Acknowledgment is made of the fact that this chapter is based in part on the last chapter of *Teaching the Language Arts in the Elementary School*, 2nd ed., by Martha Dallmann (Wm. C. Brown Company Publishers, 1971).

Books for Teachers

It is recommended that the reader supplement the listing of professional books given in this chapter by examination of the catalogues of publishers of books on the teaching of reading and related topics and by study of professional magazines (*see* page 572) in which such books are reviewed.

Books on the Teaching of Reading: A General Bibliography

In this general bibliography are not included the books listed on subsequent pages of this chapter under the more specific headings such as "Books on Linguistics" or "Books on the Culturally Different."

Anderson, Verna, *Reading and Young Children* (New York: The Macmillan Company, 1968).

Aukerman, Robert C., *Approaches to Beginning Reading* (New York: John Wiley & Sons, Inc., 1971).

Austin, Mary, and Coleman Morrison, *The First R: The Harvard Report on Reading in Elementary Schools* (New York: The Macmillan Company, 1963).

Barbe, Walter B., *Educator's Guide to Personalized Reading Instruction* (Englewood Cliffs, N.J.: Prentice-Hall, Inc., 1966).

Barbe, Walter B., ed., *Teaching Reading: Selected Materials* (New York: Oxford University Press, 1965).

Beery, Althea, Thomas C. Barrett, and William R. Powell, eds., *Elementary Reading Instruction* (Boston: Allyn and Bacon, Inc., 1969).

Berger, Allen, ed., *Speed Reading. An Annotated Bibliography* (Newark, Del.: International Reading Association, 1970).

Binter, Alfred R., John J. Diabal, and Leland K. Kise, eds., *Readings on Reading* (Scranton, Pa.: Intext Educational Publishers, 1969).

Bond, Guy L., and Robert Dykstra, coordinators, *Final Report Project No. X-001* (Washington, D.C.: Bureau of Research, Office of Education, U.S. Department of Health, Education and Welfare, 1967).

Bond, Guy L., and Eva Bond Wagner, *Teaching the Child to Read,* 4th ed. (New York: The Macmillan Company, 1966).

Bush, Clifford L., and Mildred H. Huebner, *Strategies for Reading in the Elementary School* (New York: The Macmillan Company, 1970).

Chall, Jeanne, *Learning to Read: The Great Debate* (New York: McGraw-Hill Book Company, 1967).

Cohen, S. Alan, *Teach Them All to Read* (New York: Random House, Inc., 1969).

Cordts, Anna D., *Phonics for the Reading Teacher* (New York: Holt, Rinehart and Winston, Inc., 1965).

Cushenbery, Donald C., *Reading Improvement in the Elementary School* (West Nyack, N.Y.: Parker Publishing Company, 1969).

Dale, Edgar, and Taher Razik, *Bibliography of Vocabulary Studies* (Columbus, Ohio: The Ohio State University Press, 1964).

Darrow, Helen F., and Virgil M. Howes, *Approaches to Individualized Reading* (New York: Appleton-Century-Crofts, 1969).

Davis, Bonnie M., compiler, *A Guide to Information Sources for Reading* (Newark, Del.: International Reading Association, 1972).

Dawson, Mildred A., compiler, *Developing Comprehension* (Newark, Del.: International Reading Association, 1968).

Dawson, Mildred A., ed., *Teaching Word Recognition Skills* (Newark, Del.: International Reading Association, 1970).

Dawson, Mildred A., and Henry A. Bamman, *Fundamentals of Basic Reading Instruction* (New York: David McKay Company, 1963).

Dechant, Emerald V., *Improving the Teaching of Reading*, 2nd ed. (Englewood Cliffs, N.J.: Prentice-Hall, Inc., 1970).

Dietrich, Dorothy, and Virgina H. Mathews, *Reading and Revolution: The Role of Reading in Today's Society* (Newark, Del.: International Reading Association, 1970).

Doman, Glenn, *How to Teach Your Baby to Read* (New York: Random House, Inc., 1964).

Douglass, Malcolm P., ed., *Reading in Education: A Broader View* (Columbus, Ohio: Charles E. Merrill Publishing Company, 1973).

Downing, John, *Evaluating the Initial Teaching Alphabet* (London: Cassell and Company, 1967).

Downing, John, *The Initial Teaching Alphabet* (New York: The Macmillan Company, 1964).

Durkin, Dolores, *Children Who Read Early* (New York: Teachers College Press, Columbia University, 1966).

Durkin, Dolores, *Phonics and the Teaching of Reading* (New York: Teachers College Press, Columbia University, 1965).

Durkin, Dolores, *Teaching Them to Read* (Boston: Allyn and Bacon, Inc., 1970).

Durkin, Dolores, compiler, *Reading and the Kindergarten*, rev. ed. (Newark, Del.: International Reading Association, 1969).

Ekwall, Eldon E., *Psychological Factors in the Teaching of Reading* (Columbus, Ohio: Charles E. Merrill Publishing Company, 1973).

Fay, Leo, compiler, *Organization and Administration of School Reading Programs*, Reading Research Profiles Bibliography (Newark, Del.: International Reading Association, 1971).

Frost, Joe L., ed., *Issues and Innovations in the Teaching of Reading* (Chicago: Scott, Foresman and Company, 1967).

Fry, Edward, *Reading Instruction for Classroom and Clinic* (New York: McGraw-Hill Book Company, 1972).

Gans, Roma, *Common Sense in Teaching Reading* (Indianapolis, Ind.: The Bobbs-Merrill Company, 1963).

Gans, Roma, *Fact and Fiction about Phonics* (Indianapolis, Ind.: The Bobbs-Merrill Company, 1964).

Gattegno, Caleb, *Words in Color* (Chicago: Encyclopedia Britannica, 1964).

Goodman, Kenneth S., E. Brooks Smith, and Robert Meredith, *Language and Thinking in the Elementary School* (New York: Holt, Rinehart and Winston, Inc., 1970).

Gray, William S., *On Their Own in Reading*, 2nd ed. (Chicago: Scott, Foresman and Company, 1960).

Hall, Mary Anne, *Teaching Reading as a Language Experience* (Columbus, Ohio: Charles E. Merrill Publishing Company, 1970).

Harris, Albert J., *How to Increase Reading Ability*, 5th ed. (New York: David McKay Company, 1970).

Harris, Albert J., and Milton D. Jacobson, *Basic Elementary Reading Vocabularies* (New York: The Macmillan Company, 1972).

Harris, Albert J., and Edward R. Sipay, *Effective Teaching of Reading*, 2nd ed. (New York: David McKay Company, 1971).

Harris, Albert J., and Edward R. Sipay, eds., *Readings on Reading Instruction*, 2nd ed. (New York: David McKay Company, 1972).

Harris, Larry A., and Carl B. Smith, eds., *Individualizing Reading Instruction: A Reader* (New York: Holt, Rinehart and Winston, Inc., 1972).

Heilman, Arthur W., *Phonics in Proper Perspective* (Columbus, Ohio: Charles E. Merrill Publishing Company, 1964).

Heilman, Arthur W., *Principles and Practices of Teaching Reading*, 2nd ed. (Columbus, Ohio: Charles E. Merrill Publishing Company, 1972).

Henderson, Richard L., and Donald Ross Green, *Reading for Meaning in the Elementary School* (Englewood Cliffs, N.J.: Prentice-Hall, Inc., 1969).

Herber, Harold L., *Teaching Reading in Content Areas* (Englewood Cliffs, N.J.: Prentice-Hall, Inc., 1970).

Herr, Selma E., *Learning Activities for Reading*, 2nd ed. (Dubuque, Iowa: Wm. C. Brown Company Publishers, 1970).

Herrick, Virgil E., and Marcella Nerbovig, *Using Experience Charts with Children* (Columbus, Ohio: Charles E. Merrill Publishing Company, 1964).

Hester, Kathleen B., *Teaching Every Child to Read* (New York: Harper & Row, 1964).

Howes, Virgil M., and Helen Fisher Darrow, eds., *Reading and the Elementary School Child: Selected Readings on Programs and Practices* (New York: The Macmillan Company, 1968).

Hunt, Lyman C., ed., *The Individualized Reading Program: A Guide for Classroom Teaching* (Newark, Del.: International Reading Association, 1967).

Jongsma, Eugene, *Cloze Procedures as a Teaching Technique,* Reading Instruction Series (Newark, Del.: International Reading Association, 1971).

Karlin, Robert, *Teaching Elementary Reading: Principles and Strategies* (New York: Harcourt Brace Jovanvich, 1971).

Ketcham, Clay A., ed., *Proceedings of the College Reading Association: Professional Variety in Reading,* vol. VIII (Fall 1967).

King, Martha L., Bernice D. Ellinger, and Willavene Wolf, eds., *Critical Reading* (Philadelphia: J. B. Lippincott Company, 1967).

Lee, Dorris M., and R.V. Allen, *Learning to Read through Experiences* (New York: Meredith Publishing Company, 1963).

Lillard, Paula Polk, *Montessori: A Modern Approach* (New York: Schocken Books, 1972).

McKee, Paul, *Reading: A Program of Instruction for the Elementary School* (Boston: Houghton Mifflin Company, 1966).

Mackintosh, Helen K., ed., *Current Approaches to Teaching Reading,* Elementary Instruction Service Leaflet (Washington, D.C.: National Education Associaton, 1965).

Mazurkiewicz, Albert J., ed., *New Perspectives in Reading Instruction: A Book of Readings* (New York: Pitman Publishing Company, 1964).

Moburg, Larry, *Inservice Teacher Training in Reading,* Reading Information Series (Newark, Del.: International Reading Association, 1972).

Monroe, Marion, and Bernice Rogers, *Foundations of Reading: Informal Pre-Reading Procedures* (Glenview, Ill.: Scott, Foresman and Company, 1964).

Montessori, Maria, *The Montessori Method* (New York: Frederick A. Stokes, 1912).

Morrison, Ida E., *Teaching Reading in the Elementary School* (New York: The Ronald Press, 1968).

Moyle, Donald, and Louise Moyle, *Modern Innovations in the Teaching of Reading* (Newark, Del.: International Reading Association, 1971).

National Society for the Study of Education, *Innovations and Change in Reading Instruction,* The Sixty-Seventh Yearbook of the National Society for the Study of Education, Part II, Helen M. Robinson, ed. (Chicago: The University of Chicago Press, 1968).

Otto, Wayne, and Richard J. Smith, *Administering the School Reading Program* (Boston: Houghton Mifflin Company, 1970).

Preston, Ralph C., ed., *New Look at Reading in the Social Studies* (Newark, Del.: International Reading Association, 1969).

Robinson, H. Alan, and Ellen Lamar Thomas eds., *Fusing Reading Skills and Content* (Newark, Del.: International Reading Association, 1969).

Russell, David H., *Children Learn to Read* (Boston: Ginn and Company, 1961).

Russell, David H., and Etta Karp, *Reading Aids through the Grades* (New York: Teachers College Press, Columbia University, 1953).

Sartain, Harry, compiler, *Individualized Reading*, rev. ed. (Newark, Del.: International Reading Association, 1970).

Schubert, Delwyn G., and Theodore L. Torgerson, ed., *Readings in Reading* (New York: Thomas Y. Crowell Company, 1968).

Sebesta, Sam Leaton, and Carl J. Wallen, eds., *The First R: Readings on Teaching Reading* (Chicago: Science Research Associates, 1972).

Singer, Harry, and Robert B. Ruddell, eds., *Theoretical Models and Processes of Reading* (Newark, Del.: International Reading Association, 1971).

Smith, Nila Banton, *American Reading Instruction* (Newark, Del.: International Reading Association, 1965).

Smith, Nila Banton, *Reading Instruction for Today's Children* (Englewood Cliffs, N.J.: Prentice-Hall, Inc., 1970).

Spache, Evelyn B., *Reading Activities for Child Involvement* (Boston: Allyn and Bacon, Inc., 1972).

Spache, George D., and Evelyn B. Spache, *Reading in the Elementary School*, 3rd ed. (Boston: Allyn and Bacon, Inc., 1973).

Staiger, Ralph, and David A. Sohn, eds., *New Directions in Reading* (New York: Bantam Books, 1967).

Stauffer, Russell G., *Directing Reading Maturity as a Cognitive Process* (New York: Harper & Row, 1969).

Stauffer, Russell G., *Teaching Reading as a Thinking Process* (New York: Harper & Row, 1969).

Strang, Ruth, and Donald M. Lindquist, *The Administrator and the Improvement of Reading* (New York: Appleton-Century-Crofts, 1965).

Tinker, Miles A., *Bases for Effective Reading* (Minneapolis, Minn.: University of Minnesota Press, 1965).

Tinker, Miles A., and Constance M. McCullough, *Teaching Elementary Reading* (New York: Meredith Publishing Company, 1968).

Trinker, Charles L., ed., *Teaching for Better Use of Libraries* (Hamden: Conn.: The Shoe String Press, 1970).

U.S. Department of Health, Education and Welfare, *How to Use ERIC* (Washington, D.C.: Office of Education, U.S. Department of Health, Education and Welfare, 1971).

Veatch, Jeannette, *How to Teach Reading with Children's Books* (New York: Teacher College Press, Columbia University, 1964).

Veatch, Jeannette, *Reading in the Elementary School* (New York: The Ronald Press, 1966).

Vilscek, Elaine, ed., *A Decade of Innovation: Approaches to Beginning Reading.* Proceedings of the Twelfth Annual Convention, Volume 12, Part 3. (Newark, Del.: International Reading Association, 1971).

Wallen, Carl, *Competency in Teaching Reading* (Chicago: Science Research Associates, 1972).

Witty, Paul A., Alma M. Freeland, and Edith H. Grotberg, *The Teaching of Reading: A Developmental Process* (Boston: D. C. Heath and Company, 1968).

Witty, Paul A., ed., *Reading for the Gifted and the Creative Student* (Newark, Del.: International Reading Association, 1970).

Zintz, Miles V., *The Teacher and the Learner* (Dubuque, Iowa: Wm. C. Brown Company Publishers, 1970).

Books on Literature for Children

Since "reading for enjoyment" is a highly important phase of the total reading program, books for the teacher on literature for children are listed here. Many of the books on the teaching of reading given in the preceding listing also contain chapters on means of interesting children in worthwhile reading. Source books on books for boys and girls, of value to the teacher, are given under "Sources for Book Selection" in the section on general books for boys and girls (*see* page 559).

Arbuthnot, May Hill, and Zena Salisbury, *Children and Books,* 4th ed. (Chicago: Scott, Foresman and Company, 1972).

Behn, Harry, *Chrysalis: Concerning Children and Poetry* (Harcourt Brace Jovanovich, 1968).

Burns, Paul C., Betty L. Broman, and Alberta L. Lowe, *The Language Arts in Childhood Education* (Chicago: Rand McNally & Company, 1971), Ch. VI, "Literature."

Burns, Paul C., and Leo M. Schell, eds., *Elementary School Language Arts: Selected Readings* (Chicago: Rand McNally & Company, 1969), Part Four, "Literature and Creative Writing."

Burrows, Alvina Treut, Diane L. Monson, and Russell G. Stauffer, *New*

Horizons in the Language Arts (New York: Harper & Row, 1972), Ch. 6, "Literature for Teachers," and Ch. 8, "Children's Literature in the Classroom,"

Catterson, Jane, ed., *Children and Literature* (Newark, Del.: International Reading Association, 1970).

Cullinan, Bernice E., *Literature for Children: Its Discipline and Content* (Dubuque, Iowa: Wm. C. Brown Company Publishers, 1971).

Dallmann, Martha, *Teaching the Language Arts in the Elementary School,* 2nd ed. (Dubuque, Iowa: Wm. C. Brown Company Publishers, 1971), Ch. 10, "Guiding Growth in Independent Reading."

Dawson, Mildred, ed., *Children, Books and Reading,* Perspectives in Reading (Newark, Del.: International Reading Association, 1964).

Dietrich, D.M., and V.H. Mathews, eds., *Development of Lifetime Reading Habits* (Newark, Del.: International Reading Association, 1968).

Donohue, Mildred R., *The Child and the English Language Arts* (Dubuque, Iowa: Wm. C. Brown Company Publishers, 1971), Ch. 2, "Children's Literature."

Fader, Daniel N., and Elton B. McNeil, *Hooked on Books: Program and Proof* (New York: G. P. Putnam's Sons, 1968).

Fenwick, Sara Innis, ed., *A Critical Approach to Children's Literature* (Chicago: University of Chicago Press, 1967).

Foster, Florence P., compiler, *Literature and the Young Child* (Trenton, N.J.: State Department of Education, 1967).

Freeman, La Verne, and Ruth S. Freeman, *The Child and His Picture Book* (Watkins Glen, N.Y.: Century House, 1967).

Gillespie, Margaret C., *Literature for Children: History and Trends* (Dubuque, Iowa: Wm. C. Brown Company Publishers, 1970).

Hazard, Paul, *Books, Children and Men* (Boston: Horn Book, 1960).

Hollowell, Lillian, *A Book of Children's Literature* (New York: Holt, Rinehart and Winston, Inc., 1966).

Huber, Miriam Blanton, compiler, *Story and Verse for Children* (New York: The Macmillan Company, 1965).

Huck, Charlotte S., and Doris Young Kuhn, *Children's Literature for the Elementary School,* 2nd ed. (New York: Holt, Rinehart and Winston, Inc., 1968).

Jacobs, Leland B., ed., *Using Literature with Young Children* (New York: Teachers College Press, Columbia University, 1965).

Kujoth, Jean Spealman, *Reading Interests of Children and Young Adults* (Metuchen, N.J.: The Scarecrow Press, 1970).

Painter, Helen W., *Poetry and Children* (Newark, Del.: International Reading Association, 1970).

Sawyer, Ruth, *The Way of the Storyteller* (New York: The Viking Press, 1962).

Sayers, Frances Clarke, *Summoned by Books* (New York: The Viking Press, 1965).

Smith, Dora V., *Fifty Years of Children's Books* (Urbana, Ill.: National Council of Teachers of English, 1963).

Smith, James A., *Creative Teaching of Reading and Literature in the Elementary School* (Boston: Allyn and Bacon, Inc., 1967).

Strickland, Ruth G., *The Language Arts in the Elementary School*, 3rd ed. (Lexington, Mass.: D. C. Heath and Company, 1969), Ch. 17, "Stories, Poetry, and Books."

Whitehead, Robert, *Children's Literature: Strategies of Teaching* (Englewood Cliffs, N.J.: Prentice-Hall, Inc. 1968).

Books on Creative Expression

Creative expression can serve as a means of encouraging boys and girls in reading. It can also be the satisfying result of reading. Suggestions for creative expression will be found in many of the books listed in various parts of this chapter. The reader is referred to them, as well as to the books named here, which deal chiefly with creative dramatics and choral reading.

Association for Childhood Education, International, *Creative Dramatics* (Washington, D.C.: Association for Childhood Education, International, 1961).

Baird, Bil, *The Art of the Puppet* (New York: The Macmillan Company, 1965).

Barton, Clifford, *Verse Choir in the Elementary School* (Darien, Conn.: Teachers Publishing Corporation, 1954).

Batchelder, Marjorie, *The Puppet Theatre Handbook* (New York: Harper & Row, 1947).

Batchelder, Marjorie, and Virgina Lee Comer, *Puppets and Plays—A Creative Approach* (New York: Harper & Row, 1956).

Blackman, Olive, *Puppets into Actors* (New York: The Macmillan Company, 1949).

Blackman, Olive, *Shadow Puppets* (New York: Harper & Row, 1960).

Boylan, Eleanor, *How to Be a Puppeteer* (New York: McCall Books, 1970).

Brown, Helen A., and Harry J. Heltman, *Choral Reading for Fun and Recreation* (Philadelphia, Pa.: Westminster Press, 1956).

Carlson, Bernice, *Act It Out* (Nashville, Tenn.: Abingdon Press, 1965).

Carlson, Ruth, *Literature for Children: Enrichment Ideas* (Dubuque, Iowa: Wm. C. Brown, Company Publishers, 1970).

Chambers, Dewey W., *Literature for Children: Storytelling and Creative Drama* (Dubuque, Iowa: Wm. C. Brown Company Publishers, 1970).

Crosscut, Richard, *Children and Dramatics* (New York: Charles Scribner's Sons, 1966).

Durland, Frances E., *Creative Dramatics for Children* (Kent, Ohio: Kent State University Press, 1963).

Hoben, Alice M., *Puppets and Marionettes* (Chicago: Field Enterprises Educational Publications, Inc., 1955).

Howard, Vernon, *Puppet and Pantomime Plays* (New York: Sterling Publishing Company, Inc., 1962).

Jagendorf, Moritz, *First Book of Puppets* (New York: Franklin Watts, Inc., 1952).

Kamerman, Sylvia, ed., *Dramatized Folk Tales of the World* (Boston: Plays, Inc., 1971).

Lewis, Shari, *The Puppet Book* (New York: Citadel Press, Inc., 1958).

Marksbury, Mary Lee, *Foundation of Creativity* (New York: Harper & Row, 1963).

Mearns, Hughes, *Creative Power* (New York: Dover Publications, Inc., 1958).

Menagh, H. Beresford, *Creative Dramatics in Guiding Children's Language Learning* (Dubuque, Iowa: Wm. C. Brown Company Publishers, 1967).

Pels, Gertrude, *Easy Puppets* (New York: Thomas Y. Crowell Company, 1947).

Possien, Wilma M., *They All Need to Talk* (New York: Appleton-Century-Crofts, 1969), Ch. IV, "Creative Dramatics"; and Ch. VIII, "Poetry and Choral Reading."

Pratt, Lois H., *The Puppet Do-It-Yourself Book* (New York: Exposition Press, 1957).

Raubicheck, Letitia, *Choral Speaking Is Fun* (New York: Noble & Noble Publishers, Inc., 1958).

Ross, Laura, *Hand Puppets: How to Make and Use Them* (New York: Lothrop, Lee & Shepard Company, 1969).

Severn, Bill, *Shadow Magic* (New York: David McKay Company, 1959).

Siks, Geraldine B., *Children's Literature for Dramatization* (New York: Harper & Row, 1964).

Siks, Geraldine B., and Hazel B. Dunnington, *Children's Theatre and Creative Dramatics* (Seattle, Wash.: University of Washington Press, 1961).

Taylor, Loren E., *Puppetry, Marionettes, and Shadow Plays* (Minneapolis, Minn.: Burgess Publishing Company, 1965).

Tichenor, Tom, *Tom Tichenor's Puppets* (Nashville, Tenn.: Abingdon Press, 1971).

Torrance, E. Paul, *Guiding Creative Talent* (Englewood Cliffs, N.J.: Prentice-Hall, Inc., 1962).

U.S. Office of Education, *Creative Drama: Drama with and for Children — Children's Theater*, Bulletin No. 30 (Washington, D.C.: Superintendent of Documents, U.S. Office of Education, 1960).

Ward, Winifred, *Playmaking with Children* (New York: Appleton-Century-Crofts, 1957).

Way, Brian, *Development through Drama* (New York: Longmans, Green and Company, Ltd., 1967).

Worrell, Estelle, *Be a Puppeteer: The Lively Puppet Book* (New York: McGraw-Hill Book Company, 1969).

Books Dealing with Linguistics

The subject of linguistics in relation to its application to the elementary-school reading program is discussed in parts of many of the books on the teaching of reading listed earlier in this chapter. Below are given titles of books devoted exclusively or almost exclusively to the bearing of linguistics on the teaching of reading or on the other language arts.

Anderson, Paul S., *Linguistics in the Elementary School Classroom* (New York: The Macmillan Company, 1971).

Buchanan, Cynthia, *A Programmed Introduction to Linguistics* (Lexington, Mass.: D.C. Heath and Company, 1963).

Dechant, Emerald, *Linguistics, Phonics and the Teaching of Reading* (Springfield, Ill.: Charles C. Thomas, Publishers, 1969).

Durkin, Dolores, *Phonics, Linguistics and Reading* (New York: Teachers College Press, Columbia University, 1972).

Fries, Charles C., *Linguistics and Reading* (New York: Holt, Rinehart and Winston, Inc., 1963).

Goodman, Kenneth S., *Psycholinguistic Nature of the Reading Process* (Detroit, Mich.: Wayne State University Press, 1968).

Goodman, Kenneth S., and James T. Fleming, ed., *Psycholinguistics and the Teaching of Reading* (Newark, Del.: International Reading Association, 1968).

Lamb, Pose, *Linguistics in Proper Perspective* (Columbus, Ohio: Charles E. Merrill Publishing Company, 1967).

LeFevre, Carl A., *Linguistics and the Teaching of Reading* (New York: McGraw-Hill Book Company, 1964).

LeFevre, Carl A., *Linguistics, English, and the Language Arts* (Boston: Allyn and Bacon, Inc., 1970).

Savage, John F., ed., *Linguistics for Teachers: Selected Readings* (Chicago: Science Research Associates, 1973).

Smith, Frank, *Understanding Reading: A Psycholinguistic Analysis of Reading and Learning to Read* (New York: Holt, Rinehart and Winston, Inc., 1971).

Wardbaugh, Ronald, *Reading: A Linguistic Perspective* (New York: Harcourt Brace Jovanovich, 1969).

Books Dealing with Diagnosis and Remediation

Many of the professional books listed in this chapter under "Books on the Teaching of Reading: A General Bibliography" give information on diagnosis and evaluation of children's reading and on needed remediation. Additional references are:

Barrett, Thomas, ed., *The Evaluation of Children's Reading Achievement,* Perspectives in Reading (Newark, Del.: International Reading Association, 1967).

Bond, Guy L., and Miles A. Tinker, *Reading Difficulties: Their Diagnosis and Correction,* 2nd ed. (New York: Appleton-Century-Crofts, 1968).

Brown, Frederick G., *Principles of Educational and Psychological Testing* (Hinsdale, Ill.: The Dryden Press, Inc., 1970).

Buros, Oscar K., ed., *Mental Measurements Yearbook,* latest ed. (Highland Park, N.J.: Gryphon Press).

Carter, Homer, and Dorothy J. McGinnis, *Diagnosis and Treatment of the Disabled Reader* (New York: The Macmillan Company, 1970).

Dechant, Emerald V., *Detection and Correction of Reading Difficulties: Readings and Commentary* (New York: Appleton-Century-Crofts, 1970).

Dechant, Emerald V., *Diagnosis and Remediation of Reading Disability* (West Nyack, N.Y.: Parker Publishing Company, 1968).

Delacato, Carl H., *New Starts for the Child Who Can't Read* (New York: David McKay Company, 1970).

Della-Piana, Gabriel M., *Reading Diagnosis and Prescription: An Introduction* (New York: Holt, Rinehart and Winston, Inc., 1968).

Durr, William K., ed., *Reading Difficulties: Diagnosis, Correction and Remediation* (Newark, Del.: International Reading Association, 1970).

Ebel, Robert L., *Measuring Educational Advancement* (Englewood Cliffs, N.J.: Prentice-Hall, Inc., 1970).

Ekwall, Eldon E., *Locating and Correcting Reading Difficulties* (Columbus, Ohio: Charles E. Merrill Publishing Company, 1970).

Farr, Roger, *Measurement and Evaluation of Reading* (New York: Harcourt Brace Jovanovich, 1970).

Fierson, Edward C., and Walter B. Barbe, compilers, *Educating Children with Learning Disabilities* (New York: Appleton-Century-Crofts, 1967).

Gallant, Ruth, *Handbook in Corrective Reading* (Columbus, Ohio: Charles E. Merrill Publishing Company, 1970).

Harris, Albert J., *How to Increase Reading Ability*, 5th ed. (New York: David McKay Company, 1970).

Johnson, Marjorie, and Roy A. Kress, *Corrective Reading in the Elementary Classroom* (Newark, Del.: International Reading Association, 1965).

Johnson, Marjorie S., and Roy A. Kress, *Informal Reading Inventories*, Reading Aids Series (Newark, Del.: International Reading Association, 1965).

Kaluger, George, and Clifford J. Kolsom, *Reading and Learning Disabilities* (Columbus, Ohio: Charles E. Merrill Publishing Company, 1969).

Kaphart, Newell G., *The Slow Learner in the Classroom*, 2nd ed. (New York: Schocken Books, 1971).

Leibert, Robert, ed., *Diagnostic Viewpoints in Reading* (Newark, Del.: International Reading Association, 1971).

Natchez, Gladys, ed., *Children with Reading Problems* (New York: Basic Books, 1968).

Newman, Harold, ed., *Reading Disabilities* (New York: The Odyssey Press, 1969).

Otto, Wayne, and Karl Koenke, *Remedial Teaching: Research and Comment* (Boston: Houghton Mifflin Company, 1969).

Otto, Wayne, and Richard A. McMeney, *Corrective and Remedial Teaching* (Boston: Houghton Mifflin Company, 1966).

Potter, Thomas, and Kenneth Rae, *Informal Reading Diagnosis: A Practical Guide for the Classroom Teacher* (Englewood Cliffs, N.J.: Prentice-Hall, Inc., 1972).

Ravenette, A. T., *Dimensions of Reading Difficulties* (Fairview Park, Elmsford, N.Y.: Pergamon Press, 1968).

Roswell, Florence, and Gladys Natchez, *Reading Disability: Diagnosis and Treatment*, rev. ed. (New York: Basic Books, 1970).

Schell, Leo M., and Paul C. Burns, *Remedial Reading: An Anthology of Sources* (Boston: Allyn and Bacon, Inc., 1968).

Schubert, Delwyn G., *The Doctor Eyes the Poor Reader* (Springfield, Ill.: Charles C. Thomas, 1957).

Silvaroli, Nicholas J., *Classroom Reading Inventory* second edition. (Dubuque, Iowa: Wm. C. Brown Company Publishers, 1973).

Smith, Carl B., *Treating Reading Disabilities: The Specialists' Role*, The Target Series. (Newark, Del.: International Reading Association, 1969).

Spache, George D., ed., *Reading Disability and Perception* (Newark, Del.: International Reading Association, 1969).

Strang, Ruth, *Diagnostic Teaching of Reading*, 2nd ed. (New York: McGraw-Hill Book Company, 1969).

Strang, Ruth, ed., *Understanding and Helping the Retarded Reader* (Tucson, Ariz.: University of Arizona Press, 1965).

Trela, Thaddeus M., *Fourteen Remedial Reading Methods* (Belmont, Cal.: Fearon Publishers, 1969).

Webster, James, *Practical Reading: Some New Remedial Techniques* (New York: International Publications Service, 1970).

Wilson, Robert M., *Diagnostic and Remedial Reading for Classroom and Clinic,* second edition (Columbus, Ohio: Charles E. Merrill Publishing Company, 1972).

Zintz, Miles V., *Corrective Reading* (Dubuque, Iowa: Wm. C. Brown Company, Publishers, 1972).

Books on the Culturally Different

As can be expected in an era in which there is deep concern for problems related to the teaching of the culturally different child, many books have been appearing on the market on that subject, the following among them:

Allen, Vernona L., *Psychological Factors in Poverty* (Chicago: Markham Publishing Company, 1970).

American Library Association, *Minority Groups* (Chicago: American Library Association, 1969).

Baratz, Joan C., and Robert W. Shuy, eds., *Teaching Black Children to Read* (Washington, D.C.: Center for Applied Linguistics, 1969).

Beck, John M., and Richard W. Saxe, *Teaching the Culturally Disadvantaged Pupil* (Springfield, Ill.: Charles C. Thomas, Publishers, 1969).

Bereiter, Carl, and Siegfried Engelmann, *Teaching Disadvantaged Children in the Preschool* (Englewood Cliffs, N.J.: Prentice-Hall, Inc., 1966).

Bloom, Benjamin S., Allison Davis, and Robert Hess, *Contemporary Education for Cultural Deprivation* (New York: Holt, Rinehart and Winston, Inc., 1965).

Broderick, Dorothy, *The Image of the Black in Children's Fiction* (Ann Arbor, Mich.: R. R. Bowker Order Department, 1973).

Conte, Joseph M., and George H. Grimes, *Media and the Culturally Different Learner* (Washington, D.C.: National Education Association, 1969).

Corbin, Richard, and Muriel Crosby, *Language Programs for the Disadvantaged* (Champaign, Ill.: National Council of Teachers of English, 1965).

Davis, Allison, *Social Class Influences upon Learning* (Cambridge, Mass.: Harvard University Press, 1962).

Dennison, George, *The Lives of Children: The Story of the First Street School* (New York: Random House, Inc., 1969).

Deutsch, Martin, et al., *The Disadvantaged Child* (New York: Basic Books, 1967).

Educational Policies Commission, *Universal Opportunity for Early Childhood Education* (Washington, D.C.: National Education Association, 1966).

Fantini, Mario, and Gerald Weinstein, *Making Urban Schools Work: Social Realities and the Urban School* (New York: Holt, Rinehart and Winston, Inc., 1968).

Figurel, J. Allen, ed., *Better Reading in Urban Schools* (Newark, Del.: International Reading Association, 1972).

Figurel, J. Allen, ed., *Reading Goals for the Disadvantaged* (Newark, Del.: International Reading Association, 1970).

Frost, Joe L., and Glenn R. Hawkes, eds., *The Disadvantaged Child* (Boston: Houghton Mifflin Company, 1966).

Fusco, Gene C., *School-home Partnership in Depressed Urban Neighborhoods*, OE-31008, Bulletin 1964, no. 20 (Washington, D.C.: U.S. Department of Health, Education and Welfare, 1964).

Hardy, William G., *Communication and the Disadvantaged Child* (Baltimore: The Williams & Wilkins Company, 1970).

Herndon, James, *The Way It Spozed to Be: A Report on the Crisis in Our Schools* (New York: Bantam Books, 1969).

Horn, Thomas D., ed., *Reading for the Disadvantaged: Problems of Linguistically Different Learners* (New York: Harcourt Brace Javanovich, 1970).

Jewett, Arno, Joseph Mersand, and Doris V. Gunderson, *Improving English Skills of Culturally Different Youth in Large Cities*, OE-30012, Bulletin 1964, no. 5 (Washington, D.C.: U.S. Department of Health, Education and Welfare, 1964).

Joseph, Stephen M., ed., *The Me Nobody Knows: Children's Voices from the Ghetto* (New York: Avon Books, 1966).

Kozol, Jonathan, *Death at an Early Age: The Destruction of the Hearts and Minds of Negro Children in the Boston Public Schools* (Boston: Houghton Mifflin Company, 1967).

McMurrin, Sterling M., ed., *The Conditions for Educational Equality* (477 Madison Ave., New York, N.Y.: Committee for Economic Development, 1971).

Mayerson, Charlotte Leon, ed., *Two Blocks Apart: Juan Gonzales and Peter Quinn* (New York: Holt, Rinehart and Winston, Inc., 1965).

O'Brien, Carmen, *Teaching the Language-Different Child to Read* (Columbus, Ohio: Charles E. Merrill Publishing Company, 1973).

Passow, A. Harry, *Education in Depressed Areas* (New York: Teachers College Press, Columbia University, 1968).

Passow, A. Harry, *Reaching the Disadvantaged Learner* (New York: Teachers College Press, Columbia University, 1970).

Passow, A. Harry, ed., *Developing Programs for the Educationally Disadvantaged* (New York: Teachers College Press, Columbia University, 1968).

Shuy, Roger W., *Discovering American Dialects* (Urbana, Ill.: National Council of Teachers of English, 1967).

Sleisenger, Lenore, *Guidebook for the Volunteer Reading Teacher* (New York: Teachers College Press, Columbia University, 1965).

Spache, George D., *Good Reading for the Disadvantaged: Multi-Ethnic Resources* (Champaign, Ill.: The Garrard Publishing Company, 1970).

Thonis, Eleanor W., *Teaching Reading to Non-English Speakers* (New York: The Macmillan Company, 1970).

Books for Parents

Many of the books given in previous listings in this chapter will undoubtedly be of interest to some parents. Of special value may be other books listed under "Books on Literature for Children." Valuable, too, may be the publication by a committee of The National Council of Teachers of English, of which Thomas G. Devine was chairman, entitled *Selected Reading List of Books about English Teaching for Parents and the General Public.* Attention can also be drawn to the bookmark from the Children's Book Council (free with an eight-cent postage stamp), called *Booklists for Parents,* which names and describes selected lists for help in guiding children's reading. Additional books giving information of interest to parents are:

Arbuthnot, May Hill, *Children's Reading in the Home* (Glenview, Ill.: Scott, Foresman and Company, 1969).

Artley, Sterl A., *Your Child Learns to Read* (Glenview, Ill.: Scott, Foresman and Company, 1953).

Carksehm, G. Robert, *Books and the Teen-age Readers: A Guide for Teachers, Librarians, and Parents,* rev. ed. (New York: Harper & Row, 1971).

Fusco, Gene C., *School-home Partnership in Depressed Urban Neighborhoods,* OE-31008, Bulletin 1964, no. 20 (Washington, D.C.: U.S. Department of Health, Education and Welfare, 1964).

Hechinger, Fred M., ed., *Pre-school Education Today* (New York: Doubleday and Company, 1966).

Janowitz, Gayle, *Helping Hands: Volunteer Work in Education* (Chicago: The University of Chicago Press, 1965).

Josette, Frank, *Your Child's Reading Today,* rev. ed. (New York: Doubleday and Company, 1969).

Larrick, Nancy, *A Parent's Guide to Children's Reading,* 3rd ed. (New York: Doubleday and Company, 1969).

Lorang, Sister Mary Corde, *Burning Ice: The Moral and Emotional Effects of Reading* (New York: Charles Scribner's Sons, 1968).

Love, Harold D., *Parents Diagnose and Correct Reading Disabilities* (Springfield, Ill.: Charles C. Thomas, 1970).

Meeker, Alice M., *Enjoying Literature with Children* (New York: Odyssey Press, 1969).

Mergentine, Charlotte, *You and Your Child's Reading* (New York: Harcourt Brace Jovanovich, 1963).

National Congress of Parents and Teachers and Children's Services Division, American Library Association: *Let's Read Together: Books for Family Enjoyment* (Chicago: American Library Association, 1964).

Reeves, Ruth, *The Teaching of Reading in Our Schools: Guidebook for Parents* (New York: The Macmillan Company, 1966).

Smith, B. Carl, *Parents and Reading* (Newark, Del.: International Reading Association, 1971).

Spache, George D., *Parents and the Reading Program* (Champaign, Ill.: Garrard Publishing Company, 1965).

Strang, Ruth, *Helping Your Gifted Child* (New York: E. P. Dutton & Company, 1960).

General Books for Boys and Girls

With the large number of books for boys and girls in print—some excellent, others ordinary, and still others banal—it is important for teachers and parents to know where to turn for guidance in selection.

Sources for Book Selection

With the exception of those who are experts in literature for children, few teachers are able to keep up with the great outpouring of books for children, and fewer still can judge with ease which of the new titles are suitable. Teachers are, therefore, dependent in great degree on the recommendations of the specialists. Two excellent references that discuss and list books for children are *Children and Books* by May Arbuthnot and Zena Salisbury (Scott Foresman and Company, 1972) and *Children's Literature in the Elementary School* by Charlotte Huck and Doris Young Kuhn (Holt, Rinehart and Winston, Inc., 1968). The numerous booklists now available can also be sources of valuable aids to teachers in planning their periodic requests for books.

The following are highly recommended publications, printed periodically, that evaluate currently written books for children.

The Atlantic (Atlantic Monthly Press)
The Booklist (American Library Association)
Book Review Digest (H.W. Wilson Company)
Bulletin for the Center for Children's Books (University of Chicago Press)
Chicago Sunday Tribune
Childhood Education (Association for Childhood Education, International)
Christian Science Monitor (Christian Science Publishing Society)
Elementary English (National Council of Teachers of English)
Horn Book Magazine (Horn Book, Inc.)
The Instructor (F. A. Owen Publishing Company)
Junior Libraries (R. R. Bowker Company)
New York Herald-Tribune Book Review
New York Times Book Review
Parents Magazine (Parents' Magazine Press)
Publisher's Weekly (Children's Book Number, R. R. Bowker Company)
Reading Teacher (International Reading Association)
School Library Journal (R. R. Bowker Company)
Teacher (Macmillan Professional Magazines, Inc.)
Wilson Library Bulletin (H. W. Wilson Company)
Young Readers Review (Box 137, Wall Street Station, New York, N.Y. 10005).

The following books are also excellent guides to book selection. It should be noted, however, that, as the copyright dates indicate, some of them do not include recent books. The reader is referred to page 569 for easy books for slow readers.

Adventuring with Books: A Booklist for Elementary Schools, Elizabeth Guilfoile, ed. (National Council of Teachers of English, 1965).

Aids in Choosing Books for Your Children (Children's Book Council, latest edition).

Aids in Selection of Materials for Children and Young People: Books, Films, Records (American Library Association, 1957).

American History in Juvenile Books, Seymour Metzner, compiler, (H. W. Wilson Company, 1966).

Annual List of Children's Literature (American Library Association, latest edition).

A Basic Book Collection for Elementary Grades, Miriam Snow and others, eds., (American Library Association, 1960).

Behavior Patterns in Children's Books: A Bibliography, Clara J. Kircher (Catholic University Press of America, 1966).

Best Books for Children (R.R. Bowker, latest edition).

Bibliography of Books for Children (Association for Childhood Education, International, 1968).

Booklist Books: A Selection (American Library Association).

Book Selection Aids for Children and Teachers in Elementary and Secondary Schools, Milbrey L. Jones, compiler, U.S. Government Printing Office, 1966).

Books about Negro Life for Children, Augusta Baker, compiler (New York: Public Library, 1963).

Books for Beginning Readers, Elizabeth Guilfoile (Garrard Publishing Company, 1962).

Books for Children (American Library Association, latest edition).

Books for Elementary School Libraries: An Initial Collection, Elizabeth Hodges, compiler (American Library Association, 1969).

Books of the Year for Children (Child Study Association of America, latest edition).

Children's Books, Virginia Haviland and Lois Watt, compilers, LC#65-60014 (Superintendent of Documents, U.S. Government Printing Office).

Children's Books: Awards and Prizes (Children's Book Council, latest edition).

Children's Books for $1.25 or Less, Siddie Joe Johnson and others, eds. (Association for Childhood Education, International, 1965).

Children's Books for Schools and Libraries, Phyllis Steackler, ed. (R.R. Bowker Company, latest edition).

Children's Books in Print (R.R. Bowker Company, latest edition).

Children's Books to Enrich the Social Studies, Helen Huus, compiler (National Council for the Social Studies, 1966).

Children's Books Suggested as Holiday Gifts (New York Public Library, New York, N.Y., latest edition).

Children's Books Too Good to Miss, May Hill Arbuthnot, Margaret Clark, and Harriet Long, compilers (Western Reserve University Press, 1966).

Children's Catalog, Rachel and Estelle A. Fidell, eds. (H. W. Wilson Company, latest edition).

Children's Classics, Alice M. Jordan, ed. (Horn Book).

Children's Literature about Foreign Countries (H.W. Wilson Company, 1957).

Children's Literature: A Guide to Reference Sources, Virginia Haviland and others, compilers (Library of Congress, 1968).

Distinguished Children's Books (American Library Association, latest edition).

The Elementary School Library Collection, Mary Gaver and others, eds. (The Bro-Dart Foundation, Newark, N.J., latest edition).

Fifty Years of Children's Books, Dora V. Smith (National Council of Teachers of English, 1963).

Good Books for Children, Mary K. Eakin, compiler (The University of Chicago Press, 1962).

Good Reading for Youth (New Hampshire State Library).

Growing Up with Books (R.R. Bowker Company, 1966).

Growing Up with Paperbacks (R.R. Bowker Company, 1966).

Growing Up with Science Books (R.R. Bowker Company, 1966).

Guide to Information Sources for Reading, Bonnie Davis (International Reading Association, 1972).

How-to-Do-It Books (R.R. Bowker Company, 1961).

Index to Children's Poetry, John and Sara Brewton, compilers (H.W. Wilson Company, latest supplement).

An Index to Young Readers' Collective Biographies (R.R. Bowker Company, 1970).

The Negro in Schoolroom Literature, Minnie Koblitz (Center for Urban Education, 1967).

Notable Children's Books of . . . (American Library Association, latest edition).

Paperbound Book Guide for Elementary Schools (R.R. Bowker Company, latest edition).

A Parent's Guide to Children's Reading, Nancy Larrick (Doubleday and Company, 1969).

Reading Ladders for Human Relations, 5th ed., Virginia Reid, ed. (American Council on Education, 1972).

Recommended Children's Books of . . ., reprinted from the *School Library Journal* (R.R. Bowker Company, latest edition).

Sources of Good Books and Magazines for Children, Winifred C. Ladley, compiler (International Reading Association, 1970).

Subject and Title Index to Short Stories for Children (American Library Association, latest edition).

Subject Guide to Children's Books in Print (R.R. Bowker Company, latest edition).

Subject Index to Books for Intermediate Grades, Mary Eakin (American Library Association, 1963).

Subject Index to Books for Primary Grades, Mary Eakin (American Library Association, 1967).

Subject Index to Poetry for Children and Young People, Violet Sell and others, eds. (American Library Association).

A Teacher's Guide to Children's Books, Nancy Larrick (Charles E. Merrill Publishing Company, 1960).

A Treasury of Books for the Primary Grades, Mildred A. Dawson and Louise Pfeiffer (Chandler Publishing Company, 1959).

We Build Together: A Reader's Guide to Negro Life and Literature for Elementary and High School Use, 3rd rev., Chalemae Rollins, ed. (National Council of Teachers of English, 1967).

Book Awards

The two awards in the field of literature for boys and girls that are best known are the Newbery Medal and the Caldecott Medal. The Newbery Medal has been given since 1922 when Frederic C. Melcher provided for the award to be made yearly for the book judged the most distinguished in the field of literature for children. Himself a publisher, Melcher named the award in honor of the famous publisher of books for children, John Newbery. In 1939, also through the generosity of Melcher, the first Caldecott Medal was awarded. It was named after Randolph Caldecott, well-known illustrator of books for children. This award is given annually to the book judged to be the most distinguished picture book for children published during the year. The selection of both the Newbery Medal and the Caldecott Medal books is made by members of the staff of the American Library Association.

Quite a number of additional awards are now being made. Some of these are:

The Jane Addams Children's Book Award (established by the United States Section of the Women's International League for Peace and Freedom, 345 East 46th Street, New York, N.Y. 10017, for books with constructive themes).

The Aurianne Children's Book Award (established by a bequest of Augustine Aurianne, a former librarian, to be given to writers of books for children between eight and fourteen, encouraging kindness to animals; selected by the American Library Association).

The Mildred L. Batchelder Award (established in honor of a former executive secretary of the American Library Association, to be given to the American publisher of an outstanding book for children originally published abroad in a language other than English).

The Book World Children's Spring Book Festival Awards (three given yearly for books for children on three age levels; corresponding address: The Chicago Tribune, Chicago).

The Lewis Carroll Shelf Award (given by the School of Education, University of Wisconsin, with the cooperation of state organizations).

Child Study Association of America Children's Book Award (awarded by the Children's Book Committee of the Child Study Association of America).

Thomas Alva Edison Foundation National Mass Media Awards (given by the Thomas Alva Edison Foundation National Mass Media Awards, 8 West 40th Street, New York, N.Y., for four types of books).

Charles W. Follett Award (given by the sons of Charles W. Follett, the Follett Publishing Company).

The Edgar Allen Poe Award (given by the Mystery Writers of America, for the best mystery story for boys and girls of the preceding year— providing one is considered worthy of the award).

The Laura Ingalls Wilder Award (given by the American Library Association).

The following awards are given on the basis of judgment of boys and girls:[2]

The Boys Club of America Junior Book Awards

The Dorothy Canfield Fisher Children's Book Award

The Nene Award (selected by the school children of Hawaii)

The Pacific Northwest Young Reader's Choice Award

The Sequoyah Children's Book Award

The William Allen White Children's Book Award.

Two books that give additional information on awards are *Literary and Library Prizes* (published by R.R. Bowker Company, latest edition), and *Children's Books: Awards and Prizes* (published periodically, available through The Children's Book Council, 175 Fifth Avenue, New York, N.Y. 10017).

The following are the award-winning books in the two best-known competitions, the Newbery Medal books and the Caldecott Award books:

1. *The Newbery Medal Books*, selected by the American Library Association, 50 East Huron Street, Chicago, Ill. 60611.

1923   *The Voyages of Dr. Dolittle*, Hugh Lofting (J.B. Lippincott Company).

1924   *The Dark Frigate*, Charles Boardman Hawes (Little, Brown and Company).

1925   *Tales from Silver Lands*, Charles J. Finger (Doubleday & Company, Inc.).

[2] Charlotte S. Huck and Doris Kuhn Young, *Children's Literature in the Elementary School* (New York: Holt, Rinehart and Winston, Inc., 1969), pp. 718–720.

1926 *Shen of the Sea*, Arthur Bowie Chrisman (E.P. Dutton and Company, Inc.).

1927 *Smoky, the Cowhorse*, Will James (Charles Scribner's Sons).

1928 *Gayneck: The Story of a Pigeon*, Dhan Gopal Mukerji (E.P. Dutton & Company, Inc.).

1929 *The Trumpeter of Krakow*, Eric P. Kelly (The Macmillan Company).

1930 *Hitty: Her First Hundred Years*, Rachel Field (The Macmillan Company).

1931 *The Cat Who Went to Heaven*, Elizabeth Coatsworth (The Macmillan Company).

1932 *Waterless Mountain*, Laura Adams Armer (David McKay Company).

1933 *Young Fu of the Upper Yangtze*, Elizabeth Foreman Lewis (Holt, Rinehart and Winston, Inc.).

1934 *Invincible Louisa*, Cornelia Meigs (Little, Brown and Company).

1935 *Dobry*, Monica Shannon (The Viking Press).

1936 *Caddie Woodlawn*, Carol Ryrie Brink (The Macmillan Company).

1937 *Roller Skates*, Ruth Sawyer (The Viking Press).

1938 *The White Stag*, Kate Seredy (The Viking Press).

1939 *Thimble Summer*, Elizabeth Enright (Holt, Rinehart and Winston, Inc.).

1940 *Daniel Boone*, James Daugherty (The Viking Press).

1941 *Call It Courage*, Armstrong Sperry (The Macmillan Company).

1942 *The Matchlock Gun*, Walter D. Edmonds (Dodd, Mead and Company, Inc.).

1943 *Adam of the Road*, Elizabeth Janet Gray (The Viking Press).

1944 *Johnny Tremain*, Esther Forbes (Houghton Mifflin Company).

1945 *Rabbit Hill*, Robert Lawson (The Viking Press).

1946 *Strawberry Girl*, Lois Lenski (J.B. Lippincott Company).

1947 *Miss Hickory*, Carolyn Sherwin Bailey (The Viking Press).

1948 *Twenty-one Balloons*, William Pene du Bois (The Viking Press).

1949 *King of the Wind*, Marguerite Henry (Rand McNally & Company).

1950 *Door in the Wall*, Marguerite de Angeli (Doubleday & Company).

1951 *Amos Fortune: Free Man*, Elizabeth Yates (Aladdin).

1952 *Ginger Pye*, Eleanor Estes (Harcourt Brace Jovanovich).

1953 *Secret of the Andes*, Ann Nolan Clark (The Viking Press).

1954 *And Now Miguel*, Joseph Krumgold (Thomas Y. Crowell Company).

1955 *The Wheel on the School*, Meindert de Jong (Harper & Row).

1956 *Carry on, Mr. Bowditch*, Jean Lee Latham (Houghton Mifflin Company).

1957 *Miracles on Maple Hill*, Virginia Sorenson, (Harcourt Brace Jovanovich).

1958 *Rifles for Matie*, Harold Keith (Thomas Y. Crowell Company).

1959 *The Witch of Blackbird Pond*, Elizabeth George Speare. (Houghton Mifflin Company).

1960   *Onion John*, Joseph Krumgold (Thomas Y. Crowell Company).

1961   *Island of the Blue Dolphins*, Scott O'Dell (Houghton Mifflin Company).

1962   *The Bronze Bow*, Elizabeth George Speare (Houghton Mifflin Company).

1963   *A Wrinkle in Time*, Madeleine L' Engle (Farrar, Straus & Giroux).

1964   *It's Like This, Cat*, Emily Cheney Neville (Harper & Row).

1965   *Shadow of a Bull*, Maia Wojciechowska (Atheneum Publishers).

1966   *I, Juan de Pareja*, Elizabeth Borton de Trevino (Farrar, Straus & Giroux).

1967   *Up a Road Slowly*, Irene Hunt (Follett Publishing Company).

1968   *From the Mixed-up Files of Mrs. Basil E. Frankweiler*, E.L. Konigsburg (Atheneum Publishers).

1969   *The High King*, Lloyd Alexander, illustrated by Evaline Ness (Holt, Rinehart and Winston, Inc.).

1970   *Sounder*, William H. Armstrong (Harper & Row).

1971   *Summer of the Swans*, Betsey Byars (The Viking Press).

1972   *Mrs. Frisby and the Rats of NIMH*, Robert C. O'Brien (Atheneum Publishers).

    2. *Caldecott Award Books*, selected by the American Library Association, 50 East Huron Street, Chicago, Ill. 60611.

1938   *Animals of the Bible*, Dorothy Lathrop (J.B. Lippincott Company).

1939   *Mei-Li*, Thomas Handforth (Doubleday & Company).

1940   *Abraham Lincoln*, Ingri and Edgar Parin D'Aulaire (Doubleday & Company).

1941   *They Were Strong and Good*, Robert Lawson (The Viking Press).

1942   *Make Way for Ducklings*, Robert McCloskey (The Viking Press).

1943   *The Little House*, Virginia Lee Burton (Houghton Mifflin Company).

1944   *Many Moons*, James Thurber, illustrated by Louis Slobodkin (Harcourt Brace Jovanovich).

1945   *Prayer for a Child*, Rachel Field, illustrated by Elizabeth Orton Jones (The Macmillan Company).

1946   *The Rooster Crows: A Book of American Rhymes and Jingles*, Maud and Miska Petersham (The Macmillan Company).

1947   *The Little Island*, Golden MacDonald, illustrated by Leonard Weisgard (Doubleday & Company).

1948   *White Snow, Bright Snow*, Alvin Tresselt, illustrated by Roger Duvoisin (Lothrop, Lee & Shepard Co.).

1949   *The Big Show*, Berta and Elmer Hader (The Macmillan Company).

1950   *Song of the Swallows*, Leo Politi (Charles Scribner's Sons).

1951   *The Egg Tree*, Katherine Milhous (Charles Scribner's Sons).

1952   *Finders Keepers*, William Lipkind and Nicolas Mordvinoff (Harcourt Brace Jovanovich).

1953 *The Biggest Bear,* Lynd Ward (Houghton Mifflin Company).

1954 *Madeline's Rescue,* Ludwig Bemelmans (The Viking Press).

1955 *Cinderella,* Marcia Brown (Charles Scribner's Sons).

1956 *Frog Went A-Courtin',* John Langstaff, illustrated by Feodor Rojan-kovksy (Harcourt Brace Jovanovich).

1957 *A Tree Is Nice,* Janice May Udry, illustrated by Marc Simont (Harper & Row).

1958 *Time of Wonder,* Robert McCloskey (The Viking Press).

1959 *Chanticleer and the Fox,* Barbara Cooney (Thomas Y. Crowell Company).

1960 *Nine Days to Christmas,* Marie Hall Ets and Aurora Labastida, illustrated by Marie Hall Ets (The Viking Press).

1961 *Baboushka and the Three Kings,* Ruth Robbins, illustrated by Nicolas Sidjakov (Parnassus Press).

1962 *Once a Mouse,* Marcia Brown (Charles Scribner's Sons).

1963 *The Snowy Day,* Ezra Jack Keats (The Viking Press).

1964 *Where the Wild Things Are,* Maurice Sendak (Harper & Row).

1965 *May I Bring a Friend?* Beatrice Schenk de Regniers, illustrated by Beni Montresor (Atheneum Publishers).

1966 *Always Room for One More,* Sorche Nic Leodhas, illustrated by Nonny Hogrogian (Holt, Rinehart and Winston, Inc.)

1967 *Sam, Bangs, and Moonshine,* Evaline Ness (Holt, Rinehart and Winston, Inc.).

1968 *Drummer Hoff,* Barbara Emberley, illustrated by Ed Emberley (Prentice-Hall, Inc.).

1969 *The Fool of the World and the Flying Ship,* retold by Arthur Ransome, illustrated by Uri Shulvitz (Farrar, Straus & Giroux).

1970 *Sylvester and the Magic Pebble,* William Steig (Simon and Schuster, Inc.).

1971 *A Story—A Story,* Gail E. Haley (Atheneum Publishers).

1972 *One Fine Day,* Nonny Hogrogian (The Macmillan Company).

Book Club Selections

During recent years commercially sponsored book clubs for children have gained greatly in popularity. They have the advantage and disadvantages rightly associated with book clubs for adults. A few of the clubs are named below. For a longer list and for information on each club included in the listing, the reader is referred to *Literary Market Place,* published by the R.R. Bowker Company, a copy of which is available in many libraries. Sponsors of the clubs will send details of membership to any interested person.

Arrow Book Club (Scholastic Book Services, 50 West 44th Street, New York, N.Y. 10036).

Best-in-Children's Books (A division of Doubleday and Company, 501 Franklin Street, Garden City, N.Y. 11530).

The Bookplan (921 Washington Avenue, Brooklyn, N.Y. 11225).

Calling All Girls Book Club (A division of Parents' Magazine Enterprises, 52 Vanderbilt Avenue, New York, N.Y. 10017).

Junior DeLuxe Editions Club (A division of Doubleday and Company, Garden City, N.Y. 11530).

Junior Literary Guild (247 Park Avenue, New York, N.Y. 10017).

Lucky Book Club (Scholastic Book Services, 50 West 44th Street, New York, N.Y. 10036).

Parents' Magazine's Read Aloud Book Club for Little Listeners and Beginning Readers (A division of Parents' Magazine Enterprises, 52 Vanderbilt Avenue, New York, N.Y. 10017).

See-Saw Book Program (Scholastic Book Services, 50 West 44th Street, New York, N.Y. 10017).

Teen Age Book Club (Scholastic Book Services, 40 West 44th Street, New York, N.Y. 10017).

The Weekly Reader Children's Book Club, Primary and Intermediate, one for each of these two levels, (245 Long Hill Road, Middletown, Conn. 06457).

Young America Book Club (245 Long Hill Road, Middletown, Conn. 06458).

Young Folks Book Club (1078 St. John's Place, Brooklyn, N.Y. 10013).

Young Readers of America, a branch of the Book-of-the-Month Club (345 Hudson Street, New York, N.Y. 10014).

Xerox Education Publications Book Clubs (245 Long Hill Road, Middletown, Conn. 06457).

"Easy-to-read" Books

Books referred to as "easy-to-read" books are intended not primarily for the slow reader but for the beginning reader. Among the best known of these books are those by Dr. Seuss, such as *Green Eggs and Ham* (published as one of the Beginner Book series by Random House) and *The Cat in the Hat* and *The Cat in the Hat Comes Back* (published by Houghton Mifflin Company). "Easy-to-read" books are written with a controlled vocabulary in sentences that are simple in structure. The books range in difficulty, with some on the independent reading level of boys and girls in the last half of the first grade, while others have as high as a third-grade readability level. They have become increasingly popular in schools where independent reading is emphasized even during the early years of school.

There are critics of the "easy-to-read" books who are disturbed that the books are not of higher literary value. However, some educators argue that books that beginners can read can hardly be expected to be of high literary quality, due to the necessity of controlled vocabulary. They contend that as long as the "easy-to-read" books are not of poor quality, their use should be encouraged if through them boys and girls become more interested in reading. It should be noted that in order to supplement the reading of these books by boys and girls, the teacher should read to them the classics that are the literary heritage of childhood.

The following are among the publishers, in addition to Houghton Mifflin Company and Random House (mentioned in connection with the Dr. Seuss books) who supply books of the "easy-to-read" type: American Book Company; Benefic Press (Beckley-Cardy Company); Follett Publishing Company; Grosset & Dunlap; Harper & Row; Holt, Rinehart and Winston; Kenworthy Educational Service; David McKay Company; Oxford Press; Steck Company; Southwest Regional Laboratory for Educational Research and Development (Inglewood, Cal.).

A valuable reference for the teacher is the revised edition of *Books for Beginning Readers* by Elizabeth Guilfoille, published by the National Council of Teachers of English.

Books for Retarded Readers

Although the retarded reader may enjoy some of the "easy-to-read" books, they have not been designed with him in mind. Some books written for him have long been on the market, but it is only of late that a large number have been published. Books for the retarded reader, though necessarily written with a limited vocabulary, must be on his interest level and on his intelligence level. (However, it must not be assumed that all retarded readers have low intelligence.)

Sources of information on books for the retarded reader include:

Annotated Bibliography of Selected Books with High Interest and Low Vocabulary Level (Indianapolis Public Schools).

Books for Slow Readers (Holiday House).

A Graded List of Books for School Libraries, which contains a section on books for slow learners (Harcourt Brace Jovanovich).

Gateway to Readable Books: An Annotated Graded List of Books for Adolescents Who Find Reading Difficult, Ruth Strang (H. W. Wilson Company).

Good Reading for Poor Readers, George D. Spache (The Reading Laboratory and Clinic of the University of Florida, Gainesville, latest edition).

Some of the publishers who market books with high interest-low vocabulary are:

Beckley-Cardy Company (Benefic Press)

The Bobbs-Merrill Publishing Company

Bowmar Publishing Corporation

The Children's Press

Doubleday and Company

Field Educational Publications

Follett Publishing Company

Garrard Publishing Company

Harper & Row

D.C. Heath and Company

Holt, Rinehart and Winston, Inc.

The Macmillan Company

Melmont Publishers (Children's Press)

William Morrow and Company

G.P. Putman's Sons

Random House, Inc.

Reader's Digest

Science Research Associates

Scott, Foresman and Company

Webster Publishing Company

Wheeler Publishing Company

Information on series for retarded readers can be secured from the publishers on request. Only a few of the many well-known ones are named here.

Air Space-Age series (Benefic Press, Beckley-Cardy Company).

American Adventure series (Harper & Row).

Basic Vocabulary series (Garrard Publishing Company).

Beginning-to-Read Biographies (G.P. Putman's Sons).

The Checkered Flag series (Field Educational Publications).

The Cowboy Sam series (Benefic Press, Beckley-Cardy Company).

The Jim Forest Readers (Field Educational Publications).

I Want to Be series (Melmont Publishers, Children's Press).

Landmark Books (Random House, Inc.).

New Reading for Independence series (Scott, Foresman and Company).

Pleasure Reading series (Garrard Publishing Company).

Reader's Digest Skill Builders (Reader's Digest Services).

Reading Incentive Program (Bowmar Publishing Company).

Space Age Books (Bowmar Publishing Company).

Textbooks for Boys and Girls

On the market are many excellent reading series. As indicated earlier, much of the criticism hurled by some critics against basal readers should be made of the misuse, rather than use, of the better series. On request the teacher will receive from the publishers free materials explaining a series and highlighting the points of special excellence claimed for them. Publishers will also send a list indicating their supplementary materials. The R. R. Bowker publication, revised annually, *El-hi Textbooks in Print*, lists not only textbooks but also teaching materials such as dictionaries, booklists, and maps.

Among the publishers of textbooks in reading are the following:

Allyn and Bacon, Inc.
American Book Company
The Bobbs-Merrill Company
Educators Publishing Service
Ginn and Company
Harper & Row
D.C. Heath and Company
Holt, Rinehart and Winston, Inc.
Houghton Mifflin Company
Laidlaw Brothers
J.B. Lippincott Company
The Macmillan Company
Charles E. Merrill Publishing Company
Open Court Publishing Company
Pitman Publishing Company
Science Research Associates
Scott, Foresman and Company
Silver Burdett Company

Reference Books for Boys and Girls

In today's schools much more use than formerly is made of reference books. Publishers have not been slow to meet the growing demands for dictionaries and encyclopedias for boys and girls. A valuable aid for the teacher in selecting reference books is *Children's Literature: A Guide to Reference Sources* prepared under the direction of Virginia Haviland and available from the U.S. Government Printing Office.

Picture Dictionaries

Picture dictionaries can be found on the counters of bookstores and many other stores. They are also available directly from the publishers. For a selected list of picture dictionaries the reader is referred to Chapter 5B, "Developing Skill in Word Recognition" (*see* page 153).

Other Dictionaries

A list of some widely used dictionaries, other than picture dictionaries, is given in Chapter 8A, "Locating Information and Using It" (*see* page 254).

Encyclopedias

The following encyclopedias are available for use by elementary-school boys and girls:

Book of Knowledge (Grolier Society)

Britannica Junior Encyclopedia (Encyclopedia Britannica)

The Children's Hour (Spencer International Press)

Compton's Pictured Encyclopedia (F.E. Compton and Company)

The Golden Book Encyclopedia (Golden Press)

The Golden Book Encyclopedia of Natural Science (Golden Press)

My First Picture Encyclopedia (Grosset & Dunlap)

Our Wonderful World (Spencer International Press)

Pictorial Encyclopedia of American History (Children's Press, Melmont Publishers)

World Book Encyclopedia (Field Enterprises Education Corporation)

Young People's Science Encyclopedia (Children's Press, Melmont Publishers)

PERIODICALS

Although the great storehouse for reading and for reading instruction is found in books, periodicals, too, are a treasury of printed materials for teachers and for boys and girls.

Periodicals for Teachers

Several periodicals are devoted exclusively to the teaching of reading. Three of these are published by the International Reading Association: *The Reading Teacher* (for elementary-school teachers), *The Journal of Reading* (for secondary-school teachers), and *The Reading Research Quarterly*. Many state branches of the International Reading Association also publish magazines; for example, the official organ of the Minnesota Reading Association is the *Minnesota Reading Quarterly.* The College Reading Association publishes *Reading World* (formerly known as *The Journal of the Reading Specialist*) which contains some articles of interest to the teacher of reading in the elementary school. *Elementary English,* one of the periodicals of the National Council of Teachers of English, often prints articles on elementary-school reading. Other magazines that contain articles on the teaching of reading in the elementary school are:

Teacher (Macmillan Professional Magazines, Inc.)

The Instructor (F.A. Owen Publishing Company)

Elementary School Journal (University of Chicago Press)

Childhood Education (Association for Childhood Education, International).

Magazines for the lay public, such as the *Atlantic* (Atlantic Monthly Press), as well as many newspapers, include articles on the teaching of reading from time to time.

Periodicals for Boys and Girls

The extensiveness of the use of periodicals by boys and girls is indicated by the fact that the 1970 edition of *The Dobler World Dictionary of Youth Periodicals*[3] lists nearly a thousand, with a combined circulation of more than 100,000,000.

Listings of Periodicals for Boys and Girls

The following sources are among those that list periodicals for boys and girls:

Association for Childhood Education, International, *Guide to Children's Magazines, Newspapers, Reference Books*, Nancy Nunnally, compiler (Association for Childhood Education, International).

Cundiff, Ruby Ethel, compiler, *101 Plus Magazines for Schools*, Grades 1 to 12 (Tennessee Book Company, latest edition).

Dobler, Lavinia G., and Muriel Fuller, *The Dobler World Directory of Youth Periodicals.*

Graves, Eileen P., ed., *Ulrich's Periodicals Directory* (R.R. Bowker Company, published periodically).

Ladley, Winifred C., compiler, *Sources of Good Books and Magazines for Children* (International Reading Association, latest edition).

---

[3] Davinia Dobler and Muriel Fuller, *The Dobler World Directory of Youth Periodicals,* 3rd ed. (New York: Citation Press, 1970).

Madison Public Schools, *Magazines for Elementary Grades* (Department of Curriculum Development, 545 West Dayton Street, Madison, Wis. 53703).

Martin, Laura K., *Magazines for School Libraries* (R.R. Bowker Company).

H.W. Wilson Company, *Reader's Guide to Periodical Literature* (H.W. Wilson Company).

Periodicals for Class Use

Two publishing companies that provide wide circulation of periodicals designed for class use are the American Education Publications (245 Long Hill Road, Middletown, Conn. 06457), and Scholastic Magazines, Inc., (33 West 42nd Street, New York, N.Y. 10036). The former publishes *My Weekly Reader* in the following editions:

My Weekly Reader—Surprise (for Kindergarten)
My Weekly Reader—Picture Reader (for Grade 1)
My Weekly Reader—News Reader (for Grade 2)
My Weekly Reader—News Story (for Grade 3)
My Weekly Reader—News Parade (for Grade 4)
My Weekly Reader—World Parade (for Grade 5)
My Weekly Reader—News Report (for Grade 6)

American Education Publications also publishes *Current Events* for Grades 6 to 8, and *Read* for Grades 6 to 9.

The Scholastic Magazines, Inc., publishes the following editions of its newspaper for boys and girls in the elementary school:

News Pilot (for Grade 1)

News Ranger (for Grade 2)

News Trail (for Grade 3)

News Explorer (for Grade 4)

Newstime (for Grade 5 and 6)

Other Periodicals for Boys and Girls

The following are some of the periodicals widely read by boys and girls. Some are designed for boys and girls; others, though primarily written for older people, are also read by many boys and girls in the later years of the elementary school.

American Girl, The (Girl Scouts of the United States, 830 Third Avenue, New York, 10022).

American Junior Red Cross News (American National Red Cross, 17 and D Streets, N.W., Washington, D.C. 20006).

Arts and Activities (Jones Publishing Company, 8150 North Central Park Avenue, Skokie, Ill. 60076).

Audubon (National Audubon Society, 1130 Fifth Avenue, New York, N.Y. 10028).

Boys' Life (Boy Scouts of America, New Brunswick, N.J. 08903).

Calling All Girls (The Parents' Institute of *Parents' Magazine,* 52 Vanderbilt Avenue, New York, N.Y. 10017).

Child Life Magazine (Child Life, Inc., 36 Federal Street, Boston, Mass. 02110).

Children's Digest, combined with *Humpty Dumpty's Magazine* (The Parents' Institute of *Parents' Magazine,* 52 Vanderbilt Avenue, New York, N.Y. 10017).

Children's Playmate Magazine (Children's Playmate Magazine, Inc., 3025 East 75th Street, Cleveland, Ohio 44104).

Golden Magazine (Western Publishing Company Inc., 1220 Mound Avenue, Racine. Wis. 53404).

Highlights for Children (Highlights for Children, 2300 West Fifth Avenue, Columbus, Ohio 43216).

Humpty Dumpty's Magazine, combined with *Children's Digest* (The Parents' Institute of *Parents' Magazine,* 52 Vanderbilt Avenue, New York, N.Y. 10017).

Jack and Jill (Curtis Publishing Company, Independence Square, Philadelphia, Pa. 19105).

Junior Natural History Magazine (American Museum of Natural History, Central Park West at 79th Street, New York, N.Y. 10024).

Junior Scholastic (Scholastic Magazine, Inc., 50 West 44th Street, New York, N.Y. 10036).

Model Airplane News (Air Age, Inc., 551 Fifth Avenue, New York, N.Y. 10017).

National Geographic Magazine (National Geographic Society, 17th and M. Street, Washington, D.C. 20036).

Peck-of-Fun (Clapper Publishing Company, P.O. Box 568, Park Ridge, Ill. 60068).

Plays (Plays, Inc., 8 Arlington Street, Boston, Mass. 02116).

Popular Mechanics (Popular Mechanics, 575 Lexington Avenue, New York, N.Y. 10022).

Popular Science (355 Lexington Avenue, New York, N.Y. 10017).

Summertime (Scholastic Magazines, Inc., 33 West 42nd Street, New York, 10036).

Wee Wisdom (Unity School of Christianity, Lee's Summit, Mo. 64063).

A rather unique recent addition to magazines for children is *Kids Magazine*,[4] published by Kids Magazine (777 Third Avenue, New York, N.Y. 10017). It is written by and for children.

OTHER READING MATERIALS

The market has been fairly flooded with materials—in addition to books and periodicals—that allegedly are of value in teaching reading. Some of these have stood the test of critical scrutiny by means of various evaluative procedures; others are of questionable worth.

Evaluation

Since the worth of any teaching aid is to a large degree a function of the purpose for which it is intended and the methods employed in using it, it is difficult, if not impossible, to give an appraisal of the value of many of the materials. However, a source the teacher may wish to consult is the published reports of the Educational Products Information Exchange Institute (E.P.I.E.), which attempts to present unbiased evaluations of new educational material. But in the final analysis the teacher will need to make his own evaluation of materials as he studies them and the accompanying explanatory materials made available by the publisher, and as he considers questions such as the following:[5]

1. Is it designed, according to the publicity material on it, to serve a purpose that is important to me? (Care should be exercised so that unsupported claims of publishers or distributors do not mislead the examiner in his appraisal.)
2. Is there evidence to indicate that the claimed purpose is being accomplished through use of the material?
3. Is use of the material in harmony with what we know from the field of child growth and development?
4. Is use of the material in harmony with accepted principles of teaching?
5. Is the time that needs to be spent in the use of the materials reasonable?
6. Can the materials be used without constant supervision by the teacher? (It is not necessarily a score against an aid if constant supervision is needed; however, it is important to note if a teacher is looking for an aid that can be used primarily as a "seatwork activity.")
7. Is the cost of the material in favorable proportion to its usefulness?

[4] Staff of *The Reading Teacher*, "Adults Talk about *KIDS*," *The Reading Teacher*, vol. 25, no. 2 (November 1971), pp. 60–61.

[5] Martha Dallmann, *Teaching the Language Arts in the Elementary School*, 2nd ed. (Dubuque, Iowa: Wm. C. Brown Company Publishers, 1971), p. 390.

When considering possible use of materials dealing with the development of skills in word recognition, the teacher should pay particular attention to the role that phonics plays. He will want to make certain that according to his best insights phonics is neither overemphasized nor underemphasized and that methods used in teaching it are in harmony with the teaching principles he accepts.

One further word of caution needs to be expressed. While it is important that a teacher try to justify the use of materials he selects in terms of his best understanding of educational principles and procedures, such consideration should not keep him from refusing to experiment with the new. If all teachers were reluctant to try out materials until their value has been established beyond a doubt, educational progress would be retarded.

Sources of Materials

The teacher who is using a basal textbook is advised to write to the publisher for a descriptive list of supplementary materials produced by the company. He may also wish to write for a similar list to other publishers of reading materials mentioned earlier in this chapter, as well as to some of the following:

Addison-Wesley Publishing Company

Appleton-Century-Crofts

Cambridge University Press

The Economy Company

Educational Developmental Laboratories

Educator's Progress Service

Enrichment Teaching Materials

Fearon Publishers

J.B. Lippincott Company

Longmans, Green and Company

Simon and Schuster

Society for Visual Education

Stanford University Press

Reading Laboratories

In Chapter 13, "Adapting Instruction to the Needs of the Learner," reference has been made to laboratories published by Science Research Associates (*see* page 425). That company has two very popular reading programs, the *SRA Reading for Understanding Laboratory* and the *SRA Reading Laboratory*. The *SRA Reading for Understanding Laboratory,* consisting of 4,000 selections dealing primarily with the development of comprehension skills, is planned for grades 3 through 12. The *SRA Reading Laboratory,* designed for Grades 1 through 13, places emphasis on various reading skills, including reading rates. Phonics is emphasized in the lower levels of the *SRA Reading Laboratory.* Other reading laboratories include:

Building Reading Power (Charles E. Merrill Publishing Company).

The EDL Study Skills Library (Educational Developmental Laboratories).

The Literature Sampler (Learning Research Associates).

The Reading Clinic (McGraw-Hill Book Company).

The Reading Practice Program (Harcourt Brace Jovanovich).

TESTS

For a comprehensive listing and evaluation of tests the reader is referred to the most recent edition of *Mental Measurements Yearbook* or the latest edition of *Tests in Print,* both edited by Oscar K. Buros and published by Gryphon Press (220 Montgomery Street, Highland Park, N.J. 08904).

Mental Tests

In Chapter 4A, "Readiness for Reading," a few individual, as well as group, intelligence tests are named. A more extensive list of each of the two types is given here.

Individual Tests

The following are among the mental tests designed for individual testing:

Arthur Point Scale of Performance Tests, for use with children with language handicaps (Psychological Corporation).

Detroit First Grade Intelligence Tests (Harcourt Brace Jovanovich).

Full Range Picture Vocabulary Tests (Psychological Test Specialists, Missoula, Mont.).

Peabody Picture Vocabulary Test (American Guidance Service, Circle Pines, Minn.).

Perceptual Survey Rating Scale (Charles E. Merrill Publishing Company).

Pictorial Test of Intelligence (Houghton Mifflin Company).

Slosson Intelligence Test for Children and Adults (Slosson Educational Publications, East Aurora, N.Y.).

Stanford-Binet Intelligence Scale (Houghton Mifflin Company).

Wechsler Intelligence Scale for Children (Psychological Corporation).

Group Tests

The following tests do not need to be administered to one person at a time:

The California Short-form Test of Mental Maturity (California Test Bureau).
Cattell Culture Fair Intelligence Tests (Bobbs-Merrill Company).
Goodenough-Harris Drawing Tests (Psychological Corporation).
The Kuhlman-Anderson Intelligence Tests (Educational Test Bureau)
The Lorge-Thorndike Intelligence Tests (Houghton Mifflin Company).
Otis Quick-scoring Mental Ability Tests (Harcourt Brace Jovanovich).
The Pintner-Cunningham Primary Tests (Harcourt Brace Jovanovich).
The Pintner General Ability Test (Harcourt Brace Jovanovich).
The Pintner Non-language Primary Mental Test (Teachers College Press, Columbia University).
SRA Primary Mental Abilities Test (Science Research Associates).

Reading Readiness Tests

Several reading readiness tests have been described in Chapter 4A, "Readiness for Reading" (*see* pages 65–66), namely:

Gates Reading Readiness Test (Teachers College Press, Columbia University).
The Metropolitan Reading Tests (Harcourt Brace Jovanovich).
The Lee-Clark Reading Readiness Test (California Test Bureau).
The Classification Test for Beginners (Webster Publishing Company).

Among the additional reading readiness tests are:

American School Reading Readiness Test (Public School Publishing Company).
Binion-Beck Reading Readiness Test (Acorn Publishing Company, Long Island, N.Y.).
Clymer-Barrett Prereading Battery (Personnel Press).
Early Detection Inventory (Follett Publishing Company).
Gates-MacGinitie Reading Readiness Test (Teachers College Press, Columbia University).
Harrison-Stroud Reading Readiness Profiles (Houghton Mifflin Company).
Maturity Level for School Entrance and Reading Readiness (American Guidance Service, Publishers Building, Circle Pines, Minn.).
Monroe Reading Aptitude Tests (Houghton Mifflin Company).

Murphy-Durrell Diagnostic Reading Readiness Test (Harcourt Brace Jovanovich).

Reading Aptitude Tests (Houghton Mifflin Company).

Reading Readiness Test (Steck-Vaughn Company, Austin, Tex.)

Scholastic Reading Readiness Test (Scholastic Testing Service, 3774 West Devon Avenue, Chicago, Ill. 60645).

Steinbach Test of Reading Readiness (Scholastic Testing Service).

Webster Reading Readiness Test (Webster Publishing Company).

Reading Tests

In Chapter 12, "Classroom Diagnosis of Reading Ability," reference is made to several reading tests (*see* page 401) and cautions to keep in mind in interpreting standardized tests are given. The tests named there are included in the following listing, along with a number of others—some of which are survey tests and others diagnostic. Most of them check a variety of reading skills, while others are limited to one phase of reading. It should be noted that the so-called oral reading tests check primarily silent reading skills, by means of oral reading.

American School Achievement Test: Part I, Reading, Willis E. Pratt, Robert V. Young, and Clara Cockerville (Bobbs-Merrill Company).

American School Reading Tests, Willis E. Pratt and Stanley W. Lore (Bobbs-Merrill Company).

Basic Sight Word Test, Dolch list, E.W. Dolch (Garrard Press).

Botel Reading Inventory, Morton Botel (Follett Publishing Company).

California Reading Tests, Ernest W. Tiegs and Willis W. Clark (California Test Bureau).

Davis Reading Tests, Frederick B. Davis and Charlotte Croon Davis (Psychological Corporation).

Diagnostic Reading Scales, George D. Spache (California Test Bureau).

Diagnostic Reading Tests, Guy L. Bond, Theodore Clymer, and Cyril Hoyt (Lyons and Carnahan).

Doren Diagnostic Reading Test of Word Recognition Skills, Margaret Doren (American Guidance Service).

Durrell Analysis of Reading Difficulty, Donald D. Durrell (Harcourt Brace Jovanovich).

Durrell-Sullivan Reading Capacity and Achievement Tests, Donald D. Durrell and Helen Sullivan (Harcourt Brace Jovanovich).

Elementary Reading: Every Pupil Achievement Test, Gene E. Plank (Bureau of Educational Measurement).

Flash-X Sight Vocabulary Test, George D. Spache and Stanford E. Taylor (Educational Developmental Laboratories).

Gates Advanced Primary Reading Tests (Type AWR, word recognition; Type APR, paragraph reading), Arthur I. Gates (Teacher College Press, Columbia University).

Gates Basic Reading Tests (Type GS, reading to appreciate general significance; Type UD, reading to understand precise directions; Type ND, reading to note details; Type RV, reading vocabulary; Type LX, level of comprehension), Arthur I. Gates (Teachers College Press, Columbia University).

Gates-MacGinitie Reading Tests, Arthur I. Gates and Walter H. MacGinitie (Teachers College Press, Columbia University).

Gates-McKillop Reading Diagnostic Tests, Arthur I. Gates and Anne S. McKillop (Teachers College Press, Columbia University).

Gates Primary Reading Tests (Type PWR, word recognition; Type PSR, sentence reading; Type PPR, paragraph reading), Arthur I. Gates (Teachers College Press, Columbia University).

Gates Reading Survey, Arthur I. Gates (Teachers College Press, Columbia University).

Gilmore Oral Reading Test, John V. Gilmore (Harcourt Brace Jovanovich).

Gray Standardized Oral Reading Check Tests, William S. Gray (Public School Publishing Company).

Gray Standardized Oral Reading Paragraph Tests, William S. Gray (Public School Publishing Company).

Iowa Every-pupil Tests of Basic Skills: Silent Reading Comprehension, H.F. Spitzer et. al (Houghton Mifflin Company).

Iowa Silent Reading Tests, Harry A. Greene, Ann Jorgensen, and Victor H. Kelley (Harcourt Brace Jovanovich).

Kelley-Greene Reading Comprehension Test, Victor H. Kelley and Harry A. Greene (Harcourt Brace Jovanovich).

Leavell Analytical Oral Reading Tests, Ullin W. Leavell (American Guidance Service).

Lee-Clark Reading Test, J. Murray Lee and Willis W. Clark (California Test Bureau).

Los Angeles Elementary Reading Test, Jessie E. Ingraham (California Test Bureau).

Los Angeles Primary Reading Test, Jessie E. Ingraham (California Test Bureau).

Metropolitan Achievement Tests: Reading, Gertrude Hildreth et al (Harcourt Brace Jovanovich).

Monroe Diagnostic Reading Test, Marion Monroe (C.H. Stoelting Company).

Monroe Revised Silent Reading Test, Marion Monroe (Bobbs-Merrill Company).

The Nelson-Lohmann Reading Test, M.J. Nelson and Victor Lohmann (American Guidance Service).

The Nelson Silent Reading Test: Vocabulary and Paragraph, M.J. Nelson (Houghton Mifflin Company).

Peabody Library Information Test, Louis Shores and Joseph E. Moore (Educational Test Bureau).

Phonics Knowledge Survey, Dolores Durkin and Leonard Meshover (Teachers College Press, Columbia University).

Primary Reading Profiles, James B. Stroud and Albert N. Hieronymus (Houghton Mifflin Company).

Roswell-Chall Diagnostic Test of Word Analysis Skills, Florence G. Roswell and Jeanne S. Chall (Essay Press).

SRA Achievement Series: Reading, Louis P. Thorpe et al (Science Research Associates).

SRA Reading Record, Guy T. Buswell (Science Research Associates).

Silent Reading Diagnostic Tests, Guy L. Bond, Bruce Balow, and Cyril Hoyt (Lyons and Carnahan).

Slosson Oral Reading Test, Richard L. Slosson (Slosson Educational Publications).

Stanford Achievement Test: Reading, Truman L. Kelley et al (Harcourt Brace Jovanovich).

Williams Primary Reading Test, Allan J. Williams (Bobbs-Merrill Company).

AUDIOVISUAL AIDS

Although this section deals primarily with (1.) films, (2.) filmstrips, and (3.) recordings, the teacher should not overlook the many ways in which other means of utilizing audiovisual aids can be employed; namely through viewing still pictures or slides, examining realia, listening to the radio, viewing television.

The reader is referred to the chapters in many professional books on teaching methods for ideas for using audiovisual aids effectively. In addition, the following books dealing exclusively with the subject of audiovisual education can be of great help to the teacher:

Audio-Visual Methods in Teaching, Edgar Dale (Holt, Rinehart and Winston. Inc.).

Planning and Producing Audio-Visual Materials, Jerold E. Kemp (Chandler Publishing Company).

A-V Instruction, Materials and Methods, James W. Brown, Richard Lewis, and Fred Harcleroad (McGraw-Hill Book Company).

Fundamentals of Teaching with Audio-visual Technology, Carlton W.H. Erickson (The Macmillan Company).

Films

We shall classify films of value in the teaching of reading as (1.) films for teachers, and (2.) films for boys and girls.

Films for Teachers

Two films of value to the teacher in providing background for using films in the classroom are *Choosing a Classroom Film* (McGraw-Hill Book Company) and *Film and You* (BFA).

An increasing number of films on the teaching of reading are now available. Catalogues from the audiovisual divisions of many state departments of education list not only those for viewing by the boys and girls but also some for teachers in the various disciplines. Furthermore, a letter requesting titles and terms (purchase or rental) from many of the companies listed in this section as distributors of audiovisual aids will give the reader the desired information. A few samples of such films are:

Gregory Learns to Read (produced in the Detroit Public Schools, available through Syracuse University).

How Your Child Learns to Read (produced in the Salt Lake City Schools, available from the Board of Education, Salt Lake City).

Individualizing Reading in the Classroom (Columbia University).

Readiness for Reading (McGraw-Hill Book Company).

Reading: The Language Experience Approach (Learning through Seeing, Inc., 8138 Foothill Boulevard, Sunland, Ga. 91040).

Reading and Critical Thinking (McGraw-Hill Book Company).

Reading for Pleasure (Coronet Films).

Reading Growth: Adjusting Your Reading Speeds (Coronet Films).

Reading Growth: Basic Skills (Coronet Films).

Reading Growth: Reading Creatively (Coronet Films).

Reading Growth: Understanding Word Meanings (Coronet Films).

They All Learn to Read (available through Syracuse University).

A film which provides much background information for the teacher that can also be shown with profit to older boys and girls in the elementary school is *The Lively Art of Picture Books*, distributed by Children's Services Division, American Library Association or Weston Woods Studios. It deals in an inimitable manner with some of the Caldecott Award books and with incidents from the lives of some of the artists of those books.

Films for Boys and Girls

Films for boys and girls in the area of reading can be classified as those that deal with the skills of reading and those that deal with literature for children.

The following are some of the Coronet films on skill development in reading suitable for viewing by elementary-school pupils:

Improve Your Reading

Reading for Beginners; Context Clues

Reading for Beginners: Word Sounds

Reading and Critical Thinking

Reading Growth: Understanding Word Meanings

Reading Signs Is Fun

Reading with a Purpose

What Is Active and Creative Reading?

The Who and Why of Reading

Other films include: *What Did You Read? What's in a Book? Was It Worth Reading?* (C-B Educational Films). A few titles that deal with the use of the library, filmed for boys and girls, are: *Know Your Library* (Coronet Films); *Library Story* (Encyclopedia Britannica); *You'll Find It in the Library* (Coronet Films).

A few of the big array of films for boys and girls dealing with literature for children are:

Four films of Aesop's Fables (McGraw-Hill Book Company)

The Emperor's Nightingale (McGraw-Hill Book Company)

Herman Melville's Moby Dick (McGraw-Hill Book Company)

Hiawatha's Childhood (McGraw-Hill Book Company)

Reading for Pleasure (Coronet Films)

The Shoemaker and the Elves (Golden Film Company)

Tom Thumb in King Arthur's Court (Coronet Films)

The Ugly Duckling (Coronet Films)

The Wave: A Japanese Folk Tale (BFA Educational Media, Columbia Broadcasting System)

An interesting innovation of fairly recent years is the film reader in which film is correlated with reading books. Teachers interested in film readers may wish to write for information on them to Encyclopedia Britannica, Harper & Row, or to D.C. Heath and Company. Or they may wish to consult the article, "The Film-Reader Program," in *The Reading Teacher's Reader,* Oscar S. Causey, ed. (The Ronald Press 1958), p. 326.

Filmstrips

Filmstrips have also been correlated with basal reading series. The reader may write to Harper & Row for detailed information as to how that company has used the technique with the Alice and Jerry readers. Another series of correlated filmstrips is the Taylor Associates Guided Reading Story Library with thirty filmstrip sets for six levels. Each of the sets consists of ten filmstrips which show Part B of each story, while Part A of the story is given in the accompanying study guides. Among the supplementary materials to the filmstrips and study guides are cassette playbacks. (Information on the Reading Story Library is obtainable from its distributors, Instructional Communications Technology, Inc., Huntington, N.Y. 11743.)

The following are the titles of a few of the filmstrips available on the market for use by boys and girls as part of the reading program, with some on the development of skills in reading and others on reading of literature for children:

American Folk Heroes (Encyclopedia Britannica Films).

Basic Primary Phonics (Society for Visual Education).

Better Study Habits Series: Improve Your Reading (Encyclopedia Britannica).

Filmstrips for Practice in Phonetic Skills (Scott, Foresman and Company).

Fundamentals of Reading, three filmstrips (Educational Services).

How to Read: To Understand, to Evaluate, to Use (Society for Visual Education).

How to Use an Encyclopedia (McGraw-Hill Book Company)

Landmark Books (Random House, Inc.).

Learning to Use the Dictionary, eight filmstrips (Pacific Production, 414 Mason Street, San Francisco, Cal.)

Library Services, five filmstrips (Eye Gate House).

Library Tools Services (McGraw-Hill Book Company).

Picture Book Parade Filmstrip series (Frederick Warne and Company).

Phonics, four filmstrips (Scott, Foresman and Company).

Use Your Library (Society for Visual Education).

Using a Dictionary (Webster Publishing Company).

Words: Their Origin, Use and Spelling series (Society for Visual Education).

Your Dictionary and How to Use It series (Society for Visual Education).

Your Library: A Treasure Chest (Society for Visual Education).

Records

Various series of records are now available on outstanding books. There is, for example, the well-known Enrichment Records series, which accompany some of the Landmark Books published by Random House. The National Council of Teachers of English produces a series of records of stories such as "The Elves and the Shoemaker," "Rumplestiltskin," "Aladdin and the Wonderful Lamp," "Rip Van Winkle," "Just So Stories," and "The House at Pooh Corner." Also on the market are *Folkways Records* (Folkways Records and Service Corporation), *My First Golden Record Library* (Golden Records), and various "libraries" of books, with records, distributed by *The Columbia Children's Book and Record Library* (Department CBR, 51 West 52nd Street, New York, N.Y. 10019).

Of considerable popularity are the *Newbery Award Records,* distributed by Newbery Award Record, Inc. They include titles such as *The Wheel on the School* (Meindert DeJong), *Call It Courage* (Armstrong Sperry), *Amos Fortune, Free Man* (Elizabeth Yates), *Invincible Louisa* (Cornelia Meigs). Miller-Brody Productions, Inc. (342 Madison Avenue, New York, N.Y. 10017) publishes the Newbery Award Library, which includes the books with accompanying records, cassettes, and filmstrips.

A few of the very large number of additional recordings not on Newbery Award books are:

Alice in Wonderland (with *Many Moons* and *The Eager Piano* on the reverse side; Columbia Records).

Andersen's Fairy Tales (in three volumes, with "The Nightingale," "The Emperor's New Clothes," "The Steadfast Tin Soldier" in Volume 1; Educational Record Sales).

Hänsel and Gretel (Educational Record Sales).

Make Way for Ducklings (by Robert McCloskey; Weston Woods Studios).

Records are also available on subjects indicated by these titles: "Choral Speaking for Intermediate Grades" (Educational Record Sales); "Let's Try Choral Reading" (Young America Films); "It's Your Library" (Vocational Guidance Films).

There are also recordings of stories told by famous storytellers. For example, obtainable from the American Library Association are albums of stories told by Ruth Sawyer and Gudrun Thorne-Thomsen. Recordings, too, have been made of poets reading their own work, as for example, two recordings available through Caedmon, "Robert Frost Reads His Poetry" and "Poems for Children" by Carl Sandburg.

Sound filmstrip sets, in which filmstrips are synchronized with recordings, are produced by several companies. For example, *Crow Boy* by Taro Yashima, *Petunia* by Roger Duvoisin, *Little Tim and the Brave Sea Captain* by Edward Ardizonne, and *Three Billy Goats Gruff* adapted by Marcia Brown are available as sound-filmstrips through Weston Woods Studios.

Guides to Selection

The National Information Center for Educational Media (University of Southern California, University Park, Los Angeles 90007) publishes these indices periodically:

NICEM Index to Educational Audio Tapes

NICEM Index to Educational Records

NICEM Index to Educational Video Tapes

NICEM Index to 8 mm Cartridges

NICEM Index to Filmstrips

NICEM Index to Overhead Transparencies

NICEM Index to Producers and Distributors

NICEM Index to 16 mm Educational Films

Additonal guides to selection of audiovisual aids are:

Aids in Selection of Materials for Children and Young People (American Library Association).

An Annotated List of Recordings for the Language Arts (National Council of Teachers of English).

Audio-Visual Catalog (Materials for Learning, Inc.).

Audio-Visual Materials Handbook (Indiana University, Bloomington).

Catalog of Frith Films (Frith Films).

Choosing a Classroom Film (McGraw-Hill Book Company).

CBS Audio-Visual Catalog (Children's Reading Service, Brooklyn, N.Y.).

Directory of 3,660 16mm Film Libraries, Seerley Reid, Anita Carpenter, and Annie Dougherty (U.S. Government Printing Office).

EDL Filmstrips (Educational Developmental Laboratories).

Educational Film, now on cards; in process of publication (American Library Association).

Educational Film Guide, Frederic A. Krahm; out-of-print, but still used extensively (H.W. Wilson Company).

Educational Filmstrip Catalog (Society for Visual Education).

Educational Tape Catalog (Magnetic Tape Duplicators).

Educational Television Guidebook, Phillip Lewis (McGraw-Hill Book Company).

Educational Television Motion Pictures, Descriptive Catalog (National Education Television Film Service, Audio-Visual Center, University of Indiana, Bloomington).

Educator's Guide to Free Films (Educators Progress Service).

Educator's Guide to Free Filmstrips (Educators Progress Service).

Educator's Guide to Free Slidefilms (Educators Progress Service).

Educator's Guide to Free Tapes and Recordings (Educators Progress Service).

Enrichment Filmstrips (Enrichment Teaching Materials).

Film and You (BFA Educational Media).

Film Evaluation Guide (Educational Film Library Association).

Films for Children (Educational Film Library Association).

Filmstrip Guide (The H.W. Wilson Company).

Guides to Newer Media, Margaret L. Rufswold and Carolyn Gauss (American Library Association).

National Tape Recording Catalog (National Tape Library or some state universities, among them National Tape Depository, Audio-Visual Center, University of Colorado, Boulder, 80302).

New Media Index (McGraw-Hill Book Company).

Picture Book Parade Motion Pictures, Filmstrips, and Records (Weston Woods Studios).

SVE Film and Filmstrip Catalogs (Society for Visual Education).

Sources of Information on Educational Media, John A. Moldstad (U.S. Printing Office).

The Tape Recorder in the Elementary Classroom (Minnesota Mining and Manufacturing Company).

UCLA Children's Film Series (Children's Theater Committee, Theater Arts Department, University of California, Los Angeles).

Young America Filmstrip Catalog (Young America Films).

Producers and Distributors

Visual aids can be obtained from many state universities and state departments of education. Various agencies — such as steamship lines, manufacturing companies, and consuls — are also good sources of free aids. Some book companies, too, are distributors of audiovisual materials — such as McGraw-Hill Book Company; Scott, Foresman and Company; Harcourt Brace Jovanovich. Other names of publishers or distributors of audiovisual aids include:

American Library Association (50 East Huron Street, Chicago, Ill. 60611).

American Museum of Natural History (Central Park West at 79th Street, New York, N.Y. 10023).

Audio-Visual Research (1317 Eighth Street South, Waseca, Minn. 56093).

BFA Educational Media (2111 Michigan Ave., Santa Monica, Cal. 90404).

Beltone Electronics Corporation (4201 West Victoria Street, Chicago, Ill. 60646).

Caedmon Records (461 Eighth Avenue, New York, N.Y. 10001).

Children's Press Service (1078 St. John's Place, Brooklyn, N.Y. 11236).

Children's Record Guild (27 Thompson Street, New York, N.Y. 10013).

Churchill Films (662 North Robertson Boulevard, Los Angeles, Cal. 90034).

Columbia Records, Educational Division, 799 Seventh Avenue, New York, N.Y. 10019).

Coronet Films (Coronet Building, 65 East South Water Street, Chicago, Ill. 60601).

Educational Film Library Association (250 West 57th Street, New York, N.Y. 10036).

Educational Record Sales (157 Chambers Street, New York, N.Y. 10007).

Educators Progress Service (Randolph, Wis. 53956).

Encyclopedia Britannica Films (1150 Wilmette Avenue, Wilmette, Ill. 60091).

Enrichment Teaching Materials (246 Fifth Avenue, New York, N.Y. 10001).

Eye Gate House (146–01 Archer Avenue, Jamaica, N.Y. 11435).

Folkways Records and Service Corporation (165 West 46th Street, New York, N.Y. 10036).

Frith Films, (1816 North Highland Avenue, Hollywood, Cal. 90028).

Golden Records, (239 Great Neck Road, Great Neck, N.Y. 11021).

Grover Film Productions (P.O. Box 303, Monterey, Cal. 93942).

The Jam Handy Organization (2821 East Grand Boulevard, Detroit, Mich. 48211).

Keystone View Company (Meadville, Pa. 16335).

London Records, Inc. (539 West 25th Street, New York, N.Y. 10001).

Magnetic Tape Duplicators (6766 Sunset Boulevard, Hollywood, Cal. 90028).

Materials for Learning, Inc., (1078 St. John's Place, Brooklyn, N.Y. 11123).

Modern Talking Picture Service, Inc. (3 East 45th Street, New York, N.Y. 10022).

National Council of Teachers of English (1111 Kenyon Road, Urbana, Ill. 61801).

National Educational Television (Film Library, Indiana University, Bloomington, Ind. 47401).

National Center for Audio Tapes (Bureau of A-V Instruction. Stadium Building. Boulder. Col. 80302).

Newbery Award Record, Inc. (342 Madison Avenue, New York, N.Y. 10017).

Pathways of Sound, Inc. (102 Mt. Auburn Street, Cambridge, Mass. 02188).

Popular Science Publishing Company (455 Lexington Avenue, New York, N.Y. 10017).

RCA Educational Sales (1133 Avenue of the Americas, New York, N.Y. 10036).

Society for Visual Education, Subsidiary of Graflex, Inc. (1345 Diversey Parkway, Chicago, Ill. 60614).

Spoken Arts (310 North Avenue, New Rochelle, N.Y. 10801).

Sterling Films (316 West 57th Street, New York, N.Y. 10019).

Teaching Films, Inc. (88 Lexington Avenue, New York, N.Y. 10016).

Teaching Films Custodians (25 West 43rd Street, New York, N.Y. 10036).

United States Government Printing Office (Superintendent of Documents, Washington, D.C. 20025).

University of California (Children's Theater Committee, Theater Arts Department, Los Angeles, Cal. 40524).

Vocational Guidance Films (215 East Third Street, Des Moines, Iowa 50309).

Fredrick Warne (101 Fifth Avenue, New York, N.Y. 10003).

Weston Woods Studios (Weston, Conn. 06833).

H.W. Wilson Company (950 University Avenue, Bronx, N.Y. 10452).

Young America Films (McGraw-Hill Book Company, Text-Film Department, 330 West 42nd Street, New York, N.Y 10036).

ADDRESSES OF PUBLISHING AND DISTRIBUTING COMPANIES

Since the addresses, and even names, of publishing companies and of distributors often change, the reader may find occasion to consult the latest edition of *Books in Print: Publishers' Trade List Annual,* if a copy of this index is available in a library to which he has access. It is published by R.R. Bowker Company. Another reference book, found in larger libraries, of value in locating producers of some reading materials is the *Thomas Register of American Manufacturers and the Thomas Register Catalog File* published by the Thomas Publishing Company (461 Eighth Avenue, New York, N.Y.). All of the following companies publish materials dealing directly or indirectly with reading:

Abelard-Schuman (A division of Intext Press, 257 Park Avenue South, New York, N.Y. 10010).

Abingdon Press (201 Eighth Avenue South, Nashville, Tenn. 37203).

Acorn Press (1123 West Portland Street, Phoenix Ariz. 85007).

Addison-Wesley Publishing Company (Reading, Mass. 01867).

Allyn and Bacon, Inc. (470 Atlantic Avenue, Boston, Mass. 02210).

American Book Company (450 West 33rd Street, New York, N.Y. 10001).

American Council on Education (One Dupont Circle, N.W., Washington, D.C. 20036).

American Education Publications (Education Center, Columbus, Ohio 43216; *also* 245 Long Hill Road, Middletown, Conn. 06457).

American Educational Research Association (1126 Sixteenth Street, S.W., Washington, D.C. 20036).

American Guidance Service Inc. (Publishers' Building, Circle Pines, Minn.)

American Heritage Publishing Company, Inc. (551 Fifth Avenue, New York, N.Y. 10017).

American Library Association (50 East Huron Street, Chicago, Ill. 60611).

American Optical Corporation (Mechanic Street, Southbridge, Mass. 01550).

Antioch Press, The (*see* Kent State University Press).

Association for Childhood Education International (3615 Wisconsin Avenue, N.W., Washington, D.C. 20036).

Atheneum Publishers (122 East 42nd Street, New York, N.Y. 10017).

Atlantic Monthly Press (8 Arlington Street, Boston, Mass. 02116).

Audio-Visual Research Company (1317 Eighth Street S.E., Waseca, Minn. 56093).

Aurex Company (8 South Michigan Avenue, Chicago, Ill. 60603).

Avon Books, The (A division of the Hearst Corporation, 959 Eighth Avenue, New York, N.Y. 10019).

BFA Educational Media (A division of Columbia Broadcasting System, Inc., 2211 Michigan Avenue, Santa Monica, Cal. 90404).

Bantam Books, Inc. 616 Fifth Avenue, New York, N.Y. 10016).

Barnes and Noble Books, Inc. (A division of Harper & Row, 10 East 53rd Street, New York, N.Y. 10022).

Basic Books, Inc. (10 East 53rd Street, New York, N.Y. 10022).

Beckley-Cardy Company (*see* Benefic Press).

Behavioral Research Laboratories (Box 577, Palo Alto, Cal. 94302).

Benefic Press (A division of Beckley-Cardy Company, 10300 West Roosevelt Road, Westchester, Ill. 60153).

Bobbs-Merrill Company, Inc. (4300 West 62nd Street, Indianapolis, Ind. 46268).

R.R. Bowker Company (1180 Avenue of the Americas, New York, N.Y. 10036; order department: P.O. Box 1807, Ann Arbor, Mich. 48106).

Bowmar Publishing Company (622 Rodier Drive, Glendale, Cal. 91201).

Milton Bradley Company (74 Park Street, Springfield, Mass. 01101).

Bro-Dart Publishing Company (1609 Memorial Avenue, Williamsport, Pa. 17701).

Bureau of Educational Measurement (Kansas State College, Emporia, Kan. 66801).

Burgess Publishing Company (426 South Sixth Street, Minneapolis, Minn. 55415).

Cambridge University Press (32 East 57th Street, New York, N.Y. 10022).

Center for Applied Linguistics (1717 Massachusetts Avenue, N.W., Washington, D.C. 20036).

Center for Urban Education (105 Madison Avenue, New York, N.Y. 10016).

Century House, Inc. (Watkins Glen, N.Y. 14891).

Chandler Publishing Company (A division of Intext Educational Publishers, 124 Spear Street, San Francisco, Cal. 94105).

Child Study Press (9 East 89th Street, New York, N.Y. 10028).

Children's Book Center (University of Chicago Library, Chicago, Ill. 60637).

Children's Book Council (175 Fifth Avenue, New York, N.Y. 10010).

Children's Press (1224 West Van Buren Street, Chicago, Ill. 60607).

Children's Reading Service (*see* Materials for Learning).

Christian Science Publishing Society (1 Norway Street, Boston, Mass. 02115).

Citadel Press, Inc. (222 Park Avenue South, New York, N.Y. 10003).

Claremont College Library (Claremont, Cal. 19711).

College Reading Association (Reading Center, Syracuse, N.Y. 13210).

Combined Book Exhibit, Inc. (950 University Avenue, New York, N.Y. 10052).

Committee on Diagnostic Reading Tests, Inc. (Mountain Home, N.C. 28758).

F.E. Compton and Company (A division of Encyclopedia Britannica, 425 North Michigan Avenue, Chicago, Ill. 60611).

Consulting Psychologists Press, The (577 College Avenue, Palo Alto, Cal. 94306).

Cooperative Test Division (Educational Testing Service, 20 Nassau Street, Princeton, N.Y. 08540).

Coward, McCann and Geoghegan, Inc. (200 Madison Avenue, New York, N.Y. 10016).

Criterion Books, Inc. (257 Park Avenue South, New York, N.Y. 10010).

Thomas Y. Crowell Company (666 Fifth Avenue, New York, N.Y. 10019).

Crowell, Collier and Macmillan (866 Third Avenue, New York, N.Y. 10022).

Dakon Corporation (1840 Gilford Avenue, New Hyde Park, N.Y. 11040).

Dodd, Mead & Company (79 Madison Avenue, New York, N.Y. 10016).

Doubleday and Company, Inc. (Garden City, N.Y. 11530).

Dover Publications (180 Varick Street, New York, N.Y. 10014).

Dryden Press Inc., The (A division of Holt, Rinehart and Winston, Inc., 901 North Elm Street, Hinsdale, Ill. 60521).

Duell, Sloan and Pearce (A division of Meredith Corporation, 1716 Locust Street, Des Moines, Iowa 50303).

E.P. Dutton and Company, Inc. (201 Park Avenue South, New York, N.Y. 10003).

Economy Company, The (1901 North Walnut, Oklahoma City, Okla. 74103).

Educational Developmental Laboratories, Inc. (284 Pulaski Road, Huntington, Long Island, N.Y. 11744).

Educational Resources Information Center (ERIC) (1111 Kenyon Road, Urbana, Ill. 61801).

Educational Services (1730 Eye Street, N.W. Washington, D.C. 20006).

Educational Solutions, Inc. (Box 190, Cooper Station, New York, N.Y. 10003).

Educational Testing Service (Princeton, N.Y. 08540).

Educators Progress Service (Box 497, Randolph, Wis. 53956).

Encyclopedia Britannica, Inc. (425 North Michigan Avenue, Chicago, Ill. 60611).

Enrichment Teaching Materials (246 Fifth Avenue, New York, N.Y. 10001).

Exposition Press (50 Jericho Turnpike, Jericho, N.Y. 11753).

Expression Company (Box 11, Magnolia Mass. 01930).

Farrar, Strauss & Giroux, Inc. (19 Union Square West, New York, N.Y. 10003).

Fearon Publishers, Inc. (6 Davis Drive, Belmont, Cal. 94002).

Fideler Company, The (31 Ottawa Avenue N.W., Grand Rapids, Mich. 49502).

Field Educational Publications, Inc. (2400 Hanover Street, Palo Alto, Cal. 94304).

Field Enterprises Educational Publications, Inc. (510 Merchandise Mart Plaza, Chicago, Ill. 60654).

Follett Publishing Company (1010 West Washington Blvd., Chicago, Ill. 60607).

Friendship Press (475 Riverside Drive, New York, N.Y. 10027).

Garden City Publishing Company (*see* Doubleday and Company).

Garrard Publishing Company (1607 North Market Street, Champaign, Ill. 61820; editing and sales office at Overhill Road, Scarsdale, N.Y. 10583).

General Learning Corporation (250 James Street, Morristown, N.Y. 07960).

Ginn and Company (191 Spring Street, Boston, Mass. 02173).

Golden Press (A division of Western Publishing Company, 850 Third Avenue, New York, N.Y. 10022, also 1220 Mound Avenue, Racine, Wis. 53404).

Goodyear Publishing Company (A division of Prentice-Hall, Inc., 15115 Sunset Blvd, Pacific Palisades, Cal. 90272).

Graflex, Inc. (3750 Monroe Avenue, Rochester, N.Y. 14603).

Grolier, Inc. (575 Lexington Avenue, New York, N.Y. 10022).

Grossett & Dunlap, Inc. (51 Madison Avenue, New York, N.Y. 10010).

Gruene and Stratton, Inc. (A division of Harcourt Brace Jovanovich, 111 Fifth Avenue, New York, N.Y. 10003).

Gryphon Press (220 Montgomery Street, Highland Park, N.J. 08904).

E.M. Hale and Company (1201 South Hastings Way, Eau Clare, Wis. 54701).

Hammond, Inc. Maplewood, N.J. 07040; *also* 521 Fifth Avenue, New York, N.Y. 10017).

Harcourt Brace Jovanovich (757 Third Avenue, New York, N.Y. 10017).

Harlow Publishing Corporation (532-536 N.W. Second Street, Oklahoma City, Okla. 73102).

Harper & Row (10 East 53rd Street, New York, N.Y. 10022).

Harvard University Press (79 Garden Street, Cambridge, Mass. 02138).

Harvey House (5 South Buckhout Street, Irvington-on-Hudson, N.Y. N.Y. 10533).

Hastings House (10 East 40th Street, New York, N.Y. 10016).

Hayes School Publishing Company (201 Rebecca Avenue, Wilkinsburg, Pa. 15221).

D.C. Heath Company (125 Spring Street, Lexington, Mass. 02173).

Heritage Press (A division of The George Macy Company, 6 East 39th Street, New York, N.Y. 10016).

Highlights for Children (2300 West Fifth Avenue, Columbus, Ohio 43216).

Holiday House, Inc. (18 East 56th Street, New York, N.Y. 10022).

Holt, Rinehart and Winston, Inc. (383 Madison Avenue, New York, N.Y. 10017).

Horn Book, Inc., The (585 Boylston Street, Boston, Mass. 02116).

Houghton Mifflin Company (2 Park Street, Boston, Mass. 02107).

Ideal School Supply Company (8312 South Birkhoff Street, Chicago, Ill. 60620).

Indiana University Press (Bloomington, Ind. 47401).

Initial Teaching Alphabet Publications, Inc. (A division of Pitman Publishing Corporation, 6 East 43rd Street, New York, N.Y. 10017).

International Reading Association (Six Tyre Street, Newark, Del. 19711).

Intext Educational Publishers (Oak Street and Pawnee Avenue, Scranton, Pa. 18515).

Intext Press (257 Park Avenue South, New York, N.Y. 10010).

Judy Publishing Company, The (Box 5270, Main P.O., Chicago, Ill. 60680).

Kansas State Teachers College (Bureau of Educational Measurements, Emporia, Kan. 68802).

Kent State University Press (Kent, Ohio 44242).

Kenworthy Educational Service, Inc. (Box 3031, Buffalo, N.Y. 14201).

Keystone View Division/Mast Development Company (2212 East 12th Street, Davenport, Iowa 52803).

Alfred A. Knopf, Inc. (A division of Random House, Inc., 201 East 50th Street, New York, N.Y. 10022).

Lafayette Instrument Company (52 By-Pass, Lafayette, Ind. 47802).

Laidlaw Brothers (A division of Doubleday and Company, Thatcher and Madison Streets, River Forest, Ill. 60305).

Learning Research Associates (1501 Broadway, New York, N.Y. 10036).

J.B. Lippincott Company (East Washington Square, Philadelphia, Pa. 19105).

Little, Brown and Company (34 Beacon Street, Boston, Mass. 02106).

Liveright Publishing Corporation (386 Park Avenue South, New York, N.Y. 10016).

Longmans, Green and Company, Inc. (A division of the David McKay Company, 750 Third Avenue, New York, N.Y. 10017).

Lothrop, Lee & Shepard Company (A division of William Morrow and Company, 105 Madison Avenue, New York, N.Y. 10016).

Lyons and Carnahan (A division of Meredith Corporation, 407 East 25th Street, Chicago, Ill. 60616).

McCall Books (230 Park Avenue, New York, N.Y. 10017).

McCormick-Mathers Publishing Company, Inc. (A division of Litton Educational Publishing Company, 450 West 33rd Street, New York, N.Y. 10001).

McGraw-Hill Book Company (1221 Avenue of the Americas, New York, N.Y. 10020).

David McKay Company, Inc. (750 Third Avenue, New York, N.Y. 10017).

The Macmillan Company (866 Third Avenue, New York, N.Y. 10022).

Macmillan Professional Magazines, Inc. (22 West Putnam Avenue, Greenwich, Conn. 06830).

Macrae Smith Company (225 South 15th Street, Philadelphia, Pa. 19102).

Maico Hearing Instruments (7375 Bush Lake Road, Minneapolis, Minn. 55435).

Markham Publishing Company (3322 West Paterson Avenue, Chicago, Ill. 60659).

Melmont Publishers (A division of Children's Press, 1224 West Van Buren Street, Chicago, Ill. 60607).

Meredith Corporation (1716 Locust Street, Des Moines, Iowa 50303).

Charles E. Merrill Publishing Company (1300 Alum Creek Drive, Columbus, Ohio 43216).

Julian Messner (A division of Simon and Schuster, 1 West 39th Street, New York, N.Y. 10018).

Minnesota Mining and Manufacturing Company (3M Center, St. Paul, Minn. 55101).

William Morrow and Company, Inc. (A division of Scott, Foresman and Company, 105 Madison Avenue, New York, N.Y. 10016).

National Council of Teachers of English (1111 Kenyon Road, Urbana, Ill. 61801).

National Education Association (1201 Sixteenth Street, N.W., Washington, D.C. 20006).

Thomas Nelson, Inc. (Copewood and Davis Streets, Camden, N.J. 08103).

New York Public Library (Fifth Avenue and 42nd Street, New York, N.Y 10018).

Noble & Noble (A division of Dell Publishing Company, 750 Third Avenue, New York, N.Y. 10017).

Odyssey Press (A division of Bobbs-Merrill Company, 4300 West 62nd Street, Indianapolis, Ind. 46268).

Ohio Scholarship Tests (*see* The Ohio State University Press).

Ohio State University Press, The (Hitchcock Hall, 2070 Neil Avenue, Columbus Ohio 43210).

Open Court Publishing Company (1039 Eighth Street, LaSalle, Ill. 61301).

Otarion Electronics, Inc. (Scarborough Park, Ossining, N.Y. 10562).

F.A. Owen Publishing Company (Dansville, N.Y. 14437).

Oxford University Press, Inc. (200 Madison Avenue, New York, N.Y. 10016).

Parents' Magazine Press (52 Vanderbilt Avenue, New York, N.Y. 10017).

Parker Publishing Company (A division of Prentice-Hall, Inc., West Nyack, N.Y. 10994).

Parnassus Press (2721 Parker Street, Berkeley, Cal. 94704).

Perceptual Development Laboratories (6767 Southwest Avenue, St. Louis, Mo. 63117).

Pergamon Press (Fairview Park, Elmsford, N.Y. 10523).

Personnel Press, Inc. (A division of Ginn and Company, 191 Spring Street, Lexington, Mass. 02173).

Pitman Publishing Corporation, *see* Initial Teaching Alphabet Publications (6 East 43rd Street, New York, N.Y. 10017).

Plays, Inc. (8 Arlington Street, Boston, Mass. 02116).

Prentice-Hall, Inc., (Englewood Cliffs, N.J. 07632; *also* 70 Fifth Avenue, New York, N.Y. 10011).

Psychological Corporation (304 East 45th Street, New York N.Y. 10017).

Public School Publishing Company (Test division of Bobbs-Merrill Publishing Company, 4300 West 62nd Street, Indianapolis, Ind. 46268; *also* 4 West 57th Street, New York, N.Y. 10019).

G.P. Putnam's Sons (200 Madison Avenue, New York, N.Y. 10016).

Rand McNally & Company (8255 Central Park Avenue, Skokie, Ill. 60076; mailing address: Box 7600, Chicago, Ill. 60680).

Random House Inc., (201 East 50th Street, New York, N.Y. 10022).

Reader's Digest Association (Educational Division, Pleasantville, N.Y. 10570).

Ronald Press Company, The (79 Madison Avenue, New York, N.Y. 10016).

Saturday Review Press (230 Park Avenue, New York, N.Y. 10017).

Scarecrow Press, Inc., (A division of Grolier, Inc., 52 Liberty Street, Metuchen, N.J. 08840).

Schocken Books, Inc. (200 Madison Avenue, New York, N.Y. 10016).

Scholastic Book Services (50 West 44th Street, New York, N.Y. 10036).

Scholastic Testing Service (3774 West Devon Avenue, Chicago, Ill. 60645).

Science Research Associates (A division of IBM, 259 East Erie Street, Chicago, Ill. 60611).

Scott, Foresman and Company (1900 East Lake Avenue, Glenview, Ill. 60025).

Charles Scribner's Sons (597 Fifth Avenue, New York, N.Y. 10017).

Silver Burdett Company (*see* General Learning Corporation).

Southwest Regional Laboratory for Educational Research and Development (11300 La Cienega Boulevard, Inglewood, Cal. 90304).

Spencer International Press (A division of Grolier, Inc., 575 Lexington Avenue, New York, N.Y. 10022).

Stanford University Press (Stanford, Cal. 94305).

Steck-Vaughn Company, The (A division of Intext Educational Publishers, Box 2028, Austin, Tex. 78701).

Stereo Optical Company (3539 North Kenton, Chicago, Ill. 60641

Sterling Publishing Company (419 Fourth Avenue South, New York, N.Y. 10016).

Frederick A. Stokes Company (*see* J.B. Lippincott Company).

Teachers College Press (Columbia University, 1234 Amsterdam Avenue, New York, N.Y. 10027).

Tennessee Book Company (126 Third Avenue South, Nashville, Tenn. 37202).

Charles C. Thomas, (301-307 East Lawrence Avenue, Springfield, Ill. 62717).

United States Department of Health, Education and Welfare (Washington, D.C. 20025).

United States Government Printing Office (Superintendent of Documents, Washington, D.C. 20025).

University of Arizona Press (Tucson, Ariz. 85722).

University of California Press (2223 Fulton Street, Berkeley, Cal. 94720).

University of Chicago Press, The (5801 Ellis Avenue, Chicago, Ill. 60637).

University of Florida Press (15 North West 15th Street, Gainesville, Fla. 32601).

University of Iowa (Bureau of Educational Research and Service, Iowa City, Iowa 52240).

University of Minnesota Press (2037 University Avenue, S.E., Minneapolis, Minn. 55455).

University of Washington Press (Seattle, Wash. 98105).

Viking Press, The (625 Madison Avenue, New York, N.Y. 10022).

Wadsworth Publishing Company (A division of Belmont-Tower Books, Belmont, Cal. 94022; *also* 185 Madison Avenue, New York, N.Y. 10016).

George Wahr Publishing Company (316 South State Street, Ann Arbor, Mich. 48108).

Henry Z. Walck, Inc. (19 Union Square West, New York, N.Y. 10003).

Frederick Warne and Company (101 Fifth Avenue, New York, N.Y. 10003).

Franklin Watts, Inc. (A division of Grolier, Inc., 119 West 40th Street, New York, N.Y. 10018; *also* 845 Third Avenue, New York, N.Y. 10022).

Wayne State University Press (5980 Cass Avenue, Detroit, Mich. 48202).

Webster Publishing Company (*see* McGraw-Hill Book Company).

Western Reserve University Press (2029 Adelbert Road, Cleveland, Ohio 44106).

Westminster Press, The (Witherspoon Building, Philadelphia, Pa. 19107).

Wheeler Publishing Company (A division of Harper & Row, 10 East 53rd Street, New York, N.Y. 10022).

Albert Whitman & Company (560 West Lake Street, Chicago, Ill. 60606).

Whittlesey House (1221 Avenue of the Americas, New York, N.Y. 10020).

John Wiley & Sons, Inc. (605 Third Avenue, New York, N.Y. 10016).

Williams and Wilkins Company (428 East Preston Street, Baltimore, Md. 21202).

H.W. Wilson Company, The (950 University Avenue, Bronx, N.Y. 10452).

World Publishing Company, The (110 East 59th Street, New York, N.Y. 10022).

Index